Journal of Comparative Poetics

No. 24, 2004

alif

Archeology of Literature:
Tracing the Old in the New

Editor:	Ferial J. Ghazoul
Associate Editor:	Mohammed Birairi
Editorial Coordinator:	Walid El Hamamsy
Editorial Assistants:	Sayyid Abdallah, Alia Soliman
Assistants:	Naglaa El Baz, Rana El Harouny

Editorial Advisors (alphabetically by last name):
Nasr Hamid Abu-Zayd (Leiden University)
Stephen Alter (M.I.T.)
Galal Amin (American University in Cairo)
Gaber Asfour (Cairo University)
Ceza Kassem Draz (American University in Cairo and Cairo University)
Sabry Hafez (University of London)
Barbara Harlow (University of Texas)
Malak Hashem (Cairo University)
Richard Jacquemond (University of Aix-en-Provence)
Doris Enright-Clark Shoukri (American University in Cairo)
Hoda Wasfi (Ain Shams University)

The following people have participated in the preparation of this issue:
Tamer Abdel Wahab, Randa Abou-Bakr, Kamran Ali, Roger Allen, Gian Balsamo, Aida Bamia, Hassan Al-Banna, David Dorsey, Mahmoud El Lozy, Sharif Elmusa, Ahmed Etman, Michael Frishkopf, Abdel Hamid Hawwas, Ashraf Helmy, Nicholas Hopkins, Samir Khalil, David Konstan, Suaad Al Manea, Khaled Mattawa, Mona Misbah, Abdul Rasheed Na'allah, Mohammed Omran, Abdel Hamid Shiha, John Verlenden.

Printed at: Elias Modern Publishing House, Cairo.

Price per issue: Arab Republic of Egypt: L.E. 20.00
        Other countries (including airmail postage):
        Individuals: $20; Institutions: $40
        Back issues are available at the above prices.

Earlier issues of the journal include:

Alif 1: Philosophy and Stylistics
Alif 2: Criticism and the Avant-Garde
Alif 3: The Self and the Other
Alif 4: Intertextuality
Alif 5: The Mystical Dimension in Literature
Alif 6: Poetics of Place
Alif 7: The Third World: Literature and Consciousness
Alif 8: Interpretation and Hermeneutics
Alif 9: The Question of Time
Alif 10: Marxism and the Critical Discourse
Alif 11: Poetic Experimentation in Egypt since the Seventies
Alif 12: Metaphor and Allegory in the Middle Ages
Alif 13: Human Rights and Peoples' Rights in the Humanities
Alif 14: Madness and Civilization
Alif 15: Arab Cinematics: Toward the New and the Alternative
Alif 16: Averroës and the Rational Legacy in the East and the West
Alif 17: Literature and Anthropology in Africa
Alif 18: Post-Colonial Discourse in South Asia
Alif 19: Gender and Knowledge
Alif 20: The Hybrid Literary Text
Alif 21: The Lyrical Phenomenon
Alif 22: The Language of the Self: Autobiographies and Testimonies
Alif 23: Literature and the Sacred
Alif 24: Archeology of Literature: Tracing the Old in the New

Correspondence, subscriptions and manuscripts should be addressed to:
Alif, The American University in Cairo,
Department of English and Comparative Literature,
PO Box: 2511, Cairo, Arab Republic of Egypt
Telephone: 7975107; Fax: 7957565 (Cairo, Egypt)
E-mail: alifecl@aucegypt.edu

Contents

English Section

Arabic Section

This issue of *Alif* is fondly dedicated to Doris Enright-Clark Shoukri—Professor Emerita of English and Comparative Literature at AUC—who has for decades communicated her love of literature and the humanities to students and colleagues alike.

She is as in a field a silken tent
At midday when a sunny summer breeze
Has dried the dew and all its ropes relent,
So that in guys it gently sways at ease,
And its supporting central cedar pole,
That is its pinnacle to heavenward
And signifies the sureness of the soul,
Seems to owe naught to any single cord,
But strictly held by none, is loosely bound
By countless silken ties of love and thought
To everything on earth the compass round,
And only by one's going slightly taut
In the capriciousness of summer air
Is of the slightest bondage made aware.

— Robert Frost, "The Silken Tent"

The Archeology of Literature: Tracing the Old in the New

This issue of *Alif* is inspired by Doris Enright-Clark Shoukri and her approach to literary appreciation. Steeped in the Classics and having worked on medieval Latin texts for her doctorate, she nevertheless taught and continues to teach modern and postmodern literature. She uncovers traces of the old literary heritage in the new poetry, novels, drama, and criticism. Like a dedicated archeologist, she thrives on digging and reaching beneath the surface to come in touch with concealed and buried cultural artifacts and treasures.

The contributors to this issue partake in Professor Shoukri's conviction that to appreciate the contemporary, gazing at it is not enough; you need to think of texts in their palimpsest quality and read what has been erased or covered in the process of innovating. Many of the contributors to this issue are colleagues and ex-students of hers, but some are virtual colleagues as they share in her aesthetic orientation. As Professor Shoukri constantly emphasizes the creative and the philosophical in her critical approach, this issue includes poets, novelists, and artists in their own voices as well as analytical and philosophical essays.

This issue of *Alif* investigates the different strata constituting texts, and the presence of older material (myths, classics, hymns, rituals, romance, philosophical fragments, etc.) as subtexts in literature. Articles explore the processes and modalities of such inclusions in a given work or the corpus of an author. The issue also includes critical essays on the nature of continuity and correspondence in plots, characters, and styles as well as redeployment of older motifs in modern and postmodern works.

Alif, a refereed multilingual journal appearing annually in the spring, presents articles in Arabic, English, and occasionally French. The different traditions and languages confront and complement each other in its pages. Each issue includes and welcomes original articles. The next issues will center on the following themes:

Alif 25: Edward Said and Critical Decolonization.
Alif 26: Wanderlust: Travel Literature.
Alif 27: Reception Aesthetics: The Child as Addressee.

Sahara
(For Doris Shoukri)

Desmond O'Grady

Sand, sand grained as seasalt, tawny as lionskins,
wild all that way to my horizon lashes' line.
In the swept sky's eye, its whitegold pupil centers.

Here's no sand our childhood beaches might define
where all our awful ocean couched down quiet
sometimes, nor unmapped desert children will imagine,

drowned in dream, each dreamed Arabian Night,
but all that ageless roll of hilldune, plain,
wadi crusted under this straight sun's killer light.

Desert shale and sand's my span open
sea's antithesis – tireless, endless, empty save
for me and sometimes, far off, some lone

other, proud on horseback or kindred camel drove,
clear in clean church colours – white
and black, scarlet, purple – live

in the day's relentless length and light
like one lone fisherman in his tar black
currach or some brightly painted fleet

of strung out fishing smack
come from where, you'd ask,
or headed for? Horsemen and caravan tack

their talk and desert's rise, fall and risk
as boatmen do and cross their sea. Antithesis
too in that they both boast movement, mood and mask.

The desert's constant shifts in sounds of silence,
the sea's in silent sound, when we're out in them.
Bright day unmasks night's shunt and shove of difference.

But though their each security, serenity's the same
for every restless spirit, we, in our common frame
of nature, dread them poked ferocious, plunged insane.

A Wistful Lament for an Irrecoverable Loss

Doris Shoukri

I write this in Luxor, an appropriate and agreeable place to seek out pasts, whether personal or historic; for, surely, all our searches are driven by the same nostalgia, a yearning for that irrecoverable first impression, that initial imprint staking out its territory of individual history in the collective consciousness. And the *scène primitive* for us who live in the present is primitive precisely in that it is an individualizing experience universally shared. Each of us seeks his beginnings because in our beginnings we hope to rejoin the grounds of our being, the ends beckoning to be reborn from which we spring, as though to recover a retrievable progenitor in lieu of the aimless and purposeless creator, powerless to repeat the singularity of his act in forming the one of its kind that each of us is. For always there is that in our beginnings which was underived from an end and which is irrecoverably lost in our end. Hence the immeasureable sadness of the individual death and hence the impetus to seek in the past for the long history of individual suffering reabsorbed into the universal consciousness, to comb the lived individual lives for whatever light they might shed on the individual journey, whatever spark might be shaken from past lives "like shook foil," of understanding, or wisdom, or beauty. And here in Luxor is very close indeed to where our knowledge of individual lives and communities begins.

I have been asked for a personal account of my own career with its shift of interest from the medieval to the modern and I find Luxor an appropriate place to jot down these thoughts and memories since it was to Egypt I came at the start of my teaching career where, in some ironic reversal I left the study of the past to examine the present. Upon reflection, it was perhaps more appropriate than might have appeared that in New York City, the matrix of modernity where I was born and lived, I should have sought out the past, and in Egypt, where civilization all began, I should have embraced the present and sought out the contemporary: "In our beginnings are our ends; in our ends our beginnings." It is no wonder that a New Yorker should seek her bearings in the ancient world; there is nothing surprising in that she should scurry toward the contemporary having once ascertained the presence of the past.

In all my studies I had encountered artists and scholars who had built firmly on the past, the New Learning humanist, John Colet, the subject of my Honors Paper, having steeped himself in the medieval scholastic tradition looked to the more distant past to Greek and Latin Classics for "new" knowledge. Chaucer, my major poet, saluted, in all that he wrote, the wisdom and skill of all "that han gan beforn" adding his individual talent to the great tradition. Thomas Chaundler, the subject of my PhD thesis, wrote a medieval Morality play and introduced into its dramatic form, Ciceronian Latin and classical moral virtues. The section of the thesis devoted to Sources is almost as long as the play itself and is a showcase of Intertextuality (a word not yet current when I wrote) with titles from texts and MSS in Latin, Old French, German, Old English, and Middle English. Originality had not yet become equated with ignorance of the past and Chaundler's language was larded with passages from Church Fathers, the Bible, Classical authors, etc. And so, it was predictable that when I turned to the moderns, I should not interest myself in those reinventing the wheel, however wildly they might warble, but should select Eliot, Ezra Pound, Henry James, who sought to connect the new American world to the old of Europe, and James Joyce and Virginia Woolf, and André Gide, who stood firmly upon the shoulders of past giants. It was not to turn my back upon the past but to explore its implications for contemporary life, aware as I was that there was no starting *de novo* and that the essence of the civilized is that it is incremental.

It was entirely fortuitous that on my way to Egypt, I sat one bright sunny morning in Paris at the Deux Magots, across from l'église St. Germain, comfortably basking in its beauty, and opened a slim volume I had just purchased from La Hune to allow myself the rare treat of reading for pleasure something far, I thought, from my laborious studies. "April" I read "is the cruellest month." Chaucer raced to mind and St. Augustine. And as I read on, I could have provided notes as lengthy as those of my thesis, and almost as full as Eliot's own. There was Ezekiel and Ecclesiastes, *Tristan and Isolde*, *The Golden Bough*, Baudelaire, Dante, *Antony and Cleopatra*, *The Aeneid*, Shakespeare, Marvell, Spenser, Parsifal, Tiresias, Sappho, Buddha, the Grail Legend, Arnaut Daniel, the *Upanishads*. I had no need of notes. It was all there ready in my head and Eliot had provided me the supreme delight of calling upon all that I knew "wittily dislocating his language" "to revisit the past ironically" as Eco was later to describe his ventures into the medieval world in *The Name of the Rose*. I forgot to drink my *vin rosé*! I did eventually, however, order *des oeufs au jambon* and, keeping my place with *The Wasteland* opened on the table, I nipped next door back to La Hune to buy anything they had of Eliot. *The Four Quartets* was what I read next. It was tea time when I reached my hotel, as excited by reading as I've ever been except perhaps the day I discovered the entire source for act IV of Chaundler's play in one section of St. Hugh of St. Victor's *De Anima*. I felt not only the prospect of an enchanting reading future but a deep satisfaction with all that I had done thus far as though it had been a preparation for this day. I felt ready and prepared and even worthy of Eliot! I mention this feelng because it has curiously persisted. In reading Virginia Woolf or Marguerite Duras, for instance, I have the sensation that it was for this that I schooled myself, to get myself onto their same wave-length, as though their works were written for my delight and pleasure. The upshot of my discovery of Eliot was that I decided, despite the fact that I was not an artist, to follow his injunctions. Having the whole of the Tradition in my bones, I would seek out the individual talents of my own times.

So much for the Road Taken. It now behooves me, in all candour, to speak by way of an *Apologia pro vita mea*, of the one not taken, the Cross-Cultural path I did not take. "The best that had been known and thought in the World" for me was Matthew Arnold's list— from the ancient Egyptian and Hebrew world, to the Greeks and Romans, the Medieval, the Renaissance, etc. What was I thinking, or not thinking, to spend a half-century in Egypt without learning the language and following its path? At the risk of offering a facile explanation, let me proffer one that occurs to me each time I see a fresh-faced foreign student chatting volubly and confidently in what was for me a forbiddingly difficult barrier, the Arabic language. I had, perhaps, dug myself too deeply into the roots of one culture to explore another in any less thorough way and could not face the uprooting and upheaval of being born again. On the exculpatory side, in a non-scholarly way, I was taking in a great deal since I was intimately involved with that "other world" in the persons of my husband, his family and friends. After several decades of exposure, my cultural skin became sufficiently porous so that I felt I might with some small confidence read critically—in translation—some modern Arabic fiction. Needless to say, it was too late to approach the linguistic and cultural tradition seriously. As a result, in my reading, there is no resonance of the authors' pasts, only the present which I encounter, as though I were to read in Montale's "On an Unwritten Letter," his Message in a Bottle without knowing Vigny's "*bouteille à la mer*" or that his images are redolent of Dante and Ovid, Catullus and Petrarch, the Troubadours and Pound, and that his idiom is imbued with the Platonic, the Biblical, and the Bergsonian; or Chaucer without Boccacio and Petrarch, or Shakespere without Chaucer, or Milton wihout Shakespere, or Wordsworth wihout Milton, and so on. How to appraise the individual talent without the authority acquired through an intimate knowledge of the tradition from which it springs? To savor the flavor of Eliot's "Here we go round the prickly pear," one must at least know the mulberry bush nursery rhyme, not to mind the conversational-ironic of Laforgue and Corbière. A lack of acquaintance with traditional dramatic irony can make comprehension and assessment of dramatic utterance well-nigh impossible. Witness the use by well-intentioned moralists of Polonius' platitudes displayed on school blackboards: "Neither a borrower, nor a lender be" passed on as Shakespere's words of wisdom, reducing the supreme sophistication of his wit to a grocer's list of how to run a successful shop. And so for me, the study of the present clearly required a knowledge of the past. I could, of course, have reversed the process my education had taken and allowed the modern Arabic to point my way back to its traditions, but one is given one lifetime only and so the Road Not Taken, "what might have been" remains "A perpetual possibility/Only in a world of speculation." However, what I am more and more aware of is that what sends us to the study of any literature is the same, it is the instinct to uncover the lived life, to bare its mystery and garner its experience. And what we know in the present is, again shades of Eliot, the knowledge of the past breathed in an atmosphere free of is terrors and taboos.

And so, as I sat listening in Luxor to the account of the ancient Egyptians at the *son et lumière* of Karnak Temple, I found myself admiring their use of myth in arriving at an understanding of man's place in the universe and was reminded of Aristotle's belief that the capacity for metaphor is the true sign of genius. They had found a metaphor to speak of their cosmic beliefs and it worked for them; it expressed their truth in so far as truth about the cosmos can be known or expressed. In an age without its myth, such as the present, we might learn from the past the wisdom of resorting to poetry as an alternative way of knowing. Werner Heisenberg in his fascinating account of the development of Atomic Theory, describes the uphill battle that raged among scientists before the New Physics could be accepted and he indicates that much of the difficulty was with ways of viewing Truth. One had to accept new ways of looking before even the words "complementarity" and "probability theory," "correspondences," "uncertainty principle" could be found. Scientists found themselves possessed of beliefs for which there were no words. Heisenberg wrote (in *Physics and Beyond: Encounters and Conversation* [New York: Harper & Row, Publishers, 1971], 210):

> Quantum theory provides us with a striking illustration of the fact that we can fully understand a connection though we can only speak of it in images and parables. In this case, the images and parables are by and large the classical concepts, i.e. wave and corpuscle. They do not fully describe the real world and are moreover complementary in part, and hence contradictory. For all that, since we can only describe natural phenomena with our everyday language, we can only hope to grasp real facts by means of these images.

This loosening of linguistic bonds casts new light upon the mythological world of ancient times. The appellation "mythic" ceases to be pejorative and the anthropocentrism of modern man and the puny concerns of much present day religious thought appear as glaring simplifications and egregious assumptions about the nature of Reality and man's relation to it. But, even with the Sacred Lake and the hundred pillars of Karnak before me, I had ruefully to concede that we cannot go back to the worship of Amun, no more can we look out at the world of the Greeks where Dike prevailed, nor follow Dante's spheres circling the *primum mobile*, but what we can and must do is learn from their past achievements to acknowledge metaphoric thinking as the limit of man's cosmic understanding and to know "that we can only grasp real facts by means of images." Such an acknowledgement would satisfy the contemporary need for a more flexible and plausible way of dealing with what is largely unknowable than the futile attempts at factual accounts of the cosmos, and it might provide comfort in this twenty-first century to our being in this world. We could then speak of aliens as latter-day angels or messengers of the gods and rejoin the human race!

Nietzsche spoke of nostalgia as the wistful lament for an irrecoverable loss. The loss is irrecoverable. We can never again look out at the world as the ancient Egyptians did, but the wistful lament is not irrecoverable, it has never been lost. We share it with the Egyptians, the Greeks, the Romans, among others. In their art we see it reflected, in our contemplation of it, we can encounter them searching their beginnings and pasts as we search ours in theirs. Wistfully.

Memory, Inequality, and Power:
Palestine and the Universality of Human Rights*

Edward W. Said

This is a very fraught moment to be speaking about human rights and the Middle East, and the human rights of the Palestinian people in particular; but it does seem to be in some ways a symbolically useful time for the purposes of my lecture and what I have to say. I should also say immediately that I am not a political commentator; I am not a political scientist; I don't teach Middle Eastern studies or any of that, so I speak as one of us.

The United States of America has already sent a hugely intimidating military forces to various Arab and non-Arab countries in the regions surrounding Iraq. The frankly imperial idea which my President [George W. Bush] can barely articulate is that they are there to disarm Iraq forcibly and also to change its dreadful regime. The rest of the international community, not least most of the Arab countries of the region as well as the other permanent members of the Security Council, have been expressing varying degrees of disquiet and occasionally urgent disapproval as is the case with France. Certainly it is the case that no one outside of Iraq has suggested any concern about Saddam Hussein and his government.

It is the people of Iraq who stand to suffer the most and whose doubly and triply miserable fate is of the deepest interest to people all over the world. I am sorry to say that none of this has had the slightest effect on what is a granitic will on the part of a tiny number of members of George Bush's administration to go forward with plans for a war among whose stated imperial intentions is the unilateral wish to bring American style democracy to Iraq and the Arab world, redrawing maps, overturning governments and states and modes of life on a fantastically wide scale in the process. That all of this has very lit-

---

*   This article is based on the transcription of a lecture Edward Said delivered at Ewart Hall, The American University in Cairo, on March 17, 2003. He was not able—because of his illness—to send *Alif* the final version he promised.

tle in the final analysis to do with the enhancements of human rights and democracy, in a part of the world especially rife with their abuse, is patently obvious. Were Iraq to have been the world's largest exporter of oranges and apples, there would have been no concern over its purported possession of weapons of mass destruction or its extraordinarily cruel and tyrannical regime. This is a war planned for many reasons; among them I would say the most important are resources and strategic control. And when it occurs, the United States would have then asserted its strategic dominance over the center of the world's largest known energy reserves from the Gulf to the Caspian Sea. And it plans to reshape the area by pacifying threats to its dominance in Syria, Iran, and elsewhere in the Gulf.

To threaten and soon to prosecute war with such belligerence and such a wasteful deployment of human and military resources is an abuse of human tolerance and human values. That it might in the end turn out to be only a display, rather than an actual use of force, only deepens the anxiety about the kind of world we are moving toward. By the end of the decade China will be importing as much oil as the United States and by 2025, the United States will need to import a full 75% of its oil needs from the Gulf region principally. As against those facts, when a people are prevented from getting an education, or from being allowed to move, express themselves, organize freely without fear either of intimidation, collective punishment, or straight out assassination may seem therefore like relatively humdrum if not trivial issues, but they do pertain with a frightening parallelism to both the people of Palestine and the people of Iraq. In either and both cases, my point here is to assert first of all the universal applicability of human rights to those people—given that since World War II, there has grown up an impressive, even formidable, world-wide consensus that each individual or collectivity, no matter his or her color, ethnicity, religion, or culture, is to be protected from such horrific practices as starvation, torture, forced transfer of populations, religious and ethnic discrimination, humiliation, extra-judicial political assassination, land expropriation and all manner of similar cruel and unusual punishment.

I want to affirm also that no power, no matter how special or how developed or how strong or how urgent its claims of past victimization, is exempt from accusation and judgment if that government practices such things; and finally no people or individuals can be singled out as exceptions to these general rules, so as to be considered in fact liable for such abrogation of human rights as those I have mentioned. We live in a secular historical world. History is the product of human labor, choice and will. Nothing, in my opinion, nothing transcendental or divine can supersede that truth or suspend the consequences that flow from its application. There simply is no convincing way to assert special claims whose origin is the divine whether that is done by Israel or by the United States—claims that supposedly legitimate high altitude or smart bombing or the use of 60-ton bulldozers to demolish the houses of poor and defenseless people who don't happen to belong to the correct religion or race. Yesterday, we had a tragic case of a house demolition in Gaza by a 60-ton bulldozer in which a heroic American woman [Rachel Corrie] witnessed by giving her life to that barbaric act.

Just as I feel as an American that the United States has not been divinely endowed with a special errand into the wilderness nor have its practices been endorsed by God, I feel it is my moral and intellectual duty to oppose the unjust use of its immense military economic and political power abroad for what it claims falsely to be its national security interests. I have no power so I have to resort to the tools of education, to writing and speaking. By the same token, I want to reiterate my conviction here that it is this specific case of the denial of the human rights of the Palestinian people by the state of Israel which is at the core of the Middle East conflict. This cannot at all be justified on any of the grounds routinely accepted by far too many individuals and governments who would be the first to object to similar behavior in other cases. So, far from Israel and the Palestinians being a special case of unusual exceptional circumstances, I think the exact opposite is true— that because Palestine is perhaps of all places on earth the most densely saturated with cultural and religious significance, precisely that reality makes it an instance of universality thwarted and flouted. The universality of human co-existence, the human acceptance of the Other, and the human construction of a just and fair society for all— and certainly not only for some of its residents—are all relevant principles. The point is that no State, no State at all, is in my opinion entitled legitimately to object to these formulations and certainly no leader can state unarguably, for example as George Bush has, that the United States is good and its enemies evil. Or as General Sharon has announced and I quote here that "we are placing no restriction on our operations [in the Palestinian territories]. Israel is under no pressure. No one is criticizing us or has the right to do so."

I would submit that such sweeping statement of higher purpose

and extraordinary impunity must be opposed and intellectually dismantled for the fuggish balderdash that such pronouncements really are,
specially if they are intended to cover or explain or excuse or somehow
justify barbaric devastation and vast ruin. Yet the contrast between the
immensely powerful and the relatively powerless, such as we are, is not
so simple since the great outcry all over the world against unilateral US
war, and the felt need by even US government spokespeople to reiterate a general American commitment to democracy and human rights,
does in fact reveal a profound awareness that, aside from comfort and
convenience, human beings all over the world today expect to be
respected, their requirements for a decent life met, their wish not to be
tortured or detained unlawfully in any country in the world recognized,
their concern for their children and their livelihoods accepted despite
the supposedly higher priorities asserted by great power. All these in
theory at least are rarely challenged head on and considered to be
human entitlement. Even if such terrible abstractions such as national
interest, national unity, and national security are affirmed as being more
important than individual rights, I don't think they are; I think exactly
the opposite. Human rights of the individual are much more important
in the end than national interest, national unity, and national security, I
felt this all of my life and I still feel it. This unacceptable and unattrac-
tive argument that national security is the most important thing in the
world certainly now prevails in the US where for example the education of young people in the subject of history has become a profoundly
ideological battleground between proponents of a kind of primitive
heroic white American nationalism and the much more sensible advocates of a multi-cultural, multi-racial reality—stressed, for instance, in
his work by the prominent radical historian Howard Zinn. This other
American history includes, which is I think the real history, a bitter
legacy of domestic slavery, imperial conquest, and terrible class
inequality. The universally wide-spread conviction that everyone on
earth deserves a modicum of human rights is only a symbolic moral
power perhaps too ill-endowed to take on so redoubtable a force as
American global reach and its all too numerous local henchman and the
fearsomely neo-conservative spokesmen who want American values to
rule the world—resistance and objections not withstanding.

I want to tell you today, having just arrived yesterday from
America, please do not be misled into thinking that this is a war by
America against Iraq. It is a war of a small cabal, a putsch within the
Bush administration because it is clear to me—having crisscrossed the

US in the last three months lecturing and speaking and writing everywhere—this is perhaps the most unpopular war in American history and what is tremendously important also is that this is the first war since WWII that has been opposed before the war, not during the war, as is the case with Vietnam, or after the war; but before it actually takes place. Please also note that over at least 125 municipal councils in the United States, most of the large cities including New York, Chicago, and Los Angeles have voted overwhelmingly against the war. And the demonstrations, the popular outcry, the massive assault by pro-peace activists on the population at large, I think will complicate things for the Bush administration despite the obvious appeal, which will soon appear in grotesque manners, that this is a war for patriotism and the safety of the United States and so on and so forth. So I think it is very important to keep in mind that even huge powers can still be divided up into different sectors among which we must be able to discriminate and understand them separately from the center of power. In this case, as I say, the center has illegally appropriated sweeping powers to itself—thanks to the dormant Congress, which has allowed the President to do this, in the wake of 9/11, and which it should not have done.

To speak now about the Palestinian rights in such a context may seem essentially quixotic and irrelevant and certainly the current impression that Israel and the United States have borne all before them in their hostility to full Palestinian self-determination reinforces the superficial impression of irrelevance, but I want to argue that is not at all there is to the whole truth. The processes of history and politics are much more complicated than superficial, vulgar media sound bites. There are accomplishments and realities also to be noted with positive approval and admiration. During my lifetime, Palestinians, since the climatic events of 1948 and the establishment of Israel have gone from the status of non-persons to that of a universally acknowledged national collectivity, that is, a people, by virtue not simply of force of arms but of other means some of which I want to talk about here. If for now the Palestinians are still stateless, dispossessed, and for the most part exiled, it is because by those very unmilitary means some of which are the mobilized force of memory, the power of images, and the heroism and ingenuity of sheer persistence—by all of this, Palestinians embody perhaps the most visible and certainly the most universal case of human rights abuses on earth today. There is no desire on my part to be competitive about such a claim. There are many oppressed peoples in the world today and I am not saying that the Palestinians are the most oppressed; but I am saying they are most visible, and partly because of their own activity they lay a special claim on, not only Arab, but universal attention. I want also to be able to talk about the visibility not only of their presence as victims of injustice and human rights denial, but of the equal force they present, they represent on the world stage, of a wrong that must be righted.

In an extremely suggestive lecture, the British philosopher and political scientist Ken Booth draws attention to the existence of a growing number of what he calls "trans-cultural moral and political solidarities" that have acted the part of what he calls "agents beyond sovereignty," that is to say act as institutions not bound by the borders between countries that set the international system since the peace of Westphalia in the seventeenth century. That focus seems to be an excellent way of characterizing the overall human achievement of the Palestinian people in the period after 1948 until the present. Note that in all the many amazingly different places, conditions and polities that the approximately 7.5 million Palestinians now live in as citizens of Israel, as under military occupation of the West Bank and Gaza, as refugees and stateless persons in several Arab countries including this one [Egypt], as refugees with various acquired nationalities scattered all over the world, and as members of a dispossessed people—they have developed a political and moral solidarity with each other and with other people. Nothing less, in fact than a national identity and a political constituency all over the world that it has been the goal of Israel to deny, obliterate and refuse to acknowledge.

To argue backwards for a moment, let me site only one recent example of what I mean by denial and a refusal to acknowledge. It was precisely that refusal that flawed the Oslo process from the moment it was undertaken in 1993. In this, I think, the Israelis and the United States were planning not to restore but to further postpone and deflect the fulfillment of Palestinian aspirations. I said so at the time; nobody believed me. They said: "give it a chance," but if you read the documents you would have seen that neither Israel nor the United States was moved by an acknowledgment of past injustices nor by a spirit of contrition or of reconciliation with their batteries of legal experts backed by the disproportional military weight of both countries and at the same time as more than double the pre-existing number of settlements were being created on Palestinian land and more human rights abused. Israel and the United States divided and subdivided ever-diminishing bits of Palestinian territories into smaller and less viable units for the unfortunate Palestinian authority to take over and misrule, all under the misleading—not to say willfully deceptive—rubric of the "peace process." Was there ever any other intention? No, not peace at all but pacification for a time and, I think, we are in for that now in the case of Iraq. The Oslo accords were too much of a whole with several prior decades of Palestinian dispossession, house demolitions, land expropriation and attacks on civil society. As against that, there has been, as I said, a moral and political solidarity building up between Palestinians all over the world—some of it has been evident in the past weeks of worldwide protests against the war in Iraq. People have made the connection between war by the United States against Iraq and Israel's war against the Palestinian people. This is absolutely correct; and in many countries of the world—in Europe, in the Middle East, in parts of Africa and Latin America and to some degree in America, in some of the big demonstrations that took place, for example, in New York in the middle of February, in California, where in San Francisco three or four hundred thousand people turned up—the issue of Palestine was connected with the issue of Iraq.

One of the manifestations, and perhaps not its most significant one, is that today for example, there are such things openly acknowledged as a Palestinian cinema and with it a kind of transnational visibility of a Palestinian person that would have been unthinkable three decades ago. In late January, to give a very simple example, at my University [Columbia], the head of the Middle East Studies Department who is an Iranian, Hamid Dabashi, decided—because he wrote a book on cinema; he's very interested in Iranian cinema—it would be a great idea if we had a festival of Palestinian films. This festival began on a Thursday night and between Thursday night and Sunday night about 74 films were shown in perhaps 15 or 16 sessions. Every single one of them was full; you could not get in for miles around, and now half a dozen more universities around the country are trying to do the same thing all of which attests to the power of Palestine and the visibility of the Palestinian individual as he or she appears in films. Of course, with the films went the usual threats, the picketers, the flooding of e-mails. As one of the speakers at the festival, I would get 5000 e-mail messages every day to put my e-mail out of commission. But, of course, this did not have any effect at all; people still went on and the showing of the films were all fully attended. So visual symbols have played an extraordinarily important role in the reappearance if you like of the Palestinian individual after years of absence and programmed national effacement.

I don't want to go over the steps taken by Israel inside former Palestine to obliterate systematically the centuries-old Arab presence along with its symbols and structures. I have described some of these on the juridical level so far as the taking over of land and property was concerned in my book *The Question of Palestine* which appeared more than 20 years ago, but the overall plan was to start Israel as if afresh, a state rising from nothing, to take its place among the nations. In the affirmation of its renewed millennial identity, Israel managed for quite a while to remove the traces of Palestinian life for the most part, even though, of course, a large number of these traces, remaining as a remnant of the people despite the expulsions of 1948, were there as a humbled and scarcely perceptible human presence ruled by military government inside Israel until 1966.

Even so, apparently innocent a discipline such as archeology, which is one of course of the prides of Egypt, was used in Israel and was made complicit in the making over of the land and its markers, as if there had never been any Arabs or any other civilizations there except Israel and the Israelites. This is very well described by a young Palestinian anthropologist Nadia Abu El-Haj in her recent book called *Facts on The Ground: Archeological Practice and Territorial Self-Fashioning in Israeli Society* (2002). Her argument is that in the process of providing Israel with an ancient objectivized history visible in archeological evidence, the traces of other more just as historical histories were ignored or simply moved away by trucks and bulldozers. What remained became for Israeli archeology evidence of a kind of essential "Israeliness" which gave the state an unassailable pedigree in a long distant past with the intervening cultures and peoples; myriads of people and cultures were simply pushed aside and ignored.

Moreover in a trilogy of powerful books entitled *A Land without People, The Expulsion of the Palestinians* and the third one *Imperial Israel and the Palestinians: The Politics of Expansion 1967-2000*, the Palestinian/Israeli scholar Nur Masalha has unearthed both the theory and practice of emptying the land of Israel of its indigenous inhabitants. Much of the pre-state Zionist ideology that mobilized Eastern European communities for the trek to mandatory Palestine was premised on the virtual absence of inhabitants, on what was often depicted as either completely empty or hopelessly arid land awaiting redemption by Jewish pioneers. Later on, or in some cases simultaneously with that, when the discovery of actual Palestinians could no longer be deferred or denied there was a concerted effort to devise ways of getting rid of them; it was called transfer and is still called transfer. Half the members of the present Israeli cabinet openly say that the only solution is to transfer the Arabs out of Palestine. The war of 1948 provided field commanders and Ben Gurion himself with a rich opportunity to do so. These are amply attested to in the Israeli military archive as combed assiduously by a number of Jewish as well as numerous Arab researchers including Masalha himself. Since 1967 the desire to efface and/or repress what has remained of an institutionalized Palestinian life in the cities and villages of the West Bank and Gaza has remained an often explicitly stated Israeli goal hidden inside the polemics of a war for Israel's survival and the defense against extremist terrorism. But whether its new Jewish citizens liked it or not, Israel has always been encumbered by Palestinian memory which is one of my themes here today. It is not as if a whole existence of a people can be easily wiped away like a footprint in the sand. The sheer banality of such a possibility is too obvious to require more comment and whether this was meant to put a stop to Palestinian national life, just short of full ethnic cleansing, I don't want to speculate on. But such procedures are of a piece with claims that Israel is fighting for its life and that in occupying and destroying everything possible by tanks, bulldozers, F16s and Apache helicopters, it is defending itself against terrorists who happen to have no army or viable defense or means of waging war of any description—that seems totally obvious.

In any event the great narrative of Palestinian life has not yet been achieved, or for that matter written, any more than the fulfillment of its logical national aspirations have been fulfilled. Although it seems just as obvious despite Oslo, despite what the leaders have said, there is no regression, no hesitation among Palestinians everywhere on the drive towards self-determination. A Palestinian nation exiled or in waiting has emerged with an unmistakable outline and personality of its own. The vast network of institutions—groups scattered all over the world that sustains the continuity of Palestinian national life—is an amazing thing. It is drawn not only on the mobilized energy of Palestinians everywhere but also on the dazzlingly wide-spread commitment to them of their friends, allies and comrades all over the world.

The sheer inequality between the average Palestinian and the average Israeli is breathtaking, and this has been completely shielded from the world outside. We know about it as Arabs, as Palestinians, as neighbors if you like in the Middle East, but in the West you have no idea for example when you watch a CNN broadcast—which is quite different from the CNN you watch here [Egypt] which is international CNN. But if in America you watch a broadcast about what's happened on the West Bank—let's say yesterday's events—you'll never know that there is a military occupation going on, that's never mentioned. It is simply taken out of the context.

So the great inequality between the average Palestinian and the average Israeli is simply unknown. People will then say something disapproving about those terrible suicide bombers. I always encounter that—saying well, "what about the suicide bombers?" and I'll agree. I say "yes, it's terrible"; but then one has to add how many Israelis have had to live through the demolition by bulldozing of entire villages, blocks of flats, shopping districts? How many Israelis have had to endure missile attacks by Apache helicopters or rockets from American made F16 fighter jets? How many Israelis have had to be stripped and searched at checkpoints on an hourly basis? None at all. During the first three weeks of the *Intifada*, this *Intifada*, one million bullets were fired by Israeli military personnel at Palestinians. For those of you interested in historical comparisons, neither Indians demonstrating against the British, nor South African blacks fighting against apartheid, ever faced anything like this, nor for that matter did they have to reckon with missiles, hundreds of tanks, helicopters and F16s and rocket attacks fired into civilian areas as well as refugee camps with no defenses or arms whatever.

Consider this—and I did this as a quick example on the internet—on January the 23rd, 2003 you read: 836 Muslim pilgrims to Mecca from Gaza were denied permission to leave. The Palestinian Catholic cardinal was detained at Tel Aviv airport. Some towns on the West bank have already sustained 214 days of curfew. 150 dunums of fertile agricultural land were destroyed in Gaza. Three people, two of them civilians were killed. Six homes demolished. This is all in one day in late January. 62 shops in Nazlit Isa were flattened to the ground, and that, literally, thousands of people many of them pregnant women, sick and aged men and women, children trying to get to school, doctors hoping to reach their patients their hospitals, professors and undergraduates trying to get to their classes with 3 universities closed, and ordinary human beings shopping, looking for food or work—all of them detained by the endless number of checkpoints. Over 300 checkpoints in the West Bank punctuate the existence of Palestinians in the Occupied Territories. Two or three days ago, 12 Palestinians were killed as a result of an Israeli incursion into Gaza. Today more were killed, dozens injured, tens of houses demolished in varying degrees of severity and brutality. This sort of thing has been going on there everyday for 35 years. The Israeli occupation is now the longest in modern history, the longest military occupation rivaled only by the Japanese occupation of Korea. And the settlements increase: they crowd every available hilltop.

There is one other thing I want to mention about the occupation which makes it difficult to recall or actually see, not only for outsiders so to speak but even for Israelis themselves. As Amira Hass writes in Haaretz, and I quote her: "a person could travel the length and breadth of the West Bank without ever knowing, not only the names of the villages and cities whose lands were confiscated to build the Jewish settlements and neighborhoods, but even the fact that they exist at all." I don't know how many of you have been to the Occupied Territories. I wish you would all go, you have to see it—I'll talk about that later—but the point I am trying to make is, you have no idea of, for example, the system of roads that the Israelis have built with American money. We are talking about 780 miles of roads throughout an area that is about the size of Cairo basically, I mean greater Cairo. Roads that are for Jews only. They've built roads, what Jeff Halper calls "a matrix of control," so that they connect the settlements with each other. They ban Arabs and they make it, as Amira Hass says, impossible to even see the Arabs. "Most of the names of the Arab towns," I quote her again, "cannot be found on the road signs." From a distance, the calls of the *mu'azzin* and the streets that are empty of people; after all there is nothing to go out and look for. It seems like an aesthetic decoration. A Jew traveling on the almost empty roads of the West Bank would think that there are no longer any Arabs. The Arabs do not travel on the wide roads used by Jews.

When I went to South Africa for the first time in 1991 before the end of apartheid—although Mandela had just been released from jail a few months earlier—you could drive from white centers like Cape Town to Stellenbosch, a distance of about 80 miles and never see anything of the black South Africa. It was entirely white; why? Because the road curved around in such a way that the townships, where you would occasionally see a large light, but the rest of the black population was simply made invisible. This is one of the ways that colonialism has of dissipating the existence of the other people. In addition to that now, again with the full support of the United States, the Israelis are building a wall between themselves and the Palestinians—a wall which separates villages from their lands, so that now they don't even have to, not only just see them, but they don't have to deal with the fact that their visual presence might be a problem, and all this with the support of the United States—135 billion dollars given by us. This tremendous assault on memory, to say nothing about reality, is quite without precedent or analogy in our post-modern times. Not in former Yugoslavia, not in Africa, nor elsewhere in Asia and Australia. By contrast, I want to say that none of these efforts have achieved their goal. In every possible way, the diverse affirmations of Palestinian identity, far from being a negative or passive thing have grown first and foremost a culture of human rights and democratic processes at the grass roots level that has included a sensitive register of the claims of memory, the demand for attention and justice, despite the world's indifference and a healthy awareness of the ironies of unequal power.

The other thing I'd like to note is that even though in the United States and parts of Western Europe the notion of Palestine is associated only with violence and terror; there is, as I said earlier, a serious contradiction to that superficial association in an ongoing and recognized Palestinian national life with a quite peculiar tenacity. There is today a Palestinian literature which is studied, not only in Palestinian schools and universities but in European, American, African, and Latin American countries. There is a Palestinian legal political and scholarly discourse, a Palestinian cinema, a Palestinian theatre, an oral tradition, a large number of Palestinian grass roots organizations all over the world. In short, there is a Palestinian style that invigorates and informs all aspects of this community's existence. Moreover—this is what I think is most encouraging—this Palestinian style is situated in contemporary awareness in all sorts of interesting and noteworthy ways. The habit of considering everything about Palestinian identity as basically anti-Israel does an extreme disservice to the richness of the achievement I have been discussing. As Rashid Khalidi has pointed out, in his book called *Palestine and the Palestinians,* there has been a coherent Palestinian national life well before the onset of Zionism which despite the *nakba* [disaster], and the years of dispossession, has never really been broken. Moreover, the universality of the drive for Palestinian self-determination has acquired an unbudgeable place in the world's agenda for liberation, sustainability and resistance. Every major UN conference for the past two decades, whether concerning the place of women, the environment, racism, human rights, disarmament, health, or human development has had an important place in it for the question of Palestine. Paradoxically, the Davos meetings for governmental and corporate leaders of globalization have an important component of their agenda devoted to Palestine while exactly at the same time, at the other end of the world at Porto Alegre in Brazil, the anti-globalization meetings have featured the presence of a large Palestinian delegation whose presence assures an additional progressive dimension to the debates there.

Any discussion of Middle East peace, and you notice that even in Blair's comments, two days ago [March 15, 2003], as the going expression has it, turns out inevitably to be mainly about the question of Palestine. If in the period after 1948, as part of the postwar reemergence of Europe, Israel had the status of a progressive cause, it is now Palestine that has taken that place. One need only think of the support Israel had during the 1950s and 1960s from such people as Jean-Paul Sartre and Simone de Beauvoir to gage how far from that position it has fallen today. As some of Israel's own internal critics like Amos Elon and Avishai Margalit have noted sadly since the first *Intifada* of 1987, Israel has been transformed dramatically all over the world into a symbol of oppression and injustice, lumped together with the United States for its arrogance, its supremacist attitudes and for its inhuman policies towards the Palestinians over which it has ruled for so long. Divestment campaigns in American universities—including mine [Columbia], Harvard, MIT, Berkeley, Stanford, Chicago—all the major universities of America are now conducting divestment campaigns reminiscent of the anti-apartheid movement of the 1970s and the 1980s that is to say to have university endowments divest themselves of stocks in American companies that do business or supply Israel with military equipment. This raises a whole raft of new questions about the post-cold-war political order that are quite unique in their density and difficulty.

So in conclusion, I want to talk about three such problems. I don't have pragmatic answers to these questions whatever that means, but I'll talk about them from the perspective that I can bring as a humanist and an intellectual who is deeply engaged in the matter, but who is independent and I would like to think as free of doctrinal or ideological hubbles as it is practically possible to be. Of the three issues I want to talk about the first one is the notion of victimhood. I mean there is a great deal of talk now all over the world of what do we do about the victims of the past. For a Palestinian, like myself, who has had the most fortunate and the most luxurious of lives—compared with the overwhelming number of my refugee compatriots or those who had to live under Israeli rule for decades and decades—it is still difficult for me to minimize how much more Palestinians have been sinned against than as a whole they have sinned, how much they have suffered terribly in an unacknowledged silence even today. As of this moment, not a single major Israeli political or intellectual figure, not a single one—certainly no political figure of any importance—has articulated any serious contrition the way for example Japan has expressed contrition for what it did to China and Korea. Not one Israeli politician of any stature has expressed any contrition to say nothing of accepting any responsibility at all for the disasters and sustained human suffering of the Palestinian people. I know nothing at all in contemporary history quite like this amazing stone wall of obduracy and denial and yet I must also say that the legacy of persecution, genocide, and anti-Semitism that is so much a part of Israel's history is a background that we must acknowledge and contend with just the same. Two communities of suffering, I have called them that in the past but one must, I think, make clear, that at the present time, one community has the tremendous balance of power in its favor (Israel and the Jews), the other is, so to speak, the victim of the former victim. Israeli policies as well as the meditation of many western liberals who feel a collective guilt for Christian and European anti-Semitism, nevertheless, must be able to distinguish and disentangle the past from the present to make very clear distinctions between respecting the appalling past injustices heaped on Jews historically on the one hand in Christian countries, and on the other simply excusing what the State of Israel and the State of the Jews has done to the entire Palestinian people ever since.

There is simply no earthly or divine dispensation that would excuse a State or a people for wreaking havoc upon another one while pleading the travails of its own past as an excuse. Sharon's ideas are at least clear in that he believes, like George [W.] Bush, that his people owns the land for historical, biblical reasons and that, in making every effort to appropriate all of it at present and retrospectively, Israel is neither bound nor restrained by ordinary conventions of proper justice and proportionality. My argument here has been to state that such claims don't at all correspond with universalism or the idea that human rights cannot be manipulated to accommodate what is a record of patent brutality and cruelty. Palestinians have been displaced, they have had their society shattered, they have had to live under military occupation, their lands and lives are today systematically torn apart.

There are no two ways about it I believe, which is not to say that we must simply overlook the tragic history of the Jews. On the contrary, I would always want to say that as a Palestinian, as an Arab, I should make my case to defenders of Israel on the basis of, and taking full account of, making due acknowledgment of the history of discrimination against Jews. That kind of policy, I would want to add, should never ever be visited on anyone for any reason at all, least of all by Jews in the name of their safety and independence.

The second problem that needs examination has recently taken the form of the supposed clash of civilizations especially in the Arab world where Samuel Huntington—formerly a mediocre cold warrior in republican and democratic administrations—found a new career for himself in formulating this extremely vulgar and reductive idea that civilizations clash. This and the stridently bellicose rhetoric that seems to form from it has been given a woefully inadequate formulation by politicians and demagogues within the Arab world and the Islamic world since the events of September 11th, 2001. I have always found these formulas extremely stupid, not only because they falsify and distort the notion that because cultures and nations seem to have a visible identity, they also must have rigidly policed, enforced, and defined borders and rules within them and therefore wars across those borders become inevitable. This sort of thing is completely untenable on both historical and philosophical grounds. Cultures, peoples, civilizations are not water tight inert, unchanging things. Exactly the opposite is true. And if there is such a thing as culture or nationhood at all, it is that each is, and always will be, tied in, constantly interacting and intertwined, with other cultures and nations. Allowing for differences in kind, countries cannot really be separate and stand apart from their environment. It was historically one of the great failures of British imperialism that in the Indian subcontinent, in Palestine, in Cyprus, in Africa, in Ireland, it adopted the practice of partition, or as it has been called "divide and quit." Thereby leaving matters worse off than before the separation. Building walls, therefore, is a kind of folly that ought to be exposed for exactly what it is, namely a delusion that can neither be made fully to work in theory or in practice.

Ignorance of the other is not a strategy for survival. All nationalisms at their most feverish fail this crucial test of awareness. A failure by no means limited to so-called underdeveloped or fanatical ideologies, cultures or religions. Historically, for example, Palestine is a palimpsest; a composite of an enormous number of people and civilizations—each of them has left traces and effects that last for many centuries. It must be said again and again that everything we know about ancient Palestine speaks to a rich multiplicity of peoples and tribes, not just the Israelites but also of the Canaanites, the Philistines, the Jebusites, the Moabites and many others. To extrapolate from that history, say that only one people dominated and is therefore entitled to lay exclusive claim to Palestine today, is simply a tragic misinterpretation and betrayal of something far more interesting and rich. One can therefore interpret history inclusively giving rise to complexity and universalism or far more narrowly one could interpret history as the exclusive possession of only one people and one culture and one power who prefer unending war against others to mutual recognition and coexistence.

I think this is the problem that we face today with the United States, those of us who live there. Is America going to be the unilateralist power that enters and does what it wants in the world simply because it is more powerful or, as many people, including a majority of Americans, believe that we are part of the world and have to live with the world and within the world as citizens of the world rather than as a super power. Civil wars are much more bitter and unyielding than any other kind. I think that is the essence of the problem that we face today, namely, whether some believe Palestine or America or any other country ought to become and therefore remain the principal homeland of just one dominant people or whether all these countries can become the homeland of the people who actually live there regardless of race and religion, even though for the time being they seem to be locked in mortal combat. I don't know the short term answer to that question but it seems to me that there potentially lies the universality of the appeal for Palestinian human rights. Now a second-class, dispossessed, and downtrodden people for the past century and a half, the Palestinians have been struggling for equality in that land much as the non-white people of South Africa waged the battle for liberation and equality there. It is not a matter of partition, of dividing the land. It is a matter of sharing it with equality.

I will not lie to you here and say that in all the ways they have resisted their difficult fate, Palestinians have had coexistence and sharing in mind—very far from it. For in this tale there is abundant vengeance, brutality, hatred and exterminism. Still, there is a great deal more than that as I have been arguing here. And I will say confidently that the logic of that struggle has always been inclusive against injustice and inequality for coexistence and equality and in this region of the world—the genius of this region of the world—is the fact that it is the home of many peoples and that many cultures historically have coexisted here throughout history and throughout geography. Of course there will be disagreements over how and what sort of equality, in form and method, must be achieved but that it is the desired result is as far as I am concerned the great truth of our undiminished energies as a people that has simply refused to go under and give up.

The final point I would like to mention is the antithesis between present bitter antagonism and future reconciliation. Antagonism is the structure that today binds Palestinians and other Arabs with Israelis in the land and in the diaspora. Neither people, neither the people of Israel nor the people of Palestine, has been blessed with a Mandela nor even a De Klerk. We are very far from a truth and reconciliation commission. The number of visionaries who have articulated thoughts that go beyond a wretched impoverished opposition is tiny, if they exist at all. Yes, there have been Israelis and Palestinians who have tried together to work against injustice and intolerance but they are a minority, a beleaguered out-numbered minority with very limited influence now. But that need not always be so. There are many models besides belligerence and civil strife between peoples. One model is the model of historical Andalusia where three cultures, three religions—all monotheistic—managed to coexist, with friction, with struggle, with antipathy in some cases, but always in a kind of precarious harmony, but coexisting just the same. And I would want to say that both in the Arab world and in Israel there has been a tendency to draw an iron curtain in front of one and say "they are the enemy, we are the people who are the victims, we have to be able to resist." I think in general it's true, people do want to resist, but look at the great resisters of the past— somebody who is alive today: Mandela! What was the genius of Mandela? The genius of Mandela was to understand that in order to win the struggle for liberation in South Africa, the struggle against apartheid, it was necessary first of all to formulate a strategy and a goal that never changed. It never changed for the season; it never changed during the cold war, or after the cold war. The goal was always the same: one person, one vote. Black, white, mixed, colored: one person, one vote. That is the principal of human rights and that is the strategy of a people struggling for equality and self-determination.

Now the second part of the strategy which was so important about South Africa and about Mandela was that he realized that in order to implement this he could never win the battle militarily. I mean I could give you a lecture for the next four hours on the insufficiency of military power, that military power never wins battles; I mean it wins battles but it never wins wars. I believe this passionately; that what gave the popular struggle in South Africa its ultimate victory—it is much more complicated obviously but allow me to simplify just for the sake of time—what gave the battle in South Africa its victory, was the moral high ground, that is to say, the moral high ground that Mandela and the ANC took. It was not a matter of renouncing terrorism and it was not a matter of renouncing violence; they never did that by the way. People say to the Palestinians "renounce violence, renounce terrorism." Poor old Arafat, time after time, renouncing terrorism (sometimes it sounds like tourism), but that's not the answer. Mandela, just for the record, never renounced violence, he still hasn't renounced violence to this day, but he won the Nobel peace prize. I mean a lot of shits have won the Nobel peace prize. But the idea was to define the struggle on a higher plane than that of your enemy.

Historically, Palestinians and Arabs have always done so, but unfortunately they have lost the battle because they tried to redefine it in terms of military confrontation in which in the end we are always going to lose. Our territory is first of all the land and it's very important that there has been significant cooperation between Jews and Palestinians in trying to preserve the land, in preventing house demolitions. I mean, that is where the collective struggle is; and second, the other place is in the moral principle of 'one person, one vote,' that is to say human equality based on the full realization of human rights and that—that is the final point I want to make—can never take place without two things.

One, being able directly to address your enemy as Mandela did from the court house which sent him to prison for 27 years and then again from the parliament building in 1994 when he addressed the entire nation. Always to talk to the Other. In our part of the world talking to the Other means *tanazulat* [compromises]. It does not mean that; it means you defend your point of view in a moral way, to overcome the resistance of the Other to the moral argument that you present with organization. And the second thing, of course, you can't do it just by talking, you have to do it in a mobilized and organized way, not by a group of poor people who are given arms and told to go fight while the officers sit at home and sip tea and watch television—that's immoral. Everybody is mobilized in the struggle and this is beginning to happen now, not only in Palestine but all over the world against the American war and the American Empire.

The second component is knowledge. Now, I don't think it's an accident that I speak here as an educator; you cannot deal with the Other without a profound knowledge of his or her culture, society and history. And I think this is the most important thing for us, as Arabs, who historically have had a great civilization and a great culture based upon the discovery of others. Think of Ibn Battuta, think of the discovery of Ceylon, *Sarandib* in Arabic; the word serendipity and discovery come from Arabs who were the great geographers of the east, of Africa, of Europe originally. But there has been for the last one hundred years a recoil; say that if we are afraid of *Occidentosis*, we are afraid to confront the Other because we might get an *istighrab* [westernization], by being too close to the Other. That's complete nonsense. You can look at the Other in many different ways, one is to emulate the Other and to try to imitate him, the mimic men, to try to be like one of these characters in Naipaul's novels who are just little monkeys imitating their masters. But the other way is to understand the Other better than the Other knows himself or herself. As I said about America, about Israel, there is another Israel, there is another America, there is another Europe and that is up to us to decide to have an exchange with on the basis of morality, on the basis of human rights, on the basis of collective coexistence, on the basis of sustainability.

My last point, the great failure in my opinion of what the United States is about to do in Iraq, to my great sorrow and shame as an American and as an Arab, and what Israel has been doing for the last 53 or 54 years as many Israelis have realized, is to try and win the battle through the power and military brutality. It can never work because you cannot destroy the will of a people and you can never destroy the power of an idea. And what is the idea? The idea is equality, coexistence, sustainable life, whether it's in the case of the environment, whether it's in the case of the land, whether it's in the case of society—those are the principles that we must live in and struggle by, rather than ephemeral things or illusions about returning to the past or finding the golden age somewhere else. The present is our battleground and knowledge is our main weapon.

Egypt in Greco-Roman History and Fiction*

Stephen Nimis

In the current political and intellectual context it is not necessary to explain that the portrait created by one people, such as the Greeks or Romans, of another, such as Egypt, is likely to be a "construction" more than a "representation." In his 1971 survey of the subject, C. Froidefond characterized Greek views of Egypt as a "mirage," an imaginative vision that had as much to do with who the Greeks were as it had with who the Egyptians were.[1] Edward Said's 1978 landmark work on orientalism traced how that Egyptian mirage developed and endured over the years in response to Europe's own evolving identity, and his book made a strong case for what has become a key idea in cultural studies: Power follows knowledge, and the seemingly objective and scientific study of other cultures is often an accessory to the crimes committed by empires in the name of civilization.[2] The enormous—and often nasty—controversy that swirled around the publication of Martin Bernal's *Black Athena*, with its accusation of racism in the conduct of European historiography, particularly in the treatment of the relationship between Europe and Egypt, has dealt a devastating blow to the pose of objectivity in the conduct of scholarship.[3] Despite this controversy, or perhaps because of it, the peculiar position of Egypt in the imaginations of the Greeks and Romans and its role in the classical world continue to be a subject of the greatest interest. I wish to contribute to this discussion by looking at the role Egypt plays in the so-called Greek romances, prose narratives of love and adventure that were composed during the Roman empire. I will begin by selectively sketching ideas about Egypt in Greek and Roman letters as a context for my remarks.[4]

Greek Views of Egypt

References to Egypt occur in practically every classical author, but it would not be correct to say that Egypt was "central" to the

Greco-Roman world. Indeed, marginality is paradoxically central to classical views of Egypt.[5] The most important classical source on Egypt is Herodotus' account in a long digression from his discussion of the Persian Wars, a digression that takes up the entire second book of the *Histories*. Herodotus' many factual errors have long been recognized, such as his incorrect dating of the pyramid builders by a thousand years, but these are the least of his faults. A. B. Lloyd, who has written the most thorough commentary on Herodotus' Egyptian account, concludes that Herodotus "presents a view of Egypt's past which shows no genuine understanding of Egyptian history. Everything has been uncompromisingly customized for Greek consumption and cast unequivocally into a Greek mould."[6] Indeed, as François Hartog has argued, Egypt was one of many "barbarian" countries whose customs were often defined by the Greek historian as an inversion of Greek customs: "The Egyptians seem to have reversed the ordinary practices of mankind."[7] However, since barbarians in Herodotus tend to be not only inversions of Greece but also set in contrasting relation to one another, shifting and inconsistent alignments sometimes emerge. For example, Hartog takes the Scythians as an example of the "mirror" of Herodotus, in which they are negative reflections of everything Greek. Nevertheless, these same Scythians become increasingly "Greek-like" when they are contrasted to the Amazons, in order to convey the otherness of the Amazons to his Greek audience.[8] Herodotus' report of various religious outrages committed by the Persian King Cambyses in his trip to Egypt, most likely fictitious,[9] produces a surprising affinity between Egypt and Greece, since both are the pious victims of impious Persians. Herodotus, in fact, displays a deep ambivalence towards Egypt, a place that is simultaneously fascinating and repulsive. To Herodotus, Egypt is a land of enormous antiquity, much older than Greek civilization, a land of ancient wisdom, the source of Greek religion, particularly the names of the gods, and most of all a land full of wonders: natural ones, such as the Nile river, and even more impressive man-made ones, such as the pyramids. However, as Phiroze Vasunia notes, Herodotus could conceive of no way these colossal monuments could have been executed without slave labor, which contributed to another key cliché about Egypt, its inclination towards despotism. From a political standpoint, Egypt could not for Herodotus be a school for democratic Greece.[10] At the same time, the great antiquity of Egypt is wedded to an emphasis on its immutability, so that Greece's progressiveness is frequently contrasted with the static character of Egyptian civilization. Just as Egypt is neither Europe nor Asia, but a place through which each passes on the way to the other, Egypt is also strangely out of the temporal stream in which the events of Europe and Asia lie.[11]

Two Greek tragedies centralize Greek-Egyptian comparisons, the *Suppliant Women* of Aeschylus and the *Helen* of Euripides.[12] The first involves the story of the descendants of Io, the Argive woman impregnated by Zeus. She traveled to Egypt in the form of a cow and there gave birth to Epaphus, whose descendants ruled Egypt and then founded numerous important cities in Greece. This kind of story, whose rationale seems to be the desire to make a claim of relative priority, will reappear in different guises, as will varying claims about the relative antiquity of Egypt and Europe. Aeschylus' play recounts the flight of the fifty daughters of Danaus (the Danaids) from their fifty first cousins, the sons of Aegyptus, and their supplication of the king of Árgos for protection. The sons of Aegyptus are represented in the play by a number of negative stereotypes: their blackness is emphasized and associated with death; they are savage and lustful, and, along with the Danaids, have no appreciation of the democratic institutions of Greece, expressing surprise, for example, that the king must consult a deliberative body of Greek citizens instead of simply acting on his own advice. The Argives, on the other hand, are represented as the protectors of women against these oversexed Egyptians.

The *Helen* of Euripides recounts an alternative version of Helen's whereabouts during the Trojan War, namely that she spent the 10 years of the war in Egypt. Herodotus cites an account he received from the Egyptian priests at Memphis, who claimed that Helen had been kept by the good king Proteus, the type of the generous host, until the rightful husband could come for her (*Histories* 2.113-15). In the *Odyssey*, Proteus is a mythical monster whom Menelaus encounters in Egypt on his way home from Troy. He is the Old Man of the Sea, whose wisdom is accessible only to those who can hold him fast while he changes his form (*Od.* 4.351-570). In Euripides' version when Menelaus is shipwrecked in Egypt on his way home, he discovers that the real Helen has been there all along, while Greeks and Trojans had been fighting over a phantom double. In this telling, however, Proteus' son, Theoclymenus, is king; but he turns out to be another lustful Egyptian trying to have Helen for himself. Not the generous host, but the xenophobic murderer who customarily kills strangers who land on his shore, Theclymenus is similar to the sons of Aegyptus in

Aeschylus' play, from whose rapacious grip the good Greek men must wrest their women. Such stories clearly reflect more about the anxieties of Greek men than they do about real Egyptians.

The figure of Proteus is one of many importations into the Egyptian king lists of Greek figures. Another king manufactured by the Greeks is Busiris, whose name is likely a corruption of the name of the god Osiris.[13] This Busiris was the negative image of the good host Proteus; he was reputed to kill foreigners and eat them, an instance of the notorious xenophobia of the Egyptians. Without mentioning Busiris by name, Herodotus notes the tale as an example of the silly stories Greeks make up about Egyptians (*Hist.* 2.45). Nevertheless, Egyptian xenophobia, frequently connected with cannibalism, persists as a stereotype of Egyptians to the very end of antiquity.[14] In the fourth century Isocrates makes a mock defense of Busiris, which praises him as a master administrator of the affairs of Egypt, and a model of good government for Greece:

> As for the arrangement by which they preserve their kingship and the rest of their state, they do so well that the philosophers who attempt to discuss such things and are most highly regarded choose to praise the Egyptian state, and the Spartans manage their city best when they imitate some part of the Egyptians' practice.[15]

The parodic context of this quote makes it unlikely that this uncharacteristic expression of admiration by the usually Athenocentric Isocrates is heartfelt. It is more likely, as Vasunia argues, that this represents an engagement with the ideas of Plato on good government. In the course of the fourth century, a more positive evaluation of monarchy in the philosophical tradition is reflected not only in greater praise for Sparta, but also for Egypt for displaying the stability associated with strong central rule.

Plato's own relationship to Egypt is complex and ambivalent, but certain key themes can be highlighted. In the narrative of the story of Atlantis in the *Timaeus* and *Critias*, Plato reverses the relative chronology of Egypt and Athens; but the Athenians must learn this true history from the Egyptians, because only they have the technical resources to preserve the memory of the distant past. However, superior Egyptian documentary skills do not themselves participate in Plato's own greater philosophical project, as is evident from the critique of Egyptian writing in the famous story of the *Phaedrus*.[16] Thus when Solon the lawgiver is told by the Egyptians in the *Timaeus* that the original Athens had a government that was identical to the ideal one described in Plato's *Republic*, this is Plato's way of using the "cultural capital" of Egypt to his own purposes. If Plato's own antidemocratic sentiments make the authoritarian government of Egypt an apparent ally in his ideas about kingship, it should be emphasized that neither his ideas about Egyptian government, nor those of Isocrates, reveal a genuine understanding or sympathy for contemporary Egypt, which for most of the classical period was ruled by the Persians. Although traditions about Greek intellectuals and lawgivers making trips to Egypt, where they were schooled in Egyptian wisdom, grew to include Plato himself, it is striking the degree to which Egypt was an *idea* for the Greeks, manufactured for their own purposes, rather than a contemporary reality which they confronted on its own terms.

Greeks and Egyptians in the Hellenistic Era

With the conquest of Egypt by Alexander the Great in 332 BC, the relationship between Greeks and Egyptians intensified and changed. After the death of Alexander the Ptolemaic, rulers of Egypt who succeeded him seemed to be intent on maintaining class and ethnic distinctions, but they also made significant gestures to present themselves as restorers of Egyptian institutions dismantled by the Persians and as continuers of Pharaonic traditions. In the three centuries of Ptolemaic rule the center of gravity of Greek intellectual life shifted toward Alexandria, with its famous library and generous patronage by the rulers of Egypt. Greek interest in Egypt was fueled by greater contact and greater familiarity with Egyptian sources. A number of new historical works were composed at this time in Greek, such as the *Aigyptiaca* of Hecateaus of Abdera and the *Aigyptiaca* of Manetho, both now lost except for excerpts and epitomes. The latter author was an Egyptian writing in Greek, who critiqued other Greek writers and presented accounts of events such as the colonization of Greece that were more favorable to Egypt. He also insisted on the antiquity and priority of Egypt in respect to a number of important cultural phenomena.[17] Hecataeus of Abdera centralized the story of Io and her descendants in his account, likewise reasserting the chronological priority of Egypt and emphasizing the cultural contributions that Egypt had made to world history. He was also the first to interpret Egyptian myths as the distorted records of mortal kings who were deified after their death, which is part of a more general tendency to insist on the underlying rationality of Egyptian culture.[18] This is an important development because it contributed to the sense that Egyptian tradition was a body of wisdom that needed to be interpreted allegorically, a course that would lead eventually to the hermetic corpus of literature in late antiquity.

Recent scholars have seen in the context of this intensified contact and mutual interest between Greeks and Egyptians of the Hellenistic era the development of a new aesthetic, which Susan Stephens calls "Seeing Double."[19] In this view Hellenistic Greek literature tends to straddle Greek and Egyptian audiences and cultural assumptions in certain ways that provide for a dual reading of them. The overwhelmingly Greek tradition of allusion and material found in this literature is sometimes adapted in ways that make provision for an Egyptian way of looking at things. One example Stephens gives is from the so-called *Alexander Romance*, a text that in the form that has come down to us is a compilation from the third century of the common era, but whose first chapter most scholars agree must go back to the beginnings of the Ptolemaic dynasty. This part of the narrative recounts how Nectanebo II, the last indigenous pharaoh of Egypt, travels to the Macedonian court where he ensconces himself as a magician and astrologer. By magic and ruses, he manages to sleep with Olympia, Philip's queen, convincing her that she will become impregnated by the god Ammon and give birth to a son. In time Olympia becomes pregnant with Alexander who as a man seeks out the truth about his paternity at the oracle of Ammon in Siwa. There he is confirmed to be the son of Ammon, who instructs him to found the city of Alexandria. In Memphis, however, Alexander sees a statue of Nectanebo II with an inscription predicting the fugitive king's return as a youth. Alexander recognizes himself as the fulfillment of the prophecy and explains his lineage publicly. From a Greek perspective, the fashioning of Alexander's invasion of Egypt as a "return" recalls the myths of the descendants of Io who "return" to Greece from Egypt.[20] But at the same time there seem to be too many fathers in this scenario—is Alexander the son of Ammon or Nectanebo? However, as Stephens points out, the scenario is one that is perfectly comprehensible from an Egyptian perspective, where the pharaoh is always the son of a mortal father, but at the same time a manifestation of the god on earth, the living Horus. Rather than a piece of Egyptian propaganda, as it is often thought to be, Stephens sees the story as a Greek invention to insert

Alexander into the political and religious traditions of Egypt, "a narrative that Egyptians and Greeks could recognize as possessing features not only of their own culture but of both cultures."[21]

Another interesting example is Stephen's reading of the seventeenth *Idyll* of Theocritus, which is an encomium of Ptolemy II. She again identifies a number of intriguing combinations of Greek and Egyptian themes, deployed here to clarify issues of kingship in the early Ptolemaic context. Two points are noteworthy here. First, is the emphasis on the feminine side of the family, which is not a Greek trait. The special attention given to the loving marriage of the parents of Ptolemy II derives from Egyptian ideas of kingship, wherein such unions produce true and legitimate sons (*Id.* 17 38-40). In the poem, Aphrodite is fashioned as the goddess who oversees such ideal unions, which is most likely a reflection of her identity with Isis, who is, unlike the Greek version of Aphrodite, the ideal wife. It is well-known that one of the innovations of the Greek romance is to represent true love as a mutual desire between two people of equal status, a "sexual symmetry" that eventuates in marriage and permanent happiness.[22] Although it perhaps goes too far to suggest that the origin of this idea is to be sought in Egyptian ideas about love and marriage, the least that can be said is that the interpenetration of Greek and Egyptian culture may have contributed to making the idea more acceptable to Greeks. The other noteworthy Greek theme in the poem that is enriched by Egyptian ideas has to do with revivifying unguents. Aphrodite revivifies Berenike, the wife of Ptolemy I, in ways that combine Greek themes of the miraculous preservation of corpses by the gods with Egyptian ideas of embalming as a prelude to reanimation and the arousal of erotic desire. Mummification was one of the exotic traditions which made Egyptians seem to the Greeks bizarre and excessively preoccupied with death—for Greeks, bodies were for burying or burning. Herodotus' account of the practice in a virtuoso passage includes the statement that the Egyptians had to take special steps in order to make sure that young and beautiful corpses were not subjected to necrophilia (*Histories* 2.86-9). The way that Stephens reads Theocritus' poem suggests a greater understanding among his Greek audience of the true character of Egyptian practices with regard to the dead. Although there are plenty of counter-examples which attest to hostility between Egyptians and Greeks, these gestures of accommodation between Greeks and Egyptians lay the groundwork for an Egyptian-Greek symbiosis in the context of Roman domination of the Mediterranean.[23]

Views of Egyptians in the Roman Period

The Ptolemaic era ends with the death of Cleopatra VII and the annexation of Egypt into the Roman empire as a province in 30 BCE.[24] Although Romans sometimes expressed curiosity about Egypt in the Republican era, there is a dramatic change as Egypt becomes a province. Rome's rule in Egypt was one of its most unsuccessful ventures, and there was persistent mutual hostility and mistrust between Romans and Egyptians. The Egyptians "experienced a qualitative change in repressive policy beginning with the principate of Augustus which imposed rigid restrictions on upward social mobility."[25] Literary sources from the Augustan period on tend to repeat a number of negative clichés and topoi: the treacherous murder of Pompey by Ptolemy XIII, the pernicious attack on the state by the dangerous and seductive Cleopatra, the bizarre worship of animals, Egyptians as cowardly Orientals and barbarians, etc. In his victory ode to Augustus on the defeat of Cleopatra, Horace concludes with a famous coda which seems to make the Egyptian queen sympathetic, but the middle stanzas of the poem are a catalogue of negative stereotypes of Egyptians (*Odes* 1, 37).[26] Other Augustan poets, such as Vergil and Ovid, also reference Egypt in purely negative terms, but the most outrageous attack is found in Juvenal's fifteenth satire, which is a withering example of Juvenalian *indignatio* prompted by a supposed instance of Egyptian cannibalism.[27] In these sources emphasis is often placed on the seditiousness of the Egyptians, which no doubt reflects a major context in which Romans ever thought about Egypt, for whom the province was simply a land "to be exploited methodically and efficiently."[28]

Some Greek authors of the Roman period followed suit, especially those who had achieved success in the Roman administration, such as Cassius Dio, who was a Roman senator, consul and governor in the second century of the common era; Reinhold considers him second only to Juvenal in his contempt for Egyptians. But the Greek tradition tends to be more positive toward Egypt in general. Strabo's account of Egypt in the seventeenth book of his *Geography* was written in the Augustan period and from a distinctly Roman persepective. Strabo himself visited Egypt, but after it had become part of the Roman Empire, and he sees Egypt with the eyes of an official, "noting the setting up of good Roman order."[29] The other surviving Greek description of Egypt from this period is Book 1 of Diodorus Siculus' *Library of History*. Diodorus, a compiler and epitomator, is our main source for Hecataeus of Abdera and other Hellenistic historians, although he himself visited Egypt some time between 60-56 BCE. Unlike Strabo, Diodorus is interested in the cultural and religious dimensions of Egypt. Chaeremon of Alexandria, a tutor of the emperor Nero, wrote two books on Egypt, now lost, which extended the allegorizing tendencies of Hellenistic authors in order to show that Egyptian myths were in essential agreement with the main theses of Greek philosophy. His work helped to legitimate the search for the secret wisdom of the Egyptians that was carried out in works like Plutarch's *On Isis and Osiris*, Iamblichus' *On the Mysteries of Egypt*, and the hermetic corpus.[30] In late antiquity, as Hartog notes, it was mostly the religious dimension of Egypt's profile that dominated discussion of that land.[31]

Before turning to the Greek novels, some mention should be made of the only Latin work that seems to provide a serious and positive evaluation of Egyptian religion, the eleventh book of Apuleius' *Golden Ass*, from the second century of the common era. The novel seems to be an adaptation of a Greek original that told a humorous story about a man turned into an ass, and his subsequent adventures before reassuming his human shape. The original is now lost, but an epitome survives among the works of Lucian. Apuleius has apparently added to this story a final book describing the character's redemption and initiation into the rites of Isis and Osiris. This final book is so different from the rest of the novel in tone and topic that religious scholars, like J. Gwyn Griffiths, have assumed that it is a serious representation of a true experience tacked on to an immoral tale. It is taken by these scholars to be an accurate source for details about the religion of Isis.[32] However, not everyone agrees that the ending is so serious or that the rest of the novel is so immoral. Ingenious attempts to provide a comprehensive view of the novel that would knit together its two disparate parts have so far failed to win consensus. Daniel Selden, however, has argued that the genre of the novel is typified by the figure of speech known as *syllepsis*, which is characterized by a yoking of two incompatible orders, an insistence on "both" rather than "either/or."[33] This is precisely the characteristic that Selden and Stephens have subsequently identified as animating Hellenistic poetry, there associated with the encounter by Greek poets of Alexandria with the both/and logic of Egyptian mentality.[34]

At this point, I would like to quote part of the conclusion of

Versluys' thorough discussion of Roman attitudes towards Egypt. He gives a more nuanced view of the subject by reference to the visual material available, which shows that Egypt played an important *cultural* role in Rome. That is, despite their animosity toward contemporary Egyptians, the Romans were obviously fascinated with Egyptian realia and religion. He then continues:

> In order to let Rome remain the ideal center of the world, there also had to be negative properties to counterbalance these dominant [Egyptian] influences. Amongst others for these reasons the unreliability of the Alexandrians is emphasized and not the cultural prestige of the city; the Isis cult is associated with shady amorous practices and not with the immensely popular goddess whose *Navigium Isidis* ceremony coincided with the official opening of the Roman shipping season, etc. A similar reaction can be observed with regard to the Greeks and Greek culture. The conceptualization of the Greeks, as reflected in the literary sources, is in general distinctively negative as well, and an attempt is thereby also made to have their merits have nothing to do with contemporary Greece and the Greeks in the Roman reality.[35]

In turning to the image of Egypt in the ancient novels, it is important to remember the way that, in negative stereotypes perpetuated by Romans, the Greeks often find themselves lumped together with Egyptians as "Orientals." One of the ways that Romans negotiated their own ambivalence towards the Greeks was to make a distinction between "classical" Greece and contemporary Greece, the latter having none of the fame of their ancestors, a maneuver that both Greeks and Romans frequently turned against Egypt as well. It was suggested by Moses Hadas that the ancient novel's origin could be traced to the desire of marginalized ethnic and religious groups to represent themselves in a more positive light, as an act of cultural resistance to Roman political hegemony;[36] and this has been advanced as a rationale for literary developments in the renaissance of Greek letters in the Roman period, the so-called "second sophistic," the period that is contemporary with the flowering of the novel.[37] The extant Greek novels studiously avoid making reference to the Roman political realities of their own day. They do, however, make frequent reference to

Egypt and Persia, which, like Greece, are cultural powers from the past that are now politically marginalized. Is it possible to see a latent anti-Roman sentiment expressed in the peculiar alignment of Egypt and Greece that sometimes emerges in the novels? Such an alignment is taken for granted in the many calumnies directed at "Alexandrians" catalogued by Reinhold, a term that often lumps together a variety of ethnic backgrounds in this multicultural city.[38] It is perhaps in this context that we must understand the persistence in the novels of the "herdsmen" of the Delta region, infamous as political resistors to Roman hegemony in the second century of the common era. These "herdsmen" (*boukoloi*) seem to be a privileged example of the inter-penetration not only of Greek and Egyptian sources, but also of fictional and historical texts.[39] Although it is no longer thought that the novel genre arose directly from Egyptian literature, the more modest claim that certain interpenetrations between Greek and Egyptian literature occurred in them seems much more securely established. And it is perhaps the very porousness of the novel "genre" itself (or "anti-genre," as Bakhtin calls it), its ability to absorb and juxtapose hetero-geneous elements in various "sylleptic" combinations, that makes it the privileged form for this interpenetration.

Egypt in the Greek Novels

I would like to turn now to the Greek novels that make reference to Egypt and explore in a preliminary fashion, the metaphorical reso-nances that Egypt has in them, in order to see what those resonances can tell us about the literary aims of our authors. The five extant Greek novels span the first to the third centuries of the common era. They share a handful of basic characteristics, including heroes who are beautiful and chaste young lovers, separated and reunited at the end in legitimate marriage.[40] The emphasis on fidelity and reciprocal hetero-sexual love is remarkable and has been viewed as part of a shift in cul-tural ideals.[41] Despite these similarities, aspects of plot among the individual novels, as well as tone and style, vary widely. Theories about the origin and purpose of the genre have sometimes focused on Egypt or on the mystery religions of Egypt, but these ideas have not gained wide acceptance.[42] The novels draw on a number of Greek nar-rative traditions—epic, drama, history—but it is their heterogeneity that is paramount, and the proper paternity of the novel has never been adequately identified: it may even be the wrong question to be asking.[43] Exactly how or to what extent they circulated in antiquity is also a difficult question to answer; but earlier theories that they were a "popular" literature for naive audiences (youth or women) have found no more acceptance than religious interpretations.[44] The novels have persistently proved impervious to monolithic readings of their purposes, and this multiplicity and heterogeneity is central to my own view of them. Of the extant novels Longus' *Daphnis and Chloe* does not involve travel and makes no explicit reference to Egypt. I will look at each of the other four novels in turn.[45] In general, it will be seen that Egypt retains an ambivalence in the novels: often the site of excessive cruelty and barbarism, Egypt is also the site of religious wisdom and mystery that can have a more positive valuation. It may be, as Brioso Sánchez has argued, that it is precisely this combination of popular interest in the wonders of Egypt and the shady reputations of Egyptians themselves that made Egypt an attractive locale for stories of adventure.[46] In any case, the political impotence of Egypt in Roman times, linked with its rich cultural heritage, creates a parallel to the situation of the Greeks themselves, particularly for the "Hellenized barbarians" who authored the novels.

M. Bakhtin speaks of the abstractness of space and time in these novels in the following way: "All adventures in the Greek romance are governed by an interchangeability of space; what happens in Babylon could just as well happen in Egypt or Byzantium and vice versa."[47] Chariton's *Chaereas and Callirhoe* (ca. 1st C CE) is typical of Bakhtin's point. The story begins in Syracuse near the end of the fifth century, then travels to Miletus in Asia Minor, to the capital of the Persian empire in Babylon, then to Syria and Egypt. The Persians prove to be more dangerous to the hero and heroine than the Egyptians in this story, but they are all for the most part basically Hellenic in their manners and aspirations. Certainly there is no problem acknowledged for Egyptians, Greeks and Persians in understanding each other.[48] At the end of Book 7, the "innate fear of royalty" of the Egyptian guard is referenced as an assumption that Greeks could make about Egyptians; and similar remarks are made about the servility of Persian characters as well, so there is an underlying "Hellenic bias" in the novel. Books 6-7 recount an Egyptian revolt against the Persian empire, which the hero Chaereas exploits to regain his wife from his rivals Dionysius of Miletus and the Great King of Persia. This revolt seems to draw certain details from several real Egyptian rebellions in the classical period, in some of which Greeks and Egyptians were allies against the Persians.[49]

These historical parallels make it seem natural for the Greek hero to side with the rebellious Egyptians against the "tyrannical" Persians. Prominent in the forces led by Chaereas are the 300 Dorian Greeks, who are clearly meant to recall the 300 Spartans who defended Thermopylae against the Persians in the zenith of Greek political power. However, Chaereas also leads the Egyptian fleet to victory against the Persians, and they return to Syracuse with him and are rewarded with parcels of land. Rome is not a force in the Mediterranean at the putative setting of the action in classical Greece, but nevertheless it is evoked indirectly in several ways. D. R. Edwards has argued that Chariton's representation of Aphrodite, the patron goddess of his home city Aphrodisias, as the deity "whose power encompasses even the Roman empire" is a strategy for asserting that city's prestige in the Roman world.[50] K. Haynes suggests in the conclusion of her study of the novel that the scenario of a heroine resisting overwhelming force expresses a resistance to Roman hegemony, sometimes itself expressed iconographically in sexual terms.[51] J. Alvares has identified a number of elements in the novel's cultural and political setting that would recall realities of the Roman empire. This description of Persian settings by means of Roman detail "would have encouraged some readers to see in the events narrated by Chariton a meaningful commentary on Roman-era conditions."[52] Alvares calls attention to the phrase with which Chaereas introduces himself to the Egyptian king as an especially res-onant moment (7.2.4): "The Persian King has tyrannized me too." It is unlikely that Chariton has a primarily political agenda in this story; but at the same time his choice to make a sudden, if only partially success-ful, revolt by Egyptians against an oppressive "evil empire" central to the resolution of his love story could indicate a certain enthusiasm for the discomfort of contemporary ruling powers. Even though the Egyptian revolt fails, the Greek hero gets the better of the Great King in part by strategically siding with his "enemy's enemy."

Unlike Chariton, Xenophon of Ephesus makes no effort to anchor the setting of his novel, *An Ephesian Tale*, in any particular time frame, although there are some indirect references to the author's con-temporary world of the second century Roman empire.[53] The geogra-phy of the novel is rather vague and abstract, predicated on the needs of the story rather than any strong desire for authenticity in details, although the author's knowledge of the delta region is quite accurate.[54] There are several episodes in books 4-5 that take place in Egypt, and it is easy to see why they have inspired religious interpretations of the novel. The hero Habrocomes is crucified twice, but each time he is miraculously saved by the gods of Egypt, who are called *philanthropotatos*, "most generous to men" (*Eph.* 4.2.4; 5.4.10). The heroine, meanwhile, is buried alive together with wild dogs, but survives this ordeal as well.[55] Equally significant is the account of an important secondary figure, Hippothous, who is a man of means compelled to turn to a life of crime as the result of a disastrous love affair. Although his actions in the story are thoroughly discreditable, he is associated with the hero, who joins his band temporarily at one point. Moreover, Hippothous is redeemed at the end of the novel as part of the happy ending; and therefore, unlike the hero and heroine, he is transformed by his experiences in the novel. His brigand career takes him all the way to upper Egypt, where it is specified that he and his men operate out of caves. After a number of adventures, Hippothous finally flees Egypt and gives up his brigand ways, and it is tempting to see his Egyptian career as a kind of symbolic death and resurrection parallel to that of the heroes' more literal brushes with death: "Hippothous descends into caves as though into the realm of the most dreadful abjection and death, finally emerging from this moral and social degradation to reenter society and legality and to take up a new living standard."[56] Again, the novel is not primarily a religious text, anymore than Chariton's is primarily a political one; but Egypt is emerging as a potent metaphorical element that can be deployed with complex resonances.

This is certainly the case with the most peculiar figure in the whole story: the fisherman, Aigialeus. He is a Spartan exile and a man whose story of mutual and reciprocal passion for his wife, Thelxinoe, is also a parallel of sorts to the hero and heroine. After falling madly in love and escaping Sparta together in order to flee social censure of their passion, they lived together poorly, but happily, in exile in Sicily. Now years later, he has preserved his dead wife "in the Egyptian manner," (*etethapto taphei Aigyptiai*) and "continues to speak with her and lie down with her [!], and sees her as she used to be" (*Ephesiaca* 5.1.10-11). This scene links Egyptian mummification with necrophilia, a link that goes all the way back to Herodotus, and is one of the practices that quintessentially differentiates the Egyptians from Greeks and Romans. However, Habrocomes' reaction is somewhat surprising: He sees Aigialeus as an inspiring example of love that transcends death and it spurs him on to continue seeking Anthia:

Anthia, when will I ever find you, even as a corpse? The body of Thelxinoe is a great comfort in the life of Aigialeus, and now I have really learned that true love knows no age limits. (*Eph.* 5.1.12)

Habrocomes seems to be especially capable of what Stephens calls "seeing double," able to see not only a Greek perspective, in which bodies are for burying or burning, not for preserving or having sex with, but also an Egyptian perspective, in which mummification is a preoccupation not with death, but a celebration of life. In a reciprocal gesture a few pages later, Anthia prays to Isis in Memphis either to restore her to Habrocomes or to make her "faithful to his corpse" (*Eph.* 5.3.4: *sophronousan toi nekroi*). Once again an Egyptian context sounds the theme of permanent mutual fidelity that David Konstan has argued is so central to this novel.[57] Alongside other strategies Xenophon employs to articulate this difference, we can add the introduction of this "Egyptianized Spartan" living in Sicily, whose practices can be read both as excessive and utopian.

The middle section of the novel of Achilles Tatius, *Leucippe and Clitophon*, takes place in the Delta region of Egypt, at Pelusion and then Alexandria. Achilles also avoids mention of the Romans and evokes a Hellenized Mediterranean world. Achilles Tatius is remarkable for the large number of descriptive passages he includes on the wonders of Egypt (phoenix, the Nile, crocodiles, etc.), in what seem to be digressions unrelated to the course of the story. Plazenet has argued that these descriptions must be understood in terms of the rhetorical tradition of commonplaces, so that they provide a means for Achilles Tatius to formulate a critical discourse on the writing of fiction.[58] Plazenet's reading of these scenes reminds us of the degree to which Egypt is, for both Romans and Greeks, a place of the imagination, a literary *topos*, despite the increase in real knowledge about the place from travel.

In the story, the two young lovers flee to Egypt from their parents in Tyre, together with two other characters, one of whose tragic gay love story has been recounted in the first part of the book. They encounter in their travels an Egyptian character, Menelaus, who is Egyptian only in the lightest sense. He tells his own tragic gay love story, which led to the exile from which he is now returning to Egypt after three years. His name cannot but recall his famous Homeric namesake and his episode in Egypt, where he acquired, depending on the account, either secret knowledge or his wife back. In a discourse on the relative merits of love objects, the novelistic Menelaus vigorously defends the love of boys against the love of women, wherein he shows himself to be well-versed in Greek philosophical discussions of the subject.[59] Generic considerations once again make it difficult to attach too much seriousness to this scene, but some ironies emerge when the scene is considered in the context of Greek Egyptology. Menelaus the Egyptian defends a supposedly more traditional form of love, which is, somewhat surprisingly, claimed to be something more current (*Leucippe and Clitophon* 2.35.2: *epichoiraze nun*), recalling the numerous reversals in relative chronology of Egyptian and Greek culture. At the same time, the passage suggests how Egypt has come metaphorically to represent an interior space, so that a trip to Egypt can be seen as an encounter with a prior intellectual tradition. The two sides of the debate are certainly both parts of a Greek discourse on love, but the fact that one side is given to an Egyptian gives a kind of spatial and temporal dimension to the debate. I would like to connect that possibility with the dramatic scene at the beginning of Book 5, where the city of Alexandria unfolds before the eyes of Clitophon in a remarkable adynaton that to me clearly suggests an inner journey of sorts:

> The beauty of the city struck me like a flash of lightening. The things to see outstripped my sight; the prospects lured me on. Crossing the city center is such a long journey that you would think you were going abroad though you were staying home (*endemos apodemia*).[60]

This last expression, *endemos apodemia*, juxtaposes and fuses "being at home" and "being abroad" in a way that recalls Freud's notion of the "uncanny" (*Unheimlich*). Its occurrence here in a passage of heightened emotional effusion indeed suggests the "strangely familiar" sensation produced, in Freud's account, by an encounter with a former aspect of the self that has been estranged by repression. This portrayal of Egypt as an interior space is particularly relevant in the case of Alexandria, the key point at which the Greek world penetrated the body of Egypt politically, socially and religiously. At the same time, it recalls other "uncanny" trips to Egypt, such as that of Solon in the *Timaeus*, who discovers there long-forgotten information about the past of his city. Legendary traditions about Greek wise men going to Egypt produce a tendency to make Egypt a metaphor for an interior journey to this site of religious wisdom; but literal trips into the deserts of Egypt by the holy men of late antiquity will also make this metaphor more concrete.[61]

Finally, mention must be made of the role of the *boukoloi*, the "herdsmen" of the Delta region, in the third book of the novel. Their appearance and violent actions against the heroine here are filled with stereotypes about xenophobic and seditious Egyptians, including human sacrifice and cannibalism. Attempts to clarify the relationship between these fictional herdsmen and a variety of historical, or supposedly historical, instances of brigandage in the Delta regions, have shown a complex interpenetration of fact and fiction. A famous revolt by Egyptian *boukoloi* in the second century of the common era is reported by Cassius Dio (*Roman History* 72.4), whose account bears striking resemblances to the scene in Achilles Tatius and to a substantial fragment from the *Phoinikaka* of Lollianus. It is likely that the Egyptophobe Cassius Dio spiced up his account with some typical slander from the world of fiction. But the existence of demotic material, which also involves "herdsmen" revolting against central authority and which seems to be an example of Egyptian nationalist propaganda, complicates the picture.[62] If Cassius Dio borrowed material from a Greek tradition to spice up his story, the actual rebels in the second century may have done something similar in order to set themselves in their own native tradition of heroes. This means that the novelistic representations of the *boukoloi* might require a "bicultural" interpretation, as Rutherford has shown. In Achilles Tatius, Menelaus the Egyptian, who can speak both Greek and Egyptian, who can become initiated as a *boukolos* and who also knows how to manipulate the equipment of a Homeric rhapsode, is the one who manages the heroine's escape from the herdsmen. If the *boukoloi* in this novel are portrayed negatively for the most part, the culturally diverse Menelaus is a far more attractive character than his Homeric namesake, who, according to Herodotus, really does engage in human sacrifice in order to effect his escape from Egypt.

The final text I would like to consider is Heliodorus' *An Ethiopian Tale*. Most of this novel takes place in Egypt and the parts that take place in Greece are narrated in flashback style from within Egypt, so that this is the most Egyptian of all the novels.[63] The fictive date of the story is sometime during the Persian occupation of Egypt; the opening locale of the story is precisely identified as the site of the future Alexandria. In the course of the novel, two beautiful young lovers, Charikleia and Theagenes, travel from Greece through Egypt to Ethiopia, where they are married and installed as the rightful heirs to the throne. Two Egyptian characters, Kalisiris, a priest from Memphis, and his son Thyamis, who is the leader of a group of bandits, play major supporting roles, along with an Athenian youth, Knemon, whose own unhappy story is told in the novel. Once again we have a band of desperadoes, recognizable as the *boukoloi* of Achilles Tatius and other sources. The Persian Empire is the central authority against whom they fight in Heliodorus, and their occasional success against the Persians, who are destined to be thrown out of Egypt by the Greeks, creates a vague political alignment between Greeks and Egyptians, and later between Greeks and Ethiopians as well. The novel thus poses a spatial devaluation of the center for the periphery— whether that is the politically central Persians or even Athens, represented in the novel by Knemon and his family romance—which gives a rather negative view of Athens and its institutions.[64]

Heliodorus' initial portrayal of Thyamis and his Egyptian bandits in Book 1 alludes to a number of stereotypes about Egyptians: Charikleia's beauty vanquishes the brigand heart of Thyamis, proving that nobility of appearance triumphs over even the "harshest of natures" (*Aithiopika* 1.4.3). Charikleia also chides Theagenes for entertaining the absurd notion that she might prefer a "barbarian to a Greek" (*Aith.* 1.25.5); later in Book 1, the author notes that once embarked on a course of action, "the heart of a savage brooks no turning back"; and when a barbarian loses all hope of his own preservation, "he will usually kill everything he loves before he dies" (*Aith.* 1.30.6), this again in reference to the Egyptian Thyamis. I catalogue these *sententiae* only because in the course of the novel, there is a reappraisal of Thyamis and his Egyptian friends, who become allies of the Greek heroes against the Persians.[65] And as the Egyptians in the story become rehabilitated, the Persians, particularly the degenerate sister of the Great King himself, emerge as the real enemies of everything good and true in the world. This discovery that the "other" is really the "same" in disguise has parallels in other contexts where it serves to articulate new alliances that must be redrawn due to shifting positions.[66] Whereas in Chariton, the Egyptians are settled in Greece at the end of the story, in the *Aithiopika*, Knemon the Athenian settles in Egypt, and the Greek hero Theagenes settles in Ethiopia. It is possible to see in this "decentering" a reflection of resistance against the Roman "center," even though the fictive date of the story predates Rome's preeminence by many centuries. In addition, in another reversal of the relative cultural dependence of Greece and Egypt, Homer, that central figure in Greek culture, is repatriated to Egypt by Kalisiris' account of his origins. He makes the assertion that Homer is an Egyptian, ostensibly the son of an Egyptian priest, but actually the son of Hermes himself (*Aith.* 3.14.1-4). Knemon the Athenian finds the idea quite acceptable, based on Homer's "typically Egyptian combination of concealed meanings and sheer enjoyment in his poetry" (*Aith.* 3.15.1). G. Sandy has demonstrated that this "typically Egyptian" idea is closely connected to contemporary Neoplatonic ideas.[67] It also reflects a regular assertion by Greek intellectuals, especially in this later period: barbarian wisdom is older and profounder.[68]

Also noteworthy is the way that the priest of Isis Kalisiris is a figure for the narrator himself. Morgan notes that "the performance of Kalisiris is in many ways emblematic of the whole novel, intensely self-aware, theatrical, manipulative, enigmatic . . . . He is both a solver and setter of riddles."[69] Winkler's assessment of Kalisiris as a figure of the author focuses on the way he "goes with the flow" and allows things to emerge in their own time, in contrast to characters who violently impose their own meaning upon events.[70] Clearly we have in the figure of Kalisiris a more positive valuation of certain aspects of "Egyptianness." The stereotypes of Egyptians as passive and crafty become refigured in the character of Kalisiris as an essential component of his barbarian wisdom, a wisdom which can bring about a successful conclusion to the events in the story, even against the overwhelming forces of corrupt central authority.[71]

The superiority of Kalisiris is foregrounded in the interaction between him and Knemon during the former's long flashback narrative. The naive Knemon's lack of aesthetic distance and insatiable appetite for romance is several times noted. He repeatedly interrupts Kalisiris, asking for elaborations on parts of the story that the priest deems irrelevant; he identifies with the characters in the story so completely that his emotions rise and fall with their fortunes, exclaiming at one point that Kalisiris' narrative had made the scene so real that he thought he actually saw the two heroes in the flesh. Knemon's comic outbursts confirm to Kalisiris that he is a true Athenian, intensely interested in incidental spectacle (*Aith.* 3.1.2) Knemon insists that Kalisiris continue the story deep into the night, stating that there can never be enough of love, either in its experience or in the telling (*Aith.* 4.4.3). These barbs at Knemon, the representative Athenian in the story, should be compared to the reactions of the Delphic Greeks to Kalisiris' appearance there: They ask him questions about the wonders of Egypt, for "Greeks find all Egyptian lore and legend irresistible" (*Aith.* 2.27.3). In contrast, after seeking and hearing an account of the usual wonders of Egypt, the Ethiopian king Hydaspes is unimpressed and asserts that all these supposed Egyptian wonders are actually wonders of Ethiopia, where the Nile has its origin (*Aith.* 9.22.7).[72]

There are also several instances of a contrast made by Kalisiris between true celestial Egyptian wisdom and the base magic which Egyptians are commonly asserted to have, again at the expense of the Greek characters in the story.[73] When the Egyptian Thyamis has a dream, the author clearly condemns his interpretive attempt in which he "forced the interpretation to conform with his own desires" (*Aith.* 1.18.5). But a similar criticism is voiced by Kalisiris when he describes the Delphians' attempts to extract the meaning of the oracle, "each understanding it in a sense that matched his own wishes" (*Aith.* 2.36.1). Similarly, an old crone at the end of Book 6 uses her Egyptian magic to force information from the body of her dead son and is roundly condemned by Kalisiris for practicing this base form of Egyptian wisdom. But it is precisely this baser Egyptian magic that the heroine's adoptive father, Charikles, and the lovestruck hero, Theagenes, each request Kalisiris to use in order to enact their desires for the heroine. It is this same Charikles, a priest of Delphi, who shows up at the end of the story, accusing the now dead Kalisiris of being a charlatan and demanding satisfaction from Theagenes for his daughter's theft. Heliodorus thus goes out of his way to set up this confrontation between the priests of Delphi and Isis, so that Charikles is able to find out that Kalisiris was a holy man, not a charlatan, that he was the one assisting the fulfillment of the gods' plans, against the inappropriate private designs of the Delphic priest.

Finally, it is important to note the way that Heliodorus, via his Egyptian internal narrator Kalisiris, assimilates the Homeric tradition to his novel. As we are introduced to Kalisiris and his story in Book 2, there are numerous explicit references to Homer, particularly the Scherian episode of Odysseus. Kalisiris himself seems to be occupying the position of Odysseus telling his story, for example, when he quotes directly the opening lines of Odysseus' own flashback narrative (*Aith.* 2.21.5; cf. *Od.* 9.39). And their generous host Nausikles, who is scrupulous in respecting Zeus the god of guests and suppliants, reminds us of the good host Alcinous—his name even recalls that of the Scherian king's daughter, Nausikaa. But at the same time Nausikles is characterized as a wanderer who has "visited many cities and seen into the hearts and minds of many people" (*Aith.* 2.22.3) in a reminiscence of the opening verses of the *Odyssey*. Charikleia employs Penelope-like ruses to hold off unwanted suitors, but it is also she who dons a disguise and witnesses a necromancy scene, recalling famous episodes of the hero himself from *Odyssey* 11 and 13. And yet it is Theagenes who has a distinctive wound on his thigh from a boar hunt similar to Odysseus' (*Aith.* 5.5.2). Moreover, before meeting Kalisiris, Knemon the Athenian covers himself in leaves in the manner of Odysseus just before his episode in Scheria (*Aith.* 2.20.3; cf. *Od.* 5. 481-3). Despite the density of Homeric references, the *Odyssey* is evoked as an intertext in an inconsistent way, indicating that it is no more of a clef for decoding the meaning of the novel than the philosophical ideas about Egyptian wisdom analyzed by Sandy.

Knemon compares Kalisiris to the Homeric Proteus of Pharos: "So far I have found you just like Proteus of Pharos, not that you take on false and shifting forms as he did, but you are forever trying to lead me in the wrong direction" (*Aith.* 2.24.4). This reference to the wise old man of the sea whom legend says inhabits the water near the setting of the novel, seems like a perfect figure for Kalisiris. But we perhaps hear also an echo of Herodotus' Proteus, the good king of Memphis who protects Helen until her rightful husband can come for her. There is a kind of uncanniness in the way these allusions work in the text, suggesting provocative connections that are not fully developed in the course of the novel and thus have the appearance of interpretive dead ends. Indeed, Heliodorus himself is a slippery figure like Proteus. Insofar as it is characteristic of the novel to introduce multiple and shifting perspectives which are often resistant to monolithic readings of the meaning of the work, the idea of a secret coherence underlying the entire work is something that must be alluded to periodically, by gestures that promise an ultimate illumination to come if we just keep reading, so that reading becomes a kind of wrestling match with a Proteus-like figure. When we get to the end of the *Aithiopika*, there are a lot of fireworks and epiphanies, but nothing really that could account for the elaborate journey we have taken; for it is not the arriving, but the journey itself that is important. It is in this way that Egypt is central to this novel: it is neither the beginning nor the end, but the in-between land, the land of exile and resurrection, the land of age-old wisdom as well as charlatans, the land of twists and turns of plot and fate. Egypt in this novel reflects the conceptualization of Egypt that was destined to dominate Europe from the end of antiquity on: a mystery always to be pondered and never solved, but continuously offering itself as a pretext for contemplation and self-examination.[74]

Notes

[*] A version of this article was presented at the second Rethymnon International Conference on the Ancient Novel in Crete in May, 2003. My thanks to the conference organizers and participants for their useful suggestions, as well as to my colleague Denise McCoskey and the anonymous referees of *Alif*. It is also a pleasure for me to honor with this contribution my former colleague at AUC, Doris Shoukri.

[1] C. Froidefond, *Le mirage égyptien dans la littérature grecque d'Homère à Aristote* (Aix en Provences: Ophrys, 1971).

[2] Edward Said, *Orientalism* (New York: Pantheon Books, 1978); *Culture and Imperialism* (New York: A.A. Knopf, 1993).

[3] M. Bernal, *Black Athena: The Afroasiatic Roots of Classical Civilization* (New Brunswick: Rutgers UP, 1987-1991); Mary R. Lefkowitz and G. M. Rogers eds. *Black Athena Revisited* (Chapel Hill: University of North Carolina Press, 1996); J. Berlinerblau, *Heresy in the University: the Black Athena Controversy and the Responsibilities of American Intellectuals* (New Brunswick: Rutgers UP, 1999); David Moore, ed., *Black Athena Writes Back* (Durham: Duke UP, 2001). See also the introduction to the Arabic translation of *Black Athena* by Ahmed Etman in *Atina al-sawda'*, trans. Lutfi Abdul-Wahab et al. (Cairo: Supreme Council of Culture, 1998), 13-71.

[4] This sketch relies mainly on the following recent discussions: P. Vasunia, *The Gift of the Nile* (Berkeley: University of California Press, 2000); M. J. Versluys, *Aegyptiaca Romana* (Leiden: Brill, 2000); S. Stephens, *Seeing Double* (Berkeley: University of California Press, 2003), each with comprehensive bibliographies, because they dovetail especially well with my interests in the novels. Other excellent short accounts include F. Hartog, "The Greeks as Egyptologists," ed. Thomas Harrison, *Greeks and Barbarians* (New York: Routledge, 2002), 211-28; S. Burstein, "Images of Egypt in Greek Historiography," ed. A. Lopriero, *Ancient Egyptian Literature* (Leiden: Brill. 1996), 591-604; K. A. D. Smelik and E. A. Hemelrijk, "'Who Knows What Monsters Demented Egypt Worships?' Opinions on Egyptian Animal Worship in Antiquity as Part of the Ancient Conception of Egypt," *ANR* II 17.4 (1984): 1852-2000; C. W. Müller, "Fremderfahrung und Eigenfahrung," *Philologus* 114 (1997): 200-14; M. Futre Pinheiro, "A Atracção pelo Egipto na Literatura Grega," *Humanitas*

47 (1995): 441-68. There are other works on the subject that have not been available to me, including a dissertation at the University of Athens on the image of Egypt in Greek tragedy by Tariq Radwan (1997).

[5] S. Burstein, "Hecataeus, Herodotus and the Birth of Greek Egyptology," *Graeco-Africana: Studies in the History of Greek Relations with Egypt and Nubia* (New Rochelle: A.D. Caratzas, 1994), 3-17.

[6] A. B. Lloyd, *Herodotus, Book II* (Leiden: Brill, 1975-1988); the quote is from A. B. Lloyd, "Herodotus' Account of Pharoanic Egypt," *Historia* 37 (1988): 52. For a more dialectical view of the interactions between Greek and Egyptian intellectual traditions, see I. A. Moyer, "Herodotus and an Egyptian Mirage: The Genealogies of the Theban Priests," *JHS* 122 (2002): 70-90.

[7] Herodotus, *Histories*, 2. 35. See Hartog, *The Mirror of Herodotus*, trans. Janet Lloyd (Berkeley: University of California Press, 1988).

[8] Hartog, *Mirror*, p. 224.

[9] Smelik and Hemelrijk, "'Who Knows What Monsters,'" 1864-69.

[10] Vasunia, *Gift*, 75-109.

[11] Vasunia *Gift*, 110-35.

[12] Vasunia, *Gift*, 33-74.

[13] See M. C. Miller, "The Myth of Bousiris: Ethnicity and Art," ed. B. Cohen, *Not the Classical Ideal: Athens and the Construction of the Other in Greek Art* (Leiden: Brill, 2000), 413-42.

[14] J. J. Winkler, "Lollianos and the Desperadoes," *JHS* 100 (1980): 177-80.

[15] Isocrates, *Busiris* 17. See Vasunia, *Gift*, 183-215.

[16] *Phaedrus* 274c-275b, discussed by Vasunia, *Gift*, 146-60.

[17] Burstein, "Images of Egypt," 600-01. See D. Mendels, "The Polemical Character of Manetho's *Aegyptiaca*," eds. H. Verdin et al., *Purposes of History* (Leuven: n. p., 1990), 91-110.

[18] Burstein, "Images of Egypt," 598-99.

[19] S. Stephens, *Seeing Double: Intercultural Poetics in Ptolemaic Alexandria* (Berkely: University of California Press, 2003). Cf. D. Selden, "Alibis," *Classical Antiquity* 17.2 (October, 1998): 290-412; J. D. Reed, "Arsinoe's Adonis and the Poetics of Ptolemaic Imperialism," *Transactions of the American Philological Association* 130 (2000): 319-51.

[20] Io, who journeyed to Egypt in the form of a cow, was identified quickly with Hathor/Isis, who was often depicted as a cow.

[21] Stephens, *Seeing Double*, 72.

[22] D. Konstan, *Sexual Symmetry* (Princeton: Princeton UP, 1994).

[23] See O. F. Riad, "Théocrite entre le Sicilie et l'Egypte," eds. G. P. Carratelli et al., *Roma e l'Egitto nell'antichità classica* (Roma: Istituto poligrafico e Zecca dello Stato, 1992), 305-15.

[24] Besides the comprehensive study of Versluys on Roman Egypt cited in note 4 above, see the two collections of essays from the International Congresses on Italy and Egypt: Carratelli, G. P. et al., eds., *Roma e l'Egitto nell'antichità classica* (Roma: Istituto poligrafico e Zecca dello Stato, 1992); and N. Bonacasa, et al., eds., *L'Egitto in Italia: dall'antichità al Medioevo* (Roma: Consiglio nazionale delle ricerche, 1998). A sense of the wide range of evidence that is adduced to illuminating the complex relationship between Rome and Egypt can be gleaned from the following selection of contributions:

In *Roma e l'Egitto*: F. Abou-Bakr, "The Egyptian Testament and Roman Law," 19-25; Al-Hussein Abou el-Atta, "Heracles of Alexandria," 27-39; Abdoullatif A. Aly, "Cleopatra and Caesar at Alexandria and Rome," 47-61; F. H. El-Kadi, "The 'Cives Romani' in Egypt," 123-39 (in Arabic); H. El-Sheikh, "Roman Expeditions to the Upper Nile," 157-60; M. A. Ibrahim, "The Western Desert of Egypt in the Classical Writings of the Roman Era," 209-17; M. H. Ibrahim, "Education of Latin in Roman Egypt," 219-26; M. Manfredi, "The Influence of Egypt on Rome in the Literary Field," 253-58.

In *L'Egitto in Italia*: A. Abou-Aly, "Rufus of Ephesus and Egypt," 15-22; E. Mohamed Ahmed, "La medicina egizia nella cultura e nell'arte romana," 127-34; L. A. W. Yehya, "Clement of Alexandria versus Rome," 167-74; O. Fayez Riad, "Le théâtre hellénistique à Rome," 255-62; M. G. Mokhtar, "Rome in Sinai," 303-06; N. Tayea Hussein, "The Relation between Egypt and Rome through the Ancient Roman Lamps in the Graeco-Roman Museum of Alexandria," 521-24; H. Abou el Atta, "The Doctrine of Curability in Roman Alexandria," 537-46; Y. el Gheriani, "The Cults of Alexandria," 603-10; S. R. Redwan, "L'arrivo del culto di Iside ed Osiride a Roma," 645-52.

[25] M. Reinhold, "Roman Attitudes Toward Egyptians," *Ancient World* 3 (1980): 100. A more positive view of Roman rule is given by S. A. Bari, "Economic Interests of Augustan Rome in Egypt," eds. G. P. Carratelli et al., *Roma e l'Egitto nell'antichità classica*, 69-76.

[26] See Ahmed Etman, "Cleopatra and Egypt in the Augustan Poetry," eds. G. P. Carratelli et al., *Roma e l'Egitto nell'antichità classica*, 161-75.

[27] Negative statements by other Roman authors include Propertius, *Elegies* 3.11; Vergil, *Aen.* 8.696-700; Ovid, *Metamorphoses* 15.826-31; Lucan, *Civil War* 8.542-44.

[28] Reinhold, "Roman Attitudes," 100. See M. Giusto, "Connotazioni dell'Egitto negli autori latini," eds. G. P. Carratelli et al., *Roma e l'Egitto nell'antichità classica,* 261-64.

[29] Hartog, "The Greeks," 224.

[30] Burstein, "Images," 601-04; Hartog, "The Greeks," 226-28. See especially fragment 10 on the lives of the Egyptian priests in P. W. van der Horst, ed. *Chaeremon* (Leiden: Brill, 1987).

[31] Hartog, "The Greeks," 226.

[32] J. Gwyn Griffiths, *The Isis-book of Apuleius* (Leiden: Brill, 1975). There are references to Egypt elsewhere in the novel, beginning in the first sentence, which characterizes the work as "papyrum *Aegyptiam* argutia *Nilotici* calami inscriptam" (Egyptian paper inscribed with the sharpness of a Nilotic pen).

[33] D. Selden, "The Genre of Genre," ed. J. Tatum, *The Search for the Ancient Novel* (Baltimore: Johns Hopkins UP, 1994), 39-64.

[34] Selden, "Alibis." See also I. Rutherford, "The Genealogy of the *Boukoloi*: How Greek Literature Appropriated an Egyptian Narrative-Motif." *JHS* 120 (2000): 116-18.

[35] Versluys, *Aegyptiaca*, 440.

[36] M. Hadas. "Cultural Survival and the Origin of Fiction." *South Atlantic Quarterly* 51 (1952): 253-60. Cf. S. West, "Joseph and Asenath: A Neglected Greek Romance." *CQ* 68 (1974): 70-81.

[37] E. L. Bowie, "Greeks and Their Past in the Second Sophistic," *Past and Present* 46 (1970): 3-4; B. Reardon, "The Second Sophistic and the Novel," ed. G. Bowersock, *Approaches to the Second Sophistic* (University Park, PA: American Philological Association, 1974), 23-29; S. Swain, *Hellenism and Empire: Language, Classicism, and Power in the Greek World, AD 50-250* (Oxford: Oxford UP, 1996), 101-34. E. Finkelpearl, *Metamorphosis and Language in Apuleius.* (Ann Arbor: University of Michigan Press, 1998), discusses examples of Apuleius rewriting Roman stories from a "north African" perspective.

[38] For anti-Roman sentiment in the so-called *Acts of the Pagan Martyrs*, see H. A. Musurillo, ed. *Acta Alexandrinorum* (New York: Arno Press, 1979), 256-58.

[39] J.J. Winkler, "Lollianos," 155-81; B. C. McGing, "Bandits, Real and Imagined, in Greco-Roman Egypt." *BASP* 35 (1998): 159-83; I. Rutherford, "*Boukoloi*," *JHS* 120 (2000): 106-21; R. Alston, "The Revolt of the *Boukoloi*," ed. K. Hopwood, *Organized Crime in Antiquity* (London: Duckworth, 1999), 129-53.

[40] A good overview both of the texts themselves and the critical issues raised by them can be found in G. Schmeling, ed., *The Novel in the Ancient World* (Leiden: Brill, 1996). English translations of all major texts can be found in B. Reardon, *Collected Ancient Greek Romances* (Berkeley:

University of California Press, 1989).

The fragments are collected and translated in S. Stephens and J. J. Winkler, eds., *Ancient Greek Novels: The Fragments* (Princeton: Princeton UP, 1995).

[41] M. Foucault, *The Care of the Self*, trans. R. Hurley (New York: Vintage Books, 1986); D. Konstan, *Sexual Symmetry*.

[42] Religious origin: R. Merkelbach, *Roman und Mysterium in der Antike* (Munich: Beck, 1962), restated without apology in R. Merkelbach, *Isis Regina - Zeus Sarapis* (Stuttgart: Teubner, 1995). The view is critiqued by, among others, R. Beck, "Mystery Religions, Aretalogy and the Ancient Novel," ed. G. Schmeling, *The Novel in the Ancient World*, 131-150; Egyptian origin: J.W.B. Barns, "Egypt and the Greek Romance," ed. H. Gerstinger, *Akten des VIII internationalen Kongress fur Papyrologie* (Vienna: R. M. Rohrer, 1956), 29-36; and G. Anderson, *Ancient Fiction: The Novel in the Graeco-Roman World* (London: Croom Helm, 1984); critiqued by S. Stephens and J. J. Winkler, *Fragments*, pp. 11-18. The argument has been raised again by I. Rutherford, "Kalasiris and Setne Khamwas: a Greek Novel and Some Egyptian Models," *ZPE* 117 (1997): 203-09. M. Futre Pinheiro, "A Atracção pelo Egipto," makes the more modest claim that Egypt is a favorite *mise en scene* for Greek story-telling from Herodotus to Heliodorus, a tendency which becomes fully developed in the Greek novels.

[43] S. Nimis, "The Prosaics of the Ancient Novel," *Arethusa* 27.3 (Fall 1994): 387-411. Genre questions are reviewed thoroughly in S. Swain, "A Century and More of the Greek Novel," ed. S. Swain, *Oxford Readings in the Greek Novel* (Oxford: Oxford UP, 1999), 3-35.

[44] E. Bowie, "The Ancient Readers of the Greek Novels," ed. Gareth Schmeling, *The Novel in the Ancient World*, 87-106; M. Brioso Sánchez, "¿Oralidad y literatura de consumo en la novela griega antigua?: Caritón y Jenofonte de Efeso," *Habis* 31 (2000): 177-217 and 32 (2001): 425-61, arguing against M. Fusillo, "Letteratura di consumo e romanzesca," eds. G. Cambiano et al., *Lo spazio letteratio della Grecia antica* (Rome: Salerno, 1994) I.3, 233-73.

[45] Earlier discussions of Egypt in the novels include E. M. Smith, "The Egypt of the Greek Romance," *Classical Journal* 23 (1927): 531-37; M. Brioso Sánchez, "Egipto en la novela griega antigua," *Habis* 3 (1992): 197-215, who includes extensive discussion of the fragments. L. Plazenet, "Le Nil et son delta dans les romans grecs," *Phoenix* 40 (1995): 5-22, looks care-fully at the rhetorical topos of the Nile, which provides each author with a pretext for defining his literary goals rather than for the sake of realism.

[46] Brioso Sánchez, "Egitto," 213-15.

[47] M. M. Bakhtin, *The Dialogical Imagination*, trans. C. Emerson (Austin: University of Texas Press, 1981), 100. On Chariton's Egypt in particular, see K. de Temmerman, "Institutional Realia in Chariton's *Callirhoe*: Historical and Contemporary Elements," *Humanitas* 54 (2002): 181-83.

[48] With one minor exception at 7.2.2.

[49] P. Salmon, "Chariton d'Aphrodisas et la révolte égyptienne de 360 avant J.-C." *Chronique d'Egypt* 36 no. 72 (1961): 365-76.

[50] D. R. Edwards, "Surviving the Web of Roman Power: Religion and Politics in the Acts of the Apostles, Josephus, and Chariton's *Chaereas and Callirhoe*," ed. A. Loveday, *Images of Empire* (Sheffield: Sheffield Academic Press, 1991), 200. He notes that Aphrodite's prominent role in the Julio-Claudian family is something that the city of Aphrodisias promoted in other contexts. M. LaPlace, "Les légendes troyennes dans le "roman" de Chariton," *REG* 93 (1980): 83-125, sees a political message in parallels between Roman figures, such as Aeneas, to characters in the novel.

[51] K. Haynes, *Fashioning the Feminine in the Greek Novel* (New York: Routledge, 2003), 160-61.

[52] J. Alvares, "Egyptian Unrest of the Roman Era and the Reception of Chariton's *Chaireas and Callirhoe*," *Maia* 53 (2001): 11. See also his excellent discussion of the Egyptian revolt in "Some Political and Ideological Dimensions of Chariton's Chaireas and Callirhoe," *Classical Journal* 97.2 (Dec.-Jan. 2001-2002): 113-44; and the thoughtful discussion of S. Schwartz, "Rome in the Greek Novel? Images and Ideas of Empire in Chariton's Persia," *Arethusa* 36 (2003): 375-94.

[53] J. Rife, "Officials of the Roman Provinces in Xenophon's *Ephesiaca*," *ZPE* 138 (2002): 104-07, arguing against J. O'Sullivan, *Xenophon of Ephesus: His Compositional Technique and the Birth of the Novel.* (Berlin: W. de Gruyter, 1995), who dates the novel earlier than Chariton. F. Sartori, "Italie et Sicile dans le Roman de Xénophon d'Éphèse," *Journal des Savants* (1985): 161-86, hears in Xenophon "echoes of an anti-Roman polemic."

[54] H. Henne, H., "La Géographie de l'Egypte dans Xénophon d'Ephèse," *Revue d'histoire de la philosophie et d'histoire genérale de la civilisation* 4 (1936): 97-106; J. Schwartz, "Quelques remarques sur les *Éphési-aques*," *Acta Classica* 54 (1985): 200-03. A more generous assesment of Xenophon's "documentary value" is given by F. Sartori, "L'Egitto di Senofonte Efesio," eds. L. Crisculo and G. Geraci, *Egitto e Storia Antica dal'Ellenismo all'Età Araba* (Bologna: CLUEB, 1989), 657-69.

[55] For religious interpretations of these events, see R. Merkelbach, *Isis*

Regina-Zeus Sarapis (Stuttgart: Teubner, 1995), 356-61. Brioso Sánchez, "Egipto," 204-05, argues that Xenophon represents a break in the traditional representation of Egypt by his centralization of the religious character of the place.

56 A. Scaracella, "The Social and Economic Structures of the Ancient Novels," G. Schmeling, *The Novel in the Ancient World*, 238. On the comparison and contrast between the hero and Hippothous, see J. Alvares, "The Drama of Hippothous in Xenophon of Ephesus' *Ephesiaca*," *Classical Journal* 90.4 (1995): 393-404.

57 D. Konstan, "Xenophon of Ephesus: Eros and Narrative in the Novel," eds. J. R. Morgan and R. Stoneman, *Greek Fiction: the Greek Novel in Context* (New York: Routledge, 1994), 49-63.

58 Plazenet, "Le Nil," 12.

59 S. Goldhill, *Foucault's Virginity* (Cambridge: Cambridge UP, 1995).

60 *Leucippe and Clitophon*, 5.1.1-3. This is a precis of a longer passage that I have analyzed elsewhere: S. Nimis, "Memory and Description in the Ancient Novel," *Arethusa* 31.1 (Winter 1998): 99-122.

61 P. Brown, "The Rise of the Holy Man in Late Antiquity," *JRS* 61 (1971): 80-101.

62 Rutherford, "*Boukoloi*," 113-16.

63 For the accuracy and sources of Heliodorus' descriptions of Egypt, see P. Cauderlier, Réalités égyptiennes chez Héliodore," eds. M. F. Baslez et al., *Le Monde du Roman Grec* (Paris: Presses de l'Ecole normale supérieure, 1992), 221-31.

64 For the cultural and genealogical inversions in the novel, see T. Whitmarsh, "The Birth of a Prodigy: Heliodorus and the Genealogy of Hellenism" ed. R. Hunter, *Studies in Heliodorus* (Cambridge: Cambridge UP, 1998), 93-124. For Heliodorus' treatment of Knemon and the Greeks, see D. N. Levin, "Aethiopica III-IV: Greek Dunces, Egyptian Sage," *Athenaeum* 80 (1992): 499-506.

65 Thyamis' rehabilitation is made more plausible by the fact that he is a priest who has been driven to banditry by his scheming brother, a rare example of "social banditry" in antiquity, which is parallelled in a demotic story, the *Contest for the Benefice*. See Rutherford, "*Boukoloi*," 109-13. For "social banditry" see McGing. "Bandits."

66 See F. Jameson, *The Political Unconscious* (Ithaca: Cornell UP, 1981), 118-19, for a parallel in medieval French romance.

67 G. Sandy, "Characterization and Philosophical Decor in Heliodorus' *Aithiopika*." *Transactions of the American Philological Association* 112 (1982): 141-67.

68 Hartog, "Greeks," 224.

69 J. R. Morgan, *The Aithiopika* of Heliodorus: Narrative as Riddle," eds. J. R. Morgan and R. Stoneman, *Greek Fiction: the Greek Novel in Context*, 108.

70 J. J. Winkler, "The Mendacity of Kalisiris and the Narrative Strategy of Heliodorus' *Aithiopika*." *Yale Classical Studies* 27 (1982): 130.

71 I. Rutherford, "Kalasiris," 203-09, gives a bicultural reading of Kalisiris' name and character.

72 On the significance of this passage, see Plazenet, "Le Nil," 20-21.

73 Sandy, "Characterization," gives a full account of these instances.

74 E. Hornung, *The Secret Lore of Egypt: Its Impact on the West*, trans. D. Lorton (Ithaca: Cornell UP, 2001).

Bibliography

Alvares, J. "The Drama of Hippothous in Xenophon of Ephesus' *Ephesiaca*." *Classical Journal* 90.4 (1995): 393-404.

_____. "Egyptian Unrest of the Roman Era and the Reception of Chariton's *Chaireas and Callirhoe*." *Maia* 53 (2001): 11-19.

_____. "Some Political and Ideological Dimensions of Chariton's *Chaireas and Callirhoe*." *Classical Journal* 97.2 (Dec.-Jan. 2001-2002): 113-44.

Alston, R. "The Revolt of the *Boukoloi*." Ed. K. Hopwood. *Organized Crime in Antiquity*. London: Duckworth, 1999. 129-53.

Anderson, G. *Ancient Fiction: the Novel in the Graeco-Roman World*. London: Croom Helm, 1984.

Bakhtin, M. M. *The Dialogical Imagination*. Trans. C. Emerson. Austin: University of Texas Press, 1981.

Bari, S. A. "Economic Interests of Augustan Rome in Egypt." Ed. G. P. Carratelli et al. *Roma e l'Egitto nell'antichità classica*. Roma: Istituto poligrafico e Zecca dello Stato, 1992. 69-76.

Barns, J.W.B. "Egypt and the Greek Romance." Ed. H. Gerstinger. *Akten des VIII internationalen Kongress fur Papyrologie*. Vienna: R. M. Rohrer, 1956. 29-36.

Beck, R. "Mystery Religions, Aretalogy and the Ancient Novel." Ed. G. Schmeling. *The Novel in the Ancient World*. Leiden: Brill, 1996. 131-50.

Berlinerblau, J. *Heresy in the University: The Black Athena Controversy and the Responsibilities of American Intellectuals*. New Brunswick: Rutgers UP, 1999.

Bernal, M. *Black Athena: The Afroasiatic Roots of Classical Civilization*.

New Brunswick: Rutgers UP, 1987-1991.

Bonacasa, N. et al., eds. *L'Egitto in Italia: dall'antichità al medioevo*. Roma: Consiglio nazionale delle ricerche, 1998. See note 24.

Bowie, E.L. "Greeks and Their Past in the Second Sophistic." *Past and Present* 46 (1970): 3-41.

_____. "The Ancient Readers of the Greek Novels." Ed. Gareth Schmeling. *The Novel in the Ancient World.* Leiden: Brill, 1996. 87-106.

Brioso Sánchez, M. "Egipto en la novela griega antigua." *Habis* 3 (1992): 197-215.

_____. "¿Oralidad y 'literatura de consumo' en la novela griega antigua?: Caritón y Jenofonte de Efeso." *Habis* 31 (2000): 177-217, 32 (2001): 425-61.

Brown, P. "The Rise of the Holy Man in Late Antiquity." *Journal of Roman Studies* 61 (1971): 80-101.

Burstein, S. "Hecataeus, Herodotus and the Birth of Greek Egyptology." *Graeco-Africana: Studies in the History of Greek Relations with Egypt and Nubia.* New Rochelle: A.D. Caratzas, 1994. 3-17.

_____. "Images of Egypt in Greek Historiography." Ed. A. Lopriero. *Ancient Egyptian Literature.* Leiden: Brill, 1996. 591-604.

Carratelli, G. P. et al., eds. *Roma e l'Egitto nell'antichità classica*. Roma: Istituto poligrafico e Zecca dello Stato, 1992. See note 24.

Cauderlier, P. "Réalités égyptiennes chez Héliodore." Ed. M. F. Baslez et al. *Le Monde du Roman Grec.* Paris: Presses de l'Ecole normale supérieure, 1992. 221-31.

Delia, D. "Egyptians and Greeks." Ed. B. Titchener and R. F. Moorton, Jr. *The Eye Expanded: Life and The Arts in Greco-Roman Antiquity.* Berkeley: University of California Press, 1999. 147-54.

Edwards, D. R. "Surviving the Web of Roman Power: Religion and Politics in the Acts of the Apostles, Josephus, and Chariton's *Chaereas and Callirhoe.*" Ed. A. Loveday. *Images of Empire.* Sheffield: Sheffield Academic Press, 1991. 179-201.

_____. "Pleasurable Reading or Symbols of Power? Religious Themes and Social Context in Chariton." Ed. R. F. Hock et al. *Ancient Fiction and Early Christian Narrative.* Atlanta: Scholars Press, 1998. 31-46.

Etman, A. "Cleopatra and Egypt in the Augustan Poetry." Ed. G. P. Carratelli et al. *Roma e l'Egitto nell'antichità classica.* Roma: Istituto poligrafico e Zecca dello Stato, 1992. 161-75.

Finkelpearl, E. *Metamorphosis and Language in Apuleius*. Ann Arbor: Michigan UP, 1998.

Foucault, M. *The Care of the Self*. Trans. R. Hurley. New York: Vintage Books, 1986.

Froidefond, C. *Le mirage égyptien dans la littérature grecque d'Homère à Aristote*. Aix en Provences: Ophrys, 1971.

Fusillo, M. "Letteratura di consumo e romanzesca." Ed. G. Cambiano et al. *Lo spazio letteratio della Grecia antica*. Roma: Salerno, 1994. I.3, 233-73.

Futre Pinheiro, M. "A Atracção pelo Egipto na Literatura Grega." *Humanitas* 47 (1995): 441-68.

Giusto, M. "Connotazioni dell'Egitto negli autori latini." Ed. G. P. Carratelli et al. *Roma e l'Egitto nell'antichità classica*. Roma: Istituto poligrafico e Zecca dello Stato, 1992. 261-64.

Goldhill, S. *Foucault's Virginity*. Cambridge: Cambridge UP, 1995.

Griffiths, J. Gwyn. *Apuleius of Madauros: The Isis-Book*. Leiden: Brill, 1975.

Hadas, Moses. "Cultural Survival and the Origin of Fiction." *South Atlantic Quarterly* 51 (1952): 253-60.

Hartog, F. "The Greeks as Egyptologists." Ed. T. Harrison. *Greeks and Barbarians*. New York: Routledge, 2002. 211-28.

_____. *The Mirror of Herodotus*. Trans. Janet Lloyd. Berkeley: University of California Press, 1988.

Haynes, K. *Fashioning the Feminine in the Greek Novel*. New York: Routledge, 2003.

Henne, H. "La géographie de l'Egypte dans Xénophon d'Ephèse." *Revue d'histoire de la philosophie et d'histoire genérale de la civilisation* 4 (1936): 97-106.

Hornung, E. *The Secret Lore of Egypt: Its Impact on the West*. Tran. D. Lorton. Ithaca: Cornell UP, 2001.

van der Horst, P. W., ed. *Chaeremon*. Leiden: Brill, 1987.

Johnson, J. H. *Life in a Multi-cultural Society : Egypt from Cambyses to Constantine and Beyond*. Chicago: Oriental Institute of the University of Chicago, 1992.

Luginbill, R. "Chariton's Use of Thucydides History in Introducing the Egyptian Revolt." *Mnemosyne* 53 (2000): 1-11.

Konstan, D. *Sexual Symmetry*. Princeton: Princeton UP, 1994.

_____. "Xenophon of Ephesus: Eros and Narrative in the Novel." Ed. J. R. Morgan and R. Stoneman. *Greek Fiction: the Greek Novel in Context*. New York: Routledge, 1994. 49-63.

LaPlace, M. "Les légendes troyennes dans le "roman" de Chariton." *Revue des Études grecques* 93 (1980): 83-125.

Lefkowitz , M. and G. Rogers, eds. *Black Athena Revisited*. Chapel Hill:

University of North Carolina Press, 1996.

Levin, D. N. "Aethiopica III-IV: Greek Dunces, Egyptian Sage." *Athenaeum* 80 (1992): 499-506.

Lloyd, A. B. *Herodotus, Book II.* 3 Volumes. Leiden: Brill, 1975-1988.

_____. "Herodotus' Account of Pharoanic Egypt." *Historia* 37 (1988): 22-53.

_____. "Nationalist Propaganda in Ptolemaic Egypt." *Historia* 31 (1982): 35-55.

_____. "Egypt." Ed. E. J. Bakker et al. *Brill's Companion to Herodotus.* Leiden: Brill, 2002. 415-35.

MacMullen, R. "Nationalism in Roman Egypt." *Aegyptus* 44 (1965): 180-85.

McGing, B. C. "Bandits, Real and Imagined, in Greco-Roman Egypt." *Bulletin of the American Society of Papyrologists* 35 (1998): 159-83.

Mendels, D. "The Polemical Character of Manetho's *Aegyptiaca*." Ed. H. Verdin et al. *Purposes of History.* Leuven: n. p., 1990. 91-110.

Merkelbach, R. *Roman und Mysterium in der Antike.* Munich: Beck, 1962.

Merkelbach, R. *Isis Regina - Zeus Sarapis.* Stuttgart: Teubner, 1995.

Miller, M. C. "The Myth of Bousiris: Ethnicity and Art." Ed. B. Cohen. *Not the Classical Ideal: Athens and the Construction of the the Other in Greek Art.* Leiden: Brill, 2000. 413-42.

Moore, D., ed. *Black Athena Writes Back.* Durham: Duke UP, 2001.

Morgan, J. R. "*The Aithiopika* of Heliodorus: Narrative as Riddle." Ed. J. R. Morgan and R. Stoneman. *Greek Fiction: the Greek Novel in Context.* New York: Routledge, 1994. 97-113.

Moyer, I. A. "Herodotus and an Egyptian Mirage: The Genealogies of the Theban Priests." *Journal of Hellenic Studies* 122 (2002): 70-90.

Mirhady, D. C. and Y. L. Too, trans. *Isocrates I.* Austin: University of Texas Press, 2000.

Müller, C. W. "Fremderfahrung und Eigenfahrung: Griechische Ägyptischen-reisende von Menelaos bis Herodot." *Philologus* 114 (1997): 200-14.

Musurillo, H. A., ed. *Acta Alexandrinorum.* New York: Arno Press, 1979.

Nimis, S. "The Prosaics of the Ancient Novel." *Arethusa* 27.3 (Fall 1994): 387-411.

_____. "Memory and Description in the Ancient Novel." *Arethusa* 31.1 (Winter 1998): 99-122.

_____. "The Sense of Open-endedness in the Ancient Novel." *Arethusa* 32.2 (Spring, 1999): 215-38.

Nock, A.D. "Greek Novels and Egyptian Religion." Ed. Z. Stewart. *Essays on Religion and the Ancient World.* Oxford: Oxford UP, 1972. Vol. 2. 169-75.

O'Sullivan, J. *Xenophon of Ephesus: His Compositional Technique and the Birth of the Novel.* Berlin: W. de Gruyter, 1995.

Plazenet, L. "Le Nil et son delta dans les romans grecs." *Phoenix* 40 (1995): 5-22.

Reardon, B. P. "The Second Sophistic and the Novel." Ed. G. Bowersock. *Approaches to the Second Sophistic.* University Park: American Philological Association, 1974. 23-29.

_____. *Collected Ancient Greek Romances.* Berkeley: University of California Press, 1989.

Reed, J. D. "Arsinoe's Adonis and the Poetics of Ptolemaic Imperialism." *Transactions of the American Philological Association* 130 (2000): 319-51.

Reinhold, M. "Roman Attitudes Toward Egyptians." *Ancient World* 3 (1980): 97-103.

Riad, O. F. "Théocrite entre le Sicilie et l'Egypte." Ed. G. P. Carratelli et al. *Roma e l'Egitto nell'antichità classica.* Roma: Istituto poligrafico e Zecca dello Stato, 1992. 305-15.

Rife, J. "Officials of the Roman Provinces in Xenophon's *Ephesiaca.*" *Zeitschrift für Papyrologie und Epigraphik* 138 (2002): 93-108.

Rutherford, I. "Kalasiris and Setne Khamwas: a Greek Novel and Some Egyptian Models." *Zeitschrift für Papyrologie und Epigraphik* 117 (1997): 203-09.

_____. "The Genealogy of the *Boukoloi*: How Greek Literature Appropriated an Egyptian Narrative-Motif." *Journal of Hellenic Studies* 120 (2000): 106-21.

Said, E. *Orientalism.* New York: Pantheon Books, 1978.

_____. *Culture and Imperialism.* New York: A.A. Knopf, 1993.

Salmon, P. "Chariton d'Aphrodisas et la révolte égyptienne de 360 avant J.-C." *Chronique d'Egypt* 36 No. 72 (1961): 365-76.

Sandy, G. "Characterization and Philosophical Decor in Heliodorus' *Aithiopika.*" *Transactions of the American Philological Association* 112 (1982): 141-67.

Sartori, F. "Italie et Sicile dans le roman de Xénophon d'Éphèse." *Journal des Savants* (1985): 161-86.

_____. "L'Egitto di Senofonte Efesio." Ed. L. Crisculo and G. Geraci. *Egitto e storia antica dal'ellenismo all'età araba.* Bologna: CLUEB, 1989. 657-69.

Scaracella, A. "The Social and Economic Structures of the Ancient Novels." Ed. G. Schmeling. *The Novel in the Ancient World.* Leiden: Brill, 1996. 221-76.

Schmeling, G., ed. *The Novel in the Ancient World*. Leiden: Brill, 1996.

Schwartz, J. "Quelques remarques sur les *Éphésiaques.*" *Acta Classica* 54 (1985): 197-203.

Schwartz S. "Rome in the Greek Novel? Images and Ideas of Empire in Chariton's Persia." *Arethusa* 36 (2003): 375-94.

Selden, D. "The Genre of Genre," J. Tatum, ed. *The Search for the Ancient Novel*. Baltimore: Johns Hopkins UP, 1994. 39-64.

_____. "Alibis." *Classical Antiquity* 17.2 (October, 1998): 290-412.

Smelik, K. A. D. and E. A. Hemelrijk, "'Who Knows What Monsters Demented Egypt Worships?' Opinions on Egyptian Animal Worship in Antiquity as Part of the Ancient Conception of Egypt." *Aufstieg und Niedergang der Romischen Welt* II 17.4 (1984): 1852-2000.

Smith, E. M. "The Egypt of the Greek Romance. *Classical Journal* 23 (1927): 531-37.

Stephens, S. *Seeing Double: Intercultural Poetics in Ptolemaic Alexandria*. Berkeley: University of California Press, 2003.

_____ and J. J. Winkler, eds. *Ancient Greek Novels: The Fragments*. Princeton: Princeton UP, 1995.

Swain, S. "A Century and More of the Greek Novel." Ed. S. Swain. *Oxford Readings in the Greek Novel*. Oxford: Oxford UP, 1999. 3-35.

_____. *Hellenism and Empire: Language, Classicism, and Power in the Greek World, AD 50-250*. Oxford: Oxford UP, 1996.

Tait, J. "Egyptian Fiction in Demotic and Greek." Ed. J. R. Morgan and R. Stoneman. *Greek Fiction: the Greek Novel in Context*. New York: Routledge, 1994. 203-22.

de Temmerman, K. "Institutional Realia in Chariton's *Callirhoe*: Historical and Contemporary Elements." *Humanitas* 54 (2002): 165-87.

Vasunia, P. *The Gift of the Nile*. Berkeley: University of California Press, 2000.

Versluys, M. J. *Aegyptiaca Romana*. Leiden: Brill, 2000.

Whitmarsh, T. "The Birth of a Prodigy: Heliodorus and the Genealogy of Hellenism." Ed. R. Hunter. *Studies in Heliodorus*. Cambridge, Cambridge UP, 1998. 93-124.

Winkler, J. J. "Lollianos and the Desperadoes." *Journal of Hellenic Studies* 100 (1980): 155-81.

_____. "The Mendacity of Kalisiris and the Narrative Strategy of Heliodorus' *Aithiopika.*" *Yale Classical Studies* 27 (1982): 93-158.

Valentinus et Nomina:
Saussure, Plato, and Signification

Rondo Keele

---

1. Introduction

The first two centuries of Christianity were a time of change and explosive growth in which doctrine, ritual practice, and group identification were not everywhere firmly set in orthodox patterns, regulated by ecclesiastical authority. We learn of apocalyptic groups, Essenes, and Gnostics, all of them relatively small, intense, and (in the case of the later Gnostics) intellectually elite groups of worshipers practicing the new religion sometimes openly, sometimes in secret, in ways that troubled the emerging orthodoxy. Groups of worshipers from this period of Christian history, and especially the Gnostics, have received continuing and even increased attention in the last thirty years, as scholars have begun to cope with the fertile and sometimes startling written material found in Egypt at Nag Hammadi in 1945. Among these materials are texts by the famous Gnostic preacher and theologian Valentinus. Active in Rome in the middle of the second century, the Alexandria-trained Valentinus was an innovative, charismatic and politically prominent man, whose nearly successful election as the bishop of Rome would, had it been successful, have certainly altered the course of Christianity. Valentinus' neoplatonic and mystical inclinations strongly influenced his published writings, later carefully collected and stored at Nag Hammadi. As scholars dig through these texts, working to recover and to interpret the ancient forms of worship they reveal, they have found perhaps their greatest interpretive challenges in Valentinus' many tantalizing remarks on salvation and theology.

In particular, Valentinus' works are replete with fascinating and enigmatic claims about the salvific power of *names*. In the document that scholars call *The Gospel of Truth* (henceforth 'the *Gospel*'), we find many such puzzling remarks about names: for example, Valentinus says that names are instrumental in salvation somehow;[1] that God uses names to call beings into existence;[2] and, perhaps his most obscure and celebrated remark, that "the name of the Father is the Son."[3]

Valentinus left us little context for understanding his views on names and their power. Of course we do find in the intellectual and religious life of ancient and medieval people the idea that names can have great power, for example the *nomina sacra* of early Christianity and Judaism, which had such power that they could not be pronounced and/or written fully.[4] Nor is the phenomenon confined to the elite and literate; there is a common idea that invoking the name of God can offer protection from harm. However, there is a sense in which the *nomina sacra* of literate classes are even difficult to understand, especially for modern people. I believe this is partly attributable to our post-Saussurean framework; that is, we easily take for granted that insofar as there is anything we can recover in the mysticism of the name, it must be squared with Saussure's principle of the arbitrariness of sign. This central Saussurean tenet states that the connection between any *signifier* and *signified*, which together constitute the simple linguistic *sign*, is a fundamentally arbitrary connection; thus Saussure opposes any kind of essentialism regarding names.[5] For example, there seems to be no essential reason why the sound (for Saussure, "acoustic image") 'ox' should signify to a listener the concept of an ox. But if names are in this sense conventional, it is difficult to understand them as having power inherent in them as names, and the very idea of a *nomina sacra* seems implausible or even nonsensical.

But Valentinus seems to presuppose precisely an essential connection between names and beings in the *Gospel*: he tells us that God's name "belongs" to him in some important and unique way;[6] that nonexistents cannot even have names;[7] and, most striking, that only he who becomes acquainted can answer the salvific "call" as his name "comes to him."[8] In general, Valentinus, unlike Saussure, seems to think that particular names are connected essentially and correctly to particular objects, especially persons. Thus, it is profoundly difficult to give a straight forward and consistent post-Saussurean interpretation of the mysticism of the name which underlies Valentinus' *salus per nomina* (salvation through names), as I shall call it.

These difficulties have received important attention by scholars sympathetic to both Valentinian theology and Saussurean linguistics. One such reading of name-talk in the *Gospel* is Richard Fineman's "Gnosis and the Piety of Metaphor." Fineman embraces the inconsistency instead of being embarrassed by it, and takes the natural remedy of interpreting Valentinus as having precisely the opposite views from what he seems to on the surface, a subversion which is consistent, so he claims, with the generally subversive hermeneutic of Valentinian myth construction. Specifically, Fineman argues that "the name of the Father is the Son" is a metaphor, the existence of which is made possible by God's occlusion or 'dropping out' of the metaphor when it is analyzed. Likewise, this dropping out also performs the transcendence that characterizes God in the *Gospel*. Most strikingly, Fineman argues that this hermeneutic of transcendence and occlusion also subverts the very nominal essentialism which seems to underlie Valentinus' remarks in the *Gospel*; it is as though Valentinus anticipates Saussure in a certain way.

Although Fineman's approach seems radical in the sense that it interprets Valentinus to mean the opposite of what he overtly says, there is precedent in scholarship for validly understanding the real meaning of a text as controverting or contradicting its apparent meaning, as in irony. Still, Fineman's approach encounters serious *prima facie* difficulties, making the search for an alternative highly desirable. For while his attempt is not wildly implausible, it seems only to multiply the mysteries in Valentinian theology, by explaining an apparent commitment to nominal essentialism in terms of its contradictory opposite. Moreover, it suggests that Gnosticism was more about subversion than salvation, a result which I think conflates the irreducibly religious heart of Gnosticism with its textual style.

However, the apparent alternative to Fineman does not look all that attractive either, for it would seem to involve taking Valentinus to be a nominal essentialist (or, as I shall say, a 'nomenclaturist'), which is ultimately inconsistent with Saussure. Thus, we face an unappealing dilemma in interpreting Valentinus' *salus per nomina*: we must either go with Fineman's type of analysis, and construe Valentinus as holding the polar opposite of his apparent view of names in the *Gospel*, or else we must construe him as being in conflict with Saussure's influential principle of arbitrariness, and hence as being hopelessly linguistically naive. The single motivating assumption which keeps the tension on both horns of the dilemma is that Valentinus could not possibly have meant what he seems to mean in both a straightforward and an intellectually respectable way, because he must respect Saussure in any case.

I believe that this is ultimately a false dilemma. The dilemma seems persuasive only because it presupposes the flawed assumption that in Valentinus' time there was no respectable *theoretical* view which would allow us to imagine an alternative to Saussure's dictum of arbitrariness. In fact there was such an alternative theoretical view of language, and of names in particular, whose roots can be traced to Plato, and which offers us a conception of language and of names that makes good sense of Valentinus' *salus per nomina*.

The purpose of this article is to reconstruct this theoretical view–which I shall dub *Platonic nomenclaturism*–and then to apply it to Valentinus' remarks about names in the *Gospel*, thus developing a viable and I think superior alternative to Fineman's interpretation and avoiding the dilemma mentioned above. The remainder of the article is organized into four sections. I begin by introducing some of Saussure's most basic ideas as they relate to Fineman and Valentinus, and then proceed to examine in more detail some of the shortcomings and strengths of Fineman's views. After extracting some of what is useful in Fineman's approach, I explore the possibility of a better interpretive stance by reconstructing some of Plato's views on names as developed in the *Cratylus*. The resulting Platonic nomenclaturism is immediately applied to the *Gospel* in the subsequent section, where I develop and defend a view of Valentinian soteriology and Christology completely contrary to Fineman's.[9] I will argue that this more straight-forward reading of Valentinus makes better sense of certain sections of the *Gospel*, and suggests some very provocative readings of other Gnostic material as well.

2. Fineman's Lacanian Interpretation

Although Saussure has been very influential, and his most impor-tant views are well recognized, it is important to begin with a brief sum-mary of those Saussurean tenets most relevant for this investigation. I have chosen for this purpose a summary by David Holdcroft which seems to capture most of what is relevant in an uncontroversial way:

> Saussure was root and branch opposed to nomenclatur-ism, the view that a language consists of names whose function is to label independently identifiable objects or ideas. In opposition to this view he insists that a language is a system of signs, and that the signifying features of a sign depend on its interlinguistic relations to other signs belonging to the same system rather than on its extralin-guistic relations to pre-existing objects or ideas . . . . A sign is, for Saussure, a 'two-sided entity' consisting of the union of a signifier and a signified. A signifier is an

acoustic image, so that, for example, the signifier of the
word 'cat' is not the sound made when it is pronounced,
but an image of the sound; it is thus a psychological entity. A signified is initially identified with the concept
associated with the signifier . . . . One primordial principle governing signs maintains that they are radically arbitrary. This is so because they are unmotivated. There is
nothing about the world which makes one signifier any
more appropriate for its signified than any other.[10]

I will subsequently refer to elements mentioned in this summary as issues regarding them arise; however one general point needs to
be made right away. The relation of signification is not a Saussurean
invention, nor does it fit only with a Saussurean theory; in its most
basic form the signification of a thing is simply the establishment of
the understanding of that thing.[11] This basic relation can be cashed out
in a number of ways: as calling to mind, invoking, causing to think of,
etc. Saussure has his own particular view of signification, but his
account of this important linguistic relation is one of many.

Fineman, beginning with a Saussurean background, takes
Lacan's theory of metaphor, itself profoundly influenced by Saussure,
as the basis for understanding "the name of the Father is the Son."[12]
Treating the statement as a metaphor, and inserting the terms of the
various significations and relations between the name of the Father,
the Father, and the Son into a modified Lacanian formula, Fineman
discovers that the Father himself, in the transformative process of
metaphorization, is occluded in being named, receding beyond the
reach of reference into transcendence.[13] Even though he is occluded,
dissolving at the moment he is referred to, the Father is still referred to
in a certain sense by the structure of the whole metaphor, which his
occlusion makes possible. By making the metaphor possible with his
absence, he strangely becomes the ground of everything the metaphor
involves (its language included), and of metaphor itself.[14] It is this
dual character of absence and ultimate ground which emerges from the
metaphorization in "the name of the Father is the Son."

Since the structure of metaphor itself refers us to this transcendent,
ultimate ground, the metaphorization of text becomes holy.[15] It is for these
reasons that the Valentinian seeks to make allegories of allegories: each
such creation of allegory refers us to the glory of the transcendent God.

This interpretation, although attractive in some respects,

nonetheless has difficulty explaining other, connected references to names in the *Gospel*. For example, why, if the underlying view of language here is Saussurean, can non-existents not be named, as in the *Gospel* 39:11-15? What is to prevent the signification of the unreal? Unreal things can be called to mind by names, surely. But then how do we understand this claim about non-existents? The basic view of language on which he relies, ultimately due to Saussure, has little natural ability to explain remarks such as those about non-existents and names. Only natural nomenclaturist assumptions—which insist on a natural connection between signifier and signified—could possibly hold that naming might fail because of the non-existence of an object. Since Saussurean signs consist of a signifier which is linguistic and a signified which is mental, on the terms of his theory it is not possible for the existence of objects to affect the process of signification. But if existence cannot bear on signification for Saussure and Saussureans, then Fineman's theory cannot properly explain why non-existents cannot be named, as Valentinus insists. This is not, of course, to criticize Saussure's theory *per se*, but simply to point out that its outlook does not seem *prima facie* to fit the requirements of Valentinus' text.

In an influential article addressing similar themes, Benoit Standaert likewise glosses the question of non-existents in the *Gospel* 39:11-15. For example, Standaert unproblematically relies on this fact about naming and non-existents in 39:11-15 in explaining why "the name of the Father is the Son," as though the idea that non-existents cannot be named were somehow completely well understood. He writes: "To speak of the God as Father is to name him as such. Moreover, all which exists has a name, and that which does not have a name does not exist."[16] But the idea that non-existents cannot be named is at least as puzzling as the idea that "the name of the Father is the Son." Thus Standaert, like Fineman, is guilty of serious explanatory omissions, although Standaert at least does not explicitly rely on a view of language which directly conflicts with a common-sense understanding of the *Gospel* 39:11-15.

In summary, though Standaert rightly sees that the relationship between Father and Son as important for understanding names in the *Gospel*, he tends to gloss over puzzling passages such as 39:11-15, discussed above. Similarly, Fineman is right to have seen that signification plays a crucial role in interpreting name-talk in the *Gospel*, but his interpretation is strained because he has chosen a view of signification which is alien to Valentinus, and which is flatly at odds with what the text seems most straightforwardly to assume about the nature of signification.[17]

All this suggests that we are reading back a modern view of signification into the *Gospel* anachronistically. Thus, if a view of signification could be found which actually predated Valentinus, and which could help make good sense out of the name-talk in the *Gospel*, it would be preferable on these grounds alone. In the next section I begin to explore such a view, that of Platonic nomenclaturism.

3. Platonic Nomenclaturism: *The Cratylus*

The first step to exploring Platonic nomenclaturism is to clarify a few terminological issues about the word 'nomenclaturism.' Nomenclaturism, properly so called, is simply a view of language which privileges the naming relation. Nomenclaturism is most fundamentally a tendency to analyze the world-language relation as a naming relation, and to explain languages and linguistic function in terms of names naming things.[18] We must recognize that under the broad heading of nomenclaturism many distinct theories of language are still possible; thus it is possible to view the naming relation as the fundamental linguistic relation and hold either (1) that this relation is somehow a natural one, or (2) that it is essentially an arbitrary one (though this view would be odd indeed). Likewise, one nomenclaturist might understand the 'names' in his linguistic theory to be the constituents of fully logically analyzed propositions (as did Bertrand Russell and the early Wittgenstein), or instead as some kind of basic nouns of a particular natural language (such as the common-sense view of how we begin to teach language to children).

The point is that in labeling someone a 'nomenclaturist,' while we certainly mean to exclude certain attitudes, e.g., Saussurean or later Wittgensteinian language-game views,[19] we nevertheless leave open the question of (1) how that person construes the world-name relation in his/her theory, and even the question of (2) how many types of naming relations and types of names he/she postulates.

These qualifications being made, it must be admitted that many nomenclaturists do hold the view that there is a natural, essential connection between language and the world; let us call members of this common class of nomenclaturist *natural nomenclaturists*. Still, there remains the possibility (a possibility which Plato actualized in the *Cratylus*, as I will shortly show) that a nomenclaturist might hold the naming relation to be sometimes essential *and* sometimes conventional, unmotivated or arbitrary, *provided that she also admit the existence of two distinct classes of names*. The point is simply that one might, as a natural nomenclaturist, hold that there are two types of names, one of which connects essentially to objects, the other of which connects more conventionally, in such a way that the conventional relation is an imperfect copy of the essential relation.

I will now show that Plato himself did in fact expound such a natural nomenclaturism in the *Cratylus*. I call his view simply *Platonic nomenclaturism*, waiving the question as to whether Plato himself actually held the view, since it is clearly a line of speculation which is suggested and defended by Socrates in the *Cratylus*, and this itself justifies the appellation 'Platonic,' understood loosely.[20] Since there is good evidence to suggest that the *Cratylus* was a dialogue known to Christian intellectuals in Rome shortly after Valentinus' time,[21] it seems plausible to think that Valentinus may have been influenced by Platonic nomenclaturism, and, as I shall show, the hypothesis that this linguistic theory lies behind name-talk in the *Gospel* illuminates some of its most puzzling remarks.

The *Cratylus* is an odd dialogue in certain respects, more playful and speculative in tone than many other Platonic works. The title character believes in a simple-minded kind of natural nomenclaturism, described thus by Hermogenes, the primary interlocutor in the first half of the dialogue:

> I should explain to you, Socrates, that our friend Cratylus has been arguing about names. He says that they are natural and not conventional—not a portion of the human voice which men agree to use—but that there is a truth or correctness in them which is the same for Hellenes as for barbarians.[22]

Socrates agrees to join in the ongoing discussion on this topic, in which Hermogenes has been opposing Cratylus' naive natural nomenclaturism. Hermogenes describes his reservations thus:

> [I] cannot convince myself that there is any principle of correctness in names other than convention and agreement. Any name which you give, in my opinion, is the right one, and if you change that and give another, the new name is as correct as the old .... For there is no name given to anything by nature; all is convention and habit of the users.[23]

The two opposing views above are both naive in a certain sense: so far neither one is backed by argumentation or philosophical considerations such as would make them well thought-out theoretical positions. Thus Socrates, true to form, goes to work refining both positions through dialectic. He begins by interrogating Hermogenes, exposing weaknesses and explanatory gaps in the conventionalist position from the point of view of the natural nomenclaturist. Socrates does not end up simply defending Cratylus' natural nomenclaturism as it stands, but rather ends up staking out ground between these two positions. There is some undeniable truth to conventionalism, so he believes, but it is not entirely adequate as it stands.

In fact, the deficiencies he finds with conventionalism stem directly from its failure to account for the difference between correct and incorrect speech, i.e., between the true and the false. Socrates challenges the content of Hermogenes' view thus:

> [Y]our meaning is that the name of each thing is only that which anybody agrees to call it?
> –Yes.
> –Well, now, let me take an instance. Suppose that I call a man a horse or a horse a man. You mean to say that a man will be rightly called a horse by me individually, and rightly called a man by the rest of the world . . . that is your meaning?
> –He would, according to my view.
> –But how about truth, then?[24]

Of course, absurdity looms if this kind of situation be admitted (as Socrates goes on to show). It is important to notice two things in this passage. First, Socrates has at the outset expanded the notion of name to include names in the most general sense, as a general model for language-world relations. He is not merely interested in what we would call proper names (nor is Hermogenes, or he would have objected right away), but is rather interested in names as the basic linguistic constituent, e.g., 'horse' and 'man' are to be regarded as names. Thus, the entire issue in the dialogue is couched in terms of classic nomenclaturism; the issues at stake are between two nomenclaturist positions. Second, the difficulty Socrates raises for Hermogenes is given in terms of truth (and, as the text goes on, falsehood). If we allowed that convention alone ruled the language-world relation, then the distinction between truth and falsity would collapse, and with it the possibility of assertoric speech. Most significant for us is simply the fact that Socrates ties names directly to the question of the truth or falsity of propositions. He in fact goes on to make a strange argument to the effect that as constituents of both true and false propositions, names must themselves somehow be susceptible to having the property of being either 'true' or 'false.' Strange though this argument is, it nonetheless demonstrates that for Plato names are directly linked to issues of truth and falsity.

Since Plato is thinking of names in the most general, linguistic sense, *and* as relating directly to issues of truth and falsity for propositions, Socrates appears to be developing a kind of nomenclaturist theory in which names play a role in determining the truth and falsity of propositions. This gives us a new way to understand the claims of the natural nomenclaturist: the rightness or wrongness of names should be understood in terms of how they function to make propositions true or false. Thus, if we could tease out some of Plato's views on how propositions get to be true or false, we might gain some insight into his picture of how names connect naturally with the world. This question of propositional truth and falsity is answered by Plato, unsurprisingly, in terms of the Forms, and our examination of the topic will take us on a brief digression into the *Sophist*.

In the *Sophist*, Plato faces the difficult challenge of explaining how false speech is possible. In the course of trying to define sophists as those who says things, but not true things, a character called the Eleatic Stranger runs into the puzzle of falsity: since speaking falsely seems to require saying that which is not, and saying that which is not is really saying nothing, it follows that speaking falsely is not speaking at all. Thus, false speech seems to be impossible.[25] In the interest of defining the sophist in terms of false speech, the Eleatic Stranger and Theaetetus undertake an account which will explain how false speech is in fact possible, refuting the argument sketched above.

The solution they devise is extremely complex, and much of the detailed argumentation remains obscure, but at least this much does seem clear: five privileged and important Forms, called the *megista gene* (*that which is, motion, rest, the same,* and *the different*),[26] are used to show how certain complex relationships can hold among the Forms themselves (the Forms themselves have certain properties, after all).[27] In particular, it seems that false speech is explained by the way in which other Forms are able to relate to *that which is*, and to *the different*: their interaction with *the different* against *that which is* somehow creates a de facto form of *that which is not* (as a Form in the realm of being, *that which is not* would be paradoxical otherwise understood). Somewhat cryptically, Plato concludes:

> We've also caused what turns out to be the form of *that which is not* to appear. Since we showed that the nature of *the different* is, chopped up among all beings in relations to each other, we dared to say that *that which is not* really is just this, namely, each part of the nature of *the different* that's set over against *that which is*.[28]

This solution is usually referred to as *the parts of the different*, for obvious reasons.

Without fussing much over exactly what all this means, since I have left large amounts of detail unexplained, let us only pause over one particularly relevant structural feature of the solution. Plato introduces the idea that Forms relate to each other in complex ways, in particular that certain features common to all Forms are themselves explained in terms of other Forms (as bits of *the different* are somehow 'in' each form in virtue of their multiplicity in relation to *that which is*). That Forms can interact in such complex ways will figure importantly in what follows.

At the end of the *Sophist* the parts of the different solution is applied to speech, to explain the false proposition 'Theaetetus flies.' In this section, Plato crucially develops the insight that a proposition consists of two distinct fundamental elements: names and verbs.[29] In speech, names pick out their referents and verbs predicate things about those referents. Now 'Theaetetus flies' is false, because it predicates of a flying Theaetetus that *he is*, although a flying Theaetetus in fact is *not*.[30] Though the flying Theaetetus in the proposition *is not*, the name in the proposition insures that the proposition is still *about Theaetetus*, that is, the name in this case still names Theaetetus.[31] Plato puts this by saying that the proposition, though about what is not, is still *of something*.[32] Thus, propositions can be false and still be of something, and hence false speech is possible, *pace* the argument sketched a few paragraphs above. Plato extends this analysis to belief and thought as well, counting thought as speech made silently to oneself.[33]

The significance of this for us is as follows. Because names, together with verbs, are the constituent elements of propositions, and propositions can be objectively true or false, there must be some way in which names objectively pick out their referents. 'Theaetetus flies' is false not only because Theaetetus does not participate in the form of flying, but also because the name 'Theaetetus' picks out Theaetetus, who does not in fact fly; 'Theaetetus flies' would be true if 'Theatetus' referred to some bird. Names simply cannot be merely conventional, for if they were we would have to investigate their reference each time they were used: someone who asserts in all seriousness that 'Theaetetus flies' is not using words differently, but is rather saying something false, and we would not correct such a person by shifting our language to suit his/her idiosyncratic usage (e.g., 'Theaetetus' now picks out a bird), but rather by pointing out that it is Theaetetus who is properly called 'Theaetetus.'

What all this points to is the following idea: just as the Forms in the world of being ground the predication of concepts and properties in the world of becoming, allowing those predications to be true or false, *so too the Forms ground the correctness and incorrectness of names somehow*. Unless names had some objective ground for their signification, they could not signify either correctly or incorrectly, and, if that were the case, they would not then be able to ground the correctness or incorrectness of proposition in which they occur.

Just as the Forms in the world of being correspond to properties and concepts which imitate them imperfectly in the world of becoming (Ideas corresponding to ideas), so too there must be *real names* in the world of being which correspond to the *ordinary names* of particular distinct languages in the world of becoming.[34] If such a connection between Forms and names, similar to the one we saw in the *Sophist*, can be supported textually in the *Cratylus*, this would form the theoretical basis for a uniquely Platonic theory of natural nomenclaturism which could plausibly be hypothesized to underlie Valentinian name-talk in the *Gospel*. But is there an analogous connection between Forms and names in the *Cratylus*? As it turns out, there are many such connections made in the *Cratylus*, the sum of which leads us to the idea that there are in fact two kinds of names, corresponding to Plato's two worlds of being and becoming, and hence, I will suggest, two kinds of signification.

To find this view in the *Cratylus* we must look toward the end of the dialogue, after a long and whimsical detour into etymologies. The dialogue moves back to the general theoretical discussion, with Socrates summarizing the natural nomenclaturist position a bit differently: "Have we not been saying that the correct name indicates the nature of the thing?"[35]

Given what we have discovered in the *Sophist*, this remark gives us our most critical insight into Platonic nomenclaturism. As opposed to the particular names assigned by particular languages which signify by convention (which we shall call *ordinary names*), Socrates here thinks that correct names—which we shall call *real names*—invoke not by convention but rather through the nature of the object, which is itself determined through the Forms. Thus the suggested connection with the Forms does appear to exist, although more textual evidence is needed to fill out the case.

Socrates, using Cratylus as a sounding board, begins to fill in more detail regarding the way in which a "correct name" gets at the nature of a "thing": names, like pictures, are "imitations" of the objects they name;[36] "[b]ut if I can assign names as well as pictures to objects, the right assignment of them we may call truth, and the wrong assignment of them falsehood."[37]

The 'truth' of a name is thus a function of the imitative excellence of the name, with some names imitating better than others. Does the imitative relation need to be perfect in order for the name to signify its significate? Of course not, says Socrates:

> [We] allow the occasional substitution of a wrong letter, and if of a letter also of a noun in a sentence, and if a noun of a sentence also of a sentence which is not appropriate to the matter, and acknowledge that a thing may be named, and described, so long as the general character of the thing which you are describing is retained . . . even if some of the proper letters are wanting, still the thing is signified.[38]

So far the picture analogy has held, and yet, as Socrates goes on to point out, the analogy goes seriously awry if we think of the names as literally, physically resembling the objects they represent. He uses the numbers as a counter example to the imitation analogy: how could we find an infinite quantity of names to resemble and hence represent in likeness each of the numbers?[39] This leads Socrates to suggest the possibility of a "perfect state of language," the constituent names of which really were based on a "perfectly appropriate" likenesses.[40]

This is the first in a sequence of passages in which Socrates suggests that there is a distinction to be made among names; here the distinction involves an ideal name language based on perfect likeness between name and object represented. This pattern is repeated several times. Over and over, Socrates prompts Cratylus, then drives his naive natural nomenclaturism to absurdity, finally settling on a middle position between the two extreme views. His hybrid position states that although there is sometimes conventionalism in the name-world relation, there must be at least one name-world relation which is steady and constant, if names are to be properly true or false.[41] This middle position, based on a distinction between ordinary and real names, constitutes Platonic nomenclaturism. I will briefly examine some of these passages in the sequence.

After suggesting that the origin of names might have been a name-giver, Socrates rejects the possibility on the ground that any such first-namer would have had to give names based on his own concepts, with the resulting names thus signifying merely what *he* thought of the objects. This lack of objectivity would rule out the possibility of truth and correctness of names, for unless the name-giver be perfect, he could not assure that the name given really was correct, and we would be forced to regard names as merely conventional and relative.[42]

But, interestingly, relativism would also occur even if we assume that the names the name-giver gave really defined the true nature of the things they represent, and that those name are therefore the only means to get to the true nature of things. For, if this were so, how could the name-giver get the information about the real nature of things in advance of their having names, in order that he might then name them?[43] Not even perfect convention and authority can explain the possibility of correct names. There must be something, going quite beyond mere convention, which pre-exists names and naming, and which itself grounds the correctness of names.

Socrates makes an analogy to beauty, which is often cited in connection with the Forms:

> There is a matter, master Cratylus, of which I often dream, and should like to ask your opinion. Tell me whether there is or is not any absolute beauty or good or any other absolute existence.[44]

This, of course, is again classic Form-talk. What Socrates next suggests is that these things which ground right and wrong names are themselves Forms of some kind, like beauty and goodness. Cratylus agrees that there is absolute existence (Forms), and Socrates continues:

> Then let us seek the true beauty, not asking whether a face is fair, or anything of that sort, for all such things appear to be in flux, but let us ask whether true beauty is

not always beautiful . . . . And can we rightly speak of a beauty which is always passing away, and is first this and then that? Must not the same thing be born and retire and vanish while the word is in our mouths?[45]

Cratylus agrees. But by the same reasoning, Socrates continues, we cannot suppose that ordinary names can, by themselves, account for the correctness of naming: there must be a part of reality which does not change and pass away, if words such as 'beauty' are to have any absolute assertoric force. Ordinary names, subject always to change, cannot be the same as the real names which make them possible. Socrates puts it like this:

> Then how can that be a real thing which is never in the same state? . . . [If] that which knows and that which is known exist ever, and the beautiful and the good and every other thing also exist, then I do not think that they can resemble a process or flux . . . . [No] man of sense will like to put himself or the education of his mind in the power of [ordinary] names.[46]

Thus something outside the realm of becoming grounds ordinary names; but this could only mean that the ground of ordinary names comes from the realm of being, as I have been asserting.

These considerations can lead to but one direction for Plato: it looks as though the only way for there to be name-correctness at all among ordinary names in the world of becoming is if there are some permanent, eternal entities which are *themselves* the source of knowledge about the real nature of things, and which stabilize ordinary names metaphysically and provide them a ground for going right or wrong; what it points to is the existence of models for names, if you will. These name-like models will be a likeness with perfect resemblance to beings, as in the ideal language Socrates mentioned above. Socrates suggests just such a category of models or perfect names, which I have called 'real names,' in the following excerpt:

> [If names are to be objectively right or wrong] obviously recourse must be made to another standard [other than ordinary names themselves] which, without employing [ordinary] names, will make clear which of

the two are right, and this must be a standard which shows the truth of things.[47]

Socrates invokes Form-talk to describe these entities. How else can we know things

> except the true and natural way, through their affinities, when they are akin to each other, and through themselves? For that which is other and different from them must signify something other and different from them . . . . The knowledge of things must not be derived from [ordinary] names. No, they must be studied and investigated in themselves.[48]

In summary, we have in the *Cratylus* a picture of language in which two sorts of signification and two sorts of names occur: names of the first sort are linked to being, and to the Forms; these names are connected as ideal names to objects themselves by perfect likeness. Names of the other sort are linked to becoming; these names are connected as (relatively) conventional names to our imperfect ideas of particular things. Since everything in the realm of becoming is in flux, unstable, and contingent, particular names in particular languages are also thus; though Hellene and barbarian alike do their best, they still fall short of the ideal Form-names. But, to explain how there can be right and wrong names despite the multiplicity of different ordinary names, the *one over many principle* (i.e., the doctrine that similarities in this world of multiplicity are only possible because of the reality of another world which is the ultimate unifying source and ground of becoming) must be invoked, and, just as properties in this world of change have permanent, real counterparts in the Forms, *so too do signification and names have their eternal counterpart*: the contingent names of this world model themselves (albeit imperfectly and inexactly) on names in the realm of being, which I have been calling 'real names,' and it is these real names which allow the ordinary names in this world to function despite their conventional character. The correctness of a name is thus explained in terms of how it measures up to the real name it imitates, even as the justice of a state is better or worse depending on how it matches up to Justice itself.

Furthermore–and this is especially important for our understanding of Valentinus–just as an ordinary name invokes an idea (lower case 'i') through signification, so a real name invokes an Idea, i.e., a being in-itself, as it really is. Signification, using ordinary names, invokes the concept of a thing in some particular mind, and it accomplishes only through the mediation of the real name of that thing. There must also exist signification via real names, which by contrast, invokes the thing itself in the realm of being.

4. *Salus per nomina*–When God Speaks, People Listen

In light of preceding analysis, the application of Platonic nomen-claturism to Valentinian name-talk is fairly straightforward. The real names which we discovered in the *Cratylus* map perfectly onto the very powerful names which call the elect to salvation in the *Gospel*. The story would run thus: when we humans use the ordinary names of things in the world of becoming, we have the power (made possible by the real name of that thing, of course) to invoke the concept of that thing in some particular human mind. In this way, ordinary speech functions according to our Platonic nomenclaturism. But when God calls out my real name in the ideal language which only He speaks in its entirety, He invokes not the concept of me, but the true me.

To extend the mentalism of the metaphor, as seems reasonable to do, we might say that since we are said to be in the Father,[49] and since our true self corresponds to the signified in the signified/signifi-er dyad, by the terms of the analogy we can think of ourselves as con-cepts in the mind of God. We emanate as ideas from the divine mind, having been formed and been given a real name, we are thereby given our essential nature. This kind of reading makes excellent sense out of the name-talk in the *Gospel* 27:9-28:33 where names call persons into existence:

> For who contains, if not the Father alone? All the spaces
> are his emanations. They have known that they came forth
> from him like children who are from a grown man. They
> knew that they had not yet received form nor yet received
> a name, each one of which the Father begets . . . . If he
> wishes, he manifests whomever he wishes by giving him
> form and giving him a name, and he gives a name to him
> and brings it about that those come into existence who,
> before they come into existence, are ignorant of him who
> fashioned them.[50]

And, of course, "he who does not exist has no name"[51] since without a real name signifying my being in the mind of God, I cannot be at all. The converse of this claim, which also occurs in the *Gospel*, is equally intelligible in the Platonic reading: "For what name is given to he who does not exist?"[52] Since real names invoke being on this reading, there is likewise no mystery as to why non-existents cannot have a real name: they have no essential nature to fix or describe.

Now, having been created by being *assigned* our real names, we are yet ignorant of our relationship to the divine (as the *Gospel* 28:33 says) and we must still be saved by having that name, which created us and fixed our essential nature, *called out* by God. We are existentially in limbo, and will pass away with the material if we do not heed the call when it comes.[53] We are not utterly non-existent, but we are not yet saved. What happens when God calls our names? Continuing with the mental metaphor, we could say that in having our real names called we are pulled, supposing we have the acquaintance to listen, from being a concept in the mind of God, mere potential, to being actualized as thought, and, having achieved full being as a thought of God, we cheat the destruction of merely material life.

This basic analysis of Valentinus in terms of Platonic nomenclaturism immediately suggests a very elegant account for the puzzling expression that "the name of the Father is the Son," and also accounts for the role of the Son in all of this as well. We have seen the mediating role that real names play in making possible particular cases of naming in this world. But each real name is, although perfect, nonetheless particular, and this multiplicity must, like any multiplicity in a Platonic world, be explained in virtue of a similarity corresponding to a permanent unity in the realm of being, i.e., a Form. The *one over many principle* is still in effect, and it is not unprecedented that Forms blend and relate to one another, as they did in the *Sophist*. But then there must be a form uniting all particular real names, in virtue of which they get their 'real namehood,' if you will. What could that Form of the real name be if not the name of the Father himself?

And thus, as the transcendent but ultimately real ground for real names as mediators, the name of the Father is the ultimate mediator between real names and we who are named, and is also that which makes divine signification by real names possible. For a thinker like Valentinus, who wishes to apply this structure to specifically Christian soteriology, this will immediately suggest that it is the name of the Father which ultimately makes the call, and so makes salvation possible; thus the obvious theological element Valentinus would associate with the name of the Father is the salvific figure of the Son. For Valentinus, the divine incarnate is simply this ultimate name made flesh. This is why the name is "invisible" but "[i]t is possible for the [Son] to be seen."[54] The Father's name is not spoken, of course: the ultimate name is not there to invoke or form God, who stands in no such need; rather it is there to make all real names, and hence salvation for us, ultimately possible. As such it exists solely to be manifest that people might achieve acquaintance and heed the call. It is for these reasons that "the Father's name is not spoken, but it is apparent through a Son."[55] It is this picture, I submit, which constitutes the deep structure of Valentinian Christianity's *salus per nomina*.

Notice that this analysis does not collapse the Father and the name of the Father, nor does it identify them, but rather, in line with Valentinus' actual remarks, it correctly sets up a relation of priority between the two, with the Father as the realm of being in its entirety, and the name, i.e., the Son, the Form of real names, as the mediator between the realm of being and human salvation. The Son and the Father together give salvation: the Father, because he is the source, being itself, and hence the ground, must "call" the real name of each individual, invoking them in being through their real names (for who else but God could ultimately call one to God?). But this scheme cannot function unless there is something universal, grounding the relationship between all real names, grounding their real-namehood, and hence their salvific function. This ultimate mediating thing must be the Form of the real name itself, and it is this which directly grounds the realness of the real names, and hence the power of those names to invoke the being of individual persons, and hence to bring them into Being, literally back to the Father himself.

As this ultimate mediator, the Son (= Form of the real name = the name of the Father), is a part of the realm of Being, and also very much (as much as anything) a part of the Father Himself. Hence the Son traces his being (again, as much as anything else) back to the Father as the ground of all being. What is unique about the Son is his particular role in grounding the salvific process by serving as the unifying principle of real names. Thus, in this view, the Son is as much one of the entirety as any, save he has the most important role to play in salvation.

Given this analysis we can see the remainder of the passage of "the name of the Father is the Son" as dealing with a potential objection to the doctrine: how can the Father come to be if existence is invocation through naming? The Father must, on this reading, invoke himself somehow, but this is paradoxical:

> But no doubt one will say to his neighbor: "Who is it who will give a name to him who existed before himself, as if offspring did not receive a name from those who begot them?"[56]

Valentinus' response is simple, given the theoretical machinery he has at hand. God's name, as I have shown, is of a different order of reality than the other real names which are used to invoke being; the name of God is the Form of all real names, and it alone makes the other real names possible. Valentinus describes this difference in terms of "names on loan" and God's unique "proper name":

> First then, it is fitting for us to reflect on this matter: What is the name? It is the name in truth; it is not therefore the name *from* the Father, for it is the one which is the proper name. Therefore, he did not receive the name on loan as (do) others, according to the form in which each one is to be produced. But this is the proper name.[57] (My emphasis.)

God made this name, and was not made by it, and it is this name which, as that which makes real names and hence salvation possible, is associated by a Christian with the Son.

5. Conclusion and Prospects

In conclusion, I have tried to show that Valentinian name-talk in the *Gospel* need not respect Saussure in order to be intellectually respectable. At the very least, views as theoretically complex and as anti-Saussurean as the Platonic nomenclaturism of the *Cratylus* were available to, and in use by, Christian intellectuals of Valentinus' time. Thus we need not view Valentinian soteriology as either essentially subversive or hopelessly naive. Furthermore, my interpretation of Valentinian *salus per nomina* in terms of Platonic nomenclaturism is independently plausible, and unites many of the puzzling things Valentinus says about names under a single, non-anachronistic, coherent interpretive hypothesis.

This hypothesis may shed light on other, puzzling Valentinian texts as well. For example, consider this passage from *The Gospel According to Philip* 76:6-12:

It is in the world, where power and weakness exist, that the act of joining between males and females occurs; but in the eternal realm there is a different sort of joining. Although it is with these names that we refer to things, yet other names also exist, above every current name, indeed above the most potent.[58]

Even more clearly in line with my analysis is the *Gospel* 53:23-54:4:

Names given to worldly things are very deceptive, since they turn the heart aside from the real to the unreal. And whoever hears the word "god" thinks not of the reality, but has been thinking of what is not real: so also, with the words "father," "son," "holy spirit," "life," "light," "resurrection," "church," etc., it is not the real that one thinks of but the unreal, although the words have referred to the real. The names [that one has] heard exist in the world . . . deceive. If the names were situated in the eternal realm, they would not be uttered on any occasion in the world, nor would they have been assigned to worldly things: their goal would be in the eternal realm.[59]

Indeed, these two examples alone constitute strong corroborating evidence that a straightforward Platonic reading of name-talk in the *Gospel* is ultimately closest to the native and true vision behind it.

Notes

[1] "The Gospel of Truth," *Nag Hammadi Codex I*, ed. Harold W. Attridge, trans. Harold W. Attridge and George W. MacRae, S.J., vol. 1 (Leiden: E.J. Brill, 1985), 55-122, especially 89-91 (*Evangelium Veritatis* [*Ev. Ver.*] 21:25-22:20). In subsequent citations of the *Gospel*, I will continue to include in parentheses standard chapter and line numbers from the critical edition.

[2] "The Gospel of Truth," 97 (*Ev. Ver.* 27:15-33).

[3] "The Gospel of Truth," 111 (*Ev. Ver.* 38:7).

[4] For a discussion of early textual evidence for the *nomina sacra* of Egyptian Christian communities, see Collin H. Roberts, *Manuscript, Society and Belief in Early Christian Egypt* (London: Oxford UP, 1979), chapters I and II.

5 This fundamental principle seems inoffensive enough, and yet Saussure drew profound consequences from it, consequences which influenced such later twentieth-century figures as Derrida, Lacan, Barthes and Foucault. It would be hard to underestimate Saussure's short-term impact on linguistics, social sciences, literary theory, and indeed just about any intellectual domain for which the nature of language is live issue. For a discussion of the significance of Saussure's work, see David Holdcroft, *Saussure: Signs, System, and Arbitrariness* (New York: Cambridge UP, 1991), 4-12.

6 *Nag Hammadi Codex I, v. 1*, 111 (*Ev. Ver.* 38:11-12).

7 *Nag Hammadi Codex I, v. 1*, 113 (*Ev. Ver.* 38:11-12).

8 *Nag Hammadi Codex I, v. 1*, 91 (*Ev. Ver.* 22:12-13).

9 The incompatibility between me and Fineman does not necessarily extend to any other scholarly views which hold Valentinian allegorization to be a kind of subversive treatment of texts. Consider for example chapter three of David Dawson, *Allegorical Readers and Cultural Revision in Ancient Alexandria* (Berkeley: University of California Press, 1992). Dawson gives a long and comprehensive treatment of Valentinian allegorization, beginning with the *Fragments* and moving to the *Gospel* itself. Though nothing I do here depends upon Dawson's methods or conclusions, it seems to me that no fundamental incompatibility exists between our views; Dawson's conclusions about the significance of the name of God are compatible with the results I achieve independently by considering Platonic influence from the *Cratylus*, even though Dawson deals with Platonic influence only from the *Timaeus* and explicitly views Valentinus' "allegorical interpretation as composition" to be inherently subversive to the interpreted text. If anything my conclusions are mutually reinforcing of Dawson's.

10 Holdcroft, 66.

11 Paul Vincent Spade, *Thoughts Words and Things: An Introduction to Late Mediaeval Logic and Semantic Theory* (N.p.: n.p., 1996), 61.

12 Joel Fineman, "Gnosis and the Piety of Metaphor: The Gospel of Truth," *The Rediscovery of Gnosticism*, ed. Bentley Layton, vol. 1 (Leiden: E.J. Brill, 1980), 289.

13 Joel Fineman, 297-301.

14 Joel Fineman, 297-99.

15 Joel Fineman, 305.

16 Benoit Standaert, "L'Evangile de vérité': Critique et lecture," *New Testament Studies* 22. 243-75. In the original French: "Parler de Dieu comme Père, c'est le nommer comme tel. Tout ce qui existe a d'ailleurs

un nom, et ce qui n'a pas de nom n'existe pas" (272). (Standaert explicitly footnotes the *Gospel* 39:11-16 as his source here.)

[17] Fineman digresses at one point into a discussion of something he calls the "antimimetic tradition," which he associates with Plato (304-05). How close this antimimeticism is to the Platonic nomenclaturism which I develop below is unclear, because Fineman himself says little about what he takes antimimeticism to be. Still, he recognizes the tension between the Platonic metaphysics underlying this antimimeticism and the interpretation that he himself is developing. After struggling with a fragment from Clement on Valentinus on images, Fineman admits that he has trouble explaining it. In the end, he reconciles the tension thus: "What I am suggesting is that Valentineanism accepts the metaphysical assumptions of the antimimetic tradition, but that then, in a strange reversal, it thinks its theology through the very substitution that antimimeticism deplored" (305). This kind of problem indicates, once again, the difficulty which interpreters face in forcing Valentinus to respect Saussure.

[18] This usage is common; see Roy Harris, *Language, Saussure and Wittgenstein: How to Play Games with Words* (London: Routledge, 1988), 7, and Holdcroft, 11-12. If it seems less confusing to take nomenclaturism as involving necessarily a doctrine of essential or natural connection between name and sign, then one should take my definitions as given here to be technical terminology, stipulatively defined. Nothing I say further on depends upon mere agreement of terms at this level.

[19] For an excellent discussion of the use of the game analogy in both Wittgenstein and Saussure, see Harris, especially chapters 3 and 4.

[20] The best stylometric evidence places the *Cratylus* in Plato's early period, although considerations of the total evidence (e.g. content and tone) strongly suggest it belongs in the middle period, with the *Sophist* and the *Theaetetus*. Thus there is good reason to think of the dialogue as more "Platonic" than "Socratic." See Terry Penner, "Socrates and the early dialogues," in Richard Kraut, *The Cambridge Companion to Plato*, ed. Richard Kraut (New York: Cambridge UP, 1992); also Leonard Brandwood's "Stylometry and Chronology" in the same volume.

[21] My evidence comes from John Dillon, *The Middle Platonists* (London: Duckworth, 1977): "Platonist speculations on language take their start from the *Cratylus*, particularly from such a passage as 430A-431E" (181). Dillon notes that just such passages seem to have influenced Philo of Alexandria, who predates Valentinus by perhaps a hundred years, on such subjects as names and etymology. We also learn from Dillon that there was use of the *Cratylus* in Rome just after Valentinus' time; he speculates

that Harpocration of Argos, working in Rome around 180 CE, was using the *Cratylus* in developing his theological views (259-60). This frames ancient use of the *Cratylus* right around the time of Valentinus, and in both of the two main cities where he worked. Thus it seems plausible to assume that Valentinus would have had access to the *Cratylus* and cause to consult it, as some of his contemporaries were doing.

22 *Cratylus*, 383a-b. Citation of all Platonic dialogues is by standard pagination; all translations, with a single noted exception, come from "Cratylus," *Plato: The Collected Works*, eds. Edith Hamilton and Huntington Cairns, trans. Benjamin Jowett (Princeton: Princeton UP, 1961), 421-74.

23 *Cratylus*, 384c-d.

24 *Cratylus*, 385a-b.

25 This reasoning occurs with greater detail than is here represented, in 237c-e. Extracting the precise details of the argument is not easy, but once done very illuminating parallels with false judgment in the *Theaetetus* come to light. I have argued extensively for such connections in an unpublished manuscript "The Puzzle of Falsity and the One Over Many," 1996.

26 See 254b ff, "Sophist," *Plato: The Collected Works*, eds. Edith Hamilton and Huntington Cairns, trans. F. M. Cornford (Princeton: Princeton UP, 1961), 957-1017.

27 "Sophist," 254b-d.

28 "Sophist," 258d-e. Here I have used a different translation for the excellent clarity it exhibits. See *The Sophist*, trans. Nicholas P. White (Indianapolis: Hackett, 1993).

29 "Sophist," 261e-262a.

30 "Sophist," 263b.

31 "Sophist," 263a

32 "Sophist," 263c.

33 "Sophist," 263e.

34 By "being" and "becoming" here, I have in mind the elemental Platonic distinction between the world of the Forms—changeless, perfect, and eternal—and the world of the particulars—changing, in motion, in flux, subject to generation and decay.

35 *Cratylus*, 428e.

36 *Cratylus*, 430e.

37 *Cratylus*, 431a-b.

38 *Cratylus*, 432e-433a.

39 *Cratylus*, 435b-c.

40 *Cratylus*, 435c-d.

41 Socrates seems never to give up on the original argument that, as the con-

stituents of thing which are either true or false (viz., propositions), names must also have a kind of truth or falsity. Of course it is precisely problems with this kind of compositionality that, in part, lead Wittgenstein and others to abandon nomenclaturism.

[42] *Cratylus*, 436b.

[43] *Cratylus*, 438a.

[44] *Cratylus*, 439c-d.

[45] *Cratylus*, 439d.

[46] *Cratylus*, 439e-440c.

[47] *Cratylus*, 438d.

[48] *Cratylus*, 438e.

[49] *Nag Hammadi Codex I, v. 1*, 85 (*Ev. Ver.* 19:7-10).

[50] *Nag Hammadi Codex I, v. 1*, 97 (*Ev. Ver.* 27:9-28:33).

[51] *Nag Hammadi Codex I, v. 1*, 113 (*Ev. Ver.* 39:14).

[52] *Nag Hammadi Codex I, v. 1*, 113 (*Ev. Ver.* 39:11-12).

[53] *Nag Hammadi Codex I, v. 1*, 89 (*Ev. Ver.* 21:34-22:2).

[54] *Nag Hammadi Codex I, v. 1*, 111 (*Ev. Ver.* 37:15-17).

[55] *Nag Hammadi Codex I, v. 1*, 111 (*Ev. Ver.* 38:22-24).

[56] *Nag Hammadi Codex I, v. 1*, 113 (*Ev. Ver.* 39:29-40:14).

[57] *Nag Hammadi Codex I, v. 1*, 115 (*Ev. Ver.* 39:28-40:14).

[58] Bentley Layton, *The Gnostic Scriptures: Ancient Wisdom for the New Age*, ed. and trans. Bentley Layton (New York: Doubleday, 1987), 347.

[59] Layton, 330.

The Uses of Interpretation in *Hamlet*

Leslie Croxford

T. S. Eliot called *Hamlet* "the 'Mona Lisa' of literature." It is true. No other work has presented more uncertain meanings. Interpretation has thrived. Hamlet is quite simply "the most problematic play ever written by Shakespeare or any other playwright."[1] Inconsistencies and difficulties derive from the dramatist's need to integrate his medieval and Renaissance sources. The various printed versions of the author's text have to be reconciled, but sometimes resist this. A host of deeper questions arise. Among the most celebrated are: what is the reason for the Prince's delay in revenging his father's murder; is his madness genuine or feigned; what is the true status of his feelings for Ophelia?

Most of these questions do not admit of definitive solutions. Nor will there be a search here for possible answers to the second and third. For in the case of the thematic and psychological issues there is a seemingly impenetrable ambiguity. Ambiguity is, in fact, a striking characteristic of Shakespeare's work. Hence William Empson's continuous resort to him for examples in *Seven Types of Ambiguity*. Indeed he once wrote that a given sonnet, rather than having a single meaning, is more like a musical instrument on which the critic may play a variety of tunes.

As it happens, Empson's image of the musical instrument is also used in *Hamlet*, by the Prince. It occurs on two occasions. Hamlet greets Horatio admiringly, saying what a well-balanced man he is. Those who combine passion and judgment harmoniously ". . . are not a pipe for Fortune's finger/To sound what stop she please" (III, ii, 70-71).[2] The image recurs soon after, once Claudius has burst out of the play within the play. Hamlet orders music. Then Rosencrantz and Guildenstern arrive to ask the Prince to visit his mother, distressed at his behavior. Taking one of the recorders, Hamlet says to them:

Why, look you now, how unworthy a thing you

make of me. You would play upon me, you would
seem to know my stops, you would pluck out the
heart of my mystery, you would sound me from my
lowest note to the top of my compass; and there is
much music, excellent voice, in this little organ, yet
cannot you make it speak. 'Sblood, do you think I
am easier to be played on than a pipe? Call me what
instrument you will, though you fret me, you cannot
play upon me. (III, ii, 354-63)

In each case, Hamlet rejects the idea of being used as a mere
instrument for the advancement of another's designs. But he concedes,
reluctantly, that Fortune does play him in contrast to the better-adjust-
ed Horatio. Moreover, there is an alleged mystery–the Prince–to be
recognized, even though Rosencrantz and Guildenstern use inadequate
means to "pluck" it out. So Prince Hamlet is like a pipe, a recorder, an
organ, to be played to better or worse effect. Interpretation of him is
inescapable.

Interpretation is apparently not simply a matter for scholars and
critics of the play. It is a theme that the play itself employs. It does so,
moreover, frequently, if not exclusively, through the agency of the
Prince. Interpretation is something in which other characters indulge,
as Hamlet recognizes. He too constantly interprets. The theme of interpreting is, I will suggest, a predominant one (although I acknowledge
Empson's point that more than one melody can be played on
Shakespeare's instrument). The role of interpretation in *Hamlet* may,
therefore, act as a cue to those wishing to interpret it. Furthermore,
since Shakespeare, in giving the subject this significance, had to develop previous versions of his story, we shall, in considering the issue of
interpretation in the play, also be examining a prime example of how
texts undergo alteration from period to period. We will find two specific influences on the metamorphosis of *Hamlet*: the intellectual climate in which it was written, as well as the nature of the Tudor political world. Together, they put at Shakespeare's disposal transformations of his inherited versions which are highly revealing of his creative processes.

*

Interpretation only becomes relevant where there are phenomena requiring explanation. These *Hamlet* has in plenty, thereby raising
a plethora of questions. "Hamlet's world," Maynard Mack says, "is

pre-eminently in the interrogative mood." Harry Levin quotes this, going on to say: ". . . the word 'question' occurs in *Hamlet* no less than seventeen times, much more frequently than in any of Shakespeare's other plays. Recalling that it comes as the final word in Hamlet's most famous line," ["To be, or not to be, that is the question," (III, i, 56)] "we may well regard it as the key-word of the play . . . Furthermore, besides direct inquiry, there are other modes of questioning, notably doubt and irony . . . ." [3]

Now, we may wonder whether a play of *Hamlet's* complexity and stature can be reduced to a single key-word. "Corruption" also recurs frequently. Nevertheless, so much of the play derives from the act of questioning, not only linguistically, but also, as we shall see, in terms of dramatic organization, that here we have not merely one of several repeated words. Questioning constitutes a primary structural feature of the work.

Much of the questioning is Hamlet's. Much is the other characters'. Much simply does not admit of answers. But there is a notable question that *is* settled. Let us stop to consider it since it both sets in motion and illuminates the whole theme of interpretation. It is Hamlet's, embedded in his reaction to the Ghost in the first Act.

> Be thou a spirit of health or goblin damn'd.
> Bring with thee airs from heaven or blasts from hell,
> Be thy intents wicked or charitable,
> Thou com'st in such a questionable shape
> That I will speak to thee. (I, iv, 40-44)

Although these first words on seeing the Ghost highlight his "questionable shape," the Prince, impulsively, without further ado, calls him ". . . Hamlet,/King, father, royal Dane" (I, iv, 44-45). Yet the question of who or what the Ghost is cannot be permanently ignored, given the burden he imposes on his son Hamlet. He commands him to kill Claudius.

> GHOST: Revenge his foul and most unnatural murder.
> HAMLET: Murder! (I, v, 25-26)

Is there not an ambiguity here? Does "Murder!" simply apply, as it initially and obviously appears to do, to Claudius's act? Might it not also describe what the Prince is required to do if the Ghost is not who he claims to be? Hamlet therefore soon goes on to bring his question fully into mind:

> The spirit that I have seen
> May be a devil, and the devil hath power
> T'assume a pleasing shape, yea, and perhaps,
> Out of my weakness and my melancholy,
> As he is very potent with such spirits,
> Abuses me to damn me. (II, ii, 594-99)

How, then, is the urgent question of the Ghost's identity to be resolved? The answer is through the play within the play, acting out a near parallel to Claudius's alleged murder of Hamlet's father. For:

> The play's the thing
> Wherein I'll catch the conscience of the King. (II, ii, 600-01)

It takes over two thirds of the play for Hamlet fully to acknowledge his question, devise a strategy for answering it and receive that answer unequivocally. Shakespeare could have saved himself the trouble. There is no ghost in *Hamlet's* medieval and Renaissance sources, Saxo Grammaticus and François Belleforest. Their protagonists wreak revenge without having first, elaborately, to establish the need for it. Nevertheless, given that Shakespeare did decide to use a ghost as a means of requiring Hamlet's vengeance, he could have done so much more simply. There was, after all, a precedent for such a ghost, with a white visor, in a now lost Elizabethan play, known as the *Ur-Hamlet*. Lodge refers to it in *Wit's Miserie* (1596), speaking of "the ghost which cried so miserably at the Theator, like an oyster wife, 'Hamlet, reuenge'."[4] Ghosts of this kind dated from Seneca, a collection of whose tragedies were published in 1581 to significant acclaim. But Shakespeare brilliantly undermined Elizabethan theatre-goers' expectations with his own specter. What Hamlet comes upon is no crude, bellowing apparition. He has a natural, if dramatically sepulchral, voice. It is dignified, not straining to be sensationalist. He does not provide the kind of horrific, extended report of existence in the underworld that Don Andrea's ghost offers in Kyd's earlier *The Spanish Tragedy*. Hamlet's Ghost says: ". . . I am forbid/To tell the secrets of my prison-house . . ." (I, v, 13-14). Furthermore, he is neither prologue, merely setting up the action, nor epilogue, neatly providing the meaning of the play, in the Senecan tradition. He is fully integrated into the plot, the psychology of the drama–so much so that he preserves the naturalness of his appearance in life. He wears " . . . the very armour he had on/When he th'ambitious Norway combated" (I, i, 63-64). While in the chamber of his sometime wife he comes ". . . in his habit as he liv'd!" (III, iv, 137). Yet Shakespeare's greatest advance is in the ambiguity with which he presents the Ghost. So much is clear when we compare the Ghost with that which appears to Brutus in *Julius Caesar*, written only a year or so before:

> BRUTUS: Art thou some God, some Angell, or some Devill . . .
> GHOST: Thy evil spirit Brutus. (IV, iii, 279, 282)[5]

There is no doubt as to the diabolic nature of this ghost. In *Hamlet*, however, the uncertainty is fundamental. It haunts the Prince, forcing him to interpret what manner of thing the Ghost might be.[6]

Hamlet is quite right to be dubious, according to some twentieth-century critics. L. C. Knights says: "If this ghost turns out to be one who clamours for revenge, then we have every reason to suppose that Shakespeare entertained some grave doubts about him." This is, moreover, a "Ghost whose command had been for a sterile concentration on death and evil." [7] As if to emphasize the ambiguity about the Ghost's provenance, Shakespeare has him order Hamlet to "Swear" that he will revenge him, from that hell-like "cellarage" under the stage (I, v, 163). True, revenge keeps slipping from Hamlet's mind, in favor of remembering.

> GHOST: Remember me
>
> . . .
>
> HAMLET: . . . Remember thee?
> Yea, from the table of my memory
> I'll wipe away all trivial fond records
>
> . . .
>
> And thy commandment all alone shall live . . . .
> (I, v, 91, 97-99, 102)

Revenge even slips to the margin of the Ghost's concerns when he visits his adulterous wife's chamber. He tells their son to leave her to her own conscience:

Do not forget. This visitation
Is but to whet thy almost blunted purpose.
But look, amazement on thy mother sits.
O step between her and her fighting soul. (III, iv, 110-13)

This is not the only occasion on which the Ghost urges restraint in punishing Gertrude:

But howsomever thou pursuest this act,
Taint not thy mind nor let thy soul contrive
Against thy mother aught. Leave her to heaven . . . .
(I, v, 84-86)

Such exhortation to avoid sinning, unexpected perhaps from one simultaneously urging homicide, reminds us, parenthetically, that the question of the Ghost's provenance is but one of the ambiguities surrounding him, albeit, surely, the central one. Be that as it may, it temporarily distracts him from the idea of revenge, just as Hamlet's own attention is diverted from it. And when the Prince's revenge on Claudius does finally come, it is quite unplanned. It is the impulsive result of accident and rage.

Despite all of which, the injunction to revenge can never finally be forgotten. It is even given a thematic place in the play by the parallelism of Laertes's burning desire to avenge his own father's death. The Ghost's original injunction to revenge Claudius's "foul and most unnatural murder" (I, v, 25), is simply too disconcerting in a context far remote from the primitive society of Shakespeare's source, with its talion concept of blood debt. For the Prince comes out of a Christian world in which, as he tells Laertes, "There is special providence in the fall of a sparrow" (V, ii, 215-16). In fact we can gauge how far *Hamlet* has travelled from its original by recalling that every Elizabethan parish church was required by law to put the Ten Commandments on its walls, including "Thou shalt not kill."

It is inescapable that Hamlet should—regardless of the vexed question of whether he does, or does not, have a temperamental aversion to action—establish the authority of the command he receives. It brings him back to his original dilemma: is the Ghost "a spirit of health or goblin damn'd?" Not that the Ghost himself is in any doubt. He claims, with whatever degree of veracity:

> I am thy father's spirit,
> Doom'd for a certain term to walk the night,
> And for the day confin'd to fast in fires,
> Till the foul crimes done in my days of nature
> Are burnt and purg'd away. (I, v, 9-13)

Why so? Because he was murdered, hence being denied the Church's last rites. It is a claim accepted by the Prince, at least at first: "Touching this vision here,/It is an honest ghost" (I, v. 143-44). Hamlet swears it "by Saint Patrick" (I, v, 142). This is appropriate since Saint Patrick's Purgatory was a cave in Ireland where pilgrims went to be purged of their sins and receive visions of the afterlife. In other words the Ghost alleges, and Hamlet initially accepts, that he is in purgatory. Yet inevitably the Prince soon has his doubts. *Is* the Ghost in purgatory? The question raises others. Does purgatory exist? On what basis can one know? And so, bringing the questioning full circle, how might Hamlet be sure that the Ghost is *there*?

Purgatory is a Catholic, not Protestant doctrine. Despite the official Protestantism of Elizabethan England, it has, however, been contended that Shakespeare's social milieu encouraged a continued belief in purgatory:

> Such an assimilation of Catholic belief in a purgatory denied by the Protestant faith would come easily to Shakespeare's neighbors in Warwickshire, where Catholics were thick on the ground, occupying many of the great manor houses and country estates just north and west of Stratford. It might come easily too to Shakespeare's family, where his father was or at the very least had been a practicing Catholic and the Jesuit Robert Southwell, martyred in 1595, was a distant cousin on his mother's side.[8]

What is at issue, though, is not whether the author might have been a crypto-Catholic believer in purgatory. It is, rather, by what means his protagonist can determine whether the Ghost is in such a place or not.

Hamlet, the student, intends to go "back to school in Wittenberg," (I, ii, 113). Wittenberg might seem to one critic merely to have been a favorite university for Danes studying abroad,[9] but its reputation in the sixteenth century surely rested far more on its famous sons, Luther and Melanchthon. This doubtless identifies one of its students with its brand of reformed religion. Not that Shakespeare explicitly delineates Hamlet as a Protestant. For reasons that will become apparent, the play sketches the Prince's link with Protestantism only lightly, for no other purpose than to bring out Protestant silence on the subject of purgatory.

Shakespeare therefore not only creates doubt about whether the Ghost is "a spirit of health or goblin damn'd," namely an angel or devil. He quite deliberately complicates the issue by adding the further possibility of purgatory. He does so, moreover, in an ideological context lacking the traditionally authoritative means of validating its existence and thus of ghosts claiming to hail from it. Well might Hamlet say:

> What may this mean,
> That thou, dead corse . . .
> Revisits thus the glimpses of the moon,
> . . . So horridly to shake our disposition
> With thoughts beyond the reaches of our souls? (I, v, 51-53, 54-55)

Hamlet is consequently confronted by the huge problem of how to know whether purgatory exists or not–part and parcel of the questions of how to determine if the Ghost is in it; of who the Ghost is; of whether, finally, he can be trusted and should be obeyed. The suggestion that the Ghost is from purgatory is thus considerably more than just a part of Shakespeare's novel way of presenting him as less bombastic, less unequivocally evil, more integrated into the plot than such spirits tended to be in Elizabethan theatre. It is the means, precisely, of advancing the "pre-eminently interrogative mood," launching thereby the Prince's–and play's–focus on the need to interpret. This, we shall see, serves to open up some of *Hamlet's* deepest intellectual and psychological concerns.

To be specific, Shakespeare, by introducing the idea of purgatory, puts Hamlet in the predicament of having to decide how he will go about determining who or what the Ghost is. This will be found to have a double significance: for the plot, as well as for the mental world in which the plot unfolds, be it within or without the play. That said, let us follow the steps Hamlet takes to resolve his predicament. For who can doubt that it *is* a predicament? Dilatory as Hamlet may be, he cannot turn his back permanently on the terrible command of a Ghost whose provenance and hence nature he therefore badly needs somehow to confirm. Yet how can he possibly do so, without the benefit of either Catholic or Protestant doctrine on the subject? There are only two alternatives available to the Prince.

The first is to deny the evidence of his senses, attributing his vision to distortions caused by melancholy. Horatio, for his part, begins skeptically, believing the apparition is mere illusion. This embodies what James I was to call the "damnable opinions" of Reginald Scot in his *Discoverie of Witchcraft* (1584), including "the old error of the Sadducees, in . . . denying spirits."[10] For Protestants certainly did believe in spirits, although, having no doctrine of purgatory, they held that the dead went straight to heaven or hell, crossing a "bourn/(from which) No traveller returns" (*Hamlet*, III, i, 79-80). James I's view in his *Demonologie* (1597) was that specters might be angels, but were more usually devils in the form of departed relatives.[11] Yet, for Horatio, actually seeing the Ghost becomes believing:

> Before my God, I might not this believe
> Without the sensible and true avouch
> Of mine own eye. (I, i, 59-61)

It leaves Horatio saying: ". . . this is wondrous strange" (I, v, 172). To which Hamlet replies: "And therefore as a stranger give it welcome" (I, v, 173). For Hamlet at no point denies the reality of the Ghost. It is an option he never considers, restricting himself to questioning, rather, the Ghost's identity.[12]

There is a second way open to Hamlet for confirming the Ghost's provenance and nature, without reference to doctrinal writings of any kind. It is from direct experience. Hamlet resorts to it. How? The simple answer is through the medium of the play within the play. He orders a troupe of actors to insert "a speech of some dozen or sixteen lines" (II, ii, 535), into a play based upon a murder similar to that which Claudius committed. For

> I have heard
> That guilty creatures sitting at a play
> Have, by the cunning of the scene,
> Been struck so to the soul that presently
> They have proclaim'd their malefactions. (II, ii, 584-88)

By this means Hamlet certainly does "catch the conscience of the King" (II, ii, 601). It proves to Hamlet's satisfaction the truthfulness of the Ghost's story, together with the authenticity of the Ghost himself. Not that Shakespeare goes on to work out the wider theological implications for a Protestant Prince, or an Elizabethan Anglican audience, of having the Ghost's claim to come from purgatory validated. He need not treat the question of purgatory further now that it has served its purpose of forcing his protagonist to depend on his direct experience by testing the Ghost's veracity through the play within the play. He simply dispenses with the issue, as can we, turning instead to look more closely at the nature of the test Hamlet has devised.

Three main characteristics stand out. First, Hamlet is thinking experimentally. He is consciously constructing a situation, the play within the play, on the basis of a previously acquired principle, that guilty creatures proclaim their misdeeds on such occasions. The anticipated outcome will be to test an assertion, that the Ghost's allegation of murder is true, with the logical conclusion that here is, or is not, an honest ghost whose demand to revenge must be heeded.

Secondly, Hamlet's approach to the experiment is through the senses. Of his uncle, he says: "I'll observe his looks," (II, ii, 592). He tells Horatio: "Observe my uncle," (III, ii, 80) and again: "Didst perceive?" (III, ii, 281). Yet even the operation of one's senses needs further sensory confirmation. Hamlet says to Horatio of Claudius:

> Give him heedful note;
> For I mine eyes will rivet to his face,
> And after we will both out judgments join
> In censure of his seeming. (III, ii, 84-87)

Thirdly, phenomena require interpretation. Hamlet is driven to this realization by what to him is the Ghost's originally equivocal status, although previously he had, in another context, sought to assert the primacy of the plainly authentic. He had asserted to his mother that although there is that which merely "seems" (I, ii, 75-76), "I have that within which passes show" (I, ii, 85). Now, however, there are vital matters the truth of which is far from self-evident. They badly need interpreting through the use of experiment based on the senses.

There are also two paradoxes to notice when thus describing Hamlet's way of interpreting the appearance of the Ghost. Hamlet's medium for determining factual realities is an illusion. It is drama. And:

> . . . these our actors,
> As I foretold you, were all spirits, and
> Are melted into air, thin air . . .[13]

Not that *Hamlet* lingers over the NeoPlatonic implications of these seemingly illusory underpinnings of reality, as Shakespeare does in some of his later plays. But still the interdependence of these apparently opposed categories is implicit here. In fact, the ambiguous relationship between reality and drama is a running theme in *Hamlet*, as when the Prince asks himself why the Player sheds actual tears for Hecuba, to "amaze indeed/The very faculties of eyes and ears" (II, ii, 553-54 and 559-60). While, conversely, some real events are staged, for example the encounter between Hamlet and Ophelia, set up by her father for Claudius's benefit (III, i, 90-151).

A second paradox is the outcome of the Prince's strategy for verifying facts. Does it not lend credence to the tale of a phantom; an entity whose existence, of its immaterial nature, cannot be verified by the material senses?

These paradoxes caution us against treating either Shakespeare or Hamlet as if they were practicing philosophy in a modern idiom. It is for the convenience of clarity that I have offered an analytic account of the Prince's epistemological method, as well as to highlight what, it will be argued, is his distinctive outlook. This is not to suggest that we should ignore the play's reminders that its two students have taken natural philosophy as part of the scientific curriculum at Wittenberg University. "There are," Hamlet says, "more things in heaven and earth, Horatio,/Than are dreamt of in your philosophy" (I, v, 174-75). But we remember that *Hamlet* was written between 1600 and 1601, while it was not until 1605 that Francis Bacon, the first significant early modern English philosopher, published his *Advancement of Learning*. It inaugurated his series of philosophical studies, including *Novum Organum*, drafted between 1608 and 1620, and *De Dignitate et Augmentis Scientiarum*, published in 1623. With these, Bacon closed the two and a half centuries' long lacuna since England's previous major philosopher, William of Ockham.

Shakespeare therefore worked in an as yet philosophically unsettled environment. The great Baconian, then Cartesian, crystallizations of post-medieval thought were still to come. But this does not mean Shakespeare did not have access to any of the ideas that Bacon, at least, would go on to systematize. He had a marked capacity for intellectual osmosis. An instance is when Hamlet writes to Ophelia: "Doubt that the sun doth move" (II, ii, 116). This reflects the findings of Copernicus. Shakespeare drew fully on his late Renaissance intellectual context in adapting the Hamlet story so as to make it focus on interpreting, as in the case of the Ghost. So Hamlet is hardly the first to demand that knowledge must be derived from direct observation through the senses. It was a major preoccupation for a group of sixteenth-century Italian scientific thinkers. Bernadino Telesio, the Neapolitan, published his major work, *De Natura Juxta Propria Principia*, from 1565 to 1586. He substituted for Aristotle's purely conceptual analysis of phenomena the notion that direct observation of sensory data is the sole way of understanding the natural world. Telesio's empiricism was developed by another Neapolitan, Tommaso Campanella, in his *Philosophia Sensibus Demonstrata*, (1591). He took human experience as the indispensable basis for philosophy, with the result that he was tried for heresy. There is no direct reference to him by Bacon and certainly not to either Italian by Shakespeare. But Bacon did call Telesio "the first of the moderns." He draws on the Italians' ideas in his systematic works, while Hamlet is implicitly preoccupied by the same themes.

One route by which contemporary ideas certainly did come to Shakespeare is through the writings of Montaigne. His *Essays* were translated by the Elizabethan John Florio, Sir Philip Sydney's friend and perhaps Shakespeare's. In fact, *Hamlet's* direct intellectual affinity is with Montaigne's skeptical review of humanity, rather than with the Neapolitans' observations of nature. Moreover, given that the play is no work of technical philosophy, despite the philosophical implications of many of its themes and references, the Prince's soliloquies easily adopt the *Essay's* discursive manner. Whole passages from the *Essays* are directly borrowed in *Hamlet*, though transformed by Shakespeare's needs.

Much has, of course, been written on the links between Montaigne's writings and Shakespeare's. There is no need to review the whole of that complex relationship here. We shall simply focus on what is relevant to our present argument: the parallel concern *Hamlet* and the *Essays* have with how to interpret phenomena. In "On Experience" Montaigne begins very differently from the Neapolitans by quoting Aristotle in the first book of the *Metaphysics*: "There is no desire more natural than the desire for knowledge."[14] He follows Aristotle, too, in asserting the role of reason–and yet: "When reason fails us, we make use of experience."[15] So he cites the Roman poet Manilus: "By various experiments, experience has led to art, example showing the way."[16] What, then, is the best way to interpret? Montaigne rejects the kind of interpretation that depends upon ever finer logical categories. The field in which this error becomes acute is in interpreting books. Here he concentrates on contemporary Protestant Biblical interpretations:

> And those men who think they can lessen and check our disputes by referring us to the actual words of the Bible are deluding themselves, since our minds find just as wide a field for controverting other men's meanings as for delivering its own.[17]

> Who would not say that commentaries increase doubt and ignorance, since there is no book to be found, human or divine, with which the world has any business, in which the difficulties are cleared up by the interpretation?[18]

Of Wittenberg's inaugurator of Protestantism, Montaigne says: "I have observed in Germany that Luther has left behind him as many schisms and dissensions concerning the uncertainties in his beliefs as he raised about the Holy Scriptures."[19] And Montaigne goes on to state his essential position pithily: "There is more trouble in interpreting interpretations than in interpreting the things themselves . . ."[20]

The significance of this for *Hamlet* is not only that the Prince, like his near contemporaries Montaigne, Telesio and Campanella, relies upon direct experience in "interpreting the things themselves." It is that Montaigne, from a starting point and in a mental atmosphere dissimilar to that of the Neapolitans, provides far ampler explanation than we can legitimately expect from a play of how this position is reached in the ideological climate to which Shakespeare undoubtedly had specific access. Indeed, we may extrapolate further from Montaigne what seems especially relevant to Hamlet. It is that Protestants, so Montaigne apparently recognizes, replace the authority of the Church by that of the Bible. Yet this is no real advance since scripture requires interpretation to which there is no end. Once the concept of interpretation has been introduced, however, it cannot be dispensed with, for no better reason than that it undermines efforts to center authority on the Bible. It acquires a life of its own. It puts itself at the service of a further, final, because more valid, authority: interpretation by direct experience of "the things themselves."

With this shift in mind, we can also see how Hamlet, the student from Wittenberg University, is reapplying the Protestant interpretation of scripture to the interpretation of his personal reality. That reality thereby takes on for him the solemn significance which is usually attributed to the Bible. Hamlet's life, his predicament, becomes at once a sequence to be lived and a text to be explained. This diversion of Biblical exegesis to the Prince's interpretation of his private existence carries with it an additional implication. It derived from the Protestant refusal to permit the Catholic Church and its priesthood a role as intermediary between God and man. Man's access to God was direct, through his personal interpretation of that substitute for the authority of the Church, scripture. Though how could one person's interpretation be more efficacious than another's? What authenticated this man's view rather than that man's? The response was that the interpreter had to be guided by the Holy Spirit. Nothing less sanctified the individual conscience, which must therefore be rigorously searched to prepare for and verify the influence of Divine grace. And that individual conscience it is now operating, in Hamlet's case, in his direct interpretation of his own life.

There is, then, inescapably, as much a focus on the interpreter as on the interpretation. Whereas in the case of Biblical exegesis the explicator's state of grace is indispensable, in the thought of Montaigne and Shakespeare's Prince the question of the individual's fitness to interpret his human experience becomes a conscientious sifting through of the nature and condition of the self. Such is the substance of Hamlet's soliloquies. It is the subject of that *Essay* whose author says:

> I present a humble life, without distinction; but that is no matter. Moral philosophy, as a whole, can be just as well applied to a common and private existence as to one of richer stuff . . . no man ever came to a project with a better knowledge and understanding than I have of this matter, in regard to which I am the most learned man alive; and . . . no man ever went more deeply into his subject, or more thoroughly examined its elements and effects, or more exactly and completely achieved the purpose he set out to work for. To perfect it I need only bring fidelity to my task; and that is here, the purest and sincerest that is to be found anywhere.[21]

It is important not to allow a misunderstanding to enter in at this point. We are not saying, of course, that Montaigne, in focusing on the self who interprets, no less than on what it interprets, betrays a prima-

rily Protestant pedigree. Even so, Protestantism does play a galvaniz-
ing role in his thinking, as Marc Fumaroli suggests:

> . . . it could well be that his greatest originality . . . rests
> on his successful attempt to work out a perfectly orthodox
> form of spirituality for the use of laymen and of the gen-
> try, a *liberal* spirituality quite distinct from the models
> traditionally conceived for clerics bound by constraining
> vows, inscribed within a narrow hierarchical discipline
> and thus ill suited to the specificity of an independent lay
> existence. Everything seems to show that such a need was
> keenly felt in the last third of the sixteenth century in
> Catholic circles, as an answer to the solution which the
> Protestants of the Reformation had proposed to this old
> malaise in Christendom.[22]

There is a sense in which Protestantism sets Montaigne's agenda. And in his variant answer to the questions it confronted

> he was not alone in his grasp of skepticism as an intellec-
> tual tool; skepticism was in vogue among Roman
> Catholics as a defense against Protestants who sought to
> subvert them with arguments they could not answer. In
> such cases, the only safe reaction was to demolish reason
> and scholarship entirely–both theirs and yours, while
> clinging, by faith, to the Church alone.[23]

Yet Montaigne's Catholicism is kept within strict bounds. He

> . . . acknowledged his Church's right to censor, but he also
> asserted that Theology . . . best kept her dignity by remain-
> ing apart from the mere humanities. As a humanist he
> enjoyed seeking after truth, even though truth, by human
> means alone, can seldom if ever be found within this life.[24]

What Montaigne offers is a skeptical, humanist response to
pressing sixteenth-century issues with which Protestantism's prior
answers effectively challenge Catholicism also to engage. Renaissance
issues they are, including the nature of man and scope of his knowledge; issues with wider and deeper implications than their specific the-

ological formulations by either Reformation camp. Shakespeare's Prince, no less than Montaigne, responds to these preoccupations in a manner finally emancipated from direct commitment to either ideological party, although in the Prince's case, like Montaigne's, Protestantism inaugurates the need to answer. It does so with that first, local question raised by its absence of a doctrine of purgatory.

Ultimately, though, Montaigne was a Catholic in the matter of faith, regardless of what his detractors may have claimed. What Shakespeare's religious beliefs were we cannot know for certain and it may not be worth asking. Just this much is clear: while Prince Hamlet's thinking is saturated with religious references, he cannot finally come to any settled theological conclusions. He does not accept the guidance of the Church, the Bible, or direct revelation, on the nature of "death,/The undiscover'd country, from whose bourn/No traveller returns . . ." (III, i, 78-80). As for *Hamlet*, its author omits the contemporary convention of having the Ghost reappear at the end of the drama to state and thus seal the meaning of the play. Horatio's pious words over his friend's corpse: "Good night, sweet prince,/And flights of angels sing thee to thy rest," (V, ii, 364-65), carry no weight except as an expression of Horatio's sudden need to express a personal sentiment, with whatever conventional or real force. The play itself remains steadfastly uncommitted spiritually. The ending is, ". . . in structural terms, resolutely secular."[25]

Hamlet plunges its Prince into a predicament of which he must make sense without the guidance of prior religious orthodoxy of whatever stripe. Theological props are inadequate in a world–Hamlet's world–where phenomena cannot be taken on faith, but must be assessed by the test of firsthand experience. Such interpretation finally gives dramatic voice to the late Renaissance intellectual climate in which the play was written. It reverberates with that accumulation of scientific, philosophical and transmuted religious thought to which we have been referring. It articulates it in terms of a new, open, engagement with the world, predicated on the self, to which Bacon and Descartes will, in their different conceptual ways, soon lend systematic expression.

*

What first impels Hamlet to interpret experience directly in this way is, as we have seen, the equivocal nature of the Ghost. The play within the play is his means of doing so. But the Ghost is far from being all that requires interpretation. And many other ways of enabling it are devised. For the need to interpret is a constant preoccupation in *Hamlet*, directed as much to the Prince's character as to his father's Ghost. Hence, we find intensive efforts to explain Hamlet's personality–or, more specifically, the sudden change in it noticed by others. His altered behavior dates from the time when he first encounters the Ghost, telling Horatio: "I perchance hereafter shall think meet/To put an antic disposition on" (I. v, 179-80). Ophelia describes it to her father in these terms:

> My lord, as I was sewing in my closet,
> Lord Hamlet, with his doublet all unbrac'd,
> No hat upon his head, his stockings foul'd,
> Ungarter'd and down-gyved to his ankle,
> Pale as his shirt, his knees knocking each other,
> And with a look so piteous in purport
> As if he had been loosed out of hell
> To speak of horrors, he comes before me. (II, i, 77-84)

We might well ask to what extent Hamlet is stage-managing the impression he gives, suspecting that Ophelia acts as proxy for her father and his royal master. Whatever the case, Polonius instantly offers Ophelia the interpretation to which he clings for the rest of his abbreviated life: "Mad for thy love?" (II, i, 85). And again: "This is the very ecstasy of love" (II, i, 102). Other interpretations are advanced for what Claudius calls "Hamlet's transformation" (II, ii, 5). At this point, speaking to Rosencrantz and Guildenstern, Claudius says:

> What it should be,
> More than his father's death, that thus hath put him
> So much from th'understanding of himself
> I cannot dream of. (II, ii, 7-10)

Gertrude, for her part, says: "I doubt it is no other but the main,/His father's death and our o'er-hasty marriage" (II, ii, 56-57). Nevertheless, Claudius continues trying to plumb his nephew's worrying behavior, explicitly setting aside Polonius's interpretation:

> Love? His affections do not that way tend . . .
> There's something in his soul
> O'er which his melancholy sits on brood,

And I do doubt the hatch and the disclose
Will be some danger. (III, i, 164, 166-69)

Eventually Claudius expresses in barely veiled terms what that "some-thing" is. It is Hamlet's plotting to destroy his uncle, the new King, for which Claudius seeks his nephew's death. For the

terms of our estate may not endure
Hazard so near us as doth hourly grow
Out of his brows. (III, iii, 4-6)

This debate about the correct interpretation of Hamlet's behav-ior and intentions is advanced by dramatic means similar to Hamlet's own use of the players. Again and again situations are stage-managed in which he may be observed. Claudius orders the Prince's compan-ions from youth, Rosencrantz and Guildenstern, to:

draw him on to pleasures and to gather,
So much as from occasion you may glean,
Whether aught to us unknown afflicts him thus
That, open'd, lies within our remedy. (II, ii, 15-18)

Polonius will, he tells Claudius and Gertrude:

loose my daughter to him.
Be you and I behind an arras then,
Mark the encounter. (II, ii, 162-64)

Then Polonius hides–fatally–behind the arras in Gertrude's chamber, in III, iv, to observe the conversation between mother and son. Truly, the Prince is, as Ophelia says of him in another context: "Th'observ'd of all observers" (III, i, 156).

Apparently, it is not only Hamlet who is preoccupied with inter-preting and the means of doing so. Nor is the Prince the only flesh and blood character requiring interpretation. Ophelia's distraction invites it no less than does Hamlet's:

Her speech is nothing,
Yet the unshaped use of it doth move
The hearers to collection. They aim at it,

And botch the words up fit to their own thoughts,
Which, as her winks and nods and gestures yield them,
Indeed would make one think there might be thought,
Though nothing sure, yet much unhappily. (IV, v, 7-13)

Furthermore, the practice of "lawful espials" as Claudius calls them, (III, i, 32), so fully exploited by and against Hamlet, are turned on Polonius's own family. We have spoken of the father eavesdropping on his daughter's conversation with her beloved. Polonius also orders his man Reynaldo to spy on his son Laertes in Paris, tutoring him on how to do so most effectively. While of Polonius himself, Claudius tells Gertrude "we shall sift him" for information about Hamlet (II, ii, 58).

It is not hard to suggest that the Renaissance court provides the way of rendering the theme of interpretation in dramatic form. For no less than the sixteenth-century intellectual climate, to which we have referred, the nature of contemporary politics puts at Shakespeare's disposal a means of developing earlier versions of the play through his theme of interpretation. *Hamlet* itself suggests such an Italian context when the Prince refers during the play within the play to the murder of Duke Gonzago (III, ii, 232-34), done in Urbino.[26] But despite Madariaga's suggestion that Hamlet had much in common with Cesare Borgia, not least because he regards Borgia as actually Spanish not Italian, Shakespeare had little need to look further afield than England for examples of fatally dangerous eavesdropping, trickery and intrigue at the center of power. Elizabeth I's court provided them aplenty, as did Henry VIII's. It was a lethal environment felling Essex, Mary Queen of Scots, Henry's wives, Cromwell and even that universally respected intellectual, the King's Chancellor and friend, Thomas More. While this political background can easily be seen as supplying Shakespeare with his methods of interpreting behavior and motive in *Hamlet*, it is, however, possible to press it beyond a level of mere generality. As we do so we shall find it giving the play access to a further, profounder form and method of interpretation.

Sir Thomas More was beheaded for a newly defined form of High Treason. It was "malicious silence" in refusing to give his assent under oath to the Act of Succession declaring the King's marriage to Catherine of Aragon void and that with Anne Boleyn valid. The latter union entailed a repudiation of papal supremacy which More found unacceptable, and to which he thus refused to swear. He retreated into silence: silence into which another of the King's courtiers, the poet Sir

Thomas Wyatt, withdraws.

> Now cesse, my lute, this is the last
> Labour that thou and I shall wast,
> And ended is that we begon;
> Now is this song boeth sung and past:
> My lute be still, for I have done.[27]

For with his lute, his lays, the court balladeer embodies and gives voice to the assumptions of his audience. They are the norms of a traditional face to face society with feudal bonds of honor and allegiance. But suddenly the lutanist has no place in Henry's new Machiavellian world of naked power politics. There the group is atomized into interchangeable, all-too-dispensable pawns. The lutanist and More, have been forced by the prevailing political environment into internal exile. It is silence and seclusion that now affords them the space to live conscientiously, within themselves, disengaged from what has come to pass as a "normal world."

More embraced prison life in the Tower of London. He settled down to write a Christian work: *A Dialoge of Comfort Against Tribulacion*. He told his daughter Margaret that, but for his family obligations, he would always have chosen for himself "as strait a room and staiter too."[28] Now, is this not a tone soon to be echoed by a voice we have already heard in our preceding pages? It comes from someone born two years prior to More's execution. Montaigne was to retreat from the French Wars of Religion, whose fanatical excesses destroyed all vestiges of Renaissance optimism, and were as much political as religious. He returned to his country house thirty miles away from Bordeaux, a bare year before the horrific Massacre of Saint Bartholemew. There, he retired to the library he built into one of its towers. Larger, admittedly, than More's cell, his occupancy of it has many of the same attributes:

> From this room I have three open views . . . It is a little difficult of access and out of the way, but this I like, both for the benefit of exercise and for its keeping people away from me. It is my throne, and I try to rule here absolutely, reserving this one corner from all society, conjugal, filial, and social . . . Miserable to my mind, is the man who has no place in his house where he can be alone . . . I consid-

er nothing so harsh in the life of austerity followed by our religious orders, as the rule which I found in one of their communities, by which they are required perpetually to be in company . . . I find it rather more bearable always to be alone than never to have the power to be so.[29]

Montaigne differs from More in that his seclusion was not permanent. The very civil war he shunned was to draw him in again. Then he traveled in search for a cure for the stone. He was received by the Pope in Rome. Nor was Montaigne's withdrawal enforced, which More's certainly was, even if he embraced it as part of a Christian martyrdom, contrasting, again, with the non-religious temper of Montaigne's retreat. Nonetheless, beneath these obvious differences there are points of vital continuity between the men's forms of withdrawal. They will suggest how the political experience of the century into which Shakespeare was born provides the dramatist with means to develop his theme of interpretation.

First, although Montaigne is not incarcerated in his library because of alleged High Treason, he is no less debarred from the active political world. He has discharged himself from it by the expedient of introjecting it: the library "is my throne, and I try to rule here absolutely."[30] The result is solitude, silence and internal exile. They are the preconditions for that introspective self whose genesis consequently owes so much to the political environment from which it strives to separate itself.

Secondly, More's way of experiencing the internal exile into which Henrician politics drove him was religious. He was a martyr-in-the-making, scrutinizing his soul in preparation to meet his God. Does not Montaigne's retreat embody many of these religious elements, albeit in a secularized form? His library brings to the threshold of his mind, by contrast with the kind of monastery he dislikes, his library's similarity to the sort of monastery he does approve. Rightly so, for here is the silent solitude of a chapel with those three open views like a triptych for meditation. Yet meditate he does—not pray. He has moved, in his view of the self, of *him*self, from the religious devotee overseen by God, to the solitary being, auto-reflective in the luminous after-image of his dead friend, Étienne de la Boétie.

Here we too have advanced by isolating both sets of similarities between Montaigne and More. For we are now looking well beyond the Machiavellian politics of the Renaissance court and how its cutthroat spying, suspicion and traps suggest to Shakespeare paranoid stratagems for interpreting behavior. Passing into the silence of internal exile, we have traced the emergence of a new kind of self; one that interprets, not least, itself. Earlier on, considering the intellectual underpinnings of Shakespeare's emphasis on interpreting, we met that self's Protestant forebear: the individual conscience needing to scrutinize itself in order to ensure its fitness to receive the Holy Ghost's guidance in interpreting the Bible. Now we encounter other antecedents, from an originally political perspective. Either way, the result is a self-sifting, in a non-theological vein, characterizing Hamlet as much as Montaigne. We need to show how.

We may begin by returning to Rosencrantz and Guildenstern, ordered by Claudius to watch the Prince so as to shed light on his transformation. Hamlet says that he himself will tell them why they were sent, even if he only does so implicitly. What follows is Hamlet's description of his own state of mind, albeit one in which he may be taking into account the pair of hearers through whom his words will come to the ears of that third, his uncle. In spite of which, the description might also stand as sincere, given its continuity of tone with Hamlet's soliloquies, *a priori* without an audience of *dramatis personae*. "I have of late, but where-/fore I know not, lost all my mirth . . ." (II, ii, 295-96). For although he says: "What piece of work is man . . ." (II, ii, 303), he goes on: ". . . and yet, to me, what is this quintessence of dust?" (II, ii, 308-09). Hamlet hereby expresses the transformation in his outlook that his companions seek to explain to their royal masters. In other words, Hamlet is joining all the rest who seek to interpret him, by interpreting himself.

Now, the Prince, we have already seen in the case of the Ghost, is an accomplished interpreter. Moreover, it is a role natural to him. When he gives a commentary on the play within the play, he says to Ophelia, referring to the man who explains the action in a puppet show: "I could interpret between you and your love if I/could see the puppets dallying" (III, ii, 241-42). Nevertheless, the Prince's interpretation of his own self is quite another matter. It is, furthermore, of an entirely different order from the interpretations of him offered by others. It differs in motivation, nature and significance, as we may judge not only from this instance but from numerous others.

Let us take the motivation for Hamlet's self-analysis first. He differs from the others interpreting him in that he does not seek to find thereby a simply defined key to his behavior, whether love-sickness, mourning, or murderous ambition, in order that he may be better controlled. On the contrary, we note that he is temperamentally inclined to introspection. It is a compulsive habit, not an objective requirement. He is, from the outset, melancholic. This gives him grounds for obsessive self-rumination, intensified, even before the Ghost's appearance to him, by his father's death, his mother's overhasty marriage and his forfeit of thc throne to Claudius. The atmosphere of the court world, his world, is so "rank and gross" (I, ii, 136), where nothing can "come to good" (I, ii, 158), that his human feelings cannot be openly expressed: "But break, my heart, for I must hold my tongue" (I, ii, 159). Isolation and silence are Hamlet's lot. They breed the unending self-scrutiny of psychic solitary confinement in that internal exile equivalent to More's, or Wyatt's lutanist's. Here it is aptly metaphorised by the dramatic form of the soliloquy. In fact, Hamlet will go on to say of Denmark: "To me/it is a prison" (II, ii, 250-51). To Hamlet, with his initial disaffection, the appearance of the Ghost demanding revenge for murder, adds a massive extra impulse to rumination and self-analysis. These liberate his consciousness to an extent that no other character remotely matches, certainly not in observing him. Only Ophelia, in her verbally fractured descent into madness, and Claudius, conscience-stricken after the play within the play, undergo any change of consciousness in respect of themselves, although neither experiences anything remotely comparable to the sustained surge, the sheer largeness, of Hamlet's forcibly enhanced mental vision.

How exactly does the command to revenge have its impact on Hamlet's thinking? Anne Barton says:

> Retaliation for an actual death . . . is inherently tragic, not only because blood will have blood, but because of what it does to the life and personality of the virtuous avenger: a man cruelly isolated from society by the nature of the task he has undertaken. The revenger's position, necessarily secretive, solitary, and extreme, is conducive to introspection. It encourages meditation on the anomalies of justice, both human and divine, on past time, and on the value of life and human relationships.[31]

This has an obvious relevance to Hamlet—with an important additional observation prompted by Barton's phrase "virtuous avenger." Neither the Prince nor the play ever challenge the legitimacy of the revenge. They only question, for a time, the veracity of the

Ghost ordering it. Hence John Bayley says: ". . . the duty of revenge removes from Hamlet's consciousness any question of dilemma or soul-searching. He does not have to concentrate; his mind floats freely and takes on the color of new occurrences . . . Conscience and its activities are a distraction and a relief from duty." This is ". . . the paradoxical freedom of consciousness, when confined by an unquestioned duty . . . ."[32]

Hamlet's consciousness consequently explores a multiplicity of themes. Sometimes he directly interprets his own character and its supposed defects. One example is the scene we have considered, where he tells Rosencrantz and Guildenstern of his transformation. Another is the third soliloquy: "O what a rogue and peasant slave am I!" in which he asks: "Am I a coward?" (II, ii, 543-601). On other occasions Hamlet does interpret his own disposition, although by implication. This happens while offering an account not just of himself in particular but of man, or some aspect of the human predicament, in general. The "To be" soliloquy is an instance (III, i, 56-88). There are others, including the Prince's speech to Horatio about ". . . that man/That is not passion's slave . . ." (III, ii, 56-74). For the expansion in Hamlet's consciousness results in him now interpreting all and any aspect of humanity–as he does by taking his cue from Montaigne's view of man in the Rosencrantz and Guildenstern discussion, if only to invert it. Moreover, virtually anything, no matter how accidental, becomes food for the Prince's thoughts. The passage of Fortinbras's Norwegian troops through Denmark to fight the Poles inspires the last soliloquy to consider "What is a man . . ." (IV, iv, 32-66).

Hamlet's melancholic consciousness is, then, strangely freed by the motivating command to revenge. It considers not merely Hamlet but the world. In fact, it has the capacity to include everything, relate everything, interpret everything. This driven expansiveness of his view of himself in the widest context available to him, gives Hamlet's self-analysis a radically different nature from the narrowly prosaic attempts others make to interpret him. Nor do Claudius's tormented confession and Ophelia's distracted utterances ever depart from their narrowly specific personal predicaments.

Hamlet's consciousness uncoils endlessly–but it does so from what is initially consciousness of himself. It accords centrality to his self, therefore. And in this he strongly resembles Montaigne, as we have seen. Admittedly, Hamlet is hardly at ease with himself, or with the circumstances in which he is living, in which respect he has a greater affinity with the imprisoned More than with the voluntarily leisured, self-confident Montaigne. Certainly, too, he has a more dejected view of his own being than the Frenchman. Yet not only is the self the foundation for interpreting reality in both Hamlet's and Montaigne's cases. It suffuses all it interprets with its skeptical, humane and free-floating consciousness. Above all, it does so, in either case, unconstrained by any controlling theological position–despite the fact that, in the *Essays*, such a religious stance can eventually be extrapolated, whereas Hamlet's outlook, for all its superstitious fears, remains ultimately secular.

So what, we may ask, is the significance of our protagonist's interpreting, springing, as it does, from self-reflection? It differs, we claimed, from the significance of other characters' interpretations of him. But we may best establish its cardinal quality by first reminding ourselves of the similarities between their approaches so as to see what their likenesses leave wanting. Thus the Prince's relations and associates resemble him not only in interpreting him and each other, but also in the restlessness with which they do so. It constitutes virtually their entire activity. For they all serve to express the theme of interpretation which is thereby a major preoccupation of the play, not just a concern of its protagonist. It is carried on into parts of the action, such as Polonius's family, where Hamlet is not involved. This suggests that the central character is not the be-all-and–end-all of the audience's attention. He is simply one character, among others, in a larger entity, the play, of which he and his self-interpreting form but a part. Yet what a part!

We need only remind ourselves of the divergences between Hamlet's way of interpreting and that of the rest. Its motivation and nature are, we recall, quite different. They highlight its greater range in starting from himself, yet moving to take in the rest of the world. Above all, the Prince, unlike the rest, gives us from within, over seven soliloquies and much else, one mind's engagement with the theme of interpretation. It provides, from inside Hamlet's very self, his unmediated, direct interpretation of reality, as a response to being, not just in the stiflingly corrupt world of Elsinore but in the universe as he conceives it. As such it is, by far, the most intimate, searching and sustained exploration of this preoccupation in the play. This argues so different a role for Hamlet that there is really no question of submerging his significance as a character as such, in favor of an exclusively thematic reading of the play. The theme of interpretation is advanced most fully by, and inseparably from the movement of its protagonist's qualitatively different, emphatically personal consciousness. Rooted precisely in his subjectivity, it inevitably highlights the importance of Hamlet as character. Theme and character are one.

Post-Bradleyan critical orthodoxy contrasts them, favoring the former. The play becomes a thematic poem rather than a psychological interplay between beings. It is a sterile and misleading opposition in the case of *Hamlet*, where theme and character not only co-exist but amount to one and the same, as we expect in great drama. Moreover, the tendency of some post-modern criticism to abandon both theme and character simply does not square with the experience of seeing the play in performance. The Prince's subjectivity dominates. Insofar as the protagonist of Joyce's *Ulysses* has been called the prose, the Prince's consciousness is the tragic hero of *Hamlet*.

Different, then, as may be the significance of the way in which Hamlet and the other characters interpret, we might well go on to wonder, finally: what *is* his interpretation of the world as he knows it? He gives interpretations, of course, of specific things, such as whether the Ghost is a good Ghost, or the reason for his own transformation. But a wider, fuller interpretation of reality is something he never offers. Least of all does he do so about his own self, which, if it is actually the mystery he claims, remains one that he never resolves. What we get instead is a dark mood of disaffection, seeming to some twentieth-century critics downright adolescent. It rejects the kind of Renaissance optimism to be found in Pico della Mirandola. Hamlet presents us with the temperamental inclination to radical skepticism, occasioned by specific instances of emotional urgency. He rejects complacent certainties, the banal: he questions: he does not assert positively. Caught as Hamlet is between two movements of philosophical systematization, the unraveling medieval and barely nascent early modern, he is still ill-suited to define a coherent philosophical position from the intellectual welter of his times, despite all his mentions of philosophy. Or, as Terry Eagleton puts it in Marxist terms: "His 'self' consists simply in the range of gestures with which he resists available definitions, not in a radical alternative beyond their reach. It is thus wholly parasitic on the positions it refuses . . . Hamlet is a radically transitional figure, strung out between a traditional social order to which he is marginal, and a future epoch of achieved bourgeois individualism." [33]

There is, however, another way of looking at Hamlet's failure to offer a specific interpretation of the world. Maybe it is not just the result of a disadvantageous historical position between two philosophical or social and ideological moments. Perhaps to ask what such an interpretation might be is a case of *une question mal posée*. Does Hamlet not, rather, resemble Wittgenstein who said he "holds no opinions in philosophy?" Philosophy exists to remove "a feeling of puzzlement, to cure a sort of mental cramp."[34]

Hamlet is a man ordered to revenge his father's murder without a theological means of validating the command. Reason enough, surely, to suffer from a spectacular attack of mental cramp! Is there any wonder that he draws on a constitutional inclination to worry things out? He thereby dramatizes the alternative which Wittgenstein suggests to philosophy as system-building. But he also expresses emergent secular man's reliance on the activities of consciousness as an intellectual form of mental self-cure.

Notes

[1] Harry Levin, quoted by Harold Jenkins, ed., *Hamlet: The Arden Shakespeare* (London: Thomson, 2002), 122.

[2] All references to the play are to *Hamlet: The Arden Shakespeare*.

[3] Harry Levin, *The Question of Hamlet* (New York: Oxford UP, 1959), 20.

[4] Quoted by John Dover Willson, *What Happens in Hamlet* (Cambridge: Cambridge UP, 1986), 56.

[5] *Julius Caesar: The Laurel Shakespeare*, ed. Charles Jasper Sisson (New York: Dell Publishing Company 1958), 137.

[6] For the novelty of the Ghost I have drawn on John Dover Wilson, *What Happens in Hamlet*, 55-60 and E. Pearlman, "Shakespeare at Work: The Invention of the Ghost," *Hamlet: New Critical Essays* (hereafter referred to as HNCE), ed. Arthur F. Kinney (New York and London: Routledge, 2002), 71-84.

[7] L. C. Knights, *An Approach to Hamlet* (London: Chatto and Windus, 1960), 46 and 89.

[8] Arthur F. Kinney, "Introduction," HNCE, 15.

[9] Jenkins, 436.

[10] Quoted by Dover Wilson, 64.

[11] Quoted by Dover Wilson, 62.

[12] For discussion of the sixteenth-century debate on spirits I am indebted to Dover Wilson, 60-75.

[13] *The Tempest: The New Penguin Shakespeare*, ed. Anne Barton (London: Penguin Books, 1968) IV, i, 148-50.

[14] Michel de Montaigne, *Essays*, trans. J. M. Cohen, (London: Penguin

Books, 1958), 343.

15 Montaigne, *Essays*, 343.

16 Montaigne, *Essays*, 344.

17 Montaigne, *Essays*, 344.

18 Montaigne, *Essays*, 347.

19 Montaigne, *Essays*, 349.

20 Montaigne, *Essays*, 349.

21 Montaigne, "On Repentance," 235-36.

22 Marc Fumaroli, "Foreward: Spirituality for Gentlemen," M. A. Screech, *Montaigne and Melancholy* (London: Penguin Books, 1991), xiii.

23 Screech, 3.

24 Screech, 5.

25 Pearlman, 77.

26 Here I follow Jenkins, 507, who believes that the location of the murder in Vienna is a textual mistake.

27 *Collected Poems of Sir Thomas Wyatt*, ed. Kenneth Muir (London: Routledge and Kegan Paul, 1963), 51.

28 Quoted in article on More, ed. Germain P. Marc'hadour, *The New Encyclopaedia Britannica*, Volume 8, 15th Edition (Chicago: University of Chicago, 1990), 315.

29 Montaigne, "On Three Kinds of Relationships," 263.

30 Montaigne, "On Three Kinds of Relationships," 263.

31 Anne Barton, "Introduction," *Hamlet: The New Penguin Shakespeare*, ed. T. J. B. Spencer (London: Penguin Books, 1996), 14.

32 John Bayley, *Shakespeare and Tragedy* (London: Routledge and Kegan Paul, 1981), 172.

33 Quoted by Kinney, 43.

34 Ludwig Wittgenstein, *Preliminary Studies for the 'Philosophical Investigation' Generally Known as the Blue and Brown Books* (Oxford: Basil Blackwell, 1969), 1.

Travelers from an Antique Land:
Shelley's Inspiration for "Ozymandias"

John Rodenbeck

This article concentrates on one of the greatest and most famous poems in the English language, Shelley's masterly sonnet "Ozymandias," and deals with three areas of inquiry: 1) the sources of the poem in contemporary travel literature, 2) its meaning, and 3) what its sources and meaning tell us about the nature of "poetic inspiration."

Travel literature offers experience to the entirety of a literate public and for that reason alone has historically had far greater cultural impact than the experience of mere travel itself, which can only be individual and private. To take one small and suggestive example: the two most popular manuscript texts of the late Middle Ages were probably Mandeville's *Travels* and Marco Polo's *Description of the World*. Like Herodotus' *Histories,* these two books are literary compilations, rather than simple records or observations, and as such they quite rightly include fictional elements. It was inevitable that they should have been among the earliest European best-sellers in print, anticipating by many decades the great Renaissance collections of Ramusio and Hakluyt.[1]

But what were the needs they obviously fulfilled? The question cannot begin to be answered until we bear in mind that they inspired not only More's *Utopia*—the fountainhead of an artistic lineage that includes major works of Rabelais, Cervantes, Bacon, Swift, Defoe, Voltaire, Melville, Twain, Shaw, Wells, Huxley, Orwell, Nabokov, and Calvino, not to mention V. S. Naipaul, Paul Theroux and J. G. Ballard—but also Columbus' voyage in search of the Indies.

In the case of Shelley's "Ozymandias" the fact that the poem has nothing to do with the poet/speaker's personal physical experience is announced by the first line, which tells us explicitly that the person who had the fictive experience that the poem uses as its central metaphor was not the poet-speaker at all, but "a traveler":

Ozymandias

I met a traveler from an antique land
    Who said: "Two vast and trunkless legs of stone
Stand in the desert. Near them on the sand,
    Half sunk, a shatter'd visage lies, whose frown
5   And wrinkled lip and sneer of cold command
    Tell that its sculptor well those passions read
Which yet survive—stamp'd on these lifeless things—
    The hand that mock'd them and the heart that fed;
And on the pedestal these words appear:
10 'My name is Ozymandias, king of kings:
    Look on my works, ye Mighty, and despair!'
Nothing beside remains. Round the decay
    Of that colossal wreck, boundless and bare,
The lone and level sands stretch far away."

The name *Ozymandias* is a Greek rendition of "^cUser-ma^cat-re^c," the first element in the praenomen or throne name of the ancient Egyptian king now usually known instead by his Ra-name as Ramesses II (1279-1212 B.C.). His mortuary temple was definitively identified at long last by Jean François Champollion (1790-1832) in 1829. It has been known since as the Ramesseum, and of course still stands on the West Bank at Luxor.[2] The career of this great king, however, was utterly unknown in Shelley's day. Even the name *Ramesses* would have been recognized only by readers of the Bible and then only as the Hebrew name of an Egyptian city mentioned in Genesis 47.11 and Exodus 1.11, not as the name of a king. Like all his contemporaries, Shelley thus possessed nothing that approaches an ordinary twenty-first-century schoolboy's knowledge of the pharaoh who had boasted the throne name "^cUser-ma^cat-re^c" three millennia before.

At no time before he wrote the sonnet could Shelley possibly have seen any sculptured head comparable to the one his fictional traveler describes unless he had actually gone to Egypt. In common with all the other English Romantic poets, however, either major and minor, Shelley never set foot in the Land of the Pharaohs, though many of his non-literary contemporaries did so.[3] Nor is there any record, indeed, of his ever even contemplating such a visit. It is therefore quite impossible that "Ozymandias" could have been inspired by any first-hand experience of the poet's involving either its Egyptian setting or *a fortiori* any decayed colossal sculpture within that setting. There is abundant evidence, in fact, that inspirations for his Egyptian or quasi-Egyptian allusions not only in this sonnet, but also in other works were entirely and exclusively literary.

The two most crucial lines of the sonnet and the name *Ozymandias* were borrowed from a well-known ancient Greek source, Diodorus Siculus. Among Shelley's other literary sources, the most obvious are works that were virtually contemporary: Volney's *Voyage en Syrie et en Égypte, pendant les années 1783, 1784, et 1785,* published first in 1787 and often reprinted; his *Les Ruines, ou Méditations sur révolutions des empires,* first published in 1791, an enormously influential work that circulated throughout Europe and was one of the building blocks of Shelley's mind; and Vivant Denon's *Voyage dans la Basse et la Haute Egypte,* which appeared in 1802, when Shelley was 10 and became, next perhaps to Lane's *Manners and Customs,* the most popular and successful book of Egyptology ever published, a staple of any well-furnished gentleman's library throughout the Romantic era.[4] A fourth possible source is Richard Pococke's extraordinary *Description of the East*, an important and justly famous two-volume opus that contained 178 large plates.[5] And a fifth is the celebrated *Description de l'Égypte* (1809 [1810]-1829), several volumes of which were already circulating among well-heeled enthusiasts in England.[6]

The great sonnet was published on 11 January 1818. It had apparently been written barely two weeks earlier. The occasion of its composition is now well known.[7] At his house near Marlowe on Saturday 27 December 1817, the day after Boxing Day, Shelley entertained Horace Smith (1779-1849), whom he had met at Leigh Hunt's the previous year. Smith was equally talented as a financier, a verse parodist, and an author of historical novels. The talk seems to have drifted around to Egyptian antiquity and to Diodorus Siculus, whose arrogant epitaph ascribed to Ozymandias "had become virtually a commonplace in the romantic period;"[8] and a friendly competition ensued in which each writer was to produce a sonnet on the subject of "Ozymandias, the King of Kings." Smith came up with the following:

On a Stupendous Leg of Granite,
Discovered Standing by Itself
in the Deserts of Egypt,
with the Inscription Inserted Below

In Egypt's sandy silence, all alone,
Stands a gigantic Leg, which far off throws
The only shadow that the Desert knows.
"I am great Ozymandias," saith the stone.
"The King of Kings; this mighty city shows
The wonders of my hand." The city's gone!
Naught but the leg remaining to disclose
The sight of that forgotten Babylon.
We wonder, and some hunter may express
Wonder like ours, when through the wilderness
Where London stood, holding the wolf in chase,
He meets some fragment huge, and stops to guess
What wonderful, but unrecorded race
Once dwelt in that annihilated place.[9]

Horace Smith may well have seen the depiction of just such a monumental Pharaonic leg in plate 38 of Volume I of Richard Pococke's *A Description of the East and some other Countries.* Rich and Egyptophile, he almost certainly owned a copy of this work, the most frequently cited in pioneering Egyptology.

He may also have owned copies of some of the earlier volumes of "the great French work," the *Description de l'Égypte,* which was still in the course of publication, and he may have shown them to Shelley. It is among the plates of the *Description*, for example—-a view of a colossus standing near the entrance to the hypostyle hall at Karnak—that Shelley could have found his own "vast and trunkless legs of stone."[10] Or he could, of course, simply have imagined them. What Shelley produced, in any case, was the first draft of "Ozymandias," which was published with minimal changes two weeks later on page 24 of number 524 of Leigh Hunt's *The Examiner,* where Hunt also published Horace Smith's sonnet a fortnight afterwards, on 25 January.

During that same month, January of 1818, the *Quarterly Review* (London) announced that Henry Salt's first shipment of Egyptian antiquities was on its way to the British Museum. The shipment included a colossal head that Giovanni Belzoni had extracted in 1816 from the ruins of a temple on the West Bank at Thebes and that was, the *Quarterly Review* declared, "without doubt the finest specimen of ancient Egyptian sculpture which has yet been discovered,"[11] It is this head that is commonly supposed to have inspired Shelley, who is alleged to have seen it at the British Museum before he wrote his sonnet.

The vulgar error of believing that Shelley was inspired to write "Ozymandias" by the actual vision of an Egyptian monument or work of art—and specifically by the physical sight of this particular colossal Egyptian sculptured head—has lingered in full strength as a critical commonplace to this day.[12] Based upon that defective idea about art and artists that E. H. Gombrich specifically called "a heresy,"[13] this superficially plausible folk thesis has seduced many an amateur critic and is totally fallacious. Shelley simply could not possibly have seen the head in question before he wrote his great sonnet.

The famous sculptured head that Giovanni Belzoni excavated in what he thought was the Memnonium was lowered into a boat from the West Bank of the Nile at Luxor on 17 November 1816. It took a month thereafter to float down the river to Cairo and another month to get to Alexandria, where it arrived in mid-January 1817. There it was stored in one of Muhammad ᶜAli's warehouses to await an appropriate vessel sailing for England. The wait was a long one: it lasted through most of a year—the rest of winter, all of the following spring and summer, and half of autumn, 1817. Not until 17 October 1817 could Salt assure the Foreign Minister, Lord Castlereagh, that the head had finally been embarked, aboard the transport ship *Nearchus*, and was bound for Malta.

In Malta there was presumably the normal delay of several weeks for quarantine, a stringent control exercised over all Mediterranean traffic between Europe and the Ottoman Empire. At the end of this quarantine period the head was transferred to a Royal Navy storeship, the *Weymouth*, which was also burdened with antiquities from Leptis Magna. The precise date in December 1817 or January 1818 when the *Weymouth* eventually sailed from Malta is no doubt recorded somewhere; and it is probable that the January article in the *Quarterly Review* had optimistic reference to its departure. What is certain, however, is that it did not dock in England until March 1818, at least two months after Shelley's poem had already been published The letter from the Foreign Office and the Admiralty notifying the British Museum of its arrival is dated 14 March 1818—just two days after Shelley and his entire household had left England forever to settle permanently in Italy,

The itineraries of the poet and the Egyptian head that is alleged to have been his inspiration make it clear that they never crossed paths. In

December 1817, the time when it is supposed to have influenced Shelley's poem, Belzoni's head was either stored on a ship in the harbor at Valetta or somewhere at sea. The poet could not possibly have seen the head before he wrote the poem and he probably never saw it at all.

There were, of course, still further delays. The British Museum did not bother to appoint a sub-committee to decide how to exhibit it until 9 May 1818;[14] and it was probably not actually displayed for the first time until late in 1818, while Shelley and his family were busily traveling from place to place in Italy. Not until November 1818 did Salt himself finally receive word in Alexandria that his shipment had actually arrived safely. Shelley's friend Keats, a fellow Egyptophile and a fervent habitué of the British Museum, apparently saw the head for the first time early in 1819, remarking, "I had not seen it before."[15] Shelley could conceivably have sneaked back into England sometime between then and his death in 1822 for the specific purpose of paying a visit incognito to the British Museum. But such a visit, unrecorded anywhere, seems enormously unlikely.

Shelley obviously either had no idea what Belzoni's prize looked like, moreover, or found the information irrelevant when he wrote his poem. His fictional statue has a "wrinkled lip and sneer of cold command," for example, whereas Belzoni described the real head as "smiling upon me, at the thought of being taken away to England." The head of Ozymandias in the *Description de l'Égypte,* which Shelley also might well have seen, shows the same benignly smiling countenance Belzoni describes—though probably at that point in time delighted with the idea of being taken away to France, rather than England—likewise utterly unlike the depiction Shelley describes in his poem.[16]

In any case, even if Shelley could actually have seen this head before he wrote his poem he would almost certainly not have been inspired to write a poem about it as a portrait head of Ozymandias, since almost no one among his contemporaries in England recognized it as such. Out of the deficiencies of contemporary British scholarship a mistaken identification had already arisen that would prevail among English scholars for at least 20 more years. Unable to read hiero-glyphics and badly misled by an eighteenth-century toponymical tra-dition—according to which the Ramesseum was identified as a Memnonium, a temple to the son of Tithonus by the Hellenic dawn goddess Eos—Belzoni, Salt, and the experts of the Museum itself had all decided to call the fragmentary statue "Young Memnon." It still bears this erroneous designation in the British Museum inventory list, along with its original acquisition number, 19.[17]

Publication of the sonnet was obviously timed by Hunt to capitalize on public excitement in anticipation of the arrival of Salt's collection at the British Museum; and enthusiasm for things ancient and Egyptian continued for several weeks in the circle around Hunt and *The Examiner*. "Ozymandias" had been the result of a light-hearted sonnet-writing contest arising out of this enthusiasm; and on 4 February 1818 Leigh Hunt challenged Shelley and Keats to yet another such competition on yet another Egyptian subject: "The Nile." The agreed time limit—fifteen minutes—was adhered to by Keats and Shelley, but Hunt became intrigued by his task, cheated, and worked on for several hours past the time limit. The results were a couple of perfunctory self-parodies by Keats and Shelley, who adverted, obviously uninspired, to stereotypical themes, and a somewhat better one by Hunt, which contains not only a good phrase or two, but also one delightful line characterizing Cleopatra as "the laughing queen that caught the world's great hands."

That Shelley was interested in ancient Egypt had been clearly announced years earlier in his first major poem, the lengthy verse narrative *Alastor*, with its references to pyramids, obelisks, sphinxes, and ruined temples with "stupendous columns and wild images/Of more than man, where marble daemons watch/The Zodiac's brazen mystery."[18] Pyramids reappear and are put to metaphorical use in his great philosophical poem "Mont Blanc," written the following year. And they appear yet again in *Laon and Cythna*, a political and philosophical allegory, later transformed into *The Revolt of Islam*, which he worked on between April and September of 1817, shortly before writing "Ozymandias." Similar *aegyptiaca* turn up later in his masterpiece *Prometheus Unbound*, written in 1818-1819.

Diodorus Siculus, the ancient source used by Shelley and his friend Horace Smith in their sonnet-writing contest, was a Sicilian, as his cognomen tells us, and was contemporary with Julius Caesar. He wrote his forty-volume Rome-centered history of the world in Greek, the common tongue not only of Sicily, Southern Italy, the Balkans, Asia Minor, Syria, Egypt and most of North Africa, but also of the Roman elite. Mrs. Shelley's note on the year tells us that in fact Shelley's reading throughout 1817 was "chiefly Greek." She mentions specifically the *Iliad*, Aeschylus and Sophocles, the Homeric Hymns,

Plato, and Arrian, and it is possible that he and Horace Smith found themselves reading Diodorus at the same time.[19] Nor were Shelley and Horace Smith by any means the only contemporary English readers of Diodorus, who was a cultural touchstone for their generation.[20] It is thus hardly astonishing that in contemporary issues of *The Annals of the Fine Arts*, John Elmes should have rejected the prevailing identification of the head that Salt and Belzoni had brought to England as "Young Memnon" and speculated that it might belong instead to the statue of Ozymandias that had been described by Diodorus.[21]

Elmes's quaint speculation, as it happens, was absolutely correct, since the statue to which the head belonged was indeed one of two colossi of Ramesses II that had still survived in the ruins of the structure we now call the Ramesseum.[22] Diodorus' description of the Ramesseum was composed near the end of the first century BC, over a thousand years after the temple was completed. "At the entrance," he says,

> stand three statues, each of one entire stone, the workmanship of Memnon of Sienitas. One of these, made in a sitting position, is the greatest in all Egypt, the measure of his foot exceeding seven cubits; the one standing on the right, and the other on his left, being his daughter and mother. This piece is not only commendable for its greatness, but admirable for its cut and workmanship and the excellency of the stone. In so great a work there is not to be discerned the least flaw or any other blemish. Upon it there is this inscription: "I am Ozymandias, king of kings; if any would know how great I am, and where I lie, let him exceed me in any of my works."[23]

The entire statue, more or less as described by Diodorus, was actually still intact, though prostrate, when the Danish naval officer Friderik Ludwig Norden saw it in 1738; and its lower section remains *in situ* in the Ramesseum today. The head that was brought to England by Belzoni and given by Salt to the British Museum does indeed carry the upper portions of two columns of inscriptions that are completed on this lower section.[24] The fact that neither of these inscriptions precisely matches Diodorus' text is used to argue that Diodorus himself never actually visited the Ramesseum. But on the upper-right arm, part of the lower section left behind by Belzoni, this statue carries a cartouche saying "^{C}User-ma^{C}at-re^C"—i.e., *Ozymandias*—accompanied by a laudatory epithet, "Sun of Princes," which, with reference to Egyptian beliefs, could also conceivably be translated or glossed as "King of Kings."[25]

Diodorus himself would hardly have been able to read any Egyptian inscription in any case and would therefore have had to rely either on a Greek-speaking guide or a text that purported to offer translation into Greek. The accuracy or otherwise of his version of the inscription thus neither proves nor disproves whether or not he really walked over the site. He certainly consulted a variety of written sources and seems to have visited Egypt personally and seen its major cities, as well as such monuments as were then visible.[26] And a distinguished French scholar has observed that even if he did not visit the Ramesseum personally, whatever sources he used were not only trustworthy, but quite precise.[27]

It is the words that Diodorus says were inscribed on the statue that are in any case ironically paraphrased in Shelley's sonnet as lines 10 and 11: "My name is Ozymandias, king of kings:/Look on my works, ye Mighty, and despair." Shelley's version transforms the pharaoh's declaration from the triumphant boast of a successful despot into a commentary on the transitory nature of all earthly power.

The sonnet says nothing about any temple or temple entrance, however, not even in ruins, and in fact the poet creates a natural setting altogether different from the ancient building described by Diodorus: a bleak featureless desert landscape where "lone and level sands stretch far away." This setting is vital to the poem, since its theme or meaning requires that it evoke for us a place in which, apart from the portrait statue of the tyrant, all other physical evidence of an empire shall have disappeared without a trace.

The most obvious influence at work here—thematic and philosophical, as well as topographical—is that of Constantin-François Chassebœuf, comte de Volney (1757-1820), best known to some of us as the author of a *Voyage en Syrie et en Égypte,* the book that was purportedly the chief inspiration for Bonaparte's invasions of Egypt and Syria. Volney surveys these two Ottoman provinces in terms of their political economy rather than their historical monuments and advises anyone interested in mere physical detail to read earlier European travel writers—John Greaves (1602-1652), Benoît de Maillet (1656-1738), Paul Lucas (1664-1737), Père Sicard (1676-1726), Dr. Thomas Shaw (1694-1751) Richard Pococke (1704-1765), Norden (1708-

1742), and Carsten Niebuhr (1733-1815)—and one contemporary: Claude-Étienne Savary (1750-1788).[28] So much did Bonaparte love the book that copies of it accompanied him both to Cairo in 1798 and to St. Helena in 1815.[29]

Volney's *Les Ruines, ou méditations sur les révolutions des empires*, published four years after the *Voyage*, was even more important.[30] "Said to have been the best-seller of the Revolutionary period," remarks one scholar, "it offered a strange, but characteristic blend of science, philosophy, and theology in its attack on religion and metaphysics, and in its championing of atheistic humanism as the foundation for future human happiness."[31] Shelley had read *Les Ruines* and had already absorbed it into his own intellectual being long before he wrote "Ozymandias," as is evidenced by *Alastor, w*hich he wrote in 1815. Professor Ian Jack has remarked that the hero of *Alastor* is specifically a Volneyan creation—a "child of grace and genius" who

> leaves his 'alienated home' and travels across the world,
> musing on the present and past and coming to understand
> The thrilling secrets of the birth of time.
> He is a Rasselas without a sister or an Imlac, a Rasselas
> who has read Volney's *Ruins*.[32]

The abstractly Egyptian paraphernalia of *Alastor* have nothing at all to do with the authentic history of Egyptology. Shelley's generalized references to pyramids, obelisks, sphinxes, and ruined temples clearly owe a great deal less to direct observation than they do to the ontological legacy of the Enlightenment and its concern with "general ideas," a facet of that complex of epistemological attitudes that followed naturally upon Locke's sensationalism, Hartley's Associationism, and Hume's analysis of convention. Shelley, as Professor Jack suggests, found this legacy most powerfully distilled in its French versions, especially as formulated in *Idéologie*, the official philosophy of the French Revolution.[33] Volney was one of the most prominent of the *Idéologues* and his *Ruines* is one of the primary texts of *Idéologie*.

The first edition of *Les Ruines* (Paris: Desenne, 1791) was followed the next year by publication in English as the *Ruins of Empires,* the title by which Shelley and his Anglophone contemporaries referred to it.[34] The meaning of Volney's title is explained and its theme as a whole is implied in the invocation Volney set at the head of the text:

I salute you, solitary ruins, sacred tombs, silent walls! It is you I invoke, you to whom I address my prayer! Yes! Though the sight of you may affright the gaze of the vulgar-minded with an unknown dread, in contemplation of you my heart finds the charm of deep emotion and high thought. How many useful lessons, how many tender or powerful ideas do you not afford the mind that knows how to pay heed to you! It is you, when the entire earth stood submissive and mute before tyrants, who were already at work proclaiming the truths they detest, and who, making no difference between the ultimate dispossession of kings and that of the lowest slave, bore witness to the sacred dogma of EQUALITY.[35]

Pulling together as it does several long-established cultural postures and attitudes and knitting them neatly into the political ethos of the Revolution, *Ruins of Empires* answered brilliantly a felt intellectual need and enjoyed a well-deserved Europe-wide vogue lasting at least four decades. It was central to the evolution of Romanticism from a specifically English and insular aesthetic attitude to a universal political and philosophical force. The principles Volney saw expressed in ruins were thus to re-emerge a quarter of a century later not only in poems like "Ozymandias," but in all the best of Shelley's work. In "Mont Blanc" (1816) for example, it is precisely because of its total alienation from the sentimentalities of mankind that

> The wilderness has a mysterious tongue
> Which teaches awful doubt, or faith so mild,
> So solemn, so serene, that man may be,
> But for such a faith, with nature reconciled.
> Thou hast a voice, great Mountain, to repeal
> Large codes of fraud and woes, not understood
> By all, but which the wise, and great, and good
> Interpret, or make felt, or deeply feel. (ll. 76-83)

Likewise in "Ode to the West Wind" (1819), the autumnal wind is a metaphor for that "Wild Spirit . . . destroyer and preserver," which despite repression and without revolution will inevitably bring in an ultimate era of social and political freedom and equality.

A related example of Volney's influence is provided by a well-known passage in the life and works of Byron. The first two Cantos of *Childe Harold's Pilgrimage* (March, 1812) which made Byron famous, are the versified record of the truncated Grand Tour he and John Cam Hobhouse undertook between 1809 and 1811. Compelled to circumvent French-occupied territory, Byron and his traveling companion thus also had to avoid the normal destinations of a Grand Tour, the recognized cultural capitals of Western Europe, which in those years were all in hostile hands, as French conquests or possessions. They compensated themselves by venturing around the fringes of Europe as far east as Constantinople.[36] When the two first Cantos were published they were rightly regarded as belonging to the realm of travel literature. Byron appended a full set of vivid and entertaining ethnographic, political, and historical annotations, which should never be omitted from any edition. In Canto III, however, which Byron wrote in Switzerland during the summer of 1816, a remarkable change takes place, which has been universally recognized as due to Shelley and thence to Volney.

Shelley spent the whole of that famous summer with Byron on the shore of Lake Geneva, accompanied by his own nineteen-year-old mistress, Mary Godwin, whom he would marry after the suicide of his first wife some months later, and by Mary's step-sister Claire Clairmont, one of Byron's incidental conquests and in fact pregnant since April with his lordship's second daughter. Throughout three hectically creative months Shelley enchanted Byron, who wrote Canto III of *Childe Harold* under his spell; and it was Shelley who in fact carried Byron's manuscript of Canto III back to London for delivery to his publisher, John Murray.

One of the most familiar stanzas of Canto III simply transfers a Volneyan vision of the ruins of an empire from Syria or Egypt to the battlefield of Waterloo, where a resurgent Bonaparte had been decisively defeated less than two years earlier and which Byron had just visited en route to Geneva.

> Stop!—for thy tread is on an Empire's dust!
> An Earthquake's spoil is sepulchered below!
> Is thy spot marked with no colossal bust?
> Nor column trophied for triumphal show?
> None: but the moral's truth tells simpler so.
> As the ground was before, thus let it be;—
> How that red rain hath made the harvest grow!

And is this all the world has gain'd by thee,
Thou first and last of fields! king-making Victory?
(stanza xvii: ll. 1-9)

The reference to a "colossal bust" seems almost to anticipate "Ozymandias." The next stanza introduces Byron's justly famous description of the battle of Waterloo, which opens with a brilliant allusion to the Duchess of Richmond's ball on the eve of the battle at Quatre-Bras, two days before the final clash: "There was the sound of revelry by night." It was the combination, in passages like this one, of Volneyan substance with Byron's bravura manner that excited the imagination of three generations of educated Europeans as far east as Russia, who saw in *Childe Harold* another revealed text.

Mary Shelley's classic *Frankenstein* (1818) was a product of the same summer. Not surprisingly, Volney's *Ruins of Empires* figures in it as the fundamental basis of her fictive monster's historical and moral education. It fulfills a similarly significant role in her later novel, *The Last Man*, published in 1826, four years after Shelley's death.[37] "I can conceive him," said Thomas Love Peacock, Shelley's friend and the justest and most succinct of his critics,

> if he had lived to the present time, passing his days like Volney, looking on the world from his windows without taking part in its turmoils; and perhaps . . . desiring that nothing should be inscribed on his tomb, but his name, the dates of his birth and death, and the single word 'DÉSILLUSIONÉ.'[38]

In addition to Diodorus and Volney, Shelley almost certainly knew the descriptions and drawings of Upper Egyptian ruins made between July and October of 1798 by Dominique Vivant, Baron Denon (1747-1825), diplomat, painter, pornographer, and spy, one of those figures who bridge the old and the new régimes.[39] Sprung from a family of Burgundian squires, he installed himself in Paris at the age of 25 and somehow caught the attention of Louis XV, who appointed him to the embassy in St. Petersburg. Expelled from Russia after two years, he next served the Bourbon monarchy in Sweden, Switzerland, and finally in the Kingdom of Naples, where he remained from 1776 to 1785. During these busy pre-Revolutionary years he also published the charming *conte libertin* called *Point de lendemain* in which, as Jean-Claude Vatin has said, "tout est dit, mais non décrit," and worked seriously as an artist, meanwhile holding two other lucrative and undemanding royal appointments.[40] In 1787 he was elected to the Académie de Peinture. The following year he published a *Voyage en Sicile* and retired, setting up house in Venice.

The Venetian authorities kept Denon under surveillance, however, and in 1792 he was finally expelled. He moved to Florence, but was allowed to stay only a year. In 1793 he therefore returned to France, now in the grip of the Terror, a gesture that indicated unequivocal support for the Republic, and put himself under the protection of David, who was both the chief painter of the fanatical party in power and a member of the Comité de Sûreté Générale. Denon was quite soon formally declared a good patriot and employed by the State in engraving David's designs for the official new Republican dress.

In 1798 Denon succeeded in wangling a berth among the *savants* accompanying Bonaparte's Egyptian Expedition. He was far older than most of the rest and far less clearly qualified, but his current mistress was a great friend of Joséphine de Beauharnais, the future Empress, whose circle he now belonged to; and Bonaparte no doubt found some diversion in his conversation as well as a use for his intelligence skills. A little over a year later the same influence secured him something even more advantageous, an early return from Egypt in the company of Bonaparte and two other senior *savants*. Back in Paris thus two full years before the rest of the Commission, he made excellent use of the advantage he had gained and set to work immediately to render his Egyptian experience in graphic and literary form and to organize it for personal rather than official publication.[41] Meanwhile, however, fully sympathetic with the taste of his class and time, he produced *Œuvres priapiques* and *Les Bigarrures*, a series of pornographic prints published pseudonymously.[42] Then he had a fantastic stroke of luck.

From October 1801 to 18 May 1803 an official peace reigned between England and France. Commercial relations were resumed and the French government not only extended an amnesty to *émigrés*, but also had the Calais-Paris road especially repaired and upgraded. English tourists swarmed over to Paris, where the famous Café des Anglais was created specifically for them and everything English became the fashion, while thousands of Frenchmen flocked to London and found everyone speaking French. The publication of Denon's illustrated record of his travels in Egypt in 1802—his *Voyage dans la Basse et la Haute Egypte*—became a major cultural event. In Paris quarto and duodecimo editions appeared simultaneously and in

London there were simultaneous editions in both English and French. Other French and English editions followed within twelve months and within the following year there was even an American edition.[43] Denon's success was enormous; and it is quite unlikely, given his wealth and his interests, that Horace Smith did not own a copy, either in French or English, of his *Voyage.*

Denon's influence thus appears throughout the following era much more frequently than that, for example, of the *Description de l'Égypte*, both for good or for ill. His glib misidentification of the so-called Colossi of Memnon, for example, gave support to what was already a bad toponymical tradition of reference to the Ramesseum as "the Memnonium." Contributing to decades of confusion, this same bad tradition created unnecessary difficulties for Jollois and Devilliers, the two *savants* who had the task of writing about the Colossi and the Ramesseum for the *Description de l'Égypte*. It bedeviled Egyptology for the rest of the century and is obviously the chief reason why the Ramesseum still continues to be referred to occasionally as the Memnonium even today.[44]

Like all the other *savants*, Denon could not read hieroglyphics.[45] And since he could not read hieroglyphs, he was unable to identify the building he stood in, guessing only that it might be "either a temple or a palace or both at once."[46] Erroneously, he believed the remains of the huge statue he saw—which had been correctly identified by Diodorus nearly two millennia earlier, let us recall, as representing Ramesses II—to be the famous Colossus of Memnon, a work far more celebrated in ancient times than the Sphinx.

The monument known to us and to antiquity as the Colossus of Memnon is not this statue, of course, but a completely different one in a completely different place: the northernmost of the pair of statues of Amenhotep III that are a prominent landmark on the West Bank, currently called "the Colossi of Memnon" and standing just off the road leading to Madinat Habu and the Ramesseum from the present ferry-landing.[47] They are covered with testimonial inscriptions left behind by Hellenic and Roman tourists, which identify the northernmost one absolutely as the statue that ancient visitors thought was "Memnon."

Having already decided, however, that the enormous fragments he had just seen in the ruins of the building that he could not identify otherwise had to be the Colossus of Memnon, Denon was compelled to discover a different identity for these two statues.[48] Dimly recalling that the statue of Ozymandias had been described in some ancient source—*i.e.*, Diodorus—as the center of a group of three, Denon decided that it had in fact disappeared, but must once have stood between these two seated figures, which therefore had to represent Ozymandias' mother and son.

The graffiti carved in Greek by Roman-period tourists were among the very few primary sources that Denon could possibly have read and would have corrected his mistake. His successors, in fact, made good use of them.[49] With cheerful arrogance, however, he dismissed them as nonsense.

"In the plain," he wrote,

> our attention was drawn to two great seated figures, between which, according to the descriptions of Herodotus, of Strabo, and of those who drew upon these two writers, stood the famous statue of Ozymandias, the largest of all the colossi: Ozymandias himself took such pride in the execution of so difficult an enterprise that he had an inscription carved on the pedestal of this statue in which he challenged humankind to destroy either this monument or his tomb. Such self-indulgence seems describable only as delusion. The two statues still standing are undoubtedly those of his mother and his son, who are mentioned by Herodotus; that of the king has disappeared. Time and jealousy having argued with envy over its destruction, all that remains is a shapeless lump of granite. It requires the stubborn gaze of the expert observer [*le regard obstiné de l'observateur accoûtumé à voir*] to distinguish a few features that have escaped destruction, and even those are so meaningless that they can give no idea of its dimensions.[50]

Denon's rather pompous conjectures as to what he was looking at were additionally confused not only by his rejection of available first-hand evidence, but also by his defective use of ancient secondary sources. He cites both Herodotus and Strabo, for example, as having seen and described a colossal statue of Ozymandias, but neither Herodotus nor Strabo mentions Ozymandias/Ramesses II by any name, much less his mother and his son. Nor is there any description of the Ramesseum in either of these ancient authors. Strabo is indeed the first to describe the experience of hearing the famous noise emitted by the so-called Colossus of Memnon—this gratifying occasion took place, as is well known, when he toured the West Bank at Luxor with the entourage of Aelius Gallus,[51] the third Roman governor of Egypt—but he does not actually refer to the statue by any name at all.

Perhaps Denon was attempting to recall Diodorus' description of the Ramesseum—written four centuries later than Herodotus' *Histories*, but a few years earlier than Strabo's *Geography*—which identifies the sculptor who carved the three colossi that stood in the first court as one "Memnon of Sienitas." The name *Ramesses*, in any case, like the names of most ancient Egyptian kings, had certainly meant little to Diodorus and his contemporaries and must have meant a great deal less to Denon and his compeers some eighteen centuries later. The rediscoverer of Ramesses II was Champollion who also translated as *Rhamesséion* the ancient Egyptian appellation of the building that Diodorus describes and from which Belzoni had taken the colossal head of Ramesses II in 1816, the temple we know now generally by the Latinized version of Champollion's Greek designation.[52]

All the confident ascriptions in this passage from Denon are therefore bad guesses tricked out with half-baked pseudo-scholarship. The passage may nevertheless conceivably have contributed something to the specific physical setting for Shelley's sonnet, as Nigel Leask and others have suggested, that would be conformable with its Volneyan theme.[53] This setting, where "lone and level sands stretch far away," is obviously not the ancient building described by Diodorus; and it is vital to the poem, whose meaning requires a place where all other physical evidence of empire shall have vanished without a trace. Denon's "plaine" may possibly have suggested a suitably Volneyan alternative to Diodorus. Far more familliar to Shelley and thus more likely as a source, however, was a passage from Volney himself, once again, this time from his *Voyage en Syrie et en Égypte,* describing the Egyptian landscape:

> No country looks more monotonous: always a naked
> plain as far as one can see, always a flat uniform horizon
> . . . No country is less picturesque, less suitable for the
> brushes of painters and poets: there is nothing there of
> what makes for the charm and richness of their depic-
> tions.[54]

A note in this passage by Volney refers the reader to the plates of

Norden's *Voyage d'Égypte et de Nubie*, which "make this state of things apprehensible."[55]

It would obviously be a mistake to interpret Shelley's poem as a sort of miniature travelogue, much less as some kind of anachronistic attestation to the glory of Ramesses II: that monarch's current celebrity is not even a direct inheritance from ancient times, but a recent confection based upon the intelligence, self-sacrifice, persistence, and hard work expended by a host of Egyptologists during merely the past 175 years. Nor is the poem a "claim for the power of art to survive the ruins of empire," as has recently been suggested by Nigel Leask in his wide-ranging study of travel writing during the Romantic era. Leask's assertion that Shelley's *Defense of Poetry* celebrates "the transhistorical, Platonic power of art . . . as at once the harbinger and guarantee of political liberty" is not only not supported by the text of the *Defense*, but is actually contradicted by it.[56]

Nowhere in any of his writings, indeed, does Shelley make such a claim for art, least of all in "Ozymandias" where it is clear that the survival of chunks of the colossal portrait statue of an ancient tyrant has been purely accidental. That fact, indeed, is part of the point of the whole poem. The chief principle or vision enunciated in the *Defense* and elsewhere in Shelley, moreover, is not "æsthetic" or "Platonic," but ethical and evolutionary. It is a vision concerned wholly with real life and its conduct in the world as it is. The chief elements of this vision were by no means uncommon or peculiar to Shelley alone, moreover, but were recognized by him and others as being shared with many of his contemporaries. Exemplified and enunciated certainly in "Ozymandias" and *Prometheus Unbound*, they thus also provide the intellectual framework of other great Romantic works by artists ranging from Byron, Wordsworth and Scott, to Goethe and Manzoni (in Part II of *Faust* and in *I Promessi Sposi,* neither of which he could have read), or even Beethoven (whose Ninth Symphony he could not have heard).

If Shelley had lived to complete *The Defense of Poetry,* we might have been treated to an analysis of the kind of artist among his contemporaries whom he admired. His wonderful summarizing formulation in the *Defense*—"Poets are the unacknowledged legislators of the World"—is by no means neo-Platonic or even Delphic, as some befuddled commentators have attempted to imply, but simple common sense based on a sound knowledge of the history of ideas. It deliberately echoes, in fact, that old arch-conservative, Samuel Johnson, the patron saint of common sense. In chapter X of *Rasselas,* published over 60 years earlier, Johnson's *porte-parole,* the philosopher, Imlac, describes the poet as "the legislator of mankind . . . presiding over the thoughts and manner of future generations."

In Shelley's Volneyan and evolutionary view of history, all empires are foredoomed to disappear and for a work of what we call art merely to have outlived one of them hardly signifies anything. If that work is merely a portrait of a tyrant, moreover, the value one places upon it—like the value one places on propaganda or Kitsch—may well be largely ironical, the irony being present or absent precisely to the degree that the tyranny it was originally supposed to memorialize is in fact remembered at all.

"Ozymandias" is thus a political poem, a fact that should be clear not only from the text itself, but from the kinds of things that "inspired" it: no physical experience except the reading of many other texts, which had little to do with physical experience themselves and nothing at all to do with neo-Platonic philosophy. These texts, in turn, were merely a small portion of the poet's wide reading over many years, which had given him a thorough knowledge, most importantly for this poem, of the multitudinous metaphors, living and dead, that were available to figure in contemporary political thinking. And above all, no doubt, what always echoed in his mind were the political sonnets of Wordsworth, published ten years earlier, and of Milton.

"Ozymandias" is not, in other words, the result of "inspiration" by a particular physical experience, nor of some special realization or revelation arising out of physical experience. To point out this truth is to run counter, of course, to a great many vulgar myths about art and artists. In old-fashioned Hollywood movies, for example, a sexual or quasi-sexual epiphany used to figure as the automatic explanation for virtually any creative act.[57] But "Ozymandias" is certainly not an erotic celebration. Neither is it a poem about "nature." Nor is it is in any way about "art." It has even less to tell us about nature, love, or art, indeed, than it does about ancient Egypt.

What it seeks to remind its readers, instead, is that no tyrannical power lasts forever, no matter how efficient its repressive apparatus or how deep its degree of self-deceit. And if in Shelley's day the means of tyranny available to governments were nugatory compared with the massed might that can be casually mustered by the powers-that-be in our own democratic age—an era when elected governments outdo any ancient monarchy in callousness and cruelty, in hypocrisy and mendacity, in globalized rapacity and greed—"Ozymandias" may well have more pith and relevance than ever before.

Notes

[1] Mandeville's *Travels* was recognized as an inventive compilation as early as the sixteenth century. That the same is probably true of Marco Polo's *Description* has been demonstrated by Frances Wood, who suggests that it was the result of a collaboration between Marco Polo and Rusticello of Pisa, a well-known composer of romances, who acted as ghost-writer and compiler rather than as mere amanuensis. See her *Did Marco Polo go to China?* (London: Secker and Warburg, 1995).

[2] "Ozymandias" (="CUser-maCat-reC") is not a corruption of "Ramesses" (= "Ra-messu") as has been claimed by at least one scholarly critic. An appalling invention appears in Duncan Wu's *Romanticism: an Anthology* (Oxford: Blackwell, 1994), 260, where we are assured that Ramesses' "tomb at Luxor was in the shape of a male sphinx," whatever that might be.

[3] In 1811, during one of his stays in Athens, Byron went so far as to obtain a firman allowing him to travel in Egypt, but he never made the trip.

[4] Harry James has suggested that another influence might have been William Richard Hamilton (1777-1859), whose *Aegyptiaca—Remarks on Several Parts of Turkey, Part I: Aegyptiaca, or some Account of the Ancient and Modern State of Egypt, as obtained in the Years 1801, 1802; . . .* (London: T. Payne, Cadell and Davies, 1809)—had a large British readership. An early reviewer remarks that it "will be found an excellent supplement to the more elaborate and costly work of Denon," which Hamilton himself refers to and quotes (*e.g.*, p. 142). About Diodorus, however, whom he accuses of credulity and outright invention, Hamilton was totally skeptical, with the result that he accepted Denon's identification of the Ramesseum as a "Memnonium." See Hamilton, 113, 134-137.

[5] Full citation: Richard Pococke, LL.D., FRS (1704-1765). *A Description of the East and Some Other Countries. Volume the First: Observations on Egypt* (London: Printed for the author by W. Bowyer, and sold by J. and P. Knapton, W. Innys, W. Meadows, G. Hawkins, S. Birt. T. Longman, C. Hitch, R. Dodsley, J. Nourse and J. Rivington, 1743); the second volume of this enormous work appeared in two parts in 1745. There were also editions in French (1752-1753, 1772-1773), German (1754-1755), and Dutch (1776-1786).

6 The idea of the *Description* as a possible source was negatived by D. W. Thompson in "Ozymandias," *Philological Quarterly* XVI (1937): 60.

7 For a brief straightforward account, see Nigel Leask, *Curiosity and the Aesthetics of Travel Writing 1770-1840* (Oxford: Oxford UP, 2002), 102. The story is told at greater length by Guy Davenport in "Ozymandias," *The New York Times* (May 28, 1978): 15. The date 1817, given by Peter Clayton in *The Rediscovery of Ancient Egypt: Artists and Travellers in the Nineteenth Century* (New York: Portland House, 1982), 123, is right for the composition of the poem, but not for its publication. See also *The Inspiration of Egypt: Its Influence on British Artists, Travellers and Designers, 1700-1900*, ed. Patrick Conner (Brighton: Brighton Borough Council, 1983), 76-77.

8 Johnstone Parr, "Shelley's 'Ozymandias,'" *Keats-Shelley Journal* VI (Winter 1987): 34, as quoted in Leask, 123.

9 *The Examiner* (February 1, 1818): 73; republished in Horace Smith, *Amarynthus, the Nympholet: A Pastoral Drama, in Three Acts. With Other Poems* (London: Longman, Hurst, Rees, Orme, and Brown, 1821); Facsimile edition: New York: Garland Publishing, Inc., 1977; also available on the internet at several websites, including: <www.theotherpages.org/poems/2001/smith0101. html>.

10 See *Description*, planches, *Antiquités*, III, pl. 20.

11 *Quarterly Review* XVIII (1817-1818): 368.

12 The error is repeated, for example, in all the websites (with many other errors) that deal with the poem. It also appears not only in Richard Holmes's standard *Shelley: The Pursuit* (Harmondsworth: Penguin, 1974), but also in such recent works as Christopher Woodward's entertaining collection of essays, *In Ruins* (London: Chatto and Windus, 2001), 204; Leask, 104.

13 See E. H. Gombrich, *Art and Illusion: A Study in the Psychology of Pictorial Representation, The A. W. Mellon Lectures in the Fine Arts, 1956, National Gallery of Art, Washington*, Bollingen Series XXXV, number 5 (Princeton: Princeton UP, 1961), 385.

14 For a chronology of the head's travels, see Deborah Manley and Peta Rée, *Henry Salt: Artist, Traveller, Diplomat, Egyptologist* (London: Libri, 2001), 87-99, 155.

15 See Conner, ed., *The Inspiration of Egypt*, 77.

16 *Description*, planches, *Antiquités*, II, pl. 30.

17 See Christian Leblanc, "Diodore, le tombeau d'Osymandyas et la statuaire du Ramesseum," *Mélanges Gamal Eddin Mukhtar*, II (Cairo: IFAO, 1985) [IF 630], 80.

[18] See *Alastor*, ll. 53, 107-128.

[19] Smith had received an excellent classical education and no doubt read his Diodorus, as Shelley did, in Greek.

[20] Parr (see above; note 8).

[21] See *The Inspiration of Egypt*, 77, 80.

[22] See *The Inspiration of Egypt*, 76-77, 80.

[23] From *The Library of History*, I, xlvii, as translated by the Egyptologist Sir E. T. A. Wallis Budge (1857-1934) in *The Nile: Notes for Travellers in Egypt* (London and Cairo: Thomas Cook and Son, 1905), 524-25.

[24] See Leblanc, 76-77, 80. One of the inscriptions reads: "The Horus-Re, [Bull] valiant-beloved-of-Maât, the King of Upper and Lower Egypt, rich in monuments in Thebes, Lord [of the Crowns]. Usermaatre Setepenre, son of Re. Ramses Meriamon, beloved of Amun-Re, King of Gods: may he be endowed with life!" The other reads: "Saith Amun-Re, King of Gods: 'O my son, issue of my body, my beloved, Lord of Victory, [Ramses] Meriamun! I give thee years by millions, jubilees by hundreds of thousands: all foreign countries are under thy feet.'"

[25] Leblanc, 80.

[26] The temple of Amenhotep III on the West Bank, for example, in front of which the two statues of Amenhotep that are now called the Colossi of Memnon was originally erected, had already largely disappeared in Diodorus' time, having been used as a quarry from the late New Kingdom onward. Very little, likewise, was left of Heliopolis, which had still been an important city when Herodotus visited it a mere four hundred years earlier.

[27] Leblanc, 82.

[28] See chapters I and XIX.

[29] Full title of the first edition: *Voyage en Syrie et en Égypte, pendant les années 1783, 1784, et 1785, avec deux Cartes Géographiques et deux Planches gravées, représentantes les ruines du Temple du Soleil à Baalbek, et celles de la Ville de Palmyre dans le Désert de Syrie* (Paris: Volant et Desenne, 1787; Paris: Gaulmier, Mouton, 1959). See also J. B. Rothe, *Auszug aus Volney's Reise nach Egypten* (Dresden: Gerlach, 1799; Dresden: Beyer, 1810).

[30] Paris: Desenne, 1791.

[31] Brian Riggs in *The New Oxford Companion to Literature in French*, ed. Peter France (Oxford: Oxford UP, 1995), 884. *Cf. The Concise Oxford Dictionary of French Literature*, ed. Joyce M. H. Reid (Oxford: Oxford UP, 1976), 659: "a singular mixture of picturesque description of ancient ruins and philosophical disquisition on the origin and growth of social

political, and religious institutions. [Volney] concludes in favor of the equality of all men before the law, the overthrow of despotism, and toleration and agnosticism in religious matters where truth is not verifiable."

32 Ian Jack, *English Literature, 1815-1832* (Oxford: Oxford UP, 1965), 94.

33 *Idéologie,* formalized belatedly in *Éléments de l'Idéologie* (1801-1805) by Comte Antoine-Louis-Claude Destutt de Tracy (1754-1839), is based on the notion that all ideas originate in physical sensation and is in effect a French version of Associationism, first enunciated by David Hartley (1705-1757) in *Observations on Man* (1749). *Idéologie* thus likewise derives directly from Lockean psychology, especially as interpreted by the Encyclopedist Étienne Bonnot, abbé de Condillac (1714-1780) in his *Essai sur l'origine des connaissances humaines* (1746) and his *Traité des sensations* (1754). English adherents of Associationism included not only Coleridge, Wordsworth, and Shelley, but also Priestley, Erasmus Darwin, and Godwin. Apart from Volney, Destutt de Tracy and Stendhal, notable *Idéologues* included Antoine-Nicolas Caritat, marquis de Condorcet (1743-1794), author of *Esquisse d'un tableau des progrès de l'esprit humain* (1794), Pierre-Jean-Georges Cabanis (1757-1808), author of *Rapports du physique et du moral de l'homme* (1802), and Stendhal's brilliant elder contemporary, the novelist, mémoirist, and political thinker Benjamin Constant (1767-1830). The *OED* informs us that the English word *ideology* was specifically invented to translate Destutt de Tracy's *idéologie* in 1796 and that the currently prevalent use of the same word to signify any system of convictions or ideas dates from no earlier than 1909.

34 London: J. Johnson, 1792.

35 Troisième édition, corrigée et augmentée du *Cathéchisme du Citoyren Français*, par le même auteur (Paris: Chez A. J. Dugour et Durand, Libraires, Rue et Hôtel Serpente, 1794[?]), 1-2: "Je vous salue, ruines solitaires, tombeaux saints, murs silencieux! c'est vous que j'invoque; c'est à vous que j'adresse ma prière! Oui! tandis que votre aspect repousse d'un secret effroi les regards du vulgaire, mon cœur trouve à vous contempler le charme des sentiments profonds et de hautes pensées. Combien d'utile leçons, de réflexions touchantes ou fortes n'offrez-vous pas à l'esprit qui vous sait consulter! C'est vous qui, lorsque la terre entière asservie se taisait devant les tyrans, proclamiez déjà les vérités qu'ils détestetent, et qui, confondant la dépouille des rois à celle du dernier esclave, attestiez le saint dogme d'EGALITÉ."

36 They had been notably anticipated by Thomas Hope (1769-1831) whose Grand Tour lasted from 1787 to 1795 and who lived in Constantinople for a year. His novel *Anastasius* (1819) was remarkable enough to have been

at first mistakenly attributed to Byron. See Philip Mansel, "The Grand Tour in the Ottoman Empire, 1699-1826" in *Unfolding the Orient: Travellers in Egypt and the Near East,* ed. Paul and Janet Starkey (Reading: Ithaca, 2001), 54-56.

[37] See *Frankenstein, or The New Prometheus,* chapter 13. The monster later reads Milton's *Paradise Lost*, a volume of Plutarch's *Lives,* and Goethe's *The Sorrows of Young Werther.*

[38] Quoted in Ian Jack, *English Literature*, 104.

[39] A brief biography is: Ibrahîm Amin Ghali, *Vivant Denon ou La conquête du bonheur* (Cairo: IFAO, 1986); more recent is Philippe Sollers, *Le Cavalier du Louvre* (Paris: Plon, 1995). The influence of Denon in "Ozymandias" is also discussed in Eugene M. Waith, "Ozymandias: Shelley, Horace Smith and Denon," *Keats-Shelley Journal* XLIV (1995): 22-28; in Parr, 31-35; and in Leask, 117-23. Christopher Taylor suggests that Denon served both the Bourbon and the Revolutionary régimes as a spy and that the Russian, Venetian, and Austrian authorities were justified in declaring him persona non grata. Perhaps only a career in espionage would explain both the curious range of his accomplishments and the otherwise extraordinary favors extended to him under successive French governments.

[40] Jean-Claude Vatin, introduction, *Voyage dans la Basse et la Haute Égypte, pendant les campagnes de Général Bonaparte,* by Vivant Denon (Cairo: IFAO, 1989 [reprint]), 12. First published over his initials, it has since always had a readership and has recently been republished (Paris: Gallimard, 1995) by Michel Delon, editor of the Marquis de Sade.

[41] In a woefully unresearched article, "Life Lines," *RA The Royal Academy Magazine* 48 (Autumn 1995): 59, James Putnam and Nick Tite describe the Egypt of 1798 as "this mysterious and forgotten land," then make it appear that Denon headed Napoleon's Commission. Along with Denon, Bonaparte also repatriated Claude-Louis Berthollet, Gaspard Monge, and five generals, leaving the embittered and unfortunate Kléber in command, with notice that he expected the rest of Commission to leave Egypt during the following November. See *Kléber en Égypte 1798-1800,* étude historique, présentation et notes par Henri Laurens, II (*Correspondance et papiers personnels de Kléber*) [Cairo: IFAO, 1988], 510-11.

[42] See Robert Solé, *Les savants de Bonaparte* (Paris: Seuil, 1998), 217; Gilles Néret, *Erotica Universalis* (Cologne: Benedikt Taschen, 1994), 374-89.

[43] *Voyage dans la Basse et la Haute Égypte, pendant les campagnes de Général Bonaparte* (Paris: D. Didot l'aîné, 1802; London: Samuel, 1802), two volumes, reprinted, with an introduction by Jean-Claude Vatin (Cairo: IFAO, 1989). Hereinafter *Voyage.* See Jean-Édouard Goby, "Les

40 éditions, traductions et adaptations du *Voyage en Basse et Haute Égypte* de Vivant Denon," *Cahiers d'histoire égyptienne* IV, fascicules 5-6 (décembre 1952): 290-316; Martin R. Kalfatovic, *Nile Notes of a Howadji: A Bibliography of Travelers' Tales from Egypt from the Earliest Time to 1918* (Metuchen, N.J. and London: Scarecrow Press, 1992), 73-74. Early translations of Denon include: *Travels in Upper and Lower Egypt during the Campaigns of General Bonaparte,* trans. Francis Blagdon (London: B. Crosby and Co., 1802). (Text only. The same translation was published again the following year by John Murray.) *Travels in Upper and Lower Egypt during the Campaigns of General Bonaparte,* trans. E. A. Kendal (London: Hurst, 1803). *Travels in Upper and Lower Egypt, in Company with Several Divisions of the French Army, during the Campaigns of General Bonaparte in that Country: and Published under his Immediate Patronage,* trans. Arthur Aiken (New York: Printed by Heard and Forman for S. Campbell, 1803). *Reise durch Ober- und Niederägypten während der Feldzüge des Generals Bonaparte.* Aus dem Französischen von Tiedemann (Berlin and Leipzig: Voss, 1803).

44 See Prosper Jollois and Baron René Édouard Devilliers [du Terrage], *Description de l'Égypte*, no. 10, chapître IX, sections II-III, first edition, Antiquités I (1809), 77-160: they managed to identify the monument as the Tomb of Oxymandias. Its misidentification as a "Memnonium" was first made by the Italian abbé, P. L. Pincia, whose description of a visit to the Ramesseum on 1 January 1721 is the earliest recorded by a European. See Père Claude Sicard, *Lettres et relations inédites*, présentation de Maurice Martin, *Œuvres* (Cairo: IFAO, 1982), 84, 138, 143. Pococke and Norden both remained faithful to Diodorus and consequently identified the building correctly. See Friderik Ludwig Norden [Frédéric-Louis/Frederick Lewis] (1708-1742) [toured Egypt June 1737- 38, Upper Egypt from 17 November 1837 to 21 February 1838], *Voyage d'Égypte et de Nubie, par Mr. Frederic Louîs Norden, Capitaine des Vaisseaux du Roi. Ouvrage enrichi de cartes et des figures dessinés sur les lieux, par l"Auteur même [traduit du Danois en Français par des Roches de Parthenais.]* (Copenhagen: Imprimerie de la Maison Royale des Orphelins, 1752-1755), I, 173. Savary, who cites Pococke, Sicard, Niebuhr, and d'Anville, makes the same error as Denon, though he correctly identifies the colossal head he saw in the Ramesseum with the statue described by Diodorus. See *Lettres sur l'Egypte, où l'on offre le parallèle des mœurs anciennes et modernes de ses inhabitants, où l'on décrit l'état, le commerce, l'agriculture, le gouvernment, l'ancienne Religion du pays, & la descente de S. Louis à Damiette, tirée de Joinville & les*

Auteurs Arabes, avec des Cartes Géographiques, deuxième édition revue & corrigée (Paris: Onfroi, libraire, Quai des Augustins, 1786), I, 3, II, 134-36.

[45] No textual inscription in ancient Egyptian could presumably have been correctly read by anyone; in fact, from about the fourth or fifth century A.D. until after 1822, when Champollion published the embryonic beginnings of the scheme he was evolving out of the work of Sacy, Åkerblad, and Young. Even well after 1822 the major source for knowledge of the pharaohs therefore remained a seventh-century A.D. edition of a fourth-century A.D. version of a third-century A.D. summary of the same account that Diodorus had chiefly used, which was written in Greek from Egyptian sources by an Egyptian scholar—Manetho—at the beginning of the second century B.C., a thousand years after Ramesses' accession.

[46] Denon, *Voyage,* I, 119. My translation.

[47] Denon's captions for his depiction of the statues (plate 44) note the inscriptions and refer to the statues "qu'on est convenu d'appeler les statues de Memnon."

[48] There is some confusion in Leask, 122-23, who cites an 1803 English translation of this same passage, in which he draws the reader's attention to the phrase "nothing of it remains" as a parallel to Shelley's "Nothing beside remains," and who apparently presumes that Denon's wild surmises have some Egyptological validity.

[49] They are the means by which Richard Hamilton and Denon's erstwhile colleagues in the Commission, who knew no ancient Egyptian, were in fact enabled to identify the colossi quite correctly.

[50] Denon, *Voyage*, I, 120. My translation. Denon was appointed Director of the Central Museum of Arts—the Louvre and its adjuncts—the same year his *Voyage* was published and in 1804 was made Director General of Museums. In this grandiose capacity he visited the site of almost every major Napoleonic victory, charged with the heady task of picking out works of art for removal to the Louvre as war booty. The operative principle, carried out with a vengeance, was one that the Nazi and Soviet armies would revive during World War II. Denon himself had enunciated it a decade earlier, during the Revolutionary epoch, in a single deliciously ironic sentence that summarizes all his skills and sensibilities. "The French Republic," he declared, "thanks to its strength, the superiority of its intellectuals and its artists, is the only country in the world able to offer a safe refuge to these masterpieces." Quoted in Ghali, 197: "La République Française, par sa force, la supériorité de ses lumières et de ses artistes, est le seul pays au monde qui puisse donner une asile inviolable à ces chefs-œuvre."

The major collections of Spain and Italy, including the Vatican, had already been stripped. Now Austria, Prussia, Bavaria, Saxony and the petty kingdoms and principalities of Germany were systematically pillaged. The great collection of Dresden was saved from Denon's grasp only by Talleyrand, who received a bribe of a million francs for his intervention. After the fall of the Empire Denon was compelled by the Allied victors to return over 2000 paintings, 600 sculptures, and 3000 miscellaneous objets d'art to their owners. Nothing, by the way, was sent back to Egypt. Denon himself was a classic survivor and subsequently enjoyed a decade of comfortable and happy old age, dying in 1825 at the age of 78. The famous multi-volumed *Description de l'Égypte*, to which Denon had contributed, would not be completed until 1828/9, three years afterward, six years after the death of Shelley (1822).

51 Aelius Gallus is not to be confused with the first Roman governor of Egypt, Gaius Cornelius Gallus, celebrated by Vergil in Eclogues VI and X.

52 Patterned after *Mausoleion.* See Champollion's letter of 18 June 1829 to Champollion-Figeac in his *Lettres et journaux écrits pendant le voyage d'Égypte,* recueillis et annotés par H. Hartleben (Paris: Christian Bourgeois éditeur, 1986), 308.

53 See Leask, 122-23.

54 *Voyage en Syrie et en Égypte,* I, 224: "Nul pays d'un aspect plus monotone; toujours une plaine nue à perte de vue; toujours un horizon plat et uniforme. . . Nul pays n'est moins pittoresque, moins propre aux pinceaux des peintres et poètes: on n'y trouve rien de ce qui fait le charme et la richesse de leurs tableaux."

55 Norden, *Voyage d'Égypte et de Nubie* (for full reference see note 44). There were further French editions in 1795-1798 and 1800; an English edition in 1757; 164 plates were published separately in London in 1792; a German edition, 1799.

56 Leask, 111. Note, for example, what Shelley says in the *Defense* about the necessary decay of language from being "vitally metaphoric" to being "dead to all the nobler purposes of human intercourse." Or his identification of poets with "the authors of language and music, of the dance and architecture, and statuary . . . institutors of laws, and the founders of civil society; and the inventors of the arts of life, and the teachers [of religion]."

57 Typically, in these films, the best-known works of Beethoven, Chopin, Tchaikovsky, Michelangelo, Toulouse-Lautrec, Gershwin, Cole Porter, or Shakespeare are all to be attributed equally to similar physical "inspirations," a technicolor sunset, the death of Mom, or the hero's sudden consciousness that he is in love with whomever. Tasteful exceptions among

films about artists sometimes occur, such as *Shakespeare in Love* and *Amadeus*, both based on the work of intelligent playwrights; and the early work of Ken Russell, including his black and white biographical explorations of Delius, Wagner, and George Eliot. His self-indulgent treatments of Tchaikovsky and Mahler, however, lapse into the sensational, as do two films specifically about Byron's and Shelley's famous summer together in 1816, *Gothic* and *Haunted Summer*.

From Past to Present and Future:
The Regenerative Spirit of the *Abiku*

Mounira Soliman

Our country is an abiku country. Like the spirit child, it keeps coming and going. One day it will decide to remain. It will become strong.

—Okri, *Infinite Riches*

Modern African literature, written in European languages, is characterized as being a literature that is extremely culture-specific as it relies heavily on local cultures, on African cosmology, and on oral tradition. This cultural specificity, in most cases, projects a political intention that is hard to disregard in any attempted interpretation of a literary text. On the other hand, these two characteristics of African literature have for the past fifty years or so created a kind of literature that is not quite accessible to the Western reader who, first of all, is not well versed in African local cultures and, second, is unable to perceive the political intentions of African writers. Ultimately modern African literature has come to be regarded as an exotic kind of writing but not really serious literature. The Nigerian writer, Ben Okri, sarcastically comments on the way the West perceives African literature: "[t]hey say, 'oh dear, I'm reading an African novel. Ooh dear it's bound to be a bit strange—there are bound to be rituals and things'" (Taylor 34). What the West fails to understand, in fact, is that culture specificity in this case is part of the national agenda of many African writers who are keen on promoting an exclusively African literary identity despite their awareness of the problematic and implications of writing in a foreign language as in the case of writers like Chinua Achebe, Gabriel Okara, Aye Kei Armah, among others. Indeed, Anthony Appiah explains that African intellectuals are always seeking to develop their cultures in directions that will give them a role and that, unlike the European writer, the African writer asks not "who am I?" but "who are we?" (76). Thus, the resort of African writers to their oral tradition is not simply an act of anthropological retrieval of a culture that has been intentionally confiscated by the colonizer, as Western criticism is fond of pointing out (see Cooper's discussion on this point 51-60). On the contrary, it is more of a socio-political agenda. For even though the anthropological project may have been true at a very early stage of African literature (especially West African literature) at the hands of some writers like D. O. Fagunwa and Amos Tutuola's literary production of folkloric material during the 1940s and 1950s, yet the intentions of such writers who have attempted to document African folk culture remain to a great extent debatable. In fact, it could be argued that such anthropological projects had their own socio-political agenda since the historical documentation of folkloric material has indeed contributed to the process of building up the African collective memory, which the colonial power had tried earnestly to eradicate.

The Abiku Phenomenon

This article will investigate the use of the African oral tradition to promote the socio-political agenda of African writers by focusing on the famous West African *abiku* phenomenon and its representation in three literary texts by three Nigerian writers namely, J. P. Clark-Bekederemo's poem "Abiku" (1965), Wole Soyinka's poem also entitled "Abiku" (1967) and Ben Okri's novel *The Famished Road* (1991), where the protagonist is an abiku child (see the two poems in the appendix at the end of this article). Two explanations of the abiku phenomenon will be presented, one based on common knowledge derived from the way it has been handled in various literary texts; the other based on a traditional Yoruba theory. The article will then offer a thematic analysis of the two poems and will conclude with a brief comparison with Okri's interpretation of the abiku phenomenon in *The Famished Road.*

The abiku phenomenon is quite popular in West African oral tradition especially amongst the different ethnic groups of Nigeria, particularly the Yorubas, the Igbos and the Ijos. Due to its popularity, many Nigerian and other West African writers have drawn on this rich cultural resource as a way to express their national identities. Amos Tutuola, Chinua Achebe, Goke Ajiboye, and more recently Syl Cheney-Coker, Debo Kotun; and, in francophone language, Olympe Bhêjy-Quenum are but a few of the writers who have handled the abiku notion in their writings. Also the symbolic level of the phenomenon and the fact that it embraces different beliefs—like the relationship between the physical and the spirit world, the idea of predestination, and the concept of reincarnation—have made it possible for these writers to adapt it so as to project different socio-political agendas at different times in the history of their countries. This huge corpus of literature dealing with the abiku phenomenon takes more or less as its starting point the following definition of the abiku child as:

> an individual who goes through a continuous circle of birth and death as a result of a primeval oath . . . taken in the spirit world in the presence of the creator and binding on the living. The oath is believed to be binding on the one who has taken it; the individual has to live in a particular manner throughout his or her usually short span of life. The object of the oath is hidden away from ordinary human sight and usually buried under a huge tree, in the person's palm or in other impressive places. (Maduka 18)

Because of this binding pact with fellow companions in the spirit world, the abiku child, even though it is implored by its parents and community to remain alive, refuses to do so and, at the first opportunity, returns to the spirit world. This recurrent cycle of birth, death, and rebirth involves not only the abiku but its parents as well and especially the mother who undergoes immense pain and suffering each time her child is born, knowing that she will lose it again to its spirit companions. In an attempt to break this cycle, the parents of the abiku child, with the help of priests, diviners, or the village doctor/herbalist, perform rituals to sever the relationship between the abiku and its kindred spirits. In order to do that, they have to find the spirit tokens that bind the abiku to the spirit world and destroy them. These rituals also include making scars on the body of the dead child, refusing to provide it with decent burial, and in some cases mutilating the body of the dead abiku (Maduka 18). Indeed, as Chidi Maduka explains, many people insist that they have seen abiku children reincarnated again with the same scars on their bodies which they had acquired in their former lives (18). That is why the abiku phenomenon, in the African mythic consciousness, is a terrifying experience and that—maybe partly—is the reason why this spirit child is known by different names amongst different Nigerian ethnic groups. The Yorubas, for example, use the commonly known word 'abiku' which is literally translated as "one who is born to die," but there are also other terms that refer to the same phenomenon but are rarely used nowadays like, for example, 'èré,' 'emèrè' or 'òrun' (McCabe 46).

The Igbos on the other hand prefer the word 'ogbanje' which holds the implications of a weird, capricious, callous, and sadistic kind of behavior—which is how the abikus are perceived due to the suffering which they cause to their parents and community. As a matter of fact, the word ogbanje is metaphorically used nowadays to refer to any behavior that reflects the same traits (Maduka 18; see also Ogunyemi for further discussion on the meaning of abiku and ogbanje).

Douglas McCabe, in an article on the oral Yoruba abiku texts, explains that the above-mentioned definition of the abiku phenomenon and the way it has been rendered in modern African literature is an interpretation that fails to take into consideration the anthropological and historical dimensions of the phenomenon (45). In his article, McCabe offers an alternative interpretation of the abiku phenomenon based on a traditional Yoruba theory, situating it in the context of eighteenth and nineteenth-century Yoruba society. He explains that abikus are thieves from heaven who come to the earth to steal. They form a sort of a club or a group—which in Yoruba is referred to as an 'egbé'—of heaven-people whose main purpose is to steal the riches from the houses, or the 'ilé,' of the world people. To do that, McCabe explains that

> Àbíkú further the aims of their robber-band by using children as a cover for their criminal operation. Each àbíkú is born into an ilé and poses as a child that is either sweet-natured and beautiful (and therefore likely to be lavished with good things) or sickly and disturbed (and therefore likely to be the beneficiary of expensive sacrifices). In such a way, the àbíkú quickly accumulates money, cloth, food, and livestock. Then, at a certain time and by a certain method prearranged secretly with its egbé, the àbíkú dies and takes the spiritual portion of its loot back to heaven. After dividing the spoils with its egbé, it prepares to re-enter the world and fleece the same or another ilé. (46)

In the same manner, as with the more commonly known interpretation of the abiku phenomenon, attempts can be made to fetter the relationship between the abiku and its egbé and, therefore, put an end to the continual robbing of the ilé by the abiku. To do that, the ilé must discover the oath or the sealed words that bind the abiku to its egbé and which specify the exact when, where, and how of the abiku's return to the spirit world. Having done that, the ilé then is able to break the bond between the abiku and its egbé by either blocking the circumstances necessary for its death, announcing that the abiku's oath has been found or by disguising the abiku so that it will not be found by its egbé when its members come to take it from the ilé (which they perceive as a kind of imprisonment imposed upon the child). The abiku will then be forced to stay on in the world of the living but its egbé will nevertheless continue its attempts to retrieve the child (McCabe 46).

From the above interpretation, it is obvious that there is a constant conflict between the ilé and the egbé based on the meaning and implications of both. The ilé represents the house, the village, and the ancestral city to which one is connected, not only geographically but historically as well since it constitutes one's family and origin. In other words, the ilé represents a past that extends into the present and possibly the future. The egbé, on the other hand, represents a group of people associated together not through marriage and lineage—as is the case with the ilé—but rather through a common activity which does not require them to be tied to a certain geographical location nor to a certain historical origin (McCabe 47). Therefore, the ilé and the egbé

> constitute two contrasting templates of sociopolitical organization among the Yoruba: the male-dominated ilé is based on marriage, lineage, procreation, geography, and hierarchical structures of seniority and inheritance; the male or female-only egbé is based on voluntary membership, mutual benefit, pursuit of a shared nonreproductive purpose, and group secrecy (the keeping of esoteric or specialized knowledge, practices, skills). (McCabe 48)

Despite being rivals, the relationship between the ilé and the egbé has always interpenetrated, since in many cases people had loyalties to both and, in fact, sometimes they did belong to both social structures—hence the conflict. In the eighteenth and nineteenth centuries, the ilé ideology dominated Yoruba history because it was strongly tied to the Oyo Empire which depended on the ilé social structure in its political ruling of Yorubaland. But with the increasing contact with Europeans—through the colonial experience and the rise of smaller political entities, like Ibadan and Abeokuta, whose economies depended upon the amassing of material wealth through banditry and slave trade—the hegemony of the Oyo Empire, with its emphasis on ancestral and geographical origin, was undermined and eventually gave way to the hegemony of the egbé ideology (McCabe 48-9). Now the pressing issue is to explain the reason for the use of this particular traditional Yoruba theory in the interpretation of the abiku phenomenon. What are its implications and how does it reflect the contemporary socio-political history of Nigeria?

Amongst the Nigerian people, the Yorubas, unlike other ethnic groups, have always been known for their tendency to form urban communities. Most of the larger cities today like Lagos, Ibadan, and Abeokuta are in Yorubaland, and even before it was officially included under British administration (1893-1960), Yorubaland was, in fact, divided into smaller states (see for further discussion "Nigeria Political Geography" in *The Columbia Electronic Encyclopedia*). With the rise of these smaller states, a conflict between the older traditions that governed the more rural parts of Nigeria (the ilé) and the new way of urban life (the egbé) started to become obvious. The conflict was further emphasized through the colonial experience and its aftermath which left many Yorubas in an ambivalent position, especially those of them who became the intellectuals of the nation and who were born to a rich tradition of African beliefs and concepts but bred according to imported Western ideas and concepts. Nigeria today continues to live through this conflict: with a population divided into two hundred and fifty ethnic groups, each speaking its own ethnic language, while English remains the official language of the country; half the population Muslims and about forty percent Christians, while the remainder practice indigenous religions. Significantly, Nigerian literature projects this conflict, not only that which is clearly reflected in the society but perhaps also the conflict inherent within writers themselves. The abiku phenomenon and its translation into literature is a stark example of this conflict.

In an interview, Eileen Julien comments on the potency of African literature explaining that

> [w]hat really makes this literature so extraordinarily
> vibrant is that it is extremely rooted in ethnic traditions,
> in cosmologies and legends, and often it's also taking on
> international traditions. Writers like Wole Soyinka are as
> immersed in Shakespeare and classical Greek theater as
> in Yoruba mythologies. You've got Malian writers who
> are immersed in the Dogon and its traditions as well as
> the European traditions of anthropology and sociology.
> (Englert n. pag.)

It is interesting that while Julien explains that being well versed in both traditions gives the African writer more space to negotiate both traditions—and here he touches particularly upon the situation of the exiled writer (Englert n. pag.)—he does not however comment on the conflict that sometimes exists within the writer concerning the relationship between these two traditions. Perhaps the reason why the ease of negotiating two different traditions is highlighted—also by other critics—while the conflict is sometimes overlooked is either the subtle manner in which that conflict is expressed or the fact of its seeming absence from the literary work. The case of J. P. Clark-Bekederemo's poem "Abiku" and Wole Soyinka's poem also entitled "Abiku" is a significant example.

The comparison between these two poems has been a topic for analysis in many critical studies. Perhaps the reason for this, besides the obvious fact that they both tackle the same subject, is the manner of their first publication. Both poems appeared in print for the first time in *Black Orpheus,* volume number ten in the last quarter of 1961 or the first quarter of 1962 (McCabe 57), before they were included later in anthologies. So it seems that right from the beginning there was an attempt to juxtapose these two poems that portray the abiku phenomenon as perceived by two writers coming from different Nigerian ethnic backgrounds. This is, in itself, very significant because many critics have failed to see that each writer adopts a different position and consequently advocates a different socio-political agenda. They could sense a difference of attitude, of course, but in most cases the analysis tended to show a traditional interpretation of the phenomenon by the two writers (see, for example, Porter).

Clark-Bekedermo's "Abiku"

One of the main differences between Clark-Bekederemo and Soyinka is their ethnic background. Soyinka is a Yoruba, whereas Clark-Bekederemo is an Ijo from Kiagbodo which is described by Nduka Nwosu as follows:

> Tucked away from the seat of power somewhere in the northern belt of the Burutu Local Government headquarters, bordered by the creeks of Bomadi river and a long stretch of land east of Ughelli in Delta State, is the ancient city of Kiagbodo whose sons and daughters gathered

recently to enact for posterity's sake, a befitting status for a great man of history, the legendary Ambakederemo Ogein, ninth generation descendant of Ngbile, the founder of Kiagbodo kingdom. (n. pag.)

This ancestral and geographical origin immediately brings to mind the ilé ideology explained above and sets the tone for the interpretation of Clark-Bekederemo's poem as a traditional rendering of the African oral tradition devoid of any political intention. Indeed, the poem is simply a supplication addressed to the abiku child by the father, imploring him/her to remain in the world of the living and forgo plans to return to its kindred spirits.

It is written in one stanza but internally divided into a series of movements, each portraying one of the traditional aspects of the abiku phenomenon. In the first movement, the father states the commonly known fact that an abiku is a child who is engaged in a non-ending cycle of birth, death, and rebirth "Coming and going these several seasons." Having established that, the father then puts forth an argument designed to win over the child and induce it to stay on in the world of the living:

Do stay out on the baobab tree,
Follow where you please your kindred spirits
If indoors is not enough for you. (5)

In this way, right from the beginning of the poem, the uneven relationship between the abiku and the father is established, with the abiku acknowledged as having the upper hand and, consequently, able to upset that relationship. This reminds the reader of the term ogbanje and its implications of a callous and sadistic child who disrupts the order of life and the society of people s/he comes into contact with. What follows afterwards is the father's attempt to persuade the child that "indoors" (symbolical of the house/family/world of the living) might not actually be such a bad idea since it has worked for many of the other children and could also work out for the abiku if s/he were to give it a try.

The father then goes on to describe in the following movement the poor condition of the house to which the abiku is invited to stay. For even though the roof leaks, and the bats and owls can easily find their way into the house at night, and the bamboo walls can be used to light a fire, still

it's been the healthy stock
To several fingers, to many more will be
Who reach to the sun. (5)

Having put forth his case, the father reassumes his plaintive voice,
almost begging the child to rethink its plans:

No longer then bestride the threshold
But step in and stay
For good. (5)

This introduces another aspect of the phenomenon: the rituals undertaken by the parents and the community (though not always successful) to sever the relationship between the abiku and its kindred spirits.
Indeed, the following lines highlight these rituals designed to break the
pact between the abiku and its spirit companions:

We know the knife scars
Serrating down your back and front
Like beak of the sword-fish
And both your ears, notched
As a bondsman to this house
Are all relics of your first comings. (5)

Finally, Clark-Bekederemo ends the poem with the traditional image
of the abiku's mother who is caught up in a continuous cycle of suffering and pain because of her child's refusal to remain alive:

Then step in, step in and stay
For her body is tired,
Tired, her milk is going sour
Where many more mouths gladden the heart. (5)

This traditional portrayal of the tragic experience of the abiku
phenomenon, as it has been perceived by many critics (see, for example, Maduka and Quayson) may have given the impression that Clark-
Bekederemo's intentions are purely anthropological, but this is far
from the truth. West African literature, as argued above, is characterized by two important elements: first, it is deeply rooted in the African
oral tradition; and second, that this anthropological front hides behind

it a very distinct socio-political agenda. If we were to examine John Pepper Clark or J. P. Clark-Bekederemo's (Bekederemo is the family surname which the male lineage in the family have all decided to adopt after their grandfather, chief Mbakaderemo) literary career we would understand how the anthropological project has always been firmly linked to his political agenda. As a writer, he has been engaged mostly in what could be referred to as projects of cultural nationalism. For example, in his play *All For Oil*, Clark-Bekederemo explains how the British created Nigeria for the sole reason of exploiting its resources, especially the palm oil trade which substituted for the slave trade when slave trading became illegal. He compares this period of nineteenth- and early twentieth-century Nigeria and the controlling attitude of the British toward the current conflicting situation. According to him, only one thing has changed—and that is the substitution of crude oil for palm oil; the Royal Niger Company with Shell, the Royal Anglo-Dutch Company—but "[t]he story of Nigeria is the same, the government, the foreign traders in the middle and then the people at the bottom" (Nwosu n. pag.). Commenting on the play, Clark-Bekederemo explains that his strategy has always been to revert to the past in an effort to mirror the present (Nwosu n. pag.).

Indeed, this seems to be his strategy throughout, for besides his creative writing, Clark-Bekederemo is also concerned with recording popular oral African folk epics. He has collected and translated the Ozidi Saga, one of the most popular folk epics from the Ijos of the Niger Delta. The book was first published in 1977 and won him a distinctive position in African and Western literary history. In his preface to the book, Clark-Bekederemo explains that "[t]he word epic is used here with all due deference to those scholars who doubt the existence of the genre in Africa" (Okpewho 1). His words actually take us back to his rendition of the abiku phenomenon. It is obvious that the starting point for him is always the African cultural heritage, which he tries to bring forward and shed light on, in an attempt to fight back the continual attempts to suppress African history. The fact, then, that the poem handles one of the most common phenomena in the African oral tradition in a very traditional manner is in itself a political message and very much part of Clark-Bekederemo's strategy, which is to sustain the ilé ideology that is based on a structure of ancestral hierarchy, familial origin, and extended lineage. To him, this is the only way to preserve the African identity. Therefore, the intentional absence of the egbé from this traditional picture emphasizes his belief in the ilé ideology as the one and only acceptable worldview. This is the opposite of what Soyinka does in his poem also entitled "Abiku." For the missing—or, rather, hidden—conflict between the ilé and the egbé in Clark-Bekederemo's poem is emphasized in Soyinka's poem and remains to the end unresolved.

Soyinka's "Abiku"

In his interview with Jane Wilkinson, Soyinka explains that his relationship with the abiku phenomenon goes way back to his childhood, "you have to understand that I grew up with abiku . . . Abiku was real, not just a figment of literary analysis" (107). Indeed, in his autobiography, *Aké: The Years of Childhood,* Soyinka talks about one of his playmates, a girl called Bukola, whom he describes as an abiku child who was always rebellious against her parents' authority. Bukola, he explains,

> was not of our world. . . . Amulets, bangles, tiny rattles and dark copper-twist rings earthed her through ankles, fingers, wrists and waist. . . . Like all abikus she was privileged, apart. . . . It made me uneasy. Mrs. B. was too kind a woman to be plagued with such an awkward child [a child who threatened to die if she was not given anything she wanted]. (16-18)

Soyinka's preoccupation with the phenomenon of the abiku child remained with him, maybe subconsciously, especially during his stay in London (1954-1960) which is where he composed his poem. The circumstances of its composition are indeed very significant. Soyinka explains that he was feeling very nostalgic during his stay in London and one day he entered the studio of one of his friends, the West Indian actor Lloyd Record, and saw a painting there:

> I came into his studio one day and—there it was—a painting of "Abiku"! I entered the studio, stared and shouted Abiku! He stared back at me, not knowing what the hell I was talking about. (McCabe, 58)

He admits that this feeling of nostalgia for his homeland instigated him to compose this poem:

> After all, I had been away from home—for the first time
> ever, and for over three years at that time. Any object, voice,
> smell, sky-line, was available for conversion to my cata-
> logue of missed or repressed images . . . a few weeks later, I
> consoled myself by writing the poem "Abiku." (McCabe 58)

Two things are quite significant in what Soyinka says: first, that the
reason for writing the poem was his feeling of nostalgia for his homeland—expectedly so; second, it is also interesting that the feeling of home-
sickness was translated into a literary text about a phenomenon concerning death and not really about any of the symbols usually connected with
one's country. However, resorting to the oral tradition to express feelings
of longing for Nigeria gives the impression that Soyinka thinks of his
motherland in historical terms. The historical context in this case is multi-
layered (see Osundare). There is the age-old belief in the abiku phenomenon which is part of the West African worldview; there is also the oral literary tradition of that phenomenon which Soyinka was versed in by virtue
of his Yoruba ethnic background and the long tradition of storytelling;
and, finally, there is Soyinka's own personal history with the phenomenon. Indeed, the opening lines of the poem establish this historical context
by highlighting the aspect of time, the abiku "calling for the first and the
repeated time" (28) which is the same thing that Clark-Bekederemo does
in the opening line of his poem, "[c]oming and going these several seasons" (5). This gives the impression that Soyinka's poem is going to be
another traditional interpretation of the abiku phenomenon, probably not
much different from Clark-Bekederemo's. In fact, the first two lines in
particular echo, not only Soyinka's own description of Bukola, his childhood playmate, but also a long tradition of abiku descriptions:

> In vain your bangles cast
> Charmed circles at my feet; (28)

No sooner is this traditional atmosphere established—which, like
Clark-Bekederemo's poem, recreates the ilé ideology with its emphasis on history, origin, tradition, and heritage—than it is shattered with
the introduction of an opposite ideology that advocates principles of
individualism and self-definition rather than communal definition:

> I am Abiku, calling for the first
> And the repeated time. (28)

It becomes obvious right from the first stanza then that Soyinka—who was born to an ethnic Yoruba background and brought up in urban communities like Ibadan and Abeokuta—is negotiating a personal as well as a national conflict between an old and a modern way of life, which became especially clear during the politically turbulent era preceding the independence of Nigeria from British colonialism, which is also about the time when the poem was composed (see Soyinka's Nobel lecture "This Past Must Address Its Present"). In *Infinite Riches*, Ben Okri talks about this same conflict when he describes a group of people at a dinner:

> They argued about divisions of power, tribal rivalries, territorial control. They quarreled about their loyalties, their achievements, their interpretations of the new African way, age-old disagreements surfacing. The air resounded with the clash of their myths and ideologies. (225)

Throughout the eight stanzas of Soyinka's poem, there is this ongoing conflict between the abiku, who represents the individual, and the community which has tried in vain to sever the child's connection with the spirit world but has failed. In fact, the abiku ridicules all their efforts, taunting them instead:

> Must I weep for goats and cowries
> For palm oil and the sprinkled ash?
> Yams do not sprout in amulets
> To earth Abiku's limbs. (29)

And as if that is not enough, in a typically arrogant manner, the abiku offers advice and suggests ways that might help in recognizing him/her when reborn:

> So when the snail is burnt in his shell,
> Whet the heated fragment, brand me
> Deeply on the breast—you must know him
> When Abiku calls again. (29)

It is easy to argue at this point that there is nothing unusual in Soyinka's portrayal of the relationship between the abiku and its parents and community. It is in accordance with the traditionally recognized behavior of both. And, in fact, this is true to a great extent. There is always a conflict of interest between the abiku who never wants to be born in the first place and who does his/her utmost to return to the spirit world as soon as it is feasible and, on the other hand the interest of the parents in retaining their child by trying to sever its relationship with its kindred spirits. What is exceptional though in Soyinka's interpretation of the abiku phenomenon is the self-assertive attitude of the abiku, the sense of individualism and self-adulation:

> I am the squirrel teeth, cracked
> The riddle of the palm; remember
> This, and dig me deeper still into
> The god's swollen foot. (29)

Many critics, on the other hand, have sensed that Soyinka is adopting a non-conformist attitude, as he does in many of his literary works (see, for example, Quayson 124). This non-conformity is sometimes depicted in the poem in the mixture of the genre of the riddle, which is a very popular form in African oral tradition, and the subgenre of the dramatic monologue (Maduka 25). Stylistically also, the poem has been seen as departing from the Romantic convention of expressing one's experiences in one's own voice, as McCabe explains:

> Soyinka's "Àbíkú" marks a radical break from this convention—a break toward the cryptic, compact, intricately allusive, and anti-Romantic language that would mark much of his subsequent verse and drama. (58)

Indeed, compared to Clark-Bekederemo's poem, which is straightforward and easy to understand, Soyinka's poem is very symbolic and the meaning is sometimes hard to get. In the fifth, sixth, and seventh stanzas, for example, when the abiku invokes the mother, Soyinka expresses her suffering and pain in highly symbolical images, as in "the ground is wet with mourning," implying the shedding of tears at the abiku's death, and

> . . . Mothers! I'll be the
> Suppliant snake coiled on the doorstep
> Yours the killing cry. (30)

It can be argued then that the use of such cryptic and symbolic language, as well as the combination of the oral riddle and the dramatic monologue, highlights the conflict between two traditions, African and Western. Furthermore, it highlights a conflict between two ideologies: Yoruba communal tradition and Western individualism. This becomes significantly clear if we consider the continual shift throughout the poem between the first and the third person, between the "I" and the "Abiku." The poem ends with both voices still struggling against each other. The conflict remains unresolved between the community that wants to hang on to its abiku and the ruthless spirit child who rejects their attempts to remain alive:

> The ripest fruit was saddest;
> Where I crept, the warmth was cloying.
> In silence of webs, Abiku, moans, shaping
> Mounds from the yolk. (30)

The Yoruba traditional theory of the ilé and the egbé is, therefore, clearly manifested in Soyinka's poem, projecting a community that finds its strength in holding on to its past traditions and beliefs and the individual who rejects this historical past with all its implications, moving away and adopting a modern way of life instead. It is indeed symbolical of the unresolved conflict in which Nigeria still finds itself and which is ultimately the reason why it is unable to move forward.

Talking of national cultural identities in the postcolonial era, Stuart Hall explains that

> [s]ome identities gravitate towards . . . 'Tradition,'
> attempting to restore their former purity and recover the
> unities and certainties which are felt as being lost. Others
> accept that identity is subject to the play of history, poli-
> tics, representation and difference, so that they are unlike-
> ly ever again to be unitary or 'pure.' (Qtd. in Cooper 55)

These seem to be the two positions of Clark-Bekederemo and Soyinka in their respective poems. Each poem reflects a different socio-political agenda. Whereas Clark-Bekederemo advocates history and tradition as the only way to preserve the strength of the African identity, Soyinka, perhaps by virtue of his own experience, perceives a different image, one based on conflict between past and present and the implications of this conflict upon the African identity. It is very interesting that Soyinka's poem, written almost fifty years ago, is still a true reflection of the post-independence Nigerian society as it is today. In fact, this is the starting point for Ben Okri's novel *The Famished Road*. Written in 1991, the novel tackles the same historical period covered by Clark-Bekederemo and Soyinka when they composed their respective poems, Nigeria on the verge of independence facing social and political turmoil. But Okri does not remain locked in that historical framework because his novel breaks the dilemma between past and present and moves beyond the past to project a future for Nigeria.

Okri's Abiku

Commenting on what he does in *The Famished Road*, Okri explains that the book is about hope:

> One should be very, very serious when one is going to talk about hope. One has to know about the very hard facts of the world and one has to know how deadly and powerful they are before one can begin to think or dream oneself into positions out of which hope and then possibilities can come. It's one of the steps I try to take in this book. (Wilkinson 88)

In *The Famished Road* (1991), Okri, ethnically an Urhobo, projects two abiku children: Azaro, the narrator of the novel, and his friend Ade. Azaro and Ade are opposite characters so that the hope, which Okri talks about, stems from a discrepancy in the portrayal of both characters. Ade is a typical abiku who never wanted to be born and who eventually returns to the world of the spirits in *Songs of Enchantment* (1993), the second book in Okri's trilogy. In *The Famished Road* Okri characterizes him:

> Ade did not want to stay any more, he did not like the weight of the world, the terror of the earth's time. Love and the anguish of parents touched him only faintly, for beyond their stares and threats and beatings he knew that his parents' guardianship was temporary. He always had a greater home. (486)

The attitude of Ade and his parents is typical of the abiku phenomenon, and on first encountering Azaro, the second abiku child in the book, the reader gets the impression that the situation of both children is the same. Azaro also, like other abiku children and like Ade, did not want to be born:

> There was not one amongst us who looked forward to being born. We disliked the rigours of existence, the unfulfilled longings, the enshrined injustices of the world, the labyrinth of love, the ignorance of parents, the fact of dying, and the amazing indifference of the living in the midst of the simple beauties of the universe. We feared the heartlessness of human beings, all of whom are born blind, few of whom ever learn to see. (*The Famished Road* 3)

Moreover, Azaro is born with memories of his past lives, he has very strong ties with his spirit companions, and the community looks upon him as a child with miraculous abilities. Indeed left at that point, Azaro could certainly be another typical interpretation of the abiku phenomenon. Margaret Cezair-Thompson, for example, describes him as an abiku child who is "a distinctly African archetype" (3). But Okri deconstructs this traditional image by allowing Azaro to choose life over death. In doing so, Azaro breaks the vicious cycle of birth and rebirth, which has caused much suffering for his family, and instead attempts to fulfill a social obligation toward his community. He explains that his reasons for choosing life over death

> may simply have been that I had grown tired of coming and going. It is terrible to forever remain in-between. It may also have been that I wanted to taste of this world, to feel it, suffer it, know it, to love it, to make a valuable contribution to it, and to have that sublime mood of eternity in me as I live the life to come. But I sometimes think it was a face that made me want to stay. I wanted to make happy the bruised face of the woman who would become my mother. (*The Famished Road* 5)

Having made this choice, Azaro is consequently caught up in a struggle with his spirit companions who attempt to dissuade him form the decision he has taken and when they fail to do so, try to abduct him and take him back to the world of spirits. The rest of the novel narrates the adventures of Azaro with his spirit companions which continue in the two other books of the trilogy.

Clearly Okri offers a different interpretation from both Clark-Bekederemo and Soyinka. They all start from the same historical standpoint which is the African oral tradition but whereas Clark-Bekederemo sticks to that position, and Soyinka projects an oppositional relationship between history and modernity, Okri deconstructs history and offers instead a progressive reading of the future that does not exclude the past but moves beyond it. In other words, Okri advocates history as a natural step toward a present and more importantly toward a future; and perhaps that is what he means when he describes the novel as "a flow of life." It is important to note that Okri never denies history, as a matter of fact, but he explains that in our age in particular we have to try and change our pre-concepts of what we think is history, "to alter the way in which we perceive what is valid and what is valuable, different measures and different values" (Wilkinson 87). And this is what he does in his novel when he goes beyond the traditional theory of the ilé and the egbé and the existent conflict between them, offering instead a different reading. Accordingly, Okri sees Nigeria as an abiku child, but significantly not an ogbanje, rather a resilient abiku who has taken the tough decision to remain alive (it is important to note that Azaro willfully chooses life over death and is not forced to remain alive through the rituals which his parents undertake to sever his relationship with his spirit companions). The implication is that Nigeria too can be a resilient abiku but only if it transcends a history and a present of nothing but conflict. In *Infinite Riches*, Okri states this very clearly:

> Old ways are dying.
> We who live through turbulent mysteries
> Do not know that a whole way is passing.
> We do not know the things to come. (393)

But the reader is left in doubt if such a future is indeed viable. In his own way, Okri is aware that Africa is locked in a past that has informed a present out of which deliverance seems to be a far cry from what he advocates. There is a sense of resignation in

> We go on living as if history is a dream.
> The miracle is that we go on
> Living and loving as best we can,
> In this enigma of reality. (393)

Of the three literary texts investigated in this article—J. P. Clark-Bekederemo's, Wole Soyinka's, and Ben Okri's—clearly Soyinka's poem "Abiku" remains an authentic reflection of the Nigerian socio-political dilemma. It is also clear that the abiku phenomenon is a very rich cultural resource that has lent itself to many interpretations across the years and by different writers. Given the fact that the phenomenon, as mentioned before, is about predestination, rebirth and reincarnation (and in a way the relationship between mother and child), and that African literature (although it is hard to generalize) continues to be part of a nationalist project of decolonization, it is no wonder that the mythic level of the abiku phenomenon has and continues to attract many writers who are engaged in various agendas of cultural nationalism, identity formation, and historical displacement and alienation. This article has tried to contribute to the regenerative spirit of the African oral tradition and how it continues to inform modern African literature through the investigation of one very popular example, that of the abiku phenomenon.

Works Cited

Appiah, K. Anthony. *In My Father's House: Africa in the Philosophy of Culture*. London: Methuen, 1992.

Cezair-Thompson, Margaret. "The Road of *The Famished Road* and its 'Abiku' Traveller: Irony, Dis/placement In Ben Okri's Decolonized Vision of Nigeria." Unpublished essay, 1993.

Clark, J. P. "Abiku." *A Reed in the Tide*. London: Longman, 1965. 5.

Cooper, Brenda. *Magical Realism in West African Fiction: Seeing with a Third Eye*. London, New York: Routledge, 1998.

Englert, Lucianne. "African Literature: A Topic as Vast as a Continent." *Research and Creative Activity* 21.3 (January 1999). <http://www.indiana.edu/~rcapub/v21n3/p16.html>. July 15, 2003.

Maduka, Chidi T. "African Religious Beliefs in Literary Imagination: *Ogbanje* and *Abiku* in Chinua Achebe, J. P. Clark and Wole Soyinka." *Journal of Commonwealth Literature* 22.1 (1987): 17-30.

McCabe, Douglas. "Histories of Errancy: Oral Yoruba Àbíkú Texts and Soyinka's 'Abiku.'" *Research in African Literatures* 33.1 (Spring 2002): 45-74.

"Nigeria Political Geography Articles." *The Columbia Electronic Encyclopedia*. <http://www.1upinfo.com/encyclopedia/categories/ngrageo.html>. August 4, 2003.

Nwosu, Nduka. "Bekederemo Foundation and Museum: In Kiagbodo, Bekederemo Lives." <http://www.nigerdeltacongress.com/barticles/ bekederemo_foundation_and_museum.htm>. July 18, 2003.

Ogunyemi, Chikwenye Okonjo. "An Abiku-Ogbanje Atlas: A Pre-Text for Rereading Soyinka's *Ake* and Morrison's *Beloved*." *African American Review* 36.4 (Winter 2002): 663-78.

Okpewho, Isidore. "The Art of the Ozidi Saga." *Research in African Literatures* 34.3 (Fall 2003): 1-26.

Okri, Ben. *The Famished Road*. New York: Anchor Books, 1991.

_____. *Infinite Riches*. London: Phoenix, 1998.

_____. *Songs of Enchantment*. London: Vintage, 1993.

Osundare, Niyi. "The Poem as a Mytho-Linguistic Event: A Study of Soyinka's 'Abiku'." *African Literature Today* 16 (1988): 91-102.

Porter, Abioseh Michael. "Revitalizing an Existing Cultural Phenomenon: Treatment of the Abiku in *La naissance d'abikou* and *les appels du vodou*." <http://www.obhelyquenum.com/abioseh-1.htm>. July 15, 2003.

Quayson, Ato. *Strategic Transformations in Nigerian Writing*. Oxford: James Currey, 1997.

Soyinka, Wole. "Abiku." *Idanre and Other Poems*. London: Methuen, 1967. 28-30.

_____. *Aké: The Years of Childhood*. London: Heinemann, 1981.

_____. "Nobel Lecture 1986: This Past Must Address Its Present." PMLA 102.5 (October 1987): 762-71.

Taylor, Louise. "Ambiguous Journey: Tutuola, Okri and the African Literary Canon." Diss. U of London, 1994.

Wilkinson, Jane, ed. *Talking with African Writers: Interviews with African Poets, Playwrights and Novelists*. London: Heinemann, 1992.

Appendix

Abiku[*]

J. P. Clark-Bekederemo

Coming and going these several seasons,
Do stay out on the baobab tree,
Follow where you please your kindred spirits
If indoors is not enough for you.
True, it leaks through the thatch
When floods brim the banks,
And the bats and the owls
Often tear in at night through the eaves,
And at harmattan, the bamboo walls
Are ready tinder for the fire
That dries the fresh fish up on the rack.
Still, it's been the healthy stock
To several fingers, to many more will be
Who reach to the sun.
No longer then bestride the threshold
But step in and stay
For good. We know the knife scars
Serrating down your back and front
Like beak of the sword-fish,
And both your ears, notched
As a bondsman to this house,
Are all relics of your first comings.
Then step in, step in and stay
For her body is tired,
Tired, her milk going sour
Where many more mouths gladden the heart.

---

[*] Clark, J. P. "Abiku." *A Reed in the Tide*. London: Longman, 1965. 5.

Abiku*

Wole Soyinka

Wanderer child. It is the same child who dies and returns
again and again to plague the mother—Yoruba Belief.

In vain your bangles cast
Charmed circles at my feet;
I am Abiku, calling for the first
And the repeated time;

Must I weep for goats and cowries
For palm oil and the sprinkled ash?
Yams do not sprout in amulets
To earth Abiku's limbs.

So when the snail is burnt in his shell
Whet the heated fragment, brand me
Deeply on the breast. You must know him
When Abiku calls again.

I am the squirrel teeth, cracked
The riddle of the palm. Remember
This, and dig me deeper still into
The god's swollen foot.

Once and the repeated time, ageless
Though I puke. And when you pour
Libations, each finger points me near
The way I came, where

The ground is wet with mourning
White dew suckles flesh-birds
Evening befriends the spider, trapping
Flies in wind-froth;

---

* Soyinka, Wole. "Abiku." *Idanre and Other Poems.* London: Methuen, 1967. 28-30.

Night, and Abiku sucks the oil
From lamps. Mothers! I'll be the
Suppliant snake coiled on the doorstep
Yours the killing cry.

The ripest fruit was saddest;
Where I crept, the warmth was cloying.
In the silence of webs, Abiku moans, shaping
Mounds from the yolk.

Musical Recall:
Postmemory and the Punjabi Diaspora

Ananya Jahanara Kabir

In British author Meera Syal's autobiographical novel *Anita and Me*, the narrative of a Punjabi girl growing up in an English village is interrupted at one point by memories of the Partition of India. One evening, the protagonist, Meena, overhears a musical soirée arranged by her parents and their friends turning into a heated emotional discussion:

> It was my Uncle Bhatnagar shouting. . . . "But it was a damn massacre!" he was spluttering, and then he talked in Punjabi of which I recognised a few words, "Family . . . money . . . death" and then, "They talk about their world wars . . . We lost a million people! And who thought up Partition? These 'gores' [white people], that's who!" Then everyone launched in, the whispers squeezed through the gap in the door and I could make out familiar voices saying such terrible and alien things.
>
> "My mother and I, the Hindus marched us through the streets . . . our heads uncovered . . ." That must have been Auntie Mumtaz, one of our few Muslim friends. "They wanted to do such things to us . . ." . . . there was a long pause, I thought I heard someone sniff. "All the time we were walking, mama and I, papa was lying dead, his head cut from his body. They found it later lying in the fallen jasmine blooms . . ."
>
> "We all have these stories, bhainji [sister]," Uncle Bhatnagar again, addressing her as sister. "What was happening to you was also happening to us. None of us could stop it, Mad people everywhere." There was a murmur of consensus, subdued, fearful maybe because of all the old wounds being reopened. "We were on the wrong side of the border also when the news came, none of us knew

until that moment if we would be going or staying. My
whole family, we walked from Syalcote across the border
. . . We maybe passed your family going the other way.
The bodies piled high . . . the trains pulling into stations
full of dead families. . . . Hai Ram. What we have seen. .
. ." (Syal 73)

Sisters lost to mobs, Sikhs shearing their uncut hair in trains, men's
heads chopped off as yanked-down trousers yielded evidence of circumcision—overhearing these stories, Meena realises that the past for
her parents was no sentimental journey, but "a murky bottomless pool
full of monsters . . . a deceptively still surface and a deadly undercur-
rent" (Syal 75).

Two levels of memorial recall operate here: the elders remembering what had happened, and the adult author remembering them
remembering. This memory of a memory lurks darkly beneath the
comedic vision of a diasporic subjectivity developing out of the two
strands of Meena's childhood: life outside the home, where she roams
Tollington with her white friends, and life inside the home, site of a
domestic and hospitable Punjabi culture. How do we explain this undi-
gested fragment, extraneous to the narrative task of reconciling these
strands? Holocaust scholar Marianne Hirsch's concept of "postmemory" provides a clue:

> postmemory characterizes the experience of those who
> grow up dominated by narratives that preceded their birth,
> whose own belated stories are displaced by the stories of
> the previous generation, shaped by traumatic events that
> they can neither understand nor create . . . [It is] a space of
> remembrance, more broadly available through cultural
> and public, and not merely individual and personal, acts of
> remembrance, identification and projection. (Hirsch 8)

Within Syal's narrative, however, postmemory belongs to neither the public nor the personal sphere, but to an alternative community space that is somewhere in between: a reconstituted Punjabiness
that exists behind closed suburban doors. To understand this Punjabi
postmemory taking shape in Britain, out of the very debris of the
Partition of 1947, we have to develop conceptual grids around factors
different from Hirsch's distinctions between cultural and public on the

one hand, and individual and personal on the other. From the passage cited above, we can extract some of these factors: music, bilingualism, Partition, fratricide, the somatics of religious identity, rape. Their mutual interaction—performed during moments such as that described by Syal—creates an affective matrix that revisits, from a specifically Punjabi diasporic perspective, connections between cultural trauma, collective memory, and the therapeutic powers of narrative now taken as almost axiomatic by Western scholars.

Speaking of the Carribean experience, Stuart Hall observes that diasporic subjectivity is inevitably marked by "a certain imaginary plenitude, recreating the endless desire to return to 'lost origins,' to be one again with the mother, to go back to the beginning" (Hall 32). If this is true, how is this imaginative and emotional investment in the idea of a 'motherland' impacted by that 'motherland' having been territorially divided, demographically reorganised, and scarred by extreme violence between religiously polarised groups? What impact do political configurations 'back home' have on the labels of belonging adopted by first and subsequent generations of diasporic subjects? An answer may be found in the category of 'neo-ethnic postmemory.' My use of the qualifier 'neo' is consciously weighted against the opinion that "the shattered mirror of Punjabi consciousness reflects tiny images, which refuse to coalesce into a portrait" (Grewal 52). From the evidence of memory-work produced by contemporary British Asian artists, musicians and writers, it is evident that, on the contrary, the "shattered mirror" *can* be reassembled at least for some Punjabis living in diaspora; and in ways that remain difficult, in fact, for Punjabis who continue to live within South Asia.

In this article, I first explicate this point by considering the broad contours of the Partition of India and its manifestations in the Punjab as "cultural trauma," defined as "a dramatic loss of identity and meaning, a tear in the social fabric, affecting a group of people that has achieved some degree of cohesion" (Eyerman 2). This perspective of cultural trauma further enables us to observe that the pressures of the decolonised nation state have rendered impossible any public mourning for the cultural losses occasioned by Partition. I next discuss how this work of mourning is executed in the diasporic space, and how transnational flows of cultural capital bring these works of memorialisation back to South Asia. I take my cues mostly from contemporary music created and enjoyed by Punjabis in South Asia and the diaspora: not only Bhangra music, which is most immediately identified as

'Punjabi,' but also other forms such as Qawwali and Ghazal, which, while not *per se* tied to 'Punjabiness,' gain that sense when embedded within specific contexts.

It must be emphasised at the outset that my analysis pertains to particular examples of these musical forms, and to specific artists/intellectuals using those forms within the Punjabi diaspora. Ethnographic or quantitative/qualitative analyses based on 'actual responses' of diasporic communities of listeners lie outside the article's remit. Any references made to these communities are based on my own observations of daily life both in the UK and in India, and noted as such. Rather, the methodology I employ derives from cultural and literary criticism, and is born out of the interplay between (in the words of Edward Said) the world, the text and the critic. I read music as text in order to elaborate upon that which Meera Syal hints at: music's affective power to wrench out of the ordinary and the quotidian, the very wellsprings of loss. Following the title of a book largely on memorialising the Holocaust, "cultural recall," I call this process 'musical recall' (Bal, et al.). At the same time, the concept of 'musical recall' is based on my understanding of music as oral/aural, non-narrative text. This understanding in turn suggests that music offers certain therapeutic possibilities for traumatised subjects that go beyond those offered by narrative, or the telling and reading of stories.

I

The freedom struggle in colonial India created two new nations as the British departed in August 1947. Based on the 'Two-Nation Theory,' that Hindus and Muslims comprised not one nation but separate entities with opposing interests, the Muslim League demanded the partition of the Subcontinent into a Muslim Pakistan and a Hindu India (Jalal). The Muslim majority regions of Punjab and Bengal were divided: western Punjab and eastern Bengal became West and East Pakistan, with India sandwiched in the middle (in 1971, East Pakistan seceded from Pakistan, creating a third nation, Bangladesh). This entailed a massive and violent transfer of population as Sikhs and Hindus from regions that were now in Pakistan moved into India, and Muslims moved in the opposite direction. A million people were left dead and at least seventy-five thousand women raped and abandoned; around twelve million people were displaced, countless homes abandoned or destroyed, properties, families and cultures divided as new national borders were drawn over existing ethnolinguistic identities, most obviously Bengali and Punjabi (Butalia; Bhasin and Menon).

The Partition of India exemplifies a large-scale traumatic event whose psychological and collective repercussions persist to this day, stamping identity politics between and within South Asian nations and their various diasporas (Kaul). The wound that was then inflicted on the body of the individual was also a wound inflicted on the body collective, most obviously through the rape, mutilation and abduction of women. The connection of violence with identity was heightened by the somatic markers of religious belonging, such as circumcision for Muslim men and uncut hair for their Sikh counterparts, which rendered men as well as women vulnerable to identification and subsequent assault by the 'Other.' Physical dislocation combined with violence to make not just the body, but also the body's place in the world, a site of personal and cultural trauma:

> consequent to this violence in which the most interior aspects of life were the most intruded upon—fleeing to another alien space led to a division of the self and the world according to a logic that made the self radically fugitive and the world radically fragmented. (Das 65)

This fragmented and fugitive post-Partition reality was shared by people from territorially divided regions, such as the Punjab and Bengal, as well as from regions such as Sindh, Uttar Pradesh and Hyderabad (South India) that experienced population transfer without territorial division. Nevertheless, the experience of the Punjab was particularly horrifying for the sheer scale and intensity of the violence. Images from the Punjab Partition have in fact entered the collective memory of the Indian nation as metonymic of the madness of that time: never-ending processions of people crossing the new borders in both directions; trainloads of fleeing passengers slaughtered before reaching their destination, whether Lahore in Pakistan or Amritsar in India; women being forced by their men to imbibe poison or jump into wells in preference to dishonour at the hands of the 'Other.' In further divergence from, say, the Partition of Bengal (Chatterji), an almost complete transfer of population accompanied the violence, making Indian Punjab today as nearly devoid of Muslims as Pakistani Punjab is of Hindus and Sikhs.

This near-instantaneous and violent demographic reordering, along with the concomitant fracturing of identities, destruction of sacred geographies, and necessities of rehabilitation, inevitably impacted the restructuring of Punjabi collective memory in the new nation states of India and Pakistan. Thanks to the migratory patterns of the Punjabi people, a not inconsiderable part of this restructuring has also taken place in what has been called the 'third Punjab' of the diaspora (Singh and Thandi ix). From the nineteenth century onwards, the British Empire's transnational flows of labour and capital had sent Punjabis, especially Sikhs, to Canada, East Africa, California, the UK, South-East Asia, and even New Zealand, making migration and entrepreneurship intrinsic aspects of Punjabi self-perception (Helweg; Barrier and Dusenbery; Singh and Thandi). During and after Partition, this pattern of outward movement offered Punjabis of all religious backgrounds the already established 'third Punjab' as a space of rehabilitation and reconstruction alternative to the new nations of Pakistan and India.

It is possible to view the upheavals of Partition as simply one more link in the long chain of political and economic exigencies that have shaped the worldwide Punjabi diaspora, of which a very visible part is its Sikh component. As two Punjab specialists comment,

> since the late 1940s, Sikh migration has once again become a significant world-wide phenomenon. . . . In particular the social dislocation brought about by partition was a leading push factor in the immediate post-independence era. (Barrier and Dusenbery 7)

Yet such casual references to Partition ignore its foundational, albeit often subtextually embedded, position in the memory-work of Punjabi artists and intellectuals in both South Asia and the diaspora. Taking cognisance of that evidence, I suggest that the sudden change in the territorial integrity and demographic composition of the Punjab, to the accompaniment of unimaginable levels of looting, murder, and rape are all factors that make the post-Partition diaspora function very differently within Punjabi collective memory from the remembrance of earlier migrations.

A shattered and divided motherland cannot provide the imaginative and emotional bulwark that the diasporic subjectivity often seeks as protective sheath. Punjabi literature of the Partition, whether written in English, Hindi, Urdu or Punjabi, certainly communicates this sense of a permanently altered homeland left behind in the wake of fratricide. Let us consider the eminent author Krishna Sobti's nostalgic recreation of life in a pre-Partition Punjabi village in her novel, *Zindaginama* (*Life-Chronicle*). Written in Hindi permeated with an earthy colloquial Punjabi flavour and punctuated with Persian, Urdu and Punjabi lyrics of Sufi saints and poets from the Punjab such as Bulleh Shah, the language of *Zindaginama* seeks to recuperate cultural loss through the (re)creation of an idealised, syncretistic idiom, which is then deployed in the recollection of equally syncretistic 'folk activities,' such as spinning, cotton carding, weaving and harvest rituals.

The extended prologue to *Zindaginama* provides a lyric eulogy to the Punjab itself through detailed references to key aspects of its folk culture, such as the Bhangra dance and its accompanying music. Evoking the land as mother, Sobti laments that "today from its milk-heavy breasts drips not milk but blood." The latter half of the eulogy speaks of flight, of leaving behind the "water of waters, the Punjab of five waters," and of bidding farewell to the memory of one's ancestors and the earth of childhood play (14-15). For Sobti, as for many other writers, flight from the ancestral home is equated with flight from aspects of Punjabi culture that are lost forever after Partition. From this perspective, Partition seems to have rendered every Punjabi diasporic, regardless of which of the 'three Punjabs' offered post-Partition domicile. Nevertheless, we should not ignore the specific political configurations in India, Pakistan and the diaspora proper that have impacted in very different ways the subjectivities of their respective Punjabi populations.

For Punjabis in India and Pakistan, continued territorial contact with and proximity to the Punjab, albeit a permanently altered one, was offset by nationalist agendas of both countries that required the subordination of regional identities. In post-Partition India, secularism and federalism were the two demands that the nation made on the loyalties of the citizen; in Pakistan, the Urdu language and Islamic identity exercised parallel hegemonies. In fact, the military and political dominance of people of Punjabi ethnicity within the Pakistani public sphere co-exists in some tension with the universal promotion of Urdu as the language of statecraft and high culture. In both India and Pakistan, in other words, it has been difficult to reclaim co-ordinates of collective identity—whether ethnic or religious—other than those delineated by the national master-narrative. This difficulty meant that one could only commemorate that which was lost within a private circle of communitarian belonging. In India, at least, it would seem that Punjabi subjectivity has been stamped indelibly by the need to mourn

cultural loss, as well as by the simultaneous impossibility of expressing longing or sorrow for pre-Partition Punjabiness within national
public culture. Although this partitioning of subjectivity into private
and public domains is a defining feature of any minority identity in
South Asia (Kabir, "Subjectivities"), I would like to isolate here its
specifically Punjabi manifestations within India.

Foremost among these is a rather peculiar irony: while it has
been difficult to mourn directly within India for the loss of pre-Partition
Punjab, Punjabi culture has been indirectly valorised through the circulation of television serials about post-Partition rehabilitation—most
notably the early television serials of the 1980s, *Hum Log* (*We People*)
and *Buniyaad* (*Foundations*)—as well as novels about the Punjab
Partition, and, more crucially for the popular cultural domain, through
Punjabi wedding rituals and Punjabi clothing that have spread across
India primarily through 'Bollywood' films. These discourses have projected a certain expressive Punjabi aesthetic as a representative, indeed
seductive aspect of Indian culture as a whole. This aesthetic, that one
writer and architect has termed "Punjabi Baroque" (Bhatia), has been
most recently given affectionately ironic treatment and global dissemination through 'crossover' films such as *Monsoon Wedding* (Mira Nair,
2001) and *Bend it Like Beckham* (Gurinder Chadha, 2002).

The phenomenal popularity of these films in both India and 'the
West' illustrates, furthermore, how transnational cultural flows
between 'home' and diaspora are a shaping influence on the public-
private divide in Punjabi subjectivity and therefore on Punjabi
(post)memory. As diasporic Punjabi women, Nair and Chadha know-
ingly target the family, that space where ideology is most keenly
undercut by emotional ties and kinship bonds (Brah 67-83). Although
the traditional practices of the 'Asian family' have come under liberal
and feminist scrutiny in both Britain and India, such counter-hege-
monic voices in India cannot afford the luxuries of affect and emotion
in their daily battles against the increasingly visible and militant relationship between patriarchy, religious revivalism and belligerent
nationalism. In contrast, liberal anxieties regarding multiculturalism in
the West offers the diasporic subject a space of negotiation (Singh). It
becomes possible then to recuperate from the contested site of the
'Asian family' a celebration and assertion of Punjabiness that has
shrunk to the home, but which, through film—and, as we shall see,
music—reaches India, Pakistan, and the world at large.

Such diasporic articulations of neo-ethnic postmemory must be viewed alongside the emergence of Sikh separatism in India during the 1980's through the interaction of Pakistani, Indian and diasporic Punjab (Chadda). I raise here this complex issue simply to suggest that the difficulties of mourning the Punjab Partition in India and in Pakistan and the energies and different freedoms of the diaspora resulted in what may be seen as an explosive "return of the repressed," or the demand for Khalistan—a Sikh homeland carved out of Indian Punjab, supported materially by diasporic Sikhs and the Pakistani State, whose structures, as we noted above, are dominated by Punjabi Muslims. Common wisdom attributes the crushing of that movement to the ruthless counter-terrorist measures of the Indian State. I would look also to the channels of artistic and cultural expression, increasingly carved out of Punjabi diasporic-domestic interactions since the 1990s, and offering a non-violent, cosmopolitan alternative to radical separatist politics.

II

In this circulation of Punjabi cultural capital, a crucial role has been played by different genres of music that are associated with Punjabi culture both in South Asia and the diaspora. The most obvious such genre is Bhangra, described by one commentator as

> Punjabi folk and western pop shoved into the blender at high speed . . . at least as quintessentially 'British' as it is 'Asian,' although [its] influence stretches beyond the UK to Canada and the USA, and of course the music has been re-exported back to South Asia. (Huq 61, 63)

The assertion of an urban diasporic Punjabi youth identity enabled affiliations beyond racial and intra-South Asian ethnic cleavages, but, equally, contestations through alternative British Asian sounds. More self-conscious developments in Punjabi-British dance music, termed 'post-Bhangra' by critics (Sanjay Sharma; Huq) have subsequently emerged. 'Post-Bhangra' has complicated the initial "affirmative moment in the formation of an Asian identity discourse in the early 1980s," during which Bhangra first opened up "a site for Asian youth culture acquiring a sense of identity and visibility in the public domain, and negotiating an ambivalent positionality in relation to a culturally hostile and exclusionary British nation" (Sanjay Sharma 39).

The racial politics and youth cultures articulated by Bhangra and 'post-Bhangra' have made these musical genres amenable to academic commentators interested in those wider themes, and especially in the insertion of those politics within the sanitising domains of academia (Sharma, et al.; Dudrah). The diasporic affiliations with the Punjab as homeland displayed by British Bhangra lyrics has been noted by Dudrah. I would like to develop the implications of this comment by probing the connections between diasporic Punjabi identity as formulated through trauma, and the healing capacities of Bhangra and post-Bhangra. In attempting to extract here this particular signification from these musics, I shall draw equally on other genres of South Asian music that circulate among diverse Punjabi audiences, but whose significance seems not to have been much acknowledged: the Punjabi version of Qawwali, or North Indian sufi music (Qureshi); and the Ghazal (romantic lyric), sung in Urdu, and patronized by groups across historic North India, including Punjabis (Manuel; Banerji). While Ghazal has long enjoyed popularity through South Asia and its diasporas—the soirée described by Syal within the opening citation of this article is, in fact, a Ghazal soirée—the globalisation of Qawwali owes single-handedly to the Pakistani qawwal Nusrat Fateh Ali Khan, who was, incidentally, Punjabi (Ashwani Sharma 24-25). It is not surprising, therefore, that the soundtracks of both *Monsoon Wedding* and *Bend it Like Beckham* tap into the specific affects of all these genres, weaving thereby a matrix of Punjabiness through nostalgia, homage and hope.

"Wafadar hai mitti Punjabwali/wafadar hai khoon punjabiyan da [loyal is the soil of the Punjab, loyal the blood of the Punjabi]"— this statement opens a Bhangra track by Hans Raj Hans, remixed by British Asian Punjabi DJ Bally Sagoo, and included in *Bend it Like Beckham*. Entitled "Punjabiyan di Shaan" ("Pride of the Punjabis"). It utilizes an eight-beat rhythm cycle prevalent in Indian folk music, and played on the traditional folk drum of the Punjab, the dhol (known as dholki or dholak elsewhere in northern India); signature melodic strings; strong Punjabi inflections; and traditional antiphonal punctuations ('hoi,' 'aha,' 'balle balle'). Simultaneously, electronic percussions and keyboards reproduce a spectrum of dance sounds—techno, house, drum 'n' bass and reggae. Sounds and rhythms of globalisation and Bhangra—the hybrid mix of "drum 'n' dhol" (Dudrah)—thus combine to evoke the mutual loyalty of Punjab's soil and Punjab's children. In *Monsoon Wedding*'s "Aaja Nacch Le" ("Come, Let's Dance") written by Bally Sagoo and also featuring Hans Raj Hans, similarly, techno and house sounds transform a traditional Bhangra call to dance into a flamboyant assembling of diasporic Punjabi youth.

The narrative frame into which "Aaja Nacch Le" is embedded—a Punjabi Hindu wedding in Delhi—as well as its dissemination from "Brit-Asia" to "Transl-Asia" (Kaur and Kalra 405, punning on Trans-Asia and Translation [translatia, translasia]) through the cinematic medium—foreground the transnational trajectories of Punjabiness that diasporic postmemory facilitates. The celebratory mood of Bhangra is offset in *Monsoon Wedding* by songs by the Pakistani artists—Nusrat Fateh Ali and veteran Ghazal singer Farida Khanum—which evoke sorrow, estrangement and longing. Moreover, the theme song, a traditional Punjabi lyric celebrating the monsoons, is sung by the Indian Sikh Sukhwinder Singh, who has consistently recuperated within mainstream Bollywood music the Punjabi Muslim spirituality associated with Nusrat Fateh Ali's Qawwali (Kabir "Allegories"). The cut-and-mix aesthetic of diasporic art magnifies other affects discernible in Punjabi music shops across the three Punjabs. This author has observed cassettes of Nusrat Fateh Ali Khan, Sikh religious hymns (shabads), and post-Bhangra remixes digitally mastered in Birmingham, selling cheek-by-jowl in small music shops hugging the highways of Indian Punjab; and CDs of the same genres selling in large and glitzy outlets in Manchester's "Curry Mile." In the latter case, it is often near impossible to detect, *prima facie*, the "original nationality" and religion of the shop owners beyond the obvious fact of their Punjabi origin.

In *Monsoon Wedding*, this pan-Punjabi cut-and-mix, facilitated further by the soundtrack format, is audaciously located within a narrative set in and concerned with India, precisely where, as I noted earlier, remembering Punjabiness has been complicated by the demands of nationalism. The soundtrack that recalls, like the music shops described above, the composite culture of pre-Partition Punjab thus cuts against the narrative enactment of Punjabi Hindu culture in contemporary Delhi. Ostensibly, the film has nothing to do with Sikh and Muslim cultures of the Punjab; affectively, those are the cultural and historical layers dredged up through musical recall. The soundtrack of *Monsoon Wedding* demonstrates how music offers modes of remembering and working through cultural trauma that are less contentious than narratives of Punjabiness, and, in fact, work against them. However celebratory, such narratives compulsively return to the moment of violence and rupture that overwrites "language as a precondition for experiencing history" (Van Alphen 42). Whose Punjab do we then talk about? Sikh, Hindu or Muslim? Pakistani, Indian, or

diasporic? The narrative frames that we erect to repair a world rup-
tured by trauma imply perspective, closure, rationalization. Music
heeds no such tyrannies: its affect stems not from narrative or descriptive logic, but "structures of feeling" that transmit the somatics of
memory and belonging across generations.

The transformation of traumatic memory into musical postmemory suggests that memory can become "a repository of the sub-
lime" (Van Alphen 195) only when that which is remembered is not
embedded within an overt narrative. The spatial and conceptual possibilities of diaspora encourage this freeing from story. This point is
especially pertinent for groups marginalized by the nation state and its
master narratives, and for the diasporic artist who wishes to acknowledge 'home' without necessarily participating in the displays of
nationalism that 'home' now generates. After all, it must not be forgotten that diaspora has its traditional and radical-nativist aspects,
which are often predicated on residual and reactivated caste/class posi-
tionalities and subjectivities. Nevertheless, we can claim that neo-ethnic postmemory has a certain subversive potential that resides in its
ability to undo territorial, religious and other competitive nationalisms.
To be 'Punjabi,' rather than 'Indian' or 'Pakistani,' 'Hindu,' 'Muslim,'
or 'Sikh,' can, after all, facilitate cross-border mourning with other
Punjabis that is near-impossible within South Asia itself.

This potential is most powerfully concentrated in music, which
through its oral circulation bypasses another feature of narrative today—
its transmission through the written word. This difference between
music—especially South Asian music, that, unlike Western music, is not
tied to the script of the musical score—and the written word is especially crucial in the Punjabi context. Punjabi's strong associations with
Sikhism in India means that it is written there in the Gurmukhi, or Sikh
religious script, that resembles Devanagari, the script in which Hindi is
written. Likewise, Punjabi's assimilation into the Pakistani State's
Islamicisation programme has been encouraged by its being written
there in the Shahmukhi (Persian) script. This division of script parallels
the mutual illegibility of Urdu and Hindi. Thus post-Partition Punjabis
in the different Punjabs cannot read each other's Punjabi cultural pro-
ductions. Nevertheless, they can understand Punjabi when they hear
music with Punjabi lyrics, or recognise the Punjabi accent with which an
Urdu ghazal or Persian qawwali is enunciated.

Such Punjabi music thereby embodies a transnational postmemory. Such transnationality also opens the diasporic artist to a wider

palette of creative influences, idioms and alignments, many of which range far from 'home.' This range reflects, of course, the self-conscious agenda of post-Bhangra, with its "more specific and intentional fusions of bhangra beats and South Asian instrumentations with other contemporary (dance) genres" (Sanjay Sharma 33).

> From the 1947 Partition to the 60s migration of our parents, we are the product of mass movement—this is the story of Migration: Departure, Arrival, Adaptation, Fusion. From the anguish, turmoil and pain of our parents' history comes the responsibility to build our own dreams.

These declarations on the sleeve notes of Nitin Sawhney's 1995 album, *Migration*, spell out the Punjabi diasporic artist's manifesto. A British Asian who has broken out of the 'bhangra ghetto' and is marketed as a jazz funk artist, Sawhney traces a musical trajectory of migration and remembrance that faces outward even while constantly looking back. His music echoes what Hall has described as the dialogic relationship between two vectors that defines diasporic identity: "the vector of similarity and continuity; and the vector of difference and rupture," where, "[if] one gives . . . continuity with the past, the second reminds us that what we share is precisely the experience of a profound discontinuity" (Hall 24).

The first and eponymous track of *Migration* expresses precisely this sense of continuity-in-discontinuity. Perfectly structured, its journey starts in the east—with tropical birdcall, tabla and dhol (South Asian percussion instruments, the latter bearing specifically Punjabi connotations), snake-charming bagpipe-flute or been, and a classical vocal refrain—but, as the sleeve notes describe, "the percussion stacks up gradually, building up a nice bustling groove." At midpoint, a confident jazz funk sound takes over, although one can still hear an eight-beat Indian rhythm cycle underneath; and in the final third of the track, the vocals return. This transformation through movement away from the Punjab reappears in the album's final track, "Awareness," a minute-long coda that Sawhney describes as "the end of our parents' journey and the beginning of our aspirations." These two pieces bracket six musical vignettes that are neither conclusively Indian, nor decisively 'Western,' and, ostensibly, hardly Punjabi, except for the sixth and seventh tracks, entitled "Punjabi" and "Heer Ranjha" respectively.

"Punjabi" conveys a concentrated essence of Punjabiness through minimalist yet instantly recognisable features of Bhangra: two antiphonal calls, 'hoi' and 'punjabiyan,' punctuating a keyboard rendering of a Bhangra melodic sequence to the eight-beat cycle. A tribute to the past and its postmemorial reconstruction by Bhangra artists in the UK, "Punjabi" is the emotional and musical core of the structure already demarcated by "Migration" and "Awareness." This joyous piece is balanced by the plaintive "Heer Ranjha," Sawhney's interpretation of eighteenth-century Punjabi poet Waris Shah's epic of unrequited love. Heer's refrain in this track, "call me, Ranjha, for we are one," embodies—in form and content—music's potential for healing, at least momentarily, the fissures of the Punjab. As Sobti says of the common Punjabi lyric heritage:

> Nanak, Baba Farid, Amir Khusro, Jayasi, Bulleh Shah, Waris Shah, Shah Latif—can we divide this whole lot of poets between yours and ours? No doubt we divided the territory—but tradition, art, literature are not like geographical areas: they continue to remain undivided, indivisible. (Sobti, "Interview" 51)

Sawhney's reading of Heer Ranjha is a similar one, as his sleeve notes indicate: "The story of forbidden love is as pertinent to a country divided by racial, religious and sexual politics as ever"—though one is left wondering—*which country*? This recuperative and open-ended message enables us, in fact, to read the remaining pieces of *Migration* as part of a more ambitious agenda. Old contiguities between the Punjab and the larger Islamic world are foregrounded by juxtaposing an Arabic love song by Natasha Atlas ("Hope") with *Bahaar* (*Spring*) that layers Turkish singer Denise Anyogu's wordless vocals with a recitation of an Urdu Ghazal. Sawhney thereby evokes cultural hinterlands that radiate out of South Asia from the ancestral Punjab, hinterlands which, thanks to the interventions of (geo)politics, today no longer nourish it except, possibly, in its deterritoralised diasporic incarnation. In the words of one analyst of British Bhangra:

> At the moment of technical wizardry and musical innovation, the assignment of musical instruments and sounds into easily defined nation state boundaries is impossible as one sound merges with and becomes the other. (Dudrah 370)

In the introduction to their seminal work on Bhangra, Sharma, Hutnyk and Sharma observe:

> Perhaps the new Asian dance music can be read as a cultural form that narrates diasporas, dynamically affirming, transforming and mutating both imagined and material linkages. Diaspora then may be considered a site in which music provides opportunities to formulate new alliances beyond national boundaries, rather than only as a fantasy of home affirming "tradition" or "origins." (Sharma, et al. 9)

My argument has tried to go somewhat further than these claims, largely by drawing on while modifying the work of cultural theorists of the Holocaust—such as Marianne Hirsch, Ernst van Alphen and Mieke Bal—in order to illuminate the relationship between diaspora, cultural memory and affect deriving from another, very different trauma. It has read the affirmative and transnational power of diasporic Punjabi musics, including but not merely restricted to Bhangra and post-Bhangra, as in fact undermining narratives of national origin. These musical genres perform and enable a richer, alternative and affective belonging—that of pre-Partition Punjab. Through the South Asian, and specifically Punjabi perspective, and through musical recall, I have attempted to demonstrate that where narrative falters in commemoration and healing, music can perhaps succeed better. The world that the music of the Punjab opens up is a world where all can enter, but the artist whose claims on the Punjab rest on spirit, blood and postmemory is perhaps best equipped to push open the door. In the words of E. B. Kitaj, speaking in a different but ultimately not dissimilar context, "the diasporist artist's pursuit of a homeless logic of *ethnie* may be the core of a more radical art than we can yet imagine" (Kitaj 40).

Bibliography

Bal, Mieke, Jonathan Crewe and Leo Spitzer, eds. *Acts of Memory: Cultural Recall in the Present*. Hanover: University Press of New England, 1999.

Banerji, S. "Ghazals to Bhangra in Great Britain." *Popular Music* 7.2 (1988): 207-13.

Barrier, N. Gerald and Verne A. Dusenbery, eds. *The Sikh Diaspora:*

    Migration and the Experience Beyond Punjab. New Delhi: Chanakya Publications, 1989.

Bhasin, Kamla and Ritu Menon. *Borders and Boundaries: Women in India's Partition*. New Delhi: Kali for Women, 1998.

Bhatia, Gautam. *Punjabi Baroque and Other Memories of Architecture*. New Delhi: Penguin India, 1994.

Brah, Avtar. *Cartographies of Diaspora: Contesting Identities*. London and New York: Routledge, 1996.

Butalia, Urvashi. *The Other Side of Silence: Voices from the Partition of India*. New Delhi: Penguin India, 1999.

Chadda, Maya. *Ethnicity, Security and Separatism in India*. New York: Columbia UP, 1997.

Chatterji, Joya. "Right or Charity? The Debate over Relief and Rehabilitation in West Bengal, 1947-50." *The Partitions of Memory: The Afterlife of the Division of India.* Ed. Suvir Kaul. New Delhi: Permanent Black, 2001. 74-110.

Das, Veena. "Composition of the Personal Voice: Violence and Migration." *Studies in History* 7.1 (1991): 65-77.

Dudrah, Rajinder K. "Drum N Dhol: British Bhangra Music and Diasporic South Asian Identity Formation." *European Journal of Cultural Studies* 5.3 (2002): 363-83.

Eyerman, Ron. *Cultural Trauma: Slavery and the Formation of African American Identity*. Cambridge: Cambridge UP, 2001.

Grewal, J. S. "Punjabi Identity: A Historical Perspective." *Punjabi Identity in a Global Context*. Eds. Pritam Singh and Shinder Singh Thandi. New Delhi: Oxford UP, 1999. 41-54.

Hall, Stuart. "Cultural Identity and Diaspora." *Diaspora and Visual Culture: Representing Africans and Jews*. Ed. Nicholas Mirzoeff. London: Routledge, 2000. 21-33.

Helweg, Arthur. *Sikhs in England: The Development of A Migrant Community*. Delhi: Oxford UP, 1979.

Hirsch, Marianne. "Projected Memory: Holocaust Photographs in Personal and Public Fantasy." *Cultural Recall*. Eds. Bal, et al. 3-23.

Huq, Rupa. "Asian Kool? Bhangra and Beyond." *Disorienting Rhythms: The Politics of the New South Asian Dance Music*. Eds. Sanjay Sharma, John Hutnyk and Ashwani Sharma. London: Zed Books, 1996. 61-80.

Jalal, Ayesha. *The Sole Spokesman: Jinnah, the Muslim League and the Demand for Pakistan*. Cambridge: Cambridge UP, 1994.

Kabir, Ananya Jahanara. "Subjectivities, Memories, Loss: Of Pigskin Bags,

Silver Spittoons and the Partition of India." *Interventions* 4.2 (2002): 245-64.

_____. "Allegories of Alienation and Politics of Bargaining: Minority Subjectivities in Mani Ratnam's *Dil Se*." *South Asian Popular Culture* 1.2 (2003, forthcoming).

Kaul, Suvir, ed. *The Partitions of Memory: The Afterlife of the Division of India*. New Delhi: Permanent Black, 2001.

Kaur, Raminder and Virinder Singh Kalra. "Brazen Translations: Notes for a New Terminology." *Punjabi Identity in a Global Context*. Eds. Pritam Singh and Shinder Singh Thandi. New Delhi: Oxford UP, 1999. 403-12.

Manuel, Peter. "The Popularization and Transformation of the Light-Classical Urdu *Ghazal*-Song." *Gender, Genre and Power in South Asian Expressive Traditions*. Eds. Arjun Appadurai, et al. Philadelphia: University of Pennsylvania Press, 1991. 347-61.

Kitaj, E. B. "First Diasporist Manifesto." *Diaspora and Visual Culture: Representing Africans and Jews*. Ed. Nicholas Mirzoeff. London: Routledge, 2000. 34-42.

Mirzoeff, Nicholas, ed. *Diaspora and Visual Culture: Representing Africans and Jews*. London: Routledge, 2000.

Qureshi, Regula Burckhardt. *Sufi Music of India and Pakistan: Sound, Context and Meaning in Qawwali*. Cambridge: Cambridge UP, 1986.

Sharma, Ashwani. "Sounds Oriental: The (Im)possibility of Theorizing Asian Musical Cultures." *Disorienting Rhythms: The Politics of the New South Asian Dance Music*. Eds. Sanjay Sharma, John Hutnyk and Ashwani Sharma. London: Zed Books, 1996. 15-31.

Sharma, Sanjay. "Noisy Asians or 'Asian Noise?'" *Disorienting Rhythms: The Politics of the New South Asian Dance Music*. Eds. Sanjay Sharma, John Hutnyk and Ashwani Sharma. London: Zed Books, 1996. 32-59.

_____, John Hutnyk and Ashwani Sharma, eds. *Disorienting Rhythms: The Politics of the New South Asian Dance Music*. London: Zed Books, 1996.

Singh, Arvind-Pal. "Writing Otherwise than Identity: Translation and Cultural Hegemony." *Punjabi Identity in a Global Context*. Eds. Pritam Singh and Shinder Singh Thandi. New Delhi: Oxford UP, 1999. 111-38.

Singh, Pritam and Shinder Singh Thandi, eds. *Punjabi Identity in a Global Context*. New Delhi: Oxford UP, 1999.

Sobti, Krishna. "Interview with Alok Bhalla." *Crossing Boundaries.* Ed.
    Geeti Sen. New Delhi: Orient Longman, 1997. 40-53.
_____. *Zindaginama.* Delhi: Rajkamal Prakashan, 1979.
Syal, Meera. *Anita and Me.* London: New Press, 1996.
Van Alphen, Ernst. *Caught by History: Holocaust Effects in Contemporary
    Art, Literature, and Theory.* Stanford: Stanford UP, 1997.

Discography

Danna, Mychael, et al. *Monsoon Wedding.* Milan Records, 2001.
Sawhney, Nitin. *Migration.* Outcaste, 1995.
Various Artists. *Bend it Like Beckham.* Universal/Absolute, 2002.

Filmography

Nair, Mira, dir. *Monsoon Wedding.* Universal Studios, 2001.
Chadha, Gurinder, dir. *Bend it Like Beckham.* Twentieth Century Fox, 2002.

History and Poetry

Walid Bitar

An archaeologist locates a site to unearth, classify and date artifacts. He digs up an Osiris or an Anubis. "Let sleeping dogs lie" is not his motto; he decides for them. In my work, it's up to the dogs; in that respect, historical references are no different from contemporary ones. Some dresses worn at Versailles were puce, a colour chosen to camouflage fleas. When history is invisible as Bourbon fleas, poems double as puce. There's no exhibiting past and present like identifiable thoroughbreds. They're parts of one mongrel, and sometimes parts are hard to separate. History's parts may be miscast, rewritten, simplified, manipulated or ignored. For every responsible archaeologist there are countless scams, subterfuges and acts of vandalism. Historians try to clear up the mess; poets describe it. A historian researches and analyzes, but, as Plato observes, a poet cannot explain what he is doing when composing— he's beside himself, impelled by Muses.[1] At the absurd end of the spectrum, a blind Muse leads the blind. An archaeologist is clinical and methodical. A poet doesn't catalogue the truths searched for; they form as memorable lines, not as data to be remembered. In some inexhaustible poems, lines gradually overshadow one another, and the friction lights up a pharos that shouldn't be translated back into words.

It's often retroactive guesswork, if not wishful thinking, for a person to quote historical poets and argue that they influence him or her in a particular way. I like Fernando Pessoa's heteronyms, his ability to write as different authors in different styles that transcend any one personality. But if I try to use heteronyms, they turn into my divided and ruled satraps—the exercise is a dead end. For me, Pessoa's lesson lies elsewhere. In "Autopsychography," he goes backstage to explore the theatre an audience misses if it misunderstands the nature of performance:

The poet is a faker. He
Fakes it so completely,
He even fakes he's suffering
The pain he's really feeling.

And they who read his writing
Fully feel while reading
Not that pain of his that's double,
But theirs, completely fictional.

So on its tracks goes round and round,
To entertain the reason,
That wound-up little train
We call the heart of man.[2]

Art is artifice. Pain is natural—writing about it isn't. A reader is left with fictional pain sealed off by sides of a Bermuda Triangle: the reader's real pain, the writer's real pain and the writer's faked pain. Pessoa shakes any equilibrium up into cubist planes, and this gives his work an energetic equanimity. My poem "The Breaking of Toys" pays homage to him.

In that poem I say that we play with our lives, then break the toys. A poet plays to break. For Kafka, writing is an ice pick to break the frozen sea inside us. A pick lands on a writer's subjective and objective worlds, though where one world ends and the other begins is unclear—we're in the belly of another mongrel. In theory, we're free to go ape, contact prehistory. In practice, we negotiate many boundaries, beginning with the square roots of power relationships, what it means to gaze and be gazed at, to define and be defined. Such private experiences are the building blocks without which no social identity exists—no society or nation-state either.

In Rilke's "The Panther," a poet's gaze falls on a caged cat in the Paris Jardin des Plantes. The first line speaks of "His vision"— the animal's. But the poem is about Rilke's vision:

His vision, from the constantly passing bars,
has grown so weary that it cannot hold
anything else. It seems to him there are
a thousand bars; and behind the bars, no world.

As he paces in cramped circles, over and over,
the movement of his powerful soft strides
is like a ritual dance around a center
in which a mighty will stands paralyzed.

Only at times, the curtain of the pupils
lifts, quietly—. An image enters in,
rushes down through the tensed, arrested muscles,
plunges into the heart and is gone.[3]

The panther's portrait is under Rilke's control and turns into Rilke's self-portrait. The mood described is human. Rilke, paralyzed in and by space and time—he can only experience the world in a space-time cage—lets images vanish inside him, makes no effort to interpret. But writing about it turns this passive state into an active one, a blank and pitiless epiphany. The panther embodies a recess in Rilke's nature that is being watched, and that cannot watch. A poet captures and exhibits sides of his self just as a zookeeper displays animals. Nietzsche says we only have words for what is dead inside us.[4] We have words for what we have trapped and exhibited in a sentence. A zoo is no graveyard. But a caged panther isn't fully alive. A human being content to be watched and defined by others shares the panther's fate; he doesn't tell his story, which is told by someone else, turning it into a piece of the teller's self-portrait. I often work in the no-man's land dividing portrait and self-portrait. But what's the point of exploring the "square roots of power relationships" if larger numbers are ignored?

An observer is part Don Quixote, part Sancho Panza. Sancho distinguishes between private and public spaces; Don Quixote unites them. In this sense, an artistic style is quixotic. Giorgio de Chirico's metaphysical paintings may be Surrealist, but they aren't merely private visions. They depict the early twentieth-century European city stripped of traditional meanings; it becomes a theatre whose actors resemble shadowy extras because they need time to create or recreate their own roles. Inherited lines have lost relevance, and must be reevaluated. De Chirico, like Nietzsche, was entranced by Turin's vast piazzas, their monuments dwarfed by a public space no longer commanded. Whether we live in old or modern cities, we continue to improvise in de Chirico's atmosphere. There's still no consensus on how to replace values and beliefs we used to automatically inherit. Some people fantasize about futuristic utopias. Others barge into custom-made versions of the past, usually by misrepresenting the history of others. We watch heritage-loving lords of misrule finance occupation armies, and we grow skeptical about interpreted history. It's marvelous in the chronicles of historians. In the hands of spin doctors, it goes bananas. Most of us aren't trained historians. Given a chance to choose a family tree of poetic ancestors, a person may go barking up the wrong one. Many poets would like to include Shakespeare in their trees, but, as T.S Eliot admits, a "poet of the supreme greatness of Shakespeare can hardly influence, he can only be imitated: and the difference between influence and imitation is that influence can fecundate, whereas imitation—especially unconscious imitation—can only sterilize."[5]

I'm drawn to de Chirico's alternative approach, which he explains by quoting Schopenhauer: "one has but to isolate oneself from the world for a few moments so completely that the most commonplace happenings appear to be new and unfamiliar, and in this way reveal their true essence."[6] This ahistorical attitude may capture an artist's position in time more effectively than a conscious attempt to be historical, as Wallace Stevens implies in "A Clear Day and No Memories":

> No soldiers in the scenery,
> No thoughts of people now dead,
> As they were fifty years ago,
> Young and living in a live air,
> Young and walking in the sunshine,
> Bending in blue dresses to touch something,
> Today the mind is not part of the weather.
>
> Today the air is clear of everything.
> It has no knowledge except of nothingness
> And it flows over us without meanings,
> As if none of us had ever been here before
> And are not now: in this shallow spectacle,
> This invisible activity, this sense. [7]

Memory will not reproduce the life history had while it was being made, "young and living in a live air." Stevens' poem is an example of the Schopenhauer epiphany, moments experienced "As if none of us had ever been here before/And are not now"—the cliches of the past are signed away, then those of the present. Stevens records what survives in consciousness, what is necessary and in some sense indestructible. Nothing forgettable should be memorized by rote. The more historical voices survive incognito in a poet's lines, the less destructible the lines become. But the voices are mostly unrecognizable. Poems speak for themselves when they sound as if spoken for the first time. For that to happen, a poet has to mean what he says, and also, ironically, not know what he means until after he says it. Marcel Duchamp's observations about painting apply to many poems. He says of the artist that "we must deny him the state of consciousness on the aesthetic plane about what he is doing or why he is doing it. All his decisions in the artistic execution of the work rest with pure intuition and cannot be translated into a self-analysis, spoken or written, or even thought out."[8] Francis Bacon, more open than Duchamp to self-analysis about historical influence, says "I always think of myself not so much as a painter but as a medium for accident and chance."[9] Some poems really are a series of accidents, though in a good poem the accidents were waiting to happen.

A poem that moves from private to public space will sooner or later collide with political realities. Stevens calls poetry a violence from within to counter the violence from without, but violence from within is sometimes as ugly as what provokes it. Swift's "A Satirical Elegy" was written "On the Death of a Late Famous General," the Duke of Marlborough:

> This world he cumber'd long enough;
> He burnt his candle to the snuff;
> And that's the reason, some folks think,
> He left behind so great a st- -k.[10]

Swift's works emit a life-like variety of odours. Hypocrisy, says La Rochefoucauld, is the tribute vice pays to virtue. When a satirist pays tribute, he flashes the counterfeit bills. If he tries to build a luxurious mansion on high moral ground, he sinks back into hypocrisy. Instead, the poetic theatre is reduced to a shack, or even thin air. This leaves room for many destructible elements—parts of Stevens' "invisible activity"—and a barrage of lingo to send them up.

I wrote most of my new collection, *Bastardi Puri*, in Beirut. "Pure bastards" Sicilians call themselves, a reference to the island's mixed ancestry. But any product of evolution, animate or inanimate, is a pure bastard. In Beirut the past isn't sequestered in a picturesque district. The historic streets of Solidere are also the city's most recently reconstructed and renovated ones. They are still being reconstructed, a work in

194

progress. As for other neighbourhoods, the dominant architectural styles are modern. History in the city is like history anywhere—difficult to pin down, elusive, protean. It lives in people's gestures, attitudes, customs, faiths, accents and dialects. The visible and invisible traces of several thousand years are accommodated in, and hustled into, the present. A poem can be composed of concrete block structures I pass on my walks. Near Raouche, there's a run-down shuttered establishment called Hotel Marhaba (Hotel Hello/Welcome). The English sign has lost the "M," and is now the Hotel Arhaba (Hotel He Terrorized). The building, a project from the 1950s or 1960s, is history. Though my poems often refer to life in North America, I try to give stanzas the qualities I find enigmatic in many Levantine streets—a harsh practicality, an absence of surface decoration, and, above all, humorous and chaotic traffic.

Notes

[1] Plato, "Ion," *The Collected Dialogues,* Edith Hamilton and Huntington Cairns, eds., Lane Cooper, trans. (Princeton: Princeton U P, 1980) 220.

[2] Fernando Pessoa, "Autopsychography," *Poems of Fernando Pessoa*, Edwin Honig and Susan M. Brown, trans. (San Francisco: City Lights Books, 1998) 167.

[3] Rainer Maria Rilke, "The Panther," *The Selected Poetry of Rainer Maria Rilke*, Stephen Mitchell, trans. (New York: Vintage Books, 1982) 25.

[4] Nietzsche's source is probably Schopenhauer: "The actual life of a thought lasts only until it reaches the point of speech: there it petrifies and is henceforth dead but indestructible, like the petrified plants and animals of prehistory. As soon as our thinking has found words it ceases to be sincere or at bottom serious." Arthur Schopenhauer, *Essays and Aphorisms*, R.J. Hollingdale, trans. (London: Penguin Books, 1970) 201.

[5] T.S. Eliot, *Inventions of the March Hare*, Christopher Ricks, ed. (New York: Harcourt Brace and Company, 1996) 394.

[6] Paolo Baldacci, *De Chirico: The Metaphysical Period*, Jeffrey Jennings, trans. (New York: Little, Brown and Company, 1997) 95.

[7] Wallace Stevens, *The Palm at the End of the Mind*, Holly Stevens, ed. (New York: Vintage Books, 1972) 397.

[8] As quoted in David Sylvester, *Interviews With Francis Bacon* (New York: Thames and Hudson, 2002) 104.

[9] David Sylvester, 140.

[10] Jonathan Swift, "A Satirical Elegy," *Gulliver's Travels and Other Writings*, Louis Landa, ed. (Boston: Houghton Mifflin Company, 1960) 455, ll. 13-16.

Appendix

Poems by Walid Bitar

Theatre

There are happenings into which rivers flow,
but these aren't necessarily seas.
We're outraged by liquid duplicity
we barbarize with midsection blows
splashes make fun of with elusive ease;
what we thought pure is farrago.
So when I walk along the banks of the Nile,
I withdraw into noncommittal smiles.

And I'll non-concur if you take up
the cause of H_2O's freedom to act.
I don't mind drama's cute licensed pups;
these have a crowd-pleasing right to attack
the Actaeons of the universe who peep
at box-office smash Diana's physique.
But rain and its minions are less of a draw,
with too little tragedy, too high a fall.

Still, water is sacred; without it life
would be as unthinkable as crisscrossing
oneself without a body. Any paradise
insists that its faithful be made of something
that would find fire anomalous; ice
qualifies, last of the red hot Vikings.
It and other casualties may be canonized;
to whip is human, to be whipped divine.

The Mechanics of Banality

Can we brainwash that meditating yogi?
We must find part of him that's a car
whose brakes we'll sabotage under the stars.
Get mechanics to train one of our lackeys.

A man seated like lotus is irritating.
I don't know why; it's none of my business.
I have narrow views on physical fitness,
but I close my eyes when I spot a psyche.

It may be that I love to talk,
but when others do, I grate my own nerves
in a pre-emptive strike. I won't be scratched
by people like primates in some cozy pack,

though in the wild it's supposedly grooming—
I'm mixing up human voices with ape fingers—
I couldn't care less. I'm not into singing,
or anything else except making you suffer,

whoever you are; we haven't met.
We may some day; I'm in charge of security.
There are some folks who like watching a sunset,
and others who watch them, and like opportunities.

The Breaking of Toys

Some days there are untold compositions,
then comes the odd lunation with none.
Maybe we write when we need more tombs;
is our silence, then, the praying of nuns?

We only have words for what's dead inside us,
said one man; another, deceased,
had claimed culture meant burying the dead.
Poets and gravediggers are athletic priests,

but what, I wonder, lies under my lines?
What, exactly, is no longer living?
I probably don't need to know, and besides
if it's a B-movie, there might be zombies.

To make fun of our souls is vaguely modest,
but needless to say, it's also a ploy,
a traditional way to avoid arrest;
we play with our lives, then break the toys.

An Epiphany

An epiphany in a city of concrete blocks?
Dissect your brain; it isn't any prettier,
nor are its cadaver's other neighbourhood spots—
the inner world is less picturesque than the outer

when viewed in the three dimensions that moonlight
as the Fates, so busy with these occupations
they have no time for private lives
they wouldn't enjoy, being inhuman.

But I, I'm such a social lion
I'm determined to lure them out of their state.
The Garden of Eden had its serpent,
and space must somehow deal with my hate;

its surfaces naturally take to my spying.
They'd rather not do dirty work alone,
and are always ready to donate their disguises
to the right charity, one like oblivion.

Shahrazad

Do you mind if I call you Shahrazad
as we wait for our life to turn into a story
you postpone by not telling me?

We may be hallucinated, but we're not concerned,
having friends in high places, Himalayas, anthills,
and countless speed bumps of the soul.
I'll be discreet; I won't name moguls.

Instead, I'll confess my mind has weather,
an eternal spring we Cuernavacans reside in
that won't listen to reason; it believes tsunamis
are the ecstatic ghosts of kamikazes.

Sometimes the most rigorous way to hunt
is to realize, from the beginning, there's no quarry,
but a hyperactive taking of the air, sniffing dahlias,
a mystic, for example, might perform calmly.

My mind is so crowded—not by actual mobs—
by their debris. Bits and pieces of frenzy take up
much more room than one coherent outburst.

And my skin is a bodega for lice whose thirsts
would have made me rich if they'd paid the tab
I let them run up, because I thought at the time
it was the noble thing to do; my morality
had its waiters, waitresses, maitre d',
whose existences it ignored as if to evade
wages by denying it ran a business. It did,

and made millions in silent conversations whose dialects
were the square roots of words, the creatures themselves.
See them in the Cacatua Galerita cage?
Just like them to prefer shade to high noon.
Language and I, we came from the same wilderness,
and now we've ended up in zoological gardens.

Trance: A Declassified Document

I listen to myself, can't believe what I hear,
though if I'm distracted it sounds natural.
If I were asleep, they'd be unreal,
the same phrases I nail down here as true.

Repeating over and over, I slowly
dissolve each word, syllable and letter,
except that the liquid tapped is a fetter
locking up for future use what disappears.

Kiss and make up? But whatever for?
Relations should be foreign. Besides, the lips
my own heart poisoned are now deformed.
My dears, I can't help myself—let 'em rip!

I checked with Gallup, and he/she assures me
(by the way, I'm the one called *Dark Prince*)
a jab or two of freedom fighting helium
can't hurt anybody—nab a balloon, add a pinch

of looking glass fever, and war is declared
on the air that monopolizes air; this trafficking
of an element in itself means its interest
(either cumulus or rain, that's to be determined)

is in conflict with ours. Ours is more beautiful:
behold it at work on a tree, this woodpecker
looted from a web cartoonist's portfolio—
no old fashioned Woodrow, our mascot's a predator,

though cute as the old block he's a chip off.
Habits die hard; we take life easily.
Our mentors had trench coats and Kalashnikovs.
Our bombs are dropped by the birds and the bees

we repay weekly with a real love of nature,
though we ask science to keep it in line.
To the naked eye, our venom is slime,
but under microscopes some petals flower

into objects supernatural. That rings a bell
I knelt near the other day, vowing to take
its digital photo to celebrate my awakening
from classified worlds into our leaky hell,

if you'll pardon the mild mannered theology.
The only demons I can display are gentrified,
clear their shaved throats, and leave no debris,
four comfy horsemen in my four-wheel drive.

A Disposition of the Antiquities

You know how it is with dictators and flunkies...
get as many citizens as possible involved
in the jack of all trades firing squads,
Jills too, all ages, creeds, ethnicities...

That way, with guilt, it's share and share alike.
But why serve up so jam-packed an idea?
We need a loose grip we can slip—an ear's.
Its plain, simple thugs are easiest to bribe

with babble about ideals. Call this victory.
Words are loyalists in first or last stands,
especially choreographed on shifting sands,
museums trashed, bronze poses effete,

withdrawn from a 5,000 year old account,
the Mesopotamian, a new world special,
open hearted tip of the hat to feudal
and democratic under the table body counts

whose survivors we ask how it went, looking away
to focus on nothing in particular, the distance
re-settled by the usual heroines and princes,
a landscape to some, to others eternity

but to this boy more of our enemy's gold.
Yes, we occupy what we meditate on,
frame, without painting, a scene with our brawn
lest something escape us. Our own scent grows cold,

but luckily we didn't come east to search souls,
ours or the locals'. That would be intrusive.
We're here to liberate and barter for the looters'
antiquities—re-sell them as "postmodern dolls,"

or some other code name we'll come up with
for the black markets that could be called white,
any colour in fact. Why put up a fight
when the opponent is our own rich vocabulary?

"Nothing But Little Lines"

Steffen Stelzer

For D. S.: Two Dedications

To You, in your old age. And to Philosophy.
I know, you don't take this juxtaposition to be a title of honor. Not necessarily, you would say, not necessarily an honor for you.[1]

*

I wonder, though. And I will, therefore, not separate, for the time being, not write two separate dedications. One for literature, let's say, and one for philosophy.

*

The question of What is Philosophy? *can perhaps be posed only late in life, with the arrival of old age and the time for speaking correctly.* (Deleuze/Guattari 1)[2]

*

Do you think that such things could be a matter of age? Or, to be more precise, of old age? There is an age of philosophy, and more astonishingly, there is an age for asking what philosophy is. Seriously, soberly. An age when it is time to know her or, at least, when it is time to desire to know her, finally.

*

This, at least, is what some philosophers say. They also say, or make someone say, that it is a matter of pleasures, of exchanging pleasures. And it looks, rather, like exchanging pleasantries. Remember, when Plato has those two old men, Cephalus and Socrates, dance around each other and their life's journey? "Oh yes, says Cephalus, it is marvellous, one is never left without. When the pleasures of the body fade away, the pleasures and charms of conversation increase. Oh yes, says Socrates, you know how much I love conversing, and there is nothing better than conversing with old men."[3]

*

But, Socrates, when you conversed with young men, how often did you tell them of your love of conversation? And, by the way, didn't you say at the end of your life that seeing and judging things through the lenses of pleasure and pain is the "worst evil" because it nails the soul to the body?

*

. . . There are times when old age produces not eternal youth but a sovereign freedom, a pure necessity in which one enjoys a moment of grace between life and death, and in which all the parts of the machine come together to send into the future a feature that cuts across all ages. . . . (1-2)

*

It seems to be the body. The body ages. The aging philosopher's body ages. And now will be time for two dedications. One to philosophy whose time has come, "when a figure of life has grown old"—in the words of Hegel—and one to the question: *What is Philosophy?*

*

Old philosophy, old philosophers, always old, old before their time. Oh, old philosophers, what did you do in your youth? Did you live, already then, in your old bodies and minds, thinking, wondering how the fire would go out? Extinction or exhaustion, violence or old age? One wouldn't know, at that age. And probably it didn't matter, at that age.

*

How or when the fire would die, was of no concern. One was so involved in one's plans and ideas—was just '*doing* philosophy'— that the thought, the question, never occurred. What did it matter, if one's life was going to be a life where, as you, Deleuze, put it, there is no sudden breakage, a life that just slowly goes out, or if it would, just stop? It didn't seem to matter. For a philosopher, at least, there were guarantees. In case he would have wondered, despite his youth. It went like this: If one didn't reach old age, then what one was doing—philosophy—would reach for sure old age, because it always already had, because from the beginning it had gone out.

*

Picture old philosophers in their old bodies, Kant, Socrates, Heidegger, picture the thoughts traversing these old bodies, picture what each one thinks of his old body, and what he thinks about the body itself, its concept.

*

. . . In fact, the bibliography on the nature of philosophy is very limit-
ed. It is a question posed in a moment of quiet restlessness, at mid-
night, when there is no longer anything to ask. (1)

*

Or picture a scene:
Midnight. In his dimly-lit room Gilles Deleuze, an old French philosopher, still restless, though considerably quieter than in his younger
days, goes through a sequence of dress-rehearsals, each time posing as
an old man: he first poses as the painter William Turner, then changes
costume and reappears as the French writer Chateaubriand, then
changes again and appears as the German philosopher Immanuel Kant,
in order to finally appear as himself. In the last pose, the one where
Deleuze, the old philosopher, acts the old philosopher Deleuze, I find
him most convincing. He steps forward and recites: *This is the time, at*
midnight, where there is no longer anything to ask (1). This is a
prompt. It makes a ruthless question appear on stage. Knowing no
mercy with an old man, it rushes on him, seizes him, and with a mild
smile, asks: *What is philosophy?*

*

. . . In old age Turner acquired or won the right to take painting down
a deserted path of no return that is indistinguishable from a final ques-
tion. (2)

*

Deleuze smiles vaguely, and to be given release from its terribly gen-
tle grip, he strikes a deal with it that allows him to paint. What he will
paint, he says, is a picture of philosophy, "in the manner of the late
William Turner." He intends, thereby, he says, to do to philosophy
what Turner did to painting, namely, take it *down a deserted path of*
no return that is indistinguishable from a final question. If it will ever
be finished, it will be a fine picture, one where philosophy is in the end
indistinguishable from *What is philosophy?* And it will be finished, if
the old philosopher has time to finish it.

*

Not that it wasn't already painted. It was, but is going to be repainted.
Thus, the curtain can open again. This time, it opens on something that
looks from the distance like a vast expanse of water and, on closer
scrutiny, turns out to be an immense swirl and whirl of droplets, or,
rather, sparks flashing at infinite speed, faster than light, and thus gone
when they appear.

*

. . . Art is not chaos but a composition of chaos that yields the vision or sensation, so that it constitutes, as Joyce says, a chaosmos, a composed chaos—neither foreseen neither preconceived. Art transforms chaotic variability into chaoid *variety, as in . . . Turner's golden conflagration. . . .* (204-05)

*

The name Deleuze has for what these pictures depict is an old name, *chaos*. Chaos is, not only for Deleuze, but for so many philosophers that one may be inclined to say, "for philosophy," a reasonably unsettling affair. Something threatening, something one would want to be protected against. Something whose shadow Nietzsche recognized already in Parmenides' "Being" which he understood as the ancient gods' response to Parmenides' desperate call for a piece of wood to carry him over the depth of the waters. A little something, then, to hold on to? Something graspable, a concept, or, at least, a little order so that one may find one's way through—yes, through what?

*

Not exactly disorder: *Chaos is defined not so much by its disorder as by the infinite speed with which every form taking shape in it vanishes* (118). Well, why do we then *require just a little order to protect us from chaos?* (201) Maybe, because there is more to this chaos than what would lend itself to a depiction, or even, a painting? And, maybe, because the old name and the new one are already a bit too orderly for something that is much worse (or much better, who knows?) than "chaos." For one thing, chaos cannot be located. It is as much the swimmer as the water, or, to put it more philosophically, chaos is as much the characteristic of thoughts as it is the character of "things": *Nothing is more distressing than a thought that escapes itself, than ideas that fly off, that disappear hardly formed, already eroded by forgetfulness or precipitated into others that we no longer master. These are infinite* variabilities*, the appearing and disappearing of which coincide. They are infinite speeds that blend into the immobility of the colorless and silent nothingness they traverse, without nature and thought* (201). Thoughts, without thought?

*

Deleuze/Guattari tell of three ways of struggling against chaos, or rather, of three and a half: philosophy, science, art, and, somehow unwelcome, religion. The first three deserve the name of thought. The latter doesn't, really. This is due to differences in the way the triad meets "the enemy," on one side, and "religion" does, or rather, avoids doing, on the other.

*

The scene and its setting are not very new, but that should not detract because it enhances the old heroic charm. It looks like this: the first protective layer against chaos is opinion. You will recognize an old friend (and enemy) from Socrates' time. Opinion does, however, not yield what it promises. Worse, it pretends to bring a little order into chaos while increasing it and, thus, contributes to the *misfortune of people* (206).

*

Again, Deleuze/Guattari paint an old painting using old props: *This is all that we ask for in order to* make an opinion *for ourselves, like a sort of "umbrella" which protects us from chaos* (202). The philosophical public will "understand" . . . Nietzsche's umbrella, Heidegger's *Seinsvergessenheits*-umbrella, Derrida's Heideggerian-Nietzschean umbrella, so many umbrellas, so different.

*

Our opinions are made up from all this. But art, science, and philosophy require more: they cast planes over the chaos. These three disciplines are not like religions that invoke dynasties of gods, or the epiphany of a single god, in order to paint a firmament on the umbrella, like the figures of an Urdoxa *from which opinions stem. Philosophy, science, and art want us to tear open the firmament and plunge into the chaos. We defeat it only at this price.* (202)[4]

*

Although not quite at the height of the others in the battle against chaos, religions seem to warrant a short note in this scene, maybe, because they could easily be mistaken as combatants in the old struggle against chaos. But it is clear that their characterization is not necessarily due to recognition of them as "things." It seems much more due to a function they play in the economy of what Deleuze/Guattari call "thought." They mark, so to speak, one possibility amongst a variety of attitudes towards chaos *that thought can think of.* In Deleuze/Guattari words paint, religions paint, as artists and philosophers paint (do scientists paint?). So, they seem to combat chaos. But unlike the paintings of artists and philosophers, their paintings are made *on* opinions, not through them. They leave opinions intact, making them even firmer, painting a firmament, giving the impression of stability and reliability, while chaos boils beneath.

*

Philosophy, science, and art, on the other hand, fight the enemy, chaos, by fighting the first bastion against it, opinion: *It is as if the* struggle against chaos *does not take place without affinity with the enemy, because another struggle develops and takes on more importance— the struggle against opinion, which claims to protect us from chaos itself* (203).

*

It is important to note that Deleuze/Guattari do not advocate a turning away from chaos towards opinion, although the latter seems to be the more important enemy. The attention is still focused on chaos, but in such a way that, thereby, opinion is drawn in. When philosophy, science, and art open to chaos, *plunge into it*, opinion feels attacked and, indeed, is attacked. Is opinion, then, a worse enemy, more threatening than chaos?

*

Deleuze/Guattari describe in detail the different ways in which each of the three combatants deals with its enemy. But as these lines are dedicated to you and to philosophy, I want to see how *philosophia* is painted.

*

Philosophy presents three elements, each of which fits with the other two but must be considered for itself: the prephilosophical plane it must lay out (immanence), the persona or personae it must invent and bring to life (insistence), and the philosophical concepts it must create (consistency). *Laying out, inventing, and creating constitute the philosophical trinity—diagrammatic, personalistic, and intense features.* (76-77)

*

Risking a certain degree of discourtesy and taking advantage of the slyness of old age and philosophy, I'll pass by the first two (*immanence* and *insistence*) with a short remark and concentrate on the third, (*consistency*), philosophy's creation of concepts.

*

Philosophy which intends to protect against chaos and which, pursuing this intention, does not imagine herself to be able to hover over chaos, or to construct, from above, some screen of protection, but fights by plunging into it, must in this plunge have something that stabilizes. The "raft" to which Deleuze/Guattari refer repeatedly must be created in the plunge. And, furthermore, it must float on something. What it floats on is, of course, water—the water that carries. The water that carries is not something on top of the water, something other than water. It is *the plane* of the water. Deleuze/Guattari call this plane the *plane of immanence*: *The plane of immanence is like a section of chaos and acts like a sieve* (42).

*

If this plane is, as Deleuze/Guattari put it, laid over chaos, then we have the strange phenomenon of a section of chaos over chaos. Yet, this is the meaning of *immanence*, as used by Deleuze/Guattari. Furthermore, in keeping with the image of the sieve, this section must be imagined as consisting of holes through which chaos flows (or flashes). Something like a section of space interspersed with black holes.

*

If this image overtaxes your imagination, add to it its elemental signature which I misquoted when I likened it to water: *Immanence can be said to be the burning issue of all philosophy because it takes on all the dangers that philosophy must confront, all the condemnations, persecutions, and repudiations that it undergoes. This at least persuades us that the problem of immanence is not abstract or merely theoretical. It is not immediately clear why immanence is so dangerous, but it is. It engulfs sages and gods. What singles out the philosopher is the part played by immanence or fire. Immanence is immanent only to itself and consequently captures everything, absorbs All-One, and leaves nothing remaining to which it could be immanent* (45). Immanence, then, is not water but fire, all-consuming fire. On a lighter note, one could say that immanence, as it is painted here, describes a thorough and furious refusal of any resort to transcendence. This, for Deleuze, is the most important mark of philosophy. And it is important, as we will see, for old age.

*

The other element with which philosophy takes the plunge into chaos, is the concept. For Deleuze/Guattari, philosophy is neither a matter of reflection, nor of contemplation, nor of communication. In short, not a matter of discourse. Philosophical thought is the activity of creating concepts: *In this sense the concept is act of thought, it is thought operating at infinite (although greater or lesser) speed* (21).

*

If the task Deleuze/Guattari recognized for philosophy is not carried out by some activity extraneous to chaos but within it, then the element suitable for this task must share the main character of chaos, that is, infinite speed. It must possess this quality and it must, to defeat it, possess a capacity that chaos lacks. Chaos contains *all possible particles and draws out all possible forms, which spring up only to disappear immediately, without consistency or reference, without consequence. Chaos is an infinite speed of birth and disappearance. Now philosophy wants to know how to retain infinite speeds while gaining consis-*

tency, by giving the virtual [i.e. chaos] a consistency specific to it (118). The important point in this description is that whatever is capable of giving consistency to these particles and forms must do so without slowing them down. It must itself operate at infinite speed, that is, faster than light. Deleuze/Guattari find this requirement perfectly fulfilled by thought or, more specifically, philosophical thought. Their perception of thought is common and old, and it is summed up in their quotation from Epicurus: "The atom will traverse space with the speed of thought." (38)

*

What is remarkable about this self-perception of thought is that philosophy displays with equal ease a rich tradition of the 'opposite' characterization of thought and of 'the thinker.' There, words like 'thoughtful' or 'mindful' rather invoke very slow motion. But an inquiry into the nature of thought should be wary of arguing for one side or the other. The intriguing thing regarding portraits of thought painted with speed, is that they allow for both perceptions.

*

Be that as it may, philosophical thought could not perform the task it is meant for, unless it has another trait, namely, the capacity to give consistency. This work, to bring consistency into a whirl of forms and particles traveling at infinite speed, without reducing their speed, is for Deleuze/Guattari the work, the activity of the concept.

*

The word "concept" suggests gestures like "grasping," "holding fast," "capturing," and it is the latter that renders Deleuze/Guattari's use of it best. One should, however, notice that, given the previous description of philosophical thought as plunging into chaos, concepts cannot be imagined as means to get hold of particles and forms by 'fishing them out.' In other words, conceptual thought does not stand above the swirling sea of things. Which place would it have to stand on? It does not catch things or try to 'yank' them out, even if such a move could be imagined as occurring with infinite speed: *It is as if one were casting a net, but the fisherman always risks being swept away and finding himself in the open sea when he thought he had reached port* (203). Philosophical thinking is 'in the water' or, more faithful to Deleuze/Guattari's element, 'on fire.' The word 'consistency' describes, therefore, capturing in chaos.[5]

*

To this moment, it seems that things are well with conceptual thought: it operates at infinite speed, does not slow down things and nothing slows it down. To a closer look it appears, however, that in this smoothly-running little machine one can detect from early on, and then with increasing evidence, traces of exhaustion, bother and fascination in turns. Deleuze/Guattari call these *weariness* (*fatigue*).

*

These first two aspects or layers of the brain-subject, sensation as much as the concept, are very fragile. Not only objective disconnections and disintegrations but an immense weariness results in sensations, which have now become woolly, letting escape the elements and vibrations it finds increasingly difficult to contract. Old age is this very weariness: then, there is either a fall into mental chaos outside of the plane of composition or a falling-back on ready-made opinions. . . The case of philosophy is a bit different [from the case of art], although it depends on a similar weariness. In this case, weary thought, incapable of maintaining itself on the plane of immanence, can no longer bear the infinite speeds of the third kind that, in a manner of a vortex, measure the concept's copresence to all its intensive components at once (consistency). It falls back on the relative speeds that concern only the succession of movement from one point to another, from one extensive component to another, from one idea to another, and that measure simple associations without being able to reconstitute any concept. No doubt these relative speeds may be very great, to the point of simulating the absolute, but they are only the variable speeds of opinion, of discussion or "repartee," as with those untiring young people whose mental quickness is praised, but also with those weary old ones who pursue slow-moving opinions and engage in stagnant discussions by speaking all alone, within their hollowed head, like a distant memory of their old concepts to which they remain attached so as not to fall back completely into the chaos. (214)

*

So, thought ages. There is young thought and there is weary, old thought. Or should I rather say, the thinker's body ages, and his mind ages insofar as it thinks through the body. What is this "body?" Is it the so-called " natural," or "physical" body? Is Deleuze/Guattari's philosophy, then, a kind of 'physicism' which sees the world, or rather, the cosmos, as well as thought itself, as an immense flurry of 'particles?' Is it just a clumsy kind of natural science that would be easy food for the real scientist? Not so easy. First, because such a 'natural-

ism' would be too 'natural' and, thus, not philosophical, not sufficiently thought. Second, it is because Thought and Nature, *Nous* and
Physis, for Deleuze/Guattari, are the two facets of the plane of immanence (38). That is, they are both what Deleuze/Guattari call
"prephilosophical" aspects of philosophical conceptuality. And as
such they allow for a situation where *thinking and being are said to be
one and the same. Or rather, movement is not the image of thought
without being also the substance of being. When Thales's thought
leaps out, it comes back as water. When Heraclitus's thought becomes
polemos, it is fire that retorts. It is a single speed on both sides: "The
atom will traverse space with the speed of thought."* (38)

*

Aging is, therefore, as much a matter of thought as it is of nature. But
what, precisely, does this "matter of" mean?

*

I have to revise: thought itself does not age. It ages as little as nature, or
as life. What ages is *thinking*, thinking (of) things or, for that matter, living life. And this is so because *to create is to resist* (110). As, one may
say, to live is to resist: *books of philosophy and works of art also con-
tain their sum of unimaginable sufferings that forewarn of the advent of
a people. They have resistance in common—their resistance to death, to
servitude, to the intolerable, to shame, and to the present* (110).

*

Philosophy creates concepts. Thereby, it resists. But resistance does
not only fan the fire, it exhausts it, wears it down. The age of conceptual thought, being the age of resistance, would, therefore, be neither the age of *those untiring young people whose mental quickness
is praised*, [nor the age of] *those weary old ones who pursue slow-
moving opinions* because they *can no longer bear the infinite speeds*
(214). These ages are not good news for philosophy. Yet,
Deleuze/Guattari have good news. News that is not taken from
another youth, a second wind one may wish for in one's old age, or
news from another kind of old age. No, they have news from *the
arrival of old age (quand vient la viellesse)* (1).

*

The fire of conceptual thought may certainly burn high and it may find
natures who are strong and fast enough to bear its infinite speeds. They
are Deleuzian/Guattarian heroes of thought—the philosopher, the scientist, and the artist—who *return from the land of the dead, bringing back
from chaos* (202) their trophies. But they are too heroic—and, at the same

time, not heroic enough. Their fire may have reached its apex of heat, but not its apex of exhaustion. When that moment arrives, philosophy arrives on stage, and it arrives in the form of a question, the question, *what is philosophy?* And what happens at that moment, "at midnight," at *a moment of grace between life and death* is the coming of age of old philosophy: *When Thales' thought leaps out, it comes back as water. When Heraclitus' thought becomes polemos, it is fire that retorts* (38). When Deleuze/Guattari's thought becomes *question*, it is old age that replies.

*

Is it not possible that a philosopher live past midnight? What becomes of conceptual thought when it crosses its apex of exhaustion and drifts into weaker kinds of weakness? Stagnant discussions of an old one speaking all alone within his hollowed head, like a distant memory of his old concepts to which he remains attached so as not to fall back completely into the chaos?

*

What a strange remark, after all Deleuze/Guattari said about immanence, after all their vehement attacks against transcendence, against the priests and empires! Deleuze/Guattari, at midnight, observe what happens to an old one who has passed midnight, who lost the last bit of strength required to keep up with infinite speeds, to think captively, conceptually. But this observation isn't the speech (or the thought) of an old one's thought past midnight. It is the observation of someone about something, someone who went out, above, who leaped, and, now, has no place to fall back to, not even old chaos. If Deleuze/Guattari had stayed on with the old one, we would hear an old person's thinking into the night, into the question, *What is Philosophy?* But we don't. And there is no further question, no more philosophy. Instead, someone informs us about what happens to old ones who lost the strength required for conceptual thought. That "someone," is he not the same "Deleuze/Guattari" who insisted on telling us of philosophy's glory, immanence, and who so vehemently attacked all kinds of transcendence, all priests and empires?

*

Nothing but little lines, that's how he says he conceives of an old man's project.[6] Little lines, at the hour of sobriety, when fire and fatigue meet. When one doesn't have to be someone anymore, when it's enough to be, when one doesn't have to do philosophy, when thought and life meet. When, when, when. Nothing but little lines…with little else.

*

A little difficulty. For, if the philosopher, or his thought, becomes gradually exhausted, then he must think to the point where the fatigue, the cold, is still conceptual, still allows for the creation of concepts. And, maybe, he will think up to the 'last' concept: philosophy. But that means, as a philosopher, he must *not be* past midnight and must not think past that question. Not to be past midnight signifies that thought would have to stop, at midnight. Yet, how should it stop, and who would be there to notice? How can the philosopher make sure that there will be no thinking past midnight, no thinking into the depth of the night? By making sure not to be, past that time. And, by making sure that one doesn't mistake the babble of the old ones for thought.

*

The remarkable feature of Deleuze/Guattari's question *What is philosophy?*—a feature which is reflected throughout their thought—lies in the dating of this question. That is not necessary. Questions in the form of 'what is ...?' belong to the repertoire of philosophical thought as such, whose elements can be well defined logically and irrespective of any temporal determinations. One may say that this is the case where philosophy is understood as "science," as knowledge, and Aristotle could be cited as the best witness. This definition of the three questions—which the science they are seeking, i.e., philosophy as metaphysics, must ask—makes it sufficiently clear. First, we ask, "if it [i.e., something] is," then, "what it is," and finally, "why it is." If I regard all of the three questions equally, then I will find no indication as to a particular time of life when they could be appropriately asked. And I could conclude that this is so because of the nature of 'science,' of 'scientific knowledge' which is timeless or, as the Scholastics say, "essential."

*

There is, however, already here in Aristotle, a strange duplicity which shouldn't make it so easy to relegate this question to the realm of scientific-philosophical procedure. Aristotle cannot, or does not, debate the issue of the appropriate questions for knowledge without debating the capacity, or incapacity of human beings to reach such knowledge. This debate has two aspects. One: Are human beings capable of the science, the knowledge, Aristotle is searching for and which he calls "the highest knowledge?" And another: Which 'humanity,' or which level of humanity human beings have to reach to be capable of it? One could call this, quickly, superficially, and belatedly, the transcendental condition for knowledge. In later philosophers, like Nietzsche and Deleuze, to name only two, this second aspect has become *immanent* to thought, or, to use Deleuze/Guattari's words, *immanent to immanence*. Philosophy has, for a long time, been moved and irritated by this issue, and one of its formulations is what Deleuze calls in his book on Nietzsche "the noble affinity of thought and life."[7] Once the old question is re-formulated in this way, it becomes, of course, necessary and possible to look for that time in a human being's life which would be the most suitable.

*

Deleuze/Guattari themselves are quite ambiguous on the issue of knowledge. I will outline some traits of this ambiguity, insofar as it is relevant for philosophy.

*

The understanding of philosophy as "knowledge," that is, "science" in the literal sense of this word, marks a long tradition of thought which begins with Ancient Greek philosophy and is still reflected in Hegel's thought. There is, however, a certain oscillation between versions of the concept of science. Even there—where philosophy did not hesitate to call itself by the name of 'science'—it hastened to explain, to correct, to distinguish, until the necessity for the title itself became so insignificant that it could do without. In a certain sense, it may, however, be more correct to say that philosophy has a tense relationship with knowledge. Following the course of Deleuze/Guattari's thought, one might be inclined to say that knowledge cannot be the outstanding aim of this philosophy. But the stress would, then, be on the word "outstanding." Precisely because thought is creation, for Deleuze/Guattari, knowledge can only be a feature of this activity, not an aim that it would envisage, beyond itself: *The concept is obviously knowledge—but knowledge of itself, and what it knows is the pure event* (33). In other words, knowledge is not what one tries to reach through concepts; it is the very activity of conceptual thought. This knowledge is not new for Deleuze/Guattari. They try to establish that it is already a feature of Greek philosophy: *It is often said that since Plato, the Greeks contrasted philosophy, as a* knowledge *that also includes the sciences, with* opinion-doxa, *which they relegate to the sophists and rhetors. But we have learned that the opposition was not so clear-cut. How could philosophers possess knowledge, philosophers who cannot and do not want to restore the knowledge of the sages and who are only friends?* (147)

*

The trail of knowledge, of old philosophy as a knowledge, leads into something still older, into the realm of the sage. Or, as Deleuze/Guattari call him, *the old oriental sage* (3). How, in which sense, could someone be older than old? Would he be old in a different way, in a different sense of "old?" If it was so, it would be well worth pursuing this lead, for I might have to revise what I thought I had found regarding the question *what is philosophy?* and regarding old age.

*

Such an endeavor is, however, made quite difficult through the fact that Deleuze/Guattari paint the old oriental sage in a way which suggests that its main purpose is to highlight the old philosopher, while leaving the sage in some semi-obscurity: *other civilizations had sages, but the Greeks introduce these "friends" who are not just more modest sages. The Greeks might seem to have confirmed the death of the sage and to have replaced him with philosophers—the friends of wisdom, those who seek wisdom but do not formally possess it. But the difference between the sage and the philosopher would not be merely one of degree, as on a scale: the old oriental sage thinks, perhaps, in Figures, whereas the philosopher invents and thinks the Concept. Wisdom has changed a great deal* (3).

*

Yes, maybe, a great deal. But what has changed little is the gesture, traced by Deleuze/Guattari, of this thinking: Role-distribution. Each person, each *personnage conceptuel,* is described in opposition against another. One never gets to know the sage, only the sage in distinction from, or against, the friend. Neither will one meet the philosopher alone, only the philosopher in contrast to the sage. If I were introduced to you, and you would say, 'I am a friend,' would I understand? Would I understand by looking at you, or would I have to look towards someone else? Whose rules are these? Let me know a philosopher. An old one, if you like. Or let me know a sage. Oriental, and still older, if you like.

*

Of course, the old oriental sage also thinks, Deleuze/Guattari say, only differently. And he knows, not more than the philosopher, not less, only differently. For whom is this difference so important? It seems, for the one who thinks, conceptually.

*

The philosopher is the concept's friend; he is potentiality [il est en puissance] of the concept (5). Is the older oriental sage also *en puissance*, only differently? Is there something else in his *potentiality* and potency? Deleuze/Guattari do not really say. For it is somehow much more important to understand the friends (*philo*) of the concept. Fair enough, you might say, isn't the question a question of (Greek) philosophy or of one of of its modern versions, and not (really) of old oriental wisdom? Fair enough. But I would like to know just how old this old oriental sage is.

*

For Deleuze/Guattari, "oriental" means pre-Greek, much like "pre-Socratic," or "prephilosophical." It means: one does not necessarily have to regard the sage as dead and replaced with the philosopher. The philosopher, this old person, started something new; that is important. It is not so important to ask, if the "oriental" ceased, disappeared, with the emergence of the Greek, or if it lived on, maybe, to very old age. And it is not so important to ask: In which sense is the old oriental sage old? At least, Deleuze/Guattari do not seem to think of it.

*

But I would like to know. Will you, in your old age, allow me to leave conceptual thought aside, for a moment? Let us suppose it was still possible to meet an old oriental sage, wouldn't you in your old age like to meet him? Or not anymore? Wouldn't you want to ask him about old age? Or have you heard enough?

*

I will let you read these words from someone who wouldn't mind being called 'old oriental sage,' although, I fear, he is not what Deleuze/Guattari had in mind.
And then, I will write some little lines.
And then, I will leave you—and this dedication.

*

Jalalu'ddin Rumi said:

> A little bird was hunting a worm: a cat found its opportunity and seized it.
> It (the bird) was a devourer and a thing devoured, and (being engrossed in its hunting) was ignorant of another hunter . . .
> If the herbage is drinking pure water, (yet) afterwards an

animal's belly will feed on it.
That grass is devouring and devoured: even so (is) everything that exists . . .
Every phantasy is devouring another phantasy: (One)
thought feeds on another thought
Thou canst not be delivered from any phantasy or fall
asleep so as to escape from it.[8]

*

I read: The devourer devoured. The fate of both "nature" and "thought."
Or, the fate of "everything that exists." The fate of fire. Of the plane of
immanence. Devourer devoured. In an ancient Greek version:

> However, it is to be noticed that there are two ways in
> which fire ceases to exist; it may go out either by exhaus-
> tion or by extinction. That which is self-caused we call
> exhaustion, that due to its opposites extinction. [The former
> is due to old age, the latter to violence.] But either of these
> ways in which fire ceases to be may be brought about by the
> same cause, for, when there is a deficiency of nutriment and
> the warmth can obtain no maintenance, the fire fails.[9]

If there is no escape, for everything that exists, neither from anything
that exists, nor to anything that exists, neither to life, nor to death, not
even to sleep, is there anywhere to go to? Who would be there to ask
you, where are you? At midnight, or earlier, or at any time?

*

Rumi said:

> The Elder (which is) thy intellect, has become childish
> from being a neighbour to your selfish soul (nafs) which
> is in the veil.[10]

*

I read: Yes, the "intellect" (thought, *nous*) is *old*. He will not become
young through any means. But he will take from those in whose company he is. Old people become childish in the company of children. Old
people become old in the company of the old. In whose company is the
philosopher at midnight? Either in that of the first ones or in that of the
second ones. If he is in the company of the devourer-devoured, at midnight, that is, in his own company, by himself, he has but one second.
Let him think of that moment what he will, even that it be the moment

where his thinking arrives at itself, the moment of *what is philosophy?* It is a moment of childishness, but the child is "in the veil," and so he takes it to be old.

*

Rumi said:

> Who is a "Shaykh?" An old man (*pir*), that is (to say), white-haired. Do you apprehend the meaning of this '(white) hair,' O hopeless one.
> Black hair is self-existence: (he is not "old") till not a single hair of his selfishness remains.
> When his self-existence has ceased, he is "old" (pir).[11]

*

I read: "Old" means many things and, maybe, one. Besides old nature and old thought there is old company. Who is by himself, that is, in his or her own company, whatever their age, they are children. Therefore, it is possible to *refuse* one's age, even by stressing it. The young *can* refuse being young, through stressing it or hiding it. The old *can* refuse to be old, hiding it or stressing it.

*

A philosopher can, for a moment of immense fatigue, be too tired to clown.
But in whose company will he be?

* * *

PS (From D. S. to S. S.):

Alas, here I am, at the approach of the midnight hour, both serious and sober (at least most of the time), slowing down, to be sure, from infinite speed, so that the concepts sometimes escape me and I find myself measuring simple association for the most part, swinging trapeze-like from one extensive component to the other, sensations decidedly woolly, a bit weary to be sure, and finding it increasingly difficult to contract the escaping elements and vibrations. I fear I must fall back on ready-made opinions, since I sure as hell don't want to fall into mental chaos outside the plane of composition. Like Virginia Woolf, I like to keep my feet on the strip of pavement over the abyss. Since you say I have an opinion, I think I'll refuse to be old, hiding it as long as possible and then stressing it. In any case, you'll get no little lines from me. And come to think of it, why wait for midnight to ask the question? The clock is ticking, here I go. What is Philosophy? From beyond (or beneath) all chaos, I plump for Deleuze, I reply: Philosophy is being, being is resistance, resistance is philosophy. Philosophy is philosophy. As ever, a rose is a rose.

Hopeless one that I am, I've still got a full head of hair, and I really don't mind living on opinions till I get down to a single hair of selfishness. My self-existence still hasn't ceased, but I am old whatever the oriental sage might think. Yes, I'd like to meet him, but only after midnight, when no one knows where I am.

Notes

[1] My essay begins with simple/complex questions: Philosophy sees it necessary to comprehend time. Is time only an object of philosophical thought, or is thought itself a matter of time? And is there a particular time for philosophy? These questions are triggered by a reading of Gilles Deleuze/Félix Guattari's *What is Philosophy?* The essay will, therefore, elaborate the questions as far as possible, unto the stage of Deleuze/Guattari's "philosophical theatre." For Deleuze/Guattari, philosophy is, firstly, not timeless. They describe her as "old," and they give her an even older precursor, the "old oriental sage." Thought itself has, for Deleuze/Guattari, an extremely temporal character. And thirdly, the attempt of philosophy to understand herself, or, the attempt of a philosopher to understand philosophy, has for Deleuze/Guattari also a time: old age. This attempt, indicated in the title of Deleuze/Guattari's book (*What Is Philosophy?*), is, of course, not without echoes. It echoes (or is echoed by) other philosophers, other books, other titles (e.g. Heidegger's *What is Philosophy?*). Neither is the ascription of philosophy to old age without parallels: Hegel's *Owl of Minerva* begins her flight "when a figure of life has grown old." It is, therefore, inevitable, to quickly glance sideways. This essay, however, concentrates in a second move on the "passion of thinking" as it is described in an essay Hannah Arendt wrote at the occa-

sion of a birthday of her teacher M. Heidegger ("Martin Heidegger at Eighty"). It is noteworthy that this contribution is a gift to a philosopher in his old age. It is surprising to learn to which extent this timely occasion leads her to celebrate the timeless quality of a "passion of thinking." If the pendulum can swing so easily from one side to the other, then it is advisable to ask more closely: is what is described in these philosophical texts (and in others) as "old age" a marker for philosophical thought, an extraneous signpost by which philosophy can recognize herself, or is "old age" always already defined philosophically? Are there, in other words, other concepts of "old age"? My essay suggests, in fact, that there are other ways of conceiving "old age." And it does this by referring, in the end, to "old oriental sages" that are not compatible with those hinted at in Deleuze/Guattari's thought (e.g. Rumi). For Arendt, Hegel, and Heidegger, see: H. Arendt, "Martin Heidegger at Eighty," *The New York Review of Books* 17.6 (October 21, 1971), available at <www.nybooks.com/articles/10408>; G. W. F. Hegel, "Vorrede," *Grundlinien der Philosophie des Rechts* (Frankfurt a.M.: Suhrkamp Verlag, 1970), Bd. 7, 28; M. Heidegger, *What is Philosophy?* (English and German), trans. W. Kluback and J. T. Wilde (New York: Twayne Publishers, 1958).

2   Gilles Deleuze and Félix Guattari, *What is Philosophy?*, trans. Hugh Tomlinson and Graham Burchell (New York: Columbia UP, 1994). All references to this text in the article will simply refer to this edition and indicate page numbers in parentheses. This essay calls frequently on Deleuze/Guattari's book and enters in dialogue with it. My citations from their book will be in italics followed by page numbers. Accordingly, what is originally italicized in the book will be in regular font (as customary in print). Occasionally, citations from the English translation are in this essay accompanied by phrases from the original French, to add to the precision that might have been lost in translation. Words between square brackets in the citations of Deleuze/Guattari are my own additions to clarify references. Gilles Deleuze et Félix Guattari, *Qu'est-ce que la philosophie?* (Paris: Editions de Minuit, 1991).

3   Plato. *The Republic of Plato*, trans. A. Bloom (New York: Basic Books, 1991), Book I, 328e.

4   Deleuze/Guattari are not very precise on what is torn open: once it's the umbrella, then it is the firmament which, according to his own declaration is painted on the umbrella. This seems to indicate a desire to circumvent a problem regarding those who "figure on the firmament."

5   Deleuze has found this activity in such varied areas as contemporary music

and the "rhythm that animates the State Apparatus." In the context of the latter, he speaks of the mystery "of the Binder-Gods or magic emperors. One-Eyed men emitting from their single eye signs that capture, tie knots at a distance." It would be interesting to know, if there is a way leading from those god-men to conceptual thought. There are, indeed, signs. After all, Deleuze's god-men occur in a chapter about the "State Apparatus" and philosophy has a story or two to tell about philosophers and statesmen. See Gilles Deleuze, *A Thousand Plateaus*, trans. Brian Massumi (Minneapolis: University of Minnesota Press, 1987), 424.

[6] L'Abécédaire de Gilles Deleuze, avec Claire Parnet; Gilles Deleuze's *ABC Primer, with Claire Parnet*, trans. Charles J. Stivale, II, 21. <www.langlab.wayne.edu/CStivale/D-G/ABC2.html>, September 25, 2003.

[7] Gilles Deleuze, *Nietzsche and Philosophy* (New York: Columbia UP, 1983), 101.

[8] Jalalu'ddin Rumi, *The Mathnawi*, ed. and trans. R. A. Nicholson (Cambridge: E.J.W. Gibb Memorial Trust, 1982), Book V, 45.

[9] Aristotle, *On Youth, Old Age, On Life and Death, On Breathing*, trans. G. R. T. Ross, Part. 5, The Internet Classics Archive, <http://classics.mit.edu/Aristotle/youth_old.html>, June 14, 2004.

[10] Rumi, Book V, 46.

[11] Rumi, Book III, 100.

Literary Excavations in Mahmud Darwish's Poetry:
A Reading Project of "The Hoopoe"

Mohamed Agina

This article constitutes an exploration of Mahmud Darwish's poem, "The Hoopoe," as part of a study on the relationship of myths to culture, in general, and to literature and poetry, in particular. It starts from the hoopoe as a mythical symbol pulling the text in two directions. First, a direction that relates the poem, through time, to the realms of the universe, dream, and poetry, using the language of insinuations and allusions; second, a fictional direction that makes of the the poem—through evocation of previous quest journeys, including texts by Al-Jahiz, Avicenna, Al-Suhrawardi, Al-Hallaj, Aristophanes, and Farid Al-Din Attar—a quest into the depths of the individual and the collective self. Memory, history, and language, culminate in the discovery of the mother-land. Thus, Darwish's poem may be classified as poetry, prose, drama, and epic. It is, in fact, a mixture of all these genres, as well as a literary myth narrating the story of the search for a sacred time—the time of beginnings, and of childhood.

Fate and Destiny:
An Exploration of the Interconnection
between the Old and the New

Mohammed Birairi

This article aims at uncovering certain subtexts included in modern poems dealing, in different contexts, with destiny. On another level, it also touches upon the continuing nature of destiny as tackled by poets over the ages—since Pre-Islamic time till the present. The article reaches the conclusion that modern poetry has interacted with the theme of destiny in two different ways. In the Romantic era, the author argues that the meditative, existentialist aspect prevails. On the other hand, modernist poets have brought down the theme of destiny from the level of the metaphysical to that of investigation into the dominant social and religious practices, thus constituting a rebellious critical attitude. Pre-Islamic poets have concurred with the Romantics on acknowledging the metaphysical inevitability of destiny, while taking the path of modernist poets when they manifested a strong sense of resistance and refusal to give in to destiny. It is as though the Pre-Islamic poet believes in two inevitabilities: the inevitability of destiny; and that of resistance.

History and Poetry

Walid Bitar

History is about research and analysis, it clarifies and classifies, whereas poetry describes the mess that historians try to clear up. In illustrating the difference between history and poetry, the author excavates the 'historical influence' in his own poetry: The lessons and insights acquired from such diverse sources as Fernando Pessoa's "Autopsychography," Rilke's "The Panther," Giorgio de Chirico's metaphysical paintings, Wallace Stevens's "A Clear Day and No Memories," and Swift's "A Satirical Elegy." He surmises that an ahistorical attitude may capture an artist's position in time more effectively than a conscious attempt to be historical. The author discusses the genesis of his new collection, *Bastardi Puri*, in Beirut, concluding that the city itself, like his poetry, exhibits the protean and elusive nature of history.

The Uses of Interpretation in *Hamlet*

Leslie Croxford

Hamlet is the most problematic play ever written. Inconsistencies arise from the variousness of its medieval and Renaissance sources; from discrepancies between printed versions of Shakespeare's drama; and from a host of unresolved thematic and psychological problems, such as the famous question of why the Prince delays his revenge. Hence the endless interpreting of the play. Yet interpretation is not simply a matter for scholars and critics. The Prince and virtually every other main character indulges in it. Shakespeare, in giving interpretation this significance, had to develop previous versions of the story. So when one considers the issue of interpretation in the play one is also examining a prime example of how texts undergo alteration from period to period. Specifically, there are two influences on the metamorphosis of *Hamlet*: the intellectual climate in which it was written and the nature of the sixteenth-century political world. Together, they put at Shakespeare's disposal transformations of his inherited versions that are highly revealing of his creative processes. Shakespeare gives important dramatic voice to a newly emergent form of Europe's early modern self.

Narrating and Tracing the Past:
A Reading of al-Ghitani's *Mutun al-ahram*

Ayman El-Desouky

In keeping with al-Ghitani's characteristic impulse toward autobiographical self-disclosure, early memory determines the orientation toward the Pyramids, always facing westward and straining for a clear vision, in his novel *Mutun al-ahram* (Pyramid Texts, 1994). This article seeks to explore the transhistorical and intertextual layering of word, vision, and personal destinies and ambitions, which constitute the creative principle at work in Ghitani's *Mutun* and its sequel *Sifr al-bunyan* (1998). Just as personal memory figures in his two novels, so too does Ancient Egypt reveal itself, not in all the familiar trappings of its victory over time, but as a living legacy. What al-Ghitani understands as 'living legacy,' however, is the encrustation of a historical moment that survives time, whether in written accounts, in age-honored cultural practices or in monumental architecture. Al-Ghitani's orientation is not exactly that of a reconstructive historian. Ancient Egypt becomes ultimately a trope for all that survives the forces of time and achieves monumentality. In *Mutun al-Ahram*, al-Ghitani follows in the footsteps of earlier figures, such as Abu Ja'far al-Idrisi and al-Maqrizi, and indeed all Arab scholars and historians until al-Tahtawi in the mid-nineteenth-century, by Arabizing and Islamizing the Pyramids, their history and their significance.

Recalling (Af)filiation in *Memory in the Flesh*

Ferial J. Ghazoul

The article presents the first novel of the Algerian writer Ahlam Mosteghanemi, *Dhakirat al-jasad*, 1993 (*Memory in the Flesh*, 1999, 2003), which became a best-seller. The critics' reception of the work, however, has been uneven, ranging from admiration to dismissal and even attack. The article questions the validity of the critics' accusations and analyzes the strata of the novel: (1) the story of unrequited love, (2) the story of a disappointing homeland, and (3) the self-reflexive story about writing a novel. Traces of the past float on the surface of the text and partake in the subtext in the form of *filiation*—the father figure of the woman protagonist—and *affiliation*—in the literary father figure of the author, Malek Haddad, the francophone Algerian writer, as well as the fathers of the Algerian war of independence.

Classical Arabic Music:
Its Position in Contemporary Arab Society

Scheherazade Qassim Hassan

The article delineates the major elements in the urban musical art heritage of the Arab world; then it goes on to explore the notion of artistic modernity in music and how it retains musical traditions on one hand, and on the other how it introduces the new and integrates it. The article delves into the institutional response to music in the twentieth century with emphasis on the old/new combination on the level of both conceptualization and practice. The institutions of the Establishment view heritage and modernity in binary terms, thus in their inclination to be part of the contemporary scene, they dismiss traditional music and fail to nurture its legacy.

The Music of Fingers: The Archeology of Poetic Memory

Hasab al-Shaykh Jaafar

In this autobiographical and contemplative essay, the Iraqi poet Jaafar recalls his studies in Moscow in the 1960s and his return to

Baghdad. He depicts his encounter with poets in person or through their texts—including al-Jawahiri, Tawfiq al-Hakim, Pushkin, and Alexander Blok—as well as ordinary people who made an impact on him. The poetic for him is not a matter of versification and he finds in certain passages of Chekhov, Kafka, and Tekerli sheer poetry though their writing is in prose.

Musical Recall:
Postmemory and the Punjabi Diaspora

Ananya Jahanara Kabir

The Partition of the Indian subcontinent in 1947 has profoundly altered the geopolitics and demography of South Asia, generating also large-scale diasporic movements to Britain from the regions most deeply affected thereby, such as the Punjab. Deploying paradigms from Holocaust studies, the author connects diaspora with trauma to analyze the memory-work inscribed within contemporary music produced and enjoyed by British Punjabis in Britain. Arguing that such music expresses a 'neo-ethnic' Punjabi 'postmemory' that recalls pre-Partition Punjab, the author suggests that such 'musical recall' has a redemptive and commemorative potential inherent in its ability to bypass narratives of violence and nationalism, and articulate instead post- and transnational modes of identity formation and cultural belonging.

Valentinus et Nomina:
Saussure, Plato, and Signification

Rondo Keele

The mythology of Valentinus, the Christian Gnostic, is replete with the fascinating suggestion that names have salvific power. In *The Gospel of Truth*, he says that God uses names to call beings into existence, and that "the name of the Father is the Son." This notion of *nomina sacra* has proven challenging to understand. The author of the article argues this is partly due to our post-Saussurean framework; we find it difficult to make such claims consistent with Saussure's principle of the arbitrariness of signs. Valentinus, in complete contradiction to this principle, presupposes an essential connection between names and

beings. Insofar as it relies on such essentialism, it is profoundly difficult to give a straightforward, consistent post-Saussurean interpretation of the mysticism of the name in Valentinus' *salus per nomina*.
Nevertheless many commentators have attempted such interpretations,
avoiding the tension by trying to make it a part of their reading. Such
attempts often end up obscure and desperate, clarifying little. The
author of the article critiques part of this interpretive tradition and tries
to overcome the larger difficulties by offering a reconstruction of *salus
per nomina* based on Platonic nomenclaturism, thus developing a
viable alternative interpretation in an essentialist vein.

The Mutual Gravitation of the Old and the New
in the Poetry and Poetic Theory of Nazik al-Mala'ika

Sami Mahdi

The article tackles the attitude of the Iraqi poet Nazik al-
Mala'ika (1923-) toward modernization in her poetry and poetic theory. It also explores the imprint of the old and its relationship to the
new in her poetic and critical writings. This study focuses on how foreign poetry has influenced Nazik al-Mala'ika in the renewal of her
style and prosody, highlighting her relationship to the poems of Edgar
Allan Poe and his theories on poetic structure. Poetic repetition is
exploited here as a starting point in order to uncover this connection
between the two poets, the Iraqi and the American, and to trace how
al-Mala'ika has come to revise her early revolutionism, hence her
wavering between the old and the new. The article concludes with a
reference to the ideological, individual, and social reasons that have
led al-Mala'ika to suspend her pioneering poetic experience.

Writing Out of Place:
Djebar's *L'amour, la fantasia* and Soueif's *The Map of Love*

Samia Mehrez

As narrative modes of representation, the historiographical and
literary texts can never be neutral: each, in its own way, is bound to
and by an authority against which, or on behalf of which, it militates
thereby foregrounding the relationship between ideology and narrative, power, and knowledge. It may be said that both historians and

creative writers seek to question and unsettle the dominant narratives of power that seek to moralize and narrativize reality from the dominant point of view. This article investigates the role of hybrid writers from the Arab region who, by virtue of their position 'out of place' and 'in-between,' are implicated in the production of a counter narrative that challenges both the dominant discourses of their 'indigenous cultures' as well as those of their 'host cultures.' Through a comparative reading of Assia Djebar's *L'amour, la fantasia* and Ahdaf Soueif's *The Map of Love*, written in French and English respectively, the author of the article maps out some of the new cross-cultural spaces that both authors explore in their narratives.

The Secret Thread between the Old and the New in Art: Interview with Rafa Al-Nasiry

May Muzaffar

Rafa Al-Nasiry is a contemporary Iraqi artist, well-known for his painting and graphic art. He studied painting in Baghdad, graphic art in Beijing, and engraving in Lisbon. Fascinated by the possibilities of the Arabic alphabet and Chinese brush painting, he developed a fairly abstract style with symbolic overtones. His work whether in woodcuts, etching, or in acrylic is inspired by Mesopotamian motifs and Islamic aesthetics, rendered with modern dynamism. Interviewed by May Muzaffar, Iraqi art critic and poet, al-Nasiry discusses different stages of his artistic trajectory and the subtle ways in which traces of the old figure in his art. Illustrations ranging from 1962-2002 in the interview provide a glimpse of the development of his work. He combines innovative artistic techniques with his own philosophy of design as central in plastic art.

Egypt in Greco-Roman History and Fiction

Stephen Nimis

This article sketches Greek and Roman views towards the ancient Egyptians as a prelude to examining the metaphorical resonance of Egypt in the fiction of the imperial period of ancient literature. Both the Greeks and the Romans wrote about Egypt as a way of dealing with certain anxieties and issues in their own cultures. Egypt is portrayed as the terrifying "other" of Greco-Roman culture and at the same time celebrated as an ancient site of mystery and rebirth. In the ancient novels, this ambivalence is exploited in order to make statements about contemporary relationships and realities.

Travelers from an Antique Land:
Shelley's Inspiration for "Ozymandias"

John Rodenbeck

An enduring myth about artists of all kinds is that work arises from personal physical experience. A case in point is Shelley's great political sonnet "Ozymandias," which is conventionally presumed to have been "inspired" by an ancient Egyptian sculpture. Shelley never traveled to Egypt and thus certainly never saw the landscape he describes in his sonnet. Contrary to popular belief, moreover, he likewise never saw the sculptured head allegedly described in the sonnet, which did not arrive in England until a day or two after he and his family had moved permanently to Italy and more than six months after he had published the poem. All the sources and influences visible in the poem were entirely literary and all were part of the common currency of the era. Apart from Diodorus Siculus and the political sonnets of Milton and Wordsworth, they include several classics of travel literature in English and French, most notably the work of Volney.

Memory, Inequality, and Power:
Palestine and the Universality of Human Rights

Edward W. Said

Stressing the role of collective memory in the survival of Palestinian people in the diaspora, Said argues for acknowledging the rights of the Palestinians as a people, since human rights are universal. No earthly or divine dispensation could excuse oppressing a people by pleading past victimhood. Against the reductive notion of clash of civilizations, Said espouses knowing the Other and recognizing the historical rights of Palestinians in their own country. Knowledge becomes in this quest, a tool of understanding and recognition. Said advocates replacing antagonism with reconciliation following the model of post-apartheid South Africa. For him, the Palestinian-Israeli conflict cannot be resolved by military means, but by democratic admission of equality and by inclusiveness rather than exclusiveness. The Palestinian past cannot be erased and should not be dismissed if a genuine peace is sought.

The Novel and Questioning History

Nagwa Shaaban

In this testimony, the author expresses how the budding of her awareness has been linked to the sea and her grandmother's memories of it, reminiscing about old stone buildings in her hometown, Damietta. This created in the author a sense of longing for something unknown, the untangling of which required an attachment to writing, history, and practicing journalism. Thus, she has not written the self, rather she has written on Egypt/history. In her novel *Al-Ghurr* (1998), she goes back to the last quarter of the nineteenth century when a Nubian slave is kidnapped, escapes to Egypt, and settles down in Damietta. Sixteenth-century Damietta was itself a model of the multi-national/religious Ottoman society whose creative interaction and shared concerns are highlighted in her novel *Nawwat al-karm* (2002; 2003). The Mediterranean sea enjoys a metaphysical presence and a central role in the novel, where there is piracy, and reciprocal culture and trade. The novel questions the notion that "history has the final word."

A Wistful Lament for an Irrecoverable Loss

Doris Shoukri

Reminiscing over the past while surrounded by ancient Egyptian temples in Luxor, the author of this testimonial essay reflects on the significance of the past in personal and collective consciousness. Drawing on her own experience, she views all search as inevitably linked to yearning for the irrecoverable first impression, *la scène primitive*. Her own specialization in medieval Latin literature did not conflict with her passion for modern literature. Modern texts captivate as they echo motifs from medieval, classical, and renaissance literatures. To truly appreciate the modern, one needs to recognize the richness of the past in it.

The Idea of University and My Experience with Higher Education

Doris Shoukri
(Translated by Lamis Al Nakkash)

In this valedictory speech delivered at a graduation ceremony, Shoukri—who served for more than four decades as a professor at AUC—spells out her view of the role of the university, valuing its function as a place where the minds can explore and redefine rather than a utilitarian institution attending to the immediate material needs of the society. As a faculty member of an American institution of higher learning in Egypt, Shoukri insists on the vital importance of differences of views and cultures in enlivening the debate of free minds. She focuses on literature as a means of enriching the mind and allowing young scholars to learn from the masters without limiting themselves to past visions.

From Past to Present and Future:
The Regenerative Spirit of the *Abiku*

Mounira Soliman

This article investigates the representation of the famous West African *abiku* phenomenon in three works by three Nigerian writers, namely, J. P. Clark-Bekederemo's poem "Abiku" (1965), Wole Soyinka's poem also entitled "Abiku" (1967) and Ben Okri's novel *The Famished Road* (1991). The article offers a socio-political reading of the *abiku* (the myth of a child who dies to be reborn) as handled by the three writers and based on a traditional West African world view. The article investigates how the *abiku* motif has attracted many writers who are engaged in various agendas of cultural nationalism and identity formation, and how a close reading of their work points to their aesthetic and ideological concerns.

"Nothing But Little Lines"

Steffen Stelzer

This philosophical essay—written in a non-conventional and playful way, in the form of a dialogue with a friend and with other philosophers ranging from Socrates to Gilles Deleuze—asks the elemental question of what philosophy is and why such a question is raised in old age. In the tradition of Hegel, Heidegger, and Arendt, the author explores the significance of 'old age,' while intertwining his prose with that of a book written by Deleuze and Guattari, *What is Philosophy?* (1991). The passing reference to the "oriental sage" in the book is highlighted and analyzed. Oriental thought, as expressed in Rumi's notion of the old mentor or gray-haired shaykh, is interpreted by the author as well as juxtaposed to other European notions of philosophy and old age.

Notes on Contributors
(Alphabetically by Last Name)

Mohamed Agina obtained his MA and PhD in Arabic Language and Literature. His dissertation was on Pre-Islamic Arab Myths. He translated a number of books into Arabic—including Saussure's *Course in General Linguistics* (with others)—and published a number of articles on poetry. He teaches at the University of Tunis.

Muhammad Birairi is Associate Professor of classical and modern Arabic literature at Cairo University and at the American University in Cairo. He published a book on classical Arabic poetry titled *Poetic Stylistics and Traditions: A Study in the Poetry of Hudhalis*, and several studies in the field of classical Arabic literature (poetry and prose), in addition to studies in modern Arabic literature. He has translated essays and texts in critical theory and on classical Arabic literature (from English to Arabic).

Walid Bitar spent the last two years teaching English in Beirut at the Lebanese American University. His book of poetry, *2 Guys on Holy Land*, was published in 1993 by Wesleyan University Press. A new collection, *Bastardi Puri,* will be published next year in Canada.

Leslie Croxford is Professor of Humanities at Suffolk University, Boston, and directs its Madrid Campus. He received his PhD for sixteenth-century studies from Cambridge University, where he taught, as well as at Harvard, the American University in Cairo and elswhere in Britain, America and Japan. He writes fiction and drama. His novel *Solomon's Folly* is set in Alexandria, the city of his birth. His play *Confessions* was read at Theatre Emory, Atlanta, in 2003.

Ayman El-Desouky is Lecturer in Arabic at the School of Oriental and African Studies (SOAS), the University of London. He studied Comparative Literature at the American University in Cairo and the

University of Texas at Austin, and taught Arabic Language and Literature at Johns Hopkins and at Harvard. He is currently preparing a study on the conception and practice of sacred discourse in modern Arabic literature.

Ferial J. Ghazoul is Professor of English and Comparative Literature at the American University in Cairo and author of several books and articles on medieval literature and postcolonial criticism, including *Nocturnal Poetics: The Arabian Nights in Comparative Context*. She is the editor of *Alif* and the co-editor of *The View from Within*. She has translated several texts from and into Arabic, English, and French, including writings by Althusser, Riffaterre, Ricoeur, Said, and Matar.

Scheherazade Qassim Hassan is an Iraqi ethnomusicologist specialised in the Music of the Arab Middle East. She taught at the Universities of Baghdad, Paris VIII St. Denis, and Paris X-Nanterre. She conducted field work in Iraq, Syria, Qatar, Bahrain, and the Emirates. She is the author of *Les instruments de musique en Iraq et leur rôle dans la société traditionnelle* as well as a number of articles published in French, English, and Arabic.

Hasab al-Shaykh Jaafar is an Iraqi poet who studied in Moscow and received an MA in Literature from Gorky Institute. He has published eight collections of poetry, two narrative prose works, and translations of major Russian poets. He published regularly in a monthly cultural magazine, *Amman*. He has received recently the prestigious Poetry Award of the Owais Foundation.

Ananya Jahanara Kabir teaches English Literature at the University of Leeds, UK. She has been Research Fellow at Trinity College Cambridge, and The Centre of History and Economics, Cambridge, and visiting lecturer at the Department of English, University of California at Berkeley. Trained initially as a medievalist, she now researches the relationship between conflict, trauma, cultural belonging, and imaginative expression, especially in the context of postcolonial South Asia and its diasporas. Her specific areas of interest are regions and cultures that have been partitioned in South Asia: the Punjab, Bengal (where she comes from), and Kashmir. Her current research is on literature and art arising from political conflict in Indian-administered Kashmir.

Rondo Keele is Assistant Professor of Philosophy at the American University in Cairo. His primary research interests include metaphysics, semantic theory, and logic in the late Middle Ages, especially William of Ockham. He also has interests in philosophy of religion, the history of mathematics, and modern logic. His research has appeared in *Traditio* and *Franciscan Studies*.

Sami Mahdi is an Iraqi poet who studied economics in Baghdad. He worked in the fields of journalism and culture. He was the editor of the Iraqi *Al-Thawra* newspaper. He has a number of collections of poetry including *Asfar Jadida, Awraq al-zawal, Barid al-qarrat, Hanjara Tariyya, Al-Khata' al-awwal*. He has published several critical studies including *Al-Thaqafa al-'arabiyya min al-shafahiyya ila al-kitaba* and *Al-Mawja al-sakhiba: Shi'r al-sittiniyyat fil-Iraq*.

Samia Mehrez is Associate Professor of Arabic Literature at the American University in Cairo. She is author of *Egyptian Writers between History and Fiction: Essays on Naguib Mahfouz, Sonallah Ibrahim and Gamal al-Ghitani* (1994). Her articles on Francophone and modern Arabic Literature have appeared in *The Bounds of Race* (1991), *Rethinking Translation* (1992), *Yale French Studies*, and *Alif*, among others.

May Muzaffar received her BA in English Literature from the University of Baghdad. She published four volumes of poetry, and four volumes of short stories. She has translated five books on art and literature from English, and published a large number of studies and articles on art and artists in Arabic and English. She worked as an art editor in *Iraq*, an official journal published in English by the Ministry of Education, 1980-1985; executive editor in *Thaqafat*, a bilingual journal of culture and arts (Bahrain University), 2000-2003; a researcher in The Royal Academy for Islamic Researches, Amman (Jordan), 1995-2000. A number of her poems and short stories were included in anthologies in English, French, and Italian. She now resides in Amman (Jordan).

Lamis Al Nakkash is Assistant Lecturer in the Department of English Language and Literature at Cairo University where she received her M.A. in comparative literature. Her thesis was on "Non-Fiction in the Novel: A Comparative Study of Herman Melville and Son'allah

Ibrahim." She has translated works from English into Arabic, including Beth Baron's *The Women's Awakening in Egypt: Culture, Society and the Press*.

Rafa Al-Nasiri studied painting and printmaking in Baghdad (Iraq), Beijing (China), and Lisbon (Portugal), respectively. He gave art courses at The Institute of Fine Arts (Baghdad), 1964-1989, and initiated a department for graphic arts. He had a private graphic studio in Baghdad, 1987-1991 and taught renowned painters and printmakers. He taught art in the University of Yarmouk (Jordan) and Bahrain University, respectively, 1991-2003. He held dozens of one-man shows in Baghdad and several capitals of the world, and was awarded several international prizes. He took part as a jury member in international biennales and triennales in Cairo, Paris, London, Berlin, and Fredrickstad. He published a book entitled *Contemporary Graphic Art: Horizons and Mirrors* (1996).

Stephen Nimis is Professor of Classics at Miami University of Ohio. He was Visiting Professor of English and Comparative Literature at the American University in Cairo, 2002-2003. His published research includes *Narrative Semiotics in the Epic Tradition* and several articles on the ancient novel.

Desmond O'Grady is an Irish poet who was educated at University College Dublin and Harvard. He taught in Rome, Paris, and Cairo. He has published fifteen collections of poetry and translated poems from different languages, including Welsh, Arabic, Italian, French, and Greek.

John Rodenbeck received his AB from Harvard College and his MA and PhD from the University of Virginia. He is Professor Emeritus of English and Comparative Literature at the American University in Cairo, where he taught for more than two decades, and he headed the American University in Cairo Press, 1974-1983. He has published over 100 books and articles on subjects ranging from nineteenth-century English literature to conservation of medieval architecture in Cairo. He currently lives in Languedoc.

Edward Said was educated in Jerusalem, Cairo, Princeton, and Harvard. He taught English and Comparative Literature at Columbia University and is the author of twenty books on literature, criticism, and Palestine, including his seminal book, *Orientalism*. He has received dozens of honorary degrees and awards.

Nagwa Shaaban is a cultural journalist at the Middle East Press. She has published three creative works: a collection of short stories entitled *Jada'il al-tih* (1995); a novel entitled *Al-ghurr* (1998) which was awarded the Shahrjah Girls Club prize; and another novel entitled *Nawat al-karm* (2002; 2003). She has written two studies on plastic arts in the United States. She has published articles on art criticism and the novel. She has translated a number of works in the fields of psychology, politics, anthropology, art, and history from English into Arabic.

Doris Shoukri is presently Professor Emerita and was Chair of the Department of English and Comparative Literature at the American University in Cairo. She is the editor and translator of *Liber Apologeticus de Omni Statu Humanae Naturae* by Thomas Chaundler, and has published articles on Virginia Woolf, Ionesco, Kundera, and Duras.

Mounira Soliman is Assistant Professor in the English Department at Cairo University. Her PhD dissertation was on "Magic Realism in Contemporary African and African American Fiction." She is presently working on a research project revolving around Jewish-American and Arab-American literature in the context of US culture.

Steffen Stelzer studied Philosophy and Comparative Literature at the Freie Universität Berlin and at the Ecole Normale Supérieure in Paris. He taught at the Johns Hopkins University in Baltimore and lectured at Harvard University and at SUNY, Buffalo. He is currently Professor of Philosophy at the American University in Cairo. He published a book on the temporal aspect of thought (*Der Zug der Zeit*), as well as numerous articles that deal with epistemological issues in philosophy and literature. More recently, his scholarly interests have turned towards epistemological aspects of Islamic Mysticism.

End of English Section

ألِف

مجلة
البلاغة المقارنة
العدد الرابع والعشرون، ٢٠٠٤

جفريات الأدب:
اقتفاء أثر القديم في الجديد

رئيسة التحرير:	فريال جبوري غزول
نائب رئيسة التحرير:	محمد بريري
منسق التحرير:	وليد الحمامصـي
معاونا التحرير:	عالية سليمان، سيد عبد الله
المساعدتان:	نجلاء الباز، رنا الحاروني

مستشارو التحرير (بالترتيب الأبجدي للاسم الأخير):

نصر حامد أبو زيد (جامعة لايدن)

ستيڤن ألتر (معهد ماساشوستس للتكنولوجيا)

جلال أمين (الجامعة الأمريكية بالقاهرة)

ريشار جاكمون (جامعة إكس آن پروفانس)

صبري حافظ (جامعة لندن)

سيزا قاسم دراز (الجامعة الأمريكية بالقاهرة وجامعة القاهرة)

دوريس شكري (الجامعة الأمريكية بالقاهرة)

جابر عصفور (جامعة القاهرة)

باربرا هارلو (جامعة تكساس)

ملك هاشم (جامعة القاهرة)

هدى وصفي (جامعة عين شمس)

ساهم في إخراج هذا العدد:

رندة أبو بكر، روجر ألن، جان بالسامو، عايدة بامية، حسن البنا، أشرف حلمي، عبد الحميد حواس، سمير خليل، داڤيد دورسي، عبد الحميد شيحة، تامر عبد الوهاب، أحمد عثمان، كمران علي، محمد عمران، مايكل فريشكوپيف، جون ڤيرلندن، داڤيد كونستان، محمود اللوزي، سعاد المانع، منى مصباح، خالد مطاوع، شريف الموسى، عبد الرشيد نآالله، نيكولاس هوپكنز.

الطباعة: دار إلياس العصرية بالقاهرة

سعر العدد: في جمهورية مصر العربية: عشرون جنيهاً

في البلاد الأخرى (بما فيه تكاليف البريد الجوي)

الأفراد: عشرون دولاراً أمريكياً؛ المؤسسات: أربعون دولاراً أمريكياً

الأعداد السابقة متوفرة بالسعر المذكور.

رقم الإيداع بدار الكتب: ١٩٢٠٤/.٢

الترقيم الدولي: ٥-٧٧٩-٤٢٤-٩٧٧

الرقم الدولي الموحد للدوريات: ١١١٠-٨٦٧٣

أعداد **ألف** السابقة ناقشت المحاور التالية:

المراسلة والاشتراك على العنوان التالي:

مجلة **ألف**، قسم الأدب الإنجليزي والمقارن، الجامعة الأمريكية بالقاهرة، ص. ب ٢٥١١، القاهرة، جمهورية مصر العربية.

ت: ٧٩٧٥١٠٧   فاكس: ٧٩٥٧٥٦٥ (القاهرة).

البريد الإلكتروني: alifecl@auccgypt.edu

المحتويات

القسم العربي

هذا العدد من «ألف» مهدى بكل محبة وتقدير إلى دوريس إنزيت-كلارك شكري، الأستاذة المتفرغة في قسم الأدب الإنجليزي والمقارن بالجامعة الأمريكية بالقاهرة، التي بثت لعقود عديدة شغفها بالأدب وبالعلوم الإنسانية في كل من طلابها وزملائها.

هي .. كأنها، في ساحةٍ، خيمةٌ من حرير
في الظهيرة، حيث نسيم الصيفِ المشمسِ
يجفِّف الندى، وكل حبالها تلين،
فتتمايل، في أربطتها المشدودة، في دِعَةٍ،
وعمودها الأرزي المقيم لصلبها،
الذي هو ذؤابتها المشرئبة إلى السماء،
والذي يدل على اعتداد الروح،
يبدو غير معوِّلٍ على أيٍّ من الحبال،
وفي صلابةٍ لا يَدينُ بها لأحدٍ، موصولٌ بلا قيدٍ
وبما لا يحصى من روابط الحب والفكر الحريريةِ
مع كل ما على الأرض أنَّى كانت وجهته،
وبمجرد أن يشد أحدهم وثاقه هوناً ما
في نزق هواء الصيف،
يغدو منتبهاً لأقل قيد.

– روبرت فروست، «الخيمة الحريرية» (ترجمة سيد عبد الله)

حفريات الأدب: اقتفاء أثر القديم في الجديد

يستلهم هذا العدد من **ألف** مقاربة دوريس إنزيت-كلارك شكري للتذوق الأدبي. فقد تشبعت بالدراسات الكلاسيكية وكرّست أطروحتها للدكتوراه للأدب الوسيط المكتوب باللاتينية، ومع هذا فقد درّست ولا تزال تدرّس أدب الحداثة وما بعد الحداثة. تقتفي في تعاملها مع النصوص أثر القديم والتراثي في الجديد والمعاصر من الشعر والرواية والدراما والنقد. وكمنقبة أركيولوجية، تقوم بالحفريات الأدبية كي تصل إلى باطن النص وتتواصل مع المخزون الثقافي الذي يتضمنه ويخفيه.

يشارك المساهمون في هذا العدد قناعة دوريس شكري بعدم الاكتفاء، عند تذوق الحديث، بالنظر ملياً إليه، بل بضرورة تأمل النصوص باعتبارها طروساً وقراءة ما تمّ تضمينه وتغطيته في عملية الإبداع. والكثير من المساهمين في هذا العدد زملاء أو طلاب سابقون لها، وبعضهم زملاء بالقوة – كما يقول المناطقة – حيث إنهم يشاركونها في نحوها الجمالي. وبما أن شكري تصر دائماً على البعد الإبداعي والبعد الفلسفي في الكتابة النقدية، فقد ضمّ هذا العدد شهادات شعراء وروائيين وفنانين بصوتهم الخاص بالإضافة إلى بحوث فلسفية وتحليلية.

يعالج هذا العدد من **ألف** الطبقات التكوينية المختلفة للنصوص، وما في الأدب من مواد قديمة (كالأساطير والنصوص الأدبية القديمة والشعائر والترانيم والحكايات والشذرات الفلسفية وغير ذلك) بوصف هذه الأشياء كلها نصوصاً تحتية يتضمنها الأدب. وعلى هذا فالمقالات تنقّب عن العمليات والمناهج التي تتم من خلالها تلك التضمينات، إما في عمل أدبي بعينه أو في مجموع أعمال أحد المؤلفين. كذلك يتضمن العدد مقالات نقدية حول انتقال الأغراض القديمة إلى الأعمال الأدبية الحداثية وما بعد الحداثية، وحول الطبيعة الاستمرارية لهذه الأغراض، وما يتم من تراسل بينها وبين تلك الأعمال، سواء في الحبكات أو الشخصيات أو الأساليب.

وَ**ألف** مجلة سنوية (تصدر في الربيع) وتنشر مقالات مكتوبة باللغة العربية والإنجليزية (والفرنسية أحياناً) وهي تتبع نظام التحكيم التخصصي المتعارف عليه في الدوريات الأكاديمية. وكل عدد يرحّب بمقالات نقدية أصيلة، نظرية أو تطبيقية أو مقارنة، تلقي ضوءاً على أدبيات وبلاغيات محور محدد. وستدور محاور الأعداد القادمة حول:

ألف ٢٥: إدوارد سعيد والتقويض النقدي للاستعمار.
ألف ٢٦: شهوة التجوال: أدب الرحلات.
ألف ٢٧: جماليات التلقي: الطفل مخاطباً.

تجربتي في الجامعة ورؤيتي لدورها التعليمي

دوريس شكري*
(ترجمة لميس النقاش)

الضيوف الكرام، أعضاء مجلس الأمناء، أعضاء هيئة التدريس، الطلاب المتقدمون لنيل الدرجة الجامعية، السيدات والسادة:

قبل ثلاثة أسابيع كنت جالسة وعائلتي نتناول الغداء في مطعم «البياتزا» راضية مطمئنة ناسية أن «دوام الحال من المحال»، فإذا بتليفوني المحمول الذي أقتنيته مؤخراً ولا يزال لرنينه وقع مزعج عليّ، يأتيني بصوت مدير الجامعة للشئون الأكاديمية سوليقان في طلب بسيط: أن ألقي كلمة في هذه الأمسية. ولعل هذا يبدو لكم وأنتم الجالسون في استرخاء في مواجهة هذه المنصة أمراً هيناً، ولكن فلتتأملوا عدالة القدر: فقد كان موقعي على مدى ستة وأربعين عاماً خلف المتحدثين، أرقب ساعتي وأخفي تثاؤبي أو أقرأ كتاباً نصف مصغية للحكمة التي يتلونها على الخريجين متحدثاً بعد آخر؛ كانت نواياهم جميعا طيبة، كنيتي اليوم. أما وقد بدأت أستعد لحمل خيمتي والرحيل في صمت إلى صحراء التقاعد خلسة إذ بي أجد نفسي مطالبة بالوقوف هنا ومن ورائي زملائي يقرأون ما يقرأون من كتب، وأنا أحاول بكل ما أوتيت قلباً وعقلاً أن أجلو معنى ما فعلتم هنا وأن أعبّر عن بعض الآمال لمستقبلكم - في حدود خمس عشرة دقيقة، مرت منها واحدة بالفعل! وحيث إنني خلال الأعوام الستة والأربعين التي قضيتها في الجامعة الأمريكية بالقاهرة فكرت كثيراً في أهداف هذه المؤسسة وغاياتها، فقد رأيت من الأصلح أن أستغل هذه الفرصة في الإفصاح عن تلك الأفكار عند تقاعدي. ولكن اسمحوا لي أولاً أن أشير إلى ما كانت عليه تلك الأفكار يوم جئت إلى هنا. في أحد الاجتماعات الأولى التي حضرتها في الجامعة الأمريكية بالقاهرة وكان يضم أعضاء هيئة التدريس - وكنا وقتذاك عدداً محدوداً - طُلب من كل أستاذ أن يعبّر عما يتمنى تحقيقه من خلال التدريس. بهرتني وقتها الأهداف الكبيرة المطروحة بقدر ما أثارت فزعي، وقد تنوعت بين تكوين طلاب أصحاء نفسياً إلى مواطنين مسؤولين، وزوجات وأمهات صالحات وأزواج ناجحين، إلخ.

---

* ألقت دوريس إنريت-كلارك شكري هذه المحاضرة في حفل تخرج طلاب الدراسات العليا في الجامعة الأمريكية بالقاهرة في ٢٠٠٢/٢/٥. وقد ألحق بالنسخة المطبوعة من المحاضرة هامش هذا نصه: «إنني أوظف بمواهبي المتواضعة ما التقطته من أعمال الشعراء الكبار الذين جاءوا قبلنا مع واجب الاعتراف لما أدين به إلى متحدثين سابقين مثل جيمي ريدفيلد وإدوارد سعيد، وبشكل خاص إلى أستاذتي إلينور جريس كلارك، طاب ثراهم».

وأنا، صغيرة السن، حديثة التخرج، شعرت بعجزي عن أن أكون ذلك العالم النفسي أو الأخصائي الاجتماعي أو المحلل السياسي، وإن كنت قد شعرت بالفخر وأنا أتصور نفسي كالأطلس آخذة على عاتقي حملاً ثقيلاً وأنا أقف أمام طلبتي لأدرس تشوسر Chaucer. وبحثت في أعماق نفسي، محاولة قبل كل شيء أن أكون أمينة وألا أقع أبداً في شرك الادعاء والتزييف، فلم أجد ما هو أكثر أهمية من القول إنني بتدريسي تشوسر آمل أن أزرع في طلبتي فهماً لأعمال تشوسر وحباً لها وأن أحاول ما استطعت أن أعيد الروح لرؤيته للحياة. وبسبب قولي هذا اتهمت بالنخبوية في كثير من الدوائر، ووقعت فريسة جدل دار سنوات حول الأهداف التي تسعى الجامعة الأمريكية بالقاهرة، بل وغيرها من الجامعات في العالم النامي، إلى تحقيقها. وبرز كثير من التساؤلات، كان أهمها بالنسبة لي هو ما إذا كان الأدب، وخاصة الأدب الغربي، مادة مناسبة للتدريس في بلد كمصر بما لها من احتياجات مادية. وبدا أنه مادة ستختفي من المقررات الدراسية حتى يتم حفر آخر خط مترو وتركيب آخر خط تليفون وحتى تنتهي توعية الشعب كله بوسائل تنظيم النسل! بدا وكأن الأدب من حق البلدان الغنية وحدها مثله مثله مثل اليخوت. بل إن أحد الأساتذة قال : لا ينقصنا إلا أن تطالب الدكتورة دوريس شكري بتدريس الموسيقى!

وينطوي القلق من تدريس الأدب ضمناً على قضيتين، أولاهما تتعلق بالمادة نفسها والأخرى تتمثل في الحساسيات الثقافية. ولنتحدث عن النقطة الأخيرة أولاً، فكثيراً ما أثيرت حاجة الجامعة الأمريكية إلى التقليل من التركيز على الدراسات الأمريكية والغربية، على أن يكون التركيز على كوننا في القاهرة. وجرى الحديث عن دورنا كجسر بين ثقافتين، ولكن الإحساس بالاختلاف والخوف منه خلق في بعضنا رغبة في إخفاء رؤوسنا في الرمال وإيثار السلامة بعيداً عن مناقشة أي مادة أو تدريسها بما قد يؤدي إلى صدام بين الثقافتين. ونما اعتقاد بأن أي تخاذل في الالتزام الصارم بذلك سيطلق عفريت الشقاق من قمقمه، كما لو كان الاختلاف في حد ذاته خطراً، وكأن الشرق والغرب يتنافسان، كلٌّ بما أحرز من تقدم وإنجازات، على احتكار الوصول لـ«الحقيقة» وأن أي تخل عن الحذر وأي اقتراب من لب أي مسألة وأي كشف عن أفكارنا الحقيقية سيكون مِّن شأنه بالضرورة أن يعلي كفة أحدهما على حساب الآخر. فكانت الأوامر: «نرجوكم الابتعاد عن الدين والسياسة»، فنحن مجتمع مهذب له أخلاقه. ولا شك أن ذلك صحيح، ولكن المسألة هي أننا في جامعة، والمؤكد أن الجامعة تحمل معنى يتجاوز كونها مجتمعاً مهذباً، فهي مكان تلتقي فيه العقول لتنشغل دوماً وبحرية في بحث الأفكار وفي الدفاع عن مواقف فكرية معينة ومعارضة غيرها، وفيها يتصدى المرء للقضايا الكبرى بالنقاش محاولاً سبر أغوارها، وفيها يفتح المرء عقله ويعبر عما بداخله. والمؤكد أيضاً أن الاختلافات العرقية ليست بالأمر المهم. فالقضية ليست ما إذا كان المرء يتحدث العربية أو الإنجليزية، يأكل الهامبورجر أو الملوخية ويستمع إلى البيتلز أو أم كلثوم: فليبق الشرق شرقاً والغرب غرباً و«ليحيا الاختلاف».

المطلب، إذن، ليس جسراً نبنيه بين الشرق والغرب، ولا حتى بين الشمال والجنوب، ولكن أساساً أن نحاول خلق مناخ يشعر فيه كل امرئ بضرورة تجاوز حدود رؤيته

الخاصة للعالم، ويسمح لـ «جدران عقله (والرحمة على فرجينيا وولف) بالتضاؤل» فلا تمنعه من استيعاب أي شيء، فيلتقي عقله بالآخرين ويتداخل مع عقولهم. لذلك، لم يكن المطلب الأول حقاً هو مدّ الجسور، بل حفر الأفاق ووصل كهوف بأخرى تعشش فيها المخاوف المستترة والملاذات السرية، ليدخل النور والهواء فتتفتح العقول والقلوب. إن آخر ما نحتاج إليه هو الاختباء في جيوب الغرب أو الشرق. وأول ما نحتاجه هو توضيح مفاهيمنا حول دور الجامعة ووظيفتها ومحاولة الاتفاق حول مبرر وجودها أصلاً. هناك من رأى من على الجامعة أن تسعى بكل ما أوتيت لتكون وثيقة الصلة بالمجتمع، هذا في ظل هالة التقديس التي أحاطت بالاتصال بالمجتمع وخدمته وقتها، وكان المقصود، بذلك، الصلة المباشرة بمجموعة محددة عرقياً من البشر وعلى مدى وقتي آني، وكذلك الجانب العملي والتطبيقي لخدمة المجتمع. وكان منا من عارض هذا، إذ رأى أن التعليم منذ قديم الأزل كان غير ذي فائدة من حيث الصلة بالمجتمع بمعناها الضيق هذا. وانطلقنا في دفاعنا: لقد رأى المعلم منذ زمن سقراط دور التعليم في الأخذ بيد الطالب وفي أن يكشف وأن يضيف فضاءً وبعداً لا أن يقوم بالتدريب والضبط. ويأتي دور المعلم الذي يوفر الأمان لطلبته ويشجعهم، انطلاقاً من أرضه الصلبة، على الوصول لأراض أرحب لم تزل غائبة عن الأعين. من هذا المنطلق، كانت وظيفة الجامعة دائماً أن تتولى تطوير الطالب ليكتشف الإمكانات الكامنة بداخله والتي كان يجهلها وترشده وهو يحاول تثبيت قدميه في عالم أوسع. ورأى البعض أن الإعداد للعالم الخارجي يكون بأن تتشبه الجامعة بذلك العالم، فيكون الطالب أثناء وجوده هنا منشغلاً بمهام عملية وكأنما أصبح يجلس بالفعل على مكتب ويتقاضى راتباً. ولكن فكرة الجامعة هي تحديداً كونها شيئاً آخر غير العالم الخارجي، فالجامعة مكان يمنح حق البحث والاكتشاف، مكان آمن يتحصن المرء به ليجرب ويتبنى مختلف الأفكار بحرية مطلقة. هي مكان يتكلم فيه المرء ويقرأ ثم يقرأ كل شيء. «وسيأتي وقت تلتقي فيه الوجوه» المقدر لها أن تلتقي. «سيأتي الوقت».

ذلك هو مفهوم الجامعة الذي سعينا للحفاظ عليه عبر السنوات، فقد كان علينا في سعينا لخدمة المجتمع أن نكون على وعي حتى لا نجد أحد مجالات المعرفة والإنجازات البشرية وقد أُسقطت اعتباطاً بسبب انتفاء خاصية الصلة مع المجتمع منها. إن المؤسسة التي تسعى لخدمة المجتمع عليها مواجهة إغراء دائم بالتخلي عن دور الريادة والتحرك في اتجاه رغبات المجتمع، فالاحتياجات مباشرة وعاجلة وواضحة للعيان والمشاكل ملحة يصعب معها تفادي سيكولوجية الأزمة والطوارئ وسياسة سد الخانة. ولا شك أن الحساسية التي نعانيها تجاه التطلعات الوطنية والمشروعات والأهداف المباشرة ستملي علينا تخريج طلاب قادرين بحق على خدمة قضية بلادهم وأهدافها. وهنا يكمن الخطر، ليس في فشلنا في تخريج مثل هؤلاء الطلاب، ولكن فيما يترتب على تلك الرغبة الملحة في توفير الدعم العملي من نتائج تسري عميقاً تحت السطح، إذ تنطوي على افتراض غير معلن بأن المجتمع أدرى بما يجب على الجامعة أن تقوم به. فنحن إذا ما مددنا خط هذه الفكرة على استقامته سنصل لتصور مؤداه أن الطالب زبون يأتي للجامعة كما يأتي لسوق يشتري منه بعض المعلومات والمهارات، ويسعى للتعليم كسعيه لسلعة، سلعة

جاهزة، وكأن مقاييس العلم والخبرة الحالية دائمة ولا مجال للطالب أو الجامعة لتطويرها وتنميتها، أو على الأقل كأن اتجاه ذلك التطور والتنمية مسألة مفروغ منها في مستقبل لا يمكن لأكثرنا ألمعية أن يتنبأ أو يحيط به. وكلما زادت احتياجات المجتمع المادية بدا منطقيا المطالبة بمثل تلك المؤسسة والرغبة في وجودها. وهنا كما قلت يصبح الإغراء شديداً بالنسبة للجامعة فيصبح خلق التوازن بين التجاهل التام لاحتياجات المجتمع والتخلي التام عن مفهوم الجامعة بوصفها مكاناً للتعلم أمراً يتطلب الكثير من الفكر والاجتهاد. ولقد كافحت الجامعة الأمريكية ولا تزال تكافح كل يوم للحفاظ على ذلك التوازن. وكلنا أمل في أن نكون وفقنا ولو بقدر في أن يعيش كل طالب منكم هنا تجربة تحرر يُعمل فيها عقله بصورة لا تجعله فقط قادراً على مواجهة حياته المهنية بل يتجاوز ذلك إلى القدرة على التعامل مع المشكلات التي سيواجهها في عالم يموج باستقطابات خطيرة، استقطابات لم تعد استقطابات الشرق والغرب بل واستقطابات العولمة، عالم يتحول بشكل متزايد إلى مكان «أفضل من فيه لا يملك إيماناً بشيء/والأسوأ تملؤه العواطف الجياشة». لقد سعينا، لا لتدريبكم على التوافق مع ذلك العالم، ولكن لتعليمكم كيفية خلق عالم أفضل فتنضموا بذلك إلى قوائم أصحاب العقول في مواجهة ملفقي التبريرات، لتكونوا المدافعين عن المُثل في مواجهة مروجي الدعاية، وأصحاب قناعات في مواجهة التطرف. وستدركون لحظة دخولكم ذلك العالم أن ملفقي التبريرات، أينما وجدوا في الغرب أو الشرق، من هوليوود إلى تل أبيب وحتى كهوف تورا بورا، كلهم مروجو دعاية لكونهم المؤمنين الحقيقيين، المسيطرين، الذين تملؤهم المرارة والمتبجحين باستقامتهم، لا يعرفون التسامح في دفاعهم عن التسامح ولا يعرفون العدل في دفاعهم عن العدل ويسارعون باسم الله أو الوطن أو باسم هذه القضية أو تلك إلى قتل آلاف العاملين ببرجي التجارة أو عشرات الأطفال في أوكلاهوما أو بقتل محمد الدرة في فلسطين أو أطباء عيادة تنظيم النسل في جنوب الولايات المتحدة. إنهم يعيشون في عالم من الشعارات يدور حول نفسه، عالم من المظاهر وخداع الذات، يعنيه فقط قول الشيء الصحيح وليس فعله. وللكلمة سلطة قائلها وهي قادرة، إذا ما أخذتها عنه، وتلاعبت بها بمهارة، على إخراجك من النار لتدخلك الجنة، ومن السجن إلى البيت الأبيض. والجامعة اليوم كلها أمل في أن تكون قد خلقت بكم ضرباً من البشر يستطيع أن يظهر بأفكاره وأفعاله أن «الفوضى لم تعم مجدداً» وأن الحق والعقل والوضوح والنظام أشياء لا تزال موجودة في العالم، مهما دارت الدائرة وشاء العتاة.

كانت هذه المقدمة طويلة لأصل إلى سؤالي الثاني: لماذا الأدب؟ فتحملوني بضع دقائق أخرى وسوف أحاول أن أطرح أن فكرتي. أعرف أن معظمكم سيحصل على شهادته اليوم في مجالات تحظى بمزيد من القبول في مصر - وهي المجالات العلمية والعلوم الاجتماعية - وكلها لا تحتاج إلى مسوغ. ولكن سيظل هناك من قد يسأل: لماذا الأدب؟ صحيح. فالأدب ليس هو الحياة. ولا يطعم الجائع ولا يحد من الانفجار السكاني. ولكنه مع ذلك يفضح ملفقي التبريرات والملتفين حول أنفسهم ويطرح رؤية للواقع لها فعل الدواء. الأدب مستقل بذاته لا يدين بالولاء للتنظيمات والأحزاب

وأجهزة الحكومة: فالفنان يستطيع الوصول إلى العقل الباطن، إلى حكمة البشر، وهو غير منشغل بالعلاقات الدولية ولكنه معني بالعالم في كليته. وكما يقول يونج: «إنه يرتفع بالفكرة التي يحاول التعبير عنها من مجال العارض والمؤقت إلى مجال الدوام» ويقول يونج عن الفنان إنه «ليس مجرد إنسان ولكنه الإنسان الجمعي». كما كان يؤمن أن الفن هو «جسر الإنسان للحكمة الجمعية». «فالفن يحول المصائر الشخصية إلى مصير الإنسانية». ويتيح لنا الفرصة للرجوع إلى منابع الحياة». فالفن حقا، كما رأت جماعة بلومزبري Bloomsbury Group «هو الوسيلة الوحيدة التي يستطيع من خلالها الإنسان أن يوصّل لغيره من البشر جوهر تجاربه وطبيعتها». فالفن سيظل دائماً وأبداً له أهميته.

لقد كنت أعتقد حين جئت إلى هنا، وما زلت على إيماني هذا وأنا على وشك الرحيل، أن على هذه الجامعة أن تتيح لطلابها أقصى ما توصل إليه الإنجاز البشري وكل ما يمد الإنسان بالقدرة على الحياة من أعمال فنية عظيمة وأفكار عظيمة لعقول عظيمة وبصيرة برؤيتها، في أي مجال كان، وكل ما يوفر جسراً يمتد ليصلنا بالحكمة الجمعية للإنسان، وبذا تستطيعون رؤية الحياة في أسمى صورها ويملؤكم الحماس لتقبلها واحتضانها، بكل ما فيها من تنوع جميل، مدركين كم كنتم محظوظين بلقائكم هؤلاء العمالقة والعيش بينهم والارتقاء على أكتافهم «لتروا أبعد من هؤلاء العمالقة أنفسهم» على حد قول القديس أنسلم.

وأخص الدراسات العليا هنا في ذلك الاعتماد على العملية التراكمية التي يستند فيها الباحث على إنجاز من سبقوه ويبني عليه: فأول مهام الباحث هي بالفعل دراسة الأعمال السابقة والاعتراف بها كنقطة انطلاق له. وهنا تكون الأمانة المطلقة من الأهمية بمكان وكذلك القدرة على التمييز. وأنا على ثقة من أن دراستكم العليا قد زرعت فيكم التعامل بعقل مفتوح قادر على استقبال آراء الآخرين وكذلك على رفضها. إن المضي قدماً في الاستكشاف الكامل الحر الذي لا يخشى من دحض ما يصل إليه من نتائج ولا من الوصول إلى غير ما يعتقده، ولا يخشى كذلك من أن يضطر إلى التحول عن رأيه في منتصف الطريق أثناء العمل، هو درس لابد وأنكم تعلمتموه. وتلك العادات من الدقة والأمانة والانفتاح على الأفكار هي ما تحملونه معكم وأنتم تنتقلون الآن إلى العالم الرحب. وربما لن تتاح لكم الفرصة خارج الجامعة، اللهم إلا إذا كان نصيبكم من الحظ وافراً، لمقابلة عمالقة الفكر الذين غذّت أعمالهم عقولكم في السنوات الماضية. ولكن بمقدار ما أخذتم عنهم القيم العليا والعقل والمرونة في التفكير وكذلك التواضع في تقويم النفس ستكونون قد قدمتم اعترافاً بفضل هؤلاء العمالقة الذين تقفون على أكتافهم بإسهامكم الخاص لتلحقوا بمسيرة الرجال والنساء الأمناء الذين «ينظرون للحياة بثبات ويرونها ككل» ويشكلون الأمل الوحيد للمستقبل.

تحية ووداعاً، سلاماً ومع السلامة. أحييكم وأتمنى لكم كل خير.

القضاء والقدر:
بحث في التراسل بين القديم والجديد

محمد بريري

مقدمة

تستجيب هذه الدراسة لما طرحته مجلة **ألف** في دعوتها للإسهام في هذا الإصدار من جهتين؛ فهي تسعى إلى إماطة اللثام عن بعض النصوص التحتية التي تضمنتها نصوص شعرية حديثة حين تطرّقت، في سياقات متباينة، لموضوعات بعينها، مثل موضوع القدر، ومن جهة ثانية تتلمس الطبيعة الاستمرارية لهذا الموضوع الذي تداوله الشعراء منذ الجاهلية مروراً بعصور الشعر العربي المتعاقبة.

كان لافتاً للنظر أن يستخدم مصطلح «أغراض» في الدعوة إلى الاستكتاب في موضوع «حفريات الأدب: التنقيب عن القديم في الجديد». فقد وردت العبارة الآتية في هذه الدعوة «ترحب المجلة بالمقالات النقدية حول انتقال الأغراض القديمة إلى الأعمال الأدبية الحداثية وما بعد الحداثية، وحول الطبيعة الاستمرارية لهذه الأغراض وما يتم من تراسل بينها وبين تلك الأعمال». في هذه العبارة تتم المجاورة بين مصطلح نقدي عربي عتيق هو «أغراض» من جهة، ومصطلحات الحداثة وما بعدها وحفريات الأدب، التي تشير إلى اللحظة النقدية الراهنة، من جهة ثانية. وكأن صياغة الدعوة توجهها رغبة في ألا ينفصل شكلها عن مضمونها، فلا يكون القديم، متمثلاً في مصطلح «أغراض»، منفصلاً عن المعاصر، متمثلاً في مصطلحات ما بعد الحداثة وحفريات الأدب. إن فكرة التراسل بين القديم والجديد تتضمّن معنى التفاعل بين الأطراف بحيث يعيد الحاضر تأويل الماضي والعكس بالعكس. ولعل أصحاب هذه الدعوة أرادوا لفت أنظارنا إلى أن المصطلح العربي القديم «أغراض الشعر» يمكن أن يفهم فهماً جديداً، فيصبح توارد الشعراء على غرض مثل «الغزل» نوعاً من التراسل المستمر، فيأخذ غزل بشار بن برد، في العصر العباسي، من غزل امرئ القيس في الجاهلية، ويعيد تأويله، أي يمنحه ما لم يكن فيه قبله.

غير أن الكشف عن عمليات الأخذ والعطاء هذه تتم عبر «القارئ»، فهي إذن عمليات تخضع للاجتهادات التي لا يحدها حد. ففضلاً عن اختلاف عمليات القراءة باختلاف العصور، يتباين قراءة الجيل الواحد في طرق التأويل، كل حسب الخلفية التي توجهه. وفي ظني أن هذا لا ينفي المعنى، كما يعتقد بعض المعترضين، بل يفتح باب «المعاني» على مصراعيه. إن الإصرار على أن ثمة معاني «محدودة» أو «صحيحة» أو «مشروعة» للنص الأدبي يشي برغبة في «الاستبداد» و«قهر» «المتلقين» والنصوص على

حدود يفرضها بعض «المتلقين» فلا يُسمح بتَخَطّيها.

غير أن ما أطرحه ليس دعوة إلى ما يمكن أن يُسمى «فوضى التأويل» لأن القارئ سيميّز، حسب خبرته لحظة القراءة، بين تأويل أسّسه صاحبه تأسيساً مقنعاً، وتأويل آخر يفتقر إلى مثل هذا التأسيس، فيصبح أقل اقناعاً. ولا يستبعد، مع ذلك، أن تتساوى بعض التأويلات، رغم تباينها، إذا تكافأت في قوة تأسيسها. هناك في الحالات كلها درجات متفاوتة من القدرة على الإقناع.

استئنافاً للحديث عن مصطلح أغراض الشعر، فإنه بالإضافة إلى ما سبق من أن تداول الشعراء لغرض ما يمكن عدّه تراسلاً، تخضع الأغراض هي الأخرى للقراءة، لأنها ليست محددة تحديداً قاطعاً، جامعاً مانعاً. لا تطابق أبواب الشعر كما قرأها أبو تمام في «حماسته» ما قرأه البحتري، وكلاهما يختلف كثيراً أو قليلاً مع تصورات ابن قتيبة أو ابن رشيق وغيرهما من «قراء» الشعر العربي القديم. كما أن الشعراء أنفسهم أضافوا إلى تلك الأغراض أو عدّلوها بناء على تفاعلاتهم الخاصة. فعل أبو نواس ذلك، مثلاً، حين أسس غرض الغزل بالمذكر بناءً على قراءته لما سبقه من شعر،[١] وحين جعل «الخمر» غرضًا شعرياً مستقلاً يستغرق قصائد كاملة، وحين أسس غيره موضوع الرّوضيات.

ويلاحظ في هذا السياق أن بعض نقاد الشعر العربي القديم من المعاصرين كشفوا النقاب عن أغراض جديدة. فعل ياروسلاف ستيتكيڤتش J. Stetkevych شيئاً من ذلك في دراسته الفذّة عن نجد وريح الصبا،[٢] مقارناً بينهما وما يناظرهما في التراث اليوناني. أغراض الشعر، على ذلك، باب من أبواب الاجتهاد، لم يغلقه أحد في الماضي، ومازال مفتوحاً لمن يريد أن يلجه في الحاضر.

فرضية البحث

تأسيساً على ما مضى فإن هذه الدراسة تفترض أن الشعر العربي الحديث مر بمرحلتين من حيث تناول الشعراء لموضوع القدر، مرحلة التأمل الوجودي ويغلب عليها طابع الاستسلام والعجز أمام هيمنة الأقدار بحيث لا يملك الفرد إلا أن ييأس ويشكو انعدام حيلته أمام حوادث الدهر، وأن يتشكك في إرادته وينفي حريته، وتكاد هذه المرحلة أن تستغرق المرحلة التي يسميها مؤرخو الأدب العربي الحديث المرحلة الرومانسية.

أما المرحلة الثانية فتستغرق ما يسمى فترة الحداثة، وفيها يُنزل بعض الشعراء مشكلة القدر من مستوى التأمل الميتافيزيقي إلى مستوى النظر في الممارسات الاجتماعية كما تتبدى في أنماط السلوك والقول، الفردي والجماعي، الأمر الذي أدى بهذا الجيل من الشعراء إلى اتخاذ موقف نقدي متمرد إزاء ما هو شائع في الخطابات الأدبية والشعبية والدينية من ترسيخ للاعتقاد في أن القدر قوة عليا لا يملك الناس حيالها إلا الإذعان.

وفي المرحلتين تحاول الدراسة تجلية أنماط مختلفة من التراسل بين الشعر

العربي الحديث في مرحلتيه اللتين أشرت إليهما، وما يناظرهما في التراث، وهو تراسل يصدر عن وعي من جانب الشعراء أحياناً، كما يصدر عن وعي من جانب القارئ، المشارك في صنع المعنى، أحياناً أخرى.

التراسل حول ميتافيزيقا القدر

قبل النظر في نصوص الشعر من منطلق التراسل، لابد من الإشارة إلى أن معظم مؤرخي الشعر العربي الحديث ونقاده فصّلوا فيما عدّوه تأثراً من جانب الشعراء العرب الرومانسيين بنظرائهم في التراث الغربي، بحيث يوقعون في وهم قارئ الشعر العربي أن إنجاز هؤلاء الشعراء لا يعدو أن يكون هامشاً على التراث الغربي أو محاكاة له أو سرقة منه.(٣) وحين قارن بعضهم بين هذا الشعر وتراثه العربي القديم وقع في بعض أحكام القيمة الجائرة.(٤)

أما الناقد الشهير والتر أونج Walter Ong فلاحظ شيئاً معاكساً حين قال «أفاد جبران خليل جبران في صنع شهرته من خلال تقديمه المأثورات الشفاهية القائمة على الصيغ مطبوعةً للأمريكان الكتابيين الذين كانوا يرون في تلك العبارات الشبيهة بالأمثال جدّة وغرابة، في حين أنها، طبقاً لما ذكره أحد أصدقائي اللبنانيين، شيء عادي في نظر أهل بيروت».(٥)

تنبع أهمية تعليق أونج هو بلا منازع أحد رواد الاتجاه الرومانسي، إن لم يكن رائدهم الحقيقي، وأوسعهم انتشاراً وتأثيراً، كما أن خلفيته الغربية عموماً والإنجليزية خصوصاً بلغت من العمق حد الإبداع الأدبي باللغة الإنجليزية جنباً إلى جنب مع إبداعاته العربية. ومع هذا كله فإنه لم يفلت من ثقافته العربية، التي طبعت كتاباته الإنجليزية بطابع خاص، كان سبباً في جاذبية إبداعاته للقارئ باللغة الإنجليزية.

إن أونج لفت نظرنا إلى تأثير التراث العربي الشفاهي في الأدب الإنجليزي كما صاغه جبران. أي إنه يسير في اتجاه معاكس لهؤلاء الذين جعلوا وُكدهم البحث عن تأثير التراث الرومانسي الغربي على الشعر العربي. وأغلب الظن أنه لو أتيح له أن يدرس الأدب العربي لكان حقيقاً بأن يتتبع آثار التراث الشعري العربي القديم في شعر جبران الجديد، وأن يعيد، بالتالي، تأويل هذا التراث.

وحين نوجه نظرنا نحو موضوع القدر كما عبر عنه شعراء المهجر وغيرهم من الرومانسيين العرب، فلن نجد صعوبة في إدراك أثر القديم في الجديد، إذ يكاد شعرهم في هذا الموضوع أن يشكل مع نظيره من الشعر التراثي «خطاباً» واحداً يغلب عليه طابع التأمل في معضلة القدر، الذي يكاد ينفي الإرادة الحرة، ويحيلها إلى وهم إنساني محض، يقول جبران، مثلا، مفتتحاً قصيدة «المواكب».(٦)

والشر في الناس لا يفنى وإن قبروا	الخير في الناس مصنوع إذا جبروا
أصابع الدهر يوماً ثـم تنكـسر	وأكـثر الناس آلات تحـرّكهـا

فـلا تقـولن هذا عـالم عـلـم   ولا تقولن ذاك السـيد الـوقـر

فأفضـل النـاس قطعان يسير بهـا   صوت الرعاة ومن لم يمش يندثر

كما ينهي قصيدته بالعودة إلى موضوع الدهر الذي ينفي حرية الاختيار:

العيش في الغاب، والأيام لو نظمت   في قبضتي لغدت في الغاب تنتشر

لكن هو الدهر في نفسي له أرب   فكلما رمت غاباً قام يعتـذر

وللتقادير سبـــل لا تغــيـرهـا   والناس في عجزهم عن قصدهم قصروا

وفيما بين البداية والنهاية تراوده فكرة الدهر فيقول:

فالأرض خمارة والـدهر صاحبها   وليس يرضى بها غير الألى سكروا

ويقول:

والعلم في الناس سبل بان أولهـا   أمـا أواخرهـا فالـدهــر والـقـدر

وعلى منوال قريب من هذا ينسج أبو ماضي قصيدة «الطلاسم»[7] التي تعد هي الأخرى تأملاً في لغز الوجود حيث يسير الإنسان في طريق لم يختره، بل فرض عليه فرضاً:

جئت لا أعلم من أين ولكني أتيت

ولقد أبصرت قدامي طريقاً فمشيت

وسأبقى ماشياً إن شئت هذا أم أبيت

كيف جئت؟ كيف أبصرت طريقي

لست أدري

وإذا كان إيليا أبو ماضي يجسّد في هذا الشعر حيرته وشكوكه الوجودية أكثر ممّا يعبّر عن يقين بحتمية القدر فإن عبد الرحمن شكري[8] يعلن استسلامه التام لما تأتي به الأقدار:

يا مرحبا بالـذي يأتي القضـاء به   حـظ المحكم ترحيب وإعظـام

أدر عليَّ كـؤوس العيش قاطبة   سـعد ونحس وإهـوان وإكـرام

إن كان عيش فإن العيش محتمل   أو كان موت فما لي عنه إحجـام

مما دفعه، في نبرة «علائية» واضحة، إلى المساواة بين الحياة والموت أولاً، ثم تفضيل الموت:[9]

وما الخير واللـذات إلا عواريا	وما العيـــش إلا ميتة بعد ميتة
فأفنى ولم يعنف عليَّ شتائيا	فيا ليتني كالزهر صيف حياته
وألف على مـوت يريح جِنانيا	على العيش واللـذات مني تحية

إن هذا الشعر وما يشبهه في الشعر العربي الحديث كثير، لا تسعى هذه الدراسة إلى استقصائه بقدر ما تسعى إلى لفت النظر للصلة بينه وبين أصوله القديمة في التراث العربي. قلت فيما سبق إن الشعر العربي الذي يدور حول القدر يشكل حديثه وقديمه نسيجاً متجانساً، وسوف أكتفي بضرب أمثلة قليلة من شعر أبي العلاء المعرّي الذي يعد أبرز صوت شعري قديم تجلت فيه نزعة الشك في حرية الإنسان، كما تجلت فيه أيضاً تأملات حول حتمية القضاء والقدر وما صاحبها من نزوع إلى التشاؤم بحيث تساوت لديه الأضداد، فلا فرق عنده بين الغناء والبكاء، كما تساوى لديه صوت النعي بصوت البشير:

نـوح بـاكٍ أو تـرنّـم شـادِ	غير مُجدٍ في ملّتى واعتـقادي
سٍ بصوت البشـير في كـل نـاد	وشـبيه صوت النعـيِّ إذا قيـ
نَت علــــى فرع غصنها الميّـاد	أبكت تلكـم الحمـامـة أم غنّـ

ثم يقول:

جسمُ فيها، والعيشُ مثل السهاد[10]	ضجعةُ الموت رقدةٌ يستريح الـ

وهل تختلف حيرة إيليا أبي ماضي عن حيرة أبي العلاء الذي يقول:

طـرقـاً وختهـا عـادهـا وثمودهـا[11]	وجهلت أمـري غير أني سالك

إن السير في طريق سلكها السابقون ويسلكها اللاحقون دون إرادة منهم يكاد ينفي فاعلية العقل، ويوقع أبا العلاء، في «اللاأدرية» التي وقع فيها أبو ماضي:

فمـا للجسم عـلـم بانتقـال	إذا انتقلت عن الأوصال نفسي
وقـد كان الرحيل رحيـل قال	أسير فلا أعـود وما رجوعي
كأن العقل منـــها في عقـال[12]	أمـور يلتبـسن على البرايـا

إن هذا التشابه بين أبي العلاء من جهة، وجبران وشكري وأبي ماضي من جهة أخرى، لا يقودنا إلى الظن بأن الجديد مجرد محاكاة للقديم، لكنه ينبغي أن يدعونا للتفكير في إقامة حوار بينهما، فنفهم، بالتالي، كل واحد منهما فهماً جديداً. لقد حصّل جبران، مثلاً، أنواعاً من المعرفة لم تكن متاحة لأبي العلاء، الذي ربما قد أتيح له أيضا ما لم يعد متاحاً لجبران، لكنهما يعدان تجليين لتفكير شعري عربي، أو هما، بمصطلح ابن خلدون، يصدران عن «ملكة» الشعر العربي. صوت الشاعر العربي القديم يتناغم مع الصوت الشعري الحديث، فيأخذ منه ويعطيه في آن واحد.

لقد كثر كلام منظري الرومانسية العربية، من الشعراء والنقاد، عن الثورة على مدرسة الإحياء التي مثلها الرعيل الأول من طبقة البارودي وشوقي ثم الجواهري، كما كثر الكلام عن التجديد وضرورة التمرد على القديم، لكن ما فعله الشعراء هو «إحياء» للقديم بأسلوب جديد. لقد حاكى التقليديون، في كثير من شعرهم، التراث الشعري القديم، أما الرومانسيون فقد «حاوروا» القديم فأمدوه بحياة جديدة، غير أن هذا الحوار لا يسمعه إلا قارئ يحسن الإنصات، فيدرك الأصوات والأصداء، رغم تباعد الأزمنة. إن حلم الإرادة الإنسانية الحرة راود الشاعرين القديم والجديد، واصطدم حلم كل منهما بحقيقة الدهر أو القضاء والقدر، فكان التعبير عن هذا المأزق الوجودي خطاباً شعرياً متجانس الأطراف، رغم التباين الظاهر. لا يقتصر الإحياء إذن على جماعة من الشعراء دون أخرى، فالشعر الذي يستحق هذا الاسم إحياء دائم وتأويل لا ينقطع للماضي، أي تغيير مستمر لهذا الماضي.

شعراء الحداثة والتمرد على ثقافة القدر

لعل أحداً لم يسخر من عزلة الشاعر العربي الرومانسي وعكوفه على أحزانه الفردية الخاصة كما سخر عبد الوهاب البياتي في قصيدة «أحزان البنفسج»(١٣) حيث يقول:

الملايين التي تكدح، لا تحلم في موت فراشة
وبأحزان البنفسج
أو شراع يتوهج
تحت ضوء القمر الأخضر في ليلة صيف
أو غراميات مجنون بطيف
الملايين التي تكدح، تعرى، تتمزق

في هذه القصيدة سخرية لاذعة من «المعجم» الرومانسي متمثلاً في الفراشة والبنفسج والأشرعة التي تتهادى على صفحة الماء وضوء القمر الأخضر وليالي الصيف والغراميات والأطياف وزوارق الحالمين ومناديل المغرمين. وتكاد هذه القصيدة أن تكون نقداً لقصائد بعينها لدى شعراء بعينهم. وعلى سبيل المثال فإن هذا المعجم الذي يسخر منه البياتي ورد كله تقريبا في قصيدة لعلي محمود طه.(١٤)

في مثل هذا الشعر يعلن شاعر الحداثة ثورته على ثقافة العزلة عن الملايين التي تكدح، التي لا تحلم بالفراشات وزهور البنفسج، إنما تحلم باللقمة، وهي تغني وتتألم لكنها تكابد ما لا يكابده الشاعر الرومانسي الحالم.

ولا توجد صلة مباشرة بين «أحزان البنفسج» وموضوع القدر، لكن ما يعلنه البياتي في قصيدته يعد تمرداً عاماً على هموم الرومانسيين بما في ذلك عكوفهم على تأمل مشكلة القدر، مما عزلهم عما يهم الملايين. إن موقف البياتي النقدي يتجه إلى إدانة الغيبوبة الرومانسية وما تحدثه من تخدير للوعي العام.

ولا شك أن بعض القصائد الحداثية تتراسل مع قصيدة البياتي فتفصل ما أجمله في قصيدته القصيرة نسبياً، أو هي، بعبارة أخرى، تكمل ما بدأه.

في قصيدة «خبز وحشيش وقمر»[15] لا يدين قباني ما يمكن أن نسميه الثقافة الرومانسية، مثلما فعل البياتي، بل يدين ثقافة الناس، أي يتخذ موقفاً نقدياً من الثقافة كما تتجلى في سلوك البشر في الشرق العربي. إن الغيبوبة الرومانسية التي انتقدها البياتي امتدت لتشمل جموع الناس. ومن الملاحظ أن نص قباني يتقاطع مع نص البياتي فتتكرر في النصين كلمات «قمر» و«ضوء» و«قرص» و«غناء» و«ليالي» بوصفها مخدّرات للوعي.

غير أن قباني يعقد الصلة بين غيبوبة الملايين والاستسلام للأقدار:

ما الذي عند السماء

لكسالى .. ضعفاء

يستحيلون إلى موتي إذا عاش القمر

ويهزون قبور الأولياء

علها ترزقهم رزاً .. وأطفالاً .. قبور الأولياء

ويمدون السجاجيد الأنيقات الطرز

يتسلون بأفيون نسميه قدر

وقضاء

كما يقول عن جموع الناس في الشرق العربي إنهم:

يصلون

ويزنون

ويحيون اتكال

منذ أن كانوا يعيشون اتكال

يلاحظ في قصيدة قباني أنه يتحدث عن «الناس» و«البلاد» فيقول: «يترك الناس الحوانيت ويمضون زمر/لملاقاة القمر»، كما يقول: «ما الذي يفعله قرص ضياء/بلادي/بلاد الأنبياء/وبلاد البسطاء؟» أما تعبير «في بلادي» فتكرر ثلاث مرات؛ «في بلادي .. في بلاد البسطاء»، ثم: «في بلادي/حيث يبكي الساذجون»، ثم: «في بلادي/حيث يحيا الناس من دون عيون».

أي إن القصيدة تعد حديثاً عن «الناس» في «بلادي»، وهو ما يحيل القارئ إلى قصيدة صلاح عبدالصبور التي اتخذت من «الناس في بلادي»(١٦) عنواناً لها، وكانت العبارة في الوقت نفسه عنوان ديوانه الأول. يضاف إلى ذلك أن ألفاظ التواكل والقضاء والقدر التي ذكرها قباني تمثل رابطة لفظية ومعنوية بين قصيدتي الشاعرين. وقد يغري هذا التشابه بعض النقاد بالنظر في مسألة التأثير والتأثر بين الشاعرين، بل قد يغري بعضهم بالنظر في أن اللاحق منهما يحاكي السابق، غير أن التشابه بين الشاعرين ليس تشابهاً «موضوعياً» بقدر ما هو تشابه أنتجه نشاط القراءة لا بهدف الوقوف عند واقعة التشابه بحد ذاتها، وإنما بهدف إثراء تفاعلنا مع النصين عن طريق تخصيب كل قصيدة منهما بالأخرى، بغض النظر عن السابق واللاحق.

إن الماضي يؤثر في الحاضر كما يتأثر به، النص اللاحق يجعلنا نعيد النظر في النص السابق، أي يغيره، فليس للنص الأدبي معنى ثابت. دلالته لا تكف عن التغير الناشئ عن ظهور نصوص جديدة تدفعنا إلى إعادة تأويل الماضي، وبالتالي يتغيّر هذا الماضي ويكتسب وجوداً لم يكن له.

يقول صلاح عبدالصبور في بداية قصيدته:

الناس في بلادي جارحون كالصقور
غناؤهم كرجفة الشتاء في ذؤابة الشجر
وضحكهم يئز كاللهيب في الحطب
خطاهمو تريد أن تسوخ في التراب
ويقتلون، يسرقون، يشربون، يجشأون

وهي بداية «جارحة» إذ تشمل الناس دون تمييز، وكأن القائل في القصيدة لا يستثني نفسه من الناس في بلاده، الذين وصفهم بأنهم جارحون «كالصقور». وفي إدانته للناس فإن القائل يسعى إلى إسباغ هذه الإدانة على جوهر وجودهم، إذ كل ما يصدر عنهم جارح وشرير، بما في ذلك «الغناء» و«الضحك»، بل ومجرد الخطو على الطريق، وهو فعل يفترض فيه أنه «محايد» لا يعبر عن انفعال أو تفكير من أي نوع. أما تكراره لصيغة «يفعلون» في قوله «يقتلون، يسرقون، يشربون، يجشأون»، فتعميق إيقاعي دلالي في آن واحد. تكاد هذه الأفعال أن تحيل هؤلاء الناس إلى «أيقونة» تمثل كل ما هو شرير ومقزز.

ومع هذا كله فإن هؤلاء الناس يُقال عنهم عقب ذلك مباشرة:

لكنهم بشر
وطيبون حين يملكون قبضتي نقود
ومؤمنون بالقدر

ويكاد قوله «طيبون»، و«مؤمنون» أن يكون نفياً دلالياً إيقاعياً لما أثبته قبل ذلك عنهم من أنهم «يقتلون، يسرقون، يشربون، يجشأون»، لولا أن طيبتهم مشروطة بامتلاكهم النقود كما أن إيمانهم مقيد بالقدر. إن شر هؤلاء الناس مطلق في حين أن خيرهم مشروط أو مقيد.

ومن جهة ثانية فإن وصفهم بأنهم «طيبون» لا يخلو من سخرية حين نلتفت إلى إيماءات الكلمة في العامية المصرية، التي لم تكن، في الغالب، بعيدة عن ذهن القائل. حين يقال في العامية المصرية (القاهرية خصوصاً) عن شخص ما إنه طيب فالمعنى أحياناً ينصرف إلى «ساذج» أو «مغفل» وعندئذ ينبغي أن نفكر فيما تحفل به العامية من أقوال وأمثلة تتصل بالقدر، من قبل «المكتوب على الجبين لازم تشوفه العين» أو «كله مقدر ومكتوب» أو «اجري جري الوحوش غير رزقك يا ابن آدم لم تحوش». فالرزق مقدر ولا علاقة له بالسعي. وهذا التراث الشعبي كله يمكن أن نعده إيحاءات تتضمنها عبارة «مؤمنون بالقدر». إن كون الناس طيبين ومؤمنين بالقدر لا يضيف إليهم شيئاً إيجابياً، ولذلك فإن قوله «لكنهم بشر» ليس استدراكاً على ما وصفهم به قبل ذلك، بقدر ما هو تهكّم من طرف خفي.

ومما يلاحظ أيضاً أن النص لم يمهد لفكرة «القدر» كما أن ما يأتي بعد قوله «مؤمنون بالقدر» لا يتصل بهذه الفكرة اتصالاً مباشراً، فبدا هذا القول خارجاً عن سياق القصيدة، لكننا حين نمضي في القراءة نكتشف أن هذا التعبير هو القطب الذي تدور حوله وجوه التعبير المختلفة.

يقول الشاعر عقب المقطع الأول مباشرة:

وعند باب قريتي يجلس عمي مصطفى
وهو يحب المصطفى

إن هذا الرجل الذي يجلس على باب القرية يسميه الشاعر «عمي مصطفى»، فهو إذن بلغ السن التي رشحته أن يكون حكيم القرية، وحكمته تكتسب صبغة دينية، لأنه يحب «المصطفى» وتحدث تسمية هذا الحكيم باسم مصطفى نوعاً من التماهي بينه وبين النبي «المصطفى» صلى الله عليه وسلم. إننا إذن بإزاء حكيم يجسد الدين ويبث حكمته الدينية تلك على رجال القرية:

وهو يقضي ساعة بين الأصيل والمساء
وحوله الرجال واجمون
يحكي لهم حكاية ... تجربة الحياة.
حكاية تثير في النفوس لوعة العدم
وتجعل الرجال ينشجون
ويطرقون
يحدقون في السكون

في لجة الرعب العميق والفراغ والسكون
ما غاية الإنسان من أتعابه؟ ما غاية الحياة؟

أثارت حكمة عم مصطفى عن «تجربة الحياة» أحزاناً ولوعة وشعوراً بالعدم، حتى إن الرجال واجمون أو يطرقون يحدقون في السكون والفراغ. إن حكمة الرجل تتلخص في أنه لا فائدة من تعب وأن الحياة لا غاية لها، بل هي عبث.

إن عم مصطفى الذي يحب المصطفى يفترض فيه أن يكون حكيماً مسلماً، أي أن يكون خطابه الديني إسلامياً محضاً، لكن القارئ حين يطالع قوله «ما غاية الإنسان من أتعابه؟ ما غاية الحياة؟» لابد أن يستدعي حكيماً آخر؛ سليمان النبيّ الحكيم الذي يقول في مفتتح كتاب **الجامعة** «باطل الأباطيل، باطل الأباطيل، كل شيء باطل. ما الفائدة من كل تعب الإنسان الذي يتعبه تحت الشمس؟» ويقول بعد ذلك «فأي نفع للإنسان من جميع تعبه ومكابدته العناء الذي قاسى منه تحت الشمس؟ كل أيام حياته مفعمة بالمشقة، وعمله عناء، حتى في الليل لا يستريح قلبه. وهذا أيضاً باطل» (كتاب **الجامعة**، ٢: ٢٢-٢٤).

إن ما لاحظناه من أن الرجال قد أصابهم غم عظيم جعلهم ينشجون، وأثار في نفوسهم لوعة العدم، هو من أثر حكايات عم مصطفى التي تتراسل بشكل واضح مع تعاليم سليمان الحكيم، كما وردت في العهد القديم.

وسلطة حكايات عم مصطفى إنما تنبع من توحدها مع الخطاب الديني الذي يتغذى من روافد مختلفة تصب كلها في اتجاه واحد، ذلك أن تعب الإنسان أو سعيه لا يغير من القضاء والقدر شيئاً كما تنطق حكمة عم مصطفى:

يا أيها الإله
الشمس مجتلاك، والهلال مفرق الجبين
وهذه الجبال الراسيات عرشك المكين
وأنت نافذ القضاء ... أيها الإله

إن كلمة «إله» المستخدمة في هذا النص تختلف عن كلمتي «الله» أو «الرب» في كونها أكثر عمومية، وأنها تطلق ويراد بها أي قوة ميتافيزيقية يُظن أنها المتحكمة في مصائر البشر، إن كلمتي «الله» و«رب» هما الأكثر شيوعاً في أوساط المسلمين والمسيحيين في العالم الناطق باللغة العربية، أما كلمة إله فتطلق على ما كان يعبده البشر عموماً، فتطلق على آلهة العرب قبل الإسلام والمسيحية واليهودية. ما كان يقدسه المصريون الفراعنة هو إله أو آلهة، لا «الله» أو «الرب» وشعار الإسلام يقول «لا إله إلا الله» ولا يقول «لا الله إلا الله» مثلاً.

إن عمومية كلمة «إله» تناسب معنى السلطة الدينية المطلقة، دون تخصيص دين بعينه، ويؤيد ذلك اقترانه بالشمس والقمر، اللذين كانا تجليين أو تجسيدين للإله عند الفراعنة وغيرهم، كما كانت ظواهر طبيعية أخرى تجليات عبدتها أو قدستها مجموعات بشرية متباينة على مر التاريخ.

أما معجم «الجبال الراسيات» و«عرشك المكين» فلا شك أنه يتضمّن إشارة للخطاب الديني الإسلامي، «إن ربكم الله الذي خلق السموات والأرض في ستة أيام ثم استوى على العرش» (الأعراف، ٥٤).

ومن الجلي أن الإله، كما تجسده كلمات عم مصطفى، لا ينفك وجوده عن التسلط والجبروت، فالجبال الراسيات هي عرشه، كما أن الظواهر الطبيعية هي تجلياته له، وقضاؤه نافذ. وقد يبدو أن عم مصطفى لا يخرج في هذا كله عن الصفات التي تخلعها الأديان على الخالق، غير أن الله في هذه الأديان رحيم بالناس يغفر لهم، ويقبل توبتهم إذا أخطأوا، فلا ينحصر الوجود الإلهي في كونه نافذ القضاء. استصفت كلمات عم مصطفى جانباً واحداً من جوانب الذات الإلهية وجعلته معادلاً موضوعياً لها.

ومن هنا نفهم لماذا كانت عظة عم مصطفى تثير في الناس لوعة العدم وتجعل الرجال ينشجون، ونفهم لماذا يخلو تعب الإنسان من أي غاية، فمهما سعى البشر فإن الإله «نافذ القضاء» وبالتالي فلن يغير هذا السعي شيئاً.

بعد أن قرر عم مصطفى أن الإله نافذ القضاء يستمر في بث حكمته أو فلسفته الدينية عن طريق القصص فيقول بعد قوله «وأنت نافذ القضاء أيها الإله»:

بنى فلان، واعتلى، وشيد القلاع.
وأربعون غرفة قد ملئت بالذهب اللماع
وفي مساء واهن الأصداء جاءه عزريل
يحمل بين إصبعيه دفتراً صغير
وأول اسم فيه ذلك الفلان
ومد عزريل عصاه
بسر حرفي «كن» بسر لفظ «كان»
وفي الجحيم دحرجت روح فلان
(يا أيها الإله
كم أنت قاس موحش يا أيها الإله.)

لم يكتف عم مصطفى بما قرره من أن الإنسان لا يملك إرادة، وأن قضاء «الإله» نافذ، بل عمد إلى الحكي، أو الفن القصصي، كي يرسخ من خلاله ما قرره في لغة مجردة. إن هذه الحكاية ما هي إلا تمثيل لفكرة القضاء والقدر، اللذين لا يجدي معهما أي جهد إنساني. شيّد هذا الإنسان الغني قلاعاً، وجمع مالاً، لكن هذا السـ...ـي لم يوفر له الحماية من «الموت». ولم يكن مجرد موت، بل عقاب يتسم بالقسوة، فقد ألقيت روح هذا الفلان في الجحيم بعنف وسخرية «دحرجت». ولا تتضمن الحكاية عن «فلان» هذا فعلاً يستحق العقاب من أجله. فلم يسرق أو يقتل أو يكذب، كل ما فعله أنه أراد أن يوفر لنفسه الحماية، لكن أن يبدو أن هذا الفعل عُدّ من جانب «الإله» محاولة لمقاومة قضائه الذي لا يجوز لأحد أن يفكر في أن يحمي نفسه منه، فكان أن دُحرجت روحه في الجحيم. ومن هنا يظهر

صوت القائل التخييلي في القصيدة، بعد طول غياب، حينما أفسح السبيل لصوت عم مصطفى. يظهر صوت القائل التخييلي معلقاً على صوت عم مصطفى، فيقول عن هذا الإله الذي تصنعه حكاياته «يا أيها الإله/كم أنت قاس موحش يا أيها الإله».

غير أننا نلاحظ أن هذا الإله الذي تصنعه تلك الحكايات يتراسل مع الخطاب الديني الشائع في الأوساط العربية، فهناك أولاً عزرائيل ملاك الموت، ثم إن هذا الملاك إنما ينفذ ما هو مكتوب في دفتر الموت، ينفذه بقضاء لا يملك تغييره، لأنه تنفيذ للكلمة الإلهية، وهي كلمة تجسد إرادته. «في البدء كان الكلمة، والكلمة كان مع الله، وكان الكلمة هو الله، هو كان في البدء مع الله» (يوحنا، ١: ١-٣)، يضاف إلى ذلك أن «أمره إذا أراد شيئاً أن يقول له كن فيكون» (يس، ٨٢). من هنا فإن النص الشعري حرص على أن يتضمن فعلي «كان» بصيغة الماضي و«كن» بصيغة الأمر (بسر حرفي «كن» بسر لفظ «كان»)، مشيراً إلى عمومية الخطاب الذي ترسخه الحكايات التي تستقي مادتها من المصادر الدينية الشائعة، لكنها مع ذلك تقدم قراءة خاصة تجذّر في نفوس المتلقين إيديولوجية الاستسلام للأقدار وتنذر من يساوره هاجس المقاومة بالعقاب الشديد.

ولعله لا يخفى أيضاً أن حكاية هذا «الفلان» تبدأ بأنه شيد القلاع حماية لنفسه، وهو ما يحيل القارئ بشكل مباشر إلى القرآن «أينما تكونوا يدرككم الموت ولو كنتم في بروج مشيدة» (النساء، ٧٨). يمثل فعل «التشييد» رابطة لفظية بين النص الشعري والنص القرآني، كما أن «القلاع» تكاد أن تكون مرادفاً لكلمة «بروج». يضاف إلى ذلك أن هذا الفلان «أدركه» الموت رغم تشييده القلاع وجمعه الأموال.

أما فكرة أن المال لا ينفع صاحبه مادام مآله إلى الموت، فهي من الأفكار التي تتردد كثيراً في الحض على «الزهد» في الحياة الدنيا: «فمتى كان الإنسان في سعة، لا تكون حياته في أمواله» (لوقا، ١٢: ١٥). ثم إن المسيح، عليه السلام، ضرب للناس مثلاً فقال:

> إنسان غني غلت له أرضه محاصيل وافرة، ففكر في نفسه قائلاً: ماذا أعمل وليس عندي مكان أخزن فيه محاصيلي؟ وقال: أعمل هذا: أهدم مخازني وأبني أعظم منها، وهناك أخزن جميع غلالي وخيراتي. وأقول لنفسي: يا نفسي، عندك خيرات كثيرة مخزونة لسنين عديدة، فاستريحي وكلي واشربي واطربي، ولكن الله قال له: يا غبي، هذه الليلة تطلب نفسك منك، فلمن يبقى ما أعددته؟ هذه هي حالة من يخزن الكنوز لنفسه ولا يكون غنياً عند الله. (لوقا، ١٢: ١٦-٢١)

في هذا المثل نلاحظ فكرة التشييد والبناء والمال الوفير وتخزين «الكنوز» وهذا كله يتوازى مع ما تضمنه النص الشعري عن هذا الفلان الذي ملأ أربعين غرفة بكنوز من «الذهب اللماع» لكن عزرائيل يأتيه في المساء الواهن الأصداء ليقبض روحه، تماماً كما أن الإنسان الغني في المثل الذي ضربه يسوع طلبت منه نفسه «هذه الليلة». لا تختلف «ليلة» هذا الإنسان الغني عن «مساء» ذلك الفلان الذي «جمع مالاً وعدّده، يحسب أن ماله أخلده» (الهمزة، ٢-٣).

ومما يمكن ملاحظته في النص الشعري أنه يتراسل، إلى جانب ما ذكر، مع التراث الشعبي الذي تشيع فيه قصة الغرف المملوءة بالذهب، كما أن ذكر العدد أربعين ربما يذكرنا بقصة «علي بابا والأربعين حرامي» التي ترتبط هي أيضاً بالمغارة المملوءة بكنوز من الذهب والجواهر. وإذا أثيرت الذاكرة الشعبية، أثيرت من خلالها ثقافة «القدر» والمكتوب على الجبين وما إليهما من مخزون شفوي. (١٧)

بعد تعليقه الذي يقول «يا أيها الإله .. كم أنت قاس موحش يا أيها الإله» ينتقل القائل التخييلي ليسرد «حكاية» عم مصطفى وكيف انتهى هو أيضاً:

بالأمس زرت قريتي، قد مات عمي مصطفى.
ووسدوه في التراب
لم يبتن القلاع، (كان كوخه من اللبن).
وسار خلف نعشه القديم
من يملكون مثله جلباب كتان قديم
لم يذكروا الإله أو عزريل أو حروف «كان»
فالعام عام جوع
وعند باب القبر قام صاحبي «خليل»
حفيد عمي مصطفى
وحين مد للسماء زنده المفتول
ماجت على عينيه نظرة احتقار
فالعام عام جوع

على الرغم من أن عم مصطفى لم «يبتن القلاع»، أي عاش ومات فقيراً، فإن أحداً لا يضمن له حياة طيبة بعد موته، لأن القائل التخييلي وصف الإله الذي يبثه عم مصطفى بأنه «قاس وموحش»، فلا يستبعد، في هذه الحالة، أن تتدحرج روحه في الجحيم، خاصة حين نتذكر أن الرجل الغني لم يفعل ما يستحق عليه العقاب، ومع ذلك دحرجت روحه في الجحيم.

غير أن العام الذي مات فيه عم مصطفى كان عام جوع، الأمر الذي حفز «الناس» إلى نسيان «الإله» و«عزريل» و«حروف كان»، وهي كلمات تلخص حكمته الدينية التي آل الناس بسببها إلى ما آلوا إليه من جوع. استسلام الناس للقضاء والقدر هو الذي أدى بهم إلى ما هم فيه.

ولئن كان الناس قد تناسوا أو نسوا حكمة عم مصطفى، فإن حفيده لا يكتفي بمجرد النسيان، بل يعلن ثورته على السماء، ويهددها بسواعده المفتولة معلناً احتقاره وغضبه. إنه يرفض ثقافة القدر التي كان جده يبثها للناس، وكان مع ذلك ضحية لها. يريد بالتالي أن يقوّض تلك السماء التي شيّدها خطاب جده مصطفى، ويبني بدلاً منها سماء جديدة، فما هي طبيعة تلك السماء، أو الثقافة البديلة؟

لا يحدثنا النص عن تلك الثقافة، ولا يشير إلا إلى حالة من التمرد العام، على عكس ثقافة القدر التي عبر عنها بصور مختلفة من خلال التقرير المباشر تارة، ومن خلال تراسله مع نصوص أخرى تارة ثانية.

لم يذكر النص عن الحفيد أشياء كثيرة، واكتفى تقريباً بذكر اسمه، خليل، فهل يتضمن هذا العلم ما يغني عن الكلام عنه؟ لقد اقترن اسم الجد باسم النبي «المصطفى» صلى الله عليه وسلم، الأمر الذي يمكن أن يدفعنا إلى التفكير في اقتران اسم الحفيد بنبي آخر، هو الخليل، إبراهيم عليه السلام. التشابه اللفظي بين «مصطفى» و«المصطفى» يجوز أن يدفع القارئ إلى استكمال النص باستدعاء الخليل الذي يتشابه مع «خليل»، وعندئذ نصبح بإزاء نوع من التوازن والتوازي بين «مصطفى» و«المصطفى» من جهة و«خليل» و«الخليل» من جهة أخرى.

لقد قدم مصطفى الجد عن طريق حكاياته، قراءته للمصطفى، أو تأويله الخاص للخطاب الديني، وهو تأويل رفضه الحفيد وثار عليه. ويستطيع القارئ أن يكمل النص الشعري بمجرد تذكر قصة إبراهيم، عليه السلام، كما وردت في النص القرآني، وحينئذ قد نكتشف شيئاً عن طبيعة السماء البديلة التي يرمز لها الحفيد خليل.

لقد ثار الخليل على تراث آبائه الأقدمين، وأعلن احتقاره لهذا التراث، وحطم رموزه تحطيماً، وسخر منها سخرية شديدة، مسفّهاً لها ولمن يؤمنون بها:

ولقد آتينا إبراهيم رشده من قبل وكنا به عالمين، إذ قال لأبيه وقومه ما هذه التماثيل التي أنتم لها عاكفون، قالوا وجدنا آباءنا لها عابدين، قال لقد كنتم أنتم وآباؤكم في ضلال مبين، قالوا أجئتنا بالحق أم أنت من اللاعبين، قال بل ربكم رب السموات والأرض الذي فطرهن وأنا على ذلكم من الشاهدين، وتالله لأكيدن أصنامكم بعد أن تولوا مدبرين، فجعلهم جذاذاً إلا كبيراً لهم لعلهم إليه يرجعون، قالوا من فعل هذا بآلهتنا إنه لمن الظالمين، قالوا سمعنا فتى يذكرهم يقال له إبراهيم، قالوا فأتوا به على أعين الناس لعلهم يشهدون، قالوا أأنت فعلت هذا بآلهتنا يا إبراهيم، قال بل فعله كبيرهم هذا فاسألوهم إن كانوا ينطقون. (الأنبياء، ٥١-٦٤)

ثم إن إبراهيم، عليه السلام، يقول لقومه «أفتعبدون من دون الله ما لا ينفعكم شيئاً ولا يضركم، أفّ لكم ولما تعبدون من دون الله أفلا تعقلون» (الأنبياء، ٦٦-٦٧).

والتعبير القرآني يربط بين رفض إبراهيم الخليل لتراث آبائه الأقدمين وانفعاله الشديد «أف لكم ولما تعبدون»، غير أن هذا الانفعال حلّ به بعد إعمال عقله، وبعد طول تأمل «فلما جن عليه الليل رأى كوكباً قال هذا ربي فلما أفل قال لا أحب الآفلين، فلما رأى القمر بازغاً قال هذا ربي فلما أفل قال لئن لم يهدني ربي لأكونن من القوم الضالين، فلما رأى الشمس بازغة قال هذا ربي هذا أكبر فلما أفلت قال يا قوم إني بريء مما تشركون» (الأنعام، ٧٦-٧٨).

حين أعلن الخليل إبراهيم ثورته على السماء «الكواكب، والقمر، والشمس» ورفضه لها، كان فتىً ذا سواعد قوية وعقل راجح، تمثل ذلك في إصراره على تقويض العقائد البالية، كما تمثل في حججه التي ساقها أثناء مجادلته لقومه. وهذا كله مما يغذي قراءتنا للنص الشعري الذي سمى حفيد عم مصطفى باسم خليل، وجعله شاباً قوياً ذا ذراع مفتولة نظر إلى السماء في غضب وتوعد، وهي سماء ترمز في هذا النص إلى العقيدة الناتجة عن قراءة الدين قراءة أدت إلى حصره في فكرة واحدة، هي فكرة حتمية القدر التي قادت الناس إلى الاستسلام للأمر الواقع حتى إنهم «جاعوا». وقد لاحظنا في النص الشعري أيضاً أنه لا يقتصر على إدانة الخطاب الديني هذا، بل يشير إلى التراث الشعبي والعقائد العتيقة التي أنتجت هذا الواقع الأليم.

يصح للقارئ إذن أن يكمل فهمه لغضبة خليل في النص الشعري، بقراءة غضبة إبراهيم الخليل كما وردت في النص القرآني الكريم، استناداً على التشابهات بين خليل والخليل. بعبارة أخرى، فإن البعد التأملي التفصيلي المفتقد في موقف خليل من تعاليم جده، يمكن للقارئ أن يستدركه عن طريق النظر في موقف إبراهيم الخليل، كما ورد في النص القرآني. كما أن قراءة القصيدة تلفتنا إلى إمكان قراءة النص القرآني بوعي جديد.

وبالإضافة إلى ما سبق فإن الوعي الديني المزيّف الذي أنتجه عم مصطفى يحيلنا بشكل مباشر تقريباً إلى المقولة الماركسية المشهورة «الدين أفيون الشعوب»، فقد خدّر خطاب عم مصطفى إرادة الناس في بلاده، وأحالهم إلى كائنات مستسلمة لما تأتي به الأقدار، إذ لا فائدة من السعي. كما أن محاولة تغيير الواقع عبث لا طائل من ورائه. وهو في هذا كله يدعم خطابه بتأويله الخاص للدين لأن «تجربة الحياة» كما يصوغها تتضمن إشارات للنصوص الدينية، التي سبكها في حكاياته سبكاً يوقع في نفوس السامعين اعتقاداً بتوحد تجربته مع النص الديني.

وإذا كان نص صلاح عبد الصبور لا يتضمن إشارة لفظية مباشرة تربط بين مقولة ماركس وخطاب عم مصطفى فإن نص «خبز وحشيش وقمر» يربط بينهما ربطاً مباشراً تقريباً حين يقول عن الناس إنهم:

يهزّون قبور الأولياء
علها ترزقهم رزا .. وأطفالاً .. قبور الأولياء.
ويمدون السجاجيد الأنيقات الطرز
يتسلون بأفيون نسميه قدر
وقضاء.

وقد أحال نص قباني إلى الدين في عدة مواضع فقد قال قبل هذه السطور مباشرة:

ونعيش لنستجدي السماء
ما الذي عند السماء

كما يقول بعد ذلك :

وينادون الهلال
يا هلال
أيها النبع الذي يمطر ماس
وحشيشاً ونعاس
أيها الرب الرخامي المعلق

كما يقول :

في ليالي الشرق لما
يبلغ البدر تمامه
يتعرى الشرق من كل كرامة
ونضال
فالملايين التي تركض من غير نعال
والتي تؤمن في أربع زوجات
وفي يوم القيامة
الملايين التي لا تلتقي بالخبز
إلا في الخيال
والتي تسكن في الليل بيوتاً
من سعال
أبداً .. ما عرفت شكل الدواء.

يحيلنا هذا النص إلى «الملايين» التي سبق أن تحدث عنها البياتي، كما يحيلنا إلى الناس
في بلادي، حيث الناس يتضورون جوعاً. وهذا كله أثر من آثار الإيمان المزيف الذي
يحصر الدين في حتمية القدر وفي الزواج بأربعة نساء، وقد أشار نص قباني إلى الموروث
الشعبي حين اختتم قصيدته بقوله:

شرقنا المجتر .. تاريخاً
وأحلاماً كسولة
وخرافات خوالي
شرقنا الباحث عن كل بطولة
في أبي زيد الهلالي ..

تتراسل قصائد البياتي وقباني وعبد الصبور، وتقيم معاً نصاً تتجاوب تفاصيله

التعبيرية، نصاً ينقض الوعي الذي أنتجته خطابات أخرى، شعرية وشعبية ودينية، تعوّل على فكرة أن القدر ينتج واقعاً لا سبيل إلى تغييره أو مقاومته.

الشاعر الجاهلي ومشكلة القدر

حين أراد صلاح عبد الصبور أن يعبر عن الاعتقاد العام في القدر لم يجد خيراً من الموت الذي لا يملك الإنسان أن يقاومه، فهو رسول القدر الذي لا يرد، وقديماً قال طرفة بن العبد في معلقته:

لعمرك إن الموت ما أخطأ الفتى لكالطول المُرخى وثنياه بالـــــيد [١٨]

وقال زهير في معلقته أيضاً:

ومن هـاب أسباب المنايا ينلنه وإن يرق أسباب السماء بسـلم [١٩]

غير أن الشاعر القديم يعبر أحياناً عن مغالبته للأقدار مثيراً حساً واضحاً بالمقاومة، فيقول الحارث بن حلزة في معلقته:

وكـأن المنـون تـردي بنـــا أر عـــن جـونـاً ينجاب عنه العـماء
مكفهراً على الحـــوادث لاتر توه للـدهر مؤيـــد صمـاء [٢٠]

إن الشاعر وقومه يقاومون المنية وحوادث الدهر، ولا يستسلمون لما تأتي به الأقدار، بل يصارعونها، فتعجز عن النيل منهم.
وقد ذهب الشاعر الهذلي بدر بن عامر مذهباً قريباً من مذهب الحارث بن حلزة فصرح بمعنى الصراع مع الدهر أو القدر قائلاً إن حوادث الدهر وصروفه لا تقهره، ولا تعلوه، بل يعلو هو عليها:

ولقد توارثني الحوادث واحداً ضرعاً صغيراً ثم مـــا تعلوني
فتركنني لمـا رأيـن نواجـذي في الروق مثــل معاول الزيتون [٢١]

لقد تركته حوادث الأيام لشأنه بعد أن رأت شدته في مغالبتها والصبر عليها. أما صخر الغي وهو شاعر هذلي أيضاً فله قصيدة [٢٢] يبدؤها برثاء أخيه قائلاً:

لعمر أبي عمرو لقد ساقه المنا إلى جـدث يُوزي له بالأهاضـب
لحيّـة قفر في وجار مقيمـة تنـمّى بها سوقُ المنا والجوالب

أخي لا أخا لي بعده سبقت به   منيتُه جمــــعَ الرُّقى والطبائب(٢٣)

لقد ساق القدر لأخيه حية لدغته فأودت بحياته. وعلى عادة الهذليين انتقل الشاعر من رثاء أخيه إلى الكلام عن الدهر الذي لا يبقى عليه شيء:

أعينيَّ لا يبقي على الدّهر فادر   بتَيْهورة تحت الطّخاف العصـائب(٢٤)

ويمضي فيذكر قصة هذا الوعل مع الرامي، وبعد أن ينتهي منها يقول:

ولله فَتْخاءُ الجناحين لِقْوةٌ   توسّـــد فرخيها لحومَ الأرانب(٢٥)

ويستمر بعد هذا البيت في ذكر قصة هذه اللقوة التي تسعى إلى اقتناص غزال. ويختم قصيدته بهذا البيت:

فذلـك مما أحدث الدهر أنه   له كل مطلوب حثيث وطالـب(٢٦)

إن الطالب والمطلوب نقيضان، من حيث كونهما طرفي صراع، لكنهما يتشابهان من حيث إنهما هدفان للدهر وحوادثه. وتتجلى شاعرية صخر الغي في أنه صاغ هذين النقيضين من مادة لغوية واحدة هي مادة «طلب». إن التشابه اللغوي بين طرفي الصراع يناظر التشابه الوجودي بينهما، فكل منهما هدف للأقدار. كان من اليسير على الشاعر أن يستبدل الصائد والفريسة، أو ما إليهما، بالطالب والمطلوب، لكن مدار القصيدة حول صراع بين طرفين يشبه كل منهما الآخر.

إن الوعل الذي يقدمه الشاعر في قصيدته مُسن شبهه بشيخ شفّه عقوق ذويه:

أعيني لا يبقي على الدهر فـادر	بتيهورة تحت الطخاف العصائب
تملّي بها طولَ الحيـاة فقـرنـُه	له حيـدٌ أشـرافُها كـالـرواجب
يبيت إذا ما آنس الليل كانسـاً	مبيت الكبير ذي الكساء المحارب
تدلّى عليه من بشام وأيكـة	نشاةُ فـروع مرثعنّ الـذوائب
بها كان طفلا ثم أسدس واستوى	فأصبح لِهْمـاً فـي لُهُــوم قراهب
يُروّع من صوت الغراب فينتحي	مسام الصخور فهو أهرب هـارب(٢٧)

هذه هي صورة الوعل (المطلوب)، فإذا نظرنا في صورة الرامي (الطالب) فسوف نجد أن الشاعر قد سماه «جريمة شيخ» أي كاسب شيخ، فهو صائد يكسب من أجل أبيه المسن الجائع:

أُتيح له يومـا وقد طال عـمرُه   جريمةُ شيخ قد تحنّب ساغـب(٢٨)

الطالب والمطلوب إذن يتشابهان، فقد جعل الشاعر وجودهما الشعري مرتبطاً بالشيخوخة، غير أن شيخوخة الوعل ارتبطت بالعقوق والمهانة، حين شبهه الشاعر بشيخ خاصم أهله وانتبذ بعيداً عنهم، على حين أن شيخوخة والد الصائد ارتبطت بالبر والإكرام، فالصائد لا يسعى في الحياة إلا من أجل والده:

يحامـي عليه في الشتاء إذا شتا   وفي الصيف يبغيه الجنا كالمناحـب(٢٩)

فلما رأى الوعل قال لنفسه:

...لـــــــــــــــــــه مـــــــــن رأى   مـن العصـم شـاةً قبله في العواقب

لو ان كريمـي صيد هذا أعاشـه   إلى أن يغيث الناس بعض الكواكب(٣٠)

وهنا نصل إلى مفارقة تستحق التأمل، إذ إن الصائد وإن قتل الوعل فإنه يكاد بفعله هذا أن يرد له كرامته، فالشيخوخة المهانة في صورة الوعل قد رُدّت لها كرامتها على يد كاسب الشيخ. وإذا كانت شيخوخة الوعل ترتبط بالذعر ومحاولة الهرب من الخطر:

يُرّوع من صوت الغراب فينتحي   مسامَ الصخورِ فـــهو أهـــرب ُهارب

فإن شيخوخة والد الصائد تنعم بالحماية صيفاً وشتاءً، والصائد لا يدّخر وسعاً في سبيل إعاشة أبيه المسن، كأن عليه نذراً لابد من الوفاء به، وهو يسمي أباه «كريمي».

وليست شدة السعي والمجاهدة إلا بمثابة الانتقام – شعرياً – للوعل، وإذا كان الرامي قد أحاط به وقتله:

أحـاط به حتـى رماه وقد دنا   بأسمـرَ مفتوقٍ من النـــبل صائب

فنـادى أخـاه ثم طار بشفرة   إليــــه اجتـــزار الفعفعي المناهب(٣١)

فإنه بفعله هذا قد أنصف الشيخوخة ووفر لها الحماية، والشيخوخة تنصرف إلى الوعل، كما تنصرف إلى والد هذا الصائد.

ينتقل صخر الغي بعد ذلك إلى قصة أخرى من قصص الأقدار، هي قصة العقاب والغزال، ولكنـه مـا يـزال يدور في فلك تجربة الطالب والمطلوب اللذين يتناقضان ويتشابهان في آنٍ واحد، فالعقاب (الطالب) تقوم على رعاية فرخين لها، فهي أم تسعى سعياً ناجحاً في توفير الغذاء لفرخيها وحمايتهما من الجوع:

ولله فتخاء الجنـاحـيـن لـقـوة   تـوسد فرخيها لحـوم الأرانـب

كأن قلوب الطير في جوف وكرها   نوى القسب يُلْقى عند بعض المآدب(٣٢)

أما المطلوب فهو غزال جاثم عند أمه، انقضت عليه هذه اللقوة:

فخـاتت غـزالاً جاثماً بصرت به   لـدى سـلمات عنـد أدماء سـارب(٣٣)

والأمومة هي مناط التشابه بين اللقوة (الطالب) والغزال (المطلوب). وإذا كان الشاعر قد جعل الطالب يظفر بمطلوبه في تجربة الوعل، فإنه في تجربة العقاب جعل المطلوب ينجو من طالبه:

فمـــرت عـــلى ريْد فأعنت بعضَها   فخرّتْ على الرجلين أخيبَ خائب
بمَتْلَفـةٍ قَفْـرٍ، كــأن جناحَهــا   إذا نهضت في الجو مخراقُ لاعب(٣٤)

ولئن كان الفرخان قد فقدا أمهما، فالأمومة ما تزال قائمة، لأن الغزال نجا وما يزال ينعم بأمومة الأدماء.

وانتقال الشاعر من تجربة الوعل والصائد إلى تجربة الغزال والعقاب لا يعني الانقطاع بين التجربتين، فما يزال في لغته ما يستبقي تجربة الوعل نابضة، فهو يقول مصوراً حال الفرخين بعد فقدان أمهما:

وقد تُرك الفرخان في جوْف وكرها   ببلـدةٍ لا موْلَى ولا عنـد كـاسب
فريخان ينضاعان في الفجر كلّما   أحسّا دَويّ الريح أو صوْتَ ناعب
فلـم يرها الـفرخان بعد مسائهـا   ولم يهدأ فـي عشهـا من تجاوب(٣٥)

فالفرخان مذعوران يروعهما الريح وصوت الغراب الذي ينعب، وهذا يشبه ما كان قد قاله عن الوعل:

يروع من صوت الغراب فينتحي   مسام الصخور، فهو أهرب هــارب

كما أن اللغة أيضاً تذكرنا بالصائد، فالفرخان قد تركا بلا «كاسب»، وكان الصائد قد سُمِّي «كاسب» شيخ.

نستخلص مما سبق أن القدر الذي نجّى الغزال هو نفسه الذي رصد للعقاب ما كسر جناحها ففقد الفرخان الحماية وأُسلما للذعر والتهديد. وبالمثل فإن القدر مكّن الصائد من الوعل المسن كي ينجو الشيخ من الهلاك جوعاً، كما أنه قيض لأبي عمرو الحية التي ساقته إلى جدثه. والقصيدة لذلك تخلق مواقف انفعالية تتسم بالتركيب، إذ تنتهي نهاية تخلق في نفس المتلقي إحساساً غلاباً بالتعاطف مع الفرخين اللذين ينضاعان في الفجر، وبالتالي مع العقاب التي لقيت حتفها من أجلهما، مع أن هذه العقاب نفسها كانت في لحظة من اللحظات تمثل فكرة الشر، بسبب أنها تريد أن تسلب من الظبية الأم غزالها. وما يقال عن العقاب يقال عن الرامي.

لا يعادل القدر إذن فكرة الشر دائماً، فقد كان ما نظنه شراً أصاب الفرخين خيراً بالنظر إلى الغزال؛ بل إن القتل يمكن أن ينطوي على إنصاف للمقتول، كما رأينا في قصة الوعل الذي قتله الصائد، وكان بذلك ينصف الشيخوخة المهانة التي جعلها الشاعر مصاحبة للوجود الشعري لهذا الوعل نفسه.

تنطوي هذه القصيدة على قيمة وجودية، تتمثل في سعي العقاب من أجل فرخيها وسعي الرامي من أجل شيخه، يقابلهما سعي الوعل والغزال من أجل النجاة، ولا يرتبط الحديث عن الأقدار التي لا تُرد بمعنى القهر أو الاستسلام، فهناك تلازم بين فكرة القدر وفكرة المقاومة، هناك في هذا الشعر ما يشبه التكليف بالنضال وعدم الركون إلى الدعة والاستسلام بحجة أن القضاء لا يرد؛ بل إن حتمية القدر تضفي على المغالبة مسحة بطولية نبيلة، وتخلق في نفس المتلقي تعاطفاً مع أولئك الذين يصارعون من أجل الحياة. حتمية القدر تجابهها في هذا الشعر حتمية المقاومة.

في مواجهة مشكلة القدر يتخذ الشاعر الجاهلي موقفاً مركباً، فهو يتشابه مع الشاعر الرومانسي في النزعة التأملية التي يغلب عليها طابع الحزن، لكنه من خلال هذا التأمل نفسه يثير الإحساس بالمقاومة وعدم الاستسلام، متشابهاً في هذا المنحى مع الشاعر الحداثي. إن حتمية القدر تصاحبها في الشعر الجاهلي حتمية أخرى، هي حتمية المقاومة. يضم الشعر الجاهلي في إهابه – إذن – الموقفين الميتافيزيقي والواقعي دون فصل بينهما.

خاتمة

لا شك أن كتاب الشعر العربي الحديث قد تأثروا، بطرق ودرجات مختلفة، بالثقافة الغربية عموماً، وبالشعر الرومانسي خصوصاً. وقد أولى النقاد هذا الأمر عنايتهم وفصلوا القول فيه، لكنهم لم يلتفتوا بشكل كاف إلى العلاقة بين هؤلاء الشعراء وتراثهم العربي.

وقد لاحظنا خلال قراءتنا للشعر العلاقة الواضحة بين تناول الشاعر العربي الحديث لموضوع القدر وتناول الشعراء القدماء للموضوع ذاته. ومن جهة ثانية لاحظنا أن النصوص الشعرية الحداثية تتراسل، بشكل مباشر أحياناً وغير مباشر أحياناً أخرى، مع مقولات تراثية دينية وشعرية وشعبية تتعلق جميعها بموضوع القدر. بل ولاحظنا التراسل بين هذا الشعر وبعض المقولات الفلسفية التي اتخذت من الخطاب الديني حول القضاء والقدر موقفاً نقدياً، حين يكون هذا الخطاب داعياً إلى إشاعة روح الاستسلام للأمر الواقع.

وحين نقارن بين الشعر العربي الحديث والتراث الشعري القديم، نلاحظ التقاء واضحاً بين الرومانسيين وبعض الشعراء في العصور الإسلامية من حيث النزوع الميتافيزيقي التأملي الذي يشي بميل إلى الإذعان للأقدار، الأمر الذي يحدو بهم جميعاً إلى التعبير عن حالة من الحزن والعدمية الوجودية.

أما الشاعر الجاهلي فإنه، رغم نزعته الوجودية ورغم تسليمه بحتمية القضاء والقدر، يثير لدى المتلقي إحساساً واضحاً بالمقاومة، فهو يسلم مع الشاعر الرومانسي بالوضع

الإنساني المأساوي، لكنه يلتقي مع الشاعر الحداثي في ضرورة المقاومة. إنه يعبر عن حتميتين؛ حتمية القدر، وحتمية المقاومة.

الهوامش

(١) انظر للمؤلف: «تأنيث المذكّر وتذكير المؤنّث: دراسة في الخطاب الأدبي القديم»، **ألف: مجلة البلاغة المقارنة** ١٩ (١٩٩٩)، ص ص ١٢١-١٤٣.

(٢) راجع:

Jaroslav Stetkevych, *The Zephyrs of Najd* (Chicago: University of Chicago Press, 1999).

(٣) يرى عبد القادر القط أن تسمية هذا الشعر باسم الشعر الرومانسي تفتقر إلى الدقة، لأنه على الرغم من بعض أوجه الشبه بينه وبين الشعر الغربي الرومانسي، فإنه لا يطابقه. وقد أطلق القط على هذا الاتجاه في الشعر العربي الحديث مصطلح الشعر الوجداني؛ انظر: عبد القادر القط، **الاتجاه الوجداني في الشعر العربي المعاصر** (القاهرة: مكتبة الشباب، ١٩٧٨)، ص ص ٦-٧.

(٤) قارن مصطفى بدوي، بشكل عابر، بين مطران والشاعر الجاهلي المشهور الشنفرى، من حيث تناولهما للطبيعة، فأعلى من شأن الأول على حساب الثاني! ولا وجه للمقارنة القيمية بين الشاعرين؛ راجع:

M. M. Badawi, *Modern Arabic Poetry* (London: Cambridge UP, 1975), 73.

(٥) والتر أونج، **الشفاهية والكتابية**، ترجمة حسن البنا عز الدين (الكويت: سلسلة عالم المعرفة، ١٩٩٤)، ص ٨٣.

(٦) انظر القصيدة في **المجموعة الكاملة لمؤلفات جبران خليل جبران** (بيروت: دار صادر، ١٩٥٩)، ص ص ٣٤٣-٣٥٤.

(٧) انظر القصيدة في: إيليا أبو ماضي، **من أعمال الشاعر إيليا أبو ماضي** (بيروت: دار كاتب وكتاب، ١٩٨٨)، ص ص ١٣٩-١٧٧.

(٨) **ديوان عبد الرحمن شكري**، تحقيق نقولا يوسف (الإسكندرية: منشأة المعارف، ١٩٦٠)، ص ص ٤٥٧-٤٥٨.

(٩) **المرجع السابق**، ص ٥١٢.

(١٠) **شروح سقط الزند**، تحقيق مصطفى السقا وآخرين (القاهرة: المجلس الأعلى للثقافة، الطبعة الثالثة، ١٩٨٣)، ج ٣، ص ٩٧١.

(١١) **اللزوميات**، تحقيق عبد العزيز الخانجي (القاهرة: مكتبة الخانجي، ١٣٤٢هـ)، ج ١، ص ٢٤٨.

(١٢) **المرجع السابق**، ج ٢، ص ٢٣٤.

(١٣) **ديوان عبد الوهاب البياتي** (بيروت: دار العودة، ١٩٧٩)، ص ص ٣٥٧-٣٥٨.

(١٤) يستخدم علي محمود طه هذا المعجم، الذي يسخر منه البياتي، في قصيدة «أغنية ريفية»

حيث يقول في أولها:

إذا داعب الماء ظل الشجر   وغازلت السحب ضوء القمر

ويقول فيها أيضاً:

ومرّ على النهر ثغر النسيم   يقبّل كل شراع عبر

انظر القصيدة في: **ديوان علي محمود طه** (بيروت: دار العودة، ١٩٧٢)، ص ص ٥٢-٥٣.

(١٥) انظر القصيدة في: نزار قباني، **الأعمال السياسية الكاملة** (بيروت: منشورات نزار قباني، ١٩٨٢)، ج ٣، ص ص ١٥-٢٤.

(١٦) **ديوان صلاح عبد الصبور** (بيروت: دار العودة، ١٩٨٦)، ص ص ٢٩-٣٢.

(١٧) لا يخلو المأثور الشعبي، مع ذلك، من نماذج أخرى مخالفة، من حيث التعبير عن ضرورة السعي وعدم الاستسلام لفكرة القدر. من ذلك مثلاً القول الشعبي المعروف «اسعى يا عبد وانا أسعى معاك»، أو قولهم «الإيد البطالة نجسة». ومع ذلك فإن الغالب على التعبير الشعبي التسليم بقوة القدر الغلابة. وقد أكّد بعض دارسي الأدب الشعبي تلك الظاهرة. انظر: أحمد رشدي صالح، **الأدب الشعبي** (القاهرة: مكتبة النهضة المصرية، ١٩٧١)، ص ص ١٥٥-١٥٩.

(١٨) الزوزني، **شرح المعلقات السبع** (بيروت: دار الجيل، د. ت)، ص٨٦.

(١٩) **المرجع السابق**، ص ١٢٠.

(٢٠) **المرجع السابق**، ص ٢٢٣. تردي: ترمي، جون: أسود، العماء: السحاب، ترتو: تُرخي، مؤيد: مصيبة. مجمل المعنى أن الدهر حين يصيب قومه بمصائبه فكأنه يرمي جبلاً يبلغ السحاب ارتفاعاً، فلا تؤثر فيهم مصائب الدهر. ثم يصف في البيت الثاني هذا الجبل قائلاً إنه ثابت لا تُرخيه الدواهي العظيمة التي تأتي بها حوادث الدهر.

(٢١) تمثل مشكلة القدر موضوعاً أساسياً عند شعراء هذيل. انظر للمؤلف: **الأسلوبية والتقاليد الشعرية: دراسة في شعر الهذليين** (القاهرة: عين للدراسات والبحوث الإنسانية والاجتماعية، ١٩٩٥). والتحليل التالي لقصيدة صخر الغي مستفيد من هذا الكتاب.

(٢٢) **ديوان الهذليين** (القاهرة: الدار القومية للطباعة والنشر، ١٩٦٥)، ج ٢، ص ص ٢٦٦-٢٦٧.

(٢٣) **المرجع السابق**، ج ٢، ص ص ٥١-٥٧. تتكون القصيدة من ثلاثة وعشرين بيتاً. في الأبيات الثلاثة الأولى يرثي الشاعر أخاه أبا عمرو، ثم يتناول في أحد عشر بيتاً صراع الوعل مع القدر الذي يتمثل في صائد يسعى إلى اقتناصه، وينتهي هذا القسم من القصيدة بمصرع الوعل. وفي الجزء الثالث من القصيدة، ويقع في تسعة أبيات، يسرد الشاعر قصة العقاب التي تحاول أن تصطاد غزالاً، لكنها تصطدم بحرف الجبل فينكسر جناحها وتهوي إلى الأرض تاركة صغارها للخوف والجوع. المنا: القدر، حدث: قبر، يُوزي: يُسوّى، وجار: جحر، الجوالب: المقصود ما تجلبه الأقدار، الرُّقى: جمع رقية، الطبائب: جمع طبيبة.

(٢٤) فادر: وعل مسن، التيهورة: أعلى الجبل، الطُّخاف: السحاب الرقيق، عصائب: قطع السحاب.

(٢٥) فتخاء الجناحين: ليّنة الجناحين، لِقْوة: عُقاب.

(٢٦) الطالب والمطلوب، مقصود بهما الصائد والفريسة.

(٢٧) تملّي: تمتّع، حِيَدٌ: أحرُف بارزة، أشرافها: أعاليها، الرّواجب: الأنامل، كانساً: أي داخلاً في كُناسه، والكِناس هو بيت الوعل في أصول الشجر، اللُّهْم: الكبير، أسدْس: وقعت أسنانه.

(٢٨) أتيح له: قُدّر له، تحنّب: احدودب، ساغب: جائع.

(٢٩) الجنا: ما يُجْنى من ثمر، المناحب: المجاهد.

(٣٠) كريمي: يقصد والده، الكواكب: المقصود أوان المطر.

(٣١) أسمر: صفة للنبل، مفتوق: عريض النّصل، اجتزار: قطْع اللحم، الفعفي: الجزّار، المُناهب: المُسرع.

(٣٢) القسب: التمر.

(٣٣) خاتت: انقضّت، أدماء: الظبية الأم.

(٣٤) الرّيد: حرف من الجبل، أعنت: أتلف، والمقصود كُسِر جناحها.

(٣٥) لامولي: أي حيث لا يوجد من يقوم بأمر الفرخين، ينضاعان: يتحرّكان.

الموسيقى العربية الكلاسيكية
ومكانتها في المجتمع العربي المعاصر

شهرزاد قاسم حسن

يصف هذا المقال بعض الأركان الأساسية التي تمثل التراث الموسيقي الفني العربي بصيغته التي وصلتنا من القرن التاسع عشر وبما أضيف إليه في النصف الأول من القرن العشرين.[1] وينتقل المقال إلى وصف بعض الأولويات التي تعتمد عليها الحداثة في موسيقى الشرق الأوسط العربي، عن مفهومها ومكوناتها وعما احتفظت به من الأفكار والقواعد والأصول «القديمة» من ناحية ومن ثم التساؤل عن ماهية العناصر الجديدة التي اقتبست من الغرب من ناحية أخرى.

ويتم التأكيد هنا على الإطار العام لما يمكن تسميته بالثوابت الأساسية لكل من فصيلتي التراث والمعاصرة. والمقال بهذا لا يتطرق إلى التجارب الفردية والتيارات الجديدة التي تنبثق من فصيلتي التراث والمعاصرة. كما أنه، في الحالة هذه، لا يدّعي تمثيل تعقيدات الواقع بكل تشابكاته وحركيته، الأمر الذي يستحق المعالجة بصورة منفصلة. لقد اخترت أن أركز على ما بدا لي تياراً اكتسب صفة العمومية لا يتمثل ببلد معين ولا بأشخاص معينين ومن هنا لم أجد جدوى من ذكر أسماء أو الإشارة إلى لقاءات ميدانية لدعم ما أردت أن أوصله. ويمكن أن يبدو هذا الاختيار تعميماً غير مدعم، إلا أنه في الواقع تركيب لمراقبة ميدانية امتدت أكثر من ثلاثة عقود تبلورت خلالها بعض المفاهيم المطروحة.[2]

***

إذا كان الحفاظ على استمرارية التراث الفني في تعبيراته الحيّة سمة تتصف بها المجتمعات التي نجحت فيها الحداثة، فإن وظيفة النقد لابد أن تلازم عالم التعبير الحديث لكي لا يعتبر كل جديد بحد ذاته حدثاً يجب الاحتفاء به بصرف النظر عمّا يأتي به من قيمة، ولكي لا يكون بالضرورة مرادفاً لصفات التقدم والتطور. صحيح أن الحداثة الحقّة قد تميل إلى تخطي التقاليد وإلى تغيير مسارها وصحيح أن النتاجات الفكرية والفنية التي تدخل ضمن الحديث غالباً ما تفترض وجود نوع من الانشقاق على التقاليد، لمجابهتها ومعارضتها، إلا أن هذا التمرّد لكي يكون مجدياً ينطلق عادة من قاعدة صلبة هي قاعدة التمكن من التراث ومعرفته معرفة جيدة. إضافة إلى هذا كله فإن هدف النتاج الجديد لا يمكن أن يكون إلغاء الحيّز الأقدم، ولا سيما الفني منه، ولا التلاعب به أو تغييره وفقاً لمفاهيم الذوق المعاصر السائد.

ترينا التجارب أن العالم المُعترف بحداثته يفهم جيداً سلطة موروث الموسيقى الفنية

ويسمح له بالازدهار في سياقه الاجتماعي الطبيعي كما يضع له مكانة في مؤسساته الحديثة التي تسعى إلى تعليمه لغرض الإبقاء على توارثه والحفاظ عليه حياً. ذلك لأن التراث الموسيقي، من خلال أدائه، يمثل تلك المنظومة من القيم التي يتجلى من خلالها القلب الرمزي لأي مجتمع. فالتراث الموسيقي لا يزال في عالمنا أفضل ممثل لوعي الجماعة؛ إذ إنه يجدد إحساسها بالانتماء من خلال الحدود الرمزية التي يضعها لتفصل وتميز بين ما يمثل خصوصية الجماعة التي يمثلها وينبثق عنها وما هو غريب يتأتى من نظم أخرى مختلفة عنه أو أجنبية عليه.

يمكن أن تكون هذه المقدمة مدخلاً للتساؤل عن الأسباب التي دعت الثقافة والفكر العربيين في مجال الموسيقى إلى الإحساس بعدم ضرورة المحافظة على تقاليد لا تزال حيّة وإلى عدم الاستمرار في تقديمها إلى جانب غيرها من تعبيرات الحداثة في هذا المجال. وفي الواقع إن التمعن في حالة التراث الفني العربي الذي يُقدم في الحيّز التمثيلي والمؤسساتي الحديث من مهرجانات ومؤتمرات واجتماعات وكذلك عبر وسائل الإعلام، يمكّننا من الاستنتاج بأن هذا الأخير، رغم ثرائه، لم يعد موجوداً في هذه الأوساط، إلا بصورة نادرة، إذا ما تمت مقارنته بما يماثله في بلاد شرقية إسلامية كإيران وجمهوريات آسيا الوسطى أو حتى إذا ما قورن بالاستمرارية المستديمة لأداء الكلاسيكية الأوروبية. ذلك أن هناك تصوّراً يشيع في الأوساط التعليمية والأدائية في الموسيقى، وهو أن التقديم الفعلي للتراث الفني العربي، لمنطقة الشرق الأوسط، يجب أن يمّر عبر عملية تعديل وتطوير وتغيير، لكي يكون أهلاً لأخذ موقع في الحيّز الحديث. ويؤكد الخطاب المتداول – بصيغتيه الشفهية والكتابية – في الأوساط الثقافية والموسيقية على طبيعة علاقة الحداثة مع التراث ويكشف عن أنها علاقة تسعى إلى احتواء التراث وتطويعه عبر آليات توفيقية تؤدي في الواقع إلى إزالة صفتي التعقيد والأصالة عنه. ويُبرّر هذا التطويع بضرورة وضع التراث في متناول الأيدي أولاً ومن ثم دفعه إلى حيّز الحداثة ثانياً. ويمكن أن نضيف إلى ذلك الاعتقاد الصادق الذي يسري والذي مفاده أن التغييرات التي تمثل الإيديولوجية الجمالية للحداثة، والتي تدخل على تقديم خزين التراث الفني، لا تؤثر على المعالم الجوهرية فيه. ومن ثم فإنها لا تجعله، في نظر المحدثين، مختلفاً عن الأصل الذي وصلنا به. وبهذا اتسّم التوجه الذي يشيع اليوم في الشرق العربي بالعمل على إقصاء الإنتاج الموسيقي التقليدي الفني من دائرة التداول بصيغه المتوارثة واعتبار هذا الإقصاء أمراً لا تترتب عليه أية تبعة ثقافية، حضارية أو تاريخية.

ولكن لماذا يُختزل مفهوم الإبداع والتجديد في تغيير القديم؟ وهل يمكن أن تتأسس حداثة جديرة بهذه التسمية عن هذا الطريق؟ وهل يمكن الاستنتاج بأن إشكالية الموسيقى العربية الرسمية لا تكمن في البحث عن صيغ إبداعية جديدة بقدر ما تكمن في صراع لا ضرورة له مع التراث لتملّكه وتغييره بدلاً من وضعه في مكانه الخاص به والسعي إلى إيجاد وسائل أخرى للتجديد؟ وبكلمة أخرى، هل يمكن أن نقول بأن إشكالية الموسيقى العربية الحديثة تكمن في نظرة الجديد لنفسه وموقفه من القديم؟

إن أي تأمل لموضوع الحداثة الموسيقية في المجتمعات العربية المعاصرة التي تمتلك تقاليد تاريخية عريقة، مازالت قيد الممارسة الحيّة، يجب أن يأخذ بنظر الاعتبار بعض

الحقائق التي لعبت دوراً أساسياً في التأثير على مفهوم الحداثة ونوعها في منطقة الشرق الأوسط العربية. فالعالم العربي يواجه اليوم حالة من الانزلاق الثقافي الذي يمكن أن يُعزى إلى ضغط غربي قوي امتد طيلة القرن العشرين وهو وإن كان يُمارَس على الصعيد العالمي فإنه يشتد في المنطقة العربية بفعل التقارب الجغرافي والعلاقات التاريخية لصراع القوى. كما يمكن أن يُعزى، في كثير من الأحوال، إلى فهم خاص لمفهوم الحداثة والإبداع في منطقتنا. ومع توسع الإعلام وانتشاره وطغيان سلطته بشكل لا سابقة له، حصلت انعطافة ثقافية لم يعد من السهل عدم أخذها بنظر الاعتبار. وفي مثل هذا الإطار لم يعد بمقدور أي مؤدٍّ تقليدي ولا أي باحث في أنثروبولوجيا الموسيقى ألا يتساءل عن الواقع المعاصر للموسيقى العربية، عن مفاهيمها الجمالية الجديدة وعن علاقتها بالأصول.

القديم والجديد أو التراث والحداثة

يعتمد هذا المقال، كما سبقت الإشارة، على مقاربة لصنف معين من الموسيقى التي يمكن أن نطلق عليها الموسيقى الفنية التي تشكّل جزءاً مهماً من الموسيقى الحضرية في العواصم الرئيسية العربية. ولهذا الصنف من الموسيقى بضعة مشخّصات يمكن مراقبتها في المجال الاجتماعي. ويمكن، باختصار، اعتبار التعريف الذي يرد أدناه متجاوبا مع الواقع الحضري العربي ومنطَلقا لضم جزء كبير من الخزين الموسيقي المديني إلى صنف الموسيقى الفنية التي يطلق عليها المؤلف «الكلاسيكية».[3] وتكمن مشخصات الفني «الكلاسيكي» في الآتي: ١- المكانة الاجتماعية للفن المعني ونظرة النخبة إليه، ٢- اعتماد التراث الفني على موسيقيين متخصصين يمتلكون مهارات في مجال التراث الذي يحملونه، ٣- الاعتماد على تواتر محلي للمعرفة والتقنية يشكّل جزءاً من ضرورات البنية الاجتماعية، ٤- لكل خزين فني أسلوبه الخاص الذي يظهر عند أدائه ويميزه عن خزين فني آخر، ٥- اعتماد التراث الفني على رعاية توفرها الطبقات المتمكّنة، ٦- ضرورة رسوخ خزين هذه التقاليد في محتواها وأخيراً ارتباط التراث الموسيقي الفني بمجالات ثقافية أخرى في المجتمع كالشعر (انظر Powers). ولا تزال مجمل هذه الشروط تظهر حيّة في التراث الفني لكل من مدينتي حلب ودمشق وفي تقاليد المقام العراقي في بغداد وكركوك على سبيل المثال.

وقد اختار الباحث الفرنسي في علم موسيقى الشعوب جلبرت روجيه إطلاق صفة «الأصالة» على التقاليد التي سبقت دخول الاستعمار الغربي المباشر والتي تتسم عنده بعدم تدخّل المحدثين لإضفاء طابع عصري يتناسب مع الذوق والمفاهيم السائدة (Rouget). ويتوضّح لنا أن هذا الاستخدام لا يعني بأن الفترات السابقة لدخول الاستعمار المباشر في المنطقة العربية مثلاً كانت بالضرورة منقطعة الصلة بالعالم الغربي، وأبرز مثال على ذلك هو عصر النهضة العربية وانفتاحه على مفاهيم الغرب في مجالات مختلفة. إنما المقصود هو تلك الاستعارة المباشرة التي بدأت في الانتشار والتي أسهمت في تغيّر اللغة الموسيقية العربية. وأخيراً لا يجوز الاعتقاد بأن مفهوم «الأصالة» إذا ما استخدم، يعني النظر إلى التقاليد على أنها ثابتة لا تخضع للتأثر والتغيير كما أن الحرص هنا على الحفاظ والاستمرارية لا يتمثل بدعوة إلى التوقف عن الإبداع والتجديد.

في المجال الموسيقي المعاصر يتم تداول مجموعة من المصطلحات والتسميات التي يجدر تحديد معانيها في السياق الخاص لهذا المقال. وبالرغم من أن مصطلحات كالتراث والقديم والتقاليد التي ترد هنا تأتي كلها مترادفات يقصد بها الموسيقى الفنية، إلا أن الحيّز الدلالي لهذه المصطلحات الثلاثة يتجاوز الحالة الفنية «الكلاسيكية» ليغطي أي موروث سواء كان دينياً أم شعبياً. وتشترك المصطلحات التي تمت الإشارة إليها في كونها عادة تقف بتضاد مع مصطلح الحداثة أو الجديد رغم التبدّل والتوسع الدائمين اللذين يطرآن على حيّز الحديث.

ففي كل من مصر وسوريا يطلق هواة الموسيقى أحيانا على الخزين الفني تسمية «موسيقى الطرب» لما تهدف إليه هذه الموسيقى من إيجاد تواصل مع المستمع والتأثير عليه.(٤) ويميل بعض الباحثين إلى استخدام تسمية «موسيقى عصر النهضة» (Abou Mrad; Lagrange). وكلتاهما تسميتان يجري التعارف على استخدامهما عند الإشارة إلى التقاليد السورية والمصرية. أما في العراق فمن غير المعروف تسمية الموسيقى الفنية التي تتمثل بالمقام العراقي بموسيقى الطرب أو بتراث عصر النهضة رغم أن التسمية لا تتناقض مع هذين المصطلحين من الناحيتين الوظيفية والتاريخية. يُستخدم مفهوم الحداثة بصيغته الحالية ليماثل الجديد وليعارض الموسيقى التقليدية التي باتت تُعتبر قديمة. وفي الواقع فإن مفاهيم القديم والحديث ليست حصراً على الفترة المعاصرة كما أن مفهوم الحداثة ليس مفهوما خاصاً بالغرب. فالقديم والحديث في الموسيقى كلاهما كانا مصدراً للصراع في الحضارة العربية-الإسلامية. وفي كل الأزمنة كان هناك تيار يمثل القديم وآخر يخرج عنه ليمثل الجديد. ومن الأمثلة الشائعة التي وصلتنا، من القرن العاشر عبر عدد من المصادر، هو النزاع التاريخي الذي اشتهر بين القديم الذي كان يمثله إبراهيم الموصلي (ت ٨٠٤) وابنه إسحق (٧٦٧-٨٥٠) بمقابل التيار الحديث المتمثل بشخص الأمير إبراهيم ابن المهدي(٧٧٩-٨٣٩) أخي الخليفة هارون الرشيد (الأصبهاني وFarmer).

تشير الحداثة المقصودة في سياق هذا المقال إلى التيار الذي استُحدث في القرن العشرين بهدف الربط التوفيقي بين بعض العناصر التقليدية للثقافة الموسيقية العربية وأخرى مقتبسة من الموسيقى الأوروبية. وتكمن بعض العناصر المقتبسة في استلهام التنظيم الصوتي الأوروبي، وفي النزوع التدريجي نحو النظام الصوتي المعدّل وإدخال الآلات الموسيقية الغربية وتوسيع حجم الفرقة التقليدية، ثم تغيير دور المؤدي الفردي، والعمل على تقليص مفاهيم الارتجال والتصرف الشخصي، وتشجيع الغناء الجماعي، إضافة إلى تثبيت الموسيقى عن طريق التدوين وكذلك الاستعاضة التدريجية عن المصطلحات العربية بأخرى أوروبية. تكشف اللقاءات المختلفة مع المؤدين والمختصين والمثقفين المهتمين في مجال الموسيقى أن الخزين الفني العربي المجدَّد يُصَنَّف في نظرهم ضمن التراث كما يُصَنَّف في الوقت ذاته ضمن ما يسمى بالتراث المطوّر الذي يُنظر إليه كشكل من أشكال الحداثة. وهكذا فإن «التراث المطوّر» يمثل فصيلتي التراث والحداثة في وقت واحد.

ويبدو أن جل إشكالات الحيّز الموسيقي العربي المعاصر تدور حول العلاقة بين الموسيقى الفنية التقليدية وبين متطلبات حيّز الحداثة. ويجب أن لا ينسينا التبسيط النظري أن جسوراً تمتد بين الطرفين، الأمر الذي يسمح بعبورها في الاتجاهين. فهناك الأجيال الشابة التي تأتي من العوالم التقليدية لاكتساب معارف علمية تسمح بالاعتراف وبالارتقاء الاجتماعي وهناك المؤسسات الحديثة المعنية بتنظيم الحياة الموسيقية والتي تحتاج إلى ملئها باستخدام خزين تراثي بعد أن يمرّ عبر مفاهيم الحداثة التي ذكرت أعلاه.

في الجزء الأول من القرن الماضي كان يتمتّع كل من هذين العالمين الموسيقيين – القديم والحديث – بدرجة كبيرة من الاستقلالية. ثم بدأ التقارب بينهما أولاً في مصر، التي هي الأقرب إلى التأثير الأوروبي، وانتقل منها تدريجياً إلى بلدان عربية أخرى في الفترة الواقعة بين العشرينيات والسبعينيات من القرن الماضي. حتى بدأ الاختلاف يضمحل تدريجياً بين الموسيقى «الكلاسيكية» وبين الأشكال الجديدة التي بدأت في الظهور تجاوباً مع متطلبات تلك الفترة. وتحوّل التجاور بين الأنماط المستقلة المختلفة التي كانت تتعايش سوية، بمرور الوقت إلى نمط أدائي توفيقي قضى على الكلاسيكيات المحلية. بطبيعة الحال يمكن القول إن هذا التغيير لم يكن وقفاً على الموسيقى الفنية بل إن جزءاً من التراث الموسيقي الشعبي العربي خضع لنفس عمليات التغيير، بالرغم من أن الجزء الأكبر من الخزين الشعبي يؤدى بدرجة كبيرة من الاستقلالية خارج إجراءات التطوير.(٥)

والواقع أن أولويات كل من العالمين، التقليدي والحديث، لا تتموضع في المكان نفسه. ولفهم الحالة الراهنة للموسيقى العربية في منطقة الشرق الأوسط سوف أقوم بتقسيم الحيّز الموسيقي العربي، مبسطة إياه، إلى فصيلتين متميزتين رغم وجود حركة تبادل مستمر قائمة بين الفصيلتين. فمن ناحية هناك الموسيقى التقليدية بشقيها الكلاسيكي-الحضري – التي يدخل فيها الشعبي أحيانا – ومن ناحية ثانية هناك حيّز الحداثة المتمثل بالمؤسسات التي تنظم الحياة الموسيقية وتوجهها. ما هي أولويات هذين العالمين وما هو إدراك كل منها للآخر وما هي طبيعة التفاعل بينهما؟

الاختلاف بين الحيّزين التقليدي والحديث

الحيّز الموسيقي التقليدي

رغم انحسار الكثير من العناصر المكوّنة للتقاليد الفنية العربية، كفقدانها لبعض أجزاء الخزين المكوّن لها وشيئاً من حيويتها الأصيلة أو من أسلوب أدائها إضافة إلى فقدانها لأبرز مؤديها القدماء، فإن المتبقي منها لا يزال على درجة كبيرة من الأهمية. ولهذه التقاليد في المجتمعات المدينية للشرق الأوسط، ولا سيما في سوريا والعراق، جمهورها المتُضلع في معرفة تقنياتها ووظائفها ومعانيها. وهذا الجمهور

لا يزال على صلة بهذه التقاليد ولا يزال يشعر بحاجة إليها فهي تملأ في نفسه الحاجة الجمالية والعاطفية التي تؤثر على فرديته كما تعزز عنده مشاعر الانتماء الاجتماعي. وبالرغم من التغييرات الاجتماعية الكبيرة التي طرأت على الحياة في القرن السابق فإن هذه التقاليد في مجملها مستمرة في التأثير على شعور الأفراد والجماعات.

يتضمن الحيّز التقليدي عدداً من التقاليد الفنية «الكلاسيكية» التي تتعايش مع أعداد كبيرة جداً من التقاليد الشعبية التي لم تخضع كلها إلى التعداد. وتخضع الصنوف المختلفة لهذه التقاليد إلى تقسيمات لا يمكن حصرها أحياناً داخل حدود الدول القومية الحديثة لأنها غالباً ما تتجاوزها. فالتقاليد الفنية، التي هي موضوع هذا المقال، يمكن أن تصنّف بصورة سريعة إلى نوعين: فمنها ما تشترك فيه أغلب البلاد العربية كالموشح الذي يُعرف ويُدرّس ويؤدى في المدن الأساسية، ثم هناك التقاليد الفنية المحلية المتمثلة في المراكز التاريخية الكبيرة كحلب ودمشق والقاهرة وبغداد والموصل. فلكل من هذه المدن خزين يميّزها بمحتواه أو بأسلوبه الجمالي والأدائي الخاص بها. وتجدر الإشارة إلى أن التقاليد الكلاسيكية المحلية هي ثمرة تشترك فيها دون تمييز كافة الأديان والطوائف التي تعيش في المنطقة الواحدة، علاوة على كونها، في الوقت ذاته، جزءاً من التقاليد العربية-الإسلامية في النظرية والبناء والمفاهيم الدائرة حول الأداء ودور المؤدي وعلاقة الفن بالمجتمع. ولعل هذا الواقع هو الذي يفسّر استخدام الأجيال القديمة لمصطلح الموسيقى الشرقية لتسمية كل من التقاليد الخاصة بها وتلك التي تنتمي إلى الحيّز العربي الإسلامي. وبهذا فإن الأجيال التقليدية تعبّر عن وعي عميق للانتماء إلى حيّز ثقافي شرقي إسلامي واسع كان يساعد في الوقت ذاته في التأكيد على الخصوصيات البنيوية والتقنية والجمالية الخاصة بكل من هذه التقاليد.

ولم يبدأ مفهوم الحيّز الشرقي في العالم العربي بالتقلص إلا بعد سقوط الإمبراطورية العثمانية وظهور الحركة القومية عند العرب مما أدى إلى تضاؤل تدريجي وانحسار للعلاقة التي كانت قائمة بين العالم العربي وامتداداته التاريخية في العالم الإسلامي حتى انقطعت الصلة تماماً بين العالمين. ولم تعد تعرف الكثير من الأجيال الجديدة شيئاً عن وضع الثقافات الإسلامية التي تنتمي إليها حتى إنها عندما تواجه إشكالات الحداثة لا تجد نموذجاً تستلهمه منه غير النموذج الغربي. ذلك لأن الثقافة الموسيقية في العصور الاستعمارية وضعت نفسها في موقع متناقض، فهي من ناحية توجهت نحو إقامة روابط جديدة بين الثقافة الموسيقية والقومية ومن ناحية أخرى اعتمدت اعتماداً كبيراً على النموذج الغربي لوضع أسس جديدة للثقافة الموسيقية العربية، متجاهلة بذلك العالم الشرقي الإسلامي برمته الذي كان، لقرون طويلة، مرجعاً مشتركاً لجميع الثقافات التي كانت جزءاً منه (انظر Hassan).

الاختلاف في معنى مصطلح الموسيقى واستخدامه

إن انتشار استخدام مصطلح «الموسيقى» بين الموسيقيين والباحثين والمفكرين والكتاب المعاصرين وشيوع استخدامه في وسائل الإعلام وتعميمه في كافة المؤسسات الحديثة المعنية بأمر الموسيقى، لتسمية وتعريف الأشكال المختلفة للتعبيرات «الصوتية» التي تصدر من الحنجرة أو تلك التي تؤدى بواسطة الآلات الموسيقية، يجب أن لا ينسينا أن هذا المصطلح لا يشيع استخدامه بالضرورة في مجمل العالم التقليدي اللاأوروبي الذي غالباً ما يعتمد على مسميّات أخرى للظاهرة التي نسميها نحن بالموسيقى. والتسميات التي تطلق على النوع الصوتي المؤدى، سواء انبثق من الحنجرة أو من الآلة، وتلك التي يُسمى بها المؤدي وغيرها التي تخص مجالات الأداء وتأثيره، ظاهرة متوغلة في أعماق المجتمع ومرتبطة بالمفاهيم والمعارف والممارسات الاجتماعية والفعاليات الإنسانية كالشعر واللغة والدين والطقوس وتكشف عن الارتباط المركّب للظاهرة الصوتية بأخرى غير صوتية. ولهذا فإن معظم المجتمعات القديمة والتقليدية التي تعتبر ظاهرة الموسيقى جزءاً من سياق كلي متعدد الأبعاد تجد لما يمكن أن نطلق عليه بالموسيقى مصطلحات أخرى يمكن أن تحمل كل مرة دلالة مختلفة تكيفاً مع السياق الذي تنبثق منه.

يقتصر استخدام مصطلح الموسيقى في العالم العربي-الإسلامي على التقاليد الدنيوية. ومع هذا فإن البحوث الميدانية كشفت لنا أن الكثير من حملة التقاليد الفنية الدنيوية لا يستخدمونه، أو أنهم يستخدمونه إلى جانب مصطلحات أخرى. وفي الواقع فإن جزءاً واسعاً من العالم التقليدي بما فيه المنطقة التي تُعنى بها هذه المقالة، لا يجد حاجة لاستخدام مصطلح الموسيقى. وهو في حالة معرفته بوجود هذا المصطلح لا يراه دقيقاً في التعبير عن طبيعة الفعاليات الصوتية التي يمارسها.

وهذا الواقع الذي ينطبق على الموسيقى الفنية يسري أيضا، وبدرجة كبيرة، على الموسيقى الشعبية. فالكثير من المؤدين في العالم التقليدي الفني، لا يمكن أن يفهم أننا نعتبره موسيقياً ونسمي ما يؤديه بموسيقى. وغالباً ما تسبب له معرفة ذلك اضطرابا في نظرته إلى نفسه وإلى هويته لأن دوره الاجتماعي والوظيفي مركب من عناصر كثيرة. صحيح أن الأجيال الجديدة من العالم التقليدي على علم بظاهرة الموسيقى وهي لا تمانع في أغلب الأحيان من أن تكون جزءاً منها، مضحية بتراث ثقافي ودلالي ولغوي غني، إلا أنها تقوم بذلك وهي راضية لكي تجد لها موقعاً في عالم المؤسسات الحديثة.

ولا تزال هناك في العالم التقليدي تسميات كثيرة التداول لم ينقطع استخدامها في الثقافة العربية، كما أنها تعرف وتستخدم في الثقافات الإسلامية الأخرى إلى جانب تسميات محلية خاصة بذخيرة محلية معينة. وتحلّ مجمل التسميات المحلية وتلك التي يشترك بها العالم العربي الإسلامي محلّ مصطلح الموسيقى وتلاءم مع السياق الذي تستخدم به.

فالإنشاد مثلاً من المصطلحات المتداولة التي استُخدمت منذ الفترة السابقة للإسلام. والمصطلح، في المجال الذي يخصنا، يشير أولاً إلى قراءة الشعر وإلى

قراءته بالنغم. ففي العالم الذي تتم فيه نقل المعرفة شفاهاً فإن نقل الشعر عبر اللحن غالباً ما يكون ذا فاعلية، لا سيما أن وجود الوزن والقافية يساعد على ذلك.(٦) ثم إن الإنشاد هو التسمية التي تشيع لتسمية كل ما يؤدى في المناسبات الدينية. ولكنه أيضاً، وفي الوقت ذاته، يمثل ذلك الجزء من الإنشاد الديني الذي يؤدى موقعاً من قبل الجماعة (كمثل التواشيح الدينية والأشغال التي ترد في الأذكار). وفي المجال غير الديني يشير الإنشاد إلى الجانب الموقّع الذي يؤدى من قبل المجموعة. وهكذا فإن إطلاق هذه التسمية هو أكثر دقة من استخدام مصطلح الموسيقى العام الذي لا يعتبر مرادفاً حقيقياً، لعدم تمكنه من التمييز بين الاختلافات التي وردت الإشارة إليها.

وهناك أيضاً مصطلح «القراءة» الذي يُطلق بطبيعة الحال على أنواع القراءات القرآنية دالاً على أهمية النص المقروء وعلى أولويته. وقد وجد هذا المصطلح امتدادا لاستخدامه في الذخيرتين الدينية والدنيوية وفي المجالين الفني والشعبي على حد سواء. وإلى وقت قريب جداً كان أداء المقام العراقي يسمى قراءة وكان مؤدي المقام يعرف بالقارئ. وفي المجال الشعبي يعتبر أداء الأُبوذية – وهي صيغة غنائية تميّز المناطق الجنوبية لوادي الرافدين – قراءة وليس غناء، ويسمى مؤديها بالقارئ. ويتوضح من هذين المثالين أن أداء هذه الأنواع الغنائية لم يسمى «قراءة» بسبب من أهمية الكلمة فيها. بل إن المكانة الرفيعة لهذا الفن في أعين ممارسيه، وابتعاده عن الابتذال سوية مع الأثر الذي يتركه عند السامع – الذي قد يصل إلى البكاء – هو الذي يبرر هذه التسمية. وباختصار فإن الاحترام الكبير الذي يُولى للأنواع الغنائية التي ورد ذكرها والذي قد يكون سبباً في اعتبار أدائها قراءة، يتأتى من القيم التي ينقلها ومن العواطف النبيلة التي يثيرها.

ويمكن الإكثار من الأمثلة من المجال الاصطلاحي المرتبط بالأداء الصوتي في التقاليد المختلفة التي ترينا أن كلمة موسيقى غير معروفة في عدد كبير من التقاليد. إن موضوع التسمية والمفاهيم المتعلقة بها هو موضوع حقيقي لأنه يكشف عن طبيعة العلاقة التي يقيمها المجتمع بين الاسم والمسمى. إن اختلاف المصطلح المستخدم لتعريف الظاهرة الصوتية يكشف عن اختلاف أساسي بين العالمين التقليدي والحديث وهو اختلاف يجدر التعمق في دراسته.

الموسيقى الفنية كمنظومة متكاملة

ما الذي يمكن أن نستخلصه من دراسة معمّقة لما كُتب نظرياً عن التراث الفني للموسيقى العربية-الإسلامية، وما هو الاستنتاج الذي نتوصل إليه بعد التمعن في أداء هذه الموسيقى؟ يُمكن أن نشبّه التراث الفني العربي-الإسلامي بمنظومة تتجلى عملياً عند الأداء.(٧) وتتمثل هذه المنظومة في شبكة من المفاهيم المتصلة ببعضها والتي يمكن إرجاعها إلى مجالات نظرية، تقنية، إجرائية، وظيفية، اجتماعية وجمالية متعددة تشمل: ١- نظريات التنظيم الصوتي والإيقاعي وقوانين

الصيغ الموسيقية ٢- الإجراءات والتقنيات التي يضعها التراث تحت تصرف المؤدي ليتعامل معها عند الأداء ووفق حاجته للتعبير ٣- الدور الإبداعي للمؤدي الذي يجمع بين أداء ما هو مُلزم وبين ما يضيفه شخصياً، الأمر الذي يحوله إلى مؤد-مؤلف ٤- الأداء-الإبداع المرن باختيار النقل الشفاهي الذي لا يتناقض مع وجود النظرية العربية-الإسلامية المركبة والدقيقة التي تسمح للمؤدي بتطويعها بعد استبطانها كاملة ٥- ضرورة تفاعل المؤدي التقليدي مع جمهور من أجل إيصال التعبير الصوتي والتأثير على عواطف المستمع.

ينطلق مفهوم المنظومة من فكرة الارتباط العضوي لمجالاتها المختلفة بعضها ببعض وتحرّكها سوية في وقت واحد وهو وقت الأداء. وتعتمد المنظومة على مبدأ النظام المفتوح الذي يسمح بتحريك أي جزء من أجزائها بواسطة التغيير والإلغاء والإضافة وغيرها من الوسائل. ويفرض منطق المنظومة الالتزام بأطر الصيغة، بمسارها وبقوانينها من ناحية، والسماح للمؤدي بالتعبير عن نفسه بصورة حرّة من ناحية أخرى. وبهذا يمكن القول إن قانوناً ذا أبعاد متعددة يتحكم بالنظام التقليدي ويشتمل على احترام القواعد والمسارات، على الدفع إلى الإبداع والإضافة الشخصية والتعبير عن ارتباط قوي بالجماعة التي ينتمي إليها المؤدي لإيصال التأثير إليها.

إذا كان الوصف المتكامل للأجزاء التي تكوّن المنظومة والنظر إلى العلاقات بين أجزائها ليس هو الهدف الذي بُنيت عليه فكرة هذا المقال، فإن التطرّق إلى بعض عناصر هذه المنظومة وآلياتها التي تخدم فكرة المقال يكون ضرورياً لإبراز التغيير الذي طرأ، تدريجيا، على الموسيقى الفنية في العالم العربي خلال القرن العشرين ولا سيما تلك التي تجسدت في أوائل الثلاثينيات من القرن الماضي.

الموسيقى الفنية موسيقى أداء

الموسيقى الفنية للمنطقة العربية-الإسلامية موسيقى أداء، وهذا يعني أن خصائصها التي ثُبتت نظرياً، إضافة إلى تلك التي ترد في مفاهيم الموسيقيين، تتجلى كاملة عند الاستماع إليها. وهي بهذا تعتمد على المؤدي الذي يُفترض فيه أن يكون على معرفة جيدة بالأصول وأن يتمسك بالمسار المفروض للصيغ التي يؤديها وبقوانينها المُلزمة، سواء كانت الصيغ مؤلفة كالموشح أو نصف مؤلفة كالمقام العراقي. وتُتيح آليات التراث للمؤدي التعبير عن ذاتيته بحرية تامة كما تسمح له بتطويع القطعة أو الإضافة إليها. إن الدور المنوط بالمؤدي دور صعب لأنه مزدوج يجمع بين أدائه لعمل متوارث وتقديمه لهذا العمل من خلال تأويل شخصي له عبر استخدام الوسائل التي تضعها التقاليد تحت تصرفه. وبهذا يصبح المؤدي مؤلفاً في الوقت نفسه. وهذا الدور المنوط به، من حيث إمكانية التغييرات ونوعها التي يُسمح له بإدخالها، يتجاوز الدور المعترف به للمؤدي في الحضارة الأوروبية. وتظهر البراعة التقنية للمؤدي-المؤلف في بعد آخر من الأداء التقليدي وهو تفاعله مع متطلبات اللحظة المعنية مكيّفاً إياها للمناسبة والمكان ومستوى الجمهور. نجد غالباً أن المؤدي التقليدي لا يأتي للأداء ومعه برنامج ثابت غير قابل للتغيير، بل يأتي

بمشروع برنامج يحتمل كل أشكال التكييف. وإذا ما شعر المؤدي بأن الجمهور الحاضر ليس على درجة كبيرة من المعرفة بالخزين الذي كان ينوي تقديمه، أو العكس، فبإمكانه أن يغيّر من القطع الموسيقية أو من نصها الشعري أو أن يؤديها بصورة مختصرة. كل هذا يعتمد على مدى تجاوب الجمهور ومعرفته بالخزين. لأن هدف اللحظة الحيّة للأداء يكمن في إيجاد تجاوب مع الجمهور وهو الكفيل الوحيد للوصول إلى حالة الطرب التي هي الغاية القصوى لهذه الموسيقى.

إن تكييف الخزين وإدخال تغييرات عليه عند الأداء هما اللذان يفسّران الاختلافات التي نجدها في أداء العمل الواحد، الأمر الذي يمكن أن نجده عند المؤدي الواحد للعمل نفسه. وهذه المقاربة من العمل الموسيقي لا تجد مكاناً لها عند المحدثين.

ينظر المحدثون إلى الأداء نظرة مغايرة تماماً. إذ إنهم يعتبرون حركية الأداء وانفتاح المنظومة التقليدية للتكييف من المساوئ الكبيرة للموسيقى التقليدية الفنية. بينما تكمن إحدى أهم سمات الحداثة في نظرهم في السيطرة على الاختلافات الفردية، على أمل أن تتم إعادة أداء النص الموسيقي وعند كل أداء بحد أدنى من التغيير أو التأويل. وبهذا فالمحدثون يفضلون الوصول إلى صيغة للنص الموسيقي هي أقرب إلى الثبات يتم فيها الحد من الحرية الكبيرة للمؤدي المنفرد، خوفا من الفوضى والاختلاف.

بعض تقنيات الإبداع التقليدي: الارتجال وتعدد أصوات المصاحبة

في الأوساط الثقافية العربية وفي المعاهد التعليمية الخاصة بالموسيقى العربية يسري الاعتقاد أن الموسيقى العربية موسيقى ثابتة لم تتغير عبر الأزمنة، يوازيه رأي مكمّل، وإن كان يناقضه، يقول بعدم اعتماد هذه الموسيقى على أية قاعدة لأنها لا تمتلك بنية ولا تعتمد على صيغة؛ أي أنها، بكلمة أخرى، موسيقى ارتجال كليّة، بالمعنى السلبي للكلمة.(٨) وكلا هذين الموقفين مبني على اعتقادات تعتمد على تحليل الأساس النظري ولا تنطلق من تحليل واقع الأداء الموسيقي. فالموسيقى العربية الفنية تعرف الصيغ المؤلفة كما تعرف أيضاً الأشكال الحرة وشبه الحرة. إلا أن جزءاً كبيراً من الخزين الفني العربي للمنطقة يدخل ضمن صنف وسيط تتجاور فيه خصائص الصنفين السابقين؛ أي أنه يجمع بين مسار مُلزم وبين إمكانية لإضافة شخصية. وتحتمل هذه الفصائل الثلاث، بدرجات متفاوتة، التغيير عبر مفهوم الارتجال بالمعنى العام للكلمة الذي يتضمن ١- استخدام التنويع الذي يمكن أن يدخل على أي ركن من أركان الموسيقى كاللحن مثلاً ٢- استخدام الزخرفة والتزويق ٣- الارتجال انطلاقاً من اللحن المؤدى ٤- الارتجال المقيّد والارتجال الكلي (وكلاهما يظهران في التقاسيم).

تسمح هذه الوسائل والآليات بالوصول إلى مجموعة كبيرة من التركيبات التي يمكن أن تتطوع مع حاجة المؤدي إذا ما لجأ إليها، وهي التي تسمح له بتحقيق جمالية فردية تعمل على إيصال تأثيرها إلى المستمع. فالتقسيم الذي يؤدى من قبل إحدى الآلات، ولكن ضمن فرقة تؤدي عملاً معروفاً يعتمد على لحن معين وعلى مقام

مشخص، يمكن أن يمثّل تنوعاً للقاعدة اللحنية أو الإيقاعية للعمل الأساسي. أما التقسيم الذي يعتمد في كل أبعاده على الاختيار الحر لمؤديه، فهو أكثر الأشكال تجريداً في الموسيقى الفنية العربية وهو على درجة كبيرة من الأهمية لأنه يمثل أعلى أنواع التعبير الممكن للحرية الفردية في الموسيقى رغم ارتباطه بالقواعد والأعراف التي تشكل القاعدة النظرية الأساسية له.(٩)

من الأمور المتعارف عليها في المصادر المكتوبة أن الموسيقى العربية أحادية اللحن monody أي إنها تتمثل في تتابع أفقي للأصوات. وقد تصاحب آلة موسيقية هذا اللحن الأحادي الذي يمكن أن يؤدى من قبل مجموعة غنائية تؤدي صوتاً واحداً. ولكن إذا ما تمت مصاحبة اللحن الأحادي بمجموعة من الآلات، عادة خمس أو ست آلات، فإن الناتج الصوتي يعتمد على تقنية أخرى تسمى بالهتروفونية وتصنف ضمن تعددية الأصوات. ونادراً ما تتم الإشارة إلى أهمية الهتروفونية ودورها في أوساط الموسيقى العربية، ويرجع السبب إلى طبيعة هذه التعددية التي تُعرّف على أنها غير مقصودة أو عارضة، أي أن نتائجها غير معروفة مسبقاً. وهذه التعددية تؤدّى بتزامن للأصوات يختلف عن الأداء الجماعي لصوت واحد. ورغم أن الأداء المتزامن فيها يعتمد على مادة لحنية مصدرها واحد، فإن الأصوات التي تنبثق من كل مصدر صوتي تختلف باختلاف عدد المصادر الصوتية التي تكوّن الفرقة التقليدية كالتخت الشرقي أو الجالغي البغدادي. ويعرّف بيير بوليز الهتروفونية على أنها ظاهرة تنضيد، على البنية الأولى، عدد من البنى الصوتية التي تختلف في مظهرها عن البنية الصوتية الأساسية (Boulez, 135-36). إن هذه التعددية الصوتية التي تعتمد كثيراً على لحظة الأداء والتي تختلف باختلاف تلك اللحظة، لا تُؤخذ كثيراً بعين الاعتبار في العالم العربي ولا يُنظر إليها بجدية بسبب عدم إمكانية تخمين نتاجها الصوتي النهائي بصورة مسبقة وقاطعة. إلا أن استخدامها في الأدد اء التقليدي العربي والإسلامي هو الذي أعطى هذه الموسيقى طابعها الجمالي الغني والمتميز بحركيته.

تمكّن تقنيات اختلاف الأصوات، المتمثل في الهتروفونية، عازفي الآلات الذين يصاحبون المغني من التصرف بحرية ضمن جو من التوافق الذي يقول عنه علي جهاد راسي إنه يمكن أن يكون: «أداة جبّارة لاستحضار الوجد والنشوة المتمثلتين في الطرب» ويضيف أن هناك إحساساً عاماً بـ«أن التفاعل الهتروفوني للمضمون الموسيقي ينشط الطاقة في الأداء الجماعي بما يعطي من أهمية لكل فرد في الأداء. وهو في الوقت ذاته يربط الأدوار المختلفة بعضها ببعض في وحدة عضوية» (Racy, 80-82).

وقد اهتم عالم الإثنوميوزيكولوجي الحديث بالتركيز على دراسة الأداء، في الموسيقى الفنية وفي غيرها، الأمر الذي يمكن أن يساهم في إعادة تشخيص وتسمية التقنيات المستخدمة في مختلف الموسيقات العربية التقليدية وهي كثيرة ومتنوعة ويساعد الانطلاق من مراقبة الأداء على اكتشاف الكثير من صفات التعقيد والتكامل الكامنة في الموسيقى الفنية التي يُنظر إليها غالباً بدرجة كبيرة من التبسيط.(١٠)

شفاهية النقل والحفاظ على حرية الاختلاف

إن ما يجمع بين التقاليد العربية الإسلامية قاطبة (الشعبية منها والفنية) هو تناقلها الشفاهي. ورغم اعتماد هذه التقاليد على نظرية بالغة في التعقيد فإن كلاً من تناقل هذه النظرية وتواتر تقنيات أدائها يتم عادة بصورة شفهية.

وكما يمكن أن يلاحظ هو أن الجيل الشاب المتعلم في المعاهد الموسيقية كثيراً ما يُرجع أسباب اللجوء إلى الشفاهية إلى انعدام أنظمة التدوين في الموسيقى العربية الإسلامية. ويناقض هذا الرأي بعض المخطوطات العربية التي تشير إلى نظم تدوين كانت قد عرفت منذ القرن التاسع الميلادي. ويبدو أن اللجوء إلى التدوين القديم، الذي يمكن أن نعتبره نسبياً، شأنه شأن التدوين الحديث، كان يتم في الغالب لأغراض الشرح النظري. فقد استخدم ابن المنجم (ت ٩١٢) نظام المجرى للتدوين الوصفي الذي حدد فيه مواقع الأصابع على الوتر واسم الوتر فكأنه يقال مطلق في مجرى الوسطى وعلى هذه الشاكلة يتم تحديد موقع الأصابع على الأوتار الأربعة (ابن المنجم). واستخدم الكندي(٨٠١–٨٧٣) الحروف الأبجدية لتسمية الأصوات (الكندي). علاوة على ذلك فإن بعض النصوص القديمة تكشف عن إمكانية اللجوء إلى التدوين كمصدر لنقل الاداء. فيستخدم الأصبهاني مثلاً في **كتاب الأغاني** (٨٩٧–٩٦٧) التدوين اللفظي مضافاً إليه نوع الإيقاع المستعمل. ويقول على سبيل المثال «غنى البيتين الأولين ابن محرز خفيف ثقيل أول بالبنصر على مذهب إسحاق» (الأصبهاني، جزء ١١، ص ١٦). واعتماداً على هذا النوع من التدوين تمكّن إسحاق الموصلي من أداء إحدى مؤلفات غريمه إبراهيم بن المهدي.

إن إشاعة استخدام التدوين في حضارة تعتمد على التكييف عند الأداء – وتعتَبر المؤدي مؤلفاً آنياً تفترض فيه المناورة من التمكّن في تحريك مجموعة العناصر وتغيير الأركان في الوقت المناسب – يمكن أن يكون عاملاً لتثبيت الصيغة الموسيقية المؤداة بصورة نهائية، إلا إذا تم التأكيد على اعتبار التدوين المستخدم إطاراً نسبياً. وعندئذ يمكن تقييم عملية التثبيت الكتابية للصيغ التقليدية على أنها عملية تقريبية ترتبط بمؤلَف معيّن وتعبّر عن أداء محدد في الزمان، مما لا يجوز اعتماده مصدراً لتعميم أداء ذلك العمل. ولابد من الإشارة إلى أن جوهر النقاشات، التي تدور بين الموسيقيين الجدد، تكشف أن الشفاهية، التي تتسبب في زيادة النسخ الأدائية للعمل الواحد، هي التي تزعج المحدثين لأنها تناهض رغبتهم في وضع أساس لمرجعية موضوعية واحدة وثابتة لكل قطعة موسيقية لا تتغير بتغير السياق ولا تختلف إلا بمقدار اختلاف مؤد عن آخر. ويمثل هذا الفهم إحدى المفاصل الأساسية للصراع بين الأداء التقليدي وبين طموحات المدرسة الجديدة. أما الموسيقى العربية–الإسلامية التقليدية فإنها إذا كانت قد اختارت في نموها وفي طريقة نقلها الشفاهية، شأنها شأن معظم التقاليد الكبيرة والصغيرة في العالم الخارج عن الحيز الغربي، فلأن هذا وحده يمكن أن يحمي خصوصيتها التي جاء وصفها أعلاه، ولأن الشفهية تمثل الوسيلة الملائمة لتحقيق الغايات الجمالية والتأثيرية لهذه الموسيقى. كما أن الحضارة التي تضع أولويتها في فكرة التكييف الآني في الزمان والمكان وتضع في متناول أيدي المؤدي فرصة

التعبير بحرية عبر وسائل تمكّنه من تغيير النص الموسيقي بهدف الوصول إلى حالة تفاعل آنيّ مع جمهور الحاضرين، لا يمكنها الحفاظ على المقومات ذات الأثر الجمالي إلا باعتماد الشفهية، جزئياً أو كلياً.

إن ما يحدث على أرض الواقع في يومنا هذا يرينا أن التدوين لا يزال غير كاف للتعبير عن الموسيقى الحيّة، وإن كان من يستخدمه يطمح إلى ذلك نظرياً. فالتعليم الحالي الذي يعتمد التدوين، يلجأ أيضاً في كثير من الأحيان إلى الاستماع الشفهي ليوفق بينه وبين النص المكتوب، الذي يُعتمد، في الحالة هذه، كهيكل للعمل لا غير.

عامل التأثير والطرب: تفاعل بين المؤدي والمستمع

يضع التراث تحت تصرف المؤدي، وكما سبقت الإشارة، مجموعة من الوسائل الإجرائية التي تساعده في إيجاد التفاعل مع المستمع والوصول إلى حالة الطرب المتوخاة. إذ إن المستمع العربي يتوقع من الأداء الفني أن يؤثر على مشاعره كفرد وكجماعة. وتظهر الأهمية المعطاة إلى ركن التأثير هذا، الذي يعيره محبو التراث الفني أهمية كبيرة، في شهادات كثيرة متأتية من المراقبة الميدانية أو من شهادات الأحياء التي تعزز ما ورد في الكتابات القديمة عن أهمية موضوع تأثير الموسيقى على المستمع. فإذا ما وجد المؤدي البارع أمامه جمهوراً من المتعمقين بأسرار الفن الذي يؤديه، فإن ذلك يدفعه إلى بلوغ أقصى درجات التعبير:

> في بغداد في الخمسينيات، وفي إحدى الأمسيات الخاصة التي كانت تجمع بين رئيس الوزراء ومجموعة من الوزراء وعدد من أصحاب المهن المختلفة من محبي المقام العراقي، كان أحد كبار مؤدي المقام العراقي قد وصل في غنائه إلى مقاطع تؤدى في الطبقات العليا بقي فيها طويلاً «علّق صوته». وقد أثارت هذه اللحظة درجة عالية من الانفعال والتّرقب لما سيترتب عليها، فإذا بالمجلس كله يقترب وقوفاً من المغني ويحيط به منتظراً اللحظة التي سينزل فيها بسلام من طبقته العليا. وما إن فعل ذلك حتى قبله بعض الحاضرين بينما ألصق آخرون بقطع نقدية من الذهب على جبينه (الرجب).

وقد تَغلُب على الجلسة درجة عالية من التوتّر والانفعال العاطفي الذي قد يصل إلى ذرف الدموع أو حتى إلى فقدان الوعي. فقد كان الملا عثمان الموصلي (١٨٥٤-١٩٢٣)، وهو شيخ في القراءات القرآنية، متصوف ومغن وموسيقي وشاعر، قد سمع بالمغني المصري عبده الحمولي (ت ١٩٠١) فذهب، عند زيارته مصر، للاستماع إليه. كان تأثير غناء عبده الحمولي عليه على درجة من القوة بحيث أن الموصلي فقد وعيه ثلاث مرات من فرط الانفعال: «أما عن دهشة عثمان الموصلي الذي استبطن دخائل الفن وغاص على أسراره فحدّث ولا حرج فقد مسّه الجنون ووقع مغشياً عليه ثلاث مرات وصبّ على وجهه ثلاثة أكواز ماء وكلما أفاق كان يصرخ قائلا: يا ناس ليس هذا الصوت صوت إنسان بل هو

صوت ملك آمان يا عبده كمان أنا دخيلك» (رزق، ج ٤، ص ١٠٤).

وتصاحب حالات الانفعال عادة تعبيرات وإيماءات وحركات في الرأس والوجه والجسد، يمكن تشبيهها بما يقابلها عند مغني الأوبرا، تساعد المؤدي وتمكّنه من الوصول إلى حالة التعبير التي يبحث عنها. إلا أن المحدثين عادة لا يدركون طبيعة العلاقة القائمة بين التعبير الصوتي والحركات الإيمائية التي يرونها مفتعلة ويسخرون من المؤدين التقليديين الذين يلجأون إليها. وفي الفرق الحديثة التي تؤدي التقاليد القديمة تم لفت أنظار المغنين إلى الامتناع عن الإيماءات لاعتبارها مخلّة بالذوق السليم الحديث. وليس من المستعصي الاستنتاج بحدوث خلط بين الإيماءات اللاإجمالية التي دخلت مع غناء المنوعات وبين تلك المرتبطة بالتراث الفني والتي تمثل وسيلة تقنية للوصول إلى التعبير المتوخى.(١١)

ما الذي حدث بين عصر النهضة العربية – عندما كانت الموسيقى في إحدى قممها – وبين الدخول إلى عالم الحداثة، وكيف يمكن تفسير الحاجة التي دفعت إلى رفع شعار تغيير الموسيقى الفنية العربية وهي في قمة إبداعها؟ وكيف أمكن لنماذج الحداثة العربية المستلهمة من الغرب من أن تتجذّر خلال أقل من نصف قرن في الحيّز العربي وأن تهيمن على الحيز التمثيلي (قاعات الحفلات ووسائل الإعلام) لتتحول إلى نموذج ينتظر أن يعم دافعاً بذلك التقاليد الفنية الأصيلة إلى الوراء؟

الحيّز الحديث

تعرّضت حركة الموسيقى العربية منذ أوائل القرن العشرين لعدد من التغييرات. فقد كانت الموسيقى الفنية منذ القرن التاسع عشر وحتى منتصف القرن المنصرم، في ازدهار وفي حركة نمو وتغيير داخليين إضافة إلى انفتاح على العالم الشرقي، ورغم هذا الازدهار الذي وصلتنا آثاره، فإن مفهوم عصر النهضة ونتاجه الموسيقي غالباً ما اختلط في الأذهان ببقايا عصور الانحطاط. وعند دخول الاستعمار الغربي المباشر واستقراره في العالم العربي في أوائل القرن العشرين برز مفهوم آخر للحداثة. فهو من ناحية يركّز على ارتباطه بالمفاهيم القومية – كما ورد – ومن ناحية أخرى، من الناحية الموسيقية، يمثل توجهاً توفيقياً بين التراث العربي-الإسلامي وبين استعارات مباشرة من اللغة الأوروبية في الموسيقى. وقد ساعد ذلك في ظهور أنماط موسيقية جديدة مستحدثة تواكب متطلبات السينما ووسائل الإعلام. وتميز المرحلة التوفيقية بإدخال دم جديد على التراث الفني المتوارث كانت تراه ضرورياً لبقاء الموسيقى العربية، كما جاء على لسان محمد عبد الوهاب (Al Shawwan, 52). ويتميز أبرز مؤدي هذه المرحلة، كأم كلثوم وعبد الوهاب، بانحدارهم من ثقافة تقليدية رصينة في الأداء الذي لا ينفصل عن أصول الأداء الديني وأوله القراءة القرآنية. ومن ناحية أخرى فإنهم قبلوا بالانفتاح على المتطلبات الجديدة التي ظهرت في المجتمع المصري ووفقوا بين أداء الصيغ التقليدية كالقصائد والموشحات إلى جانب الأغنيات الجديدة وأغاني الأفلام. إلا أن ممارسة التوفيقية المباشرة أدّت بعد فترة قصيرة من ظهورها، وبسبب ارتباطها المباشر بالإعلام السمعي البصري، إلى فتح الباب لاجتياح وانتشار موجة من غناء المنوّعات التي دخلت العالم التجاري في نهاية القرن الماضي واستقرت إلى حد بعيد فيه.(١٢) أما التوجه الآخر

الذي انبثق عن المرحلة التوفيقية فهو التوجه الجمالي السائد في المؤسسات التعليمية والذي يميل إلى إلباس خزين هذه المرحلة، بشقيه الكلاسيكي والمنتشر شعبياً، حلل التقنيات المستعارة من أوروبا كالتوزيع الأوركسترالي وتوسيع الفرقة وغيرها من التوجهات التي ورد ذكرها في هذا المقال. وهذه بمجملها تسعى إلى خلق كلاسيكية جديدة للموسيقى العربية.

حداثة القرن العشرين: استمرارية في ثوابت التراث وتغيير في أسلوبه وأدائه

ثبّت مؤتمر القاهرة للموسيقى العربية، الذي انعقد عام ١٩٣٢، أسس عالم حداثة القرن العشرين في الموسيقى منطلقاً من الأفكار السائدة عند أصحاب القرار وعند الموسيقيين في مصر (Recueil). ويمكن أن نستشف من النتائج الفعلية والعملية للمؤتمر أن الانعطافة الحقيقية التي كرّسها المؤتمر، والتي جاءت بناءً على طلب ملح من قبل الموسيقيين العرب أنفسهم، تكمن في الاعتماد على الموسيقى الأوروبية كنموذج يُمكن الاستعارة منه. ويبدو أن وجود مرجعية يمكن اللجوء إليها لحل المشكلات التي تجابه الموسيقى العربية كان ضرورياً، ولا سيما وأن صلة الثقافة العربية ومنها الموسيقى في تلك الفترة – على أثر تأسيس الدول القومية وهيمنة الاستعمار – كانت قد انقطعت مع العالم الشرقي أو في سبيلها إلى ذلك.

ورغم أن المؤلفين الأوروبيين الذين حضروا المؤتمر من أمثال بارتوك وهندميث، إضافة إلى باحثين كبار مثل هنري جورج فارمر، عبروا عن إعجابهم بالموسيقى العربية التي استمعوا إلى نماذج كثيرة منها في المؤتمر، ورغم أنهم عبّروا عن عدم ارتياحهم للاندفاع والحماس الذي لمسوه في التصريحات العربية ضد الكلاسيكية العربية وإلى الدعوة إلى ضرورة الاقتباس من النموذج الغربي، فإن دافع التغيير والتقليد كان قوياً جداً في تلك المرحلة عند الموسيقيين المصريين والسوريين. وفي الواقع فإن توجه المجتمع العربي آنذاك كان ينطلق من اعتماد نظرية التطوّر التي تعتبر النموذج الأوروبي هو ما يجب أن يصبو إليه العرب في كافة المجالات. وهكذا فتحت الباب أمام اقتباس أصول التنظيم النغمي الأوروبي (القواعد) وغيرها من عناصر اللغة الموسيقية الأوروبية والآلات الموسيقية على اعتبار أنها لا تؤثر على جوهر الموسيقى العربية وثوابتها. ماذا أبقت الحداثة العربية في الموسيقى من الإرث الفني وما الذي غيّرت فيه؟ ما هي العناصر التي استمرت الموسيقى الحديثة في استخدامها؟

بقاء العناصر الجوهرية المتأصلة

ينطلق المحدثون من إيمان قاطع بشمولية الموسيقى وباعتبارها لغة عالمية مشتركة بين البشر. وهم بذلك ينضوون تحت أفق موسيقي يرى أن أولوية الموسيقى تكمن في عناصرها الصوتية الثابتة والجوهرية الموجودة خارج الأطر الدينامية للأداء. والثوابت هي: استمرار الاعتماد على النص الشعري العربي بصيغتيه الفصحى والمحلية والاعتماد على أصول التنظيم النغمي وقواعده المتمثلة بـ«المقامات»، حتى وإن تحدد استخدام مقامات وتقلّص استخدام غيرها بمرور الزمن. كما أن هناك أيضاً استمراراً في استخدام الإيقاعات العربية رغم تقلص عددها ورغم الابتعاد عن استخدام النماذج الإيقاعية الصعبة والمركبة مقارنة بأول القرن السابق. وأخيراً فإن الصيغ أو القوالب الموسيقية يمكن أن تعتبر أيضاً من الثوابت التي لا تزال تستخدم إلى جانب صيغ أخرى

حديثة استجدت عبر القرن الماضي (انظر سحاب وAl Shawwan).

أي أن التمسك بالثوابت المدرجة يوازيه انفتاح لعناصر مرادفة من الموسيقى الأوروبية. فقوانين التنظيم النغمي العربي-الإسلامي لم تكن هي وحدها المستعملة بل أصبحت تتجاور مع بداية استخدام السلالم الغربية (الماجور والمينور) ومع التوجه إلى النظام الغربي المعدّل المتمثل ببعض الآلات كالبيانو والأرغن بالدرجة الأولى، رغم اختلاف هذا النظام اختلافاً تاماً عن النظام الطبيعي العربي. وإلى جانب الإيقاعات العربية بدأ يشيع استخدام الإيقاعات الغربية المبسطة ولا سيما الراقصة منها. وكذلك الحال بالنسبة إلى القوالب الموسيقية التي زاد عددها بدخول القوالب المستقاة من احتياجات المسرح والسينما ومنوعات الأغاني.

التغييرات وإيجاد ثوابت جديدة

إلى جانب هذه العناصر التي توفق بين ثبات بعض العناصر مع انفتاحها على أخرى مستقاة من الغرب، فإن التغيير الكلي الذي يقترحه الجديد ينصبّ على عناصر الأداء وإلى إضافة مفهوم الكم كأحد أهم المفاهيم التي تطرحها الحداثة في الموسيقى.

يدعو المحدثون إلى الحد من الإجراءات التي يوفرها التراث والتي تساعد المؤدي على التعبير الشخصي من ناحية وعلى السعي من ناحية أخرى إلى تثبيت العناصر الدينامية وتوحيدها على المستوى العربي. بدأ الأداء الحديث في الحفلات يميل إلى تحديد دور المؤدي المنفرد أو اقتسام دوره – جزئياً أو كلياً – مع مجموعة غنائية كبيرة، رجالية أو نسائية، أسوة بالكورس الغربي. وبطبيعة الحال فإن أي أداء جماعي لابد من أن يكون موقّعاً وبهذا فهو يستغنى عن الأداء الهتروفوني ذي التوجه التعددي الآني. ومن ناحية أخرى يميل الاتجاه الحديث إلى تحجيم الارتجال الصوتي وتحديده في موقع معين من الأداء.

وتنطبق هذه المفاهيم أيضاً على استخدام الآلات الموسيقية. فقد استعيض عن الفرقة الصغيرة بأخرى كبيرة تقارب حجم الفرقة السيمفونية تستلهم توزيع الآلات بأسلوب مقارب لهذه الأخيرة. وعليه فإن دور الآلة الذي كان يعتمد في الفرقة الصغيرة على مفهوم الأداء الهتروفوني في التنويع والتقسيم والأداء المباشر يستعاض عنه بأدوار يتحدد مكانها ويثبت مضمونها مسبقاً.

يسعى التيار الحديث في الموسيقى إلى إحلال مفهوم البراعة التقنية والدقة القصوى في الأداء والسيطرة على المادة الموسيقية محلّ مفهوم الطرب. حتى إن هذه الكلمة باتت تفسر في كثير من الأوساط الموسيقية بصورة سلبية ودونية وكأنها غير جديرة بأن تُمثّل الموسيقى الفنية التي يُطلب منها التزام الصرامة.

ولابد من الإشارة إلى أن مؤتمر الموسيقى العربية في القاهرة لعام ١٩٣٢ كان قد أكّد على نشر المؤسسات التعليمية في الموسيقى التي عليها الأخذ بنظر الاعتبار التوجه الحديث في الموسيقى وتطبيق متطلباته في المؤسسات والمعاهد التربوية.

يسعى التيار الجديد للموسيقى إلى تثبيت الموسيقى بتحجيم دور الارتجال والهتروفونية وإلغاء مفهوم التنوعات وغيرها من إجراءات المرونة المعطاة للأداء التقليدي لأن كل تنويع أو تغيير ضمن الظاهرة الواحدة أو بين ظواهر متشابهة يمثل إشكالية حقيقية،

مقلقة وغير مرغوب بها في الحيّز المعاصر. فالفكر الحداثي يميل إلى الاستعاضة عن الحركية التي تظهر في حرية الأداء بالبحث عن ثوابت جديدة تختلف عن ثوابت العالم التقليدي.

الحيّز الحديث: خلاصة التيارات

ويجدر القول بأن الموسيقى في الحيّز العربي المعاصر لا تقتصر على التيارات الكبيرة التي تم التطرق إليها في هذا المقال بل إن هذا الحيز يمتلئ بصور وتشكيلات أخرى تحاول الوصول إلى وإيجاد مكانة معترف بها. يتوجب الإشارة إلى بعضها ولا سيما تلك التي تمثل توجهاً واضحاً.

ويمكن باختصار تصنيف الواقع الأدائي إلى الحالات التالية التي تتفاوت في أهميتها الجمالية وفي مكانتها عند المؤسسات الحديثة ذات العلاقة بالموسيقى وهي تلك التي:

١ـ تعطي المكان الكامل للتراث الكلاسيكي العربي لكل منطقة كما هو وكما نقله أساتذة القرن الماضي. وهذه الحالة باتت نادرة، كما أن الخزين الذي يمثلها – الذي هو موضوع هذا المقال – هو الأكثر عرضة للاهتزاز لأن الرعاية التقليدية لهذا الفن اضمحلت إلى درجة كبيرة دون أن تحل محلها سياسة دعم مؤسساتية تدعو إلى تواصل أداء هذا التراث الفني كرمز ثقافي محلي.

٢– تعطي مكاناً للحداثة التي تستلهم التراث. وفي هذه الحالة فإن المؤدي يرتبط بمعرفته للتراث وهو مدين له بها. وإذا كان التراث الفني بشكله الأصيل يمثل حلقة ضعف حقيقي في المشهد الحديث فإن تيارين ينطلقان من معرفة بالتراث بدءاً باتخاذ موقع من هذا الحيّز. أولهما التيار المنبثق عن مدرسة بغداد للعود التي استمد ممثلوها الإلهام من التراث الفني المحلي واعتمدوا على المقومات اللحنية والنغمية للثقافة المحلية أو الشرقية وأبرزوا إلى الأمام صيغة التقسيم الحر. هذا بالرغم من أن مؤسس هذه المدرسة الشريف محي الدين حيدر (١٨٨٨–١٩٦٧) كان قد اعتمد في البدء على بعض تقنيات الموسيقى الأوروبية والمفاهيم المنبثقة عنها. إن الاستلهام من الموسيقى الغربية لا يمس هنا محتوى أو جوهر اللغة الموسيقية. كما أن التأثير الغربي لا يظهر بصورة مباشرة في الأداء الذي انتشر ليمثل في يومنا هذا مدرسة ذات طابع محلي حديث. ويمكن أن يعتبر هذا التيار فاتحة للتجديد المرتبط بالخصوصية والأصالة. وقد لاقى نجاحاً كبيراً في الأوساط الدولية وفي أوساط المثقفين المحليين. ورغم أن هذا التوجه لا يزال ممثلا ببعض المؤدين المهمين إلا أنه لم يتحول إلى مشهد قوي في الحياة الموسيقية لا سيما وأن عدداً من الشباب الذين تأثروا به بدأوا هم بدورهم ينزلقون في تيارات العولمة وفي الخلط بين أجناس متعددة مثل موسيقى الجاز وغيرها من الموسيقى الغربية.

أما التيار الثاني، وهو جديد نسبياً، فيكمن في إرجاع دور الذخيرة الكلاسيكية من مؤلفات عصر النهضة وما جاء بعده دون إدخال تغيير في أدائها وفي أسلوبها. وقد بدأت ضمن هذا التوجه مجادلات تأليفية بأسلوب المدرسة القديمة وباعتماد تقنياتها. ويمثل هذا التيار عدد قليل من الموسيقيين الذين يعيشون في بيروت وباريس والذين أعادوا التساؤل عن أهمية ومكانة التقاليد الفنية بأشكالها الأصيلة وما ينبثق منها دون التأثر بمنطق التأليف والأداء الأوروبي.

٣- المشهد المؤسساتي الذي يمثل الحداثة الرسمية وهو الأكثر شيوعاً وانتشاراً في العالم العربي. وهو يعتمد في نظرته إلى التراث على مبدأ التطوير بتغيير أدوات التراث باستلهام النموذج الغربي من منطلقات مستمدة من الأسلوب الأوروبي للقرنين الثامن عشر والتاسع عشر. وهذا التيار يؤمن بنظرية التطور الداروينية ويسعى إلى تطبيق النموذج الغربي للتحقيب التاريخي في الموسيقى معتبراً إياه نموذجاً لابد منه لتطور الموسيقى. ويسعى هذا التيار إلى وضع قواعد جديدة لحياة موسيقية منظمة تعتمد الاحتراف وتبرز في تنظيم الحفلات الموسيقية في قاعات عامة باتت مخصصة. ويخاطب هذا النتاج الموسيقي الطبقات المتوسطة الصاعدة من البرجوازية الصغيرة كما يخاطب الطبقات المثقفة.

٤- المشهد الإعلامي وهو مرتبط أصلاً بالمشهد المؤسساتي الذي يدعمه ويتوحد فيه ويساعد على تقويته. إلا أن هذا الأخير في الوقت الحاضر دخل العالم التجاري لا سيما بعد اندثار الأغنية الكبيرة التي كانت تمثلها أم كلثوم. وهو اليوم يمثل إحدى الصور الهابطة لعالم ما بعد الحداثة المفكك والذي يقبل بكل أشكال الاستعارة والتأثر بالآخر دون حدود. وتقف المؤسسات التعليمية الحديثة حائرة أمام اكتساح هذا التيار وانفلات الموسيقى وتفككها ودخولها في عالم التجارة والعولمة ضمن هذا المشهد.

٥- المشهد الكلاسيكي الأوروبي الذي يؤدى من قبل عرب متخصصين ومحترفين في إطار حياة موسيقية غربية. لقد ألهمت الصيغ الموسيقية الأوروبية عدداً من المؤلفين العرب الذين استخدموا التقنيات والصيغ الغربية في مؤلفاتهم. وهذا النتاج الموسيقي يخاطب نخبة ذات ثقافة غربية متدربة على الاستماع إلى هذا النوع من الموسيقى. وبطبيعة الحال فإن هذا التيار لا يخاطب الغالبية العظمى من الشعب الذي لا يتفاعل مع هذا النتاج النخبوي الذي يستخدم لغة أجنبية للتعبير.

ومن المهم التأكيد على أن هذه المشاهد لا تمثل بالضرورة عوالم منقطعة الاتصال ببعضها بل إنها تمثل أشكالا من التفاعل بين الاتجاهات المختلفة. ورغم أن حيز الحداثة يتميز، بحكم تعريفه من الناحية النظرية، بكونه حيزاً تعددياً يسمح باستيعاب الاختلافات التي يمكن لكل منها أن تعبّر عن نفسها بصورة مستقلة فإن الضعف الجوهري والفعلي لهذا الحيّز في العالم العربي يكمن في ميله – كما ورد – إلى إلغاء الموسيقى الفنية التقليدية التي باتت تمثل حلقة أضعف من حلقات حيّز الحداثة في عالم يراد منه أن يكون تعددياً. ويظهر جلياً من الممارسة السائدة، أن علاقة الحداثة الموسيقية بالتراث الفني هي علاقة إلغاء للوجود الطبيعي للكلاسيكية التقليدية وتكوين كلاسيكية أخرى تتماشى مع العالم الجديد المتأثر بالغرب. ويؤثر هذا الضعف على توازن الهوية المحلية وارتباطها بمفهوم الثقافة عامة كما يُمكن أن يؤدي إلى نتيجة عكسية لتلك التي تصبو إليها كل حداثة في العالم المعاصر والتي يُفترض منها أن تكون معقلاً جامعاً لكل التعبيرات الثقافية المتراكمة.

ختاما، إن انحسار الموسيقى التقليدية الفنية الذي يصاحبه انتشار سريع لموسيقى وأغاني المنوعات التي تقتبس خصائصها من الشائع التجاري، الذي يقترب أحياناً من الابتذال، زَرَع فجوة بين التقاليد الفنية الأصيلة وبين الأجيال الصاعدة التي لم تعد تعرف أصول ثقافتها. ويمثل هذا الواقع تحدياً كبيراً أمامنا وأمام المؤسسات التعليمية ويسمح بطرح

السؤال الآتي: ما هي الثقافة الموسيقية التي يمكن أن ننقلها إلى الأجيال القادمة لكي لا نجعل منهم موسيقيين بدون مقاومة أمام المتأتي من الموجات التجارية الغربية التي تتعاقب على المشهد الإعلامي والتي يمكن أن تحولهم إلى أداة استهلاكية؟ إذ إننا عندما نسمع بتلك الأعداد الكبيرة من الشباب الذي يلتحق بكل أشكال الموسيقى التجارية الجديدة بسبب من عدم وجود توجه فني يعتمد استمرارية النقل والتواتر وغير كاف لكي يعوّض عن التوجه شبه الجماعي نحو تعبيرات العولمة، يمكن أن نتساءل فيما إذا كنا بصدد فقدان فكرة الموسيقى كثقافة وكرمز حضاري وكتعبير عن الهوية وبصدد التحول إلى حيّز تجاري يماشي ويقلد الصرعات الجديدة للمنوعات التي تبثها وسائل الإعلام.

الهوامش

(١) المقصود بالتراث العربي هو ذلك التراث الذي يُنتج، يؤدى ويسمع من قبل الذين ينتمون إلى الثقافة العربية بصرف النظر عن أصولهم العرقية ومعتقداتهم الدينية. والتراث العربي الفني جزء من التراث الإسلامي، الذي يتضمن أيضاً التراث الفارسي والتركي، إذ يشتركون في قواعد اللغة الموسيقية المرتبطة بالمفاهيم المقامية والإيقاعية، بالمفردات والمصطلحات، بالأولوية المعطاة للصوت، بالعلاقة المتينة بين الغناء والشعر، بدور الآلات الموسيقية وبمفاهيم تكوين الفرق الموسيقية وكذلك بالدور الاجتماعي المنوط بالمؤدي ومكانته الاجتماعية، إضافة إلى توغل الموسيقى في سياقات اجتماعية متعددة، دينية ودنيوية.

(٢) تمت هذه المراقبة الميدانية في كل من العراق وسوريا والأردن وقطر والبحرين والإمارات العربية المتحدة واليمن ومن احتكاك مباشر مع أعداد كبيرة من الموسيقيين المؤدين، ومع هواة ذوي اطلاع في أمور التراث، ومع طلاب المعاهد الموسيقية في مصر وسوريا والعراق ومع أساتذة وعمداء المعاهد الموسيقية في كل من بغداد ودمشق وحلب والقاهرة. إضافة إلى هذا، فإن ارتياد المواسم الموسيقية أو حفلات الموسيقى العربية التي تقام بشكل مستمر ودوري في باريس في كل من معهد العالم العربي، في دار ثقافات العالم وفي مسرح المدينة ساعد على مراقبة الأداء الموسيقى العربي وعلى تغيراته. كما أن متابعتي للواقع الموسيقي، ولحفلات مهرجان القاهرة وحفلات موسيقية أخرى في عواصم عربية مختلفة تدعم هذه الاستنتاجات. ولابد لي أن أضيف إلى ذلك أن تجربتي في تدريس التقاليد الموسيقية العربية على مدى عقدين في جامعة باريس وفي نطاق علم الشعوب والتي اعتمدت فيها على نتائج الميدان والاستنتاجات الناجمة من مراقبة الأداء من ناحية وعلى التاريخ المدوّن للموسيقى العربية ومخطوطاتها مع امتداداتها الإسلامية من ناحية أخرى ساعدتني على الوصول إلى نتائج يرد بعضها في هذا المقال وقد يكون جزء منها استنتاجات شخصية أجد نفسي مسئولة عنها كباحثة.

(٣) وهو مصطلح يستخدم أيضاً في المجتمع المصري ويعتبر مرادف للموسيقى الفنية. انظر Danielson.

(٤) وردت تفاصيل وآليات الطرب وخزينه في:

Ali Jihad Racy, *Making Music in the Arab World: The Culture of Artistry of Tarab* (Cambridge; New York: Cambridge UP, 2003).

^(٥) يتضمن التراث الفني للعواصم العربية الكبرى على بعض الصيغ الشعبية التي تدخل في تركيب الخزين الأدائي الفني. وبهذا لا يمكن أن تطبق قاعدة الفصل القسري بين العالم الفني والشعبي. ويمثّل هذا التداخل إحدى صفات الفني في الحيّز العربي-الإسلامي.

^(٦) ولا يزال هذا التقليد شائعاً عند الشعراء الذين يكتبون الشعر العمودي. وقد كان الجواهري يسمي هذا النوع من التنغيم بالحدي. (يمكن مراجعة أداء الجواهري لقصيدته «يا ابن الثمانين»، وقد سُجلت على كاسيت).

^(٧) إن مفهوم المنظومة وما تمثله في هذه المقالة يعبر عن استنتاج شخصي أنا مسئولة عنه كلياً.

^(٨) مقابلات شخصية مع طلبة وأساتذة وعمداء معاهد موسيقية عربية.

^(٩) وقد برز التقسيم (والجمع: تقاسيم) في العقود القليلة الأخيرة كصنف مستقل من الموسيقى التقليدية. إن وسائل التسجيل الحديثة بدأت تلعب دوراً في تثبيت التقسيم المستقل بحيث ساهمت في تحويله إلى مؤلف ثابت، غالباً ما يعاد أداؤه نصاً وبهذا فقد ساعد التسجيل على تحويل التقسيم إلى صيغ ثابتة.

^(١٠) إن التقنيات البوليفونية المختلفة وأهمها تقنيات الديافوني والبارافوني والكانون إضافة إلى الأداء الأنتيفونالي وتقنيات المحاكاة وغيرها كثيرة الاستخدام في الأداء التقليدي للموسيقى العربية. راجع:

Collective, *Einaudi Encyclopedia della Musica* (in Press).

^(١١) ويجرنا هذا إلى ضرورة إدخال مفهوم النوع الموسيقي أو الجنس الفني genre للتمييز بين الأنواع الموسيقية في وظائفها المختلفة والتي تتجاوب معها وسائل تعبيرية مختلفة.

^(١٢) يقترح الموسيقي اللبناني نداء أبو مراد تسمية ما يسمى بمرحلة الحداثة بمرحلة الانحطاط بدلا من تلك التي سبقتها (Abou Mrad, "Musique d'art arabe").

المراجع العربية

ابن المنجم. **رسالة يحيى ابن المنّجم في الموسيقى**. تحقيق زكريا يوسف. القاهرة: دار القلم، ١٩٦٤.

أدونيس. **الشعرية العربية**. بيروت: دار الآداب، ١٩٨٥.

الديكان، غنام. **الإيقاعات الكويتية في الأغنية الشعبية**. الكويت: المجلس الوطني للثقافة والفنون والآداب، ١٩٩٥.

رزق، قسطندي. **الموسيقى الشرقية والغناء العربي**. المجلد الثاني ٣-٤. القاهرة: مكتبة الدار العربية للكتاب، ١٩٩٣. الطبعة الثانية.

الرجب، هاشم. مقابلة أجرتها شهرزاد حسن، بغداد، كانون الثاني ١٩٩٠.

الخولي، سمحة. «الارتجال وتقاليده في الموسيقى العربية». **عالم الفكر**، المجلد السادس، العدد الأول (١٩٧٥). ص ص ١٥-٣٢.

الأصبهاني، أبو الفرج. **كتاب الأغاني**. بيروت: مؤسسة جمال للطباعة والنشر، د. ت.

فارمر، هنري جورج. **تاريخ الموسيقى العربية حتى القرن الثالث عشر الميلادي**. عرّبه وعلّق على حواشيه ونظّم ملاحقه جرجيس فتح الله المحامي. بيروت: منشورات دار مكتبة الحياة. د. ت.

الكندي. «رسالة في خبر صناعة التأليف». **مؤلفات الكندي الموسيقية.** تحقيق زكريا يوسف.
بغداد: مطبعة شفيق، ١٩٦٢.

سحاب، فكتور. **أثر الغرب في الموسيقى العربية.** بيروت: دار الحمراء للطباعة والنشر، ١٩٩٨.

Works Cited (English and French)

Recueil des travaux du congrès de musique arabe. Boulac, Le Caire: Imprimerie Nationale, 1934.

Abou Mrad, Nida. "Musique d'art arabe: chronique d'un suicide." *Les cahiers de l'Orient* 8-9 (1988). 293-319.

——————————. "Tradition musicale savante et renaissance de l'Orient arabe: Esquisse d'une philologie mélodique." Thèse de doctorat en musicologie. Université Saint esprit de Kaslik, 2002.

Boulez, Pierre. *Penser la musique aujourd'hui.* Mayence: Gonthier, 1963.

Collective. "Typologies des techniques polyphoniques dans les musiques de tradition orale." *Einaudi Encyclopedia della Musica III.* (Sous presse).

Danielson, Virginia. *The Voice of Egypt: Umm Kulthum, Arabic Song, and Egyptian Society in the Twentieth Century.* Chicago: The University of Chicago Press, 1997.

Farmer, Henry George. "The Music of Islam." *New Oxford History of Music.* Vol. 1. Ed. Egon Wellesz. London; New York; Toronto: Oxford UP, 1960. 421-77.

Hassan, Scheherazade. "Tradition et modernisme: le cas de la musique Arabe au Proche-Orient." *L'homme: Revue française d'anthropologie.* (Sous presse).

Lagrange, Frédéric. "Musiciens et poètes en Egypte au temps de la Nahda." Thèse de doctorat. Université de Paris VIII-Saint Denis, 1994.

Powers, S. Harold. "Classical Music, Cultural Roots, and Colonial Rule: An Indic Musicologist Looks at the Muslim World." *Asian Music, Journal of the Society for Asian Music* XII.1 (1979): 1-39.

Racy, Ali Jihad. *Making Music in the Arab World: The Culture of Artistry of Tarab.* Cambridge; New York: Cambridge UP, 2003.

Rouget, Gilbert. *Un roi africain et sa musique du cour: Chants et danses du palais à Porto-Novo sous le reigne de Ghéfa (1948-1976).* Transcriptions musicales de Tran Quang Hai en collaboration avec l'auteur. Paris: CNRS Editions, 1996.

Al Shawwan, Salwa. "Al Musika al 'Arabiyya: A Category of Urban Music in Cairo, Egypt, 1927-1977." Diss. Columbia University, 1980.

تجاذب القديم والجديد في شعر نازك الملائكة ونظريتها الشعرية

سامي مهدي

أولا: جديد نازك الملائكة ومصادره

تعد الشاعرة نازك الملائكة أحد رواد الحداثة في الشعر العربي، وهي في هذا من السابقين إن لم تكن أسبق من غيرها.[١] فقد كتبت عام ١٩٤٧ أول قصيدة خرجت فيها على النظام التقليدي لكتابة الشعر العربي، ونعني به نظام البيت الشعري.[٢] وعدّت قصيدتها هذه، وعنوانها «الكوليرا»، مع قصيدة بدر شاكر السياب (١٩٢٣-١٩٦٤) وعنوانها «هل كان حبا»،[٣] خط شـروع لحركة جديدة في الشـعر العربي سـميت بـ «حركة الشعر الحر» وهي تسمية تقول الملائكة إنها هي من أطلقها،[٤] وهذا بغض النظر عما في هذه التسمية من خطأ أو صواب، أو تطابق مع الواقع أو عدم تطابق، أو حتى إذا اتخذنا من المصطلح الإنكليزي Free Verse أو المصطلح الفرنسي Vers Libre معيارا لها.

وقد اعترف رواد الحداثة في الشعر العربي بأنهم مدينون لاطلاعهم على الشعرِ الأوروبي، ولا سيما الإنكليزي منه، في إطلاق رؤى التحديث في الشعر العربي، ولم تشِذّ الملائكة عن ذلك، بل لعلها سبقتهم إليه، في ما كتبته في مقدمة ديوانها الثاني **شظايا ورماد** الصادر ١٩٤٩. فبعد أن تنبأت بحدوث «تطور جارف عاصف» في الشـعر العربي، وبأن هذا التطور «لن يبقي من الأساليب القديمة شـيئا»، قالت: «أقول هذا اعتمادا على دراسة بطيئة لشعرنا المعاصر واتجاهاته، وأقوله لأنه نتيجة منطقية لإقبالنا على قراءة الآداب الأوروبية ودراسة أحدث النظريات في الفلسفة والفن وعلم النفس . . . ونحن بين اثنين: إما أن نتعلم النظريات ونتأثر بها ونطبقها، أو لا نتعلمها إطلاقا».[٥] بهذا المنطق إذن حاولت الملائكة أن تسوغ تجربتها الشعرية الجديدة التي أطلقت عليها تسمية «الشعر الحر» والقصائد الأولى التي تمخضت عنها هذه التجربة، ومنها قصيدة «الكوليرا».

ومن جانب آخر، ذكرت أسـماء شعراء أعجبت بشعرهم في بعض رسـائلها الشـخصية وأحاديثها الصحفية،[٦] كما كتبت عن بعض الشعراء دراسات خاصة،[٧] وترجمت إلى العربية قصائد لغيرهم،[٨] وكانت هذه كلها علامات طريق قادت النقاد والدارسـين إلى اكتشاف بعض مصادر التأثير عليها. ومع ذلك لم يكلف هؤلاء أنفسهم عناء البحث المفصل والمقارنة الدقيقة في كشف طبيعة هذا التأثير ومواضعه. فجبرا إبراهيم جبرا مثلا أشار إلى أن الملائكة قد جاءت إلى حركة التجديد «عن طريق الشعر الإنكليزي وفهمها له في أواخر الأربعينات، وإن كان فهمها له، فيما يبدو لي، مقصورا على

شـعر القرن التاسع عشر لا العشرين»،(٩) من دون أن يقدم أية إيضاحات تدعم رأيه.

وفي إشارة أخرى قال «إن الفورم Form هو من أهم ما يميز نازك عن الشعراء المجددين الآخرين، وهو مبني على معرفتها وتذوقها الشعر الغربي، ولا سيما الشعر الإنكليزي»، وفي جملة اعتراضية أضاف «من الممتع، مثلا، أن نستقصي أثر جون كيتس في ديوان **قرارة الموجة**».(١٠)

وصفاء خلوصي أشـار هو الآخر إلى تأثرها بالشـاعر الإنكليزي جـون كيتس John Keats (١٧٩٥–١٨٢١) ولكن من دون الإتيان بأي دليل، مع أن الأدلة متوفرة للباحث المدقق. وحين أشار إلى استخدام الملائكة للرموز اليونانية ذكر من بينها خطأ «هياواثا» الذي ورد في أواخر قصيدتها «لنكن أصدقاء» في ديوانها **شظايا ورماد**، مع أن «هياواثا» هو بطل أسطورة من أساطير الهنود الحمر التي اختارها الشاعر الأميركي هنري لونغفلو Henri W. Longfellow (١٨٠٧–١٨٨٢) موضوعا لقصيدته المعنونة "Hiawatha's Childhood".(١١)

أما س. موريه S. Moreh فقد رأى في إشارة عابرة أنها تأثرت بالشكل المقطعي الموحد The homostrophic ode أو The monostrophic lyric الذي كتب به بعض الشعراء الإنكليز من أمثال غري Gray وكيتس Keats وكولنز Collins وسوينبرن Swinburne من دون أن يوضح ذلك بالمقارنة لتأييد حجته على أن قصيدة «الكوليرا» هي من هذا الشكل من الكتابة الشعرية.(١٢)

وقد قال محمد عبد الحي بتأثر الملائكة بالشعر الرومانسي الإنكليزي هو الآخر وخص بالذكر «استعمالها لصورة القمرية على غرار ما جاء عند كيتس» وأثنى على ترجمتها قصيدة غري المعروفة «مرثيـة كـتبت في مقبرة ريفية» ولا شيء أكـثر من ذلك.(١٣) وكذلك فعلت خزامى صبري (خالدة سعيد).(١٤)

أما الأكاديمي الفرنسي فنسان مونتي Vincent Monteil فقد أشـار إلى وجود عـلاقة بين قصيدة الملائكة «خمس أغانٍ للألم» وبعض الملامح في شعر الشاعرة التشيلية غابرييلا ميسترال Gabriela Mistral (١٨٨٩–١٩٥٧) التي تناولت «الألم» في قصائد ديوانها الثاني Dolor.(١٥)

وقد أشار بعض هؤلاء وغيرهم إلى تأثر الملائكة بشعر المهجريين وشعر جماعة أبولو والشاعرين علي محمود طه ومحمود حسن إسماعيل وشعراء عرب آخرين، ولكن هذا يقع خارج نطاق بحثنا هذا، فلن نتحدث عنه.

وبحسب علمنا أن سلمان الواسطي هو أول من درس أثر الشعر الأجنبي على شعر الملائكة دراسـة مفصلة مدعومة بالمقارنات والأدلة في دراسـته «المؤثرات الأجنبيـة في شـعر نازك الملائكة حتى عام ١٩٥٠».(١٦) ومما تناوله الواسطي في هذه الدراسة أثر ثلاثة شـعراء هم: إيليا أبو ماضي صاحب «الجداول» وعمر الخيام صاحب «الرباعيات» المعروفة باسمه، والشاعر الإنكليزي توماس غري Thomas Gray (١٧١٦–١٧٧١) على صورها الشعرية الثلاث التي جاءت في ديوانها **مأساة الحياة وأغنية الإنسـان**. وإذا نحينا أثر أبي ماضي والخيام جانبا، فإن الواسـطي يرى ثمة «أصداء

كثيرة) من قصيدة «مرثية كتبت في مقبرة ريفية» "Elegy Written in a Country Churchyard" قد ترددت في قصيدتها «مأساة الحياة». والمعروف أن الملائكة كانت قد ترجمت هذه القصيدة شعرا وبتصرف عام ١٩٤٥ ونشرتها في ديوانها الأول **عاشقة الليل**. بل إن الواسطي يرى أن «سيطرة أجواء مرثية غري» لم تقتصر على قصيدة «مأساة الحياة» فحسب، بل كذلك على الكثير من قصائد هذا الديوان بما في ذلك العنوان نفسه.(١٧) ثم يأتي الواسطي بمقارنات مقنعة لتدعيم رأيه.

غير أن هذا هو الآخر لا يدخل في نطاق بحثنا، برغم أنه يعطينا دليلا ملموسا على تأثر الملائكة بالشعر الإنكليزي. فنحن نحاول هنا اقتفاء أثر القديم في جديد هذه الشاعرة، وقصائد ديوانها **عاشقة الليل ومأساة الحياة وأغنية الإنسان** لا تدخل في نطاق هذا الجديد، لأنها كتبت بنظام النظم التقليدي (أي أنها قصائد عمودية)، أما جديدها فهو شعرها الحر الذي يبدأ من قصيدة «الكوليرا».

إدغار ألان پو مصدر جديد للملائكة:

إن الدراسة الفاحصة لقصيدة «الكوليرا» لنازك الملائكة التي تصور فيها مشاعرها نحو مصر خلال وباء الكوليرا(١٨) تكشف أنها قد تأثرت بأعمال الشاعر الأميركي إدغار ألان پو Edgar Allan Poe (١٨٠٩-١٨٤٩) وقصائده ومقالاته حول الشعر،(١٩) وأبرزها قصائده الثلاث التي يرى الدارسون أنها كانت وراء تعزيز مكانته الشعرية وذيوع شهرته العالمية، ونعني قصائد: «الغراب» "The Raven" و أولالوم "Ulalume" والأجراس "The Bells" ومقالتاه «فلسفة التأليف» "The Philosophy of Composition" و«المبدأ الشعري» "The Poetic Principle".(٢٠)

إن أول من نبّه إلى أثر شعر پو في شعر الملائكة وأفكارها النظرية هو الواسطي نفسه في دراسته التي سبقت الإشارة إليها. فهو يقول:

وأزعم أن مؤثرا أجنبيا لم يَنَلْ ما يستحقه من انتباه النقاد، قد كان وراء تزويدها بمؤشرات نظرية وتطبيقية التقطها ذكاؤها الحاد ووعيها المتحفز للتجديد فأحالها «بيانا»(٢١) للحداثة الشعرية العربية أطلقته نازك الملائكة في مقدمة الديوان(٢٢) بجرأة ووضوح لم يمتلكهما أي من رواد الحداثة الآخرين، ذلك المؤثر الأجنبي هو الشاعر والناقد والقاص الأميركي إدغار ألان پو.(٢٣)

وقبل أن نوضح من جانبنا هذا التأثير الذي يتحدث عنه الواسطي لنتساءل: هل اطلعت الملائكة على قصائد پو ومقالاته حتى تتأثر بها؟ الجواب: نعم، لقد اطلعت الملائكة على شعر پو ومقالاته، ولدينا الأدلة على ذلك، وسنقدم هذه الأدلة تباعا في المواضع المناسبة. ففي رسالة شخصية تحدثت الملائكة عن الشعراء الأجانب الذين يعجبونها، وقالت عن پو تحديدا إنه من الشعراء الذين

تسعد بقراءة شعرهم.(٢٤) وفي مقدمة ديوان **شظايا ورماد** أشارت الملائكة إلى قصيدتها «الجرح الغاضب» المنشورة فيه وقالت «إن الأسلوب الطريف في تقفيتها مقتبس مباشرة من الشاعر الأميركي إدغار ألان پو في قصيدته البديعة Ulalume».(٢٥) وهذا دليل على أنها قد قرأت شعره ليس من أجل الاستمتاع والإحساس بالسعادة فحسب، بل من أجل الاستفادة منه أيضا. فقد تنبهت، كما يبدو، إلى ما في بعض قصائده من محاولات تجريبية أثارت فضولها ووجدت أن بإمكانها الاستفادة منها في تطلعها إلى الجديد.

أجراس پو تلهم الملائكة في «الكوليرا»:

ثمة شيء آخر تفيدنا به إشارة الملائكة سالفة الذكر، وهو أنها كانت تقرأ پو في الفترة التي كانت في أوج تطلعها إلى الجديد ، وهي الفترة التي كتبت فيها قصائد ديوان **شظايا ورماد** ومنها قصيدة «الكوليرا». وشاءت المصادفات أن يتفشى وباء الكوليرا في الريف المصري في الفترة نفسها، فكان لهذا الاقتران تأثيره المباشر على كتابة قصيدتها «الكوليرا» بالطريقة التي كُتبت بها على ما نعتقد. هل هناك نص محدد من نصوص پو أثر عليها في كتابة هذه القصيدة؟ في الواقع هناك نصوص أثرت عليها في ذلك، وليس نصا واحدا، ولكن أحد هذه النصوص كان هو مصدر التأثير المباشر، وهو، في رأي الواسطي، ونحن معه في هذا الرأي، قصيدة «الأجراس» ، وهذا ما سنوضحه.

تتكون قصيدة پو هذه من أربعة مقاطع مثل قصيدة الملائكة. وقد نظمت على بحر التروكي Trochaic ، بينما نظمت قصيدة الملائكة على بحر «الخبب» من بحور الشعر العربي، وإيقاع هذا البحر فعلا قريب جدا من بحر التروكي إن لم يكن مطابقا له تمام التطابق عند القراءة الصائتة. وعدد تفاعيل أبيات قصيدة پو متفاوت، فهو يتراوح بين تفعيلة واحدة (وإن حدث هذا مرة واحدة فقط) وست تفعيلات، والغالب عليها التراوح بين تفعيلتين وست تفعيلات، تماما كتفعيلات أبيات قصيدة الملائكة. وثمة شيء آخر غير ما تقدم يربط بين القصيدتين، هو تكرار كلمات معينة فيهما، وخاصة تكرار كلمة «الأجراس» في قصيدة پو وكلمة «الموت» في قصيدة الملائكة. ولذا كان الواسطي على حق حين قال: إن «الإيقاع الجديد الذي عبرت به عن مأساة الموت بالكوليرا لم يأتِ من وقع أرجل الخيل التي تجر عربات الموتى (كما قالت) وإنما جاء من وقع أجراس الخيول التي تجر الزلاجات على الجليد في أميركا، كما يخلدها إيقاعيا إدغار ألان پو في قصيدة «الأجراس».(٢٦)

على أننا نرى أن المقطع الرابع من مقاطع «الأجراس» حصرا هو مصدر التأثير المباشر على قصيدة «الكوليرا». ولإيضاح ذلك ننقل في ما يأتي هذا المقطع بأبياته الأربعة والأربعين:

Hear the tolling of the bells—
Iron Bells!
What a world of solemn thought their monody compels!
In the silence of the night
How we shiver with affright
At the melancholy meaning of the tone!
For every sound that floats
From the rust within their throats
Is a groan.
And the people—ah, the people
They that dwell up in the steeple
All Alone,
And who, tolling, tolling, tolling,
In that muffled monotone,
Feel a glory in so rolling
On the human heart a stone—
They are neither man nor woman—
They are neither brute nor human,
They are Ghouls:—
And their king it is who tolls:—
And he rolls, rolls, rolls, rolls
A paean from the bells!
And his merry bosom swells
With the paean of the bells!
And he dances and he yells;
Keeping time, time, time,
In a sort of Runic rhyme,
To the paean of the bells—
Of the bells:—
Keeping time, time, time,
In a sort of Runic rhyme,
To the throbbing of the bells—
Of the bells, bells, bells—
To the sobbing of the bells:—
Keeping time, time, time,
As he knells, knells, knells,
In a happy Runic rhyme,
To the rolling of the bells—
Of the bells, bells, bells:—

To the tolling of the bells—
Of the bells, bells, bells, bells,
Bells, bells, bells—
To the moaning and the groaning of the bells.

وفيما يأتي ترجمتنا لهذا المقطع، بقليل من الاجتهاد:

اسمع قرع الأجراس——
الأجراس الحديد!
أي عالم من الرهبة تشيعه مرثاتها!

في سكون الليل
كيف نرتجف خائفين
من وعيد نغمتها الكئيب!
فكل صوت يسيل
من حناجرها الصدئة
أنين.
والناس——آه، الناس
أولئك الذين هم في البرج
وحدهم،
والذين هم يقرعون، يقرعون، يقرعون
بذلك النغم الرتيب الكظيم،
يشعرون بفخر كلما دحرجوا
حجرا على قلب الإنسان——
هم ليسوا برجال ولا نساء
ولا بهائم ولا بشر،
هم غيلان:——
ومليكهم هو من يقرع:——
وهو يردد، يردد، يردد، يردد
نشيد الأجراس!
وصدره المنشرح ينتفخ تبجحا
مع نشيد الأجراس!
وهو يرقص وهو يصيح؛
محددا الزمن، الزمن، الزمن
بنوع من قافية سحرية،
مع نشيد الأجراس——

الأجراس:—

محددا الزمن، الزمن، الزمن،

بنوع من قافية سحرية،

مع اهتزاز الأجراس—

الأجراس، الأجراس، الأجراس

مع نشيج الأجراس:—

محددا الزمن، الزمن، الزمن

بينما هو ينعي، ينعي، ينعي

بقافية سحرية سعيدة ،

في قرع الأجراس—

الأجراس، الأجراس، الأجراس:—

مع قرع الأجراس—

الأجراس، الأجراس، الأجراس،

الأجراس، الأجراس، الأجراس—

مع نواح الأجراس وأنينها.

ولكي تكون ثمة إمكانية للمقارنة ننقل في ما يأتي مقطعين من قصيدة
«الكوليرا» هـما الأول والثاني:

سكنَ الليلُ

أصغِ إلى وقع صدى الأنات ْ

في عمق الظلمة، تحت الصمت، على الأموات ْ

صرخاتٌ تعلو، تضطربُ

حزنٌ يتدفق، يلتهبُ

يتعثر فيه صدى الآهات ْ

في كل فؤادٍ غليانُ

في الكوخِ الساكن أحزانُ

في كل مكان روحٌ تصرخ في الظلمات ْ

في كل مكان يبكي صوت ْ

هذا ما قد مزقه الموت ْ

الموت الموت الموت ْ

يا حزنَ النيل الصارخ مما فعل الموت ْ

طلع الفجرُ

أصغِ إلى وقع خطى الماشين ْ

٦٤

في صمت الفجر، أصخ، انظرْ ركبَ الباكين

عشرة أموات، عشرونا

لا تحص أصخْ للباكينا

اسمعْ صوت الطفل المسكين

موتى، موتى، ضاع العددُ

موتى، موتى، لم يبقَ غدُ

في كل مكان جسد يندبه محزونْ

لا لحظة إخلاد لا صمتْ

هذا ما فعلت كف الموتْ

الموت الموت الموتْ

تشكو البشرية تشكو ما يرتكب الموتْ(٢٧)

وهكذا نجد عند المقارنة بين نص بو ونص الملائكة:

– تشابها في الإيقاع، إن لم ثمة تطابق.

– تشابها في تفاوت عدد تفعيلات الأبيات في كلا النصين.

– تشابها في تنوع القوافي.

– تشابها في تكرار كلمة معينة بذاتها، تكرار «الأجراس» لـدى بو وتكرار كلمة «الموت» لدى الملائكة. فقد ترددت كلمة الأجراس في مقاطع قصيدة بو الأربعة ٦١ مرة، وترددت في المقطع الرابع منها وحده ٢٣ مرة، بينما ترددت كلمة « الموت » في قصيدة الملائكة ٢١ مرة.

ونضيف الآن تشابها آخر هو تشابه مناخ المقطع الرابع من قصيدة بو مع مناخ قصيدة «الكوليرا». فسكون الليل، ونذر الموت، وأصداء الأنين والنواح، والمناخ الطقوسي، تهيمن كلها على النصين، نص «الكوليرا» ونص المقطع الرابع من «الأجراس».

هناك دليل آخر على أن الملائكة قد قرأت قصيدة «الأجراس» وتأثرت بها تأثرا عميقا. فثمة قصيدة أخرى كتبت عام ١٩٤٨ (أي الفترة نفسها) تفصح عن هذا التأثر، وعنوان هـذه القصيدة «أجراس سوداء».(٢٨) فالأجراس موجودة في العنوانين والقصيدتين، والسواد عنصر مشترك بين أجراس الملائكة وأجراس بو، لأن هذه الأخيرة مصنوعة من الحديد، ولون الحديد أقرب إلى السواد. كما أن المناخ العام للقصيدتين متشابه. فليست أجراس بو وحدها تنذر بالموت، بل إن أجراس الملائكة أيضا، إذ إن قصيدتها هذه هي دعوة إلى الموت الذي ينذر به دوي الأجراس:

كؤوسُ الفارغاتُ تسخر منا	لنمتْ فالحياة جفت وهذي الأ
سام عادت أجلى وأعمق لونا	وغـيوم الذهـول في أعين الأيــــ
لام لم يَبْقَ قط للعيش معنى	وسـكون الحياة في جسـد الأحـ

و فــــراغ الآهــــات أثبـــت أنّــا 　　　 قـد فـرغنا من دورنا وانتهينا

* * * * *

وعمـــيقاً في الليل نســـمع أقدا 　　　 مَ الليالي في رهبة ووجوم
ودوي الأجـــراس ينـــذرنا أنّـ 　　　 ـا انتـهينا من دورنا المحموم
أن ما في الكؤوسِ يوشـك أن ين 　　　 ـضب إلا من حفنةٍ من هموم
أن ما في العيون من عطشٍ للأحـ 　　　 ـلام أمســــى رمادَ حبٍّ قديم

* * * * *

وبــعيداً في الجـوّ تــنذرنا الأصـ 　　　 ـواتُ أنّ الحياة عادتْ جنونا
أن لـون الخيال قد حـال وارتــدَّ 　　　 شـــحوبا وواقعـاً محزونا
أن « قبل » الرجاء أصبح لا «بعـ 　　　 ـد» له فـهو فـكرة لن تكونا
أن شـــيئاً في عـمق أنفسنا يجـ 　　　 ـذبـنا للممات، شـيئاً مكينا

پو يلهم الملائكة تقنية التكرار:

وبرغم أن قصيدة پو « الأجراس» كافية في حد ذاتها للكشف عن ابتكاراته
للمطلع على الشعر المكتوب باللغة الإنكليزية، يرى الواسطي، وهو على حق، أن
الملائكة لابد من أن تكون قد قرأت مقالة پو عن «فلسفة التأليف» ، وهي المقالة التي
شرح فيها الخطوات التي كتب بها قصيدته الشهيرة: «الغراب» وأوضح كيفية
استخدامه لبحر التروكي في نظمها. فلقد خرج پو في هذه القصيدة على النظام
التقليدي للكتابة بهذا البحر، وذلك بجمعه الأشطر المختلفة في عدد تفعيلاتها في
مقطع واحد، وهذا، كما يقول هو نفسه «شيء لم يحاوله أو يقترب منه أحد قبلي»، وهو
أيضا ما فعلته الملائكة في قصيدة «الكوليرا» وفي قصائدها الحرة اللاحقة. وفي ضوء
ذلك، وضوء ما لاحظته في قصائدها الثلاث التي سبقت الإشارة إليها، راحت تصوغ
نظرية خاصة جديدة في نظم الشعر العربي ظهرت بوادرها الأولى في مقدمة ديوان
شظايا ورماد التي كانت أول وثيقة كتبت عن الحركة الشعرية الجديدة «حركة الشعر
الحر».

ثمة دليل آخر على أن الملائكة قد قرأت شعر پو وبعض مقالاته في الأقل
قراءة فاحصة واستفادت منها في كتابة شعرها والتنظير له هو: تقنية التكرار،
تكرار كلمات محورية في بعض القصائد، أو تكرار بعض القوافي، أو العبارات أو
الأبيات. إن تقنية التكرار هي إحدى التقنيات التي أهتم بها پو، واستخدمها في
قصائده الثلاث التي مر ذكرها، ونظّر لإحداها في مقالته «فلسفة التأليف»، ونعني
تكرار لازمة معينة Refrain في نهايات مقاطع القصيدة. والقصيدة التي نعنيها
هنا هي قصيدة «الغراب» "The Raven" التي كرر فيها لازمة Nevermore
كما يتضح في المقاطع الثلاثة المتعاقبة الآتية:

"Prophet!" said I, "thing of evil!—prophet still,
    if bird or devil!
By that Heaven that bends above us—by that God
    we both adore—
Tell this soul with sorrow laden if, within the distant
    Aidenn,
It shall clasp a sainted maiden whom the angels name
    Lenore—
Clasp a rare and radiant maiden whom the angels name
    Lenore."
Quoth the Raven "Nevermore."

"Be that word our sign of parting, bird or fiend!" I
    shrieked, upstarting—
"Get thee back into the tempest and the Night's Plutonian
    shore!
Leave no black plume as a token of that lie thy soul hath
    spoken!
Leave my loneliness unbroken!—quit the bust above my
    door!
Take thy beak from out my heart, and take thy form from
    off my door!"
Quoth the Raven "Nevermore."

And the Raven, never flitting, still is sitting, *still* is sitting
On the pallid bust of Pallas just above my chamber door;
And his eyes have all the seeming of a demon's that is
    dreaming,
And the lamp-light o'er him streaming throws his shadow
    on the floor;
And my soul from out that shadow that lies floating on the
    floor
Shall be lifted—nevermore!

وما لا شك فيه أن الملائكة قد لاحظت ظاهرة التكرار في قصائد بو هذه،
واستفادت منها في عدد غير قليل من قصائدها، وليس في قصيدة «الكوليرا» وحدها، كما
استفادت من تنظير بو لاستعماله اللازمة Nevermore في التنظير لتقنية التكرار في
الشعر العربي على نحو ما فعلته في كتابها **قضايا الشعر المعاصر** وخاصة في فصل «دلالة
التكرار في الشعر». (٢٩)

لقد اعترفت الملائكة نفسها، في مقدمة **شظايا ورماد** بأن أسلوب تقفية قصيدتها «الجرح الغاضب» «مقتبس مباشرة» من «الأسلوب الطريف» الذي استخدمه پو في تقفية قصيدته «أولالوم» كما ذكرنا. ويقوم أسلوب پو في تقفية هذه القصيدة على التكرار، تكرار البيت، وخاصة الكلمة الأخيرة منه، في البيت الذي يليه مباشرة، أو البيت الذي بعده، مع إجراء تغيير جزئي في كلمات حشوه. وفيما يأتي المقطع الأول من قصيدة Ulalume للإيضاح:

The skies they were ashen and sober;
The leaves they were withering and sere:
The leaves they were withering and sere:
It was night, in the lonesome October
Of my most immemorial year:
It was hard by the dim lake of Auber,
In the misty mid region of Weir:—
It was down by the dank tarn of Auber,
In the ghoul-haunted woodland of Weir.

وهذا هو المقطع الأول من قصيدة الملائكة «الجرح الغاضب»[30] للمقارنة:

أغضبُ أغضبُ لن أحتمل الجرح الساخر
جرحٌ قد مرَّ مساء الأمس على قلبي
جرح يجثم كالليل المعتم في قلبي
يجثم أسودَ كالنقمة في فكر ثائرْ
جرحٌ لم يعرف إنسان قبلي مثله
لن يشكو قلبٌ بشريٌ بعدي مثلهْ
الظلمة في أمسي المطوي أحسته
ومضت تهمس في صمت الليل : من الجاني
حتى الأبدية والآفاق أحسته
وتناسى، لم يعبأ، لم ينتبه الجاني.

غير أن اقتباس الملائكة هذا اقتباس شكلي، بينما التكرار لدى پو في قصيدة Ulalume ، كما في غيرها، يشكل جزءا لا يتجزأ من بناء كلي مدروس، مدعوم بأدوات أخرى، كابتكار أسماء وكلمات وتعابير غير موجودة في اللغة الإنكليزية أو غيرها من اللغات مثل : Ulalume وAuber وWeir وmost immemorial لغايات فنية مدروسة، موسيقية أو دلالية، لخلق جو سحري مثلا، أو لمجرد إشاعة الغموض الذي كان پو يؤمن بأنه شيء جوهري في الشعر، أو

حتى لمجرد كسر القواعد السائدة وإثارة الانتباه، وهذا أمر فعله بو في أكثر من قصيدة منها «الغراب» التي جاء فيها بتعبير Nevermore وقصيدة «إلى هيلين» "To Helen" التي جاء فيها بكلمة Nicen التي حار النقاد في تفسيرها.

وقد قامت الملائكة بتجربتين أخريين مستفيدة من تكرار لازمة Nevermore في قصيدة «الغراب»، وهاتان التجربتان جاءتا في قصيدتين مقطعيتين هما «غرباء» و«يوتوبيا الضائعة».

ففي قصيدة «غرباء»[31] جعلت من كلمة «غرباء» لازمة تكررها في نهاية كل مقطع من مقاطعها الخمسة، ولكنها لم تأتِ بغراب ليردد هذه اللازمة كما فعل بو في قصيدته، بل قالتها مرة على لسان الشاعرة، ومرة على لسان الساعة التي تدق في الظلمة، وأخرى على لسان الصمت الذي يخنق الأنفاس، ثم مرتين أخريين على لسان الشاعرة. وهذان هما المقطعان الأول والثاني من القصيدة للمقارنة مع لازمة Nevermore في المقاطع التي سبق تقديمها من قصيدة «الغراب»:

أطفئ الشـمعة واتـركنا غريبين هنا
نحن جزءان من الليل فما معنى السنا؟
يسقط الضوء على وهمين في جفن المساءْ
يسقط الضوء على بعض شظايا من رجاءْ
سميت نحن وأدعوها أنا:
مللا. نحن هنا مثل الضياءْ
غرباءْ

اللقاء الباهت البارد كاليوم المطير
كان قتلا لأناشيدي وقبرا لشعوري
دقت السـاعة في الظلمة تسـعا ثم عشــرا
و أنا من ألمي أصغي وأحصي. كنت حيرى
أسـأل السـاعة ما جـدوى حبوري
إن نكن، نقضي الأماسي، أنت أدرى،
غرباء

وقد فعلت الملائكة الشيء نفسـه في قصيدة «يوتوبيا الضائعة»،[32] إذ اتخذت من كلمة «يوتوبيا» لازمة تكررها في نهاية كل مقطع من مقاطعها العشرة ولكن لم يَنُبْ أحد عن الشاعرة في ترديد هذه اللازمة إلا مرتين: مرة الصدى ومرة الرمل.

إن تكرار اللازمة في هاتين القصيدتين يعطينا دليلا قاطعا على أن تكرار بو لازمته في قصيدة «الغراب» وشرحه سبب اختياره إياها وكيفية الاختيار في مقالته «فلسفة التأليف». نقول: إن هذا التكرار وهذا الشرح هما اللذان ألهما الملائكة في تجربتيها هاتين، نظريا وتطبيقيا.

غير أن قصيدة «يوتوبيا الضائعة» تذكرنا بقصيدتين أخريين من قصائد بو هما:
«أرض الأحلام» "Dream-Land" و«المدينة التي هي في البحر» "The City in the
Sea" لا بسبب ما يبدو من علاقة بين عناوين القصائد الثلاث فحسب، بل بسبب ما نجد
من تشابه واضح بين قصيدة الملائكة هذه وقصيدتي بو هاتين. فالمقاطع ٥ و٦ و٧ و٨ من
قصيدتها ترسم عوالم كالتي ترسمها قصيدتا بو، عوالم غريبة، موحشة، خارج المكان
وخارج الزمان، تمر بها الشاعرة خلال بحثها عن يوتوبياها وأرض أحلامها، فلا تجد هذه
الأرض، وتبقى، مثل بو، معلقة بأمل وجودها في «الماوراء». وهذا يدل على عمق الأثر الذي
تركه شعره فيها وفي موضوعاتها وثيماتها وحتى صورها في هذه المرحلة من مراحلها
الشعرية.

قصيدة الملائكة «الخيط المشدود بشجرة السرو»(٣٣) تنبئنا بأنها استطاعت
بسرعة أن تهضم «خراف» بو هضما جيدا وتتمثلها وتطوع مادتها لصنعتها الشعرية. ففي
هذه القصيدة وحدها يستطيع القارئ الفاحص أن يجد آثار أربع من قصائد بو مجتمعة
وممتزجة وطالعة في بناء جديد، هي القصائد: «أنّابيل لي» "Annabel Lee"
و«أولالوم» و«الأجراس» و«الغراب». فموضوع قصيدتها ينهل من موضوع قصيدتي بو
«أنّابيل لي» و«أولالوم»، وتكراراتها تنهل من تكرارات قصيدتيه «الأجراس» و«الغراب».
على أن أثر «أنّابيل لي» لا يكاد يبين في قصيدة الملائكة، ولكنه موجود في روحها العامة.
أما أثر «أولالوم» فهو واضح بيّن، لأن موضوعها هو موضوع قصيدة الملائكة نفسه، وبعض
تفاصيله في الأقل، ونعني به: فقدان الحبيبة عن طريق الموت.

في قصيدة «أولالوم» يسير الحبيب في ليلة من ليالي الخريف «أكتوبر» بين أشجار
السرو مع روحه التي يسميها «سايكي» Psyche وكل ما حوله ذاو وموحش وكئيب حتى
يصل إلى ضريح فيقف عنده ويسأل «سايكي» عما كتب على باب الضريح:

And I said—"What is written, sweet sister,
On the door of this legended tomb?"
She replied—"Ulalume—Ulalume!—
'Tis the vault of thy lost Ulalume!"

وقلت: ما المكتوب أيتها الأخت الحلوة
على باب هذا الضريح الأسطوري؟
فأجابت: «أولالوم - أولالوم -
هذا مدفن فقيدتك أولالوم!»

أما في قصيدة الملائكة «الخيط المشدود بشجرة السرو»، فالحبيب يسير ليلا في
شارع تصفه بأنه مظلم صامت أصم وهو في طريقه إلى بيت حبيبته التي هجرها، محدِّثا
نفسه ومعللا إياها بأن حبيبته باقية على حبه وهي ما تزال في انتظاره. ولكنه حين يصل
إلى البيت ويطرق بابه يخرج له من ينبئه بأن حبيبته قد ماتت.

غير أن ذكاء الشاعرة جعلها تتصرف بسروات پو تصرفا آخر، ولا تبقيها مجرد مكمل من مكملات المشهد، فشدت في إحداها خيطا وجعلت الحبيب المخذول يمسك به ذاهلا وهو يردد في هذيان داخلي «ماتت... إنها ماتت».

التكرار في قصيدة الملائكة هذه ينهل من قصيدتي پو: «الأجراس» و«الغراب». ذلك أنها اتخذت من عبارتي «ماتت» و«إنها ماتت» لازمة كررتها خمس عشرة مرة، ولكن ليس على غرار لازمة Nevermore في «الغراب» بل على غرار التكرار في قصيدة «الأجراس» كما نرى في هذين المقطعين المتعاقبين من القصيدة:

هي « ماتت... » لفظة من دون معنى
وصدى مطرقةٍ جوفاءَ يعلو ثم يفنى
ليس يعنيك تواليه الرتيبُ
كل ما تبصره الآن هو الخيط العجيبُ
أتراها هي شدته؟ ويعلو
ذلك الصوت المملُّ
صوت «ماتت» داويا، لا يضمحلُّ
يملأ الليل صراخا ودويا
«إنها ماتت» صدى يهمسه الصوت مليا
وهتاف رددته الظلماتُ
وروته شجرات السرو في صوت عميق
«إنها ماتت» وهذا ما تقول العاصفاتُ
«إنها ماتت» صدى يصرخ في النجم السحيق
و تكاد الآن أن تسمعه خلف العروق

* * * *

صوت «ماتت» رَنَّ في كل مكان
هذه المطرقة الجوفاء في سمع الزمان
صوت «ماتت» خانق كالأفعوان
كل حرف عصب يلهث في صدرك رعبا
ورؤى مشنقة حمراء لا تملك قلبا
و تجنّي مخلب مختلج ينهش نهشا
و صدى صوت جحيمي أجشا
هذه المطرقة الجوفاء: «ماتت»
هي ماتت، وخلا العالم منها
و سدى ما تسأل الظلمة عنها
و سدى تصغي إلى وقع خطاها
و سدى تبحث عنها في القمر

و سدى تحلم يوما أن تراها

في مكان غير أقباء الذكرْ

إنها غابت وراء الأنجم واستحالت ومضة من حلم.

وليست المحاولات التي ذكرناها هي الوحيدة التي جربت فيها الشاعرة تقنية التكرار في ديوانها **شظايا ورماد** تأثرا بپو، بل هناك محاولات أخرى. فالتكرار في هذا الديوان موجود في ١٩ قصيدة من مجموع ٣٢ قصيدة، وهذا لا يعني أنه غير موجود في القصائد الأخرى؛ فهو يكاد يكون موجودا في جميع القصائد، ولكننا اقتصرنا في إحصائيتنا هذه على التكرارات التي أخضعتها الشاعرة لنظام معين في قصائدها. فمن هذه التكرارات ما هو تكرار كلمة كما في قصيدتي «يوتوبيا في الجبال» و« ذكريات» ،(٣٤) حيث كررت كلمة «تفجري» في الأولى، وكلمات «كان» و«كانت» و« كنت» و«لم أكن» في الثانية. ومنها ما هو تكرار عبارة، كتكرار عبارة «لن يجيء» في قصيدة «الأفعوان»، وعبارة «عد بنا» في قصيدة «في جبال الشمال».(٣٥) ومنها ما هو تكرار لازمة في أواخـــر المـقـاطـع مـثـل لازمـــة «واخيبتاه» في قصيدة «جامعة الظلال».(٣٦)

وإذا صح أن نعد تكرار اللازمة في أوائل المقاطع ابتكارا قياسا على ما أخذته الشاعرة عن پو، فإنها قد فعلت ذلك في ست من قصائدها في الأقل مثل: تكرار لازمة «غدا نلتقي» في قصيدة «الباحثة عن الغد»(٣٧) وتكرار لازمة «مرت أيام» في قصيدة «نهاية السلم»(٣٨) وتكرار لازمة «لنكن أصدقاء» في قصيدة «لنكن أصدقاء».(٣٩) ويمكن أن نقسـم اللازمات التي اسـتخدمتها الشاعرة في أوائل المقاطع إلى قسمين: ثابتة كالـتي مر ذكرها، ومتغيـرة (في بعض كلماتها) كالتي اسـتخدمتها في قصيدتي «خـرافات»(٤٠) و«أنا».(٤١) ففي قصيدة «أنا» مثلا لجأت الشاعرة إلى تغيير الكلمة الأولى من اللازمة، فمرة تقول «الليل يسأل من أنا »، وأخرى تقول «الريح تسأل من أنا»، ثم «الدهر يسأل من أنا»، ثم «الذات تسأل من أنا»، الأمر الذي يذكرنا بالتغيير الذي كان يجريه پو على أبيات قصيدة «أولالوم» المتكررة .

هذه كلها مجرد أمثلة، حتى لنستطيع القول: إن تقنية التكرار أصبحت الظاهرة البارزة الثانية في ديوان **شظايا ورماد** بعد ظاهرة تجربته العروضية الجديدة. وقد امتدت هذه الظاهرة إلى ديوانها الثالث **قرارة الموجة**.(٤٢) فهناك سبع من قصائد الديوان استخدمت فيها تقنية التكرار، ولكنها اقتصرت على القصائد المقطعية Stanzaic Poems فقط، ولم تشمل القصائد الحرة، وكانت بين ترديد لازمة في أوائل مقاطع القصيدة أو في نهايات مقاطعها. والقصائد هي «الأعداء» و«نفترق» و«ماذا يقول النهر» و«لحن النسيان»(٤٣) ولازماتها في أوائل مقاطعها، و«الزائر الذي لم يجيء» و«غسلا للعار» و«هل ترجعين»(٤٤) ولازماتها في نهاية مقاطعها، ولكن صدى لازمة پو Nevermore كان يتردد في جميعها.

ومثلما قلّت تقنية التكرار في **قرارة الموجة** عنها في **شظايا ورماد**، كذلك حدث في ديوان **شجرة القمر**؛(٤٥) إذ لم نلحظ وجودها إلا في أربع قصائد هي «تحية للجمهورية العراقية» و«أغنية حب للكلمات» و«إن شاء الله» و«أغنية لطفلي» .(٤٦) واستمرت الظاهرة

في ديواني الملائكة اللاحقين **للصلاة والثورة**(٤٧) و**يغير البحر ألوانه**(٤٨) ولكنها لم تخرج عن النمط الذي استقرت عليه في ديوانها **شجرة القمر** فتراوحت بين تكرار كلمة وتكرار لازمة. وبذلك تحولت تقنية التكرار في شعر الملائكة إلى تقنية اعتيادية، عفوية، أو أقرب إلى العفوية.

إلهام نظري أيضا:

لم تكن غايتنا هنا دراسة التكرار وأنماطه وأساليبه في شعر الملائكة، وإلا لكان علينا الدخول في تحليلات ومقارنات أخرى وتقديم تفاصيل أوسع وتقويمات مسببة، بل كانت الغاية التعرف في لمحات سريعة على مدى تأثير شعر بو في شعرها، وعلى الكيفية التي استفادت بها من قراءة شعره ومقالاته النقدية. فنحن نعتقد أن قصائد بو الثلاث التي تكرر ذكرها هنا، وكذلك مقالته «فلسفة التأليف» هي التي نبهتها إلى أهمية تقنية التكرار في الشعر وإمكانياتها التعبيرية فحاولت استثمار هذه التقنية في شعرها إلى المدى الذي رأيناه، كما نعتقد أنها هي التي ألهمتها بعض أفكار المقالتين اللتين كتبتهما عن هذه التقنية بعد أن شاعت ظاهرة التكرار في الشعر العربي الحديث. والمقالتان هما: «أساليب التكرار في الشعر» و«دلالة التكرار في الشعر»(٤٩) وهذا واضح مثلا في شرح ما أسمته بتكرار التقسيم وشرح ما أسمته بالتكرار اللاشعوري.(٥٠)

ذلك أن بو قد تحدث عن شيئين جوهريين في مقالته المذكورة أولهما: الأصالة والإبداع Originality في الشعر، ويعني هنا الابتكار في موسيقاه تحديدا، فرأى أن مجال التنويع والابتكار في الإيقاع محدود بينما هما لا حدود لهما في البحر الشعري Metre وفي المقطع Stanza. ولذلك قرر خرق النظام التقليدي في نظم المقطع على بحر التروكي Trochaic وقام بجمع الأشطر التي تختلف في عدد تفعيلاتها في مقطع واحد، وهو ما فعلت الملائكة على غراره في نظم القصيدة الحرة، كما نوهنا سابقا، وحتى الشكل المقطعي Stanzaic Form الذي تمسكت به الملائكة تمسكا مبالغا فيه، وحاولت التنويع في أطوال أبياته وفي أشكال قوافيه كثيرا جدا كان، في رأينا، بتأثير ما قاله بو عن إمكانية التنويع والابتكار اللامحدودة في مقطع القصيدة المقطعية، وهو أمر يستحق، كما نعتقد، دراسة مستقلة.

أما الشيء الجوهري الثاني الذي تحدث عنه بو في مقالته هذه فهو بحثه عن وسيلة فنية حادة Artistic piquancy يمكن أن تكون مفتاح إثارة Key-note في بناء القصيدة ومحورا Pivot يدور حوله كل تركيبها. ولم يجد، بعد أن فكر بدقة كما يقول، غير اللازمة Refrain، لما في تكرارها من قيمة صوتية ودلالية (صوتا وفكرة كما يقول). وهذا لم ينبه شاعرتنا الملائكة إلى أهمية اللازمة وقيمتها فحسب، بل نبهها كذلك، مع تطبيقات بو العملية في قصائده الثلاث، إلى قيمة تقنية التكرار وأهميته وكيفيات استخدامه. ولم يكن عسيرا على شاعرة بذكائها وثقافتها التقاط هذه الأفكار والتأمل فيها وتطويرها في مجالها الخاص شاعرة وناقدة.

صحيح أن التكرار موجود في الشعر العربي الموروث منذ المهلهل بن ربيعة (أي

منذ أكثر من ألف وخمسمائة عام)، ولكنه قليل حد الندرة بحيث لا يشكل ظاهرة. كما أن التكرار في هذا الشعر لم يكن تقنية مقصودة يفكر بها الشاعر ويتعمدها لغايات فنية يريدها، بل كان وليد انفعالات لحظية عابرة، بغض النظر عما نرى فيها اليوم من دلالات لم يقصدها الشاعر وإنما ألهمتنا بها تأويلاتنا. ولذلك لم يدرس نقدنا الموروث التكرار دراسة فنية خاصة، بل علق عليها تعليقات ذوقية عابرة. وهذا ما تؤكده دراسة الملائكة نفسها في مقالها «دلالة التكرار في الشعر».

والآن، لعلنا لا نغالي إذا قلنا: إن إدغار ألان پو، شاعرا وناقدا، كان الأساس في جديد نازك الملائكة، شاعرة وناقدة. وهي لم تتخلص من أثر پو حتى بعد أن قرأت آخرين مثل ت. س. إليوت T. S. Eliot (١٨٨٨–١٩٦٥) وديلان توماس Dylan Thomas (١٩١٤–١٩٥٣)(٥١) وغيرهما من كبار شعراء عصرنا، ولا بعد أن رأت ما من تجارب مجايليها من شعراء الحداثة العربية، عراقيين وغير عراقيين.

جديد من قديم:

ترى ما معنى أن يكون پو أساس الجديد في شعر الملائكة؟

معناه، في رأينا، أن الملائكة لم تقبس نار جديدها من الجديد حقا، كما فعل مجايلوها، بل قبستها من قديم الشعر الأميركي. فليس پو سوى صاحب تجارب أولية قليلة ومحدودة في خرق تقاليد الشعر المكتوب باللغة الإنكليزية قد لا تتجاوز أصابع اليد الواحدة.

صحيح أن پو حظي باحتفاء غير عادي من لدن شعراء مثل: بودلير ومالارميه ولافورغ وأخيرا ڤاليري في فرنسا، وقسطنطين بلمونت في روسيا، وروبين داريو وغيره في أميركا اللاتينية، ولكنه ظل شاعرا ثانويا في معايير النقد الإنكليزي حتى يومنا هذا. وفي رأي موريس باورا Maurice Bowra «أن بودلير هو الذي اكتشفه وخلقه إلى حد ما»، وأن شهرته في أوروبا وأميركا اللاتينية كانت «خطأ ناجما عن عدم القدرة على تذوق الشعر الإنكليزي في قيمته الحقيقية» ولأن الأوروبيين والأميركيين اللاتينيين «لا يستطيعون فهم الشعر (الإنكليزي) مثل أهله».(٥٢)

ولا بد لنا أن نقول: إن هذا إجحاف بحق پو، فشهرة هذا الشاعر لم تأتِ من فراغ، بل من خلال شعره ونظريته الشعرية، فضلا عن قصصه. فهو أكثر من أن يكون مجرد شاعر رومانسي؛ فلديه هذا التعلق بالجمال المطلق والبحث عنه في ما وراء الواقع، ولديه هذا الشغف بالتميمة والعلامة والكلمة السحرية والزخارف الموسيقية، لديه كل ذلك وغيره مما جعله مصدر إعجاب لدى البرناسيين والرمزيين الفرنسيين. وميزة پو بين شعراء زمانه نزوعه إلى خرق التقاليد الشعرية السائدة وحرصه على ابتكار الجديد في موسيقى الشعر ولغته، وربما كان هذا هو السبب الذي جعل نازك الملائكة تميل إلى شعره في مرحلتها المبكرة.

ولكن پو، في أية حال، يبقى من شعراء النصف الأول من القرن التاسع عشر، أي من شعراء الإرهاصات الأولى التي مهدت للحداثة الشعرية، وربما انطبق عليه الوصف

الذي أطلقه أرتور رامبو على «ملك الشعراء» بودلير، ونعني قوله عنه: إنه مغال في صنعته الفنية Très artistique. وربما انطبق هذا الوصف على شاعرتنا الملائكة أيضا، فهي أيضا مغالية في صنعتها الفنية بسبب تمسكها الشديد بالوزن وقواعده واهتمامها بالتقفية وشروطها ورنين القافية وموسيقاها.

والسؤال الذي يواجهنا الآن هو: هل حافظت الملائكة على ما اقتبسته من بو وطورته، أم كان لها معه شأن آخر؟

هذا ما يجيب عنه القسم الثاني من هذه الدراسة.

ثانياً: نازك الملائكة وسطوة القديم

يستطيع دارس شعر الملائكة ونظريتها الشعرية أن يكتشف من دون عناء أن صلتها بالقديم الموروث ظلت قوية وعميقة، وأن جديدها لم يأت نتيجة قطيعة فنية معه، أو ثورة جذرية على تقاليده، بل نتيجة فورة شبابية عابرة كانت لها ظروفها وبواعثها الخاصة، ثم سرعان ما خفتت هذه الفورة وخمدت نارها وعاد القديم ليفرض هيمنته على شعرها وتفكيرها من جديد.

التراجع النظري عن الجديد:

إن من يقرأ مقدمة ديوانها الثاني **شظايا ورماد** الصادر عام ١٩٤٧ يتوقع أنها مقدمة على تغيير جذري (راديكالي) في شعرها وأفكارها، ولكنه سرعان ما سيصدم حين يتابع ما نشرته بعد هذا الديوان من قصائد ومقالات ضمها ديوانها الثالث **قرارة الموجة** الصادر عام ١٩٥٧ وكتابها **قضايا الشعر المعاصر** الصادر عام ١٩٦٢، وسيجدها وكأنها غير الشاعرة التي قالت «في الشعر، كما في الحياة، يصح تطبيق عبارة برنارد شو: 'اللا قاعدة هي القاعدة الذهبية'»، وغير التي تنبأت للشعر العربي بـ «تطور جارف عاصف لن يبقي من الأساليب القديمة شيئا» وبأن «الأوزان والقوافي والأساليب والمذاهب ستتزعزع قواعدها جميعا». (٥٣)

فالشاعرة التي قالت هذا أعطت نفسها حق وضع قواعد جديدة للشعر الجديد اعتمادا على حسها الشعري وذوقها الخاص، أسوة بالخليل بن أحمد الفراهيدي(٥٤) وقيدت نفسها بها، وطالبت غيرها من الشعراء بأن يحذوا حذوها في هذه القواعد.

والشاعرة التي تنبأت بحدوث «تطور جارف عاصف» في الشعر العربي «لن يبقي من الأساليب القديمة شيئا» وعبرت عن إيمانها بمستقبل الشعر العربي «إيمانا حارا وعميقا»، وبأنه «مندفع بكل ما في صدور شعرائه من قوى ومواهب وإمكانيات، ليتبوأ مكانا رفيعا في أدب العالم»، هذه الشاعرة وقفت على الضد من هذا التطور والاندفاع، وراحت تنتقد الشعراء المندفعين في طريق التطور وتسفه تجاربهم وتتهمهم بالتطرف والتقليد والتعصب والعناد، وتصمهم، أحيانا، بالإفساد، وغير ذلك من التهم. وصارت تتنبأ للشعر الجديد بـ «نهاية مبتذلة» والوصول إلى «نقطة الجزر» وتتوقع أن يرتد عن حركة الشعر الحر

أكثر المستجيبين لها.(٥٥)

والشاعرة التي اعتبرت ذلك «التطور الجارف العاصف» نتيجة منطقية لإقبال الشعراء العرب على قراءة الآداب الأوروبية ودراسة أحدث النظريات في الفلسفة والفن وعلم النفس، وقالت «و نحن بين اثنين: إما أن نتعلم النظريات ونتأثر بها ونطبقها أو ألا نتعلمها إطلاقا»، هذه الشاعرة صارت ترى أن التراث القديم «كان هو المنبع الذي ساق الشعراء إلى إبداع الجديد»، وراحت تتهم من تسميهم «المتطرفين» بتقليد الغرب، وتقسمهم إلى صنفين: قلة من المفسدين الكبار وأغلبية تماشي السوق.(٥٦) وهكذا ناقضت الملائكة نفسها بنفسها، وكل ذلك معبر عنه بصيغ شتى في مقالاتها وفي العديد من أحاديثها الصحفية.

ويبدو لنا أن هذه الشاعرة الموهوبة فهمت، في كتاباتها النقدية، حركة الحداثة في الشعر العربي، منذ البداية، فهما خاصا، فهم أساسه تفكير محافظ لا يرغب في الجديد إلا إذا كان تنويعا للقديم، وهذا ما يمكن أن نلمسه في مقدمة ديوان **شظايا ورماد** نفسها. فبرغم انها انتقدت في هذه المقدمة ما أسمته «طريقة الخليل» وعدتها طريقة صدئة لطول ما لاكتها الأقلام والشفاه حتى مجتها،(٥٧) برغم ذلك عدت «الشعر الحر» مجرد «أسلوب جديد لترتيب تفاعيل الخليل» و«تعديل» لطريقته، وليس «خروجا» عليها.(٥٨) وهكذا حملت هذه المقدمة في ثناياها بذرة الارتداد على الأفكار الجديدة التي جاءت فيها.

فكما لو أن الشاعرة ندمت على ما بدر منها في هذه المقدمة من أفكار تقدمية، أخذت تتراجع عن هذه الأفكار في كتاباتها اللاحقة فكرة ففكرة وتأتي بنقيضها، حتى نقضتها جميعا. وهذا ما أوضحه بدقة الناقد عبد الجبار داود البصري في كتابه **نازك الملائكة: الشعر والنظرية**.(٥٩) فقد عرض البصري في هذا الكتاب الأفكار التقدمية التي وردت في تلك المقدمة وقابلها بالتراجعات التي جاءت في كتاباتها اللاحقة، ثم نظم جدولا طريفا، ولكنه دقيق ومعبر، بثلاث عشرة فكرة وردت فيها، وقابل كلا منها بنقيضها في كتاباتها الأخرى، واستنتج أخيرا أن الملائكة «قد أتت على جميع ما ذكرته في مقدمتها بما يشبه «المحو».(٦٠)

والملاحظ أن الأفكار التقدمية التي جاءت بها الملائكة في مقدمة **شظايا ورماد** لم تكن أفكارها الخاصة فحسب بل كانت أفكار جميع شعراء الحداثة الذين جايلوها، ولكنها كانت، في الواقع، أقدرهم على صياغتها وأجرأهم وأسبقهم في إعلانها. وهذا ما جعل من حركة الشعر الحر حركة عامة بينهم، لا مبادرة خاصة صدرت عن الملائكة أو السياب أو غيرهما، وهو أيضا ما جعل تراجعات الملائكة مقتصرة، ومحسوبة، عليها ولا شأن لغيرها بها.

لقد ظنت الملائكة أن سبقها في كتابة الشعر الحر والتنظير له، يعطيها الحق بأن تضع له قواعد، وأن تلزم نفسها وتلزم الآخرين بالتقيد بها، وهذا ما يشتم من بعض صيغ التعبير في كتاباتها. بل هي أعطت لنفسها الحق بأن تعتمد قراءتها الخاصة للشعر العربي وذوقها الشخصي في وضع هذه القواعد ما دام الخليل قد فعل الشيء نفسه في وضع علم

العروض حسب رأيها، متجاهلة أن الخليل استنبط عروضه من قراءة شيء وجد قبله بأكثر من ثلاثة قرون، في حين أنها استنبطت قواعدها من شيء لم يكن عمره يزيد عن عقد من الزمان وكان ما يزال في مرحلة تحول وتكوين، وللآخرين آراء مختلفة فيه.

وهكذا اعتمدت مفاهيمها ومعاييرها الخاصة، وهي مفاهيم ومعايير ذوقية، في وضع تلك القواعد، وحاولت أن تجعل منها قواعد عامة لكتابة الشعر ونقده، وراحت تنتظر من غيرها أن يخضع لها. بل هي اصطنعت مفاهيم مبهمة وغامضة مثل «الفطرة العربية» و«قانون الأذن العربية» وأرادت أن تجعل منها مقياسا يحتكم إليه في معرفة الجميل والقبيح والصواب والخطأ والمستساغ والممجوج فإذا كل ما تراه جميلا أو صائبا تقبله «الفطرة العربية» وتستسيغه «الأذن العربية»، وإذا كل ما تراه قبيحا أو خطأ أو ممجوجا ترفضه تلك الفطرة وتمجه تلك الأذن.(٦١) بل هي لم تتردد، أحيانا، في اتخاذ شعرها معيارا للتمييز بين الجيد والرديء في شعر غيرها.

ولم تكتفِ الملائكة بذلك، بل عارضت أية محاولة للتخلي عن الوزن في الشعر، سواء جاءت بصيغة الشعر الحر Free Verse أو بصيغة قصيدة النثر Prose Poem، وعدت هذا النوع من الكتابة «نثرا اعتياديا» ومثلت له بشعر محمد الماغوط في مجموعته **حزن في ضوء القمر** واستنكرت أن تتبنى مجلة **شعر** اللبنانية «هذه الدعوة الركيكة الفارغة من المعنى» وأن تحدث حولها «ضجيجا مستمرا لم تكن فيه مصلحة لا للأدب العربي ولا اللغة العربية ولا للأمة العربية نفسها».(٦٢)

التراجع الشعري:

هذه القواعد التي وضعتها الملائكة وألزمت نفسها بها أثرت على شعرها تأثيرا مباشرا، فظل أغلبه أسير الأشكال العروضية القديمة، والأشكال المقطعية المألوفة عند پو وكيتس وغيرهما من الشعراء الرومانسيين العرب والأجانب. فلو حسبنا رصيدها من القصائد المتحررة من هذه الأشكال، لاكتشفنا كم هي قليلة بالنسبة لمجموع قصائدها. ففي إحصائية قمنا بها وجدنا الآتي:

– أن ديواني **عاشقة الليل** و**مأساة الحياة** و**أغنية الإنسان** يحتويان ٨٦ قصيدة على «طريقة الخليل» وليس فيهما أية قصيدة من الشعر الحر.

– أما ديوان **شظايا ورماد** فلم يَحْتَوِ إلا ١٠ قصائد من الشعر الحر من مجموع ٣٢ قصيدة نشرت فيه.

– و أما ديوان **قرارة الموجة** فقد احتوى ٩ قصائد من الشعر الحر فقط من مجموع ٤١ قصيدة.

– و في ديوان **شجرة القمر** لم تنشر الشاعرة سوى ٧ قصائد من الشعر الحر من مجموع ٣٠ قصيدة.

– و لكن النسبة تَغَيَّرَتْ في ديوانها **للصلاة والثورة** فَضَمَّ ١٦ قصيدة من الشعر الحر من مجموع ١٨ قصيدة.

– أما ديوان **يغير البحر ألوانه** فقد كانت جميع قصائده، وعددها ١١ قصيدة ، من

الشعر الحر.

وبذلك يبلغ مجموع ما نشرته الملائكة من الشعر الحر ٥٣ قصيدة من مجموع ٢١٨ قصيدة نشرتها في دواوينها، أي ما يساوي أقل من ربع قصائدها. أما إذا اعتمدنا صدور ديوان **شظايا ورماد** أساسا للإحصائية، بوصفه الديوان الذي صدر بعد اهتدائها إلى «الشعر الحر»، فسيكون عدد القصائد الحرة التي نشرتها ٥٣ قصيدة من مجموع ١٣٢ قصيدة، أي أقل من النصف بكثير. وعلى الرغم من هذا فأثر نازك الملائكة لا يقاس كمياً بقصائدها التي تندرج تحت «الشعر الحر» بل بقوة هذه القصائد وزخمها بما جعلها رائدة ومجددة.

ردود أفعال النقاد والشعراء:

غير أن آراء الملائكة وأفكارها ونصائحها لم يستمع إليها أحد، وعدَّها الشعراء والنقاد في حينه آراء محافظة لا تعبر عن التحولات التي أخذت تطرأ على الشعر العربي ولا تسايرها، بل تتخلف عنها. فالخروج على النظام التقليدي، الذي تسميه الملائكة «طريقة الخليل»، لم يكن من أجل إحداث تغيير جزئي شكلي بل تحقيق تحول شامل وعميق في بنية القصيدة العربية، وفتح أفق جديد ورحب لكتابة شعر حديث بإيقاعات جديدة ولغة جديدة. فهذا الخروج ليس «تعديلا» لتلك الطريقة، بل «بديل» لها، أي بعكس ما فهمت الملائكة وأرادت. ولذلك وجد الشعراء والنقاد أن الأخذ بآرائها يعوق هذا التحول ويضر بقضية الشعر نفسه، ورأى بعضهم فيها «ردة شعرية»، فحملوا على هذه الآراء حملة قاسية وفندوها في كتاباتهم، ومن هؤلاء جبرا إبراهيم جبرا، ويوسف الخال، ومحمد النويهي، وعبد الجبار داود البصري، وكاتب هذه السطور، وغيرهم. لقد انتهز هؤلاء، وغيرهم، صدور كتابها **قضايا الشعر المعاصر** الذي نظرت فيه للشعر الحر للهجوم على آرائها وتفنيدها بعد سكوت عليها دام سنوات.

فقد ساء جبرا إبراهيم جبرا ويوسف الخال هجومها على مجلة **شعر** اللبنانية التي تبنت الدعوة إلى «قصيدة النثر»، ونفيها صفة الشعر عنها وعن كل كتابة شعرية غير موزونة فانبريا يفندان آراءها، فقال جبرا: إنها تتعكز «في إبراز عيوب الشعر الحديث على مفاهيم الشعر الموروثة »، ورأى «أن الشعر الحديث قلب لهذه المفاهيم وفتح لأرض جديدة»، واعتبر نقدها لهذا الشعر «نقدا خاطئا» واستغل الواقعة في التعرض لبعض معايب شعرها، وانتهى إلى القول «لا ضير على الشعر الحديث من نقد خاطئ وتهجم من مجمدي الإبداع العربي، ففيه من العافية ما لن ينال منه النقد والتهجم. غير أنه من المحزن أن نرى النقد الخاطئ والتهجم صادرين عن قلم عرف عنه في أول عهده تجريب وخصب ومشاركة في الكشف عن أرضنا الجديدة».(٦٣)

أما يوسف الخال فوصف آراءها بالتزمت والسلفية وعبادة القديم، وعُدَّ كتابها **قضايا الشعر المعاصر** مخيبا للآمال، واعتبر الآراء التي جاءت فيه «آراء ارتدادية متزمتة خانت حركة الشعر الحر التي تدعي المؤلفة اكتشافها». وقال إن معالجتها «لبعض الموضوعات خالية من الروح العلمية والإخلاص للحقيقة، وهما صفتان حاولت المؤلفة

أن تقنع نفسها وتقنعنا بأنها تتوخاهما في بحثها هذا».(٦٤)

وأما محمد النويهي فناقش آراءها النقدية التي وردت في كتابها نقاشا مفصلا في كتابه **قضية الشعر الجديد** واستعمل في نقد آرائها كلمات مثل: الضيق والتعسف والظلم والتحامل والتسرع إلى الاتهام.(٦٥) وخلاصة رأيه أن في آراء الملائكة «كثيرا من الخطأ، وكثيرا من الضرر لو تركت دون تصحيح». والخطأ الذي يعنيه هو «خطأ في تشخيص قضية الشعر الجديد» والضرر الذي يخشاه «هو إضرار بقضية هذا الشعر نفسه وتعويق له عن أن يستمر فيما نرجو له من النمو والتطور. فلو قبلت آراؤها تلك لما كانت نتيجتها إلا أن تقعد به عن الانطلاق وتشله عن حرية التجربة وتنتهي به سريعا إلى العجز والاختناق قبل أن يؤتي خير أكله ويستغل أقصى إمكاناته، دعك من أن يمهد لما نأمله بعده من تطور جديد يزيد عليه مرونة وخصوبة».(٦٦)

غير أن الناقد عبد الجبار البصري انتظر عدة سنوات قبل أن يتصدى لآراء الملائكة ويصدر كتابه **نازك الملائكة: الشعر والنظرية**، وهو الكتاب الذي سبقت الإشارة إليه، والذي كشف فيه المؤلف تراجع الشاعرة عن جميع ما جاءت به من أفكار تقدمية حول الشعر في مقدمة ديوانها **شظايا ورماد**.

ولم يكن الجيل اللاحق من الشعراء والنقاد أقل رفضا لآراء الملائكة وقواعدها من هؤلاء الذين جايلوها، بل كان موقفه من هذه الآراء والقواعد أكثر جذرية وتصلبا، وقد كتب شعراؤه ونقاده مقالات عديدة في الصحف والمجلات للتعبير عن موقفهم، ومن هؤلاء فاضل العزاوي وعبد الرحمن طهمازي، وكذلك كاتب هذه السطور في مقالته «نازك الملائكة وعروض الشعر الحر»(٦٧) التي نشرت لمناسبة صدور الطبعة الثانية من كتابها **قضايا الشعر المعاصر**. ولذلك لم يسلم شعراء هذا الجيل من نقدها المتزمت ومن اتهاماتها، وظهر هذا بوضوح في مقالتها المعنونة «رسالة إلى الشاعر العربي الناشئ» التي نشرتها في أول عدد من أعداد مجلة **الأقلام** العراقية الصادر في أيلول (سبتمبر) عام ١٩٦٤، أي في مرحلة تكون هذا الجيل الذي كان لا ينتقد شعر نازك وآراءها بل فقط أشعار مجايليها وآراءهم معها.(٦٨)

إصرار الملائكة على تراجعاتها:

ما ذكرناه هنا عن ردود الأفعال التي قوبل بها كتاب الملائكة **قضايا الشعر المعاصر** ليس سوى نماذج من سيل من الكتابات، فقد لقي هذا الكتاب والآراء التي وردت فيه أشد وأوسع ما يلقاه كتاب من نقد واعتراض، حتى لنستطيع أن نصف ذلك بأنه حملة واسعة وقاسية. وأكيد أن الملائكة لم تكن تتوقع مثل هذه الحملة لما كان لها من مكانة محترمة لدى الجميع، حتى لدى أشد منتقديها، وأكيد أن هذه الحملة قد آلمتها وأثرت فيها. غير أن ردود أفعالها عليها لم تظهر إلا بعد حين، وظهرت أول ما ظهرت في مقالتها «رسالة إلى الشاعر العربي الناشئ» التي مر ذكرها، ثم في ورقتها المقدمة إلى المؤتمر الخامس للأدباء العرب الذي عقد في بغداد عام ١٩٦٥، وأخيرا في مقدمة ديوانها **شجرة القمر** الصادر في مطلع ١٩٦٨. وكانت جميعها ردود فعل سلبية وانفعالية، فقد زادت

إصرارا على آرائها من ناحية، وتمسكا بـ «طريقة الخليل» في شعرها من ناحية أخرى؛ ففي رسالتها إلى الشاعر العربي الناشئ، حاولت أن تريه كيف يبني نفسه وثقافته ويكتب شعره على وفق آرائها وقواعدها التي جاءت في كتابها. وقالت له: «إن الشعر الحر - في صورته المثلى - لا يهدف إلى القضاء على أسلوب الشطرين وإنما هو أسلوب مكمل له، فيه استرسال وانطلاق يجعله ملائما لموضوعات عصرنا، ومن ثم فإن الاقتصار عليه ونبذ نظام الشطرين قد يحد من آفاق الشعر المعاصر فلا يخدمه كما يرجو، وإنما يسيء إليه». وأوصته بـ «دراسة القديم العربي دراسة جدية» إذ «ما من مجدد أصيل قط، إلا وقد درس القديم، بحيث ينبثق الجديد انبثاقا عفويا فلا يفقد الصلة بالتراث العربي، ولا يقصر عن التعبير عن روح القارئ المعاصر». وبعد أن نصحته بأن يقرأ «شيئا من تراث الغرب الشعري، وتراث الأمم الشرقية المجاورة» حذرته من أن ينقل في شعره «مذاهب الغربيين وأساليبهم اللغوية ومواقفهم العاطفية» لأن ذلك لن يكون «إلا تقليدا» وهو لن ينتفع به «إلا انتفاع العبيد». وحملت بعد ذلك على «المقلدين» وصنفتهم إلى صنفين: الصنف الأول صنف الذين يقرأون الشعر الغربي بلغاته الأصلية فيتبنون مواقف شعرائه! وأساليبهم وصورهم وآراءهم، وينقلونها نقلا لا شخصية فيه، وهؤلاء قلة، وهم المفسدون الكبار لروح الشعر وعليهم يقع اللوم في تضليل اليافعين الأبرياء. والصنف الثاني، وهم الأغلبية، وهؤلاء لا يحسنون لغة أجنبية إلى درجة تمكنهم من قراءة آدابها وإنما يقرأون المترجمات المستعجلة الركيكة التي تملأ أسواقنا، وقد لا يقرأون حتى المترجمات، وإنما يستعيضون عنها بالملخصات والآراء الجاهزة العامة حول الشعر الغربي. ثم يقرأون شعر الصنف الأول بما فيه من تقليد ومظاهر أجنبية زائفة فيضطرون إلى مماشاة السوق «ويصطنعون ما هو بارز من جوانب التقليد حتى يصبح على أيديهم تيارا عاما». ^(٦٩)

أما ورقتها المقدمة إلى مؤتمر الأدباء العرب الخامس فقد كانت بعنوان «الأدب والغزو الفكري» ورأت فيها أن الأمة العربية تتعرض إلى غزو فكري لا يقتل بالنار والحديد كالغزو العسكري «وإنما يهدم بالكلمة والحرف والمعنى، وسوى ذلك من سلاح غير محسوس، فهو ينطوي على الظلم والخبث معا». وقالت إن هذا الغزو «يستهدف روح الأمة وجذورها فلا يلقيها إلا وهي أشبه بثمرة امتص رحيقها فلم يَبْقَ منها غير القشر والنوى». ورأت أن الشائع بين الناشئة العرب اليوم «إحساس ضعيف تمكَّن من نفوسهم مؤداه أن علينا إذا أردنا أن نتبنى الغربي، وماضينا جملة (وأن نتقبل) التراث الغربي دونما مناقشة أو تدبر. وعلى أساس هذا الإحساس غرق الناشئة في الأخذ والاقتباس والتقليد حتى بلغ الأمر مبلغ الخطورة». ورأت أن «مظاهر الغزو في أدبنا الحديث تكمن في أربع جهات» أجملتها بـ: موقفنا من الأخلاق، وموقفنا من الدين، وموقفنا من اللغة العربية، وموقفنا من المعنوية الغربية، ثم أردفتها بتقديم «حلول ومقترحات». ^(٧٠)

ويلاحظ أن ما ذهبت إليه في هذه الورقة كان أشد حماسة وتعصبا مما ذهبت إليه في تعاليمها إلى الشاعر العربي الناشئ، حتى بدت ورقتها هذه وكأنها «كفارة» عما قالته يوما في مقدمة ديوانها **شظايا ورماد** عن أثر الآداب والنظريات الفلسفية والفنية الأوروبية في التطورات التي حدثت للشعر العربي. وعلى أية حال، وبرغم أن الحديث عن «الغزو

الفكري» أو «الغزو الثقافي» أو «تقليد الغرب» يجد له صدى لدى شريحة واسعة من المثقفين والأدباء العرب حتى هذا اليوم، مع التفريق بين المثاقفة والغزو، فإن هذه الورقة بالذات لم تَلْقَ استحسانا إلا لدى المتعصبين والمتزمتين، في حين انتقدها الآخرون انتقادا لاذعا، ومن هؤلاء سهيل إدريس وعلي الزبيدي.(٧١)

وإذا كان ما جاء في تلكما المقالتين تعبيرا عن موقف الملائكة النظري العام، فإن مقدمة ديوانها **شجرة القمر** يعزز موقف التراجع والخضوع لسطوة القديم. فقد بدت في هذه المقدمة وكأنها تدافع عن نفسها إزاء تهمة يوجهها إليها التقليديون، فأكدت أنها لم تَدْعُ يوما إلى الاقتصار على كتابة الشعر الحر كما فعل غيرها من الشعراء الذين «تركوا الأوزان الشطرية تركا قاطعا وكأنهم أعداء لها، وراحوا يقتصرون على نظم الشعر الحر وحده في تعصب وعناء». وتدليلا على «عدم تعصبها وعنادها» وتعبيرا عن حرصها على استعمال الأوزان الشطرية «طريقة الخليل» استشهدت بديوانيها السابقين **شظايا ورماد** **وقرارة الموجة**، وقالت إنها لم تنشر في الأول سوى ست قصائد حرة (الصحيح عشر قصائد) ولم تنشر في الثاني سوى تسع. وعزت موقفها هذا إلى سببين: أولهما مزاجي في رأينا، وهو أنها تحب الشعر العربي ولا تطيق أن يبتعد عن عصرنا هذا عن «أوزانه العذبة الجميلة»، وثانيهما انفعالي (رد فعل)، وهو أن الشعر الحر يملك، في رأيها، عيوبا واضحة صورتها وكأنها عيوب أصيلة ملازمة له، أبرزها الرتابة والتدفق والمدى المحدود. وقد ظهرت هذه العيوب، كما تقول، في أغلب شعر شعراء هذا اللون. ثم تَوَصَّلَتْ إلى نتيجة غريبة مفادها أنها على يقين من «أن تيار الشعر الحر سيتوقف في يوم غير بعيد، وسيرجع الشعراء إلى الأوزان الشطرية بعد أن خاضوا في الخروج عليها والاستهانة بها». غير أنها تداركت ذلك بقولها «وليس معنى هذا أن الشعر الحر سيموت، وإنما سيبقى قائما يستعمله الشاعر لبعض أغراضه ومقاصده دون أن يتعصب له ويترك الأوزان العربية الجميلة». وبناء على ذلك لم يتضمن ديوانها هذا سوى سبع قصائد من الشعر الحر من مجموع ثلاثين قصيدة. وأخيرا عبرت عن أسفها لأنها لم تُعْنَ في شعرها الحر «عناية أكبر بالقافية» فقد كانت تغير القافية سريعا وتتناول غيرها، وهذا في رأيها، يضعف الشعر الحر. ولذا باتت تدعو «إلى أن يرتكز الشعر الحر إلى نوع من القافية الموحدة ولو توحيدا جزئيا، فبذلك نزيده موسيقى وجمالا ونحميه من ضعف الرنين وانفلات الشكل»،(٧٢) بالرغم من أنها كانت من أكثر الشعراء العرب عناية بالقافية ورنينها الموسيقي، سواء في شعرها المقطعي أم شعرها الحر.

عودة متأخرة إلى الجديد:

ومع ذلك، يبدو أن هذا الذي كتب في الرد على الملائكة وتفنيد آرائها كان شديد الضغط عليها، ولكنها، وهي الشخصية القوية المستقلة، لم تستجب له إلا بعد حين، فأدت بها هذه الاستجابة إلى إعادة النظر في بعض آرائها، وخاصة موقفها من موضوع كتابة الشعر الحر. وظهرت هذه الاستجابة في مظهرين:

الأول: قولها في مقدمة ديوانها **للصلاة والثورة**: «أنني منذ ثلاث سنوات ملتصقة

أشد الالتصاق بالشعر الحر، غير راغبة في تخطيه والعودة إلى شيء من الشطرين» وعللت ذلك بأن «لفتات الذوق تتبدل تبدلا محتوما من عصر إلى عصر».(٧٣)

والثاني: أنها لم تنشر في هذا الديوان سوى قصيدتين اثنتين من شعر الشطرين من مجموع ثماني عشرة قصيدة يضمها الديوان، وأنها لم تنشر في ديوانها اللاحق **يغير البحر ألوانه** سوى إحدى عشرة قصيدة جميعها من الشعر الحر.

لقد كان هذا نوعا من التراجع عن القديم والعودة إلى الجديد بتعليل حذر وخجول. ويخيل إلينا أن كتاب عبد الجبار داود البصري الذي سبقت الإشارة إليه كان هو السبب وراء هذا التراجع. فقد جَسَّمَ أمام الشاعرة، بما لم يفعله أي ناقد، ومن دون أي تحامل، صورة التناقض بين ما كانت عليه بدايتها في ديوان **شظايا ورماد** وما أصبحت عليه بعد عشرين سنة أو نحوها من صدور هذا الديوان، وهكذا جعلها تشعر بأنها مهددة بأن تخسر «مجد» المبادرة التاريخية التي حققتها في قصائد هذا الديوان ومقدمته، فأعادت النظر في موقفها.

غير أن أحد النقاد، وهو عبد الرضا علي، وجد تفسيرا طريفا لهذا التراجع فعزا موقفها المتزمت إلى «تعنت مزاجي» هدفه «مخالفة المهاجمين ومناكدتهم». ويوضح رأيه فيقول: أنها قد لجأت «إلى الدعوة إلى الأوزان الشطرية إمعانا في مخالفة المهاجمين لها وإغاظتهم ليس غير، لأننا وجدناها تعود إلى الشعر الحر، مدافعة عنه، داعية إليه».(٧٤) وفي أية حال كان هذا التراجع مظهرا من مظاهر التجاذب بين القديم والجديد في شـــعر الملائكة ومفاهيمها الشعرية. ومهما تكن أسبابه فإنه جاء متأخراً جداً، أي بعد أن قطع الشعر العربي شوطا بعيدا في طريق تحولاته تخلف عنه شعرها ولم يستطع بلوغه بتراجعها الجديد. ذلك أن خطأ المـلائكـة الجسيم، هذه المـرة، هو أنها فهمت اعتراضات المعترضين على شعرها ونظريتها الشعرية فهما شكليا وكميا، فظنت أنها مطالبة بالإقلاع عن نظام الشطرين فقط، في حين أنها كانت مطالبة بإحداث تحول نوعي عميق وشامل في بنية قصيدتها.

لقد كانت نازك الملائكة موهبة كبيرة فذة في الشـــعر العربي الحديث، ولكنها كبلت نفسها بيديها ومنعتها من أن تنطلق على سجيتها وتتفاعل بعمق وإيجابية مع ما يدور حولها، وسـمـحت لشعراء أدنى منها موهبة وأقل ثقافة بتجاوزها، وارتضت لنفسها «أرستقراطية شعرية» لها تقاليد لا تفرط بها، وترفع لا تتنازل عنه، وغليانات لا تسمح لها بالتفجر واختيار التقنية التي تلائمها وتستوعبها.

أسباب التردّد بين القديم والجديد:

هل لذلك من أسباب غير الأسباب الظاهرة؟ لماذا ظلت هذه الشاعرة الموهوبة الكبيرة تتردّد بين القديم والجديد وظل هذان يتجاذبانها من دون فكاك؟ لِمَ لم تعكف على تطوير تجربتها في **شظايا ورماد** وتصعد بها مع الصاعدين من شعراء جيلها؟

يخيل إلينا أن هناك أربعة أسباب جوهرية وراء هذا التردّد، أولها إيديولوجي، وثانيها أخلاقي، وثالثها ذاتي، ورابعها بيئي.

أما السبب الإيديولوجي فهو أن الملائكة من المؤمنين الثابتين بالعروبة، وقد عبرت عن هذا الإيمان في شعرها ومقالاتها بوضوح لا لبس فيه. ولذلك يهمها أمر الحفاظ على هوية الأمة العربية وتراثها القومي، ومنه الأدب العربي، من المسخ والضياع. وهي ترى أن الحفاظ على هوية الأمة وتراثها يستوجب الاستقلال الفكري والثقافي عن الغرب، وإبقاء العلاقة مع الغرب في حدود المثاقفة الرصينة والانفتاح المدروس. وهي تعتقد أن ما قام به سواها من الشعراء، وخاصة شعراء مجلة **شعر** اللبنانية، هو تقليد لشعر الغرب وأساليبه ونظرياته، وأن ما يكتبه النقاد العرب هو ترديد لنظريات النقد الغربي ومناهجه يدخل في باب التقليد ولا يدخل في باب الانفتاح والمثاقفة، وأن الأولى بها، وهي العروبية الملتزمة، ألا تتورط في ما تورط فيه هؤلاء، شعراء ونقادا. وربما كان لحمى الصراع الإيديولوجي بين القوى والتيارات السياسية العربية من ناحية، ورسوخ إيمانها الديني وتصاعد حمية هذا الإيمان مع تقدمها في العمر من ناحية أخرى، أثر في تمسكها بمعتقداتها هذه وتصلبها فيها.

هذا عن السبب الإيديولوجي، أما عن السبب الأخلاقي فنظن أن الملائكة تعتقد بأنها مسؤولة مسؤولية مباشرة عما حدث من هذا الذي ترفضه وتنفر منه في شعر غيرها من الشعراء. ففي ظنها، كما يبدو، أنها هي التي فتحت لهم الباب على مصراعيْه حينما قالت في مقدمة **شظايا ورماد**: «في الشعر، كما في الحياة، يصح تطبيق عبارة برنارد شو: اللا قاعدة هي القاعدة الذهبية»، وهي التي تنبأت بحدوث «تطور جارف عاصف» في الشعر العربي «لن يبقي من الأساليب القديمة شيئا». فالذنب إذن ذنبها قبل أن يكون ذنب غيرها. وانطلاقا من إحساسها بهذه المسؤولية أرادت أن تكفر عن هذا الذنب فعمدت إلى وضع قواعد جديدة للشعر الجديد، وراحت تنصح الشعراء بتبنيها، وبعدم ترك نظام النظم القديم تركا قاطعا، وتلوم من يخرج على قواعدها ونصائحها، وحين لم يفد نصحها مجاييلها من الشعراء توجهت به إلى الشعراء الناشئين!.

وإذا جئنا إلى السبب الذاتي، فنظنها تعتقد بأنها هي، قبل غيرها، من أطلق شرارة الشعر الجديد، بغض النظر عن مدى صحة هذا الاعتقاد. ولذلك ترى أنها أولى من غيرها بوضع قواعده وتحديد منحى تطوره. وهي تعتقد بأن ما تقوله عنه هو القول الحق، وهو القول الفصل، وعلى غيرها ألا يستمع لنصائحها فحسب، بل يأخذ بها ويفيد منها، وإلا فهو أحد اثنين: إما متطرف مقلد للغرب، أو جاهل. وربما كان للمنافسة بينها وبين غيرها من شعراء جيلها أثر في ترسيخ هذه الاعتقادات في نفسها وفي الإصرار عليها.

ويبقى السبب البيئي، ونحن نعني به محيط الشاعرة الاجتماعي، أي الأفراد الذين عايشتهم واحتكت بهم في إطارها العائلي وإطارها الجامعي. فهم فيما يبدو ذوو آراء محافظة في الشعر تهيمن عليها رواسب الموروث القديم، ذائقة ومفاهيم. وهذه الآراء كانت تؤثر فيها برغم قوة شخصيتها واستقلالها الفكري، بخاصة وأنها لم يؤثر عنها الاحتكاك بالشعراء الآخرين في مجتمعهم الذكوري والدخول في حوارات مباشرة معهم، كما لم يؤثر عنها حضور المؤتمرات والندوات والمهرجانات الشعرية إلا فيما ندر، وكان هذا يضعها في نوع من العزلة هم في منجى منها. ولذلك كانت كتاباتها دفاعا عن تهم يوجهها

إلى الشعر الجديد ذوو الآراء والأذواق التقليدية، وحاولت أن تظهر بمظهر «الاعتدال» و«التوسط» في هذه الكتابات، فهي ليست مع قديم القدماء ولا مع جديد المجددين، وإنما بين بين.

خاتمة

غير أن هذا كله لا يمحو دورها الريادي في حركة الشعر العربي الحديث، ولا ينتقص من مبادرتها التاريخية. فلقد أعطت ما كان في وسعها أن تعطيه. وإذا كانت قد توقفت في منتصف الطريق فليس عن ضعف في موهبتها، أو نقص في ثقافتها، وإنما عن خلل في قناعتها الخاصة. وكان في إمكانها أن تعطي أكثر مما أعطت لولا تمسكها بهذه القناعات وإصرارها عليها. وربما كان شأنها سيكون أفضل لو لم تنهمك بالتنظير للشعر الجديد، وتقيد نفسها بمفاهيمها وأفكارها، وتصبح ملزمة أدبيا بكتابة الشعر في ضوئها. ولكن حتى تنظيرها هذا الذي جوبه بكثير من الاعتراضات، كان رياديا في بعضه في الأقل، وكان فيه الكثير من الآراء الصائبة، وقد فتح بابا واسعا للحوار حول الشعر الحديث وكان هذا الحوار ضروريا ومفيدا جدا. وبرغم تمسكها بقناعاتها وثباتها عليها، كان فتحها الحوار دليلا على إيجابيتها وشعورها بالمسؤولية الأدبية.

الهوامش

(١) هناك خلاف حول من كتب قبل غيره قصيدة متحررة من النظام التقليدي لنظم الشعر العربي، وكانت الفتيل الأول الذي فجر «حركة الشعر الحر». وقد تنافس على هذه الأسبقية كل من نازك الملائكة وبدر شاكر السياب. اقرأ عن هذه المنافسة ما جاء في الفصل السابع في كتاب س. موريه، **الشعر العربي الحديث ١٨٠٠–١٩٧٠ تطور أشكاله وموضوعاته بتأثير الأدب الغربي**، ترجمة شفيع السيد وسعد مصلوح (القاهرة: دار الفكر العربي، ١٩٨٦). ورأي موريه قابل للمناقشة في رأينا.

(٢) تقول نازك الملائكة إنها كتبت هذه القصيدة، وعنوانها «الكوليرا»، يوم ٢٧/١٠/١٩٤٧ وأرسلتها إلى بيروت فنشرتها مجلة **العروبة** في عددها الصادر في أول كانون الأول (ديسمبر) ١٩٤٧ وعلقت عليها المجلة في العدد نفسه. راجع هامش ص ٢٣ من كتابها **قضايا الشعر المعاصر** (بغداد: مكتبة النهضة، ١٩٦٥، ط ٢).

(٣) نشرت قصيدة السياب في الطبعة الأولى من ديوانه **أزهار ذابلة** (القاهرة: مطبعة الكرنك، ١٩٤٧).

(٤) نازك الملائكة، **قضايا الشعر المعاصر**، ص ١٨٦.

(٥) نازك الملائكة، **شظايا ورماد** (بيروت: دار العودة، ١٩٧١، ط ٢)، راجع ص ص ٢٥–٢٦ من المقدمة.

(٦) تقول الملائكة في رسالة شخصية عمن أعجبت بهم من الشعراء الإنكليز والأمريكيين:

«وأولهم عندي شكسبير في مسرحياته وسونيتاته وقصائده الطويلة، فقد أحببته أشد الحب، وما زلت أجد النشوة في قراءة شعره، فهو شاعر الذروة. يليه جون كيتس الذي درسته دراسة موسعة، وحفظت كثيرا من شعره. ويليه فرانسس تومسن، وروبرت بروك، وت. س. إليوت، وييتس، ودلن توماس. ومن الشعراء الذين أحببت شعرهم جون دون، فشعره يبدو لي رائع الأعماق بحيث أجد دائما لذة في قراءته. وهناك شعراء أقل شهرة أسعد بقراءة شعرهم مثل: إدغار ألان بو، وتشيسترتن، وأوسكار وايلد، ولونغفلو، وشعراء آخرون قد أكون منهم أحببت قصيدة أو قصيدتين. أما كولردج، وووردزورث، وشـــلي، وبايرون فقد قرأت لـهم كـثيرا وأحببتهم أحيانا ولم أتحمس لهم أحيانا أخرى. وكثيرا ما راق لي شعر المجهولين الذين يختصرون اسمهم بكلمة Anon كما أحببت الشعر الإنكليزي الشعبي وحفظت الكثير من الأغاني الأميركية الفلكلورية. وكل هذا الذي أقوله مختصر، فالشعر الإنكليزي واسع وأنا لا أكف عن القراءة فيه»، نقلا عن عبد الرضا علي، **نازك الملائكة – دراسة ومختارات** (بغداد: دار الشؤون الثقافية العامة، ١٩٨٧)، ص ص ١٩-٢٠.

(٧) من الشعراء الذين كتبت عنهم الشاعران الإنكليزيان جون كيتس وربرت بروك في مقالتها «الشعر والموت» والمقالة فصل من كتابها **قضايا الشعر المعاصر**. ومن الشعراء العرب الذين كتبت عنهم دراسات خاصة علي محمود طه وقد كتبت عنه كتابها **الصومعة والشرفة الحمراء – دراسة نقدية في شعر علي محمود طه.** كما كتبت عن الجانب العروضي من مسـرحية أحمد شـوقي **مصـرع كليوباطرا** وعن شعر إيليا أبي ماضي كتبت دراستين، وهذه كلها فصول في كتابها **سايكولوجية الشعر ومقالات أخرى** (بغداد: دار الشؤون الثقافية العامة، ١٩٩٣). والملاحظ أنها لم تكتب دراسات خاصة إلا عن الشعراء الذين تأثرت بهم بقدر أو بآخر.

(٨) ترجمت لتوماس غري قصيدته «مرثية كتبت في مقبرة ريفية» ونشرتها في ديوانها **عاشقة الليل** كما ترجمت إحدى سونيتات شكسبير بعنوان «الزمن والحب». وترجمت مقطوعة «البحر» من مطولة لورد بايرون *Childe Harold's Pilgrimage* ونشرتها في ديوانها **عاشقة الليل**. ولروبرت بروك ترجمت قصيدتين نشرتهما في ديوانها **شجرة القمر.** هذا عدا قصيدة لشاعر إنكليزي لم نجد له أثرا في الأنطولوجيات المتوفرة لدينا ويدعى كريسـمـس همفريس وأخرى لشـاعر فرنسـي يدعى بروسـبير بلانشـمين ونشرتهما في الديوان نفسه. والملاحظ أن الملائكة لا تترجم من الشعر إلا ما تعجب به وتتأثر. وقد كانت جميع ترجماتها شعرية وبتصرف.

(٩) كتابه: **الرحلة الثامنة** (صيدا، بيروت: منشورات المكتبة العصرية، ١٩٦٧، ط ١)، ص ١١.

(١٠) «رسالة من بغداد»، مجلة **شعر** اللبنانية العدد ٤ (خريف ١٩٥٧)، ص ١١٣.

(١١) راجع:

Khulusi, S. A. "Contemporary Poetesses of Iraq," *Islamic Review* 38 (June 1950): 40-45 (esp. pp. 42-44).

(١٢) س. موريه، **الشعر العربي الحديث**، ص ٢٩٤.

(١٣) نقلا عن صالح طعمة في مقالته «نازك الملائكة وآثارها في بعض اللغات الغربية»، **نازك الملائكة، دراسات في الشعر والشاعرة**، كتاب تذكاري أعده وقدم له عبد الله أحمد المهنا

(الكويت: شركة الربيعان للنشر والتوزيع، ١٩٨٥)، ص ١٢٣.

(١٤) مجلة **شعر** اللبنانية، العدد ٣ (صيف ١٩٥٧)، ص ٩٥.

(١٥) راجع:

Vincent Monteil, *Anthologie bilingue de la littérature arabe contemporaine* (Beyrouth: Imprimerie catholique,1961), 99-109.

(١٦) نشرت دراسة الواسطي في كتاب: **نازك الملائكة**، سلسلة الكتاب الذهبي ١، إعداد علي الطائي (بغداد: دار الشؤون الثقافية العامة، ١٩٩٥)، ص ص ٤٢-٦٢.

(١٧) **المرجع السابق**، ص ٤٨.

(١٨) راجع ما ذكرته نازك الملائكة عن هذه القصيدة في **قضايا الشعر المعاصر**، هامش ص ٢٣.

(١٩) وهذا لا يتعارض مع ما ذكرته الشاعرة في مجادلة عائلتها: «أقسم لكم أني اشعر اليوم بأني قد منحت الشعر العربي شيئا ذا قيمة». راجع: **المرجع السابق**، المقدمة، ص ١٣.

(٢٠) تجد القصائد والمقالات المشار إليها في:

The Norton Anthology of American Literature (New York, London: W. W. Norton and Company, 1979), vol I, 1202 -1383.

و كذلك في:

Mabbot, ed., *The Selected Poetry and Prose of Edgar Allan* Poe (New York: The Modern Library, 1951).

و نحيل القارئ إلى هذين المصدرين في كل ما يرد من ذكر لقصائد پو ومقالاته في هذه الدراسة.

(٢١) استخدم الواسطي هنا وصفا للناقد عبد الجبار داود البصري وصف به مقدمة **شـــــظايا ورماد** بأنها: «البيان الأول» لحركة ثورية شعرية.

(٢٢) المقصود مقدمة ديوان **شظايا ورماد**.

(٢٣) الواسطي، **نازك الملائكة**، ص ٥٥.

(٢٤) راجع الهامش رقم (٦) في هذه الدراسة بشأن ما جاء في الرسالة.

(٢٥) نازك الملائكة، **شظايا ورماد**، ص ١٨.

(٢٦) الواسطي، **نازك الملائكة**، ص ٦٥، وقبل أن ينبهنا الواسطي إلى تأثر الملائكة في كتابة قصيدتها «الكوليرا» بقصيدة پو «الأجراس» ذهب بنا الظن مرة إلى أنها تأثرت بقصيدة والت ويتمان Walt Whitman «من المهد دائم الاهتزاز» "Out of the Cradle Endlessly Rocking" المنشورة في ديوانه الوحيد: **أوراق العشب** *Leaves of Grass*. ففي مقطع من مقاطع هذه القصيدة يكرر ويتمان كلمة الموت Death عشر مرات، مرة في بيت من المقطع، وأربع مرات في البيت الذي يليه، وخمس مرات في بيت يأتي بعده بثلاثة أبيات (لاحظ الأبيات ١٦٨ و١٦٩ و١٧٣ من القصيدة)، وبالشكل الذي تكررت فيه هذه الكلمة في قصيدة الملائكة. ولكن هذه القرينة لم تكن كافية في رأينا، فعزفنا عن إعلان هذه الملاحظة في حينها.

(٢٧) نازك الملائكة، **شظايا ورماد**، ص ١٣٦.

(٢٨) **المرجع السابق**، ص ١٠٤.

(٢٩) نازك الملائكة، **قضايا الشعر المعاصر**، ص ص ٢٤١-٢٥٧.

(٣٠) نازك الملائكة، **شظايا ورماد**، ص ٦٧.

(٣١) **المرجع السابق**، ص ١١٦.

(٣٢) **المرجع السابق**، ص ٣٥.

(٣٣) **المرجع السابق**، ص ١٨٥.

(٣٤) **المرجع السابق**، ص ص ١٥٢ و١٧١.

(٣٥) **المرجع السابق**، ص ص ٧٥ و١٢٤.

(٣٦) **المرجع السابق**، ص ٩٩.

(٣٧) **المرجع السابق**، ص ٧٢.

(٣٨) **المرجع السابق**، ص ١٠٨.

(٣٩) **المرجع السابق**، ص ١٤١.

(٤٠) **المرجع السابق**، ص ٨٢.

(٤١) **المرجع السابق**، ص ١١٢.

(٤٢) نازك الملائكة، **قرارة الموجة** (بيروت: دار الآداب، ١٩٥٧، ط ١).

(٤٣) **المرجع السابق**، ص ص ٤٨ و٧١ و٩٥ و١٣٢ بالتوالي.

(٤٤) **المرجع السابق**، ص ص ١١٨ و١٤٥ و١٨٢ بالتوالي.

(٤٥) نازك الملائكة، **شجرة القمر** (بيروت: دار العلم للملايين؛ بغداد: مكتبة النهضة، ١٩٦٨، ط ١).

(٤٦) **المرجع السابق**، ص ص ٤٣ و٨٨ و١١٣ و١٥٨ بالتوالي.

(٤٧) نازك الملائكة، **للصلاة والثورة** (بيروت: دار العلم للملايين، ١٩٧٨، ط ١). وهذا الديوان تأخر صدوره عدة سنوات بسبب ظروف الحرب في لبنان.

(٤٨) نازك الملائكة، **يغير البحر ألوانه** (بغداد: وزارة الثقافة والإعلام، ١٩٧٧، ط ١).

(٤٩) نازك الملائكة، **قضايا الشعر المعاصر**، ص ص ٢٣٠-٢٤٠ وص ص ٢٤١ - ٢٥٧.

(٥٠) **المرجع السابق**، راجع فصل :« دلالة التكرار في الشعر»، ص ص ٢٤١-٢٥٧.

(٥١) ذكرنا هذين الشاعرين لأن الملائكة ذكرتهما وحدهما من بين من ذكرت من الشـعراء المحدثين الـذين أعجبت بـهم وقرأت لهم. راجع هامش رقم (٦) في هذه الدراسة.

(٥٢) جاء هذا في الفصل الذي كتبه باورا عن پو في كتابه The Romantic Imagination الذي ترجمه إبراهيم الصيرفي بعنوان **الخيال الرومانسي**، سلسلة المكتبة العربية (القاهرة: الهيئة المصرية العامة للكتاب، ١٩٧٧)، راجع: ص ص ٢١٢ و ٢١٣ بشأن ما اقتبسناه.

(٥٣) نازك الملائكة، **شظايا ورماد**، ص ٢٦.

(٥٤) نازك الملائكة، **قضايا الشعر المعاصر**، ص ٨٠.

(٥٥) **المرجع السابق**، ص ١٣.

(٥٦) نازك الملائكة، **سايكولوجية الشعر**، ص ١١٩.

(٥٧) نازك الملائكة، **شظايا ورماد**، ص ٦.

(٥٨) **المرجع السابق**، ص ٣١.

(٥٩) نازك الملائكة، **الشعر والنظرية** (بغداد: وزارة الإعلام، مديرية الثقافة العامة، ١٩٧١)، الباب

الثالث من الكتاب.

(٦٠) **المرجع السابق**، ص ٢٣٧.

(٦١) نازك الملائكة، **قضايا الشعر المعاصر**، ص ص ١٥٢-١٥٤ مثلا.

(٦٢) **المرجع السابق**، راجع الفصل الثاني من الباب الرابع من الكتاب وعنوانه «قصيدة النثر»، ص ص ١٨٢- ١٩٦، وكذلك الفصل الأول من الباب الثالث، مبحث «قصيدة النثر»، ص ص ١٣٢-١٣٦.

(٦٣) راجع مقالة «الشعر الحر والنقد الخاطئ» المنشـور في كتـابه **الرحلة الثامنة**، ص ص ٧-٢٩.

(٦٤) «قضايا الشعر العاصر»، مجلة **شعر** اللبنانية، العدد ٢٤ (خريف ١٩٦٢)، ص ص ١٣٨-١٥٢.

(٦٥) محمد النويهي، **قضية الشعر الجديد** (القاهرة: معهد الدراسات العربية العالية [من منشورات جامعة الدول العربية]، ١٩٦٤)؛ راجع ص ٢٢٩.

(٦٦) **المرجع السابق**، ص ١٦١.

(٦٧) راجع مجلة **الآداب** اللبنانية، العدد ٣ (آذار ١٩٦٦)، ص ص ١٤٨-١٥٠.

(٦٨) نشرت المقالة فيما بعد في كتابها: **سايكولوجية الشعر ومقالات أخرى**، ص ص ١٠٣-١٢٧.

(٦٩) **المرجع السابق**. راجع الصفحات: ١١٢ و١١٥ و١١٧ و١١٨ و١١٩.

(٧٠) نشرت الورقة في: مجلة **الآداب** اللبنانية، العدد ٣ (١٩٦٥)، ص ص ٣٠-٣٤. ويلاحظ أن الملائكة لم تُعِدْ نشرها في كتبها كما تفعل عادة في مقالاتها المنشورة.

(٧١) نشرت انتقادات إدريس والزبيدي في **الآداب** العدد المشـار إليه في الهامـش السـابق، ص ص ١٢٠-١٢٣.

(٧٢) نازك الملائكة، **شجرة القمر**، المقدمة، ص ص ١٥-١٧.

(٧٣) نازك الملائكة، **للصلاة والثورة**، المقدمة، ص ص ٢٠-٢١.

(٧٤) عبد الرضا علي، **نازك الملائكة – دراسة ومختارات**، ص ص ٧٣-٧٤.

حفريات أدبية في شعر محمود درويش:
مشروع قراءة في قصيدة «الهدهد»

محمد عجينة

يقوم محمود درويش فيما يكتب منذ أكثر من عقدين من الزمن بعمل شاعر القبيلة، يغوص في لغتها وفي ثقافتها بصفتها منظومة رمزية، فيشتق من نظام اللغة كلاماً جديداً متجددا على الدوام من قصيدة إلى أخرى «ذاكرة للنسيان»،[1] وينقش من خلال تشكيل القصيدة تاريخ فلسطين على مدى آلاف السنين «في بدئه المتواصل» حركة معبرة عن تجربة الوجود بأبعادها المختلفة.

وقصيدة «الهدهد»[2] أنموذج من نماذج المطولات الشعرية[3] التي تستوقف القارئ فيسائل منها عنوانها وبنيتها ودلالتها أو على الأصح دلالاتها. ذلك أن هذه القصيدة شأن نصوص أخرى عديدة لمحمود درويش – لا سيما منذ مجموعة **أعراس** – قريبة من مفهوم «النص الجمع» أو النص القابل للقراءة وإعادة القراءة بل لإعادة الكتابة scriptible.[4] ولئن كانت القراءة وإعادة القراءة أمراً ضرورياً في مجرى العادة أثناء التعامل مع «الأدب» – ولا سيما مع الشعر الحديث بوصفه لغة من درجة ثانية أو نظاماً سيميائياً ثانياً فوق نظام اللغة الطبيعية – لا يخضع لأعراف ثابتة، لا سيما بعد التخلي عن النظرة القديمة إلى القراءة القائمة على البحث عن معنى واحد حقيقي يسعى إليه القارئ، فمن باب أولى وأحرى أن يكون ذلك مع نصوص هي في آن واحد أشبه ما تكون بطبقات الأرض وبطبقات التاريخ وبالطروس، لأنها إذ تسائل الواقع الحاضر تسائل اللغة العربية بوصفها ذاكرة جماعية وتسائل الثقافة العربية والعالمية على مر التاريخ.

وتدل كتابات محمود درويش سواء منها مقالاته أو أشعاره على أنه قارئ فذ، ولذلك تقع على عاتق من يغامر فيتصدى لقراءة أشعاره ومحاولة تحليلها وتأويلها مهمة عسيرة، ألا وهي الحفر فيها سعياً إلى تبيّن ما تتضمنِو من طبقات دلالية تنشأ بحكم طبيعة لغته الشعرية، وبحكم ما ينصب فيها من نصوص أخرى تكون مع نص محمود درويش[5] في جوار وحوار ومساءلة خلاقة ضمن عملية الإبداع بمكوناتها المتعددة.

ويتنزل بحثنا هذا الخاص بقصيدة «الهدهد» ضمن مشروع أشمل هو تدبر العلاقة بين الأساطير والثقافة عامة[6] وبين «الأدبي والأسطوري» خاصة.[7] وقد كنا بيّنا في أعمال لنا سابقة أن الأساطير وأشكال الفكر الأسطوري ليست شأناً من شؤون الشعوب العتيقة فحسب وأن خطاب الأسطورة والوعي الأسطوري ضربان من المعرفة الحدسية ومن «رؤية الكون» قد تلابسان أشكالاً من الخطابات متعددة منها خطاب التاريخ وخطاب الفلسفة وخطاب الأدب كما نبينه أسفله، وأن الأسطوري – باعتباره سمة من سمات الفكر

أو من سمات الخطاب – قد يتجلى، علاوة على شكله السردي البديهي، شكل الحكاية
تروى،(٨) في أنظمة سيميوطيقية شتى: فقد يتجلى الأسطوري في نظام اللغة من خلال
بعض الدلالات القديمة تحفظها بطون المعاجم وحتى في الاستعمال اليومي(كاقتران
اللونين الأحمر والأزرق عند العرب بمعنى الشؤم كما في قولهم: «أشأم من أحمر عاد» أو
«زرق العيون»، وشبيه بما عند الألمان عندما ينعتون يوم الاثنين بأنه يوم أزرق)، كما
يتجلى ضمن الدلالة الرمزية الأسطورية المتصلة بمختلف الموجودات والكائنات مثل
الغراب العارف المعلّم، والحية والثور – لأن كل شيء يمكن أن يستحيل إلى أسطوري
مذ يدخل مجال اللغة – كما قد يتجلى الأسطوري في سنن أخرى codes أو أنظمة
تعبيرية أخرى غير لغوية مثل الطقوس (وهي الوجه العملي من الأساطير، كالرقص
والطواف والدُوار) أو كالنحت، لأن التمثال قد يكون أسطورة متجمدة مكتوبة بلغة النحات
ويتجلى في أشكال رمزية أخرى مثل مختلف الألوان والأشكال والجهات الدالة على
الفضاء ومثل الأرقام.(٩)

وقد تأكد لنا بعد طول ممارسة الشعر العربي، قديمه وحديثه، أن الأساطير مدخل
من المداخل المفيدة إلى الشعر، بل مفتاح من مفاتيح فك المستغلق منه من خلال
الاستعانة بالرموز الأسطورية وبالأساطير، وترسخ لدينا مع التقدم في الدراسة اقتناع بأن
الصلة بين الشعري والأسطوري ليست مجرد علاقة حضور للأسطوري في الشعري، وقد
تكون أجلى صورة من صور العلاقة وأبسطها كما بين ذلك بعض الدارسين،(١٠) بل هي
علاقة أشد متانة وعمقاً لأنها تتصل بالمنشأ، منشأ كليهما وهو المخيال الجماعي، وتتصل
بالبنية، كما تتصل بالوظيفة، حتى ليتساءل المرء إلى أي مدى يمكن أن تكون العلاقة بين
الأسطوري والأدبي، ولاسيما الشعري منه، مجرد علاقة مجاورة ومحاورة، وحتى ليتساءل:
هل هما مقولتان منفصلتان حقاً بسبب ما قد يوحي بضرب من التماهي، تماهي الشعري
والأسطوري، بحيث يكون القارئ إزاء إبداع شعري أسطوري كما يقول الفرنسيون
création mythopoïétique لا سيما عندما ينشئ الشاعر/الكاتب «أسطورة
أدبية»(١١) وهو ما نحاول بيانه في بداية هذا البحث من باب التمهيد.

ليس هدفنا من هذه «القراءة» لقصيدة «الهدهد» دراسة فنية مستفيضة
نأتي فيها على جميع جوانبها ولا أن نسعى إلى استفراغ دلالاتها؛ وهل ذلك ممكن خاصة
مع طول النص وانفتاحه على أنظمة دالة أخرى حتى لكأنه مجرّة من المعاني يمكن
أن نلج إليها من سبل شتى؟ إنما هدفنا محاولة التوسل إلى عالمها الشعري من باب
الأسطورة والرمز الأسطوري وتقديم مشروع قراءة لها. ونحن نزعم أن الهدهد في قصيدة
محمود درويش رمز يتجاذب نصه في اتجاهين اثنين:

– اتجاه سياقي سردي يشده نحو الحكاية شداً أفقياً.

– اتجاه جدولي paradigmatique عمودي يشده نحو الرمز، رمزية الهدهد
ومُتعلقاتها، لما للهدهد، بصفته رمزاً، من سمات الرمز؛ ألا وهي الحسية والقدرة
الاستكشافية والكثافة الدلالية، وهو ما يؤهله للتوحيد بين مناطق من العالم مختلفة بل
حتى بين المتناقضات(١٢) وهو ما يفسر لنا اعتماد الفلاسفة إياه وسيلة من وسائل التعبير

عندما يصوغون الفكرة المجرّدة التي لم تزل غير واضحة لديهم – وهذا معنى من معاني الاستكشاف – لا في شكل خطاب جدلي منهجي منظم، ولكن في قالب سردي محسوس يخرجها عن التجريد والإبهام من خلال عرضها في مجرى الزمان.

وتتجلى مظاهر الإبداع الفني في قصيدة محمود درويش المذكورة على هذين الصعيدين بالذات، صعيد الرمز وصعيد السرد وفي صلب كل منهما:

(١) إبداع على صعيد الصور الشعرية، «استعارات حية» تتجدد بها الدلالة لا على أنها مجرد اتساع معنوي في الكلمات معزولة كما هو الشأن في البلاغة القديمة ولكن من خلال تنزيل الاستعارة في إطار الإسناد ضمن الخطاب، أي بوصفها تقوم على عملية إسناد تبدو غير وجيهة ومتباعدة الطرفين، إلا أنه تطفر على أنقاض ذلك وجاهة جديدة على صعيد الجملة بأكملها واتساع في معاني الكلمات كما في قول درويش «ياهدهد الكلمات حين تفرخ المعنى وتخطفنا من اللغة الطيور» **(أرى ما أُريد، ص ٨٤)**.

(٢) إبداع على صعيد الحبكة Intrigue من خلال عملية توليف بين عناصر شتى في حبكة واحدة وقصة واحدة يمكن للقارئ أو للسامع أن يتتبعها وأن يدركها.(١٣) ومحمود درويش في كل ذلك يشتق نصه من رحم نصوص أخرى سابقة فنرحل مع الهدهد رحلة متعددة المحطات أو «المواقف» رحلة تبدو مكررة لرحلات سابقة، ولكنها أيضا فريدة بنيةً ودلالة. تنشأ من مساءلة النصوص السابقة ولكنها لا تنفيها بل تتراكب فوقها تماماً، كما أن الهدهد نفسه من حيث هو رمز ليس له مرموز واحد بل أكثر من ذلك لأنه يجمع بين صفة الآنية والزمانية ضمن شبكة معقدة من رموز أخرى لا تقل عنه أهمية في بناء القصيدة مثل الأرض/ الأم/ والماء – والظلّ بمعنى الروح، إلخ.

الهدهد ورمزيته الأسطورية مدخلاً إلى بنية القصيدة وتأويلها

إذا كانت الثقافة بمعناها الإثنوغرافي الواسع شبكة مركبة تحتوي على المعارف والعقائد والفن والقانون والأخلاق والتقاليد وجميع ما يكتسبه الإنسان بصفته فرداً في مجتمع ما من مهارات وما يقوم به من إنجازات (كما يرى تايلور)، أو بمعناها الأنثروبولوجي، منظومة رمزية تنشئها جماعة بشرية ما بقدر ما تنشئ هي تلك الجماعة(١٤) فإن اللغة أداتها وحافظتها حتى لقد عدها بعض الفلاسفة أعظم الأشكال الرمزية على الإطلاق لأنها تحتضن في صلبها جميع ما سواها من الأشكال الرمزية.(١٥) ولما كانت اللغة بالنسبة إلى الناطقين بها منظومة بواسطتها يكون التفكير والتعبير والتواصل في الحاضر وعبر التاريخ، فإن الحفر في اللغة يمكّن من تبين طبقات دلالية قديمة قد تغطي عليها دلالات أقرب عهداً. وقد اخترنا التوسل إلى هذه القصيدة بواسطة الهدهد وإن كان عنصراً واحداً لا غير من عناصر شبكتها الرمزية كما ذكرنا آنفاً.

الهدهد: الاسم والأسطورة

أنا هدهد – قال الدليل – سأهتدي للنبع إن جف النبات.
(محمود درويش، أرى ما أريد، ٨٣)

للاسم أهمية كبرى عند الشعوب القديمة فهو جزء من الكيان يقوم مقام الكل
ولذلك كانوا يعتقدون أن التأثير فيه قد يتم بواسطة التأثير في جزء منه كالشعَر والظلّ. كما
أن التسمية وإعادة التسمية عملية خلق وفعل، تماماً مثلما يمكن أن الخلق يتم بواسطة
الكلام، لذلك كانت العلاقة بين الاسم والمسمى في الفكر الأسطوري علاقة غير
اعتباطية – مثل علاقة الدال بالمدلول في اللغة – بل علاقة مُبرَّرة شأن العلاقة بين الميزان
وما يرمز إليه من معنى العدالة، ولا سبيل إلى أن يحل بدلاً منه أي رمز سواه.

يُعرّف الهدهد في **لسان العرب** لابن منظور تعريفا لغوياً: «الهُدهد طائر معروف،
وهو مما يُقرقر، وهدهدته: صوته والهُداهدُ مثله . . .»، كما تدل المادة اللغوية التي منها
اشتق اسم الهدهد على «أصوات الجن»؛[١٦] غير أن هذا التعريف غير كاف على عادة
المعاجم العربية العامة. فإذا نظرنا في معجم مختص هو **حياة الحيوان** للدميري،[١٧] وجدنا
تعريفا يستعيد كلاماً للجاحظ في **كتاب الحيوان**:

طائر معروف ذو خطوط وألوان كثيرة، وكنيته أبو الأخبار وأبو ثُمامة وأبو الربيع
وأبو روح وأبو سجّاد وأبو عباد ويقال له الهُداهد . . . والجمع الهَداهد، وهو
طير مُنتن الريح طبعاً لأنه يبني أفحوصه في الزبل وهذا عام في جميع
جنسه، ويُذكر عنه أنه يرى الماء في باطن الأرض كما يراه الإنسان في باطن
الزجاجة. وزعموا أنه كان دليل سليمان على الماء . . .[١٨]

بهذا يكون الهدهد قد اقترن في المعاجم العربية، وفي بعض النصوص كما يرد لاحقاً، بمعنى
الدليل الهادي إلى الماء والقادر على اختراق الظاهر والاطلاع على الخفايا والبواطن.

رمزية الهدهد طائراً ذا جناح: الوساطة

وللهدهد دلالة ثانية لأنه طائر أي لأنه ذو جناح، وهي دلالة رمزية كونية يقوم
بمقتضاها كل طائر وكل ذي جناح علاوة على رموز كونية أخرى، مثل الجبل أو الشجرة،
بدور الوساطة بين عالمي السماء والأرض أو بين الأعلى والأسفل؛ ولذلك تصوروا
الملائكة في صورة كائنات ذات أجنحة. ويشترك الهدهد مع الغراب في كونه – ضمن
الفكر الأسطوري وضمن الفكر الديني القديم – من العارفين بالغيب الدالين عليه.
وحسبنا في ذلك التذكير بالغراب الذي علّم قابيل كيف يواري في التراب سوءة أخيه
هابيل، وبغراب نوح أُرسل لكنه خان الأمانة فطار ولم يعد وعادت بعده الحمامة.[١٩] ولا

شك أن الإيمان بذلك يندرج ضمن فكر أسطوري قديم في عالم يسكنه المقدس ويتكلم لساناً واحداً يفهمه الإنسان والحيوان قبل «تبلبل» الألسن في بابل، في عالم لم يحدث فيه بعد ذلك الشرخ الذي حصل بين «الأسماء والأشياء».

الهدهد ودلالاته الرمزية في المخيال العربي الاسلامي

فبينما نحن في الصعود ليلاً والهبوط نهاراً إذ رأيت الهدهد مسلماً في ليلة قمراء في منقاره كتاب صدر من شاطئ الوادي الأيمن في البقعة المباركة وقال لي: أنا أحطت بوجه خلاصكما وجئتكما من سبأ بنبأ يقين وهو ذا مشروح في رقعة أبيكما. فلما قرأنا الرقعة إذا فيها مكتوب، إنه من الهادي أبيكم وإنه بسم الله الرحمان الرحيم كم شوّقناكم فلم تشتاقوا ودعوناكم فلم ترحلوا وأشرناكم فلم تفهموا . . .

– السهروردي، «الغربة الغربية»

ولئن اشترك الهدهد مع الغراب في كونه معلّماً ودليلاً فإنه يتسم ببعض المميزات الخاصة من حيث شكله ووظيفته. ولا شك أن قنزعة الهدهد ورائحته قد كانتا سبباً فيما نسج حوله من أساطير تعليلية آلت إلى خرافات ينسبها الجاحظ إلى الأعراب ويسوقها على أنها كلام مستملح من الكذب وليس من باب الحقيقة:

وأما القول في الهدهد فإن العرب والأعراب يزعمون أن القنزعة التي على رأسه ثواب من الله عز وجل على ما كان من برّ لأمه! لأن أمه لما ماتت جعل قبرها على رأسه. فهذه القنزعة عوض عن تلك الوَهدة. والهدهد طائر مُنتن البدن من جوهره وذاته . . . فأما الأعراب فيجعلون ذلك النتن شيئاً خامره بسبب تلك الجيفة التي كانت مدفونة في رأسه . . . ويزعمون أن الهدهد هو الذي كان يدل سليمان عليه السلام على مواضع المياه في قعور الأرضين إذا أراد استنباط شيء منها.[٢٠]

إن الهدهد، في اعتبارنا، من الرموز الصميمة، أي تلك الرموز ذات الأبعاد المتعددة لاتصالها بأكثر من صعيد من أصعدة الواقع أي أنها:
أ– تضرب بجذورها في عالم الكون لأنها منتزعة من عنصر من عناصره، بناء على أن من شأن الرمز أنه محسوس وكذا شأن الهدهد، ومنتزع من عالم الحس لتجسيم غير المحسوس مما يدخل في الغامض أو المجرد أو المقدس.
ب– كما تضرب بجذورها في عالم الأحلام والرغبات، تطفو من خلال اللغة والكلام. ولذلك نجد في كتب تعبير الرؤيا الفارسية القديمة والعربية الإسلامية: «والهدهد رجل بصير في عمله كاتب ناقد، يتعاطى دقيق العلم، قليل الدين وثناؤه قبيح

لنتن ريحه، وإصابته سماع خبر خير». (٢١)

جـ- وتتصل أخيراً بعالم ثالث هو عالم اللغة، لأنها تنتمي إلى عالم الكلام والإبداع. ولذلك فإن هدهد محمود درويش منذ البداية صورة ومجاز وليس على الحقيقة أي أنه «هدهد الكلمات»: «يا هدهد الكلمات حين تفرّخ المعنى وتخطفنا من اللغة الطيور» (ص ٨٤).

غير أن ورود الهدهد في خطابات شتى يغني رمزيته، ولا سيما رمزيته الأسطورية ويجعل له - وهو بعد الرمز متعدد الأبعاد - دلالات أخرى. فالهدهد يقترن بالماء (هو دليل على المياه) في قصص سليمان الملك النبي الذي له صورة متعددة الأوجه، (٢٢) لأنها تجمع في آن واحد بين صورة النبي وصورة الكاهن، يتحدث إلى الطير ويعرف قرب الخيل (والفرس حيوان مائي شمسي في آن ضمن الرمزية العالمية)؛ ولكن الهدهد ذا الخطوط التي تذكر بأشعة الشمس وذا التاج يقترن أيضا بالشمس في قصة بلقيس - بنت الهُداهد بن شرحبيل - ملكة سبأ، (٢٣) وكان قومها - مثلما تفيد بعض الحفريات والنقوش- يعبدون الإله المقة وتنطق، Ilmukah أو Illumquh وهو الإله القمر عند عرب جنوب الجزيرة العربية. (٢٤) في حين تشير بعض النصوص إلى أن قومها كانوا يعبدون الشمس.

ومهما يكن من أمر فإن رمزية الهدهد تغتني من خلال قصة النبي سليمان وبلقيس بدلالتين اثنتين متقابلتين - وليس ذلك بالغريب عن طبيعة الرمز - هما : دلالة الماء من جهة - وهي ذات صلة بالقمر من خلال المد والجزر، وبالأنوثة لتعلقها بالدورة الطمثية - ومن جهة ثانية دلالة الشمس وتقترن بالمُلك لأنها من شارتها، فضلاً عن تلك القدرة على اختراق الحجب والأسرار. أفليس الهدهد طائر بلقيس، وطائر سليمان، وصاحب تاج يعلو رأسه؟

إن ما ذكرنا مما يتصل بالهدهد لا يستنفد بطبيعة الحال جميع دلالاته الرمزية كما سنرى في غير ما رأينا من السياقات، لا سيما إذا حفرنا في ثقافات أخرى غير الثقافة العربية الإسلامية.

دلالات الهدهد الرمزية في التراث العالمي

إن الهدهد موجود في الأساطير الهندية والإيرانية القديمة، ولكن لا علاقة واضحة لهذه الأساطير - فيما يبدو لنا - بقصيدة محمود درويش، (٢٥) بل إن أوضح ما تبين لنا من صلته إلى نصوص أخرى لابن سينا والسهروردي وفريد الدين العطار وغيرهم كما سيأتي ذكره.

وخلاصة القول أن الهدهد بؤرة دلالية كثيفة، فهو ينتمي إلى عالم الحيوان وإلى عالم الإنسان: دليلاً حاد البصر عارفاً بمنابع المياه ذا صلة بالماء والشمس والملك، ولكن أيضاً رمزاً للقلب ومعرفة العالم المحتجب كما نراه مع السهروردي وفريد الدين العطار. ومجاله الدلالي الواسع هذا مفتاح لقراءة القصيدة لأنه سيكون عنصراً وسيطاً واصلاً فاصلاً بين عوالم مختلفة وبين أصعدة من القصيدة مختلفة. ولذلك اخترنا أن

يكون الحديث عنه مدخلاً تتنزل ضمنه قراءتنا لهذه القصيدة ومفتاحاً نتوسل به إلى بنيتها من جهة وإلى المستغلق من دلالاتها من جهة ثانية.

الهدهد والقصص الأسطورية المتصلة به في بنية قصيدة «الهدهد»: التناص الأسطوري مدخلاً

إن الهدهد هو العنصر الحاضر الناظم لجهاز قصيدة «الهدهد» الخطابي على اختلاف مستويات تنظيمه من لفظي وسردي وبلاغي. ولن ندرس جميع مستويات هذا الجهاز الخطابي بل سنقصر اهتمامنا في عملية أولى وصفية على البحث عن أهم النصوص التي يمثّلها نص محمود درويش مما له صلة بالهدهد فتشكّلت منها طبقات كالطروس. ثم نبحث في مرحلة ثانية في بنية النص أو بناه، من حيث هو حكاية وسرد لرحلة ذات أطوار وكيف تصرف محمود درويش فيها على صعيد البنية والدلالة. ثم نرجع البصر في طور ثالث، في لمّية استنطاق محمود درويش لتلك النصوص و تحميلها ما حملها من الدلالات الجديدة حتى غدا نصه طبقات بعضها فوق بعض، وهو مبرر قيامنا بالحفر فيه على النحو الذي ذكرنا متسائلين عن وظيفة عملية المساءلة، مساءلة الشعري للأسطوري وذلك على الصعيدين الأسلوبي والدلالي.

النصوص الحاضرة الغائبة في بنية قصيدة «الهدهد»

يتجاذب قصيدة «الهدهد» لمحمود درويش كما ألمحنا إلى ذلك منذ البداية، شأن كل قصة شعرية تقوم على الرمز، اتجاهان اثنان:
أ- اتجاه سياقي syntagmatique أفقي، يشدها نحو الحكاية شداً فتندرج في مجرى الزمان وترتبط بقصة أو قصص رمزية نموذجية أخرى عدا القصة الحاضرة الراهنة المسندة إلى أنا فردية أو جماعية تتولى العملية السردية وتظهر من خلال الحوار مجسداً للدراما – بمعناها الأول الأرسطي أي الفعل – وذلك في مواضع شتى من النص كما في «مطلعها»:

لم نقترب من أرض نجمتنا البعيدة بعد. تأخذنا القصيدة
من خُرم إبرتنا لنغزل للفضاء عباءة الأفق الجديدة ...
أسرى، ولو قفزت سنابلنا عن الأسوار وانبثق السنونو
من قيدنا المكسور، أسرى ما نحب وما نريد وما نكون ...
لكن فينا هدهداً يملي على زيتونة المنفى بريده. (**أرى ما أريد**، ص ٨١)

ب- اتجاه جدولي paradigmatique عمودي، يتصل برمزية الطائر ذات الأبعاد المتعددة المذكورة آنفاً تطفر في كل مرة ضمن سياق مختلف مع اختلاف تشكل لغة النص ودلالاته ومختلف جهاته Modalités التلفظية وما فيها من غنائية لأن النص كما

يصرح بنفسه « نشيد»، وترد الكلمة أكثر من مرة في القسم الكبير الأخير من القصيدة.

أما على الصعيد السياقي، فالنص حكاية رحلة يظهر فيها الدليل من حين إلى آخر معلناً أنه هدهد، مشكلاً إطاراً للقصيدة، موضحاً لها ومعمّياً في آن واحد؛ لأنه إذ يظهر هذه البنية القائمة على التكرار والتنويع في آن، فإنه ينطوي على بنى أخرى تتجلى من خلال تضاعيف النص هي بنى النصوص التي منها قُدّ. وبنية الرحلة في حد ذاتها وما يشقها من حركة وما تعج به من أصوات مختلفة ناجمة عن طبيعة الخطاب الحواري:

١- أنا هدهد – قال الدليل لسيد الأشياء – أبحث عن سماء تائهة... (**أرى ما أريد**، ص ٨٢)

٢- أنا هدهد – قال الدليل لنا – وطار مع الأشعة والغبار. (**أرى ما أريد**، ص ٨٢)

٣- أنا هدهد – قال الدليل – سأهتدي للنبع إن جف النبات. (**أرى ما أريد**، ص ٨٣)

٤- أنا هدهد – قال الدليل – وتحتنا طوفان نوح. بابل .. (**أرى ما أريد**، ص ٨٤)

٥- أنا هدهد – قال الدليل – وطار منّا. طارت الكلمات –
منا، قبلنا الطوفان. (**أرى ما أريد**، ص ٨٩)

٦- أنا هدهد – قال الدليل – ونحن قلنا: نحن سرب من طيور
ضاقت بنا الكلمات (**أرى ما أريد**، ص ٩٤)

٧- هو هدهد، وهو الدليل وفيه ما فينا. (**أرى ما أريد**، ص ٩٦)

٨- من أنت في هذا النشيد؟ أنا الدليل. (**أرى ما أريد**، ص ٩٧)

٩- من أنت في هذا النشيد؟ أنا الرحيل
«يا قلب ... يا أمي» ويا أختي تدفق كي يراك المستحيل –
وكي تراه وتأخذاني نحو مرآتي الأخيرة. قال هدهدنا وطار. (**أرى ما أريد**، ص ٩٧)

تقوم هذه البنية التركيبية التي تتكرر في قصيدة «الهدهد» ثماني مرات – فتشكل بذلك «هيكلها» – على عناصر ثابتة وأخرى متحولة، وتختم في الأخيرة منها بانقلاب في صيغة القول، من ضمير المتكلم «أنا» إلى ضمير الغائب في صيغة «هو»، كما تقوم برسم ملامح الهدهد وقد غدا منذ الأسطر الأولى من القصيدة لغزاً وخيطاً ناظماً لقانون اللغز والرمز فيها. ولكنها تتأسس أيضاً على «أشلاء» نصوص أخرى يستحضرها محمود درويش ويستنطقها فتكون للقصيدة عنصراً وسيطاً على الصعيدين البنيوي والدلالي، أي أنها تكون عنصراً بنائياً تشكيلياً ولكن أيضاً بمثابة المفتاح الذي يمكّن من فك اللغز فيه.

هدهد سليمان: ذلك أن للهدهد منذ البداية شأنه في ذلك شأن «هدهد سليمان» بريداً يحمله، أو رسالة، فضلاً عن أنه:«بريد هذي الأرض» بإطلاق العبارة، فضلاً عن أنه هدهد الجماعة وحامل رسائلها منها إليها:

لكن فينا هدهداً يملي على زيتونة المنفى بريده
عادت إلينا من رسائلنا رسائلنا ... (**أرى ما أريد**، ص ٨١)

هدهد الأعراب، رواية عن الجاحظ: تحضر في صلب نص درويش أسطورة الهدهد التي حفظها لنا الجاحظ عن الأعراب المبررة لقنزعته والمخبرة عن برّه لأمه مفردة ثم مقترنة مع سليمان الحكيم الملك النبي العالم بمنطق الطير، ذاك الذي سخرت له الريح، وبلقيس ملكة سبأ الواقعة جنوب الجزيرة العربية والتي اقترن اسمها بسد مأرب:

.. كانت له أم، وكان له جنوب يستقر على هبوبه،
كانت له أسطورة الحدس المتوج بالمياه ... وفي دروبه ملك وامرأة (**أرى
ما أريد**، ص ٨٥)

...

هل عدت من سبأ لتأخذنا إلى سبأ جديدة؟ (**أرى ما أريد**، ص ٨٣)

...

هل كنتَ تعرف أي تاج فوق رأسك؟ قبر أمي
وأنا أطير وأحمل الأسرار والأخبار أمي فوق رأسي مهرجان. (**أرى ما
أريد**، ص ٩٦)

هدهد «منطق الطير» لفريد الدين العطار: يحضر هدهد فريد الدين العطار (٢٦) صاحب **منطق الطير** من خلال الإشارة في قصيدة درويش إلى رحلته وما مر به من الأودية/المواقف ومنها «وادي العشق» و«وادي المعرفة»، في غمزة إلى المعري ـ وسبيله إلى المعرفة بالعقل (٢٧) ـ وفي إشارة إلى ابن سينا صاحب **رسالة الطير** وصاحب القصيدة الشهيرة في النفس «هبطت إليك من المحل الأرفع» وسبيله إلى المعرفة بالقلب و«نور يقذفه الله في قلبه». (٢٨)

هل مسك العطار بالأشعار؟ قلنا. قال : خاطبني وغاب
في بطن وادي العشق. هل وقف المعري عند وادي المعرفة؟ قلنا. فقال :
طريقه عبث.
سألنا: وابن سينا؟ .. هل أجاب عن السؤال وهل رآك؟ (**أرى ما أريد**، ص ٩٠)

هدهد السهروردي: ويحضر في نص محمود درويش هدهد السهروردي صاحب «الغربة الغربية»، والمقصود بها النفس باعتبارها قد هبطت في غير موطنها الذي هو الشرق موطن الأنوار في الفلسفة الإشراقية المتأثرة بالأفلوطينية ولذلك فهي في شوق دائم إلى أصلها الإلهي السماوي. والسهروردي موجود في قصيدة محمود درويش «الهدهد» من خلال التنصيص على اسمه، من جهة، ومن خلال مدينته نيسابور، مدينة الحلاج وغيره من أعلام المتصوفة، من جهة ثانية، فتنعقد هكذا بين نص محمود درويش وسائر نصوص من ذكرنا صلات يتعين تدبر علاقتها بالرحلة ومختلف أبعادها، من ذلك أن رحلة الهدهد دليلاً بمن معه من الطير تتخذ بعداً ثقافياً وآخر أنثروبولوجياً كونياً كما في قوله: «فليجلس على إيوانه هذا الفراغ ليكمل البشري فينا هجرته» (**أرى ما أريد**، ص ٨٧).

بنية/بِنى قصيدة «الهدهد»

يحتار القارئ وهو يقرأ القصيدة ضمن أي جنس أو ضمن أي شكل من أشكال الكتابة يصنف النص – ومن صفات النصوص العظيمة، كما هو معلوم، أنها تستعصي على التصنيف لما فيها من خروج أو عدول على السائد المألوف –رغم أنه نص جاء ضمن مجموعة **أرى ما أريد** وتحتها علامة تفيد أنه من الشعر.

١– ذلك أن فيها – أي القصيدة – ما كان ظهر منذ مدة في شعر درويش من مزاوجة بين الشعر والنثر أو بين السردي والغنائي كما في قصيدة «الأرض» (مجموعة **أعراس**) وكما في عديد من نصوص المجموعة المذكورة نفسها – **أرى ما أريد** – وقد أعرب عن موقفه من المسألة بوضوح حين قال :«أليس الشعر هو نثر الورد على الليل ليضيء الليل؟»(٢٩)

٢– ويجد فيها القارئ ما يجعلها تتنزل في باب المسرح مأساة مثل المآسي اليونانية نعرف منذ البداية أنها تسير نحو العبث لأنها تسير منذ بدايتها نحو نهاية سطرتها الأقدار. ولا تعوزها سمات المسرح، لا سيما من خلال ذلك الحوار الذي ينعقد طوال النص بين الهدهد والجماعة. بل إن أرسطوفان أشهر كتاب المسرح الكوميدي اليوناني حاضر منذ البداية، عندما لم يفهمه الهدهد ومن خلال «تثب الوعول من الوعول على المعابد. والطيور تبيض فوق فكاهة التمثال» (**أرى ما أريد**، ص ٨٣). وليس حضور الدرامي في شكله المسرحي هذا بالأمر الغريب لأن المجموعة نفسها – **أرى ما أريد** – تتضمن قصيدة مطولة أخرى عنوانها «مأساة النرجس ملهاة الفضة».

٣– والنص ملحمي أيضاً، فهو منذ بدايته سيرة ملحمية هي سيرة الجماعة ورحلتها على مدى أجيال بل على مدى تاريخ طويل يتصل بزمن البدايات عندما علم آدم الأسماء، ويمر بزمن الطوفان وبابل والشرق القديم تتراءى من خلاله الآلهة والبلدان فتحضر كنعان والصين القديمة ومسلات مصر ومدن اليونان ونيسابور وسمرقند القديمة، وغيرها ويحضر الحاضر في النهاية: «نحن الآن ما كنّا وعدنا مكرهين إلى الأساطير التي لم تتسع لوصولنا» (**أرى ما أريد**، ص ٩٨).

٤– وأخيراً لا نعدو الحقيقة إذا قلنا إن هذا النص هو جميع ما ذكرنا: فهو نشيد وسرد وهو دراما وملحمة وأسطورة و«أصوات» شتى تتحاور. ولكن يجب أن نذكر إضافة إلى ذلك أنه «أسطورة أدبية» أنشأها محمود درويش، قدّها كما رأينا من نصوص سابقة، فكان مثلما ذكرنا في السطور الأولى ذاكرة الجماعة ومدوّن «أشيائها» الصغيرة والكبيرة.

ورغم ما رأينا من تعدد أبعاد النص وإمكانية الدخول إليه من سبل شتى، اخترنا النظر فيه من حيث هو سرد وحكاية شعرية، تفيد جملة من الحالات والتحولات بين البداية والنهاية. أي أنه من جهة «قصة» (أي جملة من الأفعال يقوم بها فاعلون)، ومن جهة ثانية «خطاب» (أي طريقة من طرق عرض القصة، منها ما يتصل بالمنظور السردي، ومنها ما يتصل بالصيغة السردية، ومنها ما يتصل بالزمان السردي وهو ما يندرج في فنّيات السرد).

وسوف نسعى في خاتمة المطاف من مشروع القراءة هذا إلى تبيّن وظيفة الأسطوري في قصيدة «الهدهد» لمحمود درويش على الصعيدين الشكلي الفني، من جهة، والدلالي، من جهة ثانية.

البداية

إذا أنعمنا النظر في بنية القصيدة من حيث هي «قصة» يمثّل الهدهد دليلها الهادي لجماعة الطير وقطبها الدلالي الجامع لشتاتها تبين لنا أولا أنها تقوم على وضع بدئي، ثم على الرحلة في حد ذاتها، ثم على خاتمة.

الوضع البدئي

تبدأ القصيدة بمقطع أول هو الأسطر الثمانية عشر الأولى، على لسان متكلم بضمير الجمع «نحن»:

لم نقترب من أرض نجمتنا البعيدة بعد
تأخذنا القصيدة من خُرم إبرتنا لنغزل للفضاء عباءة الأفق الجديدة
أسرى، ولو قفزت سنابلنا عن الأسوار وانبثق السنونو
من قيدنا المكسور، أسرى ما نحب وما نريد وما نكون ..
لكن فينا هدهداً يملي على زيتونة المنفى بريده. **(أرى ما أريد،** ص ٨١)

وهي تقوم على مفارقة، ألا وهي السعي إلى الاقتراب من «أرض نجمتنا» وكأننا في رحلة فضائية (لأنها فيما نرى فيما مِنْ منظور الهدهد)، في حال هي الأسر والأسوار والقيد والمنفى؛ ولكن الذي يلطف من ذلك هو حضور الهدهد بين الجماعة. وبهذا يتم رسم البداية ومنطلق اللغز والواسطة التي بها سيتم التغلب على هذا الوضع البدئي. ومنذ السطر الأول، تضطلع القصيدة بدور الأداة وبالوساطة فاعلة، «تأخذنا القصيدة من خرم إبرتنا لنغزل للفضاء عباءة الأفق الجديدة» وخيطاً ناظماً من خيوط النص وسننه.

الرحلة ومختلف مراحلها

فماذا عن الرحلة ووجهتها ومعناها مثلما تبدو من ظاهر النص ومنطوقه؟ يفيد النص فيما يفيد أنها رحلة عبثية كما ذكر عنها منذ البداية، «أمامنا آثارنا، ووراءنا هدف العبث»، «أمامنا آثارنا ووراءنا الصفصاف»، وأنها رحلة تُعاد وتُكرر، «سنعيد رحلتنا هناك على الظلام الخارجي»، «جسر على نهرين رحلتنا»، هي رحلة أبدية للبحث عن صفة الذي ليست له صفة، «لم تبق منا غير رحلتنا إليه». «وأمامنا آثارنا ووراءنا آثارنا». وهنا هناك. «لكن

رحلتنا إلى النسيان طالت، والحجاب أمامنا غطى الحجاب /ولعل منتصف الطريق هو الطريق إلى طريق من سحاب» (**أرى ما أريد**، ص ص ٨٢، ٨٣، ٨٥، ٨٦، ٨٨، ٨٩). وإذن فهي رحلة لغز يلفها كثير من الغموض لأنها كما سنرى رحلة متعددة الأبعاد والأصعدة والدلالات.

وهي رحلة تتألف من جملة من«المحطات» أو من «المقامات»(٣٠) تذكرنا بالأودية السبعة التي مر بها الهدهد في **منطق الطير** لفريد الدين العطار،(٣١) رحلة تتحول من صورتها السردية إلى صورة أخرى حوارية ضمن تصرف في الزمان، فتحضر محطات الرحلة أو مقاماتها لا في صيغة سردية ولكن في شكل حوار بين الهدهد ومن معه. وإذا انطلقنا من تلك «اللازمة » التي تتكرر على لسان الهدهد ثماني مرات جاز لنا أن نعتبرها مشيرة إلى جملة من المحطات هي من الرحلة بمثابة المعالم.

المحطة الأولى :هي من القصيدة بمثابة مقام الطلب أو البحث وتتفق مع «اللازمتين» ١ و٢ ويقول في الأولى: ١- «أنا هدهد – قال الدليل لسيد الأشياء – أبحث عن سماء تائهة». ويقول في الثانية: ٢- «أنا هدهد قال الدليل وطار مع الأشعة والغبار».

و هي رحلة عبثية «أمامنا آثارنا ووراءنا هدف العبث» ولذلك فهي محطة التساؤل في القصيدة عن سؤال الوجود: «من أينا جئنا؟/يسأل الحكماء عن معنى الحكاية والرحيل» (**أرى ما أريد**، ص ٨٢). والهدهد في هذه المحطة الأولى مُحفّز على الطلب: «ابحثوا عنه لكي تجدوه فيه فهو فيه» (**أرى ما أريد**، ص ٨٣).

و تنصهر الرحلة موضوع قصيدة درويش مع رحلة هدهد سليمان إلى سبأ مملكة بلقيس في الجنوب وعودته منها إليه بالأنباء: «هل عدت من سبأ لتأخذنا إلى سبأ جديدة؟»

والمحطة الثانية في القصيدة محطة جامعة بين الهدهد بوصفه خبيراً بمنابع المياه – كما في أسطورة النبي سليمان – و الهدهد على رأس جماعة الطير يقودهم إلى وادي العشق الإلهي – كما عند فريد الدين العطار؛ أي إلى مقام الفناء في الذات الإلهية وهو المقام الثاني بعد مقام الطلب وتتفق مع اللازمة عدد ٣.

أنا هدهد – قال الدليل – سأهتدي للنبع إن جف النباتُ

قلنا له: لسنا طيوراً. قال: لن تصلوا إليه، الكلّ له

والكل فيه، وهو في الكل، ابحثوا عنه لكي تجدوه فيه، فهو فيه

قلنا له: لسنا طيوراً كي نطير. فقال: أجنحتي زماني

والعشق نار العشق، فاحترقوا لتلقوا عنكم جسد المكان.(**أرى ما أريد**، ص ٨٣)

و هذه المحطة الثانية في **منطق الطير** – أي وادي العشق – محطة حاضرة لا في شكل سردي ولكن على سبيل الحوار بين الدليل والجماعة:

هل مسّك العطار بالأشعار؟ قلنا. قال : خاطبني وغاب

في بطن وادي العشق. هل وقف المعري عند وادي المعرفة

قلنا. فقال : طريقه عبث. سألنا: وابن سينا ... هل أجاب

عن السؤال وهل رآك؟ **(أرى ما أريد، ص ٩٠)**

المحطة الثالثة : يمكن أن نقول إنها تتفق واللازمة ٤ وتلمح إلى الوادي الثالث في

رحلة الهدهد ضمن **منطق الطير** وهو وادي المعرفة:

أنا هدهد – قال الدليل – وتحتنا طوفان نوح. بابل .

...

هل كنت تعرف؟ كنت أعرف أن بركاناً سيرسم صورة الكون الجديدة.

(أرى ما أريد، ص ٨٤)

وهكذا تصرف محمود درويش في بنية **منطق الطير** لفريد الدين العطار ونثر مختلف ما فيها

من مقامات على نحو آخر. ولذلك فهي لا تتجلّى – أو لم تتجل لنا نحن على الأقل – على نحو

واضح صريح أي في شكل أطوار متعاقبة، وإن كنا وجدنا أثرها في دعوة الهدهد الجماعة – عند

منتصف الطريق – إلى التخلي عن الأجساد، مع التخلّي عن الأسماء، وهو ما يغيّر من دلالة الرحلة.

لكن رحلتنا إلى النسيان طالت. والحجاب أمامنا غطى الحجاب

ولعل منتصف الطريق هو الطريق إلى طريق من سحاب

ولعلنا، يا هدهد الأسرار، أشباح تفتش عن خراب

قال : اتركوا أجسادكم كي تتبعوني واتركوا الأرض–السرابْ

كي تتبعوني. واتركوا أسماءكم. لا تسألوني عن جوابْ

إن الجواب هو الطريق ولا طريق سوى التلاشي في الضباب. **(أرى ما**

أريد، ص ص ٨٩-٩٠)

ثم يدعو الهدهد الجماعة – وقد بلغ مقام النشوة – إلى التوحد والفناء من خلال

الوصول إلى ما لا تدركه الحواس:

قال الهدهد السكران: طيروا كي تطيروا. نحن عشاق وحسب

قلنا: تعبنا من بياض العشق واشتقنا إلى أم ويابسة وأب

هل نحن من كنا وما سنكون؟ قال: توحدوا في كل درب

وتبخروا فصيلوا إلى من ليس تدركه الحواس. **(أرى ما أريد، ص ٩١)**

فترد الجماعة بأن الشوق إلى التوحد إنما هو شوق إلى الأرض أماً وأباً.

وبهذا يتجلى لنا أن بنية **منطق الطير** لئن كانت حاضرة من خلال «وادي العشق» و«وادي المعرفة» وهما من الأودية السبعة التي يمر بها الطيور في رحلتهم، ثم من خلال التلميح إلى مقامات أخرى هي وادي التوحد والحيرة والفناء، فإن حضورها في نص درويش ليس سوى حضور جزئي. كما أن الرحلة ليست مجرد رحلة أسطورية، بل هي رحلة في التاريخ: تاريخ فلسطين وتاريخ البشرية قاطبة كما ألمحنا إلى ذلك منذ البداية. ومن هنا يمكن القول إن محمود درويش وهو يسائل الأسطورة القديمة قد حوّرها وحملها دلالات جديدة.

منتهى الرحلة

ويتجلى التحويل الذي أدخله محمود درويش على أسطورة الهدهد خاصة في المحطة الأخيرة منها وهي محطة الكشف أو كما يقول «هنيهة الإشراق» (**أرى ما أريد**، ص ٩٧). ذلك أنه كشف ذو معنى يختلف عن الكشف الصوفي الذي هو التوحد مع الذات الإلهية، إنه كشف يستوعب ذلك ويحوله من المقدس إلى الدنيوي، بل يجمع بينهما في آن واحد فإذا التوحد توحد مع الأرض من خلال العود إليها أمّا أبدية للجميع.

إن المحطة الأخيرة من الرحلة تغدو هكذا محطة المكاشفة والتجلي أي اكتشاف الأرض – كما قال الآخر وجدتها وجدتها – واكتشاف أن ليس ثمة فاصل بين الطبيعة والروح، وأن الأرض روح، وهو ما يفضي إلى التحرر من «كل أجنحة السؤال عن البداية والمصير» (**أرى ما أريد**، ص ٩٢). وبذلك يكون محمود درويش قد قلب معنى الرحلة فعبّر عن رؤية جديدة وفلسفة جديدة لا تفصل بين الروح والجسد بل توحد بينهما وتضفي القدسية على الإنسان وتخرجه من وضع المستلب:

إن الطبيعة كلها روح، وإن الأرض تبدو من هنا
ثدياً لتلك الرعشة الكبرى، وخيل الريح مركبة لنا
يا طير طيري ... طيري كي تطيري فالطبيعة كلها روح ودوري
حول افتتانك باليد الصفراء، شمسك، كي تذوبي واستديري
بعد احتراقك نحو تلك الأرض أرضك، كي تنيري
نَفق السؤال الصلب عن هذا الوجود وحائط الزمن الصغير
إن الطبيعة كلها روح، وروح رقصة الجسد الأخير
طيري إلى أعلى من الطيران .. أعلى من سمائك .. كي تطيري
أعلى من الحب الكبير .. من القداسة .. والألوهة .. والشعور
وتحرري من كل أجنحة السؤال عن البداية والمصير. (**أرى ما أريد**، ص ص ٩٢-٩٣)

...

... في الأرض روح
شردتها الريح خارجها. (**أرى ما أريد**، ص ٩٥)

لقد كان الهدهد وجماعته يبحثون في جملة ما يبحثون في رحلتهم عن الأرض-الأم، وعن الأب، فإذا هي معهم أنى ساروا، ومنذ بداية الخليقة وعلى مر التاريخ. إن اكتشاف الأرض في رحلتهم «الفضائية» ورؤيتها عن بعد من خلال عيون الهدهد تفّاحة مثلما رآها الشاعر الفرنسي برتقالة زرقاء تسبح في الفضاء هو اكتشافها في نهاية الرحلة أما للجميع، هي الأرض يحملها كل في رأسه شأن الهدهد البار بأمه:

... جسد من التفاح يسبح في المجرة. والمياه له حزام
يسري مع الأبد المجسد في مدائحنا، ويرجع نحو ذاتهْ
أمّا تغطينا بغزو حنانها العاري، وتخفي ما فعلنا بالرئةْ
وبنار وردتها وتخفي حرب سيرتنا، وما صنع الحُسام
بخريطة الأعشاب حول شواطىء الزغب المقدس. أمنا هي أمنا
أم الأثينيين والفُرس القدامى أم أفلاطون زارادشت أفلوطين أم السهروردي
أم الجميع. وكل طفل سيد في أمه. ولها البداية والختام. (أرى ما أُريد، ص ٩٥)

وهو ما يفسر لنا أن هبوط الطير/البشر على الأرض – طلب سُدى – لأن الرحلة رحلة داخلية، داخل القلب «سنهبط فوق أنفسنا» (أرى ما أُريد، ص ٩٣).

إن الكشف في نهاية القصيدة تجل للحقيقة – حقيقة الجماعة – من خلال عين الهدهد، واكتشاف لحقيقة المنفى:

منفى هي الأشواق، منفى حبنا ونبيذنا منفى. ومنفى
تاريخ هذا القلب ...
واللامكان هو المكان وقد نأى في الروح عن تاريخه
منفى هي الأرض التي تنأى بنا عن روحنا نحو الغريب (أرى ما أُريد، ص ٩٨)
...
منفى هو الماضي ...
منفى هي الأفكار ...
والشعر منفى. (أرى ما أُريد، ص ٩٢)

وإذن فهو اكتشاف لمعنى الحرية. وهو أيضا تجل لحقيقة أخرى مفادها أن المطلوب في الطالب وأنه قد يرى في البعد ما لا يرى في القرب: «هل كان فيها/كل ما فيها ولم نعرف؟» (أرى ما أُريد، ص ٩٤)؛ «أعن بعد نرى ما لا نرى /في القرب» (أرى ما أُريد، ص ٩٥)؛ «هل كنتِ أنت قبيل هجرتنا ولم نعرف؟» (أرى ما أُريد، ص ٩٦)

وتنتهي قصيدة «الهدهد» نهاية تجعلها فضلاً عن كونها حكاية ومسرحية وسيرة ملحمية، نشيداً، نشيداً مقدساً ودنيوياً في آن، يسبّح بآلاء الأرض ويمجّد الهدهد فإذا هي

أقرب ما تكون إلى المدائح المقدسة في تناص مع النص القرآني ينحل معه اللغز، ويكتشف القارئ بعض ما يتعلق بالهدهد من دلالات لا سيما مع اكتشاف الجماعة توحدها وإياه فيغدو الحديث عنه في صيغة «هدهدنا»:(٣٢)

وله ... لهدهدنا خيول الماء تحت جفافه تعلو، ويعلو الصولجان
وله ... لهدهدنا زمان كان يحمله، وكان له لسان
وله ... لهدهدنا بلاد كان يحملها رسائل للسماوات البعيدة
لم يبق دين لم يجربه ليمتحن الخليقة بالرحيل إلى الإله
لم يبق حب لم يعذبه ليخترق الحبيب إلى سواه. (**أرى ما أريد**، ص ٩٧)

وبهذا يكون الهدهد قد استوى بالذات الفردية والجماعية «هو هدهد، وهوالدليل وفيه ما فينا» (**أرى ما أريد**، ص ٩٦)، ويكون محمود درويش قد صنع من قصيدة «الهدهد» «أسطورة أدبية»، أسطورة بالمعنى النبيل للكلمة في العلوم الإنسانية أي خطاباً هو خطاب المقدس وخطاب الحقيقة وخطاب الوحدة.

وهي أسطورة لأكثر من وجه: فقد انطلقت من قاع أسطوري حركه محمود درويش ذاكرةً ضد النسيان، جمع فيه بين أساطير شتى منها أسطورة الخليقة، وتعليم آدم اللغة وقصة قابيل وهابيل، قصة الراعي والفلاح، وقصة طوفان نوح وبابل، ومختلف أساطير المدن القديمة في مصر والهند: «إن الألوهة توأم الإنسان في الهند القديمة» (**أرى ما أريد**، ص ٨٨)، والصين: «إن المدينة تعبد الأجداد في الصين القديمة» (**أرى ما أريد**، ص ٨٨). فكانت الرحلة في قصيدة «الهدهد» رحلة أشبه ما تكون بالرحلات الطقوسية مثل تلك التي تجري فيها طقوس التبدئة المفضية إلى المعرفة. وهي أسطورة بزمنها الدائري عوداً على بدء، إما من خلال تكرار الرحلة والهجرة لهجرات بشرية سابقة أو من خلال تكرار لعبارات هي فيها قريبة من العبارات الطقوسية، وبزمنها الذي يعود بالقارئ إلى زمن البدايات زمن الخليقة وزمن الطفولة وزمن فاكهة الشعر يسقط من شجر الليل.

«لا أنت إلا أنت» فاخطفنا إليك إذا أذنت، ودلنا
يوماً على الأرض السريعة قبل دورتنا مع العدم العميق، ودلنا
يوماً على شجر ولدنا تحته، سراً ليخفي ظلنا
وعلى الطفولة دلّنا. وعلى يمام زافَ أول مرة لِيُذلنا
منع الصغار ولم يطيروا مثله ... (**أرى ما أريد**، ص ٨٦)

خاتمة

يمكن أن تطول رحلتنا أكثر مع هذه القصيدة محللين مختلف جوانبها البنيوية والدلالية - ولاسيما جميع العلامات ذات الصلة بالكتابة - مبينين كيف أفاد درويش من

توظيف رمز الهدهد وأساطير الهدهد ذات الأصول المختلفة من فارسية، وعربية أعرابية، وعربية إسلامية صوفية في وصف تجربة وجودية فردية وجماعية، بل كيف عبّر عن كليات بشرية هي الشبق إلى التحليق والطيران كناية عن الحرية. كما وظفها أساساً ومنذ البداية في وصف تجربة فنية، هي بناء رحلة في عالم من الكلمات على قصب الكلمات، رحلة من الأسماء إلى الأسماء، وبين الأسماء والأشياء.

لقد كان الهدهد من حيث هو رمز واسطة على صعيد العبارة وعلى صعيد الدلالة. ومثلما اكتشف محمود درويش في قصيدة «الأرض» اكتشافاً لغوياً يجسم توحده مع الأرض: «أنا الأرض والأرض أنت» فغدت انتفاضة يوم الأرض وما حدث فيها من استشهاد الفتيات الصغيرات «اشتعلن مع الورد والزعتر البلدي وافتتحن نشيد التراب» بمثابة القربان يقدم إليها للتوحد معها، كانت قصيدة «الهدهد» هي الأخرى وسيطاً فنياً بلاغياً مكن من اكتشافه للأرض يحملها الإنسان هدهداً أني حلّ، وكان ذلك بواسطة الهدهد رمزاً. وبهذا كانت قصيدة «الهدهد» عملاً فنياً إبداعياً ساءل الأساطير القديمة وبناها النموذجية والمخيال مطالباً بواقع آخر.

ولقد استعارت قصيدة «الهدهد» من الأسطورة والرمز – في عملية المساءلة تلك – طاقتهما الاستكشافية والتعبيرية والتأليفية المجسمة للمقدس من الحقائق، وللمجرد من الأفكار، والمبهم من العواطف والمشاعر والأحاسيس فاضطلعت بما تضطلع به الأساطير من دور الوساطة المتمثل في حل صعوبة منطقية ما (كما يرى ليفي ستروس). فالوساطة حقيقة تصدق بشأن الأساطير والفن معاً. إذ كلاهما أداة يتمكن بواسطتها الإنسان من حل تناقض ما. ذلك أن الشعر وكل فن إنما هو عمل يهدف الإنسان من خلاله إلى تجاوز منزلته البشرية بوصفه كائناً فانياً وإلى «التداوي من فعل الزمان» فيتغلب على الموت من خلال العقيدة الدينية والإيمان بالخلود في حياة أخرى– أو يتوهم ذلك – كما يتغلب على نقصه جنساً يحن إلى شطره، بواسطة الحب واجتماع الجنسين، ويتمكن بواسطة الإبداع الفني من السيطرة على الزمان وتثبيته أحياناً في اللوحة والقصيدة وما إليها محققاً على نحو أسطوري أو فني اجتماع الأضداد. وبذلك تكون الأسطورة في مبتدأ الأدب وفي منتهاه نشأة وبنية ووظيفة.

الهوامش

(١) انظر **ذاكرة للنسيان** (الدار البيضاء: دار توبقال للنشر، ١٩٨٧)، وتحمل عنوانين: عنواناً كبيراً «ذاكرة للنسيان» وعنواناً فرعياً «ذاكرة للحاضر».

(٢) **أرى ما أريد** (الدار البيضاء: دار توبقال للنشر، ١٩٩٠)، ص ص ٧٩–٩٩، بعد «رباعيات»، «ربّ الأيائل يا أبي»، «هدنة مع المغول أمام غابة السنديان»، «جملة موسيقية»، «مأساة النرجس ملهاة الفضة». ظهرت المطولات قبل ذلك في قصيدة «الأرض»، مجموعة **أعراس** (بيروت: دار العودة، ١٩٨٤)،ص ص ٦٨–٩٤. وقد أضفنا قصيدة «الهدهد» في ملحق هذه المقالة.

(٣) وتمثل تحولاً في شعر محمود درويش يطرح تساؤلات تتصل بالمنحى الذي نحاه، كما في

قصيدة «الأرض»، في المزاوجة بين الغنائي والسردي الحامل للدرامي بمعناه الأول الأرسطي (الدراما = الحركة) والمعبر عن الملحمي (كما في قصيدة «الأرض») وعن المأساة والملهاة كما في ديوان **أرى ما أريد**. وليس من باب الصدفة أن إحدى قصائده، تحمل عنواناً مزدوجاً هو «مأساة النرجس ملهاة الفضة» وتصل الشعري بالدرامي.

(٤) كما يقول رولان بارط. انظر كتابه:

Roland Barthes, *S/Z* (Paris: Seuil, 1970), 11-12.

(٥) ومن شأن النصوص العظيمة أن تتمثل نصوصاً أخرى وتصهرها وهو ما فعله المعري مثلاً في **رسالة الغفران**. انظر: عز الدين المدني، مقدمة مسرحيته **ديوان الزنج** (تونس: الشركة التونسية للتوزيع، ١٩٨٣)، ص١٩: «النص المسرحي العظيم وكل نص عظيم يستحوذ، يبتلع، يهضم النصوص الأخرى».

(٦) انظر بحثنا: **موسوعة أساطير العرب عن الجاهلية ودلالاتها** (بيروت: دار الفارابي؛ تونس: العربية،١٩٩٤)؛ وكانت أطروحة دكتوراه دولة أُجزت بالجامعة التونسية ونوقشت سنة ١٩٩١.

(٧) «خطاب الأدب خطاب الأسطورة» درس افتتاحي قدمه صاحب هذا المقال في المعهد العالي للغات بتونس، أكتوبر ٢٠٠١ (قيد النشر)، ونشير إلى بعض نتائجه في هذا العمل.

(٨) الأسطورة بوجه عام قصة: انظر تعريفنا لها وللأسطوري في **موسوعة أساطير العرب عن الجاهلية ودلالاتها**، ص ص ٦٣- ٧٦. ومن أفضل تعريفاتها في اعتقادنا تعريف جيلبار دوران: «هي نظم لوقائع رمزية في مجرى الزمان» انظر كتابه:

Gilbert Durand, *Les structures anthropologiques de l'imaginaire* (Paris: Bordas, 1969), 411.

وتـعـريـف پـول ريـكـور Paul Ricoeur لـهـا فـي **المـوسـوعـة الـعـالمية أونيفرساليس** *Encyclopaedia Universalis* ج ٩، مادة Hermeneutique، ص ٢٦٣: «الأسطورة حكاية تقليدية تروي وقائع حدثت في بداية الزمان وتهدف إلى تأسيس أعمال البشر الطقوسية حاضراً، وبصفة عامة تهدف إلى تأسيس جميع أشكال الفعل والفكر التي بواسطتها يحدد الإنسان موقعه من العالم. فالأسطورة تثبّت الأعمال الطقوسية، ذات الدلالة وتخبرنا عندما يتلاشى بُعدها التفسيري(Etiologique) بفضل ما لها من مغزى استكشافي وتتجلى من خلال وظيفتها الرمزية أي في ما لها من قدرة على الكشف عن صلة الإنسان بمقدساته. وإذن فهي قصة مؤسسة للحقائق المقدسة، هي خطاب الحقيقة وخطاب المقدس وخطاب الوحدة، وحدة العالم». وانظر تعريفات أخرى عند ليفي ستروس:

Claude Levi-Strauss, *La pensée sauvage* (Paris: Plon, 1962), 38.

وهي إذن كلام من درجة ثانية وحداته الرموز ويختلف الرمز عن الدليل من حيث هو مبرر.

(٩) انظر: **موسوعة أساطير العرب عن الجاهلية ودلالاتها**، ج١، ص ص ٦٣- ٧٦.

(١٠) يوسف حلاوي، **الأسطورة في الشعر العربي المعاصر** (بيروت: دار الآداب، د. ت).

(١١) قد تكون الأسطورة الأدبية مشتقة من أسطورة قديمة سابقة كما هو الشأن بالنسبة إلى أسطورة أوديب وما فعله بها الكتاب ومنهم أندريه جيد وتوفيق الحكيم وعلي أحمد باكثير، أو

أسطورة برومثيوس، وأَساف ونائلة وما فعله بهما الكاتب المسرحي محمود المسعدي في **السد** وغيره، أو تكون إبداعاً صرفاً على غير منوال سابق.

(١٢) انظر:

Paul Ricoeur, *Finitude et Culpabilité, II: La symbolique du mal* (Paris: Seuil, 1971), 18; Gilbert Durand, *L'imagination symbolique* (Paris: PUF, 1968), 9 ff.; Jean Chevalier et Alain Gheerbrant, *Dictionnaire des symboles* (Paris: Robert Laffont/Jupiter, 1982), v-xxxii.

ويستفاد منها أن من شأن كل رمز أنه كوني بمعنى منتزع من عناصر الكون، ومحسوس، وأنه عنصر جمع وتوحيد بين عناصر مختلفة من الواقع، شأن الطائر مثلاً أو الجبل في أنه عنصر وصل بين الأسفل والأعلى، بين السماء والأرض، بين عالم الإنسان «طائراً لا يطير» وعالم الطيور. كما أن له علاقة بعالم الأحلام والرغبات وبعالم الإبداع والإنشاء وجميعها عوالم كما سنرى حاضرة في قصيدة درويش.

(١٣) انظر:

Paul Ricoeur, *Temps et récit*, t. 2 (Paris: Seuil, 1984), 100.

(١٤) انظر:

Paul Ricoeur, "Poétique et symbolique," *Initiation à la pratique de la théologie*, publié sous la direction de Bernard Lauret et François Refoulé (Paris: Cerf, 1987), 37-61.

(١٥) انظر:

Ernst Cassirer, *La philosophie des formes symboliques*, t.2, traduit par Ole Hansen-Love et Jean Lacoste (Paris: Les éditions de minuit, 1924), 8.

(١٦) ابن منظور، **لسان العرب**، مج ٦، ص ص٧٨١-٧٨٢، أعاد بناءه على الحرف الأول من الكلمة يوسف خياط (بيروت: دار الجيل؛ دار لسان العرب، ١٩٨٨).

(١٧) الدميري، **حياة الحيوان الكبرى**، ج ٢ (بيروت: دار إحياء التراث العربي، ١٩٨٩)، ص ص ٤٧٩-٤٨٤.

(١٨) الجاحظ، **كتاب الحيوان**، تحقيق عبد السلام محمد هارون (بيروت: دار الجيل؛ دار الفكر للطباعة والنشر، ١٩٨٨)، ج ١، ص ص ٩٧-٩٨ (ضمن حديث عن الكتاب والكتابة وتبليغ الرسالة المكتوبة)؛ ج ٣، ص ٥١٣ (هدهد سليمان) و٥١٢؛ ج ٦، ص ٣١٠ (معرفته بمكاسن المياه).

(١٩) انظر: **موسوعة أساطير العرب عن الجاهلية ودلالاتها**، ج١، «الطير في الأساطير»، ص ص ٣٢٢-٣٢٩؛ وكذلك:

Toufic Fahd, *La divination chez les arabes* (Paris: Ed. Sinbad, 1987), 507.

(٢٠) الجاحظ، **كتاب الحيوان**، ج ٣، ص ٥١٢ (باب القول في الهدهد)؛ والنويري، **نهاية الأرب**، نسخة مصورة بالأوفست عن طبعة دار الكتب (القاهرة: المؤسسة المصرية العامة للتأليف والترجمة والطباعة والنشر، وزارة الثقافة والإرشاد القومي، د.ت.)، ج ١٠، ص ص ٢٤٦–٢٤٧.

(٢١) ابن سيرين، **تفسير الأحلام الكبير** (لبنان: دار الكتب العلمية، ١٩٨٥)، وكتب الأحلام مصدر نفيس آخر من مصادر البحث عن مخيالنا الرمزي؛ وانظر كذلك:

Jean Chevalier et Alain Gheerbrant, "Huppe," *Dictionnaire des symboles*, 513.

(٢٢) انظر تحليلنا لذلك في: **موسوعة أساطير العرب عن الجاهلية**، ج ١، ص٣٣٣.

(٢٣) انظر مقال «بلقيس»، **دائرة المعارف الاسلامية**، الطبعة الفرنسية الجديدة:

Encyclopédie de l'Islam (Leiden: Brill, 1960), vol. 1, 1256.

وقصتها مع النبي سليمان لدى الثعلبي في **قصص الأنبياء** (بيروت: المكتبة الثقافية، د. ت)، الموسوم بـ«عرائس المجالس»، ص ص ٢٧٦–٢٧٩؛ والنويري، **نهاية الأرب**، ج ١٠، ص ص ٢٤٦–٢٤٧، رواية عن الكسائي صاحب **قصص الأنبياء**.

(٢٤) جواد علي، **المفصل في تاريخ العرب قبل الإسلام** (بيروت: دار العلم للملايين، ١٩٧٠)، ج٦، ص٥١ وما بعدها؛ وانظر:

Jamme, "Le panthéon Sud-arabe pré-Islamique," *IBLA* Nº 11 (1948): 42.

(٢٥) هو يرمز عند الإيرانيين القدامى إلى طائر السيمورغ الأسطوري كما يرمز في أسطورة إيرانية إلى امرأة متزوجة كانت تمشط شعرها أمام المرأة عندما دخل عليها أخو زوجها فانقلبت طائراً وطارت والمشط في رأسها. انظر: مقالة "Huppe"، المذكورة سابقاً، ص ٥١٣.

(٢٦) عاش بين٥١٣هـ–٥٨٦هـ/١١١٩م–١١٩٠م؛ انظر **دائرة المعارف الإسلامية**، ج ٢، ص ٧٧٥.

(٢٧) لا شك أن استحضار شاعر المعرة وصاحب **رسالة الغفران واللزوميات** ههنا إنما هو باعتباره شاعراً له موقف من المعرفة وطرق تحصيلها.

(٢٨) صاحب **حي بن يقظان ورسالة الطير** التي كانت منطلقا لما كتبه السهروردي. انظر ما كتبه عنهما هنري كوربان:

Henry Corbin, *Avicenne et le récit visionnaire* (Téhéran: Département d'ira-nologie de l'institut franco-iranien, 1954); *Suhrawardi, le livre de la sagesse orientale* (Paris: Verdier-Lagrasse, 1986).

وقد نشر أحمد أمين الرسالتين مع **حي بن يقظان** لابن طفيل (القاهرة: دار المعارف، ١٩٥٢).

(٢٩) «لم يعلن شاعر كما أعلنت انحيازي للنثر لأنه أكثر من القصيدة استيعاباً للوردة والبستان معا، ولكن وردة واحدة قد تكتنز أكثر بالكثافة والشمس حين تكون وحيدة في غرفة. ولعل ذلك ما يحاول الشعر أن يقوله وما يحاول النثر أن يشرحه. أليس النثر هو حقل الشعر المفتوح؟ أليس الشعر هو نثر الورد على الليل ليضيء الليل؟»، **عابرون في كلام عابر، مقالات مختارة** (الدار البيضاء: دار توبقال، ١٩٩١)، ص ١١٦.

(٣٠) «كل مقام في طريق الله تعالى فهو مكتسب ثابت، وكل حال فهو موهوب غير مكتسب غير ثابت». محي الدين بن عربي، **الفتوحات المكية** (القاهرة: الهيئة المصرية العامة للكتاب، ١٩٨٥)، ج٢، ص ١٧٦.

(٣١) فريد الدين العطار، **منطق الطير**، ترجمه من الفارسية غارسين دي تاسّي:

Farid al-Din Attar, *Le langage des oiseaux*, traduit du persan par Garcin de Tassy (Paris: Albin Michel, 1996).

ومفاد القصة باختصار أن الطيور اجتمعت ذات يوم ورأت أنها تفتقر إلى ملك، فأشار عليهم الهدهد بالسيمورغ ملكاً، فدلهم إليه فرحلوا مع الهدهد دليلاً، وعبروا أودية سبعة هي على التوالي: ١- وادي الطلب ٢- وادي العشق ٣- وادي المعرفة ٤- وادي الاستغناء ٥- وادي التوحيد ٦- وادي الحيرة ٧- وادي الفناء. وهلكوا جميعاً ما عدا ثلاثين منهم انتهى بهم الأمر إلى إدراك أن الإله قد حل فيهم وبلغوا الفناء النهائي من خلال توحدهم مع السيمورغ الطائر الإلهي عند الفرس القدامى. و يرى بعض الدارسين أن له علاقة بطائر الفنيق. انظر **دائرة المعارف الإسلامية**، مقال «عنقاء»، لشارل بلا، ج ١، ص ٣٢٤.

(٣٢) في **عابرون في كلام عابر، مقالات مختارة**، ص ٤٢، يتحدث عن هدهد آخر:

كـالغبار المرّ مروا أينما شئتم ولكن
لا تمروا بيننا كالحشرات الطائرة
فلنا في أرضنا ما نعمل
ولنا قمح نربيه ونسقيه نـدى أجسادنا
ولنا ما ليس يرضيكم هنا:
حجر أو حجل
فخذوا الماضي إذا شئتم إلى سوق التحف
وأعيدوا الهيكل العظمي للهدهد إن شئتم
على صحن خزف
فلنا ما ليس يرضيكم: لنا المستقبل
ولنا في أرضنا ما نعمل.

وهكذا تختلف رمزية الهدهد باختلاف توظيفها في صلب النص فليس لها معنى مطلق.

الهدهد*

لم نقترب من أرض نجمتنا البعيدة بعد. تأخذنا القصيدة
من خُرم إبرتنا لنغزلَ للفضاء عباءة الأفق الجديدة ...
أسرى، ولو قفزت سنابلنا عن الأسوار وانبثق السنونو
من قيدنا المكسور، أسرى ما نحب وما نريد وما نكون ...
لكن فينا هدهداً يملي على زيتونة المنفى بريده.
عادت إلينا من رسائلنا رسائلنا، لنكتب من جديد
ما تكتب الأمطار من زهر بدائي على صخر البعيد
ويسافر السفرُ–الصدى منّا إلينا. لم نكن حَبَقاً –
لنرجع في الربيع إلى نوافذنا الصغيرة. لم نكن ورقاً –
لتأخذنا الرياح إلى سواحلنا. هنا وهناك خطٌّ واضح
للتيه. كم سنة سنرفع للغموض العذب موتانا مرايا؟
كم مرّة سنحمّل الجرحى جبال الملح كي نجد الوصايا؟
عادت إلينا من رسالتنا رسالتنا. هنا وهناك خط واضح –
للظلّ. كم بحراً سنقطع داخل الصحراء؟ كم لوحاً سننسى؟
كم نبيّاً سوف نقتل في ظهيرتنا؟ وكم شعباً سنشبه كي نكون –
قبيلة؟ هذا الطريق – طريقنا قصبُ على الكلمات يرفو
طَرف العباءة بين وحشتنا وبين الأرض إذ تنأى، وتغفو
في زعفران غروبنا. فلننبسط كيدٍ لنرفع وقتنا للآلهة ...
أنا هدهد – قال الدليل لسيّد الأشياء – أبحث عن سماء تائهة.
لم يبق منّا في البراري غيرُ ما تجد البراري
منا: بقايا الجلد فوق الشوك، أغنية المحارب للديار
وفم الفضاء. أمامنا آثارنا. ووراءنا هدف العبث ...
أنا هدهد – قال الدليل لنا – وطار مع الأشعة والغبار
من أين جئنا؟ يسأل الحكماء عن معنى الحكاية والرحيل
وأمامنا آثارنا، ووراءنا الصفصاف. من أسمائنا نأتي إلى
أسمائنا ونخبئ النسيان عن أبنائنا. تثبُ الوعول من الوعول
على المعابد. والطيور تبيض فوق فكاهة التمثال. لم نسأل لماذا
لم يولد الإنسان من شجر ليرجعْ؟ أنبأتنا الكاهناتْ
أن المسلة تسند الأفق المهدَّد بالسقوط على الزمان. وأننا
سنعيد رحلتنا هناك على الظلام الخارجي. وأنبأتنا الكاهناتْ
أن الملوكَ قُضاتنا، وشهودنا أعداؤنا. والروح يحرسها الرعاة
جسر على نهرين رحلتنا. ولم نولد لتمحونا وتمّحي الحياة ...
أنا هدهد – قال الدليل – سأهتدي للنبع إن جفَّ النباتُ

قلنا له:لسنا طيوراً. قال : لن تصلوا إليه، الكل لهْ
والكلّ فيه، وهو في الكل، ابحثوا عنه لكي تجدوه فيه، فهو فيه
قلنا له: لسنا طيوراً كي نطير. فقال : أجنحتي زماني
والعشق نار العشق، فاحترقوا لتلقوا عنكم جسد المكان
قلنا له: هل عدت من سبأ لتأخذنا إلى سبأ جديدة؟
عادت إلينا من رسائلنا رسالتُنا ولم ترجع ... ولم ترجع
وفي اليونان لم تفهم أرسطوفان. لم تجد المدينة في المدينةِ
لم تجد بيت الحنان لكي تدثّرنا حريراً من سكينة
لم تدرك المعنى فمسّك هاجس الشعراء: «طيري
يا بنت ريشي! يا طيور السهل والوديان، طيري
طيري سريعاً نحو أجنحتي وطيري نحو صوتي»، إن فينا
شبقاً إلى الطيران في أشواقنا. والناس طير لا تطيرُ
يا هدهد الكلمات حين تفرّخ المعنى وتخطفنا من اللغة الطيور
يا ابن التوتر حين تنفصل الفراشة عن عناصرها ويسكنها الشعورُ
ذَوِّب هنا صلصالنا ليشقّ صورة هذه الأشياء نورُ
حلّق لتنفتح المسافة بين ما كنّا وما سيكون حاضرنا الأخيرُ
نأى، فندنو من حقيقتنا ومن أسوار غربتنا
وهاجسنا العبورُ
نحن الثنائي السماء-الأرض، والأرض-السماء. وحولنا سورُ وسورُ
ماذا وراء السور؟ علّم آدم الأسماء كي يتفتّح السر الكبيرُ
والسرُّ رحلتنا إلى السرّي. إن الناس طيرٌ لا تطيرُ
أنا هدهد - قال الدليل - وتحتنا طوفانُ نوح. بابل .
أشلاءُ يابسة. بخار من نداءات الشعوب على المياه. هياكلُ
ونهايةٌ كبداية لنهاية. حلّق لينسى القاتل
قتلاه. حلّق فوقنا.حلّق لينسى الخالق المخلوق
والأشياءَ والأسماء في أسطورة الخلق الذي نتبادلُ
- هل كنت تعرف؟ - كنتُ أعرف أن بركانا سيرسم صورة -
الكون الجديدة. - لم تقل شيئاً وأنت بريد هذي الأرض - كنتُ أحاول ...
فيه من الأشباح ما يكفي ليبحث في المقابر عن حبيبه
... كانت له أم، وكان له جنوب يستقرّ على هبوبه
كانت له أسطورة الحدس المتوّج بالمياه ... وفي دروبه
ملك وإمرأة ... وجيش يحرس الصبوات في الجسدين من نمّامنا
ولنا من الصحراء ما يكفي لنُعْطِيَهُ زمام سرابنا وغمامنا
ومن الهشاشة ما سيكفي كي نسلّمه منام منامنا
خذنا، لقد هدّ اللسان فكيف نمتدح الذي طلب المديح
ومديحه فيه. وفيه الكلّ للكل . اعترفنا أننا بشر، وذبنا

في هذه الصحراء حباً. أين نخلتنا لنعرف في التمور قلوبنا؟
والله أجمل من طريق الله.لكن الذين يسافرون
لا يرجعون من الضياع لكي يضيعوا في الضياع. ويعرفون
أن الطريق هو الوصول إلى بدايات الطريق المستحيل
يا هدهد الأسرار، جاهد كي نشاهد في الحبيب حبينا
هي رحلة أبدية للبحث عن صفة الذي ليست له
صفة. هو الموصوف خارج وصفنا وصفاته. حلّق بنا
لم تبق منّا غيرُ رحلتنا إليه. إليه نشكو ما نكابد في الرحيل
دمنا نبيذُ شعوبه فوق الرخام وفوق مائدة الأصيل
«لا أنت إلاّ أنت» فاخطفنا إليك إذا أذنتَ، ودلّنا
يوماً على الأرض السريعة قبل دورتنا مع العدم العميق، ودُلّنا
يوماً على شجر ولدنا تحته، سراً ليخفي ظلنا
وعلى الطفولة دلّنا. وعلى يمام زاف أول مرة ليُذلنا
منع الصغار ولم يطيروا مثله. ياليتنا. ياليتنا. ولعلنا
سنطير في يوم من الأيام ... إن الناس طير لا تطير
والأرض تكبر حين نجهلُ، ثم تصغر حين نعرف جهلنا
لكننا أحفادُ هذا الطين، والشيطان من نار يحاول مثلنا
أن يدرك الأسرار عن كثب ليحرقنا ويحرق عقلنا
والعقل ليس سوى دخان، فليضع! إن القلوب تدلنا
خذنا إذن يا هدهد الأسرار نحو فنائنا بفنائه.حلّق بنا
واهبط بنا، لنودّع الأم التي انتظرت دهوراً خيلنا
لتموت غب النور أو تحيا لنيسابور أرملة تزيّن ليلنا
هي «لا تريد من الإله – الله إلا الله» ... خذنا!
والحبّ أن لا يُدرَك المحبوب. أرسلَ عاشق لفتاته
فرس الغياب على صدى النايات واختصر الطريق: «أنا هي»
وهي «الأنا» تنسلّ من يأس إلى أمل يعود إليّ يأساً
لا تنتهي طرقي إلى أبوابها ... طارت أناي فلا أنا إلا أنا ...
لا تنتهي طرقي إلى أبوابها، لا تنتهي طرق الشعوب –
إلى الينابيع القديمة ذاتها. قلنا. ستكتمل الشرائع –
عندما نجتاز هذا الأرخبيل ونعتقُ الأسرى من الألواح –
فليجلس على إيوانه هذا الفراغُ ليكمل البشريّ فينا هجرته ...
عمّن تفتش هذه النايات في الغابات؟ والغرباء نحن
ونحن أهل المعبد المهجور مهجورون فوق خيولنا البيضاء –
ينبتُ فوقنا قصب وتعبر فوقنا شُهب ونبحث عن محطتنا الأخيرة
لم تبق أرض لم نعمّر فوقها منفى لخيمتنا الصغيرة

هل نحن جلدُ الأرض؟ عمّن تبحثُ الكلمات فينا
وهي التي عقدت لنا في العالم السفليّ محكمة البصيرة
وهي التي بنت المعابد كي تروّض وحش عزلتها بمزمار وصورة
وأمامنا آثارنا. ووراءنا آثارنا. وهنا هناك. وأنبأتنا الكاهناتُ
أن المدينة تعبد الأجداد في الصين القديمة. أنبأتنا الكاهنات:
الجدّ يأخذ عرشه معه إلى القبر المقدس، يأخذ –
الفتياتِ زوجات وأسرى الحرب حراساً له. قد أنبأتنا الكاهناتُ
أن الألوهة توأم الإنسان في الهند القديمة. أنبأتنا الكاهنات
ما أنبأتنا الكائنات به ... «وأنت تكون أيضاً مَن هو»
لكنا لم نعل تينتنا – ليشنقنا عليها القادمون من الجنوب
هل نحن جلدُ الأرض؟ كنّا إذ نعض الصخر نفتحُ –
حيّزاً للفل. كنّا نحتمي بالله من حُرّاسه ومن الحروب
كنا نصدّق ما تعلّمنا من الكلمات. كان الشعر يهبطُ –
من فواكه ليلنا، وقيود ماعزنا إلى المرعى على درب الزبيبْ
الفجرُ أزرق، ناعم، رطب. وكنا حين نحلم نكتفي
بحدود منزلنا: نرى عسلاً على الخرّوب، نجنيه. نرى
في النوم أن مربّعات السمسم اكتنزت، فننخلها.
نرى في النوم ما سنراه عند الفجر. كان الحلمُ منديلَ الحبيبْ
لكننا لم نعل تينتنا ليشنقنا عليها القادمون من الجنوب
أنا هدهد – قال الدليل – وطار منّا. طارت الكلمات –
منا. قبلنا الطوفان. لم نخلع ثياب الأرض عنا –
قبلنا الطوفان. لم نبدأ حروب النفس بعد. وقبلنا
الطوفان. لم نحصد شعير سهولنا الصفراء بعد.
وقبلنا الطوفان. لم نصقل حجارتنا بقرن الكبش بعد.
وقبلنا الطوفان. لم نيأس من التفاح بعد. ستنجب
الأم الحزينة إخوة من لحمنا لا من جذوع الكستناء ولا
الحديد. ستنجب الأم الحزينة إخوة ليعمّروا منفى
النشيد. ستنجب الأم الحزينة إخوة كي يسكنوا
سعف النخيل إذا أرادوا أو سطوح خيولنا. وستنجب
الأمّ الحزينة إخوة ليتوجوا هابيلهم ملكاً على عرش التراب
لكن رحلتنا إلى النسيان طالت. والحجاب أمامنا غطى الحجابْ
ولعلّ منتصف الطريق هو الطريق إلى طريق من سحابْ
ولعلنا، يا هدهد الأسرار، أشباح تفتّش عن خرابْ
قال: اتركوا أجسادكم كي تتبعوني واتركوا الأرض-السرابْ
كي تتبعوني. واتركوا أسماءكم. لا تسألوني عن جوابْ

إن الجواب هو الطريق ولا طريق سوى التلاشي في الضباب
هل مسّك «العطار» بالأشعار؟ قلنا. قال: خاطبني وغاب
في بطن وادي العشق. هل وقف المعرّي عند وادي المعرفة
قلنا. فقال: طريقه عبث. سألنا: وابن سينا ... هل أجابَ
عن السؤال وهل رآكَ؟ - أنا أرى بالقلب لا بالفلسفة
هل أنت صوفيّ إذن. أنا هدهد. أنا لا أريد. «أنا أريدُ
أن لا أريد» ... وغاب في أشواقه: عذّبتنا
يا حب. من سفر إلى سفر تسفّرنا سدى. عذبتنا،
غربتنا عن أهلنا، عن مائنا وهوائنا. خربتنا. أفرغت
ساعات الغروب من الغروب. سلبتنا كلماتنا الأولى.
نهبت شجيرة الدراق من أيامنا، وسلبتنا أيامنا. يا
حبّ قد عذبتنا، ونهبتنا. غربتنا عن كل شيء واحتجبت
وراء أشجار الخريف. نهبتنا يا حب. لم تترك لنا شيئاً
صغيراً كي نفتّش عنك فيه وكي نقبّل ظله، فاترك
لنا في الروح سنبلة تحبّك أنت. لا تكسر زجاج
الكون حول ندائنا. لا تضطرب. لا تصطخب. واهدأ
قليلاً كي نرى فيك العناصر وهي ترفع عرسها الكلّي
نحوك. واقترب منا لندرك مرة: هل نستحقّ
بأن نكون عبيد رعشتك الخفية؟ لا تبعثر ما
تبقّى من حُطام سمائنا. يا حبّ قد عذبتنا، يا
حبّ، يا هبةً تبددنا لترشد غيبنا فيهب ...
هذا الغيب ليس لنا وليس لنا مصبّ النهر،
والدنيا تهب أمامنا ورقاً من السرو القديم ليرشد
الأشواق للأشواق. كم عذبتنا يا حب، كم غيبتنا
عن ذاتنا، وسلبتنا أسماءنا يا حب ...
قال الهدهد السكران: طيروا كي تطيروا. نحن عشاق وحسبْ
قلنا: تعبنا من بياض العشق واشتقنا إلى أم ويابسة وأبْ
هل نحن من كنا وما سنكون؟ قال: توحدوا في كل دربْ
وتبخّروا فَصِلُوا إلى من ليس تدركه الحواس. وكلّ قلبْ
كونٌ من الأسرار. طيروا كي تطيروا. نحن عشاق وحسبْ
قلنا، وقد متنا مراراً وانتشينا: نحن عُشاق وحسب.
منفى هي الأشواق. منفى حبّنا. ونبيذنا منفى. ومنفى
تاريخ هذا القلب. كم قلنا لرائحة المكان: تحجري لننام. كم
قلنا لأشجار المكان تجرّدي من زينة الغزوات كي نجد المكانْ
واللامكان هو المكان وقد نأى في الروح عن تاريخه

منفى هي الروح التي تنأى بنا عن أرضنا نحو الحبيبْ
منفى هي الأرض التي تنأى بنا عن روحنا نحو الغريبْ
لم يبق سيفٌ لم يجد غمداً له في لحمنا
والإخوة-الأعداء منّا أسرجوا خيل العدوّ ليخرجوا من حلمنا
منفى هو الماضي: قطفنا خوخ بهجتنا من الصيف العقيم
منفى هي الأفكارُ: شاهدنا غداً تحت النوافذ فاخترقنا
أسوارَ حاضرنا لنبلغه فأصبح ماضياً في درع جنديّ قديم
والشعر منفى حين نحلم ثم ننسى حين نصحو أين كنا
هل نستحقّ غزالة؟ خذنا إلى غدنا الذي لا ينتهي
يا هدهد الأسرار! علّق وقتنا فوق المدى. حلّق بنا
إن الطبيعة كلها روح، وإن الأرض تبدو من هنا
ثدياً لتلك الرعشة الكبرى، وخيل الريح مركبة لنا
يا طيرُ طيري ... طيري كي تطيري فالطبيعة كلها روح. ودوري
حول افتتانك باليد الصفراء، شمسك، كي تذوبي واستديري
بعد احتراقك نحو تلك الأرض، أرضك، كي تنيري
نفق السؤال الصلب عن هذا الوجود وحائط الزمن الصغير
إن الطبيعة كلها روح، وروحٌ رقصة الجسد الأخير
طيري إلى أعلى من الطيران ... أعلى من سمائك ... كي تطيري
أعلى من الحب الكبير ... من القداسة ... والألوهة ... والشعور
وتحرري من كل أجنحة السؤال عن البداية والمصير
الكونُ أصغر من جناح فراشة في ساحة القلب الكبير
في حبة القمح التقينا، وافترقنا في الرغيف وفي المسير
من نحن في هذا النشيد لنسقف الصحراء بالمطر الغزير؟
من نحن في هذا النشيد لنعتق الأحياءَ من أسر القبور؟
طيري بأجنحة انخطافك، يا طيور، على عواصفَ من حرير
لك أن تطيري مثل نشوتنا. يناديك الصدى الكونيّ: طيري
لك ومضة الرؤيا. سنهبط فوق أنفسنا ... سنرجع إن صحونا
سنزور وقتاً لم يكن يكفي مسرّتنا ولا طقسَ النشور
من نحن في هذا النشيد لنلتقي بنقيضه باباً لسور
ما نفع فكرتنا بلا بشر؟ ونحن الآن من نار ونورِ؟
أنا هدهد - قال الدليل - ونحن قلنا: نحن سربٌ من طيور
ضاقت بنا الكلمات أو ضِقنا بها عطشاً وشرّدنا الصدى
وإلى متى سنطير؟ قال الهدهد السكران: غايتنا المدى
قلنا: وماذا خلفه؟ قال المدى خلف المدى خلف المدى
قلنا: تعبنا. قال: لن تجدوا صنوبرة لترتاحوا. سدى

ما تطلبون من الهبوط، فحلّقوا لتحلّقوا. قلنا: غداً
سنطير ثانية ... فتلك الأرضُ ثدي ناضح يمتصه هذا الغمامُ
ذهب يحُكُ الرعشة الزرقاء حول بيوتنا. هل كان فيها –
كل ما فيها ولم نعرف؟ سنرجع حين ترجع كي نراها
بعيون هدهدنا وقد مسّت بصيرتنا. سلامٌ حولها ولها السلام
ولها سريرُ الكون مفروش بقطن الغيم والرؤيا. تنام
وتنام فوق ذراعها المائي سيدة لصورتها وصورتنا. لها
قمر صغير مثل خادمها يمشّط ظلها. ويمرّ بين قلوبنا
خوفا من المنفى ومن قدر الخرافة، ثم يشعله الظلامُ
سهراً لحال النفس قرب المعجزات. أمن هنا ولد الكلامُ
ليصير هذا الطين إنساناً؟ عرفناها لننساها ونسى
سمك الطفولة حول صرتها. أعن بعد نرى ما لا نرى
في القرب. كم كانت لنا الأيامُ أحصنة على وتر اللغة
كم كانت الأنهار نايات ولم نعلم. وكم سجنَ الرخامُ
منا ملائكة ولم نعرف. وكم ضلّت هنا مصرٌ وشامُ
للأرض أرضٌ كان هدهدنا سجيناً فوقها. في الأرض روح –
شردتها الريحُ خارجها. ولم يترك لنا نوحُ الرسائل كلها
ومشى المسيح إلى الجليل فصفقت فينا الجروح. هنا اليمامُ
كلماتُ موتانا. هنا أطلال بابلَ شامةً في إبط سيرتنا. هنا
جسد من التفاح يسبح في المجرة. والمياه له حزامُ
يسري مع الأبد المجسّد في مدائحنا. ويرجع نحو ذاته
أما تغطينا بغزو حنانها العاري وتخفي ما فعلنا بالرئة
وبنار وردتها، وتخفي حربَ سيرتنا، وما صنع الحسامُ
بخريطة الأعشاب حول شواطئ الزغب المقدس. أمنا هي أمّنا
أم الأثينيين والفرس القدامى أم أفلاطون زارادشت أفلوطين أم السهروردي
أم الجميع. وكل طفل سيد في أمه. ولها البداية والختام
وكأنها هي ما هي الميلاد إن شاءت، وإن شاءت هي الموت الحرام
أطعمتنا وأكلتنا يا أمنا كي تطعمي أولادنا يا أمّنا، فمتى الفِطام؟
يا عنكبوت الحب. إن الموت قتل. كم نحبّك كم نحبّك فارحمينا
لا تقتلينا مرة أخرى ولا تلدي الأفاعي قرب دجلة ... واتركينا
نسري على غزلان خصرك قرب خصرك، والهواءُ هو المُقام
واستدرجينا مثلما يُستدرج الحجل الشقيّ إلى الشباك، وعانقينا
هل كنت أنت قبيل هجرتنا ولم نعرف؟ يغيّرنا الغرام
فنصير مثل قصيدة فتحت نوافذها ليحملها ويكملها الحمام
معنى يعيد النسغ للشجر الخفيّ على ضفاف الروح فينا ...

طيري، إذن، يا طير في ساحات هذا القلب طيري
ما نفع فكرتنا بلا بشر ... ونحن الآن من طين ونور؟
- هل كنتَ تعرف أي تاج فوق رأسك؟ - قبر أمي
وأنا أطيرُ وأحمل الأسرار والأخبار أمّي فوق رأسي مهرجان ...
هو هدهد ، وهو الدليل وفيه ما فينا، يعلّقه الزمانُ
جرساً على الوديان. لكن المكان يضيق في الرؤيا وينكسر الزمان
ماذا ترى ... ماذا ترى في صورة الظل البعيدة؟
- ظلٌّ صورته علينا فلنحلّق كي نراه، فلا هو/إلا هو ...
«يا قلب... يا أمّي» ويا أختي ويا امرأتي تدفق كي تراهُ
وله ... لهدهدنا عُروش الماء تحت جفافه تعلو ويعلو السنديانُ
للماء لون الحقل يرفعه النسيم على ظهور الخيل فجراً
للماء طعم هديّة الإنشاء وهو يهبّ من بستان ذكرى
للماء رائحة الحبيب على الرخام تزيدنا عطشاً وسُكراً
للماء شكل هنيهةِ الإشراق حين تشقنا نصفين: إنساناً وطيراً
وله لهدهدنا خيول الماء تحت جفافه تعلو، ويعلو الصولجان
وله ... لهدهدنا زمان كان يحمله، وكان له لسانُ
وله ... لهدهدنا بلاد كان يحملها رسائل للسماوات البعيدة
لم يبق دين لم يجرّبه ليمتحن الخليقةَ بالرحيل إلى الإله
لم يبق حبّ لم يعذبه ليخترق الحبيبَ إلى سواه
وهو المسافر دائماً. من أنت في هذا النشيد؟ أنا الدليل
وهو المسافر دائماً. من أنت في هذا النشيد؟ أنا الرحيل
«يا قلب ... يا أمي» ويا أختي تدفق كي يراك المستحيل -
وكي تراه وتأخذاني نحو مرآتي الأخيرة. قال هدهدنا وطار
هل نحن ما كنّا؟ على آثارنا شجر وفي أسفارنا قمر جميلُ
ولنا حياة في حياة الآخرين هناك. لكنا أتينا -
مكرهين إلى سمرقند اليتيمة. ليس في أجدادنا ملكٌ نعيدُهْ
تركت لنا الأيام إرث الناي في الأيام ... أقربه بعيدُهْ
ولنا من الأمطار ما لشُجيرة اللبلاب. نحن الآن ما كنا وعدنا
مكرهين إلى الأساطير التي لم تتّسع لوصولنا، لم نستطع
أن نحلب الأغنام قرب بيوتنا، ونرتّب الأيام حول نشيدنا
ولنا هناك معابد، ولنا هنا ربٌّ يمجده شهيدُهْ
ولنا من الأزهار «مسك الليل» يوصده نهارٌ لا يريده
ولنا حياة في حياة الآخرين. لنا هنا قمح وزيتٌ -
نحن لم نقطع من الصفصاف خيمتنا، ولم نصنع من -
الكبريت آلهة ليعبدها الجنود القادمون. لقد وجدنا -

كل شيء جاهزاً: أسماءنا مكسورة في جرّة –
الفخار ... دمعَ نسائنا بقعاً من التوت القديم على
الثياب ... بنادق الصيد القديمة ... واحتفالاً سابقاً لا نستعيدُهْ
القفر مكتظ بآثار الغياب الآدمي. كأننا كنّا هنا
وهنا من الأدوات ما يكفي لننصب خيمة فوق الرياح
لا وشم للطوفان فوق تجعد الجبل الذي اخضرت حدودُه
لكنّ فينا ألف شعب مرّ ما بين الأغاني والرماحْ
جئنا لنعلم أننا جئنا لنرجع من غياب لا نريدُهْ
ولنا حياة لم نجرّبها، وملح لم يخلدنا خلودُهْ
ولنا خطى لم يخطُها من قبلنا أحد ... فطيري
طيري، إذن، يا طيرُ في ساحات هذا القلب طيري
وتجمعي من حول هدهدنا، وطيري ... كي ... تطيري.

* محمود درويش، «الهدهد»، **أرى ما أريد** (الدار البيضاء: دار توبقال، ١٩٩٠)، ص ص ٧٩-٩٩.

القص والاقتصاص بين قديم اللحظة وجديد التاريخ:
قراءة في رواية «متون الأهرام» للغيطاني (١)

أيمن الدسوقي

﴿ لا تستدعي الذاكرة لحظةً ما إلا مُقترنةً بوضع ما ﴾

﴿ يستحيل العشق بدون معرفة ﴾

﴿ الأمر دائماً نسبي ﴾

﴿ للبدايات شأنٌ عظيم، والبدايات لا تتكرر أبداً ﴾

﴿ يولَد النهار من الليل، ويخرُج الليل من النهار ﴾

﴿ إنها للزيارة، ليست للإقامة ﴾

﴿ أحياناً ترى البصيرة ما لا يراه البصر، وأحياناً يرى البصر ما لا تدركه البصيرة ﴾

﴿ هل كان بإمكانك مشاهدتها ليلاً؟ ﴾

﴿ ما يبدو واضحاً في حين، يغمض في حين آخر، وما يكون غامضاً في وقت، ينجلي في وقت ﴾

﴿ السائل جاهل، لكن ... هل المجيب عالم؟ ﴾

﴿ من يثابر يصل، ومن يعبر حاجز الوقت تكتمل له الرؤية ﴾

﴿ بلوغ المراحل نسبي ﴾

﴿ كلمة، أو نظرة، أو إيماءة ... ربما تُحيد بمصير وتغير مسار حياة ﴾

﴿ كل شيء من لا شيء ﴾

﴿ لا يدري الإنسان أنه مسافر دائماً، إنْ في حركته أو ثباته ﴾

﴿ الوافد من بعيد في نظر القوم غريب، وهم بالنسبة إليه كذلك، فالكافة غرباء ﴾

﴿ البقاء في الفناء، والفناء في البقاء ﴾

﴿ ما يكون قصياً في البداية، يصبح قريباً بحكم الوقت وقانون المدة ﴾

﴿ بالمداومة تقع الإحاطة، شرط الالتزام ﴾

﴿ ما لا يُدرَك بالنظر، يَنفُذ إليه القلب ﴾

﴿ تبدو الجبال ثابتة، صماء، لكنها تذوي كل لحظة ﴾

﴿ الأمر نسبيٌّ، الأمر نسبيّ ﴾

﴿ الإنسان راجلٌ، والوقت راكب، فكيف يلحق العابر بالأبدي؟ ﴾

﴿ الألفة في غير الوطن تُذهِب باليقين ﴾

﴿ كلُّ نفس تائقة ﴾

﴿ كلُّ طريقٍ يؤدي حتماً إلى طريق ﴾

متون الأهرام

أبو جعفر الإدريسي (توفي ٦٤٩هـ/١٢٥١م) هو صاحب أول دراسة مستفيضة تتناول، في منطق منهجي سليم، ذكر كل ما يخص الأهرام ويأتي ذلك بالخبر والمعاينة وتحقيق الرواية وصحة المصادر وبتوقيف الأعجوبة وبالقياس على الواقع. وهذه الدراسة هي بحق الأولى من نوعها قبل عصرنا الحديث، في اللغة العربية أو في غيرها، وقد أطلق عليها عنوان **كتاب أنوار عُلوي الأجرام في الكشف عن أسرار الأهرام**. ويروي لنا أبو جعفر الإدريسي في كتابه أن أحد من يثق بهم حدثه فيما يخص ذكر الأهرام أن رجلاً من العجم جاءه يوماً بذكر أن لديه علماً في أحد مهاوي الهرم الأكبر لم يسبقه أحد إليه من قبل فاتفقا على المضي فلما تعمقا في الداخل، بعد الخوض في «المهاوي المهولة»، انتهيا إلى:

بيت مربع ليس بالواسع فيه حوض كالحوض الذي في البيت المكعب الذي بأعلى الهرم، وقد قلع غطاؤه وهو فارغ. وحوله نقض من آثار حفر،/وحصير حلفاء بالية، وسُدة جريدة نخرة – أنا إلى الآن لم أقض العجب من أمرهما، وأفكر: إن كان دخل بهما داخل مثلنا، فمن أين دخل بهما؟ وما المراد بهما؟ وإن كانا من حين بناية الأهرام هناك، فكيف أبقت الأيام والليالي على ما بقي من رميمهما؟ ورفعت رأسي إلى السقف فأجد فيه مكتوباً بالمُغْرة العراقية بقلم جليل كقلم الطُّومار: ورد ورد فأما الأعجمي فضرب يداً على يد، وحوقل، واسترجع، وقال لي: إلى هنا انتهى علمي.(٢)

ويسترسل الصديق الثقة فيروي أنه لما أُسقط في أيديهما راجعيْن من حيث أتيا وقد هابا أن يأتيا المزيد من غير علم يسترشدان به. وهنا يتدخل أبو جعفر فيشرح لصديقه الذي بعده لا يزال يتعجب مما رآه:

فقلت له أنا: أما الكتابة التي رأيتها في السقف فإنّ الذي سبقكما إلى الدخول إلى ذلك الموضع، وفتح ذلك الحوض، وأخذ ما كان فيه، فكان اسمه وَرْداً، فكتب: وَرَدَ – يعني من الورود – وَرْدٌ – يعني نفسه، أنه ورد إلى هذا الموضع الذي ما ورد قبله من أبناء جنسه واردٌ –/وردّ – أي رجع من طريقه التي ورد منها –، وأبقى ذلك أثراً من بعده يخبر كلُّ واردٍ بعده إلى ذلك المكان أنّه قد سبقه بالورود إليه، والاطّلاع على ما لم يتفق له الاطّلاع عليه.

فاستحسن ما قد تفطنت له من ذلك هو وجميع من سمعه مني، وكُتِب في جملة ما يكتب من لمح الملح عني.(٣)

هذه الرواية هي في الحقيقة ملحة ذات مغزى وقد أوردها الإدريسي في جملة ما أورده في الفصل الثالث من تحقيق كيفية الوصول إلى الأهرام والطرق المؤدية إليها متوخياً في ذلك المعاينة الشخصية إلى جانب صحة الرواية فيما قد سُبِق إليه من العلم عنها. أما صفة هذه

الرواية الشخصية كملحة فواضحة لما تخبر به عن شخصية الإدريسي وعن تفطنه لوجه المفارقة في الموقف. ووجه المفارقة هنا يزداد في عمقه التاريخي بالنسبة لنا إذا ما انتبهنا إلى أن الذي ادعى الأسبقية هنا هو أعجمي، ثم إلى ما جاء بعد ذلك من ذهوله بعد أن تحقق من أن أحداً قد سبقه إلى الموضع، وذلك أن علم المصريات سينشأ بعد ذلك بستة قرون تقريباً على يد أعاجم كان لهم السبق وصعب بعدهم ورود المصريين لفترة طويلة.(٤)

أما المثير في تلك الرواية فليس فقط أن الوارد الذي ورد وسبق كان عربياً وإنما أنه سجل سبقه بالحرف العربي غير المُشكَّل على عادة القدماء وأنه اتفق واستخدم حروفاً متقطعة تماثل في أشكالها أشكال «قلم الطير» أو «الطلسمات الكاهنية» كما كانت الرسوم الهيروغليفية تُعرف عند العرب وفي المصادر العربية حتى القرن التاسع عشر، وهكذا جاءت الحروف غير مُشكَّلة، على ما نجدها في الهيروغليفية، أي حروف سواكن (متقطعة) ليس عليها شكل الحركات تتكرر في الترتيب وتتطلب فك طلاسمها تمامًا كما حدث مع الهيروغليفية في مطلع القرن التاسع عشر على يد العالم الفرنسي شامبليون، والذي كان أيضاً مستشرقاً ومتمكناً من اللغة القبطية. وكما نعرف الآن، فإن علماء المصريات وفقه اللغات السامية يعدون اللغة الهيروغليفية من ضمن عائلة اللغات السامية (وفيها أيضاً بعض ملامح اللغات الحامية)، وإن كانت تشكل فرعاً خاصاً بها. والفطنة التي أدت بأبي جعفر الإدريسي إلى تخمين معاني الحروف العربية، على نسق أسلوب فك الطلاسم، هي خير مثال على سلامة منهجيته التي اتبعها في تحقيق كل ما يخص الأهرام.

هذه الرواية التي اقتصصتها من كتاب **أنوار عُلوي الأجرام في الكشف عن أسرار الأهرام** تمثل إلى حد ما طبيعة اللحظة التاريخية، بما فيها من كشف شخصي، التي تزخر بها كتب التراث العربي والتي اتخذ منها جمال الغيطاني مدخلاً لنظريته في «فن القص الإسلامي». وأهمية مثل تلك اللحظة التاريخية لا تقل عن أهمية مصدرها وأسلوب روايتها وشخصية راويها وأساليب القص التي تخرج إلينا به من سياقها التاريخي إلى لحظتنا المعاصرة. وما يجدر الالتفات إليه هنا في رواية الإدريسي وخروجها إلينا في شكل عربي ومنطق عربي للقص وتقصي الأثر في الخبر والكلمات وفي شخصية الرواة هو أنها في كل ما تقدمه لنا إنما تقدم لنا أيضاً شخصية الإدريسي نفسه ومنطقه في التفكير وطموحه فيما سعى إليه في أعماله، وهذا إنما هو جوهر ما استقاه الغيطاني من التراث العربي، وبالأخص من أعمال ابن إياس ومن شخصيته المتكشفة من خلالها على ما يردد الغيطاني نفسه في أكثر من موضع. وهذا المنهج في القص – أو الاقتصاص الروائي من المصادر كما سأوضحه في موضعه - يعتمد البحث في طبيعة شخصية من الشخصيات (راوية كانت أم مروية) من خلال استرجاع اللحظات الماضية من سجلات الذاكرة الشخصية أو الجماعية، في عبارة موحية وألفاظ منتقاة من أساليب عدة للقص، تنتهي بنا إلى تكوين الشخصية في سياق العمل الأدبي بتنميطها على أنساق السيرة وقص الرواية في أعمال التراث. والإدريسي في كتابه يعتمد هذا الفرق بين قص الروايات والاقتصاص منها ويستجلبه في موضعه عند الإشارة إلى مصادره التي يوردها أو يرد بنا إليها بطريق السرد أو الرواية عن نفسه.

وعلى مثل هذا تخرج إلينا رواية **متون الأهرام**، فهي تخرج في شكل عربي سليم وإن كان محتواها ينزع إلى رغبة المصري القديم في حفظ لحظته التاريخية التي هي أيضاً قوام

صوته المتفرّد وشخصيته التي عاش بها، وذلك بتسجيلها في حروف مقدسة تتغلب على «تاريخية» اللحظة بقوة اللغة ونموذجية تراكيبها وأساليبها الموروثة.(٥) الراوي في **متون الأهرام** يردُّ بكل شخصية إلى الهرم حيث تمر بتجربتها الفريدة وتكتشف أو يُتكَشَّف لها عن كنه غموض قدرها الذاتي، ثم هو يردّ بها إلينا، في شكل التأريخ أو أدب الحوليات وأنساق تراثية أخرى، وقد سجلها على بنية الهرم أو بنيانه والذي يشكل بدوره بنية الرواية. الشخصية في الرواية هي أيضاً المتن والنص والكلمة وإن كان الراوي لا يحاول فك طلاسمها، كما يفعل الإدريسي، وإنما يقدمها في غموض قدرها الذاتي وأبعاد حياتها التي لا تتكرر من حيث تاريخيتها وخصوصيتها. وكما سأوضح، فإن اللحظة المصيرية الحاسمة التي تتمحور حولها الشخصية هي في ذاتها قديمة منتظمة في نمط وجودي ومعرفي يؤكد إمكانية الاستمرارية ويُفعّله مبدأ الاقتصاص الفني، وإن كانت الشخصية فريدة في حاضرها ومتجددة في تاريخيتها. والشخصية وإن خرجت إلينا في خصوصيتها فإنها لا تزال تمثل بعداً من تكوين أكبر، هو الهرم، يحفظها في لحظتها من «صيرورة الزمن المخيفة» (والعبارة هنا للغيطاني). والشكل الهرمي هنا هو بنيان في حركة دائمة، وهذه أيضاً نظرية الغيطاني في المعمار وفي المعمار الإسلامي بشكل خاص: حركة دائمة وتناسق ارتقائي للحظات وأشكال وحروف. وتشكل روايته الأخرى **سفر البنيان** تعبيراً روائياً عن مثل تلك النظرة للفن المعماري.(٦) أما في **متون الأهرام** فهو يحيل الأقدار الشخصية على تلك الحركة في تناسقها الارتقائي في محاولة تكاد تنم عن رؤية للتاريخ ذاته كعمل فني إسلامي!

ومن كل هذا أخلص إلى قصدي من هذا البحث ألا وهو محاولة تتبع أثر القديم، الذي هو قديم اللحظة، والتي تأتي بدورها في شكل ذكرى شخصية مرتبطة بموضع بعينه، في جديد التاريخ. فهذا هو ما يشكل في أعمال الغيطاني خصوصية الذات التي يعرضها، والتي يستوحيها من طموحه الغالب الذي لا يخفيه إلى الحفاظ على ذاته وخصوصية لحظته، بل وخصوصية التكوين الفني. فنحن نرى الشخصية في أعمال الغيطاني على تنوعها أبداً باحثة في ذاكرتها أو مندفعة إلى مصيرها بفعل الاستعادة للحظة بعينها تكشف لها عن نفسها وقدرها، هذه اللحظة تأتي دائماً مرتبطة بموضع بعينه. واللحظة والموضع في مثل هذه العملية الإبداعية لا يشكلان أداتين لعرض الشخصية وتأطير حركة السرد فقط، وإنما يعلوان إلى مقام المبدأ الفني الذي يحفظ تكوين العمل الأدبي، وينطبق هذا بالأخص على روايتي **متون الأهرام** و**سفر البنيان**. وفي تاريخ الفكر الإنساني عامةً ليس أدل على تلك النزعة إلى الحضور في التاريخ من الشكل الهرمي، ليس فقط كبنيان معماري له خصوصيته ورمزيته الشديدتان، وإنما كسفر يحوي بين دفتيه متن حياة فردية تُلغز الزمن بطموحها إلى حفظ لحظتها التاريخية في نفس الوقت الذي تتخارج فيه من محدودية التاريخ والزمن. ولا يجب هنا أن ننسى دور اللغة ذاتها في الوساطة بين الفرد واللحظة والتاريخ.

أما عن تمحور أعمال الغيطاني حول لحظات أصيلة تأتي من تضاعيف حياة الشخصية وزمنها وذكرياتها فإن ما يشكل تلك اللحظة هو الحضور القوي لوعي مأزوم ينزع إلى التأصل في حاضر هو أبداً مولّ وبالتالي يتبلور الصراع حول جوهر الزمن واللحظة الماضية، كما نشاهد في **تجليات الغيطاني** أو في **رسالة البصائر في المصائر** وفي أعمال أخرى.

وقد يتكشف هذا الوعي في سياق لحظة تاريخية بعينها، كما نشاهد في رواية **الزيني بركات** حيث اللحظة الفاصلة قبل الاحتلال العثماني والتي تتجلى في سيرة شخصية حاضرة- غائبة هي شخصية الزيني بركات. وهذا الوعي المتأزم في اللحظة وباللحظة يخرج إلينا متماهياً مع وعي تاريخي-تسجيلي هو وعي الراوي الذي يتماهى بدوره مع وعي المؤرخ ابن إياس. وهذه الجدلية وإن جاءت في شكل علاقة بين لحظة قديمة ووعي حاضر فإن ما يجمع بينهما في الحقيقة يبدو وكأنه حضور اللغة ذاتها وأساليب القص التي يخرج بها ومن خلالها الحدث. وهذه العلاقات المتداخلة في زمن اللغة ووعي الراوي لا تخفى على قُراء الغيطاني ونُقاده على السواء. فكما يذكر فيصل درّاج في كلماته الموجزة: «يتحدد إشكال الغيطاني الأساسي بسؤال: الزمن والكتابة، إذ للكتابة هوية، وإذ للكتابة-الهوية زمن أصلي، لا يجب الخروج عنه، لأنه يؤمِّن طمأنينة الروح ويُقصي عنها الضياع والهزيمة».(٧) وعلى ما في هذه العبارة من إيجاز، قد يجمع بين الآراء المختلفة والمتضاربة في أعمال الغيطاني ومشروعه الروائي، فإن إسقاط فيصل دراج لزمن أصلي للكتابة وبالتالي إحالة هذا الزمن على مبدأ الأسبقية الدائمة على كل ما يلحقه من كتابة وأزمان (هي أصوات الراوي والشخصيات على تتابعها وتداخلها وتناصها التراثي في البنية السردية)، يعني أن هذا الزمن الأصلي إنما يجيء دائماً متماهياً مع زمن الكتابة الحاضر وبالتالي مُفكِّكاً لتفعيل هذه الكتابة الزمني ولأنساقها المعنوية، فهي بذلك لا تعدو كونها مجازاً استعارياً لحالة معرفية، ويصير فعل اللغة هنا بلاغياً محضاً ويصير هذا الزمن الأصلي نفسه مجرد إسقاط استعاري لبلاغية هذه اللغة. وهذا الإسقاط متجذر في رؤية النقد التفكيكي Deconstructionism وقد استفاض الناقد الأمريكي، الفرنسي الأصل، پول دو مان Paul de Man في عرضه وتطبيقه في دراساته حول أليغورية فعل القراءة، وقد أطلق عليه مصطلح «الأسبقية المُتغيِّبة أبداً» "forever unreachable anteriority".(٨) وعلى ما في هذه الرؤية من عمق في فهم العلاقة بين اللغة وزمن الكتابة وبينهما وفعل القراءة، إلا أنها تحيل المعنى على أنساق اللغة وتراكيبها أكثر منه على لحظة الكاتب النفسية والإبداعية المعقدة والمركبة، وإن كانت تلك اللحظة لا تنفصل عن صياغاتها اللغوية. وهذه اللحظة ترد في سياق أعمال الغيطاني دائماً في صيغة السيرة الذاتية،(٩) إما في شكل تسجيلي ذاتي مباشر حين يذكر لنا الغيطاني في حوارات ومقابلات ومقالات متعددة أصل اللحظة في حياته وتجربته الشخصية أو حينما يتم تفعيلها في العملية السردية حيث تتأصل في تركيب إحدى الشخصيات وبالتالي تُفعِّل الإشارة قبل العبارة أي تعطي اللحظة أولوية معنوية في تركيب الشخصية تسبق في أهميتها العبارة والتراكيب اللغوية ولا تُحال إلى زمن روائي سابق. واللحظة دائماً «حاضرة» في النص وإن جاءت «قديمة» بتراكيبها وأنماطها.(١٠)

والواقع أن رؤية الغيطاني للغة والتاريخ والذات، والتي تنصب على العلاقة مع الزمن وعلى قدرة استخلاص الفنان أو القصاص للحظة المولية أبداً من ذاكرة النسيان، هذه الرؤية، على عكس فرضية القراءة لزمن أصلي، تفترض أن ثمة ما هو خارج اللغة وخارج الزمن وإن تكشَّف ذلك وجودياً بفعل اللغة ومن خلال نفوذ اللحظة المصيرية الحاسمة. وهذا الذي يتخارج على اللغة وعلى الزمن (السردي أو التاريخي) فيجمع بين الغيطاني في

زمنه وابن إياس في زمنه، على ما يرى الغيطاني، وعلى وعيه بما بينهما من اختلاف في اللحظة التاريخية وفي النظرة أو التوجه الشخصي، ذاك هو ما يرتبط في النهاية بما يطلق عليه الغيطاني «الجوهري» في الإنسان أو في التجربة الإنسانية. والتوجه هنا مستقبلي في أساسه.

وانطلاقاً من هذه الإشارات التمهيدية يمكننا أن نبدأ الحديث عن رواية **متون الأهرام** بالإحالة على ذكرى شخصية قديمة للغيطاني عندما كان في الثالثة من عمره تعود إلى الغرفة التي عاشت فيها أسرته في حارة درب الطبلاوي:

> غرفة في الطابق الخامس يمتد أمامها سطح فسيح. كنت أرى عبر أسواره التي كان ارتفاعها يحاذي بالكاد رأسي أفق المدينة التي لم تعرف بعد العمارات العالية، كانت أعلى عمارة تقع إلى جهة الشمال، في غمرة، وفي المساء يبرق فوقها إعلان عن مشروب الكوكا كولا. أما الآن فتُعَد عمارة قزمة. أما إلى الغرب فكان ممكناً رؤية الأهرامات، خاصةً بدءاً من العصر وحتى اكتمال المغيب.(١١)

وانطلاقاً من مبدأ الكشف الذاتي عند الغيطاني autobiographical self-disclosure، والذي هو مبدأ حداثي في توظيفه الإبداعي المنعكس على الذات خارج «السيرة الذاتية» كجنس أدبي، وكذلك انطلاقاً من استعادة اللحظة كمبدأ فني، فإن هذه الذكرى القديمة، وإن جاءت شخصية بحتة، تندرج تحت تاريخ طويل من التوجه الشخصي صوب الأهرام للرحالة العربي القديم أو ساكن القاهرة المقيم. وهي في ذات الوقت تؤصل توجه الشخصيات جميعها **في متون الأهرام** وتؤطر حركة القص وانفعال الشخصية بمصيرها الغامض والمحتوم. ونشاهد كذلك كيف تستهل رواية **سفر البنيان** بأقصوصة تحوي نفس التوجه إلى ناحية الأهرام («مصطلح: باب»، ص ص ٩-١٢) أما **متون الأهرام** فتستهل في المتن الأول «تشوّف» بسيرة الشيخ تهامي الذي يتوجه بكلّيته تجاه الغرب ويثبت على ذلك حتى تحل اللحظة الحاسمة: «هكذا، قام ساعياً إلى الأهرام في ليلة هادئة، باردة، أبطأ صقيعها إيقاع مرور الوقت، جاء الهرم الأكبر من الشرق، كان على يقين أن ثمة شيئاً إنسانياً في تلك الأحجار التي تبدو صماء. وأنه لو تكلم فسوف يسمع من يخاطبه» (ص ٢١). والإشارة إلى إنسانية الهرم هنا لها مغزاها على ما سأوضح في موضعه. وهذه اللحظة السردية ترد متواترة في مصادر التراث العربي، وقد خصها بالذكر المقريزي وابن إياس، أما الإدريسي فقد جمعها وأفرد لها فصلاً خاصاً بعنوان «في التعريف بالناحية المخصوصة بها من أرض مصر وبالطرق المسلوكة إليها، وما يخصها من الحدود والصفات المُطّلَع بطريقي الخبر والمعاينة عليها».(١٢) وهي في لغتها وأسلوب سردها تأتي إما لتحديد التوجه المكاني أو التوجه المصيري، الاندفاع تجاهها بدافع غامض ووازع مقيم لا يهدأ به حال الشخصية إلا في كنفها أو في الحوم حولها أو الولوج في فتحاتها.

والمغزى هنا سن ذكر هذه الواقعة الشخصية هو تبيان كيف أن اللحظة أو الذكرى الشخصية، تجربة الغيطاني الخاصة غير المتكررة والتي من الواضح أنها تركت انطباعاً ما قوياً في أعماقه، هي على خصوصيتها تحمل تاريخاً خاصاً في هذه الحالة تم تسجيله في التراث العربي.

والواقع أن هذه التجربة هي في النهاية مُيسَّرَة ومتكررة في تلك المنطقة من أحياء القاهرة القديمة على مدار تاريخها الطويل، وهي أيضاً ما دفع الغيطاني للاهتمام فيما بعد بأعمال ابن إياس وغيره من المؤرخين وبأدب الخطط كذلك، إلى جانب اهتمامه بالفن المعماري المتوفر في المنطقة.

ومن هنا فالشخصي والتاريخي يجتمعان في تجربة خاصة يغلب عليها عنصر الزمن والتوجه المكاني والوعي بالمصير، وهذه الأبعاد كلها تخرج إلى حيز المعنى التاريخي في لغة مرهونة باللحظة وإن كانت في ذات الوقت متوالدة بأساليبها ومغزاها. وهكذا، فإن الصوت الروائي في **متون الأهرام** ينتقل بين اللحظة الشخصية المرتبطة بزمن ما وبموضع ما إلى جديدها التاريخي المتوالد في العبارة التراثية المشيرة بدورها إلى اللحظة الحاضرة والمتجددة بالواقعة الشخصية التي لها خصوصية وجودية لا تتكرر: «للبدايات شأن عظيم، والبدايات لا تتكرر» (ص ١٠). وما يجمع بين هذه البدايات أو المصائر عبر حواجز الوقت والتاريخ هو الحضور في اللغة الذي هو في الوقت ذاته الحضور في بنية الهرم بخصوصية رمزيته وصموده وإلغازه للزمن. فكما كُتبت المصائر لأصحاب الأهرام على جدرانها وحُفظت بقوة اللغة والعقيدة يعيد الراوي كتابة مصائر كثيرة لأزمان متباعدة في لحظة زمانية مكانية متجسدة هي متن وبنيان. أو بمعنى استعاري آخر، الراوي يحيل الشروح المتراكمة تاريخياً على ديمومة متن نص واحد – هو الهرم الذي يتخذ صفة المبدأ الإلهي في نهاية المتن الأول – معتمداً في ذلك على قوة اللغة وحركية المعنى/البنيان الدائمة، وبذا يعيد كتابة التاريخ في شكل سِيَر أو تراجم قد غلّبها على «صيرورة الزمن المخيفة». ولعل هذا المنطق في تكوين النص ورسم الشخصيات والذي تتميز به الرواية يشكّل السمة الرئيسية التي تربطه بالفكر المصري القديم، فما عداها يخرج في منطق عربي وتراثي يتناول مصر القديمة والنظرة إليها وإلى آثارها وبراريها من منطلق التجارب والمفاهيم التي تسبق فكّ رموز الهيروغليفية – فهي تحتفظ بعبق «الطلسمات الكاهنية» – وبداية المعرفة التاريخية الموثّقة لمصر الفرعونية. وهذه الصفة تركز الاهتمام على التجربة الشخصية أكثر منه على المعرفة التاريخية.

بنية الرواية الشكلية: المتن والموضع والبنيان

تتخذ **متون الأهرام** شكل «المتتالية الروائية»، فهي تنقسم إلى أربعة عشر متناً كل منها يشكل وحدة سردية متكاملة، إما في الشكل الروائي المتعارَف عليه أو فيما تحيل إليه المقولات المأثورة أو الترانيم المستقلة في المتون الخمسة الأخيرة. يتناول كل متن سيرة أو ترجمة شخصيةٍ واحدة أو عدة شخصيات اجتمعت على مصير مشترك، وكلها يرتبط مصيرها – والمعنون على ماهيته بمصطلح خاص يتصدر المتن – بالأهرام ونواحيها، الرمز الجامع للمتون والمصائر. هذا من ناحية التقسيم الشكلي، أما على مستوى حركية السرد فالمتون تتدرج في الطول، مع تباينها في أساليب القص والاقتصاص من أشكال التراث الفنية المستخدمة فيها، حتى تصل بنا إلى المتن العاشر حيث تختفي العناوين ويتقلص النص إلى مقولة واحدة ما تكون بترنيمات متون الأهرام الأصلية وعندما نصل إلى المتن الرابع عشر والأخير نجد عبارة واحدة فقط تتكرر ثلاث مرات في شكل عمودي: «لا شيء لا شيء لا شيء» (ص ١١١). وتشكّل هذه العبارة في تكرارها عمودياً وموضعتها في خاتمة المتتالية الروائية قمة الهرم النصي المتصاعد.

.

.

.

.

.

﴿ تَشَوُّف ﴾

وهكذا فمن الواضح أن تكوين المتون وتدرّجها مُشاكل في بنيانه بنية الهرم ذاتها (انظر الشكل السابق)، فنبدأ من القاعدة وأطول متن ونتدرج في التصاعد وفي النظرة/القراءة المستشِفّة إلى الهرم في محاولة للوصول إلى قمته التي هي نقطة التماس بين البنيان والفضاء اللامرئي. وما يجمع النصوص في بنيتها الداخلية والخارجية هي علاقة الجزء بالكل، الذي هو الشكل الهرمي المتكامل. والكل لا نراه ولا يشمله اللحظ أو تحيط به النظرة، وإنما نرى القاعدة ويتدرج بنا النظر إلى أعلى. وهذا بالطبع يتوقف على قرب المسافة أو بعدها، أو حميمية النظرة وقوة الإدراك أو وهنهما. فعندما يقوم الشيخ تهامي في المتن الأول «تشوّف» ساعياً إلى الهرم وقد أتاه من الشرق متحركاً بتشوفه ويقينه «أن ثمة شيئاً إنسانياً في تلك الأحجار التي تبدو صماء. وأنه لو تكلم فسوف يسمع من يخاطبه» (ص ٢١)، تتكشّف له الإلهامات التالية والتي تعنونها ترنيمة تحوي مغزاها:

«تبدو الجبال ثابتة، صماء، لكنها تذوي كل لحظة»
في تلك الليلة أدرك أموراً عديدة بعضها يمكن التصريح أو التلميح إليه فمنها:
- استحالة إدراك الأهرام بالنظر عند الوقوف بالقرب منه، في مدى ظله، أما رؤيته عن بعد فوهمٌ، لأنه لا يبدو على حقيقته.
- استيعاب الارتفاع بالنظر مستحيل، التطلع من أي نقطة يتعارض تماماً مع زوايا ميل الأهرام.
- البناء أشمل من إدراكه بنظرة واحدة، لذلك أينما وقف الإنسان، أينما تطلع فإنه لا يدرك إلا جزءاً من كل . . . (ص ٢١)

وهنا تجدر الإشارة إلى أن فعل القراءة لمتون الرواية يشاكل فعل التطلع للشكل الهرمي. فإن كان فعل الكتابة السابق هنا بزمنه ولغته يؤطر مسيرة حياة، فإن فعل القراءة يخرج بهذه الحياة إلى مصيرها وإلى ديمومة الحركة وصيرورة الزمن والتماس بين المرئي واللامرئي. والمفاهيم التي تعنون المتون، وهي على التوالي: «تشوّف»، «إيغال»، «تلاش»، «إدراك»، «نشوة»، «ظلّ»، «ألق»، «صمت»، «رقصة»، هذه المفاهيم تجمع بين مسيرة الحياة ومصيرها، بين فعل الكتابة والتأصيل وفعل القراءة والإدراك. وهذه المفاهيم ذات رموز صوفية لا تخفى على القارئ وتعكس توجه لغة المتون خطابياً نحو التناص مع لغة الصوفية ومفاهيم التصوف ومقاماته وأحواله. فهي تشكل مقامات ومراحل البلوغ المصيري إلى قمة الهرم أو قمة الإدراك للنفس والعلاقة مع الزمن.

وتبدأ حركة التطلع ويبدأ فعل القراءة بالترجمة لسيرة مريد صوفي من المغرب قد عنّفه شيخه لأنه خرج إلى الحج ولم يعرج في الطريق لرؤية الأهرام، فيشد المريد الرحال عائداً إلى مصر متشوفاً للقاء مصيري مع الهرم الأكبر. ووزن كلمة «تَشَوُّف» يفيد بترداد الحركة وتواتر الرغبة وتوالي البدايات حتى تحصل الرؤية وتبدأ رحلة الولوج إلى الداخل أو «الإيغال» ثم إلى تماهي الطالب والمطلوب في حضور المعنى أو «التلاشي» ثم حصول «الإدراك» وإقبال «النشوة»

ثم البقاء في «ظل» أو في كنف الكل (ظل الهرم) ثم «ألق» الحضرة وأدب «الصمت» في حضرة الكل، وأخيراً «رقصة» كونية تعبر عن الحركة الدائمة للجزء في الكل وللكل في فضاءاته اللامتناهية. وهكذا، فإن كل مفهوم أو مقام هنا هو عنوان لمتن يحوي سيرة حياة ويوضعها في علاقة جزء مع كل هو بنيان الهرم الذي يخرج بها من لحظتها التاريخية إلى علاقة مصيرية مع الزمن. والشخصيات في المتون تنتمي إلى حقب تاريخية مختلفة ومصائر شخصية وأقدار متباينة جمع بينها الهرم: «وكأنهم على ميعاد، وإن باعدت بينهم الأماد» (المتن العاشر، ص ٩٥). ومن هذا المتن الذي يبدأ معه اختفاء العناوين وتوحد المصائر أو تجمع السير في مقولة واحدة موحدة تبدأ حركة الارتقاء إلى الذروة (انظر ص ١٠٣).

والملاحظ أن هذا التقسيم لفصول الرواية أو متونها أيضاً يشاكل إلى حدٍ ما التنظيم الشكلي لمتون الأهرام الأصلية والتي كانت تهدف إلى الوصول بالملك (وبالنبلاء ثم العامة في العصور التالية على الأسرة الخامسة، تحت عنوان «متون الكفن») إلى السماء حيث يتخلد بين الآلهة. والمتون الأصلية تأتي في شكل ترانيم أو شذرات مستقلة ذات أساليب مختلفة تعكس أقدم الأجناس الأدبية في التاريخ الفرعوني من صلوات جنائزية وترانيم ونصوص أسطورية/لاهوتية وطلسمات سحرية ونصوص طقسية وسِيَر ذاتية وتاريخية وغيرها. وعلى ما تعكسه المتون في رواية الغيطاني من أساليب تراثية عربية مختلفة، فإنها لا تحوي أية محاولة للتناص مع النصوص الفرعونية القديمة، وإن كانت هذه النصوص أيضاً تستخدم صيغة الغائب وتشير إلى صاحب الهرم باسمه وليس بصيغة الأنا. ومجاميع النصوص التي تُعرف الآن بعنوان «متون الأهرام» تعود إلى الفترة ما بين الأسرة الخامسة والأسرة السابعة (٢٤٩٤-٢١٧٥ ق.م.)، وهي تلك التي نجدها في هرم الملك أوني آخر ملوك الأسرة الخامسة وفي الأهرام التابعة لملوك الأسرة السادسة وملكاتها: الملك تيتي والملك بيبي الأول والملك ميرنَرَع والملك بيبي الثاني، ثم أُضيفت إليها نصوص الأهرامات التابعة للملكة أودجيبتين والملكة نيت والملكة أبوييت (زوجات الملك بيبي الثاني) ثم أخيراً هرم الملك إبي من الأسرة السابعة. وكل هذه الأهرامات تم بناؤها تقريباً بين عامي ٢٣٥٠ و ٢١٧٥ قبل الميلاد. وهذه المتون في مجموعها ربما كان أصلها شفاهياً وهي لا تشكل نصاً متكاملاً.(١٣) وعلى علاقة المصري القديم بالحياة واللغة والتاريخ فربما من المهم ذكر أن هذه العلاقة أيضاً أدت إلى تطور أدب السيرة الذاتية، كما نشاهد في رؤية الغيطاني الذاتية لعلاقة الأنا بالمجموع وبالزمن، في نفس الفترة التاريخية التي تنتمي إليها متون الأهرام. وأدب السيرة الذاتية هو أقدم الأعمال الأدبية في التاريخ الفرعوني.(١٤)

ومن ثم فرواية متون الأهرام للغيطاني، وإن جاءت مشاكلة من ناحية منطق السيرة والنزوع إلى البقاء والبقاء في ظل «أفق الأبدية» (كما كان يطلق على الأهرام في بعض النصوص القديمة) للمتون الأصلية إلا أن المتاليات السردية ومنطق الحبكة وعلاقة الجزء بالكل إنما تأتي كلها في الحقيقة من نظرية الغيطاني في «فن القص الإسلامي» ورؤيته الخاصة بين الكلمة والفن المعماري الإسلامي. وذلك على الرغم من أن العلاقة بين الكلمة والصورة أو الشكل الفني والبنيان المعماري هي في صميم الإبداع المصري القديم وتشكل جانباً من أعمق جوانب الفكر والإبداع الفني في العصور الفرعونية. فكما أن الغيطاني يرى

في كل متن في الرواية وحدة معنوية متكاملة تتماهى كجزء مع الكل الذي هو الرواية وتتشابك في التراكيب والإشارات وفنون القص والسرد والاقتصاص من نصوص عربية بعينها، كل هذه الجوانب التي يستقيها من التراث العربي الإسلامي إنما يراها تأتي من وحدة الآية القرآنية وعلاقتها بالنص القرآني ككل، والتي هي على ما يراها أصل الفن الإسلامي، سواء كان أدبياً لغوياً أو معمارياً فنياً:

ثمة رؤية كامنة تحد أطر الفن الإسلامي، والنثر الأدبي أيضاً.
وبداية لا بد من الإشارة إلى المرجع الأول الذي يحدد أساس هذه الرؤية، أي القرآن الكريم.
يتكون القرآن الكريم من سور، وتتكون السور من آيات، كل آية تعتبر وحدة نثرية متكاملة، يمكن أن نقرأها ونكتفي بها لكنها متصلة بالآية التي تليها أيضاً، ومن مجموع الآيات تتكون السور، سورة البقرة أطولها وتتكون من مائتين وستة وثمانين آية. وأصغرها قصار السور، عدد سورة الناس ست آيات فقط.
ما بين الآية والسورة تكمن الرؤية، ما بين علاقة الجزء بالكل، والكل بالجزء. هذا ما نجده في فن الزخرفة العربي، وفي فن القص العربي أيضاً.(١٥)

هذه الرؤية الإسلامية التي تجمع فنون الزخرفة والقص العربية يراها الكاتب في صميم خصوصية فن النثر العربي الذي يسبق فن الرواية. ويسعى الغيطاني من هذا المنطلق إلى تأصيل لغة سردية نموذجية تستوحي أنماطها من هذا التراث ومن هذه الرؤية الفنية (والكونية في مرجعيتها إلى النص القرآني). وعلى هذا فالكلمة والشكل الفني، الآية والسورة، المنمنمة والتصميم، هذه العلاقات التي هي في أساسها علاقة جزء بكل في حركة دائمة هي في أصلها علاقة دائمة مع الزمن، فإن كل سرد هو حركة دائمة للكلمة والمعنى في الزمن كما أن كل بنيان هو في حركة دائمة وإن بدا صامداً. وخير ما تتجسد هذه الرؤية الفنية، في مشاكلة الكلمة بالفن المعماري في إطار سيرة شخصية، إنما تتجسد في رواية **سفر البنيان**؛ فكما يذكر الراوي: «كل بناء من حامل ومحمول . . . فما دام الأمر احتوى على حامل لمحمول فلابد من حركة. لابد من انتقال، لابد من سفر، فالتحميل لا يكون إلا عند الرحيل، من هنا فإن كل حامل ومحمول تأهب لمغادرة، وكل بناء يبدو للأحداق العوابر ثابتاً، جامداً إنما هو في حركة» (ص ٢٧). وفي الحكاية السابقة، وكلتا الحكايتين تخصان ذكر الأهرام، يذكر الراوي: «هذا البناء (الأهرام) ليس عمارة، إنه توق، إنه تذكرة، إنه مسعى الحروف التي ستبقى بعد فناء كل شيء عند بلوغ تلك الذروة - قمة الهرم/أفق الأبدية» (ص ١٩). أما فيما يخص البنيان وعلاقته بالحكايات والروايات والأحاديث فيقول على لسان حال حور محب الفرعون الأعظم المتسائل: «ما يرتبط بالبنيان من حكايات صغيرة، ورواية أحداث، أبقى وأشمل من رص الأحجار وضبط الزوايا، والحد من حرية الميل، وصون القدرة على الارتفاع!» (ص ٣٣).

وفي الواقع إن تحديد الرؤية الفنية وراء فن القص الإسلامي أو النثر العربي بين الآية والسورة أو الجزء والكل إنما هو في صميم الرؤية الدينية للعلاقة بين الذات والآخر أو الذات والكون كما تبدى في الفكر المصري القديم وفي التراث الإنساني الديني بشكل عام فهي أيضاً في الفلسفة اليونانية التي ستظهر بعد ذلك في فلسفة القديس توما الإكويني الذي سيضعها في إطار مسيحي ويحدها، أي في علاقة الجزء بالكل، في مبدأ فني جمالي سيتأثر به بعد ذلك الكاتب الأيرلندي المشهور جيمس جويس ويستخدمه كمبدأ فني في أعماله الأولى وكرؤية مؤسِّسة للفنان الشاب ستيفن ديدالوس.(١٦) وعلى نمط آخر ومن خلال الفلسفة الألمانية سيطور تلك الفكرة كمبدأ للعمل الفني وللرواية بالتحديد المفكر والناقد الروسي باختين في مقالاته الفلسفية الأولى وبالأخص في مقاله «العلاقة بين المؤلف والبطل في الحركة الإبداعية (١٩٢٠/١٩٢٣)».(١٧) ويطور باختين هذه العلاقة في إطار العمل الفني تحت مبدأ فن «النسقية» أو ما يعرف بـ architectonics التي يعارض بها فكرة الفن المعماري الذي يستخدم أشكالاً مسمطة. ففن «النسقية» يعتمد على العلاقة المنفتحة بين الجزء والكل الذي بدوره في حالة صيرورة. وعلى هذا ففن المعمار Architecture وفن الجمال Aesthetics إنما هما شكلان من أشكال فن «النسقية» الذي يحول الأجزاء المتناثرة في كل متحرك – هو الوجود بذاته – إلى حدثٍ ذي معنى أو إلى نص متكامل. وفي غضون عرضه لطبعة **ألف ليلة وليلة** كنص عربي إسلامي، يعترف الغيطاني بأن الوحدات التي يتشكل منها المعمار الإسلامي، بل والمدينة الإسلامية، هي متأصلة في ثقافات متعددة وعلى هذا فخصوصيتها تأتي من رؤية الفنان المسلم الجديدة «التي تنتقل بحرية بين هذه الوحدات الزخرفية (أو الفنون السردية) لتخلق عالماً خاصاً به».(١٨) وفيما يخص فن النثر العربي فهو يستمد خصوصيته من المزج الحُر والمبدع بين الأشكال الفنية وأساليب القص المختلفة ليعبر عن لحظة تاريخية بعينها في شكل فني واضح يمكن تعيينه بفن السيرة أو التأريخ أو الخطط أو الأخرويات وغيرها من فنون الكتابة التراثية. ويأتي دور الغيطاني ومشروعه الأدبي في محاولة خلق لغة نموذجية للرواية تسبق فن الرواية العربية، على ما يراه ويمارسه، تعتمد على التوظيف للأشكال الفنية العربية (في الأغلب في سياق سيرة شخصية أو ذاتية) هو ما عرّفه أبو جعفر الإدريسي بأسلوب الاقتصاص بطريق الرواية والخبر والمعاينة في مؤلفه عن الأهرام كتاب **أنوار عُلوي الأجرام في الكشف عن أسرار الأهرام**.

وعودة إلى رواية **متون الأهرام**، فإن المتتاليات السردية تعتمد مبدأ الاقتصاص (من التجربة الشخصية للراوي أو بطريق السماع والرواية أو الإشارة إلى نصوص بعينها) بينما الكل الذي تنفتح عليه يسري بأسلوب القص السردي المبني على رؤية معمارية تجمع بين الأجزاء ومصائر الشخصيات في بنيان شديد الرمزية هو الشكل الهرمي: «باستمرار، سيكون ما يستعصي على الإدراك، وأوله .. تلك الأهرام، بتمام ظهورها يكون الاختفاء» (**سفر البنيان**، ص ٦١). وهذا عين ما توصل إليه الشيخ تهامي، طالب العلم في المتن الأول «تشوّف»: «ورغم انتظاره، والمنتظر قلق دائماً، غير مستقر، فإنه ظل شاخصاً دائماً إلى ناحية الأهرام، وكثيراً ما تأخذه رجفة يجتهد لإخفاء أعراضها إذ يقوى عليه حضور هذا البناء، المهيمن، المشرِف، الملغِز، المحيط، الدالّ، الجلي، الغامض، الراسخ، الصامد، الثابت الساري،

القريب في بعده، البعيد في قربه» (ص ٢٤) هذا التوصيف للهرم يحيله إلى رمز لقدس الأقداس، ويحيل الأوصاف إلى أسماء حسنى، حتى يبدأ مجموعة من الفتية في المتن الثاني «إيغال» الدخول في جوف الهرم الأكبر مستحضرين في رغبتهم الشديدة قصة «الفتية الذين آمنوا بربهم» كآية قرآنية ووحدة نثرية متكاملة المعنى.

والتعبير العربي «متن» للإشارة إلى جسم النص يوحي بالعلاقة بين المتن والشروح. وعلى هذا فكل متن أو سيرة حياة في الرواية ينتظر شروحه كما تنتظر مومياء الملك في الهرم الانتقال إلى العالم الآخر بعد مرورها بمراحل ما بعد الموت وخلوصها إلى عتبات أفق الأبدية حيث يتم إعلانها «مُصَدَّقَة الصوت» وهو الحكم الأخير قبل اجتيازها عتبات الخلود. وكذا فإن كل متن في الرواية يمنح صوتاً روائياً للشخصية التي ارتبط مصيرها بالهرم والتي تنتهي إلى المرحلة التي تجسد فيها المقام الذي يعنون للمتون «تشوّف»، «ألق»، إلخ. أي إنها قد صُدِّق عليها واجتيز بها إلى البنيان الذي هو رمز الخلود.

بنية الرواية الداخلية: الشخصية واللحظة والتاريخ

ينسق كل متن في الرواية ويجمع ما بين الخطوط التي تؤطر حياة شخصية أو مجموعة من الشخصيات والتي تتمحور حول علاقة مصيرية غامضة بالأهرام. وكل متن يخرج وكأنه إعادة كتابة لتلك الحياة في ظل الهرم-الكل-الرمز المنفتح وكأنه يمنح الحياة لتلك الشخصية ويغلِّبها على «صيرورة الزمن المخيفة»، تماماً كما كان الهدف من الترانيم التي تشكل متون الأهرام القديمة. وتجدر الإشارة هنا إلى أن هذه الشخصيات في مجموعها تنتمي إلى حِقَب تاريخية مختلفة ومواطن ومدن مختلفة - أي إنها تنتمي إلى لحظات تاريخية مختلفة تجسد كل شخصية فيها علاقة الأنا بالواقع في تلك اللحظة بعينها. وما يجمع بين هذه المصائر المتباينة زمنياً ومكانياً هو التقاؤها في الشكل الهرمي بشكل يتحدد معه مصيرها وكأنهم اتفقوا على ميعاد عبر الأزمنة والأمكنة، كما يعلن المتن العاشر ويخرجها حقيقةً من اللفظ إلى حيز الرؤية بقوة العبارة وغموضها وجزالتها.

وإذا عدنا إلى علاقة المتن بالشرح، أو علاقة مومياء الملك بمعاني أسمائها المختلفة المسجَّلة على جدران الهرم والتي توحِّد بينها روح الملك التي ستنطلق إلى عالمها فيما بعد بقوة اللفظ ومصداقية الصوت، نجد أنها تشكل مجازاً استعارياً لحركة تنميط الشخصية في الرواية وترهينها بأنماط تأتي من التراث على مستوى السيرة ومستوى العبارة المستخدمة في فنون السيرة والقص العربي المختلفة. فهناك النمط-المتن الذي يشكل لحظةً ما مصيرية في حياة شخص وتجربة إنسانية قد ولت بزمنها، وهناك الشروح التي هي بمثابة حيوات أخرى تلت في العصور المختلفة والتي تنجذب إلى الهرم بقوة مصيرية غامضة تنتهي بها إلى سيرة ذاتية منمَّطة على متن-أصل (كما في أدب السيرة الذاتية الفرعونية)[١٩] وإن أضافت بعداً تاريخياً يُعَد شرحاً تاريخياً وإنسانياً لنمط اللحظة المصيرية الحاسمة. فتناول الشخصية في روايتي **متون الأهرام وسفر البنيان** يأتي على أسلوب الغيطاني المميز في النزوع إلى أسطرة الشخصية إما بعرضها في لغة تتداعى إلى مفاهيم صوفية وأساليب تراثية في العرض كما في **الزيني بركات** أو في **التجليات** أو بترهينها على أنماط إنسانية نموذجية وعرضها في لغة

مناسبة للنمط النموذج كما في شخصية الزويل.[٢٠] ولنأخذ مثالاً على ذلك المتن الأول «تشوّف» والذي تستهل به الرواية متونها ويشكل كذلك قاعدة الهرم السردي.

يبدأ «تشوّف» المتن الأول بصوت روائي غير محدّد الهوية يعلن عن معرفته بشخص آخر في نمط التوقيف على خبر ورواية كما يعلن أن تمام الإحاطة بالخبر لم يتم إلا بعد انتفاء إمكانية اللقاء أو المخاطبة، أي بعد الموت: «عرفه أول سعيه، غير أنه لم يحط بخبره إلا بعد التمام. وما بين البداية والنهاية استغرق الأمر سنوات طوالاً ما تزال أصداؤها سارية، ممتدة، كذلك وجوده. حتى وإن أصبح غير ماثل مع تمام اليقين بانتفاء إمكانية اللقاء والمخاطبة» (ص ٢٩). المعرفة وإن تمت في أول السعي، في ظل البداية التي لا تتكرر (انظر ص ١٠) كما يؤكد الراوي مراراً في المتون، لا تضمن الإحاطة بالخبر، أي تحقيق الفهم والإدراك. ما يضمنها هنا هو بقاء الأصداء السارية من ذكريات وروايات ترتبط بأحداث بعينها تحوي الذكرى وتمنح قوة الحضور والتواجد، فالأصداء الممتدة تضمن كذلك امتداد الوجود وهكذا يتبلور جوهر التجربة وتتحدد إمكانية الإحاطة وحصول المعرفة بالمقولة أو الترنيمة الفاصلة التي تتبع بداية المتن والتي تشكل الأولى من سلسلة ترنيمات سوف تتشكل حولها ومن معانيها سيرة الشخصية في المتن الأول: «لا تستدعي الذاكرة لحظة ما إلا مقترنة بوضع ما» (ص٩). وتشكل اللحظة المقترنة بالموضع في كل المتون مبدأ معرفياً من ناحية العلاقة بالذات وإمكانية المعرفة وموضعة المعروف تاريخياً، كما تشكل مبدأ فنياً لعرض السير المختلفة في بقية المتون، فالشخصيات دائماً تستعيد حياتها في ذاكرة الراوي التي تستدعي الشخصية في لحظتها المصيرية الحاسمة. ففي المتن الثاني «إيغال» تستولي على ثالث الفتية أول هبات الحنين والتذكر في الحجرة المربعة حيث:

هلت على فؤاده رائحة شجرة عتيقة تتدلى أطراف أغصانها لتلامس مياه ترعة عميقة. كان يعبرها يومياً ويتذوق ثمارها، لمحة عابرة، مارقة، لم تعن شيئاً في البداية، لحظة وقوعها. لكنها صارت فيما بعد محطة غير مرئية، يطيل الركون إليها كلما أوغل يكتشف من خلال استعادتها ما لم يقف عليه لحظة وقوعها. هنا .. في هذا الحيز الضيق، المحدود في الظاهر، يدرك ما لم يستوعبه بالنظر المباشر في الخارج. كثيراً ما لا يكون الاستيعاب لحظة السماع أو النظر إنما يتم الأمر كله عند الاستعادة بالخيال، ويبدو التفسير الذي استعصى أمره زمناً، يبرق مع اللحظة المستعادة من بين ثنايا الذاكرة، ترسخ ذلك مع تقدمهم، إيغالهم. (ص٣١)

وهكذا فإن مبدأ الاستعادة للحظة والموضع يشكل مبدأ القص الذي سيجمع بين المتون. وهو يحدد أيضاً العلاقة مع الزمن فيحول اللحظة المصيرية في حياة الشخصية إلى أسطورة بالمعنى الأصلي، أي حياة مُسَطَّرة تصل بالخبر والرواية إلى تمام الإخبار وإن ظلت الحركة المصيرية منفتحة على التساؤل ومندفعة إلى الذروة حيث التماس بين المرئي واللامرئي. وهكذا تظهر الشخصيات أنموذجية في لحظتها الحاسمة، تاريخية في جديد خبرها، أسطورية

في مغزاها وتعبيرها الشخصي. والقاص هنا أبداً مستعيد للرؤية من بين ثنايا الذاكرة (الشخصية أو التاريخية/القصصية) وهو أبداً مقتص للخبر بالرواية أو المعاينة تماماً على نمط ابن إياس والمقريزي والإدريسي والجبرتي. فالتاريخ يتبدى دائماً في شكل لحظات حاسمة تُنتزع من «صيرورة الزمن المخيفة» والذي ينتزعها هو المؤرخ أو الفنان أو الراوي.(٢١) وهكذا فالحدث التاريخي يخرج دائماً في شكل لحظة في حياة الشخصية أو في حياة الراوي أو المؤرخ. فحادثة الخليفة المأمون مع الهرم الأكبر على سبيل المثال، وما كان من أمره بفتح نقب فيه تعاد صياغتها من وجهة نظر «ابن الشحنة» الذي تشهد له وعليه رمزية اسمه الصوفية وطاقاته الشخصية فهو ذو «شحنة» أو طاقة روحية تنصبّ على معرفة أسرار الهرم وتنتهي بالاتحاد مع قمته والفناء فيها «لحظة دورانه جهة الغرب» (ص٦٣).

وهكذا، فشخصية الشيخ تهامي التي يحويها المتن الأول هي شخصية طالب العلم الذي جاء من المغرب يقصد الأهرام، تتجمع خيوطها مع استعادة الراوي للمواضع التي ارتبطت به وارتبط بها وأهمها الجامع الأزهر وميدان الحسين. يرتبط الشيخ تهامي في ذاكرة الراوي بلحظة بعينها، وإن كان لا يتذكر أول مرة شاهده فيها وهذه اللحظة تحوي جوهر شخصية الشيخ تهامي طالب العلم فهو «يبدو خلالها مبتسماً بهدوء، قامته ممتلئة، مستقيم الظهر، بارز الصدر لم يغير جلسته طوال أعوام، كذا وجهة عينيه، ونظراته، حتى عند حديثه إلى آخرين، أما تعبير الدهشة فمبادر دائماً، كأنه يطالع أمراً عجباً للتو» (ص ٩). ونكتشف فيما بعد أن لُبّ الشيخ تهامي قد أُخِذ صوب الغرب، تجاه الأهرام، ويصل بنا المتن في علاقة متدرجة بين الراوي والشخصية تعنون مراحلها ترنيمات جزلة قوية الإيحاء والعبارة إلى أن تصل إلى اللحظة الحاسمة في حياة الشيخ تهامي والتي تعنونها ترنيمة: «كلمة، أو نظرة، أو إيماءة .. ربما تحيد بمصير وتغير مسار حياة» (ص ١٥). فالشيخ تهامي قد اختلف لطلب العلم منذ طفولته إلى شيخ ذي قدم قد «طاف بلاد المشرق، ودخل أقطار الزنج». وفي صدر شبابه أراد تهامي الخروج في ركب الحج فأذن له الشيخ. وعند عودته سعى إلى شيخه «ليقص عليه ما كان من أمره». ولكن الشيخ:

بعد أن أصغى طويلاً سأله فجأةً:
حدثني عن الأهرام وما رأيته منها؟
تلجلج، تردد:
ما عندي من المعاينة ما أرويه، ولا أقدر أن أسوق حديثاً صحيحاً عنها.
أشاح بوجهه قائلاً:
أخْسِس بهمةٍ طالبِ علم وحكمة، لا يتشوق، لا يتشوف ، إلى معاينة ما يكمن من عجب .. ألم تعبر القاهرة مرتين؟
أومأ مجيباً. قال الشيخ:
ألم يكن بينك وبينها إلا ركضة راكب، أو دفعة قارب؟ إذا لم يكن ذلك سقوط همة، فماذا تسميه؟
ثم أدار ظهره إليه، وأطرق، فلم يكن بوسعه إلا الانصراف والمغادرة، لكن

.. منذ تلك اللحظة لم يطب له مقام، ولم تلن له ضجعة، أدرك أن مقامه في مسقط رأسه انتهى، وأن سنوات استقراره ولت، وأنه يجب أن يرحل. (ص ص ١٥-١٦).

ويقضي الشيخ تهامي بقية حياته في رحيل دائم صوب الغرب وتشوّف دائم للأهرام ينتظر معه الإذن بحصول المراد، وقد انكشف له مع المداومة ووقوع الإحاطة الكثير من العلم عنها. ولكنه انتهى إلى محاذاة جامع الأزهر يعمل في بيع الكتب وينتظر من يجيء له بمخطوطة قد جاءته حولها إشارات عديدة تحوي الشرح والتفسير لكل ما استعصى عليه من حروف غامضة بانت له مع مداومته التطلع إلى الأهرام. وينتهي المتن بشخوصه الدائم في اتجاه الأهرام، والذي صار متحجباً وراء مجموعة من الصفات التي يسوقها الراوي تقترب من الأسماء الحسنى وتُظهر الأهرام كسر إلهي تحجّب وراء أسمائه وصفاته (ص ٢٤).

وشخصية التهامي وما يمثله تتكرر الإشارة إليها وهي تأتي من ذكريات طفولته وشبابه في منطقة ميدان الحسين والجمالية وما حولهما. وهي تبدو نمطية حين تظهر ملامحها في شخصيات أخرى مثل شخصية «عم عاشور» في **رسالة البصائر في المصائر**. وفي مقولة مباشرة للغيطاني يذكر بصدد خصوصية أعماله وتكوينه الفني والفكري أنه كان يختلف إلى رصيف الأزهر ويقرأ كل ما كانت تقع عليه يداه من كتب التفاسير والأحاديث والتاريخ والسير، ويسترسل قائلاً: «كنت في هذه الفترة أظل جالساً على الرصيف حتى صلاة العشاء أقرأ في نهم، ودون تحديد مقابل نصف قرش يأخذه مني الشيخ 'تهامي' صاحب المكتبة التي شكلت وجداني وعقلي».(٢٢) أما الشخصية ذاتها التي تظهر في المتن الأول فروايتها تأتي على ما جاء من ذكر طالب علم مغربي وعلاقته بالهرم في **كتاب أنوار علوي الأجرام في الكشف عن أسرار الأهرام** للإدريسي. وتجدر الإشارة هنا إلى أن مبدأ التأليف الذي اتخذه الإدريسي في مؤلفة يطابق ما أمر به الشيخ مريده، فهو مبدأ التحقق من مكنون العجيبة وفهم أسرارها والذي يعلو به الإدريسي في مقدمته إلى مقام المبدأ الإسلامي المعرفي ويؤكد به على ضرورة فهم الآثار والبرابي والحفاظ عليها ويربطها بتعاليم القرآن وتقديس الصحابة لها بزيارتها.(٢٣) ومن الناحية التطبيقية، فالإدريسي أيضاً يسير على المنهج الذي يكشف عنه المريد نظرياً ألا وهو مبدأ تحقيق المعرفة إما بالمعاينة أو بالرواية الصحيحة. ورواية الإدريسي تأتي في هذا السياق على ما يعرضه في الفصل الثاني الذي موضوعه: «فيما جاء عن العلماء في التعجب من العجب والسعي لمعاينته من الأثر المسموع، وفيما نقل من إجماعهم على أنها أعجب ما على/بسيط الأرض من البناء المرفوع». ورواية الإدريسي تأتي بأسلوب الحديث حيث تبدأ بـ«حدثني صاحبنا الفقيه الزاهد تقي الدين أبو التقي صالح بن صارم بن مخلوف الأنصاري القوصي. . . قال: جمع بيني وبين رجل/من فضلاء المغاربة بمصر، مجلس أبي زكريا البياسي الحكيم. . .»، ثم يصل الإسناد إلى «فحدثنا ذلك الرجل الفاضل الواصل من المغرب إلينا، الوافد الوارد علينا، قال: . . .»، وهنا يقص المغربي حكايته مع شيخه والتي تطابقها في تفاصيلها ولغتها حكاية الشيخ تهامي على ما وردت في المتن الأول. والجدير بالذكر أن التركيز في رواية المغربي، كما أوردها الإدريسي،

يأتي على المعاينة أكثر من الرواية والأثر المسموع فهو يقول: «حدثني عن أهرام مصر بما رأيته، واضرب صفحاً عما من أخبارها رويته». فالدرس للمريد هنا يركز على «التشوق» و«التشوف» و«معاينة ما يمكن معاينته من عجب كامناً».[24] وإسقاط الشخصية التراثية على شخصية من واقع تجربة الراوي المعاصرة – أو العكس – يشكل أحد أهم أساليب القص التي يتبعها الغيطاني في مشروعه الروائي.[25]

وهنا نأتي إلى إسلامية رؤية الغيطاني على ما أراد تحديدها بإشارته للآية والسورة وعلاقتهما بالنص القرآني. فالآية القرآنية على جزالتها تمثل وحدة سردية متكاملة من حيث إنها قد تختزل حياة بأكملها أو جانباً معيَّناً ومعرِّفا لتلك الحياة، وذلك على عكس أسفار التوراة والأناجيل التي تعتمد بشكل أساسي على العنصر القصصي السردي وربما لا عجب في أن القُصّاص الأوائل في التاريخ الإسلامي كانوا في معظمهم من الذين تحولوا من اليهودية أو المسيحية إلى الإسلام وقد كان لهم دور ذو شأن في تعليم القرآن وتفسيره للعامة في بدايات الإسلام الأولى بما كان لديهم من معرفة بقصص الأنبياء والأولين وبداية الخلق.[26] وتتضح هذه الخاصية للرؤية الإسلامية المعرفية للذات وعلاقتها بالواقع وبالغيبي على السواء مع بدايات التراث العربي في أدب السيرة والطبقات، وبعدها في أدب السيرة الذاتية، وأذكر هنا بالأخص سيرة السيوطي الذاتية **التحدث بنعمة الله** كنموذج مثالي لهذه العلاقة وللمفاهيم العربية الإسلامية التي تعكسها وتنعكس عليها. ومن العنوان ذاته يمكننا الاستدلال على المبدأ الذي اتبعه السيوطي في تأليف سيرته، فمغزى حياته قد اختُزل في عبارة «التحدث بنعمة الله»، وما يبرز هذا المغزى للوجود أو على الأقل لحيز المعنى وتمام الإخبار عن الذات هو فعل التحدث. ومن هذا المبدأ نستدل كذلك على أن فهمه لحياته هو ذاته قراءة لتلك الآية/النموذج، وكذا فإن ممارسة حياته هي بمثابة كتابة أو إعادة كتابة لها. وعلى هذا المبدأ يسير السيوطي في عنونة فصول سيرته أو مراحل حياته وجوانبها المختلفة. وهنا أحيل القارئ بالأخص إلى الفصل الذي يتناول «ذكر المجدِّدين المبعوثين على رأس كل مائة» والذي يشكل خير مثال على محاولة قراءة السيوطي لذاته في ظل تراث طويل من الأحاديث التي يسوقها بإسنادها والتي تعود إلى الحديث النبوي المعروف. وبعد التأويل والتفسير ينتهي السيوطي إلى إمكانية كشف ذاته في معناها، وعلى ما يمارسها ويصبو إليه، كالمجدِّد المشار إليه على رأس المائة التاسعة.[27]

وبتصاعد فعل القراءة وتتابع الروايات تنتقل النظرة مع المتن الثاني «إيغال» إلى داخل الهرم الأكبر، ويبدأ المتن بأسلوب الحوليات: «وفي هذه السنة شاع أمر فتية الأهرام، قيل إنهم سبعة عُرفوا بتقاربهم، وامتزاج أهوائهم، وترحالهم صحبةً، وشروعهم معاً» (ص ٢٧). وهذا التوصيف لفتية الأهرام يذكرنا بالفتية الذين آمنوا بربهم في النص القرآني، وكما ورد في الروايات المتوارثة عنهم فإن الروايات تختلط أيضاً فيما يخص ذكر فتية الأهرام وتتضارب الأحاديث حولهم وإن اتفق على أنهم السابقون في إقدامهم وإن «مضوا بدون أي فكرة مسبقة» (ص ٢٧). ومع الإيغال في العمق ينفرط عقد الذوات وتنصبّ التجربة على التوحد الفردي وتبدأ العلاقة بين كل منهم على حدة وبين فراغات العمق والتي تمثل «فضاء التفرد» في عرف القوم (الصوفيّة) حيث «كافة الاحتمالات قائمة» (ص ٣٢).

وهكذا مع انفراط العقد واختفائهم واحداً بعد الآخر يدخل كلُّ منهم في تجربة خاصة فريدة وخيالات مؤرقة وزمان وجودي خاص به وينتهي أولهم وحيداً وقد «أوغل في الأهرام، وعين الولوج تدركه، ما هو إلا ذرات مكونة. هو هو. وهنا هناك. وهناك هو. تكتمل استدارته، فتلتقي النقطة بالنقطة. وتكون الالتفاتة إلى الالتفاتة» (ص ٤٣). وفي قمة التوحد والتي رُمز إليها بقمة الهرم المُجتاز المُعتاد إليها من الداخل حيث لا مكان والزمان مغاير وحيث تتجه الرؤية إلى داخل الذات ينتهي الراوي بقوله «من يصل إلى هنا لابد أن يكون وحيداً، منقطعاً، تلك اللحظة، هذه المسافة من غور الأهرام .. لا تحتمل الرفقة» (ص ٤٤).

وينتقل القص إلى المتن الثالث «تلاش». وفي هذا المتن تتبدى اللحظة المصيرية مع الميلاد، مع الميلاد لوحيد في أسرة قديم وعَلاقتها بالأهرام معروفة شائعة قد خُطَّت في مخطوطات لم تُطبع بعد. فقد ولد الوحيد «دائم التطلع إلى جهة الأهرام، إلى الغرب. لو حملته أمه يستدير، إذا حادت به يرتفع صراخه» (ص ٤٨). وهنا تظهر شخصية مغربي مرابط من أهل الوقت والحضرة ليخبر الأم بأن وليدها موعود. ويبدو موعود الوليد، والذي لم يفسره المغربي، وثيق الصلة بحضور الأهرام الدائم المهيمن المستدعي لدوام التساؤل: «ما وراء هذا التكوين؟ لماذا جاءوا بهذا الشكل؟ كيف تتصل المادة بالفراغ؟» (ص ٥٤). وباتجاه هذا الكيان الشخصي كلِّية إلى الهرم ومع ارتقاء التكوين إلى القمة حيث تتصل المادة بالفراغ يبدأ الإدراك الشخصي: «لم تكن حركة الدائريّة، المتّوثبةُ تلك، إلا تمهيداً لتلقّي تلك البغتات من الإشراقات المفاجئة المتوالية والتي أخذته من كلّ جانب، تخلّلته، اجتاحته، دَفَعَت به وإليه مُسْتَقَرّ النغم. ومصدر كُل حُلم، جذر كل تَوُقٍ، سِرّ اندلاع الرغبةِ وانطفائها، والدافع لميل الغصنِ وفراقِهِ عن الجِذعِ ..» (ص ٥٦). فما وصل إليه مُقَدَّم الفتية السبعة في داخل الهرم يصل إليه الساعي هنا على قمة الهرم من الخارج، فتتوحد التجربة وإن اختلف الأصل والمصير.

ثم ينتقل القص إلى المتن الرابع «إدراك»، وتندفع حركة القص في شكل متدرّج يرتقي من درجة إلى درجة من المعرفة عن الهرم والتي هي وعيٌ بالنفس وإدراك لِلمصير الشخصي المحتوم. ومن ثم تنتقل حركة القص بالمصائر الشخصية عبر فترات التاريخ المتباينة - وهنا يخرج التاريخ على ما يعرّفه الغيطاني كتجربة خاصة مع الزمن - من «إدراك» إلى «نشوة» إلى «ظل» إلى «ألق» إلى «صمت» ثم إلى «رقصة» كونية حول نقطة المركز ما بين الشرق والغرب، والتي «تبدو لمن صبر وحاول وجاهد وأفنى فتمكن، لا يحيد موعدها» (ص ٩١). ونجد تعبيراً تفسيرياً عن تلك الحركة المتدرّجة في الباب الخاص بعنوان «مصطلح: درج» في رواية **سفر البنيان:**

الدرج مرقاة، فهو توق، وهذا لا يكون إلا لصعود أو انتقال من سُفلٍ إلى
عُلو، ومن هنا تكون المحاولة، فالانتقال من موضع إلى موضع مساوٍ لهُ في
الأفقية يقتضي بذل الجهد، فما البال إذا كان مضاداً للقوة الحَافظة،
الماسكة لكل ما هو حي أو نبات ينمو أو طير يحوم أن يفلت ويتوه في
فراغات الكون. وتلك القوة القابضة لا نراها، ولا نلمسها، ولا يمكن

تعيينها، أو وصفها، أو إرجاعها إلى عناصرها الأولى، تماماً شأن كل ما يؤثر في مصائرنا، الزمن مثلاً، نرى أعراضه ولا ننفذ إلى جوهره ولا نقف على ما يجري في مساره، ولا يمكننا تحديد أوله، وبالتالي آخره، فكل ما تدرك بدايته يمكن تحديد نهايته، وليس الأمر إلا بحث وتقص وازدياد.

للصعود زهوة، وجلوة، وما الدرج إلا مساعد، فالمسافة إلى أعلى تُقطع بميل. كل درج مائل مع أنه مؤدٍ إلى أعلى. (ص ١٤٧)

ومع تبدّي درجات الميل تبدأ الترنيمات المتصاعدة إلى قمة الهرم وقد اتخذت حركة القص سمات التجربة الصوفية:

متنٌ عاشر: وكأنّهم على ميعاد، وإن باعدت بينهم الآماد (ص ٩٥).
متنٌ حادي عشر: البداية نقطة، والنهاية نقطة (ص ٩٩).
متنٌ ثاني عشر: عند الذروة .. يقع الفناء (ص ١٠٣).
متنٌ ثالث عشر: كلُّ شيء .. من .. لا شيء (ص ١٠٧).
متنٌ رابع عشر: لا شيء لا شيء لا شيء (ص ١١١).

وتستمر الحركة حتى نصل إلى حيث تتصل المادة بالفراغ وتفنى الحركة، أو تستمر أبداً في بنيان لامرئي، في ترنيمة «لا شيء لا شيء لا شيء».

فصٌّ حكمة حامية في قول كلمة سامية: فن السيرة العربي بين الأسطرة والقَصص
يأتي على لسان الراوي في سفر البنيان أنه قد «جرى النطق بالحروف الحامية، ومشت الأرتال ترى وسجد الكهنة ومشاهدو المعاني» («حكاية: عاقبة»، ص ٣٣). وهذه إنما تأتي من الإشارات القلائل التي توحي بجو مصري قديم، وإن كانت الحروف المصرية القديمة ليست حامية تماماً، فاللغة المصرية القديمة هي حامية-سامية تحوي صفات من عائلتي اللغتين القديمتين.(٢٨) وفي نفس الموضع والحكاية يؤكد لنا الراوي، والإشارة هنا إلى الأهرام، أن «ما يرتبط بالبنيان من حكايات صغيرة، ورواية أحداث، أبقى وأشمل من رص الأحجار وضبط الزوايا، والحد من حرية الميل، وصون القدرة على الارتفاع». وهكذا فالبنيان في تاريخيته إنما يتحقق في ما يَمْثُل للتجربة الإنسانية عبر التاريخ، وهذه تتمثل في الحكايات ورواية الأحداث، وتلك إنما يأتي ذكرها في نصوص التراث العربي، وبالأخص في تضاعيف أشكال السيرة وانعطافاتها الأسلوبية. فالقيمة التاريخية هنا عند الراوي وعند الغيطاني لا تكمن في تاريخ البنيان ذاته أو تاريخيته (موضعته في عصره) وإنما في معناه أو مغزاه العابر لحواجز الزمن والمتماثل للوعي الطالب له.

إن محاولة أسطرة الوعي باللحظة التاريخية ونمطيها عبر أشكال القص والتعبير التراثية في شكل حياة أو تجربة إنسانية تتخذ شكل السيرة أو السيرة الذاتية إنما هو متجذر بوصفه رؤية أو ممارسة نصية في التراث العربي الإسلامي. هذا كما أن له تأصيلاً في نظريات

النقد الأدبي الحديث. أما من ناحية التراث فالرؤية الفنية وراء هذه الممارسة ترتبط أيضاً بمرجعية الفنان والقصّاص الرئيسية، من وجهة نظر الغيطاني، إلى النص القرآني. وبالتحديد، فإن المرجعية على مستوى الرؤية، أي على مستوى علاقة الجزء بالكل المنفتح، إنما تتجذر في تأصيل القرآن للاختلاف بين الأسطورة والقَصص. الإشارات القرآنية إلى «أساطير الأولين» (انظر على سبيل المثال: سورة المطففين، الآية ١٣ وسورة القلم، الآية ١٥) في الماضي المغاير للعقيدة ولمَن حمل لواءها من الأنبياء، وإلى الحاضر المغاير المعاكس لرؤية النبي والتنزيل في «نون والقلم وما يسطرون» (سورة القلم، الآية ١) تشير إلى أهمية الرؤية المؤصّلة في النظر إلى الحياة النموذجية والتي تظهر في النص القرآني في سِيَر الأنبياء والمرسَلين. وهنا يقيم النص القرآني الحد بين السيرة على ما نُقِلت قبل الرؤية القرآنية والسيرة على ما يعرضها بإقامة الحد بين الأسطورة وبين «القصص الحق» (انظر على سبيل المثال: سورة آل عمران، الآية ٦٢ وسورة يوسف، الآيتين ٣ و١١١). فمن اللافت للنظر أن الآيات المرتبطة بالقصص والقصص الحق وما يقصه القرآن وما لم يقصصه كلها تشير إلى ذكر الأنبياء وسِيَرهم، وذلك على ما نرى في سوَر يوسف ومريم وآل عمران والأنبياء بالأخص.

وعلى أساس هذا التفريق التأويلي والعقائدي والفكري بدأ تشكُّل الكتابة التاريخية كما نشاهد بالأخص في تاريخ الطبري والذي يعرض فيه ما جمعه من سير الأنبياء مما جاء ذكره في القرآن وما لم يجئ معتمداً مبدأ القصص الحق طالما أنه قد أسس رؤيته التاريخية والتفسيرية على أساس الرؤية الإسلامية. ومن الأمثلة على ذلك ذكره بالشاهدة للأبيات الشعرية التي أنشدها آدم عليه السلام بالعربية في الجنة، وتقديم ذلك في الجزء المؤطر لعمل تأريخي. وهذا المبدأ يسري أيضاً على أدب «قصص الأنبياء» وأعمال التفسير وأدب الطبقات وما شاكلها. وهذه الإشكالية المبنية على تأصيل الرؤية المعرفية والدينية للاختلاف بين الأسطورة والقصص جدّ شائكة ومثيرة ولا تزال بعد في حاجة إلى دراسة نقدية تحليلية وتأويلية متأنية وشافية. وإنما قد أشرت إليها هنا بشكل مبدأيّ لإمكانية تأصيل رؤية الغيطاني للتاريخ وللوعي الشخصي باللحظة التاريخية في مثل هذه الرؤية العربية الإسلامية. وإن كانت الرؤية ذاتها للأنبياء والصالحين ولإمكانية ترهين حياة الفرد التاريخية بالأطر الأساسية التي تؤطر حياة مثالية حياة النبي أو القديس قد تم تأصيلها أيضاً في اللاهوت المسيحي وبالأخص في أدب المذهب البروتستانتي تحت عنوان Typology. وقد بدأ هذا المفهوم أساساً كمبدأ تفسيري تأويلي يجمع ما بين العهد القديم والعهد الجديد على مستوى الرؤية واللغة والحدث والشخصيات، ليصل إلى تاريخ واحد متصل يبدأ بسفر التكوين وينتهي برؤيا يوحنا ومن ثم يرهن تاريخ العالم Weltgeschichte بنمطية تاريخ الخلاص Heilsgeschichte كذلك. ومن ناحية الإمكانية الأدبية لمثل هذا المبدأ فقد تناولها الناقد الكندي نورثروب فراي Northrop Frye في آخر مشاريعه النقدية.(٢٩)

أما تأثر الغيطاني بأعمال الشيخ الأكبر محيي الدين بن عربي الصوفية فواضح ومعروف ويظهر أكثر ما يظهر في **تجليات الغيطاني**، حيث تظهر شخصية ابن عربي نفسها كدليل لشخصية الغيطاني والإشارات في الأعمال الأخرى كثيرة. وفيما يخص **متون الأهرام**، فقد جاءت أسطرة الحيوات التاريخية المتباينة التي تمثلها الشخصيات في ارتباطها المصيري بالأهرام

في شكل التجربة الصوفية التي تترقى في المقامات والأحوال التي تعنونها المتون، حتى تصل إلى إمكانية الاتحاد مع البنيان. وتوصيف البنيان في نهاية المتن الأول بصفات تكاد تكون إلهية يخرج بالمتون من حيز الأسطرة إلى إمكانية القصص على مستوى الرؤية وإمكانية إخراج حياة الشخصية بإحالتها على الجامع الواحد بفعل التدوين وبفعل نمطية اللحظة المصيرية والتي تعنون لها شخصية أو رواية لشخصية مقتصة من التراث بلغته وأساليبه الموحية. وهذا المبدأ اتبعه ابن عربي على مستوى الحقيقة الإنسانية وتعبيرها عن الحقيقة الإلهية في كتابه **فصوص الحِكَم**، حيث تظهر شخصية كل نبي كفصّ حكمة أو تعبير متفرد عن جانب من جوانب الحقيقة الإلهية قد اختص بها هذا النبي. وعلى أساس هذا المبدأ فكل حياة فردية تُظهر في إضمارها وإخبارها وطموحها وتجاربها بعض ملامح من جانب الحقيقة الخاص الذي يعنون عليه نبي من الأنبياء، فإن هذه الحياة الفردية في ممارستها واستكشافها لمعناها تنتظم في علاقة مصيرية مع نموذجها المثالي المتمثل في هذا النبي. فإن أظهرت مثلاً جانب التفويض للأعلى والتسليم المطلق ونحر الذات فقد انتظمت بذلك في نموذج فص الحكمة الإسماعيلية الذي يجسده النبي إسماعيل (أو النبي إسحق في التراثين اليهودي والمسيحي).

ولعله تكمن هنا رؤية الغيطاني الإبداعية على مستوى خلق الشخصيات أو إعادة كتابتها بتنميط مصيريتها في لحظة ما وموضع ما بين الأسطرة والقَصص، على مستوى الرؤية، وبين القص والاقتصاص على مستوى اللغة والبنية السردية.

القص والاقتصاص: قراءة في أساليب استيحاء مصادر الرواية

في المتون التسعة الأولى، وبعد أن يؤطر الراوي للعلاقة بينه وبين الشخصية المعاصرة له في المتن الأول، تبدأ المتون في عبارة تراثية تعكس أسلوب الحوليات ورواية التاريخ ورواية الأحداث وتمتد حركة القص بأسلوب تحقيق الرواية وذكر تضارب الروايات في السماع ونقل الخبر، وذلك في لغة تراثية مرهونة بأسلوب القص العربي الإسلامي (فهي، على سبيل المثال، لا تعكس أساليب القص القبطية العربية والتي نذكر منها، مثالاً لا حصراً، أساليب الوصف والتمثيل والتنميط على حيوات القديسين التي نجدها في أعمال الشهداء، أو الجمع بين هذه وبين أسلوب أدب الحوليات على ما نشاهد في **كتاب السُّنْكِسار**). وفي المتن الرابع «إدراك» فقط، والذي يتناول ذكر الخليفة المأمون وعلاقته بالأهرام في سياق سيرة شخصية باسم «ابن الشحنة»، يبدأ المتن بذكر مصدر الرواية: «حدثنا الناصري محمد أحمد بن إياس الحنفي المصري فقال . . .» (ص ٥٩). وفي مواضع أخرى قليلة من المتون يأتي ذكر مباشر لمصادر أخرى مثل المقريزي (ص ٤٧) ولكنها لا تؤطر لحركة القص في المتن. وعلى الرغم من أن بعض الشخصيات معاصرة مثل الشيخ تهامي أو المرأة الأجنبية في المتن الخامس «نشوة» أو الشاب في المتن الثالث «تلاش» أو الراوي في المتن الثامن «صمت» إلا أن أسلوب القص وكذا الروايات التي تؤطر اللحظة المصيرية الحاسمة في حياة كل شخصية تأتي كلها من مصادر تراثية سابقة على القرن التاسع عشر.(٣٠) فهي بذلك لا تعتمد اكتشافات علم المصريات منذ فك رموز الهيروغليفية في بدايات القرن التاسع عشر ولا إنجازاته من بعد ولا التحقيق العلمي للنصوص المصرية القديمة الأدبية أو التاريخية. وهي لا تعتمد حتى أول

تأريخ باللغة العربية لمصر القديمة والذي ضمّنه رفاعة الطهطاوي في كتابه **أنوار توفيق الجليل في أخبار مصر وتوثيق بني إسماعيل** والذي أصدره في عام ١٨٨٦ واعتمد في تدوينه وفي تقسيم العصور والأسرات وتحقيق أهم الإنجازات على أحدث المصادر الفرنسية في ذلك الوقت.(٣١) ومن ثم فرواية **متون الأهرام** لا تعتمد متون الأهرام الأصلية لغةً ولا أسلوباً وإن تشابهت معها على ما ذكرت آنفاً في التركيز الشكلي (مع اختلاف الرؤية) على السيرة الشخصية وعلاقتها باللغة، وفي النزعة إلى التغلب على الزمن، وفي أشكال المتون الخمسة الأخيرة التي تعتمد شكل الشذرة أو الترنيمة المستقلة أو المتكررة. وكذلك لا نشاهد أي أثر للأشكال الأخرى للأدب المصري القديم، ولا بعد ذلك لأشكال الأدب القبطي العربية من أعمال الشهداء أو قصص القديسين المتداولة منذ الفتح العربي لمصر وحتى عصرنا هذا.(٣٢)

وربما تعليل هذا الأمر يأتي من صميم مشروع الغيطاني الروائي وأيضاً من صميم رؤيته للتاريخ، أو بالتحديد للعلاقة مع الزمن، ولطبيعة اللحظة التاريخية. فطبقاً لرؤية الغيطاني أهمية اللحظة التاريخية لا تكمن في خصوصية حقبة تاريخية بعينها وإنما تكمن فيما تكشف عنه من المصائر والأحداث وفي طبيعة هذا الكشف، أي في التعبير المتجاوز لحدود الزمن والمتكشِّف بالكلمة أو بالشكل المعماري. ولهذا فالغيطاني لا يكتب روايات تاريخية بالشكل المتعارَف عليه ولا يكمن اهتمامه في إعادة كتابة الماضي ولا في تقديمه في شكل رمزي أو أليغوري. وهذه النظرة تنطبق على تاريخية مصر القديمة، وهو يعترف بذلك ولا يخفيه:

> لقد تعلمت الكثير من التراث العربي، وكان أكبر متعة لي قراءة كتابات المؤرخين الذين كتبوا عن مصر المملوكية، لأن مصر الفرعونية لم ترق لي، ولم أشعر بأي رغبة في مواصلة قراءاتي عنها. قد يكون ذلك لبعد الزمن، أو اختلاف اللغة والعادات والتقاليد، أو أي سبب آخر، ولكنني وجدت نفسي في كتابات «ابن إياس»، وغيره من مؤرخي مصر المملوكية.(٣٣)

وهنا تكمن المفارقة ليس فقط في اهتمام الغيطاني باستمرارية التاريخ وواقعه الحي المتناقل بين الأجيال وفي التراث الشعبي في نفس الوقت الذي يعتمد فيه مصادر مدوّنة، بلغتها وأساليبها، وإنما أيضاً في عنوان الرواية ومحتواها ومضمونها المغايرَيْن. ففي النهاية تخرج مصر القديمة بأهرامها في حلة مجازية عربية إسلامية تتفق في رؤيتها مع ما بدأه الإدريسي في كتاب **أنوار عُلوي الأجرام في الكشف عن أسرار الأهرام** واستكمله الطهطاوي في **أنوار توفيق الجليل**، على اختلاف المرجعية والنظرة التحليلية وعلى ما سأبين في موضعه.

وبالرجوع إلى المصادر المملوكية وغيرها يتبع الراوي واحداً من أسلوبين للاقتصاص المباشر، فهو يذهب إلى اقتصاص اللحظة الحاسمة وروايتها على ما هي عليه كما في حادثة الشيخ تهامي مع شيخه الصوفي والتي وردت بأكملها في **كتاب أنوار عُلوي الأجرام في الكشف عن أسرار الأهرام** واقتصها الراوي بلغتها وأساليبها ودرامية لحظتها وكشفها لمصير الشخصية، وإن أسقطها على شخصية معاصرة.(٣٤) أما أسلوب الاقتصاص الآخر فيأتي

بالذكر المباشر للواقعة ومصدرها، كما أتى في ذكر المأمون، بأسلوب رواية الحديث وبهدف التأطير لسيرة ابن الشحنة والتي لا يرد ذكرها في ابن إياس ولا في الإدريسي على شمولية الأخير في تناول الروايات ومصادرها.(٣٥) ثم إنه يورد أوصافاً بلغتها وتراكيبها في الروايات التي ترد حول عجائب الأهرام وخاصةً ما يتعلق بروحانيتها (الأرواح أو الأشباح الحافظة والتي شوهدت تحوم حول كل هرم على ما أتى في الروايات) والتي اقتصها الراوي من ابن إياس، وهي ترد أيضاً في الإدريسي والسيوطي والمسعودي، على سبيل المثال لا الحصر.(٣٦) ونجده أحياناً يعيد صياغة بعض الروايات في سياق معاصر، وإن احتفظ بالتراكيب التراثية، كما في المتن الخامس «نشوة» حيث تعاد صياغة الروايات حول محاولة الإتيان والجِماع داخل الأهرام والتي تنتهي في أغلبها بتفحم الذين تجرأوا على إتيان الفاحشة داخل الأهرام (انظر أيضاً ص ٨٧). وهي في هذا المتن تأخذ شكل علاقة حميمية مصيرية غامضة بين وافدة أجنبية وشاب وسيم يبدو «وكأنه خارج للتوّ من جدار معبد لم تتغير ألوانه ورسومه» (ص ٦٨) قد دُفعا دفعاً للقاء داخل الهرم، وينتهي المتن بحالة نشوة لا انتهاء لها «إنما اتقاد مستمر، متصاعد».(٣٧) وهذا الأسلوب الأخير من التناص وإعمال الخيال في إشارات النصوص التراثية يشكل أيضاً المبدأ الفني للقص في رواية **سفر البنيان**.

وهكذا فالقَص هنا كمبدأ فني يعتمد على إعادة كتابة الرواية/الأسطورة والتي تم اقتصاصها بأساليب مختلفة يأتي من إعمال الرؤية العربية الإسلامية في علاقة الجزء بالكل عبر أزمنة متباعدة، ومن ثم إعادة صياغة اللحظات القديمة وترهين تاريخيتها على مصداقية الرؤية ذاتها. والسؤال الذي يطرح نفسه الآن ليس فقط تاريخية هذه الرؤية وتجذرها في الحاضر، وإنما أيضاً تاريخ الأسبقية في الورود إلى عمق التاريخ والردّ بهذه الرؤية.

فالواقع أنه منذ بدايات علوم التفسير والحديث وأعمال التاريخ ثم ما تلا ذلك من كتب الحوليات والرحلات وما شاكلها لا تخلو المصادر العربية الرئيسية من الإشارة إلى أرض مصر وعجائبها وبرابيها وبركة نيلها وخصوبة أرضها وتخطيط مدنها وأعمال كوراتها وذكر مَن زارها من الأنبياء في القديم ومن الصحابة إبان الفتح العربي وغير ذلك مما اختصت به النظرة لمصر. ومن أهم هذه الأعمال **تاريخ الطبري** (توفي ٩٢٣م) و**مروج الذهب وأخبار الزمان** للمسعودي (توفي ٩٥٦م)، والمسعودي بالأخص قد أكد تحقيق الخبر بالمعاينة ولم يكتف بالرواية الصحيحة، فقد سافر جنوباً إلى أعالي النيل حتى أسوان وتحدث إلى كثير من المصريين وجمع ما توصل إليه في مؤلفاته. وقد ذكر عبد اللطيف البغدادي (توفي ١٢٣١/١٢٣٢م) برابي مصر وآثار القدماء. ومن أهم المؤلفات بعد ذلك تاريخ ابن إياس **بدائع الزهور في وقائع الدهور** في القرن السادس عشر الميلادي والذي يشير إليه الغيطاني كثيراً لارتباطه به. ومن أهم المصادر أيضاً حسن **المحاضرة في أخبار مصر والقاهرة** للسيوطي (توفي ١٥٠٥م) و**أخبار مصر والمغرب** لابن عبد الحكم ومن أدب الرحلات هناك **رحلة ابن بطوطة** الشهيرة من القرن الرابع عشر الميلادي و**كتاب الرحلة** للأندلسي ابن جبير (توفي ١٢١٧م). ومن أدب الخطط كتاب **خطط المقريزي** الشهير (توفي ١٤٢٢م)، وبعده في القرن التاسع عشر الميلادي **الخطط التوفيقية** لعلي مبارك والتي يشير إليها الغيطاني في مواضع عدة (خارج الرواية) وإن لم يشر إلى روايته الشهيرة **علم الدين** (١٨٨٢) والتي تُعد من

أول الأعمال الأدبية التي تتناول مصر القديمة بالذكر فهي تتضمّن نقاشاً طويلاً ومثيراً حول تاريخ مصر القديمة وأهميته وأهمية الآثار الفرعونية(٣٨) وهذه المراجع يشير إليها الغيطاني في أعماله الروائية وغير الروائية إما بالتصريح أو بالتلميح ويستمد منها ما قد عرّفه على أنه «أشكال فنية جديدة» للرواية تستمد من أساليب القص التي وردت في كتب التراث على اختلاف أجناسها الأدبية ومقاصد تأليفها.

ومن كل هذه الأعمال ينفرد المسعودي والسيوطي والمقريزي وابن إياس بذكر مستفيض لبرابي مصر، وبالأخص الأهرام، وللحكايات التي شاعت حولها بين العامة والخاصة. وهنا نأتي إلى ذكر الإدريسي وكتاب **أنوار عُلوي الأجرام في الكشف عن أسرار الأهرام** والذي يمثل أحد أهم المصادر حيث يشمل كل ما يخص ذكر الأهرام في أعمال جميع من سبقه إلى ذكرها، ثم هو يضيف إليها ما حققه بطريق المعاينة الشخصية بعدما يتثبّت من صحة الرواية ويقيم الحجة بالرجوع إلى المصادر المتاحة بما فيها الترجمات العربية للمصادر اليونانية وغيرها. ويُعَد كتاب الإدريسي أول دراسة تاريخية موثَّقَة في منهجيتها، فنحن نراه مثلاً يُجنّب كل الحكايات والروايات الشعبية التي شاعت حول الأهرام وطلاسمها وأعاجيبها وروحانيتها ويُفرد لها فصلاً خاصاً بها. ثم هو أيضاً يقيم الحجج في الرد على من يقلل من شأن الأهرام مستعيناً في ذلك بالقرآن والأحاديث على ما اعتاد السابقون عليه، ولكنه أيضاً يرجع إلى أعمال الفلاسفة والمؤرخين اليونانيين ويستفيض في الإشارة إلى التوراة والإنجيل. ثم يضيف إلى مادته فصلاً في الطرق المؤدية إلى الأهرام وما حولها على غرار أدب الخطط، كما يفرد فصلاً يختتم به يحوي المأثور من القول والشعر حول الأهرام. وفي كل هذا يتوخّى منهجية صارمة في تحقيق الرواية وإخراجها صحيحة بإسنادها أو في التحقق بالمعاينة. وما ينبغي ذكره أن الإدريسي يقدم لنا أيضاً سجل تاريخي لمقاييس الأهرام الصحيحة، فهو يسبق بعدة قرون أول محاولة في الغرب والتي قام بها عالم الرياضيات والمستشرق الإنجليزي جون غريفز John Greaves والذي كان يعمل أستاذاً في جامعة أوكسفورد، وقد عرض خلاصة أبحاثه في مؤلفه الشهير Pyramidographia or a Discourse of the Pyramids in Aegypt وذلك في عام ١٦٤٦. والإدريسي أيضاً كان من أول من أكّد الترجيح بأن الأهرام كانت بمثابة مدافن ملكية، مستشهداً على ذلك ببعض المصادر اليونانية والرومانية وهو يسوق الروايات المختلفة حول أصل الأهرام والغرض منها.(٣٩)

ورؤية الإدريسي المؤطِّرة لمنهجيته البحثية والمؤصِّلة لنظرته إلى الأهرام تنكشف لنا في موقفه الذي يثبت عليه خلال عرضه لها، ألا وهو تأكيده على «إسلامية» الأهرام في عظمة بنيانها والمعنى المتبدي من خلالها للمتفكر المتأمل. فهو يُضمِّن معناها في الآيات القرآنية الخاصة بالأولين ثم يضيف عليها الآيات الحاثّة على السياحة في الأرض والتفكر في عظمة الخلق، ويؤكد ذلك بالأحاديث النبوية، وعلى أساس ذلك ينتهي إلى دعوته للحفاظ على الأهرام بوصفها مصدراً للتأمل المعرفي والتدبُّر المنصوص عليهما في القرآن. وهو لا يكتفي بذلك، فهو يذهب إلى الدعوى بقدسية موقعها التي قد اكتسبتها بزيارة بعض الصحابة وآل البيت لها.(٤٠) وفي نفس الموقع يروي الإدريسي كذلك أن «أحد

أكابر المؤرخين» قد ذكر أن الصابئة كانوا يحجون إلى الأهرام وأنهم كانوا يُجلّونها كما يجل المسلمون الحرمين. والمثير هنا أن الطهطاوي في **أنوار توفيق الجليل** يذكر في غضون الإضافات التي أضافها على مصادره الفرنسية أن الديانة المصرية القديمة كانت على مذهب الصابئة، ومثل هذه الإشارة تفيد بأن المصريين القدماء كانوا من أهل الكتاب وتُعَد هذه أول محاولة في العصر الحديث لتأكيد استمرارية الهوية المصرية، ليس من وجهة النظر التاريخية فحسب بل من وجهة النظر الدينية كذلك.

ونظرة الغيطاني لمصر القديمة بمنظور عربي إسلامي بحت إنما تأتي في إثر تاريخ طويل من الممارسة يبدأ بتاريخ الطبري ويتأصل في رؤية الإدريسي الواعية ويمتد في نظرة الطهطاوي الشاملة. ومن الجدير بالذكر أن تفسير الغيطاني لهذه النظرة ببُعد الحقبة التاريخية يجيء مخالفاً لما يسميه «الجوهري» في الإنسان والذي يتجاوز في رأيه تاريخية الزمان والمكان ويجمع بينه وبين ابن إياس.

قديم اللحظة وجديد التاريخ: مفهوم الاستمرارية التاريخية عند الغيطاني

وهكذا تأتي رواية **متون الأهرام** (وبعض الفصول من رواية **سفر البنيان**) كمحاولة فريدة من نوعها تختلف تماماً عما سبقها من محاولات لمعالجة التاريخ روائياً. فهي على سبيل المثال لا تأتي في شكل الرواية التاريخية كما نجده في روايات علي أحمد باكثير أو روايات نجيب محفوظ الأولى **عبث الأقدار** ورادوبيس و**كفاح طيبة،** أو حتى في قصص محمد حسين هيكل القصيرة ذات الطابع التاريخي والتي يتناول بعضها أحداثاً وشخصيات من مصر القديمة. كما أنها تختلف عن المعالجات الرمزية التي نجدها في رواية نجيب محفوظ **أمام العرش** أو في **العائش في الحقيقة،** أو في معالجات معاصرة كما نجد في أعمال بهاء طاهر. معالجة الغيطاني الروائية تعتمد على الرواية عن المخطوط أو المدوّن العربي الإسلامي للتعبير في النهاية عما يؤمن به من استمرارية حية للتاريخ تستمد مصداقيتها من الممارسات الثقافية والشعبية على ما خبرها في مراحل تكوينه الفكري والفني وفي المناطق التي ارتبطت بها. وقد دون رؤيته تلك في أكثر من موضع.(٤١)

أما من ناحية عناصر الاستمرارية فهو يذكر على سبيل المثال إمكانية استمرارية مفهوم الثالوث المصري القديم، المرموز له بشخصيات الآلهة أوزيريس وإيزيس وحورس، في مبدأ الثالوث المسيحي (وحتى الآن نرى آثار ذلك على جدران بعض المعابد ومحاولات تحويل قدس الأقداس إلى هيكل مسيحي). أما من ناحية الثقافة العربية الإسلامية المصرية فنجد هناك تشابهاً بين المفهومين وبين النظرة إلى الإمام علي والسيدة فاطمة (أو السيدة زينب) والإمام الحسين. ويركز الغيطاني كذلك على أسطورة المحاكمة في الحياة الأخرى في شكلها القديم والتي استمرت في شكل اللجوء إلى السيدة زينب والتضرع إليها بصفتها «رئيسة الديوان». وعلى مستوى الممارسات التاريخية فهناك تقارب في شكل وسياقات ممارسة اللجوء إلى الإلهة إيزيس واللجوء إلى السيدة العذراء والسيدة زينب.(٤٢) ويذكر الغيطاني كذلك ظاهرة انتشار أضرحة «سيدي الأربعين» في قرى مصر وإمكانية تفسيرها على أنها تعود إلى محاولة إحياء الأجزاء الأربعين لجسد أوزيريس، وإن اختلفت الروايات

في ذلك.(٤٣) والتركيز على عناصر الاستمرارية هذه يعبر عن مفهوم خاص للتاريخ ليس في شكل عصور وحِقَب متمايزة بأحداثها وشخصياتها وإنما في شكل لحظات ومفاهيم عبرت حواجزها التاريخية وأتت في ارتباطها بمسيرة حياة إنسانية على ما دوّنها الأولون أو على ما استقرت في الممارسات الأدبية أو الفنية أو الثقافية أو الشعبية. وهو يعبر عن ذلك في غضون تفسيره لضرورة خلق أشكال فنية للرواية تستمد عناصرها من التراث:

ربما كان السبب الكامن وراء ذلك اهتمامي المبكر منذ فترة بعيدة بالتاريخ، ونشأتي في منطقة القاهرة القديمة المزدحمة بالمساجد والأسبلة والبيوت القديمة، والأهم من ذلك علاقات الناس التي لا تزال في جوهرها تمتّ إلى زمن آفل، ثم سبب آخر وهو إحساسي القوي بالزمن، هذه القوة التي لا راد لها، الزمن في صيرورته المخيفة، واستمراريته، وسيولته التي لا تتجمد أبداً، كان إحساسي بالزمن هو أساس مفهومي للتاريخ، التاريخ بالنسبة لي هو الزمن، ليس مفهومي للتاريخ أنه عصر معين محدد بعلامات رمزية وضعها الإنسان، أقصد السنوات والشهور والدقائق والثواني، هذه اللحظة التي أتحدث فيها الآن ولّت إلى غير رجعة. . . .(٤٤)

وهذه الرؤية التي تركز على صيرورة الزمن الذي يولي دائماً إلى غير رجعة لا بد وأن تحيل واقع التاريخ على لحظات الرؤية العميقة القادرة على تحدي الزمن. ويرى الغيطاني أنه «لا حقيقة في التاريخ»، فكل شيء حتى الحقائق الكبرى هو في تبدل وتغير مع صيرورة الزمن، وحتى الغد أو الآتي في الزمن إنما هو «تاريخ مستقبلي مُتخيّل».(٤٥)

ومن هنا فإن انتقال اللحظات العميقة من الزمن المولّي إلى الآتي المتخيّل يرتبط بأشكال الوعي الإنساني والتي تتغلب على الزمن بقوة الفن المتخيّل وقدرة الفنان، أي بقوة الرؤية التي تؤصل اللغة أو نسقية الشكل المعماري في علاقة للجزء مع كل منفتح على المستقبل المتخيّل، أو على مبدأ الإمكانية الوجودية وليس على مبدأ الضرورة الوجودية أو التاريخية. وهكذا فالغيطاني يؤكد أن:

الفنان الحقيقي هو الذي يصون مسافة زمنية معينة من العدم، إن الفنان يسجل ما لا تذكره سطور المؤرخين، أو صفحات الجرائد، أو سجلات الحوليات، إنه ينفذ إلى جوهر الواقع، إلى اللامرئي، واللامحسوس، هنا أعتبر أن الفنان مؤرخ من نوع فريد، لأنه يصون جوهر مسافة زمنية معينة من العدم، من التلاشي في هذا الفراغ الكوني الرهيب المسمى بالزمن، وجوهر المسافة الزمنية أقصد به جوهر الواقع الذي لا يرصده إلا الفنان ويعيد خلقه من خلال رواية، أو قصة، أو شعر، أو لوحة. لولا اللوحات التي نُقِشت على جدران المعابد الفرعونية، ولولا القصص التي وصلتنا على أوراق البردي لما أمكن لنا أن نستعيد هذه المسافة الزمنية المسماة بالعصر الفرعوني.(٤٦)

والمبدأ الفني الفاعل هنا هو أن الصيانة لمسافة زمنية معينة لا تتم بصيانة الواقع التاريخي ذاته، وإلا صار هذا الفن محض سجل تاريخي، وإنما بصيانة «جوهر» هذا الواقع، وهو على ما تتيحه الرؤية الإبداعية للفنان. وصيانة الجوهر في هذه الرؤية، وفي ممارسات الغيطاني الروائية المرهونة عليها، لابد وأنها تكمن في مبدأ الإمكانية الوجودية، على ما أسسه في استخراج شخصية الزيني بركات من واقعها التاريخي ومن توصيفها النصي إلى إمكانيتها الوجودية المنصَبَّة على الماضي والحاضر في آنية قصصية، أو على ما فعل مع الشيخ تهامي وإحالة شخصيته على إمكانية وجودية مدوَّنة.

ومثل هذه الإمكانيات الوجودية المُعَبَّر عنها في رؤية فنية تستحيل مع قوة الرؤية (أو ضعفها) إلى إمكانية معرفية للذات ولموقعها من الزمان والمكان. وهذا الانتقال في العلاقة مع الزمن من الضرورة إلى الإمكانية الوجودية ثم إلى الإمكانية المعرفية (في تركيب الشخصية وتعبيرها عن نفسها أو في وعي القارئ) بطريق اللغة وبأساليبها الفنية التي هي أيضاً أساليب للتلقي لانطباع ما أو لمعرفة ما أو لإحساس ما، هذا الانتقال المتأسس على مبدأ الإمكانية هو من جوهر الرؤية الحداثية للزمن وللإبداع الفني. ومن هنا فرؤية الغيطاني حداثية وإن اتخذت شكل الأساليب التراثية، ومن هنا نرى أيضاً بشكل أعمق الاختلاف، على سبيل المثال، بينه وبين ابن إياس على مستوى الرؤية وموضعتها التاريخية وإن اتسقت جدلية التناص في أسلوب السرد التاريخي أو في أسلوب عرض الشخصيات.

فمسيرة الشيخ تهامي على ما يعرضها الراوي في المتن الأول تأتي في المقام الأول كتجسيد إنساني لمفهوم «التشوف» ولحال «المعاينة» المؤسِّس لجوهر طالب العلم أو طالب المعرفة كنمط إنساني. ثم بعد ذلك تتواتر في شكل مقولات جوهرية أو ترانيم تعنون معاني الجوانب المختلفة للشخصية، وكأنما قوام الشخصية في هذا الجانب من جوانبها هو في تعبيرها وجودياً عن معنى تلك المقولة النموذج. وعلى هذا فقراءة تلك المقولة هي في الوقت ذاته قراءة للذات بشكل أساسي، وممارسة الذات لحياتها هي بمثابة إعادة كتابة لتلك المقولة. ومن ثم، فمقولة «كلمة، أو نظرة، أو إيماءة .. ربما تحيد بمصير وتغير مسار حياة» هي كلمة تملك قوة التفعيل الوجودي وتعبر عن اللحظة الحاسمة في حياة المغربي الذي جاء خبره في رواية الإدريسي وفي حياة الشيخ تهامي على السواء. ومن ثم فهي تجمع بين الحياتين وتؤطر لهما على بعدهما الزماني والمكاني، كما يدعو منطق القص في **متون الأهرام** وكما يتكشف لنا في المتن الفاصل، المتن العاشر. ومن الجدير بالذكر أنه في متون الأهرام الأصلية وفي أدب السيرة الذاتية الفرعوني وأيضاً في النصوص التي تندرج تحت **كتاب الموتى** (أو ما يُعرف بكتاب **السعي في وضح النهار**) نرى كيف تصبو الحياة الشخصية التاريخية إلى أنموذجية الحياة المثالية التي لا تتخارج إلا في جوهر اللغة وسلطتها على التحول بالواقع التاريخي إلى المثال الإنساني، ومن ثم قدرتها على الخلق. وتتجذر رؤية المصري القديم في النظرة الدينية المنبثقة من الأسطورة الأونية للإله آتوم الذي أوجد الخلق بفعل نطقه للأسماء ومن ثم بقوة اللغة.

وأسلوب الغيطاني لا يخلو من الإشكالية للناقد والمتلقي وإن كان المبدع له حرية الإبداع المطلقة. فمما لا شك فيه أن عرض شخصية من الواقع المعاصر في لغة تراثية ونمط

إنساني مخالف تاريخياً وإن كان مطابقاً للإمكانية الوجودية لا بد وأن يهدف إلى خلق حس جديد للمتلقي المعاصر يعتمد بشكل أساسي وقوي على الإيمان من جانب الراوي/القاص بوحدة الرؤية بينه وبين المتلقي/السامع، وهذه الرؤية هنا تشكل أداة معرفية على مستوى الفكر وعلى مستوى الحس الإبداعي كذلك. وهي في سياق مشروع الغيطاني رؤية عربية إسلامية تكمن في العلاقة بين الآية والسورة، بين الجزء والكل، وهي متجذرة في التراث وتظهر أكثر ما تظهر في العلاقة مع التاريخ، أو التصور العربي الإسلامي للعلاقة بين الذات والآخر زمانياً ومكانياً، وتأتي العلاقة بوساطة اللغة وحضورها المؤثر فكرياً وعقائدياً وشعورياً.

الهوامش

(١) يعتمد هذا المقال على محاضرتين قد ألقيتهما سابقاً، الأولى في جامعة هارڤارد في مؤتمر حول العلاقة بين الرواية العربية والتاريخ كنت قد قمت بإعداده إبّان فترة عملي هناك بالاشتراك مع الزميل وليم غرانارا في عام ١٩٩٩. أما المحاضرة الثانية، والتي ركزت فيها على مفهوم اللغة المقدسة، فألقيت استجابةً لدعوة من مركز بحوث الفنون وبحوث العلوم الإنسانية (AHRB) للاشتراك في سلسلة المحاضرات التي ينظمها سنوياً بكلية الدراسات الشرقية والأفريقية (SOAS) بجامعة لندن، وذلك في عام ٢٠٠٢ بترتيب من الزميلة ونشن أويانغ، فلها جزيل الشكر. وأشكر الزملاء والذين حضروا على تعليقاتهم وحسن تجاوبهم. وهذا المقال في شكله الأخير مُهدى إلى الأستاذة الدكتورة دوريس إنريت-كلارك شكري، رئيسة قسم الأدب الإنجليزي والمقارن بالجامعة الأمريكية في القاهرة، والتي شملتني بكامل رعايتها وخصتني باهتمامها وحسن توجيهها منذ بداية سعيي كطالب للأدب المقارن. فتقديري لها ولاهتمامها الذي شملتني به، واحترامي لشخصها ولعمق تفكيرها، واللذان كنتهما لها آنذاك ولم أخفهما عليها إنما قد ازدادا مع مرور السنين.

(٢) أبو جعفر الإدريسي، كتاب **أنوار عُلوي الأجرام في الكشف عن أسرار الأهرام**، تحقيق أُلريش هارمان (بيروت: المعهد الألماني للأبحاث الشرقية في بيروت، ١٩٩١)، ص ٧١.

(٣) **المرجع السابق**، ص ٧٢.

(٤) راجع الدراسة التالية حول تاريخ المصريين بعد نشأة علم المصريات:

Donald M. Reid, "Indigenous Egyptology: The Decolonization of a Profession?," *Journal of the American Oriental Society* 105.2 (April-June 1985): 233-46.

راجع أيضاً دراسته حول العلاقة بين مصر القديمة وعلم المصريات والحركة الوطنية في مصر:

Donald M. Reid, "Nationalizing the Pharaonic Past: Egyptology, Imperialism, and Egyptian Nationalism, 1922-1952," *Rethinking Nationalism in the Arab Middle East,* eds. James Jankowski and Israel Gershoni (New York: Columbia UP, 1997), 127-49.

(٥) أرجع في هذا البحث إلى طبعة شرقيات الأولى، جمال الغيطاني، **متون الأهرام** (القاهرة: دار شرقيات، ١٩٩٤). كل الإشارات والاستشهادات في متن النص تحيل إلى هذه الطبعة ويتبعها رقم الصفحة أو الصفحات بين قوسين. هذا مع العلم بأن هناك طبعة أخرى صدرت عن دار الشروق في عام ٢٠٠٢.

(٦) في إشاراتي للرواية سأرجع إلى الطبعة التالية: جمال الغيطاني، **سفر البنيان** (القاهرة: دار الهلال، ١٩٩٧). كل الإشارات والاستشهادات في متن النص تحيل إلى هذه الطبعة ويتبعها رقم الصفحة أو الصفحات بين قوسين.

(٧) راجع فيصل درّاج، **نظرية الرواية والرواية العربية** (بيروت: المركز الثقافي العربي، ١٩٩٩)، ص ٢٣٦. وحول هذه الإشكالية بشكل عام، راجع دراسة سعيد يقطين، **الرواية والتراث السردي: من أجل وعي جديد بالتراث** (بيروت: المركز الثقافي العربي، ١٩٩٢)، ومقال سيزا قاسم، «القص العربي المعاصر»، **فصول**، المجلد الثاني، العدد الثاني (يناير–مارس ١٩٨٢)، ص ص ١٤٣–١٥١، وفي نفس العدد راجع مقال سامية أسعد، «عندما يكتب الروائي التاريخ»، ص ص ٦٧–٧٤. انظر كذلك دراسات محمود أمين العالم والتي جُمعت في مجلد بعنوان **أربعون عاماً من النقد التطبيقي: البنية والدلالة في القصة والرواية العربية المعاصرة** (القاهرة: دار المستقبل العربي، ١٩٩٤)، راجع المقدمة العامة، ص ص ١٣–٣٩ وفيما يخص الغيطاني، ص ص ١٤٢–٢٠٤.

(٨) انظر بالأخص قراءته لأعمال الشاعر الألماني ريلكه والكاتب الروائي الفرنسي مارسل بروست في الدراسة التي أشرت إليها وهي:

Paul de Man, *Allegories of Reading: Figural Language in Rousseau, Nietzsche, Rilke, and Proust* (New Haven: Yale UP, 1979).

(٩) في قراءته للغيطاني التي أشرت إليها آنفاً يحدد فيصل دراج أيضاً علاقة الوعي بالأزمة والسيرة الذاتية فيذكر أنه في أعمال الغيطاني «يرد الوعي بالأزمة، في علاقة الأنا بالواقع، إلى صيغة السيرة الذاتية، ويحيل الوعي بالأزمة، في علاقة الأنا بالمجموع، على الهوية المؤرقة، أي على الكتابة الأصل. يطمح الغيطاني المستجير بتاريخ جماعي ملتبس، إلى دمج الكل في واحد وإلى ترحيل الأزمنة إلى زمن أساسي وإلى تخليق لغة نموذجية سابقة على اللغة الروائية، أي أنه، وقد ذهب في مغامرة روائية فريدة، يطمح إلى رواية مغايرة، تبني فضاءها الروائي بمواد غير مرئية، رغم التباس العبارة»، **نظرية الرواية والرواية العربية**، ص ٢٣٧. وينبغي الإشارة هنا إلى أن هذه المقولة جاءت في معرض الحديث عن رواية **الزيني بركات** وبالتالي فمفهوم السيرة الذاتية هنا ينطبق على الصوت الروائي في الرواية أكثر منه على تفعيل الغيطاني لبعض تجاربه الشخصية، هذا وإن جاءت الرواية بأكملها كتفعيل رمزي للحظة الكاتب التاريخية.

(١٠) انظر على سبيل المثال رواية **سفر البنيان**، ص ص ١٥٣–١٥٤. وفي هذا الموضع من الفصل بعنوان «حكاية: بربا» يذكر الراوي في «صيغة الغائب» تذكر الشخصية لصوت الأب واحتفاظها بتسجيل لصوت الأم وما يترتب على ذلك من العلاقة بالأصل وبالزمن المولّي. وهذه التفصيلات تتكرر بشكل يجعل منها تيمة شبه أساسية في رواية **تجليات الغيطاني**، ومنها تسهل الإحالة على سيرة الغيطاني الذاتية، وإن وجب اتخاذ الحذر النقدي في مثل هذه العمليات الإحالية.

(١١) يسرد الغيطاني هذه الواقعة الشخصية في مقال له بعنوان «إشارات . . إلى معرفة البدايات» (دون مرجع)، وقد قام بتوزيعه في مؤتمر للرواية العربية تم تنظيمه تحت إشراف جامعة جورجتاون بالولايات المتحدة الأمريكية في عام ٢٠٠٢. راجع أيضاً **متون الأهرام**، المتن التاسع «صمت»، حيث ترد الواقعة في سياق ذكرى شخصية كذلك.

(١٢) انظر **كتاب أنوار عُلوي الأجرام في الكشف عن أسرار الأهرام**، ص ص ٤٩-٧٦.

(١٣) عالم المصريات الفرنسي ماسبيرو كان أول من حقق هذه النصوص ونشرها في ترجمة فرنسية، ثم جاء بعده العالم الألماني سيث الذي أصدر أول طبعة محققة لمتون الأهرام. أما أحدث طبعة للمتون وأصحها من ناحية التحقيق والترجمة والشرح هي طبعة فوكنر التالية:

R. O. Faulkner, *The Ancient Egyptian Pyramid Texts: Translation into English* (Oxford: The Clarendon Press, 1969; 1998).

وهذه الطبعة لها ملحق خاص يحوي النصوص الهيروغليفية، وقد اعتمدت الطبعتين الفرنسية والألمانية وكذلك أول طبعة إنجليزية في أربعة مجلدات مع التعقيب والشرح، وهي طبعة ميرسر:

Samuel A. B. Mercer, *The Pyramid Texts in Translation and Commentary*, 4 Volumes (London: Longmans, Green and Co., 1952).

ولهذه الطبعة أيضاً ملحق للنصوص الهيروغليفية، وقد أتبعها ميرسر بدراسة نقدية مطولة للجوانب الأدبية واللغوية لمتون الأهرام تعد من أولى الدراسات الأدبية للمتون وللأدب الفرعوني بشكل عام:

Samuel A. B. Mercer, *Literary Criticism of the Pyramid Texts* (London: Luzac & Company Ltd., 1956).

وعلى ما أعلم، ليست هناك طبعة كاملة ومحققة لمتون الأهرام باللغة العربية، وإن جاءت بعض المقتطفات في موسوعة سليم حسن للحضارة المصرية القديمة، وفي أعمال قليلة أخرى تفتقر إلى المصداقية البحثية.

(١٤) راجع:

Miriam Lichtheim, *Ancient Egyptian Literature, Volume I: The Old and Middle Kingdoms* (Berkeley: University of California Press, 1973; 1975), 3-5.

(١٥) الاستشهاد هنا من مخطوطة بيد الكاتب في خمس صفحات بعنوان «فن القص الإسلامي .. بين الخصوصية المحلية والرؤية الكونية: **ألف ليلة وليلة** نموذجاً» (ص ١). والاستشهاد هنا من مقدمة هذه المخطوطة، وإن كان بقيتها قد نُشِر في دراسته **منتهى الطلب إلى تراث العرب: دراسات في التراث** (القاهرة: دار الشروق، ١٩٩٧). انظر بالأخص مقدمة الكتاب، ص ص ٥-١٦، والفصلين بعنوان «زخرفة ألف ليلة» (ص ص ١٢١-١٢٤) و«مدينة **ألف ليلة وليلة**» (ص ص ١٢٥-١٢٨).

(١٦) انظر الدراسة التي قام بها الناقد والكاتب الإيطالي أمبرتو إكو والتي تتناول تأثر جويس بفكر القديس توما الإكويني في تشكيل نظرته الإبداعية، وبالأخص في بدايات أعماله:

Umberto Eco, *The Aesthetics of Chaosmos: The Middle Ages of James Joyce*, trans. Ellen Esrock (Cambridge, Mass.: Harvard UP, 1982).

(١٧) انظر الترجمة الإنجليزية:

Mikhail M. Bakhtin, *Art and Answerability: Early Philosophical Essays*, eds. Michael Holquist and Vadim Liapunov, trans. Vadim Liapunov (Austin: University of Texas Press, 1990).

(١٨) انظر **منتهى الطلب**، ص ص١٢٢-١٢٣.

(١٩) راجع مقال صافيناز-أمل نجيب حول أدب السيرة الذاتية الفرعوني: «تمثيل الذات: السيرة الذاتية والهوية في مصر القديمة»، ترجمة لميس النقاش، **ألف**، العدد الثاني والعشرون (٢٠٠٢)، ص ص ٣٤-٤٣.

(٢٠) انظر على سبيل المثال دراسة وليد منير «حول توظيف العنصر الأسطوري في الرواية المصرية المعاصرة»، **فصول**، المجلد الثاني، العدد الثاني (١٩٨٢)، ص ص ٣١-٣٨. انظر بالأخص مناقشته لشخصية «زويل الكبير» كشخصية أسطورية تجمع بين نموذج السيد المسيح عليه السلام ونموذج المهدي المنتظر، ص ص ٣٥-٣٦.

(٢١) انظر مقال الغيطاني بعنوان «بعض مكونات عالمي الروائي»، **الآداب**، المجلد ٣٨، العدد ٤-٦ (أبريل - يونيو ١٩٩٠)، ص ١١٣.

(٢٢) انظر «مشكلة الإبداع الروائي عند جيل الستينيات والسبعينيات»، **فصول**، المجلد الثاني، العدد الثاني (١٩٨٢)، ص٢١٣. ومقولة الغيطاني تأتي في حوار ندوة هذا العدد الخاص بالرواية وفن القص، وقد اشترك معه في الحوار كل من صبري موسى وصنع الله إبراهيم ويوسف القعيد واعتدال عثمان ومحمد بدوي.

(٢٣) انظر كتاب **أنوار عُلوي الأجرام في الكشف عن أسرار الأهرام**، ص ص ٥ -١٢.

(٢٤) **المرجع السابق**، ص١٤.

(٢٥) يعترف الغيطاني على سبيل المثال بأن «هناك وجوه اتفاق بين حياتي وواقعي، وحياة ابن إياس وواقعه. ولكن هناك وجوه اختلاف وتباين كذلك. وهناك ما أسميه 'وحدة التجربة الإنسانية' بمعنى أن ثمة أشياء تتجاوز الزمان والمكان لتكون 'الجوهري' في الإنسان»، انظر «مشكلة الإبداع الروائي عند جيل الستينيات والسبعينيات»، ص ٢١٣.

(٢٦) انظر على سبيل المثال الدراسة التي قام بها روبرتو توتولي:

Roberto Tottoli, *Biblical Prophets in the Qur'an and Muslim Literature*, trans. Michael Robertson (Richmond: Curzon Press, 2002).

انظر بالأخص ص ص ٨٦-٩٦.

(٢٧) راجع سيرة السيوطي **التحدث بنعمة الله** في الطبعة التي حققتها الدكتورة إليزابيث سارتن:

Elizabeth Sartain, ed., *Jalal al-Din al-Suyuti, "Al-Tahadduth bini'mat Allah"*, Volume II (Cambridge: Cambridge UP, 1975).

راجع بالأخص الفصل التاسع عشر «ذكر المجددين المبعوثين على رأس كل مائة»، ص ص ٢١٥- ٢٢٧.

راجع أيضاً: دراسة كريستين بروستاد حول أنماط التمثيل في سيرة السيوطي الذاتية:

Kristen Brustad, "Imposing Order: Reading the Conventions of Representation in al-Suyuti's Autobiography," *Edebiyat* n.s. 7.2 (1997): 327-44.

وحول أدب السيرة الذاتية العربي ما بين القرنين التاسع والتاسع عشر، راجع الدراسات التي قام بها مجموعة من الأساتذة وأعدها للنشر دوايت رينولدز:

Dwight F. Reynolds, ed., *Interpreting the Self: Autobiography in the Arabic Literary Tradition* (Berkeley: University of California Press, 2001).

وفيما يخص سيرة السيوطي الذاتية، راجع ص ص ١-٥؛ ٦٥-٦٧؛ ٨٧-٨٨؛ ٢٠٢-٢٠٣؛ ٢٧٢.

(٢٨) قام عالم المصريات الإيطالي أنطونيو لوبرينو بإعداد أول دراسة مستفيضة للغات المصرية القديمة من منظور علم اللغويات:

Antonio Loprieno, *Ancient Egyptian: A Linguistic Introduction* (Cambridge: Cambridge UP, 1995).

(٢٩) راجع بالأخص دراساته التالية:

Northrop Frye, *The Great Code: The Bible and Literature* (New York: Harcourt Brace Jovanovich, Publishers, 1982); *Words with Power* (New York: Harcourt Brace Jovanovich, Publishers, 1990).

وقد اعتمد فراي كذلك على مشروع المفكر وعالم اللاهوت الألماني رودولف بولتمان Rudolf Bultmann والذي يرتبط مشرعه باللاهوت الوجودي والظواهراتي وبالأخص بمشروع التخلص من أسطرة الإنجيل Demythologizing the New Testament.

(٣٠) انظر على سبيل المثال روايات الإدريسي في **كتاب أنوار عُلوي الأجرام في الكشف عن أسرار الأهرام**، ص ص ١٤-١٦؛ ٣٠؛ ٣١-٣٥؛ ٣٧؛ ٦١؛ ٦٤-٦٥؛ ١٣٣. وهذه الروايات قد جمعها الإدريسي من المصادر السابقة عليه وحققها وأضاف عليها، ومن ثم فقد اكتفيت بالإشارة إليه بهدف الاختصار.

(٣١) راجع مؤلَّف الشيخ رفاعة رافع الطهطاوي **أنوار توفيق الجليل في أخبار مصر وتوثيق بني إسماعيل**، في **الأعمال الكاملة لرفاعة رافع الطهطاوي**، المجلد الثالث، تحقيق محمد عمارة (بيروت: المؤسسة العربية للدراسات والنشر، ١٩٧٤). وقد قام الطهطاوي أيضاً بالإشراف على أول ترجمة (عن الفرنسية) لتاريخ مصر القديمة وكتب لها مقدمة خاصة، **بداية القدماء وهداية الحكماء**، وقد ترجمها بعض تلامذته وهم عبد الله أبو السعود ومصطفى الزواربي ومحمد عبد الرازق (القاهرة: مطبعة بولاق، ١٨٣٨، طبعة ثانية ١٨٦٥). وحول هذا الموضوع راجع دراسة دونالد ريد:

Donald M Reid, *Whose Pharaohs? Archaology, Museums, and Egyptian National Identity from Napoleon to World War I* (Berkeley: University of California Press, 2002).

راجع بالأخص ص ص ١٠٨-١١٢، والهامش رقم ٣٢٩.

(٣٢) ويؤكد الغيطاني بأنه قرأ في الأدب المصري القديم، فيذكر موسوعة سليم حسن في الحضارة المصرية القديمة وسيرة سنوحي المصري الذاتية. ويذكر على سبيل المثال قراءته لرواية بعنوان **وردة** لكاتب ألماني تدور أحداثها في مصر القديمة، هذا إلى جانب بعض الأعمال من الأدب القبطي

وروايات نجيب محفوظ الأولى: **عبث الأقدار** (١٩٣٩) و**رادوبيس** (١٩٤٣) و**كفاح طيبة** (١٩٤٤)، راجع جمال الغيطاني، «جدلية التناص»، مقابلة أُجريت معه ونُشرت على صفحات **ألف**، العدد ٤ (١٩٨٤)، ص ص ٧١-٨٢.

(٣٣) انظر «مشكلة الإبداع الروائي عند جيل الستينيات والسبعينيات»، ص ٢١٢.

(٣٤) انظر كتاب **أنوار عُلوي الأجرام في الكشف عن أسرار الأهرام**، ص ص ١٤-١٥.

(٣٥) راجع ابن إياس، **نزهة الأُمم في العجائب والحِكَم**، تحقيق محمد زينهم محمد عزب (القاهرة: مكتبة مدبولي، ١٩٩٥)، ص ص ١٥٢-١٥٤. انظر كذلك **كتاب أنوار عُلوي الأجرام في الكشف عن أسرار الأهرام**، ص ص٣١-٣٥. وقد أورد الإدريسي ذكر كل ما يتعلق بحادثة المأمون مع الأهرام ولا يذكر أي شخصية باسم ابن الشحنة، بل إنه يذكر رواية عن الوصيفي في تاريخه وأبي الصلت الأندلسي والوزير الأسعد بن ممّاتي المصري أن المأمون «كان ذا نفس بمطالعة غرائب العلوم متعلّقة، وذا همة إلى الاطلاع على عجائب الحِكَم متسلّقة، وفي زمانه بأمره تُرجمت كتب العلوم الفلسفية من اللغة اليونانية إلى اللغة العربية - وإنه لما دخل مصر وعاين الأهرام، ولم يجد مَن يُشفي بحديثه عنها من شغفه بالوقوف على حقيقة حديثها الأسقام، أمر بنقب الهرم الأكبر ليطلع على ما فيها من الأسرار التي طال ما كانت الأيام على الأنام تخفيها»، ص ٣٤. فمن ثابت الرواية إذن أن المأمون لم يجد مَن يعينه على فهم أسرار الأهرام، وربما أتى الغيطاني هنا على معالجة الحادثة خيالياً كما فعل مع الإشارات البسيطة لشخصية الزيني بركات في تاريخ ابن إياس.

(٣٦) يشير الغيطاني أكثر ما يشير إلى تاريخ ابن إياس الشهير **بدائع الزهور في وقائع الدهور**، ويورد ابن إياس في جملة ما يورد ذكر «عجائب مصر وما بها من الطلسمات والبرابي»، انظر طبعة الكتاب تحقيق محمد مصطفى، الجزء الأول، القسم الأول (القاهرة: الهيئة المصرية العامة للكتاب، ١٩٨٢)، ص ص ١٣-١٧. وذكر الأهرام يأتي في الجزء الأول، القسمين الأول والثاني، في الطبعة الكاملة، ١٢ مجلداً (Wiesbaden: Franz Steiner 1975-1992). انظر كذلك **نزهة الأُمم في العجائب والحِكَم**، حيث يُفرد ابن إياس ثلاثة أقسام للأهرام يرد فيها وصف الروحانيات وغيرها من عجائب الأهرام وطلسماتها، انظر بالأخص ص ص ١٤١-١٥٨، وفيما يخص الروحانيات، ص ١٤٨. انظر أيضاً الأقسام الخاصة بذكر الأهرام في **حُسن المحاضرة في أخبار مصر والقاهرة** لجلال الدين السيوطي، وفي **مروج الذهب ومعادن الجوهر** للمسعودي، وبالأخص انظر القسم الخاص بروحانيات الأهرام، والذي يعود إليه السيوطي والإدريسي وابن إياس، بعنوان «بناء الأهرام وأخبارها وروحانياتها» في **كتاب أخبار الزمان**، لأبي الحسن المسعودي (القاهرة: مطبعة عبد الحميد أحمد حنفي، ١٩٣١)، ص ص ١٣٣-١٤٣.

(٣٧) انظر الإدريسي، **كتاب أنوار عُلوي الأجرام في الكشف عن أسرار الأهرام**، ص ٣٠ ومواضع أخرى.

(٣٨) فيما يخص نظرة علي مبارك لمصر القديمة وللأهرام في **الخطط التوفيقية وعلم الدين**، راجع الدراسة التالية:

Darrell Dykstra, "Pyramids, Prophets, and Progress: Ancient Egypt in the Writings of Ali Mubarak," *Journal of the American Oriental Society*, 114.1 (January-March 1994): 54-65.

^(٣٩) راجع دراسة دونالد ريد السابق ذكرها *Whose Pharaohs?*، ص ص٢٢-٣١.

^(٤٠) انظر الإدريسي، **كتاب أُنوار عُلوي الأجرام في الكشف عن أُسرار الأهرام**، الفصل الأول والفصل الثالث. راجع كذلك مقالات أولريش هارمان، مُحقّق مخطوطة الإدريسي، التالية:

Ulrich Haarmann, "In Quest of the Spectacular: Noble and Learned Visitors to the Pyramids around 1200 A. D.," *Islamic Studies Presented to Charles J. Adams*, eds. Wael B. Hallaq and Donald Little (Leiden: E. J. Brill, 1991), 57-68, and "Regional Sentiment in Medieval Islamic Egypt," *Bulletin of the School of Oriental and African Studies* 43.1 (1980): 55-66.

^(٤١) هناك إشارات متعددة في مقالات الغيطاني تخص فكرة الاستمرارية التاريخية، وقد جمعها في الفصل بعنوان «عناصر الاستمرارية في الثقافة المصرية» في **منتهى الطلب إلى تراث العرب**، ص ص ١٧-٢٢.

^(٤٢) انظر **المرجع السابق**، حيث يرد ذكر هذه الأمثلة وغيرها.

^(٤٣) هناك مَن يردد تفسير الغيطاني لأضرحة سيدي الأربعين، انظر على سبيل المثال ذكر هذه الأسطورة في رواية تتناول أيضا ذكر مصر القديمة حيث يُبعث رمسيس الثاني، كتمهيد لبعث جمال عبد الناصر، كمجاز استعاري وفي محاولة رمزية لإحياء بعض «القيم المصرية» تحت مفاهيم «الإيزيسية»، وهذه الرواية هي لبكر الشرقاوي بعنوان **وقائع ما حدث في يوم القيامة بمصر** (القاهرة: مكتبة مدبولي، ١٩٨٧)، انظر بالأخص ص ٢٩٣ وص ٢٩٤. وهناك تفاسير أخرى مخالفة لأصل الأضرحة وقد ورد أحدها في دراسة حسن الشامي:

Hasan M. El-Shamy, ed. and trans., *Folktales of Egypt* (Chicago: The University of Chicago Press, 1980).

راجع ص ص ١٤١-١٤٣. وفي الحكاية التي يسجلها الشامي أُقيمت الأضرحة لأربعين شيخاً كانوا في الأصل من اللصوص وقُطّاع الطرق ثم تابوا على يد الإمام الرفاعي الذي يظهر لهم في هيئة ولي من الأولياء. وفيما يخص النظرة للسيدة زينب كرئيسة الديوان، انظر ص ص ١٥١-١٥٣. وكما هو معروف، فإن رواية **أمام العرش** لنجيب محفوظ هي بمثابة معالجة رمزية لأسطورة محاكمة ما بعد الموت الفرعونية.

^(٤٤) انظر جمال الغيطاني، «بعض مكونات عالمي الرواي»، ص١١٣.

^(٤٥) **المرجع نفسه.**

^(٤٦) **المرجع نفسه.**

الكتابة خارج المكان:
«الحب والفانتازيا» لآسيا جبار و«خارطة الحب» لأهداف سويف

سامية محرز

I

إن القاسم المشترك بين رواية التاريخ والرواية الأدبية يتمثل في كونهما شكلين قصصيين، أي قص أحداث واقعية أو متخيلة، تجمع بينهما خصائص مشتركة قد يكون على رأسها الاشتقاق اللغوي سواء في اللغة العربية أو في اللغات الأوروبية.[١] وقد ظلت الحدود بين رواية التاريخ ورواية الحكايات حتى العصر الحديث شديدة الإبهام. وذلك لأنهما يهتمان بالواقع والحياة وإعادة تشكيل ذلك الواقع وتلك الحياة. ويذهب بعض المؤرخين المعاصرين إلى أن نسيج التاريخ يماثل لما نسميه في الأدب بـ«الحبكة»، أي تصميم الوقائع والأحداث وترتيبها وتنظيم الأفعال في النص، سواء كان ذلك في النص التأريخي أو النص الأدبي.[٢]

فالمؤرخ مثل الروائي يقتطع من كليّة الواقع عناصر محددة يربطها معاً وفقاً «للحبكة» التي يختارها. فالأحداث ليست أشياء أو مواد صلبة بل هي تقطيع وتفصيل وانتقاء وحذف وفقاً للإيديولوجيا أو الخطاب الذي يريد أن يستخلصه المؤرخ أو يفرضه على الأحداث. فالماضي إذن – والواقع أيضاً – يجري تحويله من جانب التأريخ مثلما يحدث مع الأدب الروائي فيعاد بناؤه من وجهة نظر ما أو موقف إيديولوجي ما. فالوقائع التاريخية ما هي في الواقع إلا «المادة الخام التي يعمل عليها لإعدادها المؤرخ والروائي على السواء»، مثلهما مثل «المهندس المعماري تتمثل عبقريته في تصميم الواقع وإعادة بنائه».[٣]

ويطرح السؤال نفسه إذن: لماذا يعاد بناء الواقع ولماذا يجري تحويله في كل نص مفرد بقلم مؤرخ أو روائي في روايته للتاريخ أو روايته عن التاريخ؟ وكيف يتحقق ذلك ونحن في الحالتين أمام قصة أو «حبكة»، أمام بنية تعطي معنى للأحداث المختارة؟

إن القصة الرسمية عن التاريخ ووقائعه مرتبطة دائماً بالسلطة وبنظامها وقيمها بشكل عام، سواء كانت قيماً سياسية أو اجتماعية أو ثقافية أو جمالية، فعلاقة الإيديولوجيا بالقص هي علاقة السلطة بالمعرفة. فالسلطة إذن دائماً ما تكون وراء القصة أو بالأحرى وراء «الحبكة».

إن هيمنة القصة/الحبكة الرسمية على المعرفة تضع المؤرخ والأديب معاً في موقع الاختيار والاختبار. إما أن يخضعا لسلطة الحبكة الرسمية فتتطابق روايتهما/حبكتهما معها وتتوافق مع قيمها ورؤاها للواقع والحياة. وإما أن يثورا عليها فيتعارض إنتاجهما للحبكة مع القصة الرسمية. وفي الحالة الأخيرة – حالة التعارض مع القصة الرسمية – تصبح رواية

التاريخ والرواية الأدبية بمثابة خطاب بديل للخطاب الرسمي. ويجد ذلك الخطاب العكسي المناهض لسلطة القص الرسمية نفسه في محاولة دائمة لإعطاء ثغرات الصمت في خطاب السلطة لساناً تنطق به.

وبالنظر إلى مجتمعاتنا العربية نجد أن الحقل الثقافي وإنتاجه لا يزال تابعين للسلطة العربية – أو لنقُل السلطات – السياسية والاجتماعية والدينية. فالقصة الرسمية هي المهيمنة على تمثيل الواقع وحبكته، أي أن الحقل الثقافي لا يزال مفتقداً لاستقلاليته بوصفه حقلاً معرفياً بالمقارنة مع مجتمعات أخرى تحققت فيها تلك الاستقلالية على مستويات متباينة.(٤)

ويجد الكاتب المناهض للقصة الرسمية نفسه، على الرغم من المحاذير والمخاطر، في موقع المواجهة مع سلطة الخطاب الرسمي ليقع عليه عبء أن يصبح «ضمير الأمة» وأن ينتج ذاكرتها الجمعية البديلة.(٥)

ونظراً لهذه العلاقة الملتبسة بين القص والسلطة، الإيديولوجيا والمعرفة في عالمنا العربي على وجه الخصوص، فقد وجدت الرواية العربية نفسها مشتبكة مع القصة الرسمية وحبكتها في غالب الأحيان هاجس مناهضة التاريخ الرسمي هاجساً أساسياً في الكتابة الإبداعية الحديثة، انطلاقاً من أعمال الكاتب الكبير نجيب محفوظ الذي تشكل أعماله مجملة تاريخاً مغايراً لتاريخ مصر الحديث ووصولاً إلى إبداعات «جيل التسعينيات» في مصر (على سبيل المثال) الذي عكف على كتابة الذات المهمشة من قِبَل القصة الرسمية. وأزعم من منظور قراءتي أن غياب الأحداث التاريخية الكبرى عن أعمال التسعينيين والتركيز على الذات وحدها في مواجهتها مع العالم، يعتبر في حد ذاته مناهضة للتأريخ الرسمي الذي يكتب، على حد تعبير الأديبة مي التلمساني، «بمعزل عن المثقف المصري».(٦)

وعلى صعيد آخر، وبحكم التجربة الاستعمارية والهيمنة الإمبريالية والوجود الصهيوني في المنطقة العربية فقد أفرز الأدب العربي الحديث أدباً عربياً آخر ناطقاً بلغات أجنبية عديدة على رأسها الفرنسية والإنجليزية والألمانية والعبرية.(٧) وقد ارتبط هذا الأدب في بادئ الأمر بالوجود الكولونيالي ثم تجاوز ذلك في العقود الأخيرة من القرن العشرين فأصبح مرتبطاً بالشتات والهجرة التي فُرضت فرضاً على كثير من الشعوب العربية خاصة في حالة الشعب الفلسطيني. وهناك المئات من الأدباء في العالم العربي يبدعون أدباً بغير لغتهم الأم. وفي الآونة الأخيرة ازداد حجم الإبداع مزدوج الثقافة من العالم العربي ومناطق أخرى عاشت التجربة الكولونيالية بحيث أصبح ظاهرة عالمية تطلق عليها مسميات مختلفة مثل: «الأدب الهجين» Hybrid Literature أو «الآداب العالمية» World Literature أو «أدب ما بعد الكولونيالية» Postcolonial Literature.

وعلى الرغم من أن حجم هذا الإبداع محدود بالطبع بالنسبة لما يكتب باللغة العربية فهو جدير بالاهتمام والدراسة لأنه في كثير من تجلياته يسهم إسهاماً فعالة في مواجهة الهيمنة الثقافية والسياسية وأحادية الخطاب التي تنفي الآخر وتعمل باستمرار إما على تهميشه أو على عولمته. أي أن هذا الأدب مزدوج الثقافة مواجه هو الآخر بقصة/حبكة رسمية (كولونيالية/إمبريالية) يقوم بزحزحتها وإعادة بنائها.

وبطبيعة الحال فإن العلاقة التي تربط المبدعين العرب مزدوجي الثقافة بالحقل الأدبي في ثقافتهم الأم أو في ثقافتهم المكتسبة تختلف عن ذات العلاقة التي تربط بين معاصريهم في العالم العربي بالحقل الأدبي. وذلك لأن «أدب ما بعد الكولونيالية»، بشكل عام، يتم إنتاجه في حقل ثقافي غربي فاز بالفعل باستقلاليته عن السلطة التي لا تزال تهيمن على الحقل في المجتمعات العربية الأم. وهذا الموقع الجديد الذي يتمتع به الكتّاب مزدوجو الثقافة يمدهم بمساحة واسعة من الحرية في مواجهتهم للحبكة الرسمية سواء كانت تلك التي تتسلط على الثقافة الأم أو تلك التي تسيطر على الثقافة المكتسبة/المضيفة.

وفي واقع الأمر فإن هذه المساحة من الحرية قد تقود المبدعين مزدوجي الثقافة في اتجاهين مختلفين: إما أن يختاروا الانصياع إلى القيم الإبداعية والفنية المهيمنة على حقل الثقافة المكتسبة فينأون بإبداعهم وهواجسه عن الثقافة الأم، وإما أن يقتنصوا مساحة الحرية المتاحة لهم في موقعهم الجديد لإنتاج خطاب بديل يسائل الحبكة الرسمية على الضفتين ويشتبك معها في الثقافة الأم والثقافة المكتسبة في آن.

إلا أن هذا المسلك الأخير محفوف بالمخاطر فهو يضع المبدعين مزدوجي الثقافة «خارج المكان»، في موقع الـ«بين–بين» the in-between حيث تتشكل المواجهة مع الحبكة الرسمية على جبهتين فتصبح المعركة معركتين. وفي الوقت نفسه، ومن منظور أكثر إيجابية، تسمح هذه الكتابة «خارج المكان» للمبدعين بتفكيك ثنائيات الحبكة التقليدية من علاقة الأنا بالآخر، والمستعمِر والمستعمَر، والفردي والجمعي، والموروث والحديث، والقديم والجديد، إلخ. هي نوع من القراءة الجديدة للتاريخ الكولونيالي وما بعد الكولونيالي، قراءة تعتمد في الأساس لا على إسكات الماضي وطمسه وإنما على استنطاقه والكتابة من داخله، قراءة أكثر رحابة وأكثر انفتاحاً وحرية، تقبل وتستوعب الانخلاع متعدد المستويات الذي تفرضه الكتابة من «خارج المكان».

إن هذا الموقع في الكتابة يضع المبدعين مزدوجي الثقافة في منطقة تسمح لهم بالتحرر من الحدود: حدود الهوية القومية، والانتماء القومي بالمفهوم الضيق المُكَبِّل في الإبداع، حدود المكان، حدود اللغة وحدود التعبير. فتصبح الكتابة في الـ«بين–بين» نقطة انطلاق لكيان آخر، كيان هجين، يشتبك مع الاختلاف بدون أحكام مسبقة وبدون كهنوتية.(٨) وفي إطار تلك الكتابة خارج المكان يبدو مفهوم «الثقافة القومية» المتجانسة والمتكاملة مفهوماً يستدعي إعادة النظر والمراجعة. وفي الوقت نفسه تطالب كتابة الـ«بين–بين» بنقد يقف هو الآخر خارج المكان: يستقي أحكامه وآلياته وأدواته لا بالقياس على معايير «الثقافة القومية» وهيمنتها وإنما من منطلقات تتوافق مع موقع الكتابة نفسه.

ومثلما تخلخل الكتابة خارج المكان مفهوم الثقافة القومية المتجانسة الأحادية وتسائله فإنها تضع العالم الكولونيالي في موقع المواجهة مع تاريخه الكولونيالي لا بوصفه تاريخ الآخر المستعمَر وإنما بوصفه تاريخ الذات، أي سرداً داخلياً لا يتجزأ عن صميم قوام هوية المستعمِر نفسه.(٩)

II

وقد اخترت التركيز في هذا المقال على نموذجين لكاتبتين عربيتين تكتبان خارج المكان: آسيا جبار من الجزائر وأهداف سويف من مصر. الأولى تكتب بالفرنسية والثانية بالإنجليزية. آسيا جبار تكتب بين الجزائر وفرنسا وأمريكا حيث تقيم وتعمل الآن، وأهداف سويف تكتب بين مصر وإنجلترا حيث تقيم وتعمل هي الأخرى.

والقارئ للأدب العربي «ما بعد الكولونيالي» يعلم جيداً أن هذين النموذجين من أكثر النماذج تميزاً في هذا الحقل وأن الكاتبتين قد حظيتا بقدر وافر للغاية من الكتابات النقدية سواء بالفرنسية أو بالإنجليزية أو بالعربية حتى بدا أن الكتابة عنهما، خاصة وقد أسهمتُ إسهاماً متواضعاً في قراءة أعمال كل منهما على حدة، ما هي إلا إعادة كتابة.(١٠) ولكنني انتبهت في مراجعتي للكم الضخم من الكتابات النقدية (خاصة في حالة آسيا جبار) إلى أن أحداً لم يجمع بين النموذجين من قبل.

فقد تناول النقاد و(أنا منهم) أعمال كل منهما على حدة في سياق الكتابة عن الأدب المغاربي/الفرانكوفوني بالنسبة لآسيا جبار والأدب المصري/الأنجلوفوني بالنسبة لأهداف سويف. وقد يكون في إصرارنا هذا على تحليل كل نموذج دليلاً قاطعاً على قراءتنا المجزوءة لهذا الإنتاج الإبداعي العربي «ما بعد الكولونيالي». وبدلاً من أن نجمع بينهما في إطار مقارن يمكننا من رسم خارطة عامة للكتابة خارج المكان والتنقيب عن سمات تلك الكتابة وآلياتها بوصفها نموذجاً لزحزحة الحبكة الرسمية في الثقافة الأم والثقافة المضيفة، أَثرنا قراءة محدودة مكبّلة بحدود الثقافة القومية والانتماءات القومية فغابت عنا الصورة الأوسع في قراءة تاريخ الكولونيالية بشكل عام، سواء كان في مغرب العالم العربي أو مشرقه، فرنسياً كان أو إنجليزياً.

وفي واقع الأمر فإن الجمع بين آسيا جبار وأهداف سويف قد أبرز بشكل واضح مجموعة من العناصر والسمات التقنية والإبداعية المتوازية لدى الكاتبتين بحيث تتبدى لنا بعض حفريات الكتابة خارج المكان بشكل عام من هذا الموقع الـ«بين-بين». ومن خلال قراءة مقارنة بين نص **الحب والفانتازيا** (١٩٨٥) لآسيا جبار و**خارطة الحب** (١٩٩٩) لأهداف سويف تتبلور أمام أعيننا محاور المشروع المشترك الذي أقدمت عليه كل من الكاتبتين، مشروع يتسم بالتنقيب والتفكيك والخلخلة لثنائية الأنا والآخر، كما عهدناها في معظم الكتابات عن تلك العلاقة الإشكالية الشائكة.

وقبل الدخول إلى النصين المطروحين أمامنا قد يكون من المفيد محاولة رصد سمات موقع الكاتبتين خارج المكان من خلال تتبع مقارن لمسيرتيهما الحياتية والعملية. أي أننا نبدأ أولاً بالتنقيب عن تاريخ الكتابة «بين-بين».

وعلى الرغم من اختلاف طبيعة التجربة الكولونيالية بين المغرب والمشرق في العالم العربي بالإضافة إلى فارق الجيل وتجربته بين آسيا جبار الجزائرية وأهداف سويف المصرية فإن الكاتبتين تتشابهان في عناصر أساسية في التكوين الأول ستترك بصمتها بُوضوح على إنتاجهما الإبداعي وتطوره فيما بعد.

بادئ ذي بدء نجد أن الكاتبتين تنتميان إلى محيط عائلي، طبقي، ثقافي متشابه؛ فآسيا جبار من طبقة متوسطة عمل والدها مدرساً بالمدارس الفرنسية الكولونيالية بالجزائر حيث كانت تدرس آسيا. وتعلّمت والدتها اللغة الفرنسية أيضاً وارتدت الملابس الأوروبية، أي أن الطفلة عرفت الاختلاف منذ البداية. وبالنظر إلى خلفية أهداف سويف نجدها هي الأخرى من عائلة مصرية ليبرالية مثقفة، سافرت مع أهلها إلى إنجلترا وهي في الرابعة من عمرها ودخلت المدارس الابتدائية في لندن وتعلمت الإنجليزية «كما يتعلمها أطفال الإنجليز»(١١) أي كما تعلمت آسيا اللغة الفرنسية. وتظل علاقة الكاتبتين باللغة الأم أي اللغة العربية علاقة شفاهية (في حالة آسيا جبار)/مؤسساتية (في حالة أهداف سويف). فآسيا تجيد اللهجة الجزائرية من ناحية وتعلمت اللغة العربية الفصحى أثناء أعوامها الأولى في الكتّاب. وعلاقة أهداف سويف باللغة العربية بوصفها اللغة الشفاهية الحياتية الأولى من ناحية ولغة المؤسسة التعليمية من ناحية أخرى لا تختلف كثيراً عن علاقة آسيا جبار باللغة نفسها. وحيث إن القراءات القصصية الأولى للكاتبتين كانت بلغة «الآخر» يصبح التكوين «الأدبي»، «الثقافي» تكويناً أدبياً فرنسياً في حالة آسيا وإنجليزياً في حالة أهداف. وهذا الانغماس شبه الكامل في ثقافة «الآخر» منذ الصغر سيحدد ملامح علاقة الكاتبتين بلغتهما المكتسبة وموروثها الثقافي وتوظيفهما لتلك المعرفة الحميمة في أعمالهما الإبداعية بشكل عام.

وعلى صعيد آخر تتجلى علاقة الكاتبتين باللغة الأم الحياتية/الشفاهية/المؤسساتية في أعمالهما الأدبية من خلال الكمّ الهائل من «الأصوات» ومستويات اللغة المحكية التي تسكن أعمالهما، خاصة الأصوات النسائية منها.

والمتتبع لسيرة آسيا جبار وأهداف سويف يكتشف أن علاقتهما بالتاريخ وتفتّح الوعي السياسي والفكري لديهما متوازيان إلى حد كبير. فالوعي السياسي لدى آسيا يتفتح على لحظة انتفاضة تاريخية في الجزائر هي حرب التحرير (١٩٥٤-١٩٦٢). أما أهداف فيتشكل وعيها من خلال انتكاسة تاريخية هي هزيمة ١٩٦٧. واللحظتان في آخر الأمر، على الرغم من اختلافهما، تشكلان نقطتين على مفترق الطريق: أسئلة الهوية والانتماء القومي ورؤية الماضي والمستقبل.

وستتمكن الكاتبتان من اقتفاء آثار هذه الأسئلة بشكل مكثّف من خلال العمل الإبداعي بحكم تكوينهما العملي: فآسيا جبار قد درست التاريخ في فرنسا ثم عملت أستاذة للتاريخ في جامعة الرباط بالمغرب وجامعة الجزائر بعد الاستقلال في ١٩٦٢. وأهداف سويف حاصلة على دكتوراه في علم اللسانيات من إنجلترا ثم عملت أستاذة للأدب الإنجليزي بجامعة القاهرة (١٩٧١-١٩٨٤) وجامعة الملك سعود بالرياض (١٩٨٧-١٩٨٩). وعلاوة على هذا المشترك الأكاديمي لدى الكاتبتين فقد عملت الاثنتان بمجال الصحافة والكتابة الصحفية والترجمة، حيث ترجمت آسيا جبار رواية نوال السعداوي **امرأة عند نقطة الصفر** من العربية إلى الفرنسية في ١٩٨١، وترجمت أهداف سويف نص مريد البرغوثي **رأيت رام الله** من العربية إلى الإنجليزية في ٢٠٠٠. فليس بالغريب إذن أن تطغى النزعة البحثية، التنقيبية، الأنثروبولوجية (في كثير من الأحيان) على أعمال هاتين الروائيتين.

وفيما يخص التاريخ الإبداعي للكاتبتين تنشر آسيا جبار روايتها الأولى **العطش** La soif عام ١٩٥٧ في باريس وتصدر لأهداف سويف مجموعتها القصصية الأولى بالإنجليزية **عائشة** Aisha عام ١٩٨٣ في لندن. وعلى الرغم من عدد السنوات التي تفصل بين الحدثين سنجد أن استقبال العملين والكاتبتين في الثقافة المضيفة ينم عن دلالات في غاية الأهمية فيما يخص الكتابة خارج المكان. منذ اللحظة الأولى يحظى العملان الإبداعيان بترحاب واسع، لكنه ترحاب ينبئ بتشكّل موقع ملتبس للكاتبتين في الثقافة المضيفة: فآسيا توصف بأنها فرانسواز ساجون Françoise Sagan جديدة.(١٢) أما أهداف فتُشبَّه قصصها الحديثة بـ«حكايات شهرزاد»،(١٣) أي أنه في كلتا الحالتين تُطمس هوية الكاتبة الفردية وعلاقتها بتاريخها المعاصر ومساهمتها الأدبية بوصفها مبدعة معاصرة.

وتتسم الأعمال الأولى لآسيا وأهداف بنوع من البراءة. إنها أعمال «الطفولة» الإبداعية، على حد تعبير أهداف سويف،(١٤) أي أنها أعمال يغيب عنها بشكل ملحوظ الوعي السياسي والتاريخي الذي يصبح السمة الرئيسية في أعمال الكاتبتين اللاحقة، وعي يفجره إدراك لاحق على براءة الأعمال الأولى بخطورة موقع الكتابة خارج المكان مصحوب بفهم ناضج لعلاقة الكاتبة بالتاريخي والسياسي، الشخصي منه والجمعي. فتؤكد أهداف سويف، على سبيل المثال، أن انخلاعها الجغرافي قد يكون ملهمها في المواضيع التي تتناولها في رواياتها، حيث فرض عليها الوجود خارج الوطن التفكير في أسئلة الهوية الفردية والجمعية، التاريخ الفردي والجمعي.(١٥) ومن المنطلق نفسه نجد النقد الأدبي يقرأ أعمال آسيا جبار منذ العقد الثمانيني من القرن العشرين بوصفها أعمالاً موغلة، بشكل موجع، أحياناً، في التنقيب.(١٦)

ومثلما يتبلور إدراك الكاتبتين بموقعيهما خارج المكان يتبلور أيضاً وعيهما بتفعيل الكتابة بلغة الآخر. فهناك الاكتشاف الأول بأن الكتابة بلغة الآخر قد تعطي مساحة أوسع من الحرية وتسمح بمستويات من البوح لن تسمح بها اللغة الأم خاصة في سياق كتابة المرأة. ولكن هذا المستوى الأول من الحرية سريعاً ما يصبح أكثر تركيباً. فلغة الآخر يمكن تطويعها في مساحات جديدة للمواجهة وللمساءلة سواء مع الذات أو مع الآخر.

III

يمثل نصا **الحب والفانتازيا** لآسيا جبار(١٧) و**خارطة الحب** لأهداف سويف(١٨) فترة النضج عند الروائيتين. ويحتل كلٌّ من النصين موقعاً خاصاً في السياق الإبداعي العام للكاتبتين. فنص **الحب والفانتازيا** هو الجزء الأول من رباعية روائية ملحمية تتشابك فيها خيوط السيرة الذاتية بالسيرة الجمعية.(١٩) ويأتي هذا النص بعد حوالي ثمانية عشر عاماً على صدور آخر روايات المرحلة الأولى عام ١٩٦٧.(٢٠) وتعتبر هذه الفترة الطويلة مرحلة انتقالية في علاقة آسيا جبار بالكتابة بلغة الآخر. فهي تعلن بعد استقلال الجزائر أنها لن تكتب بالفرنسية بعد ذلك. ثم تتجه إلى الأفلام التسجيلية عوضاً عن الكتابة مسجلة من خلال الفيلم الأول

شهادات النساء الجزائريات أثناء حرب الاستقلال ومن خلال الفيلم الثاني تاريخ المغرب خلال فترة ١٩١٢-١٩٤٢،(٢١) أي أن فترة «الصمت» التي تفصل بين روايات آسيا جبار هي في الواقع فترة تنقيب وتأريخ مرتبطة بشكل واضح بعملها كمؤرخة داخل الأكاديمية وبأسئلة الهوية التي تفجرها لحظة الاستقلال وما بعدها من «ردّة» سياسية واجتماعية واقتصادية وثقافية في الجزائر. فتعود آسيا مرة أخرى إلى فرنسا وإلى الكتابة بالفرنسية.

ونص **خارطة الحب** عند أهداف سويف له هو الآخر موقع مهم في مسيرتها الإبداعية. فهي الرواية الطويلة الثانية بعد روايتها الأولى **في عين الشمس** (١٩٩٢)، يفصل بينهما حوالي ست سنوات قد تعتبر فترة مراجعة على عدة مستويات، من أهمها محاولة الربط بين الذاتي والجمعي، الحاضر والماضي. تقول أهداف عن هذه النقلة النوعية في الكتابة:«لا أتصور أن الهم الأساسي في **في عين الشمس** هو الشرق والغرب أو الأنا والآخر. أتصور أنها رواية تعالج أساساً مسألة نضج فتاة/امرأة. . . . أما **خارطة الحب** فهي تعالج إشكالية الشرق/الغرب بشكل مباشر».(٢٢)

وتصبح إذن رواية **خارطة الحب** هي ردها على السؤال الذي تطرحه على نفسها: «أين نحن من التاريخ؟ ما الذي تغير؟ وما الذي ظل على حاله؟»(٢٣)

في **الحب والفانتازيا** تتضافر مقاطع السيرة الذاتية الشعرية مع تاريخ احتلال الجزائر من خلال مجموعة شهادات ورسائل، مكتوبة وشفاهية، قديمة ومعاصرة، للجنود الفرنسيين والنساء الجزائريات، بالفرنسية وبالعربية، بالفصحى وبالعامية، كلها منقولة ومترجمة على يد الراوية مجهولة الاسم.

وفي عنوان النص إشارة واضحة إلى موسيقيته. فالفانتازيا نوع من التأليف الموسيقي يطلق العنان للخيال ويغلّبه على متطلبات الشكل التقليدي. وفي العنوان مستوى آخر من الدلالة يشير إلى تقليد قديم لدى قبائل البربر يستعرض فيه الفرسان مهاراتهم على الخيل مصحوبة بطلقات نارية من بنادقهم والتقليد مرتبط تاريخياً بلحظات النصر العسكري والفخر القبائلي.

وتلجأ **خارطة الحب** إلى استراتيجيات موازية للسرد المركب. فهذه الرواية أيضاً تبدأ في الحاضر (عام ١٩٩٧) ثم تعود بالقارئ حوالي قرن من الزمان في تاريخ مصر وتستمر في تضفير الحاضر بالماضي من خلال صندوق أوراق الليدي آنا ونتربورن (التي كانت قد جاءت إلى مصر مع مطلع القرن العشرين وتزوجت من شريف باشا البارودي، أحد رموز الحركة الوطنية المصرية في الرواية)، ذلك الصندوق الذي عثرت عليه حفيدتها الكبرى، الأمريكية إيزابيل بركمان، في آخر القرن العشرين، فحملته معها إلى القاهرة حيث قبعت على فك طلاسم أوراقه مع أمل (أخت خطيبها المصري-الفلسطيني، عمر الغسراوي، المقيم بنيويورك) التي تؤدي دوراً محورياً في النص للربط بين الحاضر والماضي. وكما في نص **الحب والفانتازيا** يجد القارئ نفسه في رواية **خارطة الحب** أمام تجربة إبداعية تشحن ألواناً متعددة وشديدة التميز من تقنيات البنية الروائية وتطويع اللغة الإنجليزية وتطعيم النص باللغة العربية مترجمة الفصحى منها والعامية. فتتدرج اللغة الإنجليزية في النص من إنجليزية أدبية (خطابات الليدي آنا ومذكراتها) تحاكي تراث كتابة رحلات الاستشراق في القرن التاسع

عشر إلى إنجليزية أمريكية معاصرة؛ ومن لغة عربية فصحى مترجمة (مذكرات ليلى البارودي) إلى لهجة مصرية عامية منسوخة بالحروف اللاتينية أحياناً ومترجمة إلى الإنجليزية (المعرّبة/الحرفية) في أحيان أخرى حتى تكاد اللغة العربية بمستوياتها المتعددة تشف أمام القارئ من خلال النص المكتوب بالإنجليزية.

وفي النصين تذهب الكاتبتان إلى إعادة قراءة حوالي قرن من الزمان وإعادة كتابته: العقد الثالث من القرن التاسع عشر حتى أواخر القرن العشرين، سواء في الجزائر أو في مصر، حيث يبدأ بتاريخ الكولونيالية الفرنسية وسقوط الجزائر عام ١٨٣٠ في المغرب العربي وتاريخ الاحتلال الإنجليزي في مصر في أواخر القرن التاسع عشر وينتهي الإطار التاريخي للروايتين في فترة ما بعد الاستقلال في الجزائر ومصر وصعود المدّ الثوري ثم انتكاسه وتردّي الحلم القومي وتمادي قمع الأنظمة السلطوية وتبعيتها للإمبريالية الأمريكية المهيمنة على النظام العالمي الجديد. ومن خلال التوازي الذي يخلقه النصان بين الماضي والحاضر، الكولونيالية الفرنسية/الإنجليزية والإمبريالية الأمريكية والغطرسة والاستكبار في حكم الشعوب واستلاب حقوق المواطنة من قِبَل السلطة «الشرعية» الحاكمة بين منتصف القرن التاسع عشر وحتى أواخر القرن العشرين (في الروايتين) تتوجه الكاتبتان إلى القارئ الغربي والعربي في آن لتحكيا له «حكايتنا معهم من وجهة نظرنا نحن».(٢٤) ويتبدى للقارئ فجأة بعد دورته في هذا الإطار التاريخي أنه يدور في حلقة تاريخية مفرغة؛ ففي نص **الحب والفانتازيا** تصبح صيحات «الفانتازيا» القبائلية المنتصرة هي صيحات الموت. وينتهي النص على «عزف ناي [حزين]»، مقطع أخير تتنبأ فيه الراوية مجهولة الاسم «باللحظة القادمة لا محالة حين تدعس حوافر الخيل [خيل فرسان الفانتازيا] كل امرأة تجرؤ على الوقوف حرة».(٢٥) وفي مقابل هذه النبوءة عند آسيا جبار نرى أمل – قارئة الماضي والحاضر في **خارطة الحب** – تقذف بالصحيفة اليومية في سلة الأوراق المهملة بعد أن أدارت شريط التاريخ في رأسها دورة كاملة على مدار مائة عام:

مونيكا لوينسكي وفستانها الأزرق تشغل صفحتين، لا يجب تقسيم السودان – كلينتون يقسم أن تنتقم أمريكا من بن لادن، أولبرايت تهدد بضرب العراق – التعذيب في سجون فلسطين.

[...]

كتبت أنا منذ مائة عام: لا أجد مفراً من الاقتناع بأننا نعيش في عصر فظيع الوحشية – ونحن لا نملك إلا – تدخل أمل التغيير الطفيف – الانتظار إلى أن يدور التاريخ دورته.(٢٦)

وينزع النصان إلى رؤية شبه دائرية للتاريخ. ففي كلتا الحالتين لا يتوقف النص عند المرحلة الكولونيالية وإنما يتعمد الخوض في ما بعد «رحيل» المستعمِر عن المغرب والمشرق. ومن خلال هذه الدورة الطويلة تستطيع الكاتبتان استكمال معالم الصورة من خلال الربط بين الماضي والحاضر وعلاقتهما الجدلية في تكوين الذات والآخر.

وفي النصين تختار الكاتبتان أن تقرأ الماضي من منظور الحاضر، أي أن الشخصية التي يعهد إليها بالسرد في النصين شخصية معاصرة، موقعها موقع الشاهدة والقارئة، المنسقة والمرتبة لمجموع الأوراق والشهادات – التاريخية منها أو المعاصرة – التي تطرحها أمام القارئ. والشخصيتان (شخصية الراوية مجهولة الاسم في **الحب والفانتازيا** وشخصية أمل في **خارطة الحب**) متوازيتان من حيث السن (منتصف العمر) والتجربة العملية (الحياة بين الشرق والغرب) والتجربة الشخصية (الانفصال عن الدائرة العائلية) والتجربة الاجتماعية (التواصل مع قطاعات أعرض من المجتمع) والتجربة الروائية (موقف الناظر إلى الحدث لا المشارك فيه). وكل هذه الاختيارات عند جبار وسويف تمكنهما من إعادة قراءة التاريخ وكتابته من منظور جديد يطرح علينا «حبكة» جديدة تتعارض مع الحبكة الرسمية سواء كانت من «عندنا» أو من «عندهم». لذا لا يمكن قراءة هاتين الروايتين بوصفهما روايات تاريخية بالمعنى التقليدي للمصطلح وإنما يجب قراءتهما بوصفهما نصوصاً تعيد قراءة الرواية التاريخية الرسمية من منظور معاصر يتميز في الحالتين بأنه خارج الزمان وخارج المكان.

واللافت للنظر عند الروائيتين أنهما تلجآن إلى الآليات نفسها في صياغة تلك «الحبكة» المعارضة للحبكة الرسمية. فالنصان يدخلان إلى التاريخي من الأبواب الخلفية، أي أن الكاتبتين تستدعيان وتستنطقان نصوصاً غير «رسمية» استُبعدت من قِبَل الحبكة الرسمية. ففي **الحب والفانتازيا** تعكف الراوية مجهولة الاسم على البحث في مجلّدات مرصوصة على أرفف المكتبات في صمت وقد تراكم عليها التراب، تقرأ مراسلات الجنود الفرنسيين من القرن التاسع عشر وشهود العيان المنسيين والمقالات والمذكرات المكتوبة بالفرنسية والعربية. وتصف الراوية فعلها هذا بالصورة الآتية: «أنسلّ إلى الغرفة الخارجية the antechamber لهذا الماضي القريب كالزائر المتطفل. أخلع نعلي، كما هو التقليد، أحبس أنفاسي، أتصنت على كل شيء . . .»(٢٧)

والغرفة الخارجية التي توظفها آسيا في وصفها لعلاقة الراوية بالمادة التاريخية هي، في السياق المعماري، غرفة صغيرة تؤدي إلى الغرفة الكبيرة الأساسية. ونحن القراء ننفذ معها من هذه الإطلالة على الرسائل والشهادات والمذكرات المنسية إلى غرفة التاريخ الكبرى.

أما أمل في **خارطة الحب** فتنفذ إلى أوراق الماضي من خلال صندوق، صندوق الليدي آنا ونتربورن:

تبدأ القصص من أغرب الأشياء: مصباح سحري، نتفة من حديث وقع على الأذن، خيال يتحرك على حائط. أما قصتنا هذه فتبدأ بصندوق، صندوق قديم من الجلد البني جف وتشقق . . . .(٢٨)

[...]

هذه ليست قصتي، هذه قصة وجدتها في صندوق. صندوق جلدي قديم، جاء من لندن إلى القاهرة، ثم عاد وسكن سندرة منزل في نيويورك لسنوات قبل أن يجد طريقه مرة أخرى إلى القاهرة فيستقر على أرض غرفة معيشتي في يوم من أيام الربيع عام ١٩٩٧.(٢٩)

وتعكف أمل في النص على ترتيب أوراق الصندوق «صندوق من العجائب كأنه كنز»،(٣٠) لتساعد الأمريكية إيزابيل باركمان في فك طلاسم أوراقه لأن الأخيرة تدرك أن «جزءاً من تاريخها موجود بهذا الصندوق»، «جزء من قصة أكبر».(٣١)

صحيح أن نص **الحب والفانتازيا** يعتمد في الأساس على نصوص وثائقية تاريخية بينما تعتمد أهداف سويف على تضمين التاريخي داخل نصوص وثائقية متخيلة (أي أن الكاتبة الروائية تقوم بخلقها محاكاة أنماطاً تاريخية من الكتابة مثل رسائل المستشرقين وكتب رحلاتهم في الشرق) إلا أن الكاتبتين تتوحدان في رؤيتهما للتاريخ: فالتاريخ في النصين يُكتب لا من خلال الأحداث الكبرى وإنما من خلال ما قد استبعد منها: تاريخ أفراد مجهولين وعلاقاتهم الإنسانية ورؤيتهم للحظة التاريخية التي يسكنونها. والتاريخ في النصين ليس تاريخ تسلسل الأحداث وإنما هو تاريخ يكتب من خلال استقراء التقابل والتقاطع بين الوثائق والترادف والتجاور بين المذكرات والشهادات الموظفة في النص سواء كانت مكتوبة أو شفاهية، تاريخية أو متخيلة، قديمة أو معاصرة، فرنسية أو إنجليزية أو عربية. وينأى النصان عن أنماط التأريخ الرسمي بكل مستوياته ويطلقان العنان للراويتين في التخييل والتخيل: تنقبان في الأوراق والوثائق، تستنطقان لحظات الصمت فيها وتملآن الفراغات لتصوغا رواية مغايرة عن التاريخ. يغدو التاريخ إذن لا بوصفه نسقاً متسقاً، إنما فهماً للماضي قائماً على التراكم الشخصي والعلاقة الجدلية بين الماضي والحاضر، الفردي والجمعي.

ومثلما تتقاطع الوثائق والمذكرات والأصوات في النصين تتقاطع أيضاً مستويات توظيف اللغة وتقابل. ومن خلال كل هذا الزخم الوثائقي في النصين وتعددية الأصوات الشاهدة على الماضي والحاضر في آن تُكتب الذات، ذات الراوية مجهولة الاسم في **الحب والفانتازيا** وذات أمل قارئة أوراق صندوق الليدي آنا ونتربورن ومترجمتها ومنسقتها في **خارطة الحب**: ذات هجينة تاريخها الحاضر يستحيل فك طلاسمه إلا من خلال إعادة قراءة أوراق الماضي التي تتضافر، على مستوى بنية الروايتين، مع السيرة الذاتية للشخصية الممسكة بزمام التنقيب والسرد في النصين.

وفي ظل كل هذا التنقيب والتأريخ تطرح أهداف سويف سؤالاً محورياً: «ما هي إمكانية اللقاء الحقيقي عبر الحضارات؟ وما هي المساحة التي يسمح بها التاريخ والسياسة والمجتمع للحياة الفردية والعلاقات الشخصية؟»(٣٢) وفي اعتقادي أن الإجابة عن هذا السؤال قد تكمن في عنواني الروايتين. فالحب قاسم مشترك بينهما. وفي واقع الأمر فإن الحب في النصين يتجلى على عدة مستويات على الرغم من التاريخ الدموي العنيف الذي تؤرخ له الكاتبتان. ففي نص **الحب والفانتازيا** يهيمن الحب على الكلمة المكتوبة في النص: هناك أول خطاب حب يصل إلى الراوية ليقع في يد الأب وينتهي في سلة مهملات، تلتقطه يدها وتجمع أجزاء المقطوعة وتعيد قراءته. وهناك خطابات الجنود الفرنسيين المحتلين الذين وقعوا في حب الجزائر، البلد التي استباحوها لأنفسهم، وهناك خطابات الحب التي ترسلها وتتلقاها شابات جزائريات معزولات داخل الحريم، ثم خطاب «الحب» الذي يرسل به الأب إلى أم الراوية. وعلى صعيد آخر تتقابل كلمات «الحب» التي تنطق بها الفتاة الفرنسية، جارة الراوية، لتدليل خطيبها، مع كلمات التدليل العربية التي تستخدمها النساء الجزائريات بينهن.

وفي المقابل نجد أن تاريخ مصر الحديث في **خارطة الحب** مكتوب من خلال خطابات ومذكرات شخصيات إنجليزية ومصرية بالإنجليزية وبالعربية أفرزتها قصص حب بين أبطال الرواية. فـ**خارطة الحب** تتناول التاريخ الكولونيالي وما بعد الكولونيالي من خلال قصتي حب متداخلتين، أبطالهما من الشرق والغرب: واحدة في مقتبل القرن العشرين (بين ليدي آنا وشريف باشا البارودي) والثانية في آخره (بين إيزابيل باركمان وعمر الغمراوي). وتستهل الكاتبة نصها بشجرة للعائلة تتتبّع من خلالها النسب الهجين الذي يربط بين الليدي آنا وأمل وإيزابيل على مدار قرن وفي ثلاث قارات.

هل من باب المصادفة إذن أن يحمل عنوانا الروايتين كلمة «حب» ونراها توظف توظيفاً مركباً عند هاتين الكاتبتين اللتين تكتبان من خارج المكان؟ أم أن هذه الرؤية المطروحة تطمح إلى استكشاف معالم جديدة، «حبكة» جديدة في إمكانيات كتابة اللقاء عبر الحضارات؟ هاجس مؤرق ومشروع محفوف بالمخاطر؛ فالموقع الذي تسكنه الكاتبتان، موقع «البين–بين»، ليس متاحاً للجميع بل هو موقع استثنائي مرتبط في الأساس بسيرتهما الشخصية وتكوينهما العملي ووجودهما، في آخر الأمر، خارج المكان، تلك المساحة التي استكشفها وسكنها وحدد معالمها الراحل الكبير إدوارد سعيد:

بين الحين والحين أحس أنني لفيف من التيارات المتدفقة. أؤثر هذه الفكرة عن نفسي على فكرة الذات الراسخة: فكرة الهوية التي يتمسك بها الكثيرون . . . إنه ضرب من ضروب الحرية كما يحلو لي أن أتصور على الرغم من أنني لست مقتنعاً تماماً بذلك. هذا التشكيك في الثوابت التي أتشبث بها. ومن خلال حياتي المليئة بالأصوات المتنافرة تعلمت أن أؤثر ألا أكون سوياً تماماً وأن أظل خارج المكان.(٣٣)

الهوامش

(١) لمناقشة وافية عن العلاقة بين رواية التاريخ والرواية الأدبية، انظر على سبيل المثال: Samia Mehrez, *Egyptian Writers between History and Fiction: Essays on Naguib Mahfouz, Sonallah Ibrahim and Gamal al-Ghitani* (Cairo: AUC Press, 1993).

(٢) انظر: إبراهيم فتحي، «الرواية المصرية والتاريخ: الوقائع لا تتحدث عن نفسها»، **أخبار الأدب** (١٠ أبريل ١٩٩٤)، ص١٠. والمقال قراءة مكثفة ووافية للأفكار المطروحة في المرجع السابق لسامية محرز.

(٣) **المرجع السابق**.

(٤) لقراءة وافية عن الحقل الأدبي في مصر وعلاقته بالحقل السياسي انظر: ريشار جاكمون، **بين كتبة وكُتّاب**، ترجمة بشير السباعي (القاهرة: دار المستقبل العربي، ٢٠٠٤)؛ ومحمد برادة، «الأدبي والسياسي: جدلية معاقة»، **لطيفة الزيات: الأدب والوطن**، تحرير سيد البحراوي

(القاهرة: نور، دار المرأة العربية ومركز البحوث العربية، ١٩٩٦)، ص ص ٣٩-٤٩.

(٥) انظر كلاً من: ريشار جاكمون، **بين كتبة وكُتّاب**؛ و
Samia Mehrez, *Egyptian Writers between History and Fiction.*

(٦) مي التلمساني، «الكتابة على هامش التاريخ: مصر-الغياب»، **لطيفة الزيات: الأدب والوطن**، ص ص ٩٧-١٠٦.

(٧) على سبيل المثال خصصت **ألف: مجلة البلاغة المقارنة** عدداً من أعدادها لموضوع «النص الإبداعي ذو الهوية المزدوجة: مبدعون عرب يكتبون بلغات أجنبية»، العدد العشرون (٢٠٠٠).

(٨) لمناقشة وافية حول موقع الكاتب والكتابة «بين-بين» انظر: هومي ك. بابا، **موقع الثقافة**، ترجمة ثائر ديب (القاهرة: المجلس الأعلى للثقافة، ٢٠٠٤).

(٩) **المرجع السابق**، ص ص ٥٠-٥١.

(١٠) انظر:

Samia Mehrez, "The Subversive Poetics of Radical Bilingualism," *The Bounds of Race*, ed. Dominick Lacapra (Ithaca: Cornell UP, 1991), 255-77; "Translation and the Post-Colonial Experience," *Rethinking Translation: Discourse, Subjectivity, Ideology*, ed. Lawrence Venuti (London: Routledge, 1992), 120-38.

وانظر: سامية محرز، «خارطة الكتابة: حوار مع أهداف سويف»، **ألف: مجلة البلاغة المقارنة** ٢٠ (٢٠٠٠)، ص ص ١٦٨-١٨١.

(١١) سامية محرز، «خارطة الكتابة: حوار مع أهداف سويف»، ص ١٧٥.

(١٢) انظر: العدد الخاص من *World Literature Today* عن آسيا جبار بمناسبة منحها جائزة نوستاد العالمية للأدب عام ١٩٩٦؛ وعلى وجه الخصوص:
Evelyne Accad, "Assia Djebar's Contribution to Arab Women's Literature: Rebellion, Maturity, Vision," *World Literature Today* (Autumn 1996): 801-12.

(١٣) هكذا وصفت أهداف سويف استقبال عملها الأول *Aisha* **عائشة** (١٩٨٣) في الأوساط الثقافية الإنجليزية أثناء محاضرة ألقتها حول مجمل أعمالها في الجامعة الأمريكية بالقاهرة، ٢٢ أكتوبر، ٢٠٠١.

(١٤) **المرجع السابق**.

(١٥) سامية محرز، «خارطة الكتابة: حوار مع أهداف سويف»، ص ١٧٩.

(١٦) انظر:

Winifred Woodhull, *Transfigurations of the Maghreb: Feminism, Decolonization, and Literatures* (Minneapolis: University of Minnesota Press, 1993), 81.

(١٧) انظر:

Assia Djebar, *L'amour, la fantasia* (Paris: Jean-Claude Lattès, 1985; reédi-tion Paris: Albin Michel, 1995); English translation: *Fantasia: An Algerian Cavalcade*, trans. Dorothy S. Blair (Portsmouth, NH: Heinemann, 1993).

(١٨) انظر:

Ahdaf Soueif, *The Map of Love* (London: Bloomsbury, 1999).

والترجمة العربية: أهداف سويف، **خارطة الحب**، ترجمة فاطمة موسى (القاهرة: الهيئة العامة للكتاب، ٢٠٠١). الاقتباس في هذا المقال مأخوذ عن نص الترجمة العربية.

(١٩) الأجزاء الثلاثة الأخرى من رباعية آسيا جبار صدرت بالفرنسية كالآتي:

Assia Djebar, *Ombre sultane* (Paris: Jean-Claude Lattès, 1987) [*A Sister to Scheherazade*, trans. Dorothy S. Blair (London: Quartet Books, 1989)]; *Loin de Médine: Filles d'Ismaël* (Paris: Albin Michel, 1991) [*Far from Madina*, translated from the French (London: Quartet Books, 1994)]; *Vaste est la prison* (Paris: Albin Michel, 1995) [*So Vast the Prison*, trans. Betsy Wing (New York: Seven Stories Press, 1999)].

(٢٠) المرحلة الأولى من روايات آسيا جبار تتضمن:

Assia Djebar, *La soif* (Paris: Julliard, 1957) [*The Mischief*, trans. Frances Frenaye (New York: Simon and Schuster, 1958)]; *Les impatients* [*The Impatients*] (Paris: Julliard, 1958); *Les enfants du nouveau monde* [*Children of the New World*] (Paris: Julliard, 1962); *Les alouettes naïves* [*The Naïve Larks*] (Paris: Julliard, 1962; reédition 1967).

(٢١) الفيلم التسجيلي الأول لآسيا جبار عنوانه *La Nouba des femmes du mont Chenoua*. أخرجته عام ١٩٧٧ ونالت عنه جائزة النقاد العالمية في مهرجان فينيسيا عام ١٩٧٩. أما الفيلم الثاني فعنوانه *La Zerda et les chants de l'oubli* وأخرجته عام ١٩٨٢.

(٢٢) سامية محرز، «خارطة الكتابة: حوار مع أهداف سويف»، ص ١٧٧.

(٢٣) **المرجع السابق**، ص ١٨٠.

(٢٤) **المرجع السابق**، ص ١٧٦.

(٢٥) انظر:

Assia Djebar, *L'amour, la fantasia*, 226.

(٢٦) أهداف سويف، **خارطة الحب**، ص ٤٥٧.

(٢٧) انظر:

Assia Djebar, *L'amour, la fantasia*, 8.

(٢٨) أهداف سويف، **خارطة الحب**، ص ١٥.

(٢٩) **المرجع السابق**، ص ١٩.

(٣٠) **المرجع السابق**، ص ١٤.

(٣١) **المرجع السابق**، ص ١٥.

(٣٢) سامية محرز، «خارطة الكتابة: حوار مع أهداف سويف»، ص ١٨٠.

(٣٣) إدوارد سعيد، **خارج المكان**، ترجمة فواز طرابلسي (بيروت: دار الآداب، ٢٠٠٠)، ص ٣٥٩. الاقتباس في المقال من الترجمة العربية بتصرف بسيط.

ذاكرة الأ(د)ب في «ذاكرة الجسد»

فريال جبوري غزّول

التلقي المتباين للرواية

شكّلت رواية أحلام مستغانمي[1] الأولى، **ذاكرة الجسد**، ظاهرة لم يسبق لها مثيل في مجال الرواية العربية الحديثة. فبعد أن نشرت دار الآداب اللبنانية الطبعة الأولى منها في عام ١٩٩٣، ونشرتها دار موفم للنشر الجزائرية في العام نفسه، تبعتها طبعات متتالية تقترب من خمس عشرة طبعة، وقد تجاوزت مبيعات هذه الرواية خمسين ألف نسخة،[2] هذا على الرغم من سوء توزيع الكتاب في العالم العربي وعزوف المواطنين العاديين عن القراءة عامةً، وعن اقتناء الكتاب الأدبي خاصة. فما تكاد هذه الرواية تأخذ مكانها على رفوف مكتبات البيع حتى تتخاطفها أيدي المشترين، مع العلم أن أعمالاً روائية متميزة لا تبيع في أحسن الأحوال أكثر من ثلاثة آلاف نسخة، مع أن مؤلفيها نجوم في حقل الرواية العربية.

ومن اللافت إزاء جماهيرية هذه الرواية اختلاف النقاد حولها اختلافاً بيناً، فمنهم من لم يكتف بالانصراف عنها فقرر إدانتها لاعتبارات كثيراً ما كانت خارجة عن موازين النقد ومعاييره. وهناك من فتنوا بها وأشادوا بقيمتها. ولعبت الصحافة دوراً في الانتقاص من قيمة هذا النجاح الهائل، فزعم البعض أن مستغانمي انتحلت هذا العمل، ولكن اختلفوا فيمن يكون صاحبه الأصلي (وهذا الزعم في ذاته يشير إلى التفوق الأدبي الذي لا يمكن في نظر البعض أن تتميز به روائية ناشئة). فمرة يشار إلى الشاعر العراقي سعدي يوسف ومرة أخرى إلى الشاعر السوري نزار قباني، ومرة ثالثة إلى الروائي الجزائري واسيني الأعرج (ربما لأنه أيضاً يكتب الرواية الشعرية مثل مستغانمي)، ومرة رابعة إلى الروائي السوري حيدر حيدر، إلخ. فعوضاً عن الابتهاج بعمل أدبي يقبل القراء عليه، تسابقت الأقلام في استدعاء آباء غير شرعيين لهذه الرواية، وأطلق البعض عليها «الكتابة بالجسد» عوضاً عن «**ذاكرة الجسد**»، مما يتجاوز التلويح بالتزييف إلى التشهير بالكاتبة نفسها. وأما أحلام مستغانمي فقد تعالت على هذا الاغتياب الرخيص، وأطلقت على هذه الكتابات ذات الطابع النميمي التي تدور حول **ذاكرة الجسد** تعبير «ذاكرة الحسد»، وطالبت بنقد أمين يصحح ويقيم ولا ينحدر إلى مستوى الترهات، فلا مانع عندها من أن يكون لها خصوم على شرط أن يكونوا شرفاء.[3]

ومع أن هذه الإشاعات المغرضة حول رواية **ذاكرة الجسد** قد تمّ تكذيبها، فقد

استمرت الصحف في التنديد بكاتبتنا مستغانمي، مستكثرين عليها النجاح والتقدير. فقد كذّب سعدي يوسف ما قيل عن دوره في كتابة هذه الرواية وذكر بالنص «الخبر غير صحيح وهو إساءة إلى أحلام وإليّ»،[٤] كما امتدح واسيني الأعرج أحلام مستغانمي باعتبارها «ظاهرة تستحق التأمل والقراءة».[٥] وقد نفى سهيل إدريس صاحب دار الآداب بشكل قاطع أي دور لنزار قباني في كتابة ذاكرة الجسد في مقالة في جريدة الحياة. وفي شهادة أخرى له عن الموضوع، ذكر كيف أنه حدّث نزار قباني عن رواية ذاكرة الجسد وأهداه نسخة منها، بعد أن رفضت المؤلفة أن تفعل ذلك منعاً للحرج، فشغف قباني بها وعكف على قراءتها وكتب كلمة على غلاف طبعتها الثالثة.[٦] وقد قام الناقد رجاء النقاش بتحليل رواية حيدر حيدر وليمة لأعشاب البحر[٧] من جانب ورواية ذاكرة الجسد من جانب آخر ليجد تشابهاً مفرطاً يوحي له بأن مستغانمي نقلت عن حيدر حيدر وسرقت من روايته.[٨] فهو يرى تناظراً بين العملين وإن كان يقرّ بأن ذاكرة الجسد تتفوق أدبياً على سابقتها وليمة لأعشاب البحر. والتفوق في الأسلوب، حسب رأيه، لا ينفي الاقتباس لأن التيمات تتشابه إلى درجة عدم إمكان ورودها إلا من باب استعارة من نص سابق. ويعطي النقاش عشرة أدلة على ذلك، أولها تشابه الخلفية العامة للروايتين وآخرها تشابه شكلي، ففي كليهما يحمل البطل اسم خالد. ولكن خالد – كما هو معروف – اسم دارج في الوطن العربي، فوروده في أكثر من رواية ليس بدليل على الإطلاق على سرقة، بل بالعكس لو كانت هناك سرقة فعلاً أدبية ما فالأولى بالسارق أن يخفي فعلته باستخدام اسم آخر. وأما التشابه في الخلفية العامة وفي وصف ما يجري في الجزائر من تفسخ القيم الثورية، فهذا بدوره لا يعني على الإطلاق نقل رواية عن أخرى، وإنما يعني أن المرجع العيني واحد، ألا وهو الواقع الجزائري. فتماثل الروايتين كما يقدمه النقاش بدقته، وبما يطلق عليه «أدلة وبراهين»، لا يعني أخذ الرواية اللاحقة عن الرواية السابقة، بقدر ما يعني تدهور الوضع الإنساني في الجزائر الذي نعرفه جميعاً، والذي يجعل الروايات المكتوبة عنه تتماثله. ولو راجعنا روايات أخرى عن الجزائر المعاصرة لوجدنا هذا التشابه أيضاً على مستوى الأجواء والأحداث، وهذا أمر طبيعي. ففي الروايات المكتوبة، على سبيل المثال، عن الحرب الأهلية اللبنانية نجد الكثير من التقاطع في الوصف والمقاربة؛ لا لأن هناك قناة ناقلة، وإنما لأن التجربة بعنفها وفوضاها واحدة.

وقد فسّرت مستغانمي هذه الاتهامات العديدة تفسيراً اجتماعياً ونسوياً. فهي باحثة في قضايا الكتابة والمرأة في وطنها الجزائر وتخصصت في دراستها العليا بهذا الموضوع. إنها ترى علاقة قوية بين النسق الاجتماعي السائد وحملة التشهير بها، فتقول: «المسألة ليست مسألة ذاكرة الجسد ولا القضية قضية أحلام مستغانمي وإنما كوننا ننتمي إلى مجتمع ذكوري يرفض الأنثى ويحتقر النساء حتى إنه ما ظهرت كاتبة أو شاعرة عربية إلا وجاء من يقول إن رجلاً يكتب لها».[٩]

ويجب أن لا يجعلنا هذا التشويه نتصور أن حق مستغانمي قد هضم، فقد أشاد بها الكثير من النقاد، وقام آخرون بتحليل عملها، قبل حصولها على جائزة نجيب محفوظ وبعده، ومنهم علي الراعي،[١٠] وعلي خفيف،[١١] وصبري حافظ،[١٢] وبيتر كلارك،[١٣] وعايدة بامية،[١٤] وكيم جانسن.[١٥]

وأما الشاعر والروائي والناقد عبده وازن فيبتعد عن التحليل وينحاز للإثارة الصحفية، مطلقاً إدانته لهذا العمل على مختلف المستويات. فهو يرى أن الرواية «لا تنتمي إلى الحركة الجزائرية مقدار انتمائها إلى الأدب الرائج أو 'الجماهيري' الذي يتخطى كل التصنيفات والانتماءات الوطنية وسواها».(١٦) ومع هذا فهو يناقض نفسه في مقالة أخرى عندما ينفي إمكانية أن يكون سعدي يوسف وراء هذه الرواية فيقول: «من الصعب على شاعر عراقي أن يلمّ بما أوردت الروائية من تفاصيل جزائرية صرف ومن معالم بيئية لا يدركها سوى الجزائري نفسه».(١٧) وفات عبده وازن أن حتى الأدب «الجماهيري» يتسم بمعالم الثقافة التي أنتجته، فرواية جماهيرية أمريكية غير الرواية الجماهيرية العربية أو اليابانية، وهو ما يشير إليه ضمناً عندما يتحدث عن الحس الجزائري في الرواية. وينطلق عبده وازن في استعلائه على الذوق الجماهيري، قائلاً: «لعل أجمل وصف أطلق على الرواية [**ذاكرة الجسد**] هو ما وصفته بها إحدى الصحف في أنها تنتمي إلى أدب المسلسلات 'المكسيكية' الرائجة جماهيرياً».(١٨)

وعلى عكس هذا التعالي النخبوي، نجد مقالة صبري حافظ تبحث في أسباب هذا الرواج من منطلق سوسيولوجي، ومع أن حافظ لا يرجع إلى المفكر جرامشي وكتاباته عن رواج الرواية الفرنسية المترجمة والمنشورة مسلسلةً في الصحف الإيطالية، فإن تحليله يتضمن ما توصل إليه جرامشي ويتقاطع معه. رأى جرامشي أن الإقبال الإيطالي على روايات فرنسية مترجمة ومنشورة كأدب مسلسلات (مثل رواية **الكونت دي مونت كريستو**) يرجع إلى أن النزعة الرومانسية فيها تتجاوب مع النزعة الوطنية الإيطالية الصاعدة حينذاك (نهاية القرن التاسع عشر ومطلع القرن العشرين)، ومن هذا المنطلق يمكن تفهم انصراف القارئ الإيطالي عن أدبه المتمثل في كتابات بيرانديلو ودانونزيو، والتي لم تكن تحقق رومانسية نزعته القومية.(١٩)

يفسّر صبري حافظ سر شعبية هذه الرواية في «عربيتها، وشاعرية لغتها وبلاغتها التقليدية، وبساطة بنيتها التي تردنا إلى مرحلة النشأة والتأسيس في الرواية».(٢٠) فهو يرى، أولاً، إحالة الرواية إلى الوضع العربي العام على الرغم من ارتباطها بالجزائر بشكل خاص؛ فهي «رواية العذاب الذي يعانيه الذين يخلصون في حب الوطن».(٢١) وهذا أمر أتفق معه وأضيف: إنها الرواية التي تعبر عن هول الواقع مخالفة بذلك الخطاب الرسمي المنشرح والمنافق والمدّعي بإنجازات وهمية على الرغم من الخراب المقيم. في رواية مستغانمي تحرير للحزن المكبوت في كل مواطن، فالأسباب تتعدد والخيبة واحدة. وثانياً، يرى حافظ سر رواج العمل في أسلوبه الشعري الإنشائي وجاذبيته التقليدية؛ وهنا أختلف شيئاً ما مع حافظ. فالأسلوب شعري غنائي، وليس إنشائياً، وهو جذاب لا لأنه تقليدي بل لأنه يعتمد على استعارات في متناول القارئ العادي، تبتعد عن التجريد والتعقيد؛ كما أن الأسلوب يتوسل الأمثال الشعبية والأقوال المأثورة. و**ذاكرة الجسد** ليست رواية تقليدية: إنها استرجاع عبر مونولوج داخلي لما كان ولما لم يكن، وكما في عملية التذكر، نقع على شذرات وإلماعات، على القارئ أن يجمعها ليشكل منها حبكة الرواية. وهذا التبعثر والابتعاد عن حبكة مرسومة ومخطط لها من بداية ونهاية وما بينهما، تجعل من العمل

تحدياً للقارئ واستدراجاً له ليدخل في لعبة القراءة. وإن كان القارئ العادي ينصرف عن مجهود الربط والتأويل، فهو هنا ينخرط في ذلك تماماً مع عالم الرواية. وفي المقام الثالث يرى حافظ أن رواج الرواية يرجع لكونها رواية نشأة وتأسيس «تطرح المرأة كمعادل للوطن كما فعل حسين هيكل في روايته **زينب**».(٢٢) وهنا أختلف مع حافظ، فكون المرأة معادلاً للوطن أمر لا يقتصر على رواية التأسيس، بل يتجاوزها ليكون قاسماً مشتركاً في الأدب العالمي بدءاً من **أوديب ملكاً** لسوفوكليس الإغريقي إلى رواية **نجمة** لكاتب ياسين الجزائري التي قال عنها صاحبها: «لقد أردت أن أعطي من خلالها صورة للجزائر من خلال صور المرأة فيها».(٢٣) كما أن بنية رواية مستغانمي، كما يذكر حافظ نفسه، تعتمد على «لعبة التقديم والتأخير في تناولها للزمن، وأنها تلجأ كذلك إلى لعبة النص داخل النص»،(٢٤) مما يختلف جذرياً عن فجر الرواية العربية وبنيات تأسيسها.(٢٥)

ويجدر أن أذكّر القارئ، في هذا السياق، بأنّ هناك أعمالاً كثيرة في تاريخ الرواية والسرديات كانت رائجة شعبياً ومهملة من المؤسسة الثقافية. فهناك صفوة أدبية ترفض الجماهيري باعتباره أدباً رائجاً لا صنف له ولا انتماء، وتبتهج لوقوعها على تصنيف جاهز (أدب المسلسلات) لتستعلي عليه. كما أن هناك أعمالاً شاعت جماهيرياً وتجاهلها النقاد أو هاجموها، لكنها فيما بعد أخذت مكانتها بين عيون الكتب وأمهات الروايات. وعلى سبيل الذكر، لا الحصر، رواية الأديبة الإنجليزية شارلوت برونتي، **جين إير** (١٨٤٧). ويقال إنها الرواية الأكثر انتشاراً في العالم الأنجلو سكسوني.(٢٦) وحتى منتصف القرن العشرين، كان النقاد والأكاديميون يدينون هذه الرواية - على عكس قرّائها وقارئاتها - باعتبارها عملاً مبتذلاً تنقصه «الكفاءة الروائية».(٢٧) وتجلى استعلاء المؤسسة الأكاديمية والنخبة النقدية على هذه الرواية في تجاهلها أحياناً وتحقيرها أحياناً أخرى. وأما الآن، فقد أصبحت هذه الرواية نموذجاً في الدراسات العليا ومحكاً للنظريات الجديدة، فقد تناولتها أقلام النقد النسوي والنقد ما بعد الكولونيالي من أمثال شوالتر وجلبرت وجوبر وسبيفاك. وأما بالنسبة لتراثنا، فهناك **ألف ليلة وليلة** التي تخاطب ذائقة العامة والتي تجاهلها وأدانها النقد العربي القديم باعتبارها عملاً غثاً؛ وأصبحت الآن محط أنظار النقد الرفيع، شرقاً وغرباً، وتقام الندوات والمؤتمرات من أجل دراستها، وتدخل في سياق تنظير كبار النقاد من أمثال فوكو وتودوروف، عبد الفتاح كيليطو ومحسن مهدي.

ومن الاتهامات التي وجهها عبده وازن لرواية مستغانمي كونها بعيدة كل البعد عن الحركة الروائية العالمية، بعد أن زعم أنها أيضاً بعيدة كل البعد عن الرواية الجزائرية: «فهي لم تستطع أن ترث الروائيين الجزائريين الكبار ولا أن تنطلق من تراثهم المهم لتبني عالمها الخاص».(٢٨) وهذا أغرب ما يمكن أن يقال في الرواية، فأحلام مستغانمي تتواصل مع الأدباء الجزائريين، بل تصر في هذه الرواية على حبكها مع روايات الروائي والشاعر الجزائري مالك حداد (مما سيأتي تفصيله فيما بعد). وفي دراسة الناقدة الفلسطينية عايدة بامية، المتخصصة في الأدب الجزائري، تحليل للعلاقة الحميمة والقرابة الأدبية بين **ذاكرة الجسد** وروايات أدباء جزائريين من أمثال محمد ديب وكاتب ياسين والطاهر وطار وآسيا جبار. وأما «انقطاع» مستغانمي عن الرواية العالمية فيستدل عليه وازن من إشارات في

رواية **ذاكرة الجسد**، فيقول: «أما أن تذكر الكاتبة في روايتها الروائي الفرنسي مارسيل پانيول والروائية الإنجليزية أغاثا كريستي وأن تورد أسماء مونترلان وپول إيلوار وسواهما فهو دليل ساطع على انقطاعها عن العالمية . . . فمارسيل پانيول روائي مدرسي بامتياز وأغاثا كريستي رواية شعبية ولا مكانة لها في الحركة الروائية العالمية».(٢٩)

إن نقد وازن، في حقيقة الأمر، دليل ساطع على انقطاع صاحبه عن التيارات العالمية في النقد والأدب (أو تجاهلها عن عمد)، وليس بدليل على انقطاع مستغانمي عنها، كما سأوضح. بدءاً، نقول إن الإشارات إلى روائيين مدرسيين أو جماهيريين (أي من درجة أدنى فنياً) يعني في سياق الرواية توصيفاً للشخصيات التي يتضمنها العمل، فأن نقول إن فلاناً يقرأ أغاثا كريستي أو يحضر في مونولوجه الداخلي پانيول، لا ڤيرجينيا وولف ولا جيمس جويس مثلاً، ليس إلا تقنية تعريف، كأن نقول فلانة تلبس المقياس (سوار جزائري تقليدي) في معصمها أو تتزين بعقد من تيفاني (المتخصص في بيع الحلي الغربية والمجوهرات الحديثة). صحيح أن مرجعية الشخصية، لو اقتصرت في تفكيرها على پانيول وكريستي، لكانت فقيرة أدبياً وسطحية فلسفياً. ولكن ألا يوظف هذا في سياق الرواية لإلقاء الضوء على جوانب سطحية وتقليدية في الشخصيات؟ إن بطلي الرواية خالد وحياة/أحلام (للبطلة اسمان أو اسم مزدوج) لا يُقدمان باعتبارهما نموذجين للاحتذاء بهما (وبالتالي فالبعد الأمثولي في الرواية يضيء أيضاً الجوانب السطحية والتقليدية في الوطن نفسه). فالبطلة ترضخ للتقاليد والصفقات العائلية وتوافق، ربما على مضض وربما عن تواطؤ، بالزواج من رجل متزوج، من الأثرياء الجدد. وأما البطل خالد فقد لعب دور الرقيب وطلب من الشاعر الفلسطيني زياد، الذي جاء بديوانه ليطبعه في مؤسسة النشر في الجزائر، حذف ما هو تهجمي على الحكومات العربية. وحتى لو افترضنا أن هناك تماهياً بين المؤلفة أحلام وقرينتها حياة/أحلام، فهذا لا يعني غياب نقد الذات. وقد فعل ذلك من قبل فلوبير عندما رسم شخصية سطحية (وإن كانت تشير ضمناً له في سيرة ذاتية روائية) في فردريك مورو في رائعته **التربية العاطفية**، وبذلك انتقد ذاته بذاته. ففي رواية مستغانمي رومانسية ونقد للرومانسية في آن واحد. ومن جانب آخر، فإن الرواية العالمية – رغم أنف النقاد النخبويين – قد تأثرت كثيراً بالرواية الشعبوية وتحديداً الرواية البوليسية من النوع الذي تكتبه أغاثا كريستي، ويتجلى هذا في تلقيح القص بعامل التحري في أعمال إدجار آلان پو، أمبرتو إيكو، خورخي لويس بورخيس، وپول أوستر. بل إن التلاعب بالاسم وتطابق اسم المؤلف واسم الشخصية الرئيسية، كما يرد في **ذاكرة الجسد**، نجده أيضاً في الجزء الأول من **ثلاثية نيويورك** المعروف بعنوان **مدينة الزجاج**، حيث المؤلف پول أوستر وكذلك بطل الرواية يحمل الاسم ذاته.(٣٠) إن من يتابع الحركة الروائية العالمية سيجد تزاوجاً بين الرواية التي يُطلق عليها 'الأدب الرفيع' مع الرواية الجماهيرية الرائجة، بل إن مفهوم ما بعد الحداثة والنقد الثقافي (كما جاءت به مدرسة النقد الثقافي الإنجليزية) يأخذ بنظر الاعتبار والجدية أثر الثقافة الجماهيرية والشعبوية على الأدب.

قد يكون هناك أكثر من سبب في الإقبال على رواية **ذاكرة الجسد**، كثفها صبري حافظ في «قدرتها على لمس وتر حساس في القارئ العربي في كل مكان».(٣١) وهذا يقترب

مما تقوله مستغانمي نفسها: «ما شكّل **ذاكرة الجسد** هو هذه الحالة من الآلام والأحلام، ثم هذه الحالة من الانكسارات المفجعة؛ ثمة رهان جماعي على خيبات عربية متداخلة وليست جزائرية فقط . . . قمة المأساة أن ننتمي إلى أوطان نشعر بواجبنا تجاهها، لكنها لا تمنحنا أية حقوق».(٣٢) إن رواج هذه الرواية لا يرتبط – كما يزعم البعض – بجمال صاحبتها وشبابها ـ فالمبدعات الجميلات والشابات كثر ولم يحققن جماهيرية تذكر – ولا بقدرتها على التسويق (كما تزعم زليخة أبو ريشة)؛(٣٣) ولا لتقديمها الممنوع والمحرمات، فليس هناك مشهد جنسي واحد، بل أقصى ما تصل إليه علاقة الحب بين البطل والبطلة هو قبلة يتيمة. كما أن رواجها لا يأتي من إحالتها على أشخاص في الواقع المعيش – كما يحدث في روايات تتناول شخصيات سياسية مقنّعة – وإنما تقدم الرواية أنماطاً من الشخصيات التي أفرزتها الجزائر في مراحل تاريخها المختلفة، بدءاً من انتفاضة الأربعينيات (١٩٤٥) في شرق الجزائر ضد الاستعمار وانتهاءً بانتفاضة الثمانينيات (١٩٨٨) ضد الغلاء والظروف الاقتصادية. واستحضار ماض مشرق في الرواية ليس من باب النوستالجيا السنتيمنتالية وإنما من باب النوستالجيا النقدية التي نظّر لها الناقد الإنجليزي الماركسي رايموند وليامز، والتي تستدعي ماضياً كريماً لتنتقد حاضراً هابطاً وتستجوبه.(٣٤)

رؤية تأويلية لتيمات الرواية ونسيجها

تقدم **ذاكرة الجسد**، سواء كان ذلك تخطيطاً واعياً من المؤلفة أو إبداعاً حدسياً، علاقات مركبة ومتشابكة تسمح بقراءات متعددة وعلى مستويات مختلفة، لكنها تتضافر جميعها في استدراج القارئ إلى اقتفاء أثر القديم في الجديد أو الماضي في الحاضر. فهناك حكاية حب غير متحقق، وهناك حكاية وطن مفقود، وهناك حكاية الحكاية مطروحة في صيغة تساؤلية؛ أي كيف ومتى ولماذا نكتب الرواية. ففي حكاية الحب غير المكتمل بين خالد وحياة/أحلام نجد البعد الرومانسي، لكننا نجد أيضاً ما هو أعمق، ألا وهو استبطان معنى العشق واحتواؤه على علاقات القرابة الحميمة من أمومة وأبوة، ومن بنوة وأخوة. وهذا يؤهل الرواية لدراسات تجمع بين النقد الأدبي والتحليل النفسي. وحكاية الوطن المفقود بوجهي الفقدان – عندما نغترب عنه وعندما نغترب فيه – تُعالج متمثلة في خالد الرسام الجزائري المقيم في باريس، وناصر، أخي حياة/أحلام، المقيم في قسنطينة. في هذا المستوى من العمل، نجد البعد التاريخي والوطني، الذي يثير سؤالاً جوهرياً: لماذا أُحبط المشروع الوطني وكيف وهل كان بالإمكان مسار آخر وأفضل؟ إن الثورة الجزائرية على خلاف الثورات العربية الأخرى، لم تكن انقلاباً عسكرياً، بل تعبئة شعبية. كانت كفاحاً خارقاً كلّف الشعب الجزائري مليون شهيد. وأصبحت التجربة الجزائرية نموذجاً من الكفاح المسلّح ضد المستعمِر، عُرفت لا على الصعيد العربي فقط، بل على صعيد العالم. وقام المفكرون الثوريون بالتنظير حول المقاومة بناء على هذه التجربة التاريخية الفذة،(٣٥) وأبرزهم فرانز فانون. وبالتالي فهناك تساؤل مبطن وأحياناً نغرانز يُلوّح به: كيف يمكن لكل هذه التضحيات والبطولات أن تنقلب لتصبح الجزائر وطناً مستحيلاً

لمواطنيه، يُستبعد فيه المجاهد أو يُتاجر باسمه؟ وكيف استطاع المرتزقة ورجال الصفقات الهيمنة على الوطن فلا يبقى للمواطن إلا الالتجاء إلى الدين في صورته المتطرفة أو الارتحال إلى المنفى الاختياري؟ في ظل الرقابة الفكرية والتبجح الحكومي وتهميش المثقف العضوي بقيت هذه الأسئلة تراود أهل الضمائر دون أن تجد جواباً شافياً في البحث، بل دون أن تُطرح كأسئلة مع أنها تهم كل مفكر، وبشكل خاص كل مفكر عربي، وبشكل أخص كل مفكر جزائري. وفي مقطع من الرواية يتساءل خالد:

هل هناك من فرق بين القتلة؟
على يد الفرنسيين مات سي الطاهر .. وعلى يد الإسرائيليين مات زياد ..
وها هو حسّان يموت على يد الجزائريين اليوم.
فهل هناك درجات في الاستشهاد؟ وماذا لو كان الوطن هو القاتل
والشهيد معاً؟ (ص ٣٩٦)

ومن زاوية أخرى، **ذاكرة الجسد** عمل عن الذاكرة والكتابة. لماذا نكتب وكيف نكتب؟ ولماذا نختار كتابة الرواية لا القصيدة أو العكس؟ ولماذا في الفن يختار البعض الصورة وآخرون الكلمة؟ إن الرواية تسائل نفسها بنفسها مما درج على تسميته بالعمل العاكس لذاته. ونجد هذا الانعكاس الذاتي عند بيرانديلو وفيلليني، عند مالارميه ويبول أوستر وسلمان رشدي. وتحاول مستغانمي عبر شخصيات روايتها أن ترد على هذا التساؤل، ولهذا نجد مقولات الكثير من الأدباء (وليس بانيول وكريستي فقط) ومن الفنانين.
ذاكرة الجسد عمل يتناول العلاقات الفردية والتاريخية والأدبية، التي يمكن قراءة كل منها منفصلة أو متصلة وفي شبكة علاقات. وسأتناول كلاً منها على حدة.

حكاية الحب في الرواية

ظل العشق مستعصياً على الفهم والإدراك. عالجه العديد من الفلاسفة والفقهاء والأطباء والنقاد وكتب عنه الأدباء والشعراء، وعرفه معظم الناس وإن بقي حتى لغزاً لمن عايشه. كتب عنه أفلاطون في محاورة **المأدبة** وابن حزم الأندلسي في **طوق الحمامة** ورولان بارت في **شذرات من خطاب في العشق**. ويفترض بارت في كتابه غير التقليدي أن العشق مستحيل التحقق لأنه في حقيقة الأمر الرغبة الكامنة في التوحد مع الأم: «باستثناء الاقتران (ولنلق بالمخيلة إلى الجحيم) يوجد هذا العناق الآخر الذي يعتبر ارتباطاً ثابتاً: إننا مفتونان ومسحوران راقدان من دون سبات. إننا في لذة النعاس الطفولية. إنها لحظة الحكايات ولحظة الصوت الذي يأتي ليسكنني ويصفعني. إنها العودة إلى الأم».(٣٦) ويستطرد بارت ليقول إن في هذه العلاقة شيئاً من عشق المحرمات يتوقف فيها الزمن والقوانين والممنوعات.
وتقدم الرواية حكاية حب بين خالد وحياة/أحلام من هذه الزاوية فهو بشكل ما

أبوها، قام مقامه عندما سجلها باسم أحلام وهي طفلة بعد أن كانت أمها قد أطلقت عليها اسم حياة وهي في تونس؛ كما أنها بالنسبة له الأم والبنت في آن واحد. كان سي الطاهر مشغولاً بمسئولياته في المقاومة ففوّض صديقه ومرؤوسه في الجهاد خالد كي يقوم بهذه المهمة: «لو وضعت في جيبك عنوان العائلة في تونس وشيئاً من الدراهم . . . لو قدّر لك أن تصل إلى هناك .. أتمنى أن تذهب لزيارتهم حين تشفى وتسلم هذا المبلغ إلى (أما) لتشتري به هدية للصغيرة، وأود أيضاً أن تقوم بتسجيلها في دار البلدية» (ص ٣٦). الاسم المزدوج يحمل أيضاً دلالات مختلفة فالأم بتسمية ابنتها حياة اختارت لها اسماً يدل على الحاضر لشيوعه، بينما والدها اختار لها اسماً غير مألوف «أحلام» دلالة على المستقبل، وهي كما تقول في الرواية لو أن جدتها سمّتها لكان الاختيار «السيدة» وذلك «تيمناً ببركة السيدة المنوبية» (ص ١١٠)، وهم اسم يحمل في ثناياه الماضي والتقليدي.

وتتخذ حياة/أحلام وظائف مختلفة في مخيلة خالد، فهي الأم والابنة والحبيبة. فعندما يلتقي خالد لأول مرة بحياة/أحلام في باريس بعد ربع قرن من تسجيلها رسمياً في تونس، يقع نظره على سوارها فيتمثل أمه (أما) كما يتمثل عبرها مدينته قسنطينة التي يحب، وهي كناية عن الجزائر:

وقبل أن تصلني كلماتك .. كان نظري قد توقف عند ذلك السوار الذي
يزين معصمك العاري الممدود نحوي. كان إحدى الحليّ القسنطينية
التي تعرف من ذهبها الأصفر المضفور، ومن نقشتها المميزة. تلك
«الخلاخل» التي لم يكن يخلو منها في الماضي، جهاز عروس ولا معصم
امرأة من الشرق الجزائري.
مددت يدي إليك دون أن أرفع عيني تماماً عنه. وفي عمر لحظة، عادت
ذاكرتي عمراً إلى الوراء، إلى معصم (أمّا) الذي لم يفارقه هذا السوار قط.
(ص ٥٣)

هكذا نجد في تعلق خالد بحياة/أحلام رغبة في العودة إلى الأم، وفي هذه الحالة بديلتها التي لا تتطابق معها، لكنها تتقاطع معها في ذلك السوار رمز الأمومة. وهي بالنسبة لخالد، كما يقول في مونولوجه الداخلي: «إنها امرأة كانت دائماً على وشك أن تكون حبيبتي» (ص ٧٦). وتبادل الأدوار القرابية الحميمة واضح عندما يقول خالد لنفسه: «كنت هنا أعرض عليك أبوتي، وكنت تعرضين علي أمومتك. أنت الفتاة التي كان يمكن أن تكون ابنتي والتي أصبحت دون أن تدري .. أمي!» (ص ١١٨).

وهكذا نجد بارت معيناً لنا في فهم هذه العلاقة، لا من منطلق نشوئها فحسب، بل أيضاً لماذا بقيت هذه العلاقة احتمالية، على وشك أن تكون دون أن تكون: إنها علاقة عصية على التحقق لأنها في التحليل الأخير تتطلع إلى التوحد المستحيل مع الأم.

وفي المقابل تتعلق حياة/أحلام بخالد الذي يرتبط بوالدها لا عن طريق القرابة البيولوجية بل عن طريق القرابة الروحية، فقد عملا معاً في المقاومة السرية. لم تلتق

حياة/أحلام بوالدها - الذي استشهد وهي طفلة صغيرة - إلا مرات معدودة، فعرفته بالسمعة والشهرة، فهي تفتقد المعرفة الحميمية التي أسقطتها على خالد، الذي يقول لنفسه: «وربما كان هذا سر تعلقك بي؛ أنا الذي أعرف الحلقة المفقودة من عمرك، وأعرف ذلك الأب الذي لم تره سوى مرات قليلة في حياتك . . . أنت التي تعلقت بي لتكتشفي ما تجهلينه. . . . كان (سي الطاهر) طرفاً ثالثاً في قصتنا منذ البدء» (ص ٤٣).

تقدم الرواية العائلة وعلاقاتها على مستويين: قرابة الدم وقرابة الفكر، أي قرابة النسب والانتساب. وقد فصّل الناقد إدوارد سعيد في الفصل الأول من كتابه **العالم والنص والناقد** نمطين من العلاقات والروابط أحدهما مبني على علاقات القرابة الحرفية والثاني على علاقات القرابة المجازية. وأشار إلى أن النوع الأول من العلاقات يتبع النسق التراتبي العمودي والثاني النسق التجاوري الأفقي. ففي الأول علاقة طاعة وفي الثاني علاقة حوار. (٣٧) ومن هذا المنطلق السعيدي، يمكننا أن ندرك لماذا فضلت حياة/أحلام زياد الشاعر الفلسطيني على خالد الرسام الجزائري، فالأول بمثابة الند والزميل والآخر بمثابة السلطة الأبوية. وكل من زياد وحياة/أحلام مشدودان إلى الكلمة مما أوجد بينهما علاقة انتساب، علاقة مبنية على التبادل الأفقي. والرواية لا توضح لنا نوعية العلاقة بين زياد وحياة/أحلام، فنحن نتعرّف عليها عبر الراوي خالد. هل هي علاقة تواطؤ فكري وأدبي أم تتجاوز ذلك إلى تواطؤ نفسي وجسدي؟ هل هي الغيرة وأوهامها في ذهن خالد أم هناك اعتراف ضمني بأن العلاقات الأبوية (العمودية) لابد أن تنزاح لتعطي مكاناً للعلاقات الندية (الأفقية)؟ فالنسب - حتى في صيغته المجازية - ينزاح مفسحاً المجال لعلاقات الانتساب، في صيغتها المجازية أيضا.

إن إهداء المؤلفة الرواية إلى أبيها الحقيقي وإلى مالك حداد، أبيها المجازي، في ذاته يؤكد على نوعين من القرابة: قرابة الدم وقرابة الروح، وعندما تقول في إهدائها لأبيها إن كتابها هو كتابه (ص ٥)، فهي تعبّر عن كونها امتداداً له، وأن أثر الأب حاضر على الرغم من غيابه. إنها لا تتماهى معه وإنما تستحضره وتتمثله أدبياً. وسواء كان والد أحلام مستغانمي - المؤلفة - هو نموذج سي الطاهر والد البطلة - حياة/أحلام - في الرواية أو لم يكن، فالأمر سيان. المهم هو هذا الحنين إلى الأب الغائب، وهذه الاستمرارية بين الماضي المتمثل في الأب المزدوج - بوجهيه الحقيقي والمجازي - وبين الحاضر المتمثل في البنت الكاتبة، دون أن تشكل هذه الاستمرارية تطابقاً أو تكراراً.

حكاية الوطن في الرواية

إن تماهي البطلة حياة/أحلام مع الوطن أمر لا يختلف عليه اثنان، فهي الجزائر، وهي الوطن العربي بكل مآسيه وكوارثه وإحباطاته وقصوره. وربط المرأة بالوطن لا يقتصر على رواية التأسيس، كما سبق ذكره، حيث نجده في أعمال ما بعد مرحلة التأسيس، في **ذات** لصنع الله إبراهيم، على سبيل المثال، حيث البطلة ذات تمثل الانهيار المصري والتراجع في حقبة الانفتاح الاقتصادي. كما نجد المرأة مجازاً للوطن في قصائد محمود

درويش ومحمد عفيفي مطر وغيرهما، كما نجدها هكذا في التراث الشعبي وفي الأدب الرفيع. ومع هذا فهي في **ذاكرة الجسد** امرأة من لحم ودم بالإضافة إلى كونها رمزاً للوطن.

وقد استغرب البعض تقليدية البطلة (التي تمثل الوطن) وكيف أنها لا تبدي تمرداً نسائياً أو إنسانياً على وضعها واستخدامها في آخر الأمر كسلعة بشرية، فتقبل الزواج من رجل فاسد وثري، لتكون زوجته الثانية. ولكن في تقليدية البطلة إشارة ونقد ضمني للمشروع الوطني بعد الاستقلال الذي أثبت عبر نهجه التقليدي والمتخلف عدم قدرته على إحداث ثورة حقيقية، بل بالعكس قمع الثوار واستغل سمعة المجاهدين. تختزل حياة أحلام في الرواية جمالية الثورة الوطنية وأيضاً ما جرى لها من تقهقر وتراجع.

تكشف الرواية عن كيفية استغلال سمعة من جاهدوا في حرب التحرير الجزائرية وانحدار القيم بصورة عامة وتبلور تيارات إسلامية أصولية متطرفة كرد فعل للفساد والضغوط المتراكمة المؤدية إلى انفجارات. فالمواطن العادي لا يجد أماناً إلا في ركونه إلى العقيدة في وجهها السلفي والرافض، كما يتمثل ذلك عند ناصر، الأخ الأصغر للبطلة حياة/أحلام. وتكشف الرواية عن المساوئ في استخدام السلطة في الجزائر والإثراء السريع على حساب الشعب وخلط الأوراق بين المجاهدين الحقيقيين والمنتفعين الجدد. وعم البطلة سي شريف نجح في التأقلم مع الوضع فتم تعيينه ملحقاً في السفارة في باريس، بينما خالد اضطر إلى القطيعة مع وطنه مختاراً المنفى الفرنسي لعدم قدرته على التأقلم، والجسور التي يرسمها ما هي إلا محاولة للتواصل ولاستحضار جسور قسنطينة المحروم منها.

هناك ثلاثة أنماط في الشخصيات في **ذاكرة الجسد**: سي الطاهر الذي مات شهيداً، وسي خالد رفيقه ومرؤوسه في حرب التحرير الذي بترت ذراعه في المعارك ضد المحتل والذي أصبحت ثوريته مستحيلة في الجزائر المستقلة، فكان عليه إما أن يتنازل عنها ليخدم الطبقة الحاكمة فيعمل رقيباً على المصنفات الفنية والأدبية، أو يرحل بعيداً ويكون حراً. والنمط الثالث هو سي شريف الذي عايش الطبقة الجديدة من الأثرياء، وإن لم يمارس فسادهم، لكنه بارك زواج ابنة أخيه الشهيد لواحد منهم. وكأن الرواية تقول – دون أن تقول – للمناضل الحقيقي خياران: الموت أو المنفى. والمنفى أيضاً «موت» بمعنى ما، كما أن بتر الذراع ليصبح خالد معوقاً «استشهاد» جزئي لو صح التعبير. ففي باريس التي هاجر إليها خالد، محترفاً الرسم باليد السليمة، تحقق فنياً لكنه بقي مغترباً. وليس أدل على ذلك من علاقته مع عشيقته الفرنسية كاترين، فبينهما رابطة جسدية لا يواكبها تفاهم نفسي أو تواطؤ وجداني. كاترين تمثل فرنسا بالنسبة للمغترب: تحقق له، بشكل ما، متطلباته الآنية دون أن تمنحه الشعور بالانتماء. لهذا عندما تقع عينا خالد على حياة/أحلام نجده منبهراً بها لأنها صورة من الوطن الأم: «يا امرأة متنكرة في ثياب أمي .. في عطر أمي وفي خوف أمي عليّ ..» (ص ٣٧٧).

من هذا المنطلق يبدو الوطن جذراً لا نستطيع أن نقطع صلتنا به وإن كنا لسنا قادرين على العيش فيه. ويتخذ الوطن صورة نموذجية، بل أسطورية، يكون فيه القائد بطلاً: «كان مصادفة وجودي مع (سي الطاهر) في الزنزانة نفسها شيء أسطوري بحد ذاته،

وتجربة نضالية ظلت تلاحقني لسنوات بكل تفاصيلها، وربما كان لها بعد ذلك أثر في تغيير قدري. . . . كان (سي الطاهر) استثنائياً في كل شيء .. لقد خلق ليكون قائداً، كان فيه شيء من سلالة طارق بن زياد، والأمير عبد القادر» (ص ٣٢).

ويكشف هذا عن رغبة خالد وهو في السادسة عشرة عاماً من عمره (وهو في سجن الكديا)، «إثر مظاهرات ٨ ماي ١٩٤٥ التي قدمت فيها قسنطينة وسطيف وضواحيهما أول عربون للثورة» (ص ٣٠)، في أن يجد القائد المخلّص، مكثفاً بهذا رغبة جماهيرية عارمة ورومانسية في أبوة تقود وتحنو في آن واحد.

حكاية الحكاية في الرواية

هناك مستوى أدبي نقدي في الرواية يتعلق مباشرة بمساءلة فن الكتابة. ماذا يعني أن تكتب ولماذا؟ وما الفرق بين التعبير بالصورة (الرسم والفن التشكيلي) والتعبير بالكلمة (الأدب الروائي والشعر). وعلى الرغم من زعم النقد الصحفي أن مستغانمي تشير إلى كتّاب في الطبقة الأدنى أدبياً من أمثال بانيول وكريستي، فإنها في حقيقة الأمر تشير إلى مجموعة كبيرة من الأدباء الفطاحل والعاديين، كما تشير إلى عدد من الرسامين والفنانين والموسيقيين. وليس هذا من قبيل الاستعراض المعرفي، بل لأن أبطال الرواية مبدعون، فخالد رسام تشكيلي وحياة/أحلام روائية وزياد شاعر، فليس من الغريب أو العجيب أن تكون مرجعيتهم فنية وأدبية.

تقدم مستغانمي أنماطاً بشرية بتطلعاتها وهواجسها، إلا أنها تقدمهم من الداخل فنتعرف عليهم وعلى عالمهم ليصبحوا مألوفين كما نألف أصدقاءنا، بحسناتهم ومساوئهم. وبالتالي فهي تخلق حميمية بين القارئ وشخوصها الروائية، مما يفسر جانباً من الإقبال على عملها، فنحس وكأننا نعرف زوربا ولماذا رقص بين أنقاض الخراب.

ولكن هناك أديباً يطغى على بقية الأدباء ويتخذ موقع الأب الأدبي لمستغانمي وهو مالك حداد. فهي تفتتح روايتها بإهدائها له (ثمّ لأبيها):

إلى مالك حداد
ابن قسنطينة الذي أقسم بعد استقلال الجزائر ألا يكتب بلغة ليست لغته ..
فاغتالته الصفحة البيضاء .. ومات متأثراً بسلطان صمته ليصبح شهيد اللغة العربية، وأول كاتب قرر أن يموت صمتاً وقهراً وعشقاً لها. (ص ٥)

وقد خصصت أحلام مستغانمي جائزة للرواية العربية في الجزائر باسم مالك حداد تكريماً له، وقالت إنه «أول من شجعها على الكتابة» والجائزة كما تقول هي استنطاق للصمت: «عساني أثأر لصمته بقلمي وأواصل نيابة عنه كتابة ما مررنا بمحاذاته».(٣٨) تقوم مستغانمي في روايتها عبر الإهداء والتناص مع حداد بتحرير أديبها المفضل وأبيها الأدبي

من منفاه اللغوي (الفرنسية)، بتضفير شذرات من أقواله المكتوبة أصلاً في الفرنسية أصلاً في عملها بعد ترجمتها إلى العربية وكأنها تؤكد حضور السابق في اللاحق، حضور الأديب الجزائري الفرانكوفوني في نص الأديبة الجزائرية العربي، وتشير مباشرة إلى استحضار القديم في جديدها. فتكتب في الهامش الوحيد في الرواية: «الجمل المكتوبة بخط مميز مأخوذة من تواطؤ شعري في روايتي مالك حداد 'سأهبك غزالة' و'رصيف الأزهار الذي لم يعد يجيب'» (ص ٣٠).

فعلى الرغم من اكتظاظ الرواية بأسماء روائيين وشعراء من أمثال كاتب ياسين وغسان كنفاني ونزار قباني والسياب والحلاج وبودلير وهمنجواي ومورافيا وإيلوار ولوركا وخليل حاوي وكوكتو وغيرهم، فإنها تحدد انتماءها وامتدادها لكاتب وشاعر جزائري عُرف بقصائده وبنثره الغنائي وأسلوبه الشعري في رواياته (المكتوبة كلها بالفرنسية)، ولا تحدد مستغانمي من أي صفحة من أعماله انتقت هذه الاستشهادات وإن كانت تميزها بالبنط الغامق، لتستدرج القارئ إلى مطالعة أعمال مالك حداد. وهنا يخدم التناص خط الاستمرار بين الأدب الفرانكوفوني الجزائري والأدب العربي الجزائري، فمثلاً تستحضر مستغانمي حداد فيما يلي: «إذا صادف الإنسان شيء جميل مفرط في الجمال .. رغب في البكاء» (ص ٦٧). وهو نص مأخوذ من مطلع رواية **سأهبك غزالة** لمالك حداد.[٣٩] وحتى عندما تستشهد بأندريه جيد في **ذاكرة الجسد**، «كيف نسيت تلك المقولة الرائعة لأندريه جيد 'لا تهيئ أفراحك!'» (ص ١٩٣)، فهي تشير ضمناً إلى ما ذكره خالد بطل **رصيف الأزهار لم يعد يجيب** لمالك حداد عن أندريه جيد.[٤٠] ويمكن أن نقرأ في هذا التناص «إيماءة لأهمية الحوار الثقافي واللغوي في الجزائر كخطوة أولى لكسر الأسوار»[٤١] التي تقف حاجزاً بين الجزائريين الذين يتكلمون الفرنسية والجزائريين الذين يتكلمون العربية.

وخلاصة القول، تثير **ذاكرة الجسد** أسئلة متعددة كما تفعل كل الروايات الكبيرة، ولكونها تسرد الأحداث على مستويات مختلفة، فهناك من سيقرأها كحكاية حب، وآخر سيقرأ فيها حكاية الوطن، وثالث سينشدّ لها لما تطرحه بخصوص الكتابة ذاتها؛ وأما الناقد – أو القارئ المتخصص – فسيجد متعة في كيفية تشابك هذه المستويات في الرواية وفي اقتفاء أثر الإرث الأدبي والأسري في هذا العمل واستدعاء التاريخ في ثناياه.

الهوامش

(١) أحلام مستغانمي من مواليد الجزائر العاصمة عام ١٩٥٣. وقد نالت البكالوريوس في الأدب العربي من جامعة الجزائر عام ١٩٧٦. وفي مطلع السبعينيات أسهمت في تقديم الشعر في الإذاعة الجزائرية شفاهياً وفي جريدة **الشعب** تحريراً. وبعد تخرجها، سافرت إلى باريس حيث أكملت في عام ١٩٨٠ بحوثها ونالت شهادة الدكتوراه في العلوم الاجتماعية من جامعة السوربون. وقد نشرت رسالتها المكتوبة بالفرنسية بتقديم المستعرب جاك بيرك عام ١٩٨٥ وعنوانها «الجزائر: المرأة والكتابة». راجع:

Ahlem Mosteghanemi, *Algérie: Femme et écritures* (Paris: L'Harmattan, 1985).
ولها مجموعتان شعريتان، **على مرفأ الأيام** (الجزائر: الشركة القومية للنشر والتوزيع، ١٩٧٣)؛ **الكتابة في لحظة عري** (بيروت: دار الآداب، ١٩٧٦)، بالإضافة إلى ثلاث روايات: **ذاكرة الجسد** (بيروت: دار الآداب، ١٩٩٣)؛ **فوضى الحواس** (بيروت: دار الآداب، ١٩٩٧)؛ **عابر سرير** (بيروت: منشورات أحلام مستغانمي، ٢٠٠٣). وقد نالت روايتها الأولى جائزة نجيب محفوظ عام ١٩٩٨، وترجمت إلى الإنجليزية عام ٢٠٠٠ ثم أعيد نشر الترجمة منقحة عام ٢٠٠٣ (صدرت الطبعتان عن دار نشر الجامعة الأمريكية بالقاهرة)، كما ترجمت إلى الفرنسية (دار ألبان ميشيل)، عام ٢٠٠٢، وهناك مشروع نقل الرواية إلى الشاشة. وكل الإشارات إلى صفحات رواية **ذاكرة الجسد** في المقالة ترجع إلى طبعة دار الآداب الأولى.

(٢) راجع:

The New York Review of Books 50.18 (Nov. 20, 2003): 32.

(٣) ذكرت أحلام مستغانمي هذا في ندوة «المرأة والكتابة» التي عقدت في الرباط (نقلاً عن عادل حمودة، «البحث عن أعداء شرفاء» ، **الأهرام**، ٢٠٠٠/٧/٨، ص ٢٤). وعبرت مستغانمي في الندوة عن أزمة الكاتب العربي قائلة: «أي قدر هو قدر الكاتب العربي الناجح، الذي يقف في مسافة وسطية بين القتلة والمرتزقة، فهو بالنسبة للأولين متهم بالكتابة وليس بما يكتب، والذين يعادونه، والذين قد يقتلونه، لم يقرأوه ولم يحاولوا أن يفهموه أو أن يناقشوه، إنما هم يحاسبونه على اختلافه عنهم، لا على اختلافه معهم. أما إذا نجا من هؤلاء، فمرتزقة الصحافة يتربصون به ويريدون جثته ممددة على صحائفهم الصفراء للتمثيل بها، لا بتهمة الكتابة، وإنما هذه المرة بتهمة نجاحه فيها، فالنجاح هو أكبر جرم يرتكبه كاتب عربي اليوم»، أحلام مستغانمي، «روايتي تدافع عن نفسها»، **الحياة**، ٢٠٠٠/٥/٢٦، ص ١٦.

(٤) سعدي يوسف، «أساءوا إليّ وإلى أحلام مستغانمي»، **الحياة**، ٢٠٠٠/٦/١٥، ص ١٦.

(٥) واسينـي الأعرج، «فـداحـة الأجـوبـة في مـجتمـع متـنـاقـض وشبـه مـعطـل»، **الحياة**، ٢٠٠٠/١٢/١٩، ص ١٦.

(٦) «سهيل إدريس عن قضية مستغانمي: ينبغي إنهاء هذه المعركة»، **الحياة**، ٢٠٠٠/٧/١٣، ص ١٦. كما يختتم شهادته في عدد لاحق بالقول: «وأنا أقدم اليوم هذه الشهادة لكي تكون شهادة أدبية تضع حداً – حاضراً ومستقبلاً – للجدل غير النزيه والتلميحات غير البريئة التي تصنع منها بعض المجلات بين الحين والآخر أغلفتها. . . . أو يرددها البعض فيبادرون إلى التشكيك في أبوتها. . . . بنسبها كل مرة إلى كاتب بما في ذلك نزار قباني نفسه»، سهيل إدريس، «شهادة أخرى في **ذاكرة الجسد**»، **الحياة**، ٢٠٠٠/٩/١٠، ص ١٢.

(٧) حيدر حيدر، **وليمة لأعشاب البحر** (القاهرة: الهيئة المصرية العامة للكتاب [آفاق الكتابة]، ٢٠٠٢ [الطبعة الأولى ١٩٨٣]).

(٨) رجاء النقاش، **قصة روايتين: دراسة نقدية وفكرية** (القاهرة: دار الهلال، ٢٠٠٠).

(٩) أحلام مستغانمي، «روايتي تدافع عن نفسها»، ص ١٦.

(١٠) ذكر علي الراعي في عرضه لرواية **ذاكرة الجسد**: «إن الكاتبة الجزائرية أحلام مستغانمي

هي نور يلمع وسط هذا الظلام الكثيف»، واحتفى بالدلالة الرمزية للرواية؛ راجع: علي الراعي، «الأم والحبيبة والثورة وأحلام مستغانمي في **ذاكرة الجسد**»، **الأهرام**، ١٩٩٧/١١/١٦، ص ٢٥.

(١١) راجع علي خفيف، «سيمائية المكان في رواية **ذاكرة الجسد** لأحلام مستغانمي»، **التواصل** ٨ (جوان ٢٠٠١)، ص ص ٢٢٥-٢٣٦؛ حيث يقول في خاتمة دراسته: «تبعث الشخصيات الحياة في المكان، فيأخذ حالاتها النفسية، ويمتزج معها بشكل تفاعلي مذهل، فتكون النتيجة الهائلة 'أنسنة المكان'» (ص ٢٣٥).

(١٢) يحلل الناقد صبري حافظ أسباب شعبية رواية **ذاكرة الجسد**، ويرجع ذلك إلى استدعاء قيم باتت منقرضة. راجع صبري حافظ، «أغرودة حب الوطن وحنين للقيم العربية القديمة»، **إبداع** ١٧: ٨/٧ (يوليو / أغسطس ١٩٩٩)، ص ص ١٢٤-١٣٢.

(١٣) يشيد الناقد الإنجليزي بيتر كلارك برواية **ذاكرة الجسد** ويرى أنها تستحق الشهرة التي نالتها فهي عمل متميز. وقد قام بمراجعة الترجمة الإنجليزية في طبعتها الثانية (٢٠٠٣). راجع: Peter Clark, "Despair, Religion and Exile: The Only Escape Routes," *Banipal* 7 (Spring 2000): 78.

(١٤) تقوم دراسة عايدة بامية على تحليل استخدام مستغانمي في روايتها **ذاكرة الجسد** لتيمات قديمة بشكل جديد. راجع:
Aida A. Bamia, "*Dhakirat al-jasad* (The Body's Memory); A New Outlook on Old Themes," *Research in African Literature* 28. 3 (Fall 1997): 85-93.

(١٥) في عرض كيم جانسن للترجمة الإنجليزية لرواية **ذاكرة الجسد**، تأكيد على أن الرواية تتجاوز قصة الحب لتشكل أمثولة عن القدر الجزائري. راجع:
Kim Jensen, "A Literature Born from Wounds," *Aljadid* 8.39 (Spring 2002): 12, 25.

(١٦) عبده وازن، «الذاكرة المثقوبة»، **الحياة**، ١٩٩٨/١٢/٢٣، ص ١٨.

(١٧) عبده وازن، «ذاكرة 'الزنجي'»، **الحياة**، ٢٠٠٠/٦/٢٢، ص ١٦.

(١٨) عبده وازن، «الذاكرة المثقوبة».

(١٩) راجع:
Antonio Gramsci, *Selections from Cultural Writings*, ed. David Forgacs and Geoffrey Nowell-Smith, trans. William Boelhower (London: Lawrence and Wishart, 1985), 203-12.

(٢٠) صبري حافظ، «أغرودة حب الوطن وحنين للقيم العربية القديمة»، ص ١٣١.

(٢١) **نفس المرجع**.

(٢٢) **المرجع السابق**، ص ١٣٢.

(٢٣) «كاتب ياسين: منفى اللغة»، **الحياة**، ٢٠٠٤/١/٢٤، ص ١٨.

(٢٤) صبري حافظ، «أغرودة حب الوطن وحنين للقيم العربية القديمة»، ص ١٣٢.

(٢٥) كُتب على غلاف الرواية: «**ذاكرة الجسد** هي أول عمل نسائي باللغة العربية في الجزائر»، وقد يكون هذا السبب في ربط صبري حافظ بين هذه الرواية ونزعة التأسيس (نسائياً وعربياً في

هذه الحالة). وقد نبهت الناقدة الجزائرية شهرزاد العربي إلى أن زهور ونيسي الجزائرية كتبت رواية بالعربية قبل مستغانمي، بعنوان **يوميات مدرّسة حرّة** (١٩٧٨) راجع: شهرزاد العربي، «ليست الرواية النسائية الأولى في الجزائر»، **الحياة**، ٢٣/١٢/١٩٩٨، ص ١٨. وقد اعتمد البعض على هذا لاتهام مستغانمي بتزوير الحقيقة، إلا أن مسألة الريادة في الرواية عامة ــ وفي الرواية العربية تخصيصاً ــ مسألة خلافية. فموقف حمدي السكوت وخياراته في الريادة الروائية يختلف عن موقف جابر عصفور على سبيل المثال، وكلاهما يختلفان مع ألفت الروبي التي ترى أن أول رواية عربية تعود لامرأة. والتضارب يأتي من أن البعض لا ينظر إلى بعض الأعمال السردية باعتبارها «رواية». فقد لا يرى البعض رواية في يوميات، وقد لا يرى آخرون رواية في سرد غنائي متدفق. المهم في كل هذا أن رواية ونيسي لم تُعرف، وبقيت مجهولة. ومن عرّف القراء بالرواية الجزائرية العربية بقلم امرأة هي دون شك أحلام مستغانمي.

(٢٦) راجع:

Michael Mason, "Introduction," Charlotte Brontë, *Jane Eyre* (London: Penguin, 1996), xi.

(٢٧) **المرجع السابق**، ص vii.

(٢٨) عبده وازن، «الذاكرة المثقوبة».

(٢٩) **نفس المرجع**.

(٣٠) راجع:

Paul Auster, *The New York Trilogy* (New York: Penguin, 1990), 20, 79.

(٣١) صبري حافظ، «أغرودة حب الوطن وحنين للقيم العربية القديمة»، ص ١٢٥.

(٣٢) أحلام مستغانمي (مقابلة مع عماد الغزالي)، «أسكن مدينة اسمها باريس وتسكنني قسنطينة»، **الوفد**، ٢٦/٢/١٩٩٨، ص ٩.

(٣٣) نقلاً عن رجاء النقاش، **قصة روايتين: دراسة نقدية وفكرية**، ص ٢٥.

(٣٤) راجع:

Raymond Williams, *The Country and the City* (New York: Oxford UP, 1973), 36.

(٣٥) راجع:

Franz Fanon, *L'an V de la révolution algérienne* (Paris: Maspero [nouvelle édition], 1960).

(٣٦) الترجمة العربية من فقرة استشهاد في مقالة عرض للترجمة العربية للأصل: نقولا زيادة، «شذرات من خطاب في العشق»، **الحياة**، ٢٤/١٢/٢٠٠٣، ص ١٥. راجع الأصل الفرنسي:
Roland Barthes, *Fragments d'un discours amoureux* (Paris: Seuil, 1977), 121.

(٣٧) راجع:

Edward W. Said, *The World, the Text, and the Critic* (Cambridge, MA: Harvard UP, 1983), 1-30.

(٣٨) «رسالة الجزائر: جائزة مالك حداد للرواية العربية المُعبرة في الجزائر»، **الرافد** ٤٨

(أغسطس ٢٠٠١)، ص ١٢٣.

(٣٩) راجع رواية حداد التي نشرت لأول مرة عام ١٩٥٩:

Malek Haddad, *Je t'offrirai une gazelle* (Paris: Union Générale d'Editions, 1978 [René Julliard, 1959]), 25.

(٤٠) راجع:

Malek Haddad, *Le Quai aux fleurs ne répond plus* (Paris: René Julliard, 1961), 8.

وهي ترد هكذا في الأصل الفرنسي:
"Un mot de Gide lui revint à l'esprit: 'Ne prépare pas tes joies..'."

(٤١) خليفة قرطي، «رواية البحث عن تقاطعات أزمنة الجزائر الهاربة»، **الحياة**، ٢٩/١٠/١٩٩٧، ص ٢٠.

عَزْفاً على أصابع اليد:
حفريّات في الذاكرة الشعرية

حسب الشيخ جعفر

استحضارات

قد تنطفئ السيجارة كما تنطفئ الروح أو الشمعة، ومن الممكن تجديد السيجارة أو الشمعة غير أننا لا نستطيع أن نجدد «اللحظة الروحية» التي قد أتيحت لنا في يوم من الأيام، إنها تذهب مع الريح وليس من النافع أن نندم أو نتحسر على ذهاب اللحظة الروحية التي أضعناها نحن بأيدينا. إنني أتذكر، الآن، وجهاً روسياً، وجه أستاذة شابة، كنت أتطلع إلى قوامها ووجهها البديعين طيلة عامين، ولم أتفوه أول الأمر بحرف واحد، على الرغم من أنها أتاحت لي أن أتقرب منها، بل وتقربت هي إليّ.

ذات يوم كنت في القاعة الدراسية التي تخص طلبة آخرين، وأقبلت هي كي تلقي محاضرة لها، فأبعدتني مازحة عن القاعة، وأغلقت الباب، إلا أنني فتحته مازحاً أيضاً، فتحته قليلا. فجاءت إليّ وأخرجت وجهها فقط من الشق، وشدتني إليها بنظرة سعيدة عميقة جداً وطويلة، أحسست معها أننا غدونا كأننا واحد، وهذا ما أدعوه باللحظة الروحية. لقد عشت طويلاً في الصحاري الباردة، كما عشت طويلاً في الغابات الثلجية المشتعلة، وبين برد الصحراء واشتعال الثلج قد يبدو قوس قزح «اللحظة».

لا أظن أن عربياً واحداً يجرؤ على القول إنه حر تماماً في ما يقول أو يكتب، إلا إذا كان مستعداً لأن يدفع ثمن هذه الحرية، وهو دائماً باهظ جداً، في العالم العربي قد يتاح لك أن تكتب غير أنك لن تستطيع أن تنشر ما تريد في معظم الأحيان.

حقاً لست راغباً بالأضواء الإعلامية .. يربكني، بل يرعبني أن أقرأ أمام الناس. أنا لا أملك هذه الموهبة الخارقة، ثمة قدرة هائلة لا نجدها عند هذا الشاعر أو ذاك. أعني قدرة الخروج علناً إلى الآخر، قدرة التماس مع الآخر، قدرة أن تتجرأ على فضح الدواخل، وتعرية القلب بعيداً عن عزلتك وأوراقك الخاصة، أما بعدئذ، بعد أن تكون قد كتبت، فلا خوف أو وجل من أن تنشر كل شيء .. عارياً ..

لماذا يريد الشاعر أن يتشبه بمطرب العصر؟ وأي جدوى من ألاعيبه أو حيله، ورغبته المحمومة باجتذاب الأضواء؟ لم يعش الشعر إلا في الظل، وفي الظل تتوهج الروح وتتعرى .. فما الفائدة من الارتماء في الجحيم التلفازي؟ طالما صفق بعضهم للشعر الخاوي!

لم أتقصد يوماً، الانتقال من مرحلة شعرية إلى أخرى، إنما هي هذه التضاريس الروحية إن أمكن القول، وهو التنقل السري في مسارب التجربة الإبداعية الذي يذكرنا

برحلة الينابيع الخفية في أغوارها السحيقة. قد تتشعب الينابيع في تنقلاتها عبر الأغوار الأرضية. وقد تلتقي هذه الفروع أو التشعبات وتتدفق ينبوعاً جديداً. فأنا كما يتراءى لي لم أكن، في تنقلاتي، إلا شاعراً واحداً .. أو قطرة ماء واحدة .. غير أن الزمن والتجربة قد يدفعان بهذه القطرة صفراء أو خضراء من هذه الفوهة الينبوعية أو تلك، وبالطبع سيجد القارئ ألواناً شتى مثل ألوان الطيف الضوئي .. وما هي، في حقيقة الأمر، إلا لون واحد .. ولم يمنع هذا يوما الفكرة المركزية من أن تتبلور وتتعمق وتتجدد أيضاً.

وصلت موسكو في شهر سبتمبر/أيلول ١٩٦٠ وقبل ذلك كانت هناك في ذهني صورة وردية عن موسكو .. كنت أتصور أنني سأجد نفسي في عاصمة مرحة «سعيدة» تبني الاشتراكية وهي تغني وتضحك .. غير أن هذه الصورة المتخيلة سرعان ما تهشمت حال هبوطي من الطائرة. كان البرد قد بدأ .. وكانت العتمة جاثمة على الأرض، وبدا كل شيء حزيناً وموحشاً.

وحين عدت إلى بغداد صيف ١٩٦٦ كنت أتلهب حنيناً إليها، وكنت مثقلاً أيضاً بالتجارب الموسكوفية، وحال وصولي أحسست بخيبة مريرة كتلك التي أحسستها ليلة وصولي موسكو للمرة الأولى، فالجو حار والوجوه كالحة، والرقيب العسكري في المطار يظن صورة تشيخوف صورة لينين، وانعكست الحال .. **هناك** كان الحنين إلى قريتي .. وها أنا **هنا** أتقد حنيناً إلى **هناك** .. تلك كانت غربة الطير العائد .. غربة حفّارة في القلب والروح، ولعلها كانت وراء كل ما كتبت من قصائد. أتذكر حجرة الخان المتقشرة رطوبة، ونزهة الوطواط الليلية بينما كنت أشم بعيداً رائحة الغابات، والقرنفل باقة أحملها باحتراس، تحت الثلوج الناعمة، في انتظار صاحبة لي عند محطة مترو الجامعة.

في «الكهف» الشعري

كان نيتشه، فيما أعلم، أول من أشارَ إلى الوجه والوجه الآخر من الشعر .. وبعدئذ أشارَ إليهما الفيلسوف الوجودي المسيحي الروسي بيرديائيف .. والناقد الإنجليزي بورا .. أي إلى الوجه الأپولوني للفن (ولننقل، هنا، للشعر) .. والوجه الباخوسي (الديونيزي) له .. وتعني الأپولونيةُ الإشراقَ والوضوحَ والصفاءَ في التأمل والبناء الشعريين .. بينما تعني الباخوسيةُ الغموضَ والتشابكَ (الفوضى) والقتامة. فعندما ننظر إلى الشعر العربي، مثلاً تمشياً مع هذا المنطلق، نجد الأپولونية في شعر شوقي والجواهري .. ونجد الباخوسية في شعر السيّاب وعبد الصبور .. فإذا انتقلنا إلى الشعر الروسي بدا لنا الوجهُ الأولُ واضحاً تمامَ الوضوح في شعر پوشكين وأخماتوڤا .. أما الوجه الآخر فيبدو جلياً في قصائد بلوك وتسيڤيتايفا. هنا التأمل القاتم والشرود واجتيازُ آفاقٍ غير واضحة المعالم .. وهناك التأمل الصافي والتحليق الوضيءُ والكشفُ عن هذا «العالم» .. فإذا أردنا أن نكون أكثر قرباً من هذه الفكرة .. فمن الممكن أن نشيرَ إلى أن الوجهَ الأولَ هو وجهُ الكلاسيكية والواقعية معاً .. أما الوجهُ الآخر فهو، أبداً، وجه الرومانتيكية والرمزية .. والتجريب. أهي «الأعالي» و«الأعماق»؟ ربما! قال نيتشه، مرة: «ليست الأعالي هي التي تخيفنا، إنما هي الأعماق» ..

غير أن الأعالي قد تغدو انطلاقاً من هذه الفكرة، أعماقاً، وتُمسي الأعماقُ أعالي. إن السماء في شعر بوشكين صافية تماماً، مقارنةً بالسماء في شعر بلوك. نحن عند بوشكين أمامَ زوبعةٍ ثلجيةٍ حقيقية .. بينما زوابع بلوك الثلجية ليست إلا ظلالَ زوابعَ من عوالم «الليلكية» أخرى. في قصائد السيّاب، أحياناً، قد لا ندري من هي المرأة، ومن هي عشتار – بينما المرأة هي المرأة في شعر الجواهري – في الواقع – في شعر الجواهري أو بوشكين، مثلاً، تلوح لنا الأنثى كما لو أنها منعكسة في الغدير الساكن الصافي .. أما في الرمزية أو في شعر بلوك مثلاً، فتلوح لنا مترجرجةً في مرايا من الزرقة والضباب!

* * *

من السهل جداً أن نقول إن الشعر هو جماليةُ اللغةِ موزونةً .. أي هو ما قال (شعرياً) المتنبي وحافظ شيرازي وبودلير مثلاً .. أو هو هذه المجاميع أو الدواوين الشعرية الجيدة الملقاة على ناصية الشارع .. أو المصفوفةُ في واجهاتِ المكتباتِ التجاريةِ والشخصية. لكننا نجد «الشعر» في لوحةٍ أو تمثالٍ تشكيليين .. كما نجده في فيلم سينمائيٍ أو سيمفونيةٍ ما .. (لا أظن الموسيقى إلا قصائدَ لم تجد، بعدُ، أو لن تجدَ الطريقَ إلى اللغةِ المنطوقة) .. (أو هي، ربما، لغة الأكوان أو الأفلاك الخفية ..) لماذا تبدو لي بعض الصفحات عند كافكا أو تشيخوف أعمقَ شعريةً من العديد من المجاميع المنظومة؟ لماذا أكاد أسمعُ تمثال حواء لرودان ناطقاً، وأراه متموجاً حياةً ودفئاً ورغبةً .. بينما لا أجد العديدَ من «الدواوين» إلا ركاماً؟

* * *

تقول الشاعرة التشيلية غابرييلا ميسترال :
أبوابٌ هي قشرياتٌ مكتئبة
لا مدَّ يأتيها، وبلا رمال
أبوابٌ هي سحابة قاتمة، عاصفة
فوق أرض سعيدة، كبيرة
أخذة في استقامتها
هيأةَ موتٍ لا مفرَّ منه
وأنا أنحني أمامها
مثلَ قصبةٍ في مهب الرياح ..

لا تتحدث الشاعرةُ، هنا، عن «موت البحر» فقد تحدثت عنه في قصيدةٍ أخرى .. بل هي تتحدث عن «الأبواب» .. الأبوابِ المقفلة على روح العالم المهجورة .. على روح الشاعر أو الفنان .. الروح التي خلّفتها حُطاماً تجربةُ حُب مدمرة أو خيبة سياسية أو «وجودية» .. يستيقظ الإنسان، فجأةً، فإذا هو في «القفص»، في «الزنزانة» .. إلا أنه يرى كل شيء عَبْرَ الجدار الصلد، عَبْرَ الباب المغلق .. يرى السماءَ والعالم كما يرى خطوطَ راحتيه .. ألم تتجول يوماً، صديقي أو صديقتي القارئة، وقد ضاقت بك الطرقاتُ ذرعاً، في حدائقَ أو مدائنَ من خطوط راحتي يديك؟ قد تتصدع «الصخرة» وتصحو الكوابيسُ من تحتها .. من الحفائر والظلمات .. يقال إن الجمال مرعب، وقد يقبضُ على القلب أو النفس كما يقبض بيتُ العنكبوت على فريسته.

* * *

ألا يبدو، لنا، موتُ هاملت التراجيدي «جميلاً» بينما يبدو موتُ العجوز كرمازوف مقزِّزاً؟ . .

* * *

أنا أقرأُ القصيدةَ الجيدةَ، أحياناً، وكأنني أتأمل امرأةً رائعة، قد أخذت زينتها منذ حين، وهي في الطريق إلى موعدٍ .. إلى لقاء، في معطفٍ من الفرو الناصع، تحت الثلوج المتراقصة في ضوء الشارع، كالفراشات كما يقول باسترناك .. وأقرأ القصيدةَ الجيدةَ الأخرى وكأنني أتأمل امرأةً رائعة، ممددةً على سرير مستشفى، ملتفةً بالبياض، تتنفس ببطء، أو هي تهذي في قبضة الحُمّى .. أو هي تتنزّه في حديقةٍ خريفيةٍ .. حديقةِ مقبرةٍ ما .. وحيدةً، متشحةً بالحداد. أنا أعرف السيدةَ الأولى .. ربما كانت جارةً لي، ربما كانت صديقةً أو ممثلةً معروفةً ما .. أما السيدةُ الثانية فلا أعرف لها عنواناً أو اسماً .. ولا أذكر بوضوح أين رأيتها من قبل .. ربما في كابوس أو حلم «تشكيلي» .. أو في «لوحةٍ» قد أزالت الأمطارُ ملامحَها، وعلاها الغبار .. ليست إلا ظلاً باهتاً أو ذكرى لوحة!

شيء عن الجواهري

بغداد: ١٩٥٩

تلك هي المرة الأولى التي أرى فيها الجواهري الكبير. حضرت حفلاً أقيم في قاعة الشعب إحياءً لذكرى الرصافي .. وقد قرأ الجواهري قصيدة قصيرة عن صديقه الرصافي أولها:

لغزُ الحياة وحيرة الألبابِ   أن يستحيل الفكر محضَ ترابِ

وكان الزعيم الراحل عبد الكريم قاسم حاضراً الحفل.

بغداد: ١٩٦٢

كنت عائداً من موسكو في العطلة الصيفية .. وكنت أتردد على اتحاد الأدباء .. في إحدى المرات حضر الزعيم زائراً اتحاد الأدباء .. وقد استقبله الجواهري ودعاه إلى الحديقة ليلقي كلمة على الأدباء، وقد حاول الزعيم أن يختار أقرب المفردات إلى الجو الأدبي. لم يلق الجواهري كلمة ولم يتحدث بشيء.

موسكو: ١٩٦٣

دُعيت لأقرأ قصيدةً في حفل أقامه اتحاد الكتاب السوفييت .. في قاعة هي أكبر قاعات موسكو وأكثرها عراقةً .. وعند المنبر الذي ألقى منه كبار الشعراء الروس (ألكساندر بلوك .. ماياكوفسكي .. أخماتوفا) ألقى الجواهري قصيدة .. بعده قرأ الشاعر الكبير البياتي وأنا والشاعر السوداني جيلي عبد الرحمن وشاعرتان روسيتان .. وقد بعث الشاعر التركي ناظم حكمت برقية معتذراً عن الحضور لسوء حالة قلبه .. (وقد قرئت قصائدنا مترجمة إلى الروسية أيضاً) .. ووقف الجواهري الكبير معانقاً إياي، قائلاً لي: «أنت يا ابني كوكب طالع»

.. كنت صديقاً لابنه (الدكتور فلاح الجواهري الآن) .. وقد دعا فلاح أباه إلى غرفته في منزل مجاور للمنزل الذي كنت أقيم فيه .. وقد اقتصرت المائدة على أربعة شخوص: الجواهري وابنه وأنا وجيلي عبد الرحمن. أتذكر أن الجواهري تلا بيتين للمتنبي:

ذراني والفـلاة بـلا دليـل   ووجـهـي والهجير بلا لثام
فإني أسـتريح بذي وهذا   وأتعب بالإناخةِ والمـقـام

واستدرك قائلاً: «لم يقل شكسبير شيئاً أعظم من هذا فيما أظن ..»

بغداد: ١٩٧١-١٩٧٨

كان الجواهري رئيساً لاتحاد الأدباء .. وكنت عضواً في الهيئة الإدارية .. كلما حضر الجواهري اجتماعاً للهيئة الإدارية كنت أراه بالطبع .. وقد تضمنا بعد الاجتماع مائدة مشتركة .. أحياناً، بعد الحادية عشرة من الليل، كان الشاعر سعدي يوسف، ساعة انصرافنا من نادي الاتحاد، يقترح عليّ زيارة الجواهري في منزله .. في المرة الأولى قلت له:

– في مثل هذه الساعة المتأخرة؟

– لم تبدأ سهرته بعد .. سترى.

كنا نتصل خلال التليفون .. ونجده يتمشى في حديقة منزله منتظراً إيانا. مرة كان الشاعر عبد الوهاب البياتي معنا. كان الجواهري يُسرّ بزياراتنا هذه سروراً واضحاً .. كان يبهجه أن نتحدث إلى ساعة متأخرة من الليل عن الشعر العربي .. عن قصائده خاصة حين يسمع منا مقاطع أو أبياتاً منها .. نحن أصحاب القصائد الحديثة!

دمشق: ١٩٧٩

كنت حاضراً مؤتمراً للأدباء العرب .. حالما عرفت بحضور الجواهري أسرعت أحييه وأسأل عن صحته.. في اليوم التالي سمعت من يقول لي : «الجواهري عاتب عليك قائلاً: كيف لم يحضر فلان ويسلم عليّ؟» وحين أخبرته أنني كنت معه بالأمس .. اعتذر متعللاً بضعف بصره. قرأ الجواهري قصيدته البديعة «أيها الأرق» .. ولمّا ذكّرته بمقالة لي عنها نُشرت في جريدة **الثورة العراقية** أخبرني أنها قرئت عليه .. فحروف الجرائد الناعمة تؤذي عينيه. تلك كانت آخر مرة رأيت فيها الجواهري الكبير .. الذي أحببت شعره حباً عظيماً منذ صباي .. طالما قرأت أشعاره حافظاً العديد من المقاطع .. محاكياً، متعمداً، أولَ عهدي بالشعر، قصائدَ معروفةً له .. «أخي جعفر» .. «جرّبيني» .. «القرية العراقية» وغيرها من غرر الشعر العربي ..

يقال إن هناك أدباءَ (تولستوي مثلاً) لم يمرّوا بما يمرُّ به الأديب، عادةً، حين يبدأ النشر .. أي البداية غير الناضجة .. الجواهري واحد من هؤلاء الأدباء .. كان متميزاً منذ أولى قصائده .. للجواهري غرر عديدة لا تقل جودة عن أعظم القصائد العربية (منذ المعلقات .. مروراً بأبي تمام وأبي الطيب ..) ولعل «المقصورة» و«أنيتا» هما ذروتاه أو معلقتاه إذا ما أتيح لأروع القصائد العربية أن تُعلّق في أحد بيوت الشعر العربي .. في الشارقة مثلاً!

شيء عن توفيق الحكيم

كان يحلو له أن يرتدي المعطف الأسود الطويل والقبعة السوداء العريضة .. أن يظهر بمظهر الفنانين .. في باريس أواخر العشرينيات .. باريس الضاجة بأجرأ الصيحات الفنية الجديدة .. بعث به أبوه القاضي ليحصل على دكتوراه الحقوق وكان يقضي يومه في المتحف أو قراءة المسرحيات. وعاد إلى الإسكندرية دونما شهادة .. ممتلئ الذهن بموسيقى القرن التاسع عشر .. وفي الحقيبة رواية ومشروعات مسرحية. لم تكن المخطوطة إلا رائعة الرواية العربية الأولى **عودة الروح** .. ولم تكن المشروعات غير **أهل الكهف وشهرزاد** رائدتي المسرح العربي الجاد.

وبينما كان «نائباً في الأرياف» نأى بنفسه عن الفن والفنانين .. كان القدر آخذاً بيديه إلى أضواء الشهرة الفنية الساطعة ثم وجد نفسه (دون قبعة ومعطف أسودين) علماً من أعلام مصر .. فناناً تتصدر أنباؤه الصحف .. حيث يكثر الحديث عن بخله وعدائه للمرأة. ولم ينف عن نفسه صفة البخل .. فالبخل عنده هو الحرص والبعد عن التبذير. ولم يكن في عدائه للمرأة جاداً كما يبدو لي .. بل وجد «التهمة» فرصة لمزيد من الشهرة والإعلان .. فأمعن في الغلو والمعابثة .. غير أنني أجد أو أتلمس (في الأصح) سرّاً تحت هذه «الضجة» .. سرّاً لم تزل نفسه الجبارة منطوية عليه مذ كان طالباً في الثانوية وحتى آخر العمر .. .

كان خائباً في حياته القلبية .. خائباً في الحب. وهو أحد عظماء «الشعراء» المتعبدين على أعتاب هيكل الجمال الإنساني. لم يكن يرتضي من النساء غير شهرزاد أو إيزيس .. وأين هي المرأة «العصرية» التي تهدهد الملك النمر فينعس بين يديها طفلاً من الأطفال .. أو تلك التي تذرع وادي النيل بحثاً عن رفات ملك مقتول؟

في حياته كلها، وهو المتعطش إلى الجمال، لم يعشق الحكيم إلا ثلاث أو أربع مرات (في اعترافه هو) .. لم يشتعل جوىً إلا بأربعة وجوه: سنية وسوزي وريم وراقصة المعبد. سنية في **عودة الروح** .. وكانت عروساً ولم يكن هو إلا صبياً. وسوزي الباريسية بائعة تذاكر الأوديون في **عصفور من الشرق** .. ولم تكن ريم إلا فلاحة لاح له وجهها في مرة واحدة في ضباب جريمة قتل .. في **يوميات نائب في الأرياف** .. مثلما تظهر النيازك لمحة وتختفي إلى الأبد. آخر مرة كان متولهاً براقصة أوروبية .. وفرّ منها خائفاً، مجروح الفؤاد. لم يذكر الحكيم في سيرته أو قصصه أنه أحب غير هؤلاء النساء الأربع. وأي حب غريب؟ ترى من يعشق امرأة لم يرها إلا مرة واحدة غير المجانين من الشعراء والفنانين؟ هو الذي لم تلح له ريم الفلاحة إلا فجراً في زحمة التحقيق والبحث عن خفايا جريمة! ولم تكن سنية إلا اخضرار ثوب أو ضحكة وجه جميل هائم بحب رجل آخر. أما سوزي المتيمة برئيسها المشرف على إدارة المسرح .. فلم يعش معها إلا ليالي معدودة وصفتها هي في رسالة إليه بليال «ليتها لم تكن» .. في الوقت الذي اعتبرها هو أياماً فردوسية، ولم يخرج منها إلا خروج آدم من الجنة.

كان من أوائل الأدباء الذين قرأت وأحببت. وما انفككت أعيد قراءة عدد من كتبه

بين مرحلة وأخرى من عمري.. قرأته كله تقريباً.. عدا كتابين أو ثلاثة من كتبه غير الأدبية. بل وجدت نفسي عاماً بأكمله لا أقرأ كاتباً غيره! اكتشفته بنفسي دون أن يهديني إلى قراءته أحد من الناس.. في الوقت الذي كنت فيه مترع النفس بأنفاس جبران الربيعية وارتعاشات قلبه الإلهي! فكنت متردد الخطى بين الكلمة المجنحة والحوار الذهني التأملي! في رأي جورج شحادة أنه كان من الممكن أن يصبح من أعظم فناني البشرية لولا أنه شغل نفسه بالشواغل الإعلامية.. بالكتابة الصحفية وبالتنظير الفني.. بالتعادلية والخوض الزائد في المعترك السياسي. ولم يكن الحكيم سياسياً إلا أنه رمى بنفسه جرياً فيما يصطخب حوله من الحياة السياسية. وكانت **أهل الكهف** عند شحادة من أرقى المسرحيات في التاريخ المسرحي. اختيرت روايته **يوميات نائب في الأرياف** بين خمسين (أو مائة؟) كتاباً وقع عليها الاختيار بين آلاف الكتب المؤلفة في النصف الأول من القرن العشرين. ومن غرائب هذا القرن أنه لم يمنح جائزة نوبل مع أنها منحت لمن هم أدنى قامة منه! للسابحين في مياه الشواطيء بينما هو السباح الموغل بعيداً في المحيطات! وهو الذي استوعب الفكر العالمي مسرحاً ورواية وفلسفة وموسيقى وفنوناً تشكيلية، لم يجد مصدراً له إلا في القرآن الكريم.. وفي **ألف ليلة والعقد الفريد** وسواه من كتب التراث. ومن هذه المصادر العظيمة انطلق بأروع أعماله.. **أهل الكهف** من القرآن الكريم.. **شهرزاد** من **ألف ليلة.. السلطان الحائر** من التراث.

من منا لم يخفق قلبه مرتعداً، مقبوضاً عليه بروعة **عصفور من الشرق وزهرة العمر**؟

لم يكن يريد من الفن إلا ما يُشبه المعبدَ الإغريقي: أعمدةً رائعة، متناسقة في العراء ولا شيء آخر. ربما وجد بغيته في الأخريات من كتبه.. حيث لم تعد المفردة تجري غير جريان الماء العذب.. الصافي! وكأنه لا يكتب.. كأنه يقول بلسان «لغة» أدركت آخر ما يدرك من الصفاء واللين.. وكأنه النيل يجري هادئاً فسيحاً بين القرى والأرياف! كان الجاحظ عنده صاحبَ لغة جديدة.. لغة «شعبية» مثل لغة دانتي في الأدب الإيطالي. من هنا جاء بحثه عن «لغة» جديدة.. اهتدى إليها.. أو هي التي وضعت نفسها بين يديه في أعماله الأخيرة **سجن العمر** مثلاً. أنت هنا لا تقرأ كتاباً مكتوباً بأساليب الأدباء.. بل تجد الكلمة سائلة بين يديك سيلان الماء!

في الطريق إلى بلوك

مرةً، وأنا أتسكعُ في الحديقة العامة، رأيتُ امرأةً جالسةً على مصطبة.. وبين يديها كتاب تقرأ فيه.. كان واضحاً أنه ديوان شعر.. حيّيتُ المرأةَ بلطف وقلت:

– أنا أيضاً أُحبُّ الشعر.. هل يمكنني الجلوسُ إليكِ قليلاً؟

قالت المرأة متفحصةً ملامحي الأجنبية:

– لن تضيقَ المصطبةُ باثنين.

قلت، وقد أغلقت المرأةُ الكتاب، وبدا الغلاف ظاهراً لي:

– وأنا أيضاً أحبُّ الشاعر ألكساندر بلوك.

قالت المرأةُ ناظرةً إلى أوراق الشجر الصفر المتساقطة:

- هل تعجبك الرمزية الروسية؟

- لم أجد بين شعرائها شاعراً مهماً جاداً غيرَ بلوك .. الآخرون لم يكتبوا إلا قصائدَ ظلالية باهتة .. بعضهم أغرقته «الصوفية» المصطنعة في تهاويلها الغامضة .. ولم تكن «الأفلاطونية المحدثة» كما أخرجها الفيلسوف الروسي سولڤيوف (وهو شاعر أيضاً) .. لم تكن إلا استغراقاً في اللامحدود .. انتظاراً لعالم بنفسجي يتفتح عن «زهرة» الجمال المطلق .. لم يكن كلُّ ما قيل إلا حُلماً تائهاً!

- ألم ينتظر بلوك «سيدتَه الجميلة» هو الآخر؟ ولم تكن هي إلا زائرةً «غريبةً» في المطعم .. وجهاً مقنّعاً بخمار!

- حدثَ هذا في المنتصف من طريقه الشعري .. في البداية كانت «السيدةُ» ظلاً كنائسياً .. أو ملمحاً أيقونياً .. ألهمته إيّاه صديقةُ صباه (وقد تزوجها فيما بعد) .. وكثيراً ما تساءلت النساء كيف أمكن فتاة غيرَ جذابة، خشنةَ الملامح .. «أرضية» تماماً أن تقودَ الشاعرَ إلى تلك الرؤى النورانية!

- هي غيرة من بعض ممن أردن التقرّبَ منه.

- ربما .. غير أن «غريبتَه» وقد انتصفَ الليل البنفسجي الشعري لم تعد محضَ طيفٍ سماوي .. إنها آخذةٌ الآن حالتين: الرؤيويةَ والأرضيةَ .. في «الأعالي» هي نجمةٌ جديدة .. وفي المطعم أو في الشارع هي امرأة تبحثُ عن «الشاعر» .. وسريعاً ما تعود إلى العُلى وقد أيأسَها منه أنه صامت منزوٍ .. متأخرٌ عن القبض على دفئها «الأرضي» .. مكتفياً بحرارة الحلم.

- وماذا تقول في قصائده عن الخمرة الثلجية وأقنعتها؟

- تلك كانت قصة حُبٍّ عاشها مع ممثلةٍ مسرح .. لم تكن إلا النصفَ الأرضيَّ من الغريبةِ الجميلةِ .. مثلما هو الأمر في قصيدته الطويلة **الدمُ الأسود** .. لم يعد لديه من الرمزيةِ غير «البحثِ الدائب» عن الفكرة الجمالية .. إنها هي الآن متجسدةٌ بامرأةٍ ما .. ما هي بأكثرَ من ظلٍ ..

- إلا أن خيبتَه كانت مبكرة .. أتذكرُ مسرحيتَه القصيرة **عرضٌ هزلي**؟

- لم تكن مبكرة كما تظنين .. لم يكتبها إلا بعد الخسران.

- تعني في «المنتصف» من الطريق كما ذكرت؟

- تقريباً .. ألم تتكشف «الجميلةُ» أخيراً عن دمية كرتونية؟

- فهي، إذن، انقطاع عن التعلّق بأذيال الرمزية .. أو «بأجنحتها المتكسرة» كما يقول عنوانُ روايةٍ من قصائدِ جبران.

- أو هي أجنحةُ إيكاروس!

- ومسرحُه الشعري؟

- كان قصائدَ أكثرَ منه عملاً مسرحياً .. لقد اعتذرَ المخرجُ البارع ستانسلاڤسكي عن إخراج عمله المسرحي المركزي **أغنية القدر**. لم تكن شخصياتُها إلا وجوهاً شاحبة .. وقد أفرغَ الاستغراقُ في «الحُلمية» عروقَها من الدفق الحي .. كانت روسيا تترنح تحت العاصفة .. ولم يعد، ثمة، حيّزٌ «للحُلم الجمالي» .. ورياحُ التغيير تهبُّ كانسةً الشوارعَ من هذه الأوراق الصفر المترامية كما ترين!

- وعندئذٍ لم يجد الشاعر بُدًّا من اللحاق بالواقعية.

- في هذه المرحلة الأخيرة من الطريق الشعري .. لم يكن واقعياً تماماً .. كانت الواقعيةُ لديه مضبّبةً، غائمة .. كان من الصعب جداً عليه أن ينفلتَ نهائياً من المسوح «الليلكية» .. ألم يضع في مقدمة «الإثنا عشر» الثائرين وجهاً نورانياً هو أبعد ما يكون عنهم وعن تطلعاتهم الأرضية؟ لم تكن رمزيةُ بلوك إلا آخرَ صيحةٍ رمزيةٍ في بدايات القرن!

- وهي رمزية أخرى كما يلوح لي .. غيرُ رمزية الفرنسيين.

- كان أقربَ إلى سترندبيرغ .. لم يكن متأثراً به .. بل كان صديقاً روحياً له .. وربما كانت مسرحيةُ سترندبيرغ **الطريقُ إلى دمشق** هي مدخلُ بلوك إلى عالم المسرحي السويدي .. حيث تتشابك أطيافُ الرمزيةِ الجماليةِ بالواقعيةِ السوداء.

- لم يكن بلوك سوداوياً فيما أظن.

- كانت العاصفةُ أقربَ إلى وجدانه المتفجر .. كانت المنفذَ الوحيدَ من الكابوس .. وكان صادقاً في التمسك بأردان العاصفة .. فقد جاءت قصيدتُه الطويلة **الإثنا عشر** ذروةً شعرية .. آخذةً المركزَ من تجربته الفنية .. وهي العمل الشعري الأول والأبرع الذي جاءَ مناقضاً **للأرض الخراب** .. وجمالياً كان قريباً جداً من المرتفعات الشعرية التي حاولت قصيدةُ إليوت أن تقتربَ منها!

في «الطاقة» الشعرية

أحياناً أجدُ «الشعريةَ» في قصة قصيرة جيدة .. أكثرَ مما أجدها في قصيدة .. أجد الشعريةَ في قصة «كآبة» لأنطون تشيخوف أكثرَ مما أجدها في الكثير من قصائد الشاعر الروسي نكراسوف .. وتتألق «الشعرية» في قصص فؤاد التكرلي – «الدمّلة» – مثلاً – بينما هي تخبو في الكثير من قصائد الزهاوي .. مع أن النثرية هي العباءة في القصتين المذكورتين .. إلا أن النبض الشعري هو «المحرّك» .. النسغ الدافق .. مثل هذه «الجوّانية الشعرية» نجدها في بعض قصص كافكا – «حُلُم» مثلاً – أو في بعض قصص همنغواي .. «مكان نظيف .. حَسَنُ الإضاءة» مثلاً .. أين تكمن العلّة؟ إنها تكمن في الرؤيا والأسلوب. في كلتا الحالتين تتقاطع الطرقُ والمنافذ .. يتخلّى الشاعر عن منطقته الشعرية قصوراً وتراخياً .. فيضلُّ السبيل إلى الركاكة .. إلى النظم .. ويتسلل النائر إلى المنطقة الشعرية آخذاً خطوات برومثيوس!

***

في **رباعيات أربع وأربعاء الرماد** .. يبدو إليوت شاعراً صافياً أو خالصاً .. بينما يبدو في «اليباب» مثقلاً بالكشوفات النثرية.. وكأنما هو قصّاص بارع .. يجيد النظم إجادة عظيمة .. كان تماماً مثلَ معلّمه دانتي ..لقد وقعَ «صافياً» في «التجريد» .. أو في النزوع إلى «البياض» .. مثلما وقع دانتي.. يظهر دانتي في **الجحيم** شاعراً أعظم .. وتتأتى عظمته من «واقعيته النثرية» .. وقد توهجت بين يدي الشاعر المبدع توهجاً شعرياً عالياً .. ويظهر في **الفردوس** تجريدياً ضائعاً في «البياض» .. هكذا هو إليوت .. في «الشارعية» .. في ابتلاله بأمطار الأزقة وضبابها كان «قصصياً» .. شاعراً يقبض على الطين بيدين ملتهبتين .. فيمنحه ما يجعل منه فخّاراً .. وفي «صفائه» الشعري كان بارداً .. كان «بياضاً» لا غير!

***

يقال في النقد الأدبي العربي الحديث .. إن «العذرية» أو مرحلة الشعراء العذريين هي رومانتيكية الشعر العربي .. لماذا القول باتجاه رومانتيكي، في الشعر العربي، في غير أوانه أو مكانه؟ لقد سبقت «العذريةُ» العربيةُ الرومانتيكية الغربية بمراحل زمنية طويلة .. وكانت أسبابها غيرَ تلك الأسباب المعروفة التي عجّلت بانبثاق الاتجاه الرومانتيكي .. كانت الثورتان الصناعية والفرنسية و«روح» نابليون وراءَ الرومانتيكية .. وقبلهما كان جان جاك روسو .. ووراءَ «العذرية» كانت الطهرانية والحِسّ البدوي الرفيع .. أين هي الصلة أو الخيط الممدود بين كيتس وبايرون .. وجميل بثينة؟ ربما كان النقاد يقصدون الفردانية والوجدانية .. ربما نجد الخيط العذري ممتداً إلى غنائية التروبادور الفرنسية .. لم تكن «العذرية» رومانتيكية .. كانت عشقيةً «بطوليةً» .. أو نزوعاً «صوفياً» مبكراً .. فإذا كانت هناك رومانتيكية عربية .. فهي الاتجاه الذي اتخذه علي محمود طه شاطئاً يتجول بين مرابعه .. مقمراً أحياناً .. أو هو شاحب بأضواء الشموع!

***

في التنظير الشعري الغربي .. بعد **فن الشعر** لأرسطو .. فيما أعلم .. لم يُكتب كتابٌ نقدي في مثل قوة كتاب الناقد الأميركي ماثيسون عن إليوت .. كان ماثيسون يسارياً .. على العكس من إليوت إذا اعتمدنا النعوت الفكرية المعهودةَ في عالم اليوم .. مع هذا كان ماثيسون أبرعَ من أدرك أسرارَ إليوت الشعرية .. لقد تلمّس بأصابعه الحاذقة تلك «النثريةَ» المتوهجة في شعر إليوت .. «النثرية» التي هي الروح الجديدة «المحرّكة» للمسار الشعري الغربي .. آخذةً طريقها من «زقاقية» بودلير .. لا أظن أن كتاباً آخرَ يُضيء الممرَّ إلى «كواليس» إليوت مثل كتاب ماثيسون!

***

لماذا «النثرية» في الروح الشعرية الجديدة؟ إنها تقليم أظافر العصر الآلي .. إنها تعرية الوجه الملطخ بالأصباغ .. ولابد من أن تتلطخ الأصابع الشاعرة في محاولتها انتزاعَ الصبغة الفاقعة عن الوجه .. وقد تخلّى عن جماليته الرائقة مفضّلاً زينةً كثيفةً، زائفة .. وكأننا في السيرك .. وكأننا نحاول ترويض النمور! كان الشاعر أحمد عبد المعطي حجازي رائداً في قصيدته «مرثية لاعب سيرك» .. لم يكن اللاعب السائر على الحبل إلا شاعراً .. العملُ الشعري كالسير على الحبال .. بين قطبين أو منطقتين: الشعرية واللاشعرية .. القادر الأبرع

هو من يجد «الشعرية» في «النثرية» .. في أيامنا الرديئة هذه كما أظن، لم يعد العالم إلا نثرا .. قال عبد الصبور، مرة، عن بودلير: شاعرٌ أنتَ والكون نثر .. وهو يعني بالكون العصرَ. لقد خبت النزعة «التصوفية» مثلما تصفرُّ الزهرة في الإصيص اليابس .. قد يُقبض على الرياح .. إنما هو القبض على الرمال أيضاً .. كان المتنبي بارعاً في القبض على الحالتين: الرملية والرياحية .. مثلما كان بوشكين وغوته!

❋ ❋ ❋

لا ريب أن الإيقاع العروضي «الرتيب» .. لا يثير إلا المللَّ والرتابة .. من هنا ركب الشعراءُ ناصية النثر الشعري .. إلا أن الحركة الكونية موزونة .. بالسر الكوني الإيقاعي .. وقد يحدث الانفلات فتسقط الشهب وتضيع الأجرام .. لتخبو وتتبدد .. لتعود موزونةً، من جديد .. من خلال الثقوب السوداء كما يقال .. فهل ستضيع القصائد، وقد خلت من الريش .. متحررةً من حكمة الكون الإيقاعية؟

الرواية ومساءلة التاريخ

نجوى شعبان

في شهر مسرى/أغسطس بينما تميل شمس العصاري، كانت النسائم القوية تذرو الرمال الناعمة وتفتُّتات الأصداف لتلقيها على مصبٍّ أنشأته إنشاء، وهي الكثبان الرملية الهلالية في مصيف «الجربي» بدمياط، حيث ستبدأ جدتي دفن جسمها في حمام الرمل لعلاج الروماتيزم. استأنفت الجدة حكايتها وهي تنضو بعض ثيابها في حجرة حفرت في بطن الكثيب .. تجتر ذكرى مواسم الفيضان العفية الزاخرة بأسراب سمك السردين السمينة، مع مؤانستي لها تلتمع عيناها حنيناً، يتصبب وجهها وجسدها عرقا في الدفن .. تقول كطفلة فرحة أنها رأت «الدرافيل» في موسم السردين الذي يعكس أضواء خافتة على سطح كل من البحر والنهر على حدة وأيضاً بعد اختلاط مياههما في لسان رأس البر، وتحكي عن طيور النورس التي تظهر في سماء دمياط فقط في هذا الموسم.

أسألها أن نذهب بالطفطف – الذي يشبه مقطورات الملاهي – إلى لسان رأس البر حتى أرى ومضات السردين تحت الأمواج وأرى الدلافين والنورس، غير أنها أكدت لي للتهرب من ملاحقتي لها .. وقد أثقل الروماتيزم حركتها: رأيت ذلك في عرض البحر، ألحف: متى سأكون في عرض البحر؟

وإذ تتمتم جدتي بالتسبيح أثناء حمام الرمل، أحدق في الرياح التي تنبسط رمالاً وتتكوم كثباناً، ناحتة أشكالاً بديعة تتراءى لخيالي تكوينات سحرية لا ينقصها سوى التعويذة ..

ولدت بمدينة دمياط حيث لا تزال شوارع ضيقة مرصوفة بأحجار البازلت التي قد تنبعج وتتآكل، لكنها تقاوم العدم بإصرار. بين البازلت وبضعة مبان حجرية قديمة والبحر والنهر والبحيرة، استقرت مهاد أحلامي وتأملي، لأنها هي المفعمة بالقديم والحديث في آن. في طفولتي كنت مولعة بقصص كامل الكيلاني للأطفال التي أطلقت في خيال يتحرى المنطق حتى لو تحدث عن الجنيات، وبالراديو ومذيعاته وجرس أصواتهن في لغة عربية رصينة، تمنيت أن أصبح مذيعة وأعلنت هذا على الملأ من أقارب ومعلمات المدرسة. لكني يوماً حملت الجريدة اليومية إلى معلمتي لتدلني عن معنى: أ .ب، ي .ب في مقدمة أخبار الصفحة الأولى؛ فقالت لي:

– إنه يعنى أن الخبر بثته «أسوشيتد برس» أو «يونيتد برس».

– ما معناهما؟

- يعني أنهما وكالتا أنباء.

- ما اختلافهما عن الجريدة؟

- إنها الأسرع، فهي تغطي الأنباء وتبثها دقيقة بدقيقة.

لحظتها قررت أن أكون صحفية، وتركت دمياط وأنا في السابعة عشرة من عمري للالتحاق بكلية الإعلام، جامعة القاهرة .. ولما تخرجت عملت بصحف ومجلات عدة، ولم أستقر بعد في مؤسسة صحفية، حتى أعلنت وكالة أنباء الشرق الأوسط عن مسابقة لتعيين محررين ومترجمين، تقدمت للمسابقة كمحررة، غير أني وجدت أني قد عينت كمترجمة/محررة. وهنا بدأ معي رحلة معرفية جميلة، ما كانت لتتوافر لي لو عملت محررة فقط، وهي التعامل مع اللغة الإنجليزية لست ساعات يومياً، لأني تعلمت في مدارس حكومية، لم تزد علاقتي باللغتين الفرنسية والإنجليزية عن الصحبة الصامتة، غير أنها علاقة أتاحت لي أن أقرأ مؤلفات عالم النفس الإنسانى إيرك فروم من مكتبة الجامعة الأمريكية، وأن أحصل معارفي في الفن التشكيلى الحديث والمعاصر من كتالوجات المكتبة نفسها ومن مكتبة المركز الثقافي الفرنسي بالمنيرة قبل توجهي إلى الولايات المتحدة في منحة دراسية عام ١٩٩٣، لأجد أني أحطت بأغلب حركات وفناني أمريكا عبر هذه الكتب، والجديد أن أرى اللوحات أو التجهيزات في الفراغ وغيرهما مباشرة دون وسيط طباعي.

ثم أكتب قصة «متاهات كوردوفا» في المجموعة القصصية **جدائل التيه** التي صدرت عام ١٩٩٥، استلهم فيها علاقتي بالفنانة التشكيلية الأمريكية المشرفة على بحثي، والحوار الثري الذي كان بيننا، وكانت تتجول معي في معارض خارج بوسطن – رغم حملها في الشهر السابع – إلى أن قاربنا الوصول إلى منطقة طبيعية جميلة، وأخذت بجمالها وصحت «إن لم تكن هذه الجنة، فماذا تكون؟ ردت: إنها كوردوفا، قلت: أه، كوردوفا، تعنى قرطبة»،[١] وتأتى روايتي **الغُر** (١٩٩٨) **ونوة الكرم** (٢٠٠٢) وبهما شخصيتان تكرسان حياتهما لفنهما: في الأولى يوهان الأرمني الذي يمارس التصوير الزيتي، وفي الثانية الخزاف في القرن السادس عشر، حينما استُنزفت مصر من فنانيها وعلمائها.

في عام ١٩٩٥ قررت أن أكرس حياتي لمشروع كتابة ما، ليست بالضرورة مشابهة للكتابات السائدة، فأنا لا يزعجني أن أحفر في منطقة تتطلب صبراً، وأنا ابنة مدينة جل سكانها من صناع الأثاث ومنهم حرفيون فنانون يحفرون على خشب الموبيليا قصصاً مصورة من العصور الوسطى وحتى القصص الشعبية. هنا تراءى لي دمياط كمدينة تكتنز الكثير من الأسرار والتاريخ، وإذا كانت جدتي تنتظر النوارس في موسم الفيضان والسردين، فكان طائري الذي تعلقت به هو الغُر، طائر مهاجر ألوانه بين الأبيض والأسود يأتي من شمال أوروبا إلى سواحل مصر الشمالية سعياً للدفء، ومنه فصيل مقيم في البرك والبحيرات في الدلتا، ومع توقي لمشاهدة أسرابه كنت أخشى أن يقع ضحية إرهاق طيرانه آلاف الأميال فيجري صيده بسهولة ببنادق الرش أو شباك الصيد بنبات المُخَّيط الذي يفرز مادة صمغية يلتصق بها الغُر الذي اتخذته عنواناً لروايتي الأولى كرمز إلى

الارتحال والاستقرار معاً؛ وكل شخصيات الرواية كذلك: مهاجرة، مرتحلة، ومقيمة.

كانت والدتي رحمها الله تحب أيضاً طائر الغُر لتزامن قدومه مع اجتماع العائلة حول «منقد» الفحم، تستدفئ وتقشر الفول السوداني والحكايات التي تحلو في عز شهر طوبة.

كان لابد في الفصل الأول من روايتي الغُر أن أعود بالزمن ما يربو على مائة عام، حين أصدر الخديوي إسماعيل قانون إبطال تجارة الرقيق ويتم تهريب صافيا وهي جارية تلخصت في دمها عدة أعراق، لتصل بعد رحلة طويلة إلى دمياط .. حيث تؤسس هذه «السرية» التي تلقت فنون السرير، لعائلة خشنة وإن كانت رؤيوية، لها اهتياج المرح رغم سوداويتها. كانت صافيا الجدة قادرة على أن تشع إنسانية على من حولها، وذات حضور وعطاء وتواصل مع أهل دمياط الذين كانوا لا يزالون متعددي الجنسيات والديانات في الربع الأخير من القرن التاسع عشر.

في الغُر اهتممت بشخصيات لم تنتزع فقط من أوطانها، بل وليس ثمة أمل في العودة إليها، مثل الصديقة الأرمنية لصافيا الجدة التي كانت تعمل بالتطريز الذي يمنحها مأثرة معرفة الوضع الاجتماعي والاقتصادي للمرأة من درجة تطريز ملابسها .. وتناولت الاجتياح الإسرائيلي لجنوب لبنان ١٩٨٢ وأسر أحد أحفاد صافيا وعودته إلى مصر وفق اتفاقية تبادل الأسرى. بالرواية أيضا شخصية فلسطيني وكردي إضافة إلى جالية الأرمن في مصر الذين تعايشوا مع المصريين ولكنهم لم يندمجوا أبداً بالمجتمع خلافاً للأتراك والمغاربة وحتى اليونانيين الذين أقاموا كمواطنين في مصر.

كانت الغُر هي محاولتي الأولى في استدعاء الغائب لا من صفحات المؤرخين، ولكن من خلال التخييل لمجتمع لم أشهده. ويجدر بي الاعتذار عن هذا الخوض والإبتعاث المنهكين في مقتبس **أوديب في كولون** في بداية الفصل الأول «تعالين يا بنات الظلام القديم أيتها الملاح». ويرد الكورس: «إنه رجل مسن . . . وإلا ما وطئت قدماه الغابة المقدسة التي تقيم بها الصبايا اللائي نرتاع من ذكرهن ونغض أبصارنا ونكمم أفواهم إذا جاورنهن»،(٢) والتاريخ الاجتماعي يقول الكثير عن أربع تجارة في ذاك الوقت وقبله بما يربو على ثلاثة عشر قرنا، وهي تجارة قوامها الأول الآدميون بعد أن يجردوا من صفة الآدمية. تنتفي الآدمية، فلا يد للعبد أو الأمة في صياغة مصيرهما، لتتحدد ملامح صك البيع:

بسم الله الرحمن الرحيم وبعد . . . فمن عبدي ربهما محمد إدريس وعبد المجيد خليل، أن الفرخة الموصوفة بعالية فهي ملكنا، أي عبد الله محمد عثمان. خالية الشبهة والغنيمة. والآن أجرينا مبيعها إلى ستنا بت مكي بمبلغ مائة ريال مجيدي لسداد ثمن الأقمشة المأخوذة منها، وسلمناها الآدمية تتصرف فيها كيف شاءت، وحررنا لها هنا للاعتماد وعدم المعارضة فيها. وذلك بشهادة حسان عبد الكريم وأحمد محمد البشير وحسين بلال في ١٢٩٢ هجرية.(٣)

ومن هنا كان رعب صافيا الجدة من كلمة حرية؛ هي بالنسبة لها مضللة، وقد تنتهكها

خلافاً للعبودية التي عرفت ملامحها واستدمجتها في نفسها، لذا عندما تضع قدميها لأول مرة في حذاء تشعر كما لو أنها أصيبت بالعمى:

انتشت بما لبست حتى جاء الدور على قدميها الحافيتين، وانتعلت الحذاء لأول مرة في حياتها، أصابها اضطراب فلم تعرف كيف تمشي به، وحين جاهدت لتمشي ظنت أنها باتت عمياء. فقد فقدت ما يساوي نصف حواسها، قدمان عميّاوان، إنها استوعبت بقدميها الحافيتين القصر داخلها، الملمس الأملس للرخام الوردي للسلالم الأمامية، ولدفء الباركيه الكاتم لأسرار الخطوات... (ص ٣٦)

ولم تسترد بصرها حتى عاودت الحفاء «.. فخلعت صافيا الحذاء، لا حاجة بها له.. تريد أن تتذوق ملمس أحجار البازلت المرصوف بها الطريق إلى القصر .. أحبت ذلك كله وأحبت باطن قدميها المبصرتين» (ص ٣٧) .. ولن تكون ذاتاً فاعلة سوى في منطقة «التضحية».

سألت نفسي مثل ما يوجه لي من أسئلة دائماً عن سبب ابتعادي عن الكتابة الذاتية، والحقيقة أني كتبت قصة قصيرة وحيدة بها قدر طفيف جداً من ذاتي وهي «دوائر متماسة»، نالت حينها اهتماما من الناقد الراحل غالي شكري، لكني لم أكرر هذه التجربة. أشعر أن مثل هذه الكتابة قد تحدق بي كسياج سجن، مدركة أني لو كتبت عشرات القصص والروايات سأظل أكرر قصة واحدة ووحيدة، بالرغم من إدراكي للنمو والنضج النفسي والروحي، والتجارب التي يخبرها المرء ناهيك عن الولادات المتكررة للنفس .. فأنا في الحقيقة ليس لدي ما أقوله غير أسئلة معلقة تستنفر طاقتي لئلا تكل حتى أجد إجابة ما، جزئية نعم!، هي عندي أفضل من الادعاء بمعرفة تنتالوسية، تومئ ولا تقترب، تقترب ولا تشبع ذهناً أو روحاً.

لا أجد صعوبة في إبعاد ذاتي عند كتابة موضوعات تتعلق بالناس والتاريخ مع معرفتي في الوقت عينه أنه ما أسهل أن يتخفى الكاتب وراء أقنعة عدة شخصيات ذكورية كانت أم أنثوية. وقد أسدت لي روايتاي صنيعاً بديعاً يتجاوز بكثير مجرد البوح، والإحساس بالراحة بعد الفضفضة. عادة أبدأ الكتابة وأنا في حالة سكونية «ظاهرياً» وبعيداً .. خافياً عني تمور الأعماق .. كل واحدة من شخصيات الرواية أخذت مني وأخذت منها، خلت أنني خالقتها، فإذا بها تحرث في روحي، تطلق بريتها، نزوعها للشمشمة والفضول، سخريتها، مرارتها، ولعها بكل هذا الجمال وبتذوق الحياة.

لقد تقلبت التربة إذن .. وواجهت شمس الحياة.

الخنثوية شغلتني لأنه ما من حضارات مجيدة وقديمة إلا ولها أساطيرها عن الخنثى، وزاد من ولعي لاستيعاب معنى ودلالة هذه الفكرة المتكررة في العقل الإنساني، ورودها في فترة لا يمكن أن توصف بأنها فترة طفولة عقل الإنسان، فالآلهة الكبرى في مصر الفرعونية كانت خنثوية (آتوم-نيت)، (شو-تفنيت)، (أوزيريس-إيزيس)، أي أن الإلهي يجمع في ذاته قطبي الذكورة والأنوثة، لأن الولادة وتكرار الحياة يتطلبان ذكراً

وأنثى. لذا كان من الطبيعي أن تكون أقنعة الملك الفرعون، رجلاً كان أم امرأة مثل حتشبسوت، أقنعة مزدوجة الجنس. والأسطورة الإغريقية تشير إلى أن الإنسان الأول كان رجلاً وامرأة في جسد واحد ورأسين، شقهما إله غيور .. تعرضت في **الغُر** لرواية **أورلاندو** لـفرجينيا وولف التي كانت معزوفة جديدة للحن قديم قدم الحكيم نصف الإلهي تيريسياس .. وبدا لي أن الأخيلة التفسيرية القديمة ذات عمق بالغ من الحقيقة، فمبدأ الخنوثة هنا ليس أمراً يمس الأخلاق، لكنه قراءة مستبصرة للنفس الإنسانية وأبرزتْ في قوالب مختلفة من الأسطورة. ويأتي التحليل النفسي المعاصر الذي ينوه بأن رمز الخنثى ينطوي على رغبة عميقة وعسيرة وهي الكمال والاكتمال، ويقول إن كلاً من المرأة والرجل، كلاهما يحمل «الأنيما/نفس المرأة» و«الأنيموس/نفس الرجل» وآملين أن يتفاهم الجزآن من أجل علاقة طيبة مع النفس ومع الآخر .. وقد حوت **الغُر** إشارات إلى ذلك الحلم بالتناغم مع العالم، فصافيا الحفيدة تعلن عن رغبتها المستحيلة في أن تكون الفرس والجواد معا، وفي آخر الرواية يهديها صديقها الأرمني/المصري يوهان لوحة رسمها عنوانها «الخنثى/هيرمافروديتي القرن الحادي والعشرين»، فكتبت صافيا الحفيدة خلف اللوحة: «الآن أخوض في الغابة» (ص ٢٢٩) .. ومعناه المباشر أن ستخوض في معمعة الحياة. هذا صحيح جزئياً، غير أن صافيا الصغيرة لن يكون بمقدورها إنجاز هذا الأمر إلا بدخول الغابة المقدسة كما في نص **أوديب في كولون** التي تعنى الخافية من النفس الإنسانية التي تمتلك إمكانات تبهر وتسعد، وجحيم لا يشقه إلا إنسان شجاع .. حينما تقترب صافيا من لاوعيها وتدركه، فلا خوف عليها من خوض معتركات الحياة.

أتذكر في طفولتي بدمياط أني صعدت سلالم حجرية مرهقة لبيت حجري عتيق وعال يعود إلى قرون مضت، دلفت إلى شرفة في الدور الأعلى، فشعرت بشيء غريب: تتغلغل فيّ بهجة ساكنة وإحساس لم أسمه يومها – الحرية – وبأني أعرف أشياء لم يسبق لي أن سعيت لمعرفتها حقا .. وأن هذه اللحظة لن تتكرر كثيراً. ولأني أفكر بمنطقية اعتبرت أن المشهد البانورامي لمدينة دمياط الذي يبدو واضحاً من الشرفة هو السبب. غير أني بدأت السؤال والاستفسار والقراءة، ولم يكذب حبوري آنذاك فخلفي في هذا المشهد كانت تقع قصبة الثغر في القرن السادس عشر ومسجد البحر والوكالات والقسياريات التجارية والخانات ومكاتب القناصل الأوروبية بدمياط وبمحاذاة النيل البيوتات الثرية لأعيان دمياط: كبير التجار، القاضي، كبير الصاغة، يهودي الجمرك، أرمني الصرافة، قبودان ثغر دمياط، وعلى مدى النظر «سوق اللبن» القديم وبه كنيسة مار جرجس التي بنيت في القرن السابع عشر تضم عظام القديس مار جرجس مزاحم.

عن يساري يقع سوق الحسبة الذي لا يزال يحمل اسمه حتى الآن، حيث كان المحتسب وشيوخ الطوائف كافة، هذه الطوائف التي اقتضتها الحاجة من قبل الحرفيين في مصر، والتي كانت تعد شكلاً أولياً لممارسة ديمقراطية من بيئتنا. وفي البعيد تربض أوقاف السلطان قنصوه الغوري فوق جزيرة القصبي التي طمرتها الفيضانات .. وثمة خليج يخاصر المدينة ويصب قرب قرية شطا .. البيت الحجري في طفولتي أعاد لذهني الأحجار الضخمة التي ألقاها الظاهر بيبرس لإغلاق مدخل مصب دمياط أمام السفن التجارية

الكبيرة تحسباً من أية هجمات حربية بعد الصليبيين، فدمياط هي مفتاح النيل الموصل لقلب مصر .. في هذا كله أحب دمياط التاريخ، إذ كانت مدينة كوزموبوليتانية تضارع مدينة البندقية أنذاك، تعرف بنسيجها الدقيق كالحرير والقباطي وكسوة الكعبة المشرفة، وقلعة عسكرية حصينة صدت الكثير من هجمات الصليبيين التي أرّخ لها، وغارات القراصنة التي لم تسجل بوضوح فهي في حكم المهمل والمهمش، ولأن الأهالي من البحارة هم من يتصدون منذ ما قبل الميلاد وحتى عصر الحكم العثماني للقراصنة .. فليس من المستبعد أيضاً أن يكون من بين سكان المدينة قراصنة، وبخاصة أن حركة القرصنة في بحر الروم كانت تعكس بدقة مدى توازن أو اختلال القوى لدول في حوض البحر المتوسط، ولا ننسى الأصول الشامية (الفينيقية) والقبرصية واليونانية لأهل دمياط.

وأتذكر أمثلة عن الشهور القبطية سمعتها مغناة من نساء العائلة، كما تغنيها ليل وأمونيت المغتربتان في جزيرة رودس في رواية **نوة الكرم**: واحشني مية طوبة، ولبن برمهات، وتين بؤونة، وسمك كيهك، ورطب توت، وعنب مسرى .. إلخ.

أينما وليت وجهك تجد المياه تضمك فأنت في دمياط، التي نحت اسمها من «الماء» باللغة الهيروغليفية «تم أتي» أي مدينة المياه أو مدينة مجرى المياه .. وقبل قرون كانت ذات ثغرين: نهري وبحري كشبه جزيرة يحدها شمالاً بحر الروم/البحر المتوسط، نهر النيل، بحيرة المنزلة، ويالثرائهم جميعاً، في **الغُر** كان الصيادون القدامى يرتجفون فرقاً لدى انبثاق نافورة من النيران على فترات متباعدة في بحيرة المنزلة ويرون هذا من أعمال الجن والشياطين، غير منتبهين إلى أن رائحة النيران تشير إلى النفط المخبوء في قاع البحيرة. وقبل أشهر في الملتقى الثقافي الأول لمدينة دمياط في سبتمبر ٢٠٠٣ يؤكد نيافة الأنبا بيشوي مطران دمياط وكفر الشيخ أن نيل دمياط مكتنز بالآثار القبطية.

أما البحر فهو انفتاح على العالم ومكمن التعرض للغزو والغارات.

لما تراجعت قيمة ميناء دمياط بعد حفر ترعة المحمودية سنة ١٨٢٠ على أيام محمد علي، تكاثفت الخسارة بحفر قناة السويس وقيام مدن بور سعيد والإسماعيلية، لكن تاريخ دمياط وجغرافيتها يرشحانها كمكان لا يتطلب الضعف واليأس والاستسلام فأبدعت عقول أهل دمياط صناعات جديدة كصناعة الحلوى والأحذية وتحول كل بيت إلى مصنع صغير لغزل الحرير، وحتى التربة استفادوا من عيوبها بزراعات غير نمطية .. إنها مصر مصغرة .. ولنرى تحايل البطلة ليل كي تكسب عيشها في ظل ظروف اقتصادية ضاغطة .. وإذا طفح الكيل تتمرد شخصيات الرواية وناس دمياط عبر النقش بالأنامل وبالروح، بالنقش سواء على المخبوزات، على الخزف، على أقدام الناس وعظامهم، بالكتابة وصناعة الأحبار، كبعد وجودي، وإن لم يؤتيا أثرهما الفوري أو القريب، تمردوا عبر النزق كما في ليلة يوم القيامة في الخرابة التي حاصرتها المياه فيما بعد لتندثر. في هذه الليلة سخر الدمايطة بخيالهم الصافي من السلطان والوالي وكبار العسكر العثمانية بتقليد لبسهم الخلع السلطانية من فرو السمور، وأبرز المشوهون عيوبهم الجسمانية بفخر لا يدانيه سوى عشق نرسيس لجسده وجماله، ولم ينسوا الرقصات المعربدة في ضوء القمر الفضي .. ثملوا و«انسطلوا» .. عاشوا لحظة

خارج زمان الوعي والمنطق، لحظة في بؤرة منطقة الظل والعتمة في الجماعة: لاشعورهم .. هؤلاء هم الذين يحتملون الحياة، ويبنونها، يحافظون ويعيشون ويحبون الحياة، حتى لو قامت القيامة فإنهم سيقيمون في «الخرابة» لاستحلاب المباهج، لا ينسحبون من الحياة رغم إزاحتهم، حتى وهم مُزاحون راغبون بالحياة، لأن مصر حضارة تعرف قيمة الحياة وبناءها والاستمتاع بها.

ميتافيزيقا البحر تغمرني بتجلياتها اللانهائية في شعابه وفي أعماقه، في طيات تياراته، في صخب وسكون أمواجه، رياحه، وأنوائه، فهل دخلت عرض البحر بعبر مياه المعتمة أحياناً؟ أم كررت لفظة البحر خمساً وستين مرة عبر صفحات الرواية؟ علني أتوحد مع موسيقاه الأداجو والكريشندو في حركة الأمواج، أصف أنواء الكرم:

موجة واحدة كالجبل داهمت سفن القافلة فردمتها، بعثرتها، أهاجتها ففقدت الاتجاه والتوازن، انفتح كهف داخل الأمواج، فظلت تدور حول بعضها، حتى توقفت الرياح والأمطار واصطخاب الأمواج مخلفة البرد القارص، أحدث ارتطام سفن القافلة ببعضها البعض خسائر أفدح من أنواء الكرم نفسها، تتطوح سفينة لتأخذ اتجاه العرض فتأتي أخرى مندفعة تضربها في منتصفها لتتحطم وتغرق في حين تتهشم مقدمة الثانية وتتسرب المياه إلى جوف السفينة .. كانت سفينتنا الأحسن حظاً، إذ لفظت إلى البحر كل مئونتها والبضائع في الخُن وبعض البحارة والتجار ثم استوت متوازنة ثم مالت يميناً فانزلقت اندفاعات الأمواج إلى البحر من جديد.(٤)

وفي الحلم الرئيسي في الرواية يعن للبحر أن تُرسم خطوط القدر عبره:

أمال غياث الدين رأسه في إغفاءة مباغتة، فزع منها وقد ظنها أعواماً، رأى نفسه يطفو على سطح البحر وحيداً، والطريق إلى رودس لا يزال طويلاً، طويلاً، هل سيقطع هذه المسافة سباحة في هذا الشتاء القارس؟ يرتجف من صقيع المياه .. هاهو الآن في رودس يبحث عن نور الدين، النار تلتهم الجزيرة، ما إن تقع عيناه على مبنى حتى تدكه النيران، يترك الحي المحترق مخلفاً وراءه أسواره وبوابته وقد ضربتها الصواعق، يتجه إلى جبال قريبة: إنه الطريق، البيوت مخفية وسط تدرجات الجبل، حتى هذه تشتعل .. ورأى داراً صغيرة ذات قبة باقية على حالها، يقف على بابها صبي، أشاح بوجهه إلى جهة أخرى، ثم صرخ: كيف لم أعرفه؟ إنه نور الدين، عاد ولم يجد الدار ولا الصبي. (ص ١٦)

وفي هدوء قبل الكارثة:

على صفحة ماء ساكن بلا زبد، ضربت مجاديف سفينتنا على غير هدى في الظلام، السمع الرهيف للمجدفين أيقظهم من سبات الاطمئنان، أبلغوا الربان .. أمر بدوره بإيقاظ الأعور الذي صعد إلى سطح السفينة، رغم أن له عيناً واحدة، كان ذا قدرة لا توصف على الإبصار في الظلام، إذ ينظر إلى الشيء من جانب عينه مما يعطيه صورة أوضح من توجيه النظر المباشر للشيء .. نظر الأعور في اتجاه الظلمة البعيد، وحرك عينه المبصرة الوحيدة ذات اليمين وذات اليسار وإلى أعلى وإلى أسفل، ثم توجه إلى القائد. (ص ٨٨)

وكما نصح جدي حفيده ذات يوم بعيد في طفولتي، استدعى غياث في نوبة إغمائه الترجمان مع أصداء التراتيل، شأنه شأن معلم . يقول :

يا ولدي الموج أنواع ثلاثة مثل مواقف الحياة الصعبة، موجة عالية، عالية كجبل تظنها غادرة، تتراجع إلى الوراء فتضربك بعنف، فقط لو وقفت مكانك، فإنها ستتجاوزك، ويتلاشى هياجها وتصبح ساجية حال مرورها بك .

حاول غياث الوقوف في الماء، شعر كأن دوامة تسحبه إلى أسفل، ففزع وجدف بطاقة الهلوع.

يا ولدي، ثمة موجة عالية، إذا تراجعت للوراء أكلتك، ولو قذفت بنفسك داخلها، وتركت نفسك للتيار ستنجو حتماً، اقتحمها واسبح مع التيار، ليس ضده.

فعل غياث ما أوصاه به الترجمان فوجد نفسه مبتعداً كثيراً عن سفينة القراصنة والتي تراءت كمنقذ وحيد، ودونها حتف محتوم.

يا ولدي، الموجة الأخيرة صاخبة عنيفة كالقدر الذي لا مفر منه، فارم صيدك من السمك وأدوات صيدك، ركز اهتمامك على الحفاظ بيديك على دماغك ورقبتك، ستفصد الموجة العنيفة دمك، ستصدمك بالصخر ويمتلئ جسمك بالجروح والرضوض، لكنها لو تعرف: أقل الخسائر.

يا ولدي، لا ترفس في البحر، الرفس إنهاك للطاقة وإهدار لها، وثمن فعل هذا جد باهظ. (ص ٩٢)

ويشف الماء والبحر في أحلام ليل عن رغبة إيروتيكية:

في تلك الليلة حلمت ليل أنها عطشى للغاية، ومعها كوز ماء فارغ، تبحث عمن يملأه لها، هناك من يقترح أن تحصل على ماء القلة البارد في الطابق

الثاني، لما وصلت قالوا لها إن الماء الساقع في مكان آخر .. تتراجع ليل عن رغبتها في الماء البارد، مجرد ماء عادي من السبيل، وحتى ماء السبيل لم تحصل عليه. (ص ١٠٣)

واللايقين هي الكلمة التي أعتبرها مفتاحاً لنصوصي، من بداية رواية **نوة الكرم** وأنا أشير إلى اللايقين عبر اقتباسات قيلت في أزمنة وأماكن متعددة، ولم يقتصر هذا على بداية الرواية، بل كمقدمة لبعض الفصول، فنقلت عن التراث الفرعوني قول إيزيس «أنا ما كان، وما هو كائن، وما سيكون، وما من إنسان بقادر على رفع برقعي» (ص ٩) وتساءلت أنا «أليست الحقيقة نفسها كذلك؟!» (ص ٩)، ونقلت عن ديورانت قوله: «معظم التاريخ ظن وتخمين والبقية الباقية تحامل وهوى» (ص ٩) وعن جاك دريدا «الوهم أشد رسوخاً من الحقيقة، بل إنه متجذر فيها بالدرجة التي يضحى فيها متطابقاً معها ومطابقاً لها تماماً» (ص١٣٩).. لذا أرى أن الراوي العليم بكل شيء وببواطن الأمور، لا يناسبني كتركيبة شخصية، ومن ثم لا يناسبني فنياً لأنني اخترت الابتعاد عن التاريخ الرسمي، لهذا كانت الأصوات الثلاثة الراوية: الذات الراوية غير محددة الهوية والترجمان «الشاهد على العصر» وحفيدته المعاصرة .. وفي **الغُر** كانت كل شخصية تسرد الأحداث من منظورها الشخصي مما يعني نسبية الحقيقة لدى كل منها، ومن ثم فالحوار قائم دوماً بينها، ليضيء روافد الخبيئة الماضية في نهاية القرن التاسع عشر وبين الحاضر يمتد منذ ثمانينيات القرن العشرين وحتى الآن. وكتبت شخصية يمنى، تلك الشخصية القلقة والمقلقة في آن، تعلن عن نفسها بجلاء: «أنا لا أنتمي لأحد، لا أحد ينتمي إليّ» (ص ٢٢٤) مستلهمة فيها تجربة حياتية لصديقة رحلت هي أروى صالح ذات التجربة اليسارية المتوهجة في فترة السبعينيات، والغريب أن أحداً من أصدقاء أروى الكثر لم ينتبه إلى أن يمنى هي أروى، فيما عدا ناقد مرهف الحدس هو ياسر طلعت كتب مقالاً في **الأهرام المسائي** يربط بين التصريح السابق ليمنى، وفقرات من كتاب أروى صالح الأشهر: **المبتسرون**.(٥)

لقد كتبت الروايتين عن مدينة دمياط مدينة/التاريخ، ليس لأنها مدينة طفولتي التي تختلف كثيراً عما قلته آنفاً، فتاريخ على هذا النحو يأتي بحمولته من الغواية بالحرية وارتياد لمنطقة خصيبة غير مجرَّفة في فن الرواية .. وأهداني مولد الست دميانة/سانت دميانة .. وبعض ممارسات الورع أو الهوس الديني الذي يصل حد الإغماء، أهداني بعض مفاتيح لشخصية المتطهرة آمونيت في **نوة الكرم** .. وإذا كان التاريخ لا يعيد نفسه إلا لمن لم يقرأه جيداً، من هنا أرادت هذه الشخصية أن تبتعث الأجلّ والأجمل والأجدى، حتى لا نعاني مجدداً من القطيعة المعرفية عن ماضينا التي أرهقتنا ولا تزال، لنتساءل كل يوم عن هويتنا! أصرت آمونيت على أن يدون الترجمان العامية القبطية وفق ما تنطقه امرأة عجوز في الصعيد ونقل هذه إلى العامية العربية، أو بشكل أدق العامية المصرية.

وهنا أستعير وصف ثناء أنس الوجود في وصفها لدمياط في الرواية بأنها «واسطة عقد»(٦) من حيث المكان، ففي لحظة تاريخية في القرن السادس عشر يمتد فضاء الحكي من دمياط إلى المشرق وتمتد إلى الصحراء في الغرب وإلى القسطنطينية وإلى البحر المتوسط (بحر الروم)، وتنزل ناحية الجنوب في الصحراء حيث القبائل الذاهبة للتجارة شمالاً وجنوبا، وحيث قبائل الحجيج .. في مسعى لفتح نوافذ الحكاية على أكثر من هواء لكي يدخل، لاقتناص اللحظة ومحاولة الاحتفاظ بها .. هل اللحظة مهددة حتى أستطيع أن أقتنصها؟ إن الوجود مهدد، ومهدد في العمق، والحضارة موجودة ولكن عملية النقش تعمقها.

وقد أشار صلاح السّروي إلى محاولة استنطاق اللحظة التاريخية في كتابتي الروائية،(٧) كما أن محيي الدين اللاذقاني يرى أنني وكاتبات جيلي نتعامل مع «التاريخ الكامن»،(٨) و أضيف من ناحيتي أنني أستعين بالتاريخ بوصفه خطاباً اجتماعياً لأناس عاديين، ليسوا هامشيين بالمعنى المتعارف عليه. هؤلاء الناس هم صناع التاريخ وبناؤوه، المقهورون الذين يقع عليهم ثقل وعبء القرارات الخاطئة للحكام، وهم وحدهم الذين يشيدون في حال القرارات السديدة؛ هم صناع التاريخ الذين لم يكتبوا التاريخ أبداً، بل كتبه مؤرخون رسميون لذوي النفوذ والسلطة، يضخمون إنجازاتهم الهزيلة ويزيفون كما يتراءى لهم، لتبقى الذاكرة الحقيقية خاوية أو مليئة بالأباطيل .. التاريخ الحقيقي صنعه هؤلاء، فمن يكتب عنهم؟ لذا بدت شخصية الترجمان كمؤرخ يكتب بالحبر السري تاريخ هؤلاء، فهو الشاهد على عصره ذو الضمير الحي.

في كتابتي الروائية لم يحدث أن كان لها بطل واحد، بل هم عدة أبطال تتواصل وتتوازى مصائرهم وخياراتهم في الحياة. هذا يتيح لي أن أظهر تعددية المجتمع الدمياطي بين مسلم ومسيحي - بكنائسهم المختلفة - ويهودي، وأيضاً شخصية لا تزال تخايلها بعض ممارسات وثنية من الكرنفالات الأوروبية السلافية .. لكني أرى أن المايسترو في نوة الكرم المتحكم والمسيّر لنغمات الشخصيات ونجواها - من أطراف أنامله - هو المطراوي ذو الحنين القهري إلى جنة طفولته المفقودة.

وتحزنني مقارنة وقائع الرواية بما هو معيش حالياً، فأنا لا أرى أن التاريخ يكرر نفسه كما يقول البعض، أرى أننا - من حيث العقلية الجمعية - لا نزال «محلك سر»، سأورد مثالا لذلك: اتصل بي أحد الأصدقاء، كنت أيامها راقدة لمرض ولا أقرأ الصحف، وقال لي افتحي روايتك نوة الكرم على الصفحة رقم ١١١ حيث كتبت: «حدثان هامان في يوم واحد، أعلن الكشاف وقوع فتنة طائفية وحذر مناديه من مغبة الفتنة وسوء عواقبها على الجانبين، زاعماً أن القبط أعادوا بناء أجزاء من كنيسة بدلاً من ترميمها، وأنهم يسعون لضم أراض مجاورة لها وإعلاء قبة الكنيسة كي تطاول المئذنة» (ص ١١٧).

ولما أنهيت قراءة الفقرة سألته عن غرضه من ذلك قال: هذا بالضبط ما حدث في مغاغة ٢٠٠٢، فتنة طائفية لأن هناك من أشاع أن مسيحيي مغاغة يسعون إلى بناء قبة

تطاول مئذنة مسجد بالبلدة. تنهدت وقلت لحالي : ستمائة عام مرت على مثل هذه الأحداث في مصر العثمانية ولم يتغير تفكير الناس .. ماذا يعني ذلك؟

أن أكتب عن امرأة من القرن السادس عشر معناه أن أحدس أيضاً بمشاعرها الحسية، . . لذا كتبت عن ليل الفتاة المكافحة التي تعول أخوتها الصغار بعد وفاة والديها. ليل أيضا مشاغبة لها شقاوات لا تخلو من براءة، وائدة لأنوثتها التي لن تتفجر إلا في مرحلة لاحقة من عمرها، عمر الجدات آنذاك، وتحايلها وهي صغيرة على المعيشة بارتداء ثياب الغلمان في أوقات صدور قرارات – وقتية أو لحظية أو مزاجية – بمنع خروج النساء من بيوتهن، فإذا بزيها الغلماني يفضح تهتك مجتمع يعاني الاضمحلال، حين يتجه بعض الرجال إلى الجنسية المثلية، مدركين أو غير مدركين، أنهم يتعالون حتى على المرأة كجسد.

والرواية تسائل التاريخ عن مسار ومصير الحضارة العربية والإسلامية. وتسأل: هل نحن نحتضر؟ ومن آيات الأفول ما جاء على لسان صاحب سفينة أجنبية قبيل إبحارها «كما أني لا أستغل الشح في قمحكم» (ص ١٥) ويعترف أئمة الجوامع في صلاة الجمعة «. . . بالرغم من شح القمح الآن» (ص ٤٤)، ولذلك حرّمت السلطات العثمانية على الغريب أن ينقل قمحاً إلى خارج البلاد المصرية أو عبر هذا الثغر، لكن التلاعب سار من قبل قبودان الجمرك وكبير تجار دمياط معاً. وقد ظلت اللحظة التاريخية التي شح فيها القمح مسيطرة حتى نهاية الرواية، ربما لهذا السبب جعلت البطلة ليل تعمل في صناعة الكعك «كحكية» وهي الصناعة التي لا تتوافر إلا مع الرخاء.

أما اللغة فقد نهلت من العامية المصرية المعاصرة جملها الثرية بالمجاز الشعبي الذي ينطوي على شاعرية لا تنفد، وتضمينها بعض المفردات والجمل التي كانت سائدة في القرن السادس عشر لدى الشعب المصري. أعتقد أن الالتزام بالفصحى على طول الرواية هو نوع من المخاتلة، لأن الألفاظ والجمل العامية لأبطالي سواء كانوا مصريين أو وافدين، تحمل شحنة أصدق في الدلالة ووقعها الشفاهي .. ومن الثراء الاعتراف بهذا التعدد في اللهجات وتفاعلها، فهذا من قبيل الانفتاح على الآخرين داخل أنفسنا.

الهوامش

(١) جدائل التيه (القاهرة: دار الثقافة الجديدة، ١٩٩٥)، ص ٢٨.

(٢) سوفوكليس، أوديب في كولون، ترجمة وتقديم علي حافظ (الكويت: وزارة الإعلام، ١٩٧٢)، ص ص ١١٤ و١١٥.

(٣) الغُر (القاهرة: الدار المصرية اللبنانية، ١٩٩٨)، ص ١٣. وكل الاستشهادات من الرواية تحيل إلى أرقام الصفحات بين أقواس داخل المتن.

(٤) نوة الكرم (القاهرة: دار ميريت، ٢٠٠٢؛ الطبعة الثانية: القاهرة: مكتبة الأسرة، ٢٠٠٣)، ص ٢٧. وكل الاستشهادات من الرواية تحيل إلى أرقام الصفحات الطبعة الثانية بين أقواس داخل المتن.

(٥) ياسر طلعت، «شخصيات تأسر القلب وتوجعه .. **الغُر** شهادة عن جيل مسكون بالخوف»، الأهرام المسائي (٨ ديسمبر ١٩٩٩).

(٦) ثناء أنس الوجود، «**نوة الكرم** بين النقش بالروح والمجاز الشعبي»، **أدب ونقد**، السنة الثامنة عشرة، العدد ٢٠٧ (نوفمبر ٢٠٠٢)، ص ١١٩.

(٧) صلاح السّروي، «**نوة الكرم** تستجلي الحقيقة تحت ركام الأوهام»، **ميدل إيست أونلاين،** <www.middle-east-online.com>. ٧ فبراير ٢٠٠٤.

(٨) محيي الدين اللاذقاني، «أساليب تعامل الرواية النسوية مع الذاكرة التاريخية العربية»، **جريدة الشرق الأوسط** (٣١ أكتوبر ٢٠٠٣).

الخيط السري بين القديم والحديث في الفن:
مقابلة مع رافع الناصري

مي مظفر

مقدمة

ينتمي الفنان رافع الناصري (١٩٤٠-) إلى جيل الستينيات، تبعاً لتقسيم الحركات الأدبية والفنية إلى أجيال. وتشكل مجموعة الستين الجيل الثالث من الحركة الفنية الحديثة في العراق إذا ما اعتبرنا الجيل الأول هو الجيل المؤسس. ولدى الحديث عن نشأة الحركة الفنية الحديثة وتطورها في العراق لا يمكن لأي باحث تجاهل الدور التاريخي للفنانين الذين أسهموا فيه. فمع قيام الحكم الوطني في العراق (١٩٢١) عاد نفر من الضباط العراقيين الذين درسوا فنون التصوير وفق المناهج الأوروبية ضمن دراستهم للعلوم العسكرية في إسطنبول، عاصمة الدولة العثمانية آنذاك. فقد كان العراق، لغاية تفكك الحكم العثماني مع انتهاء الحرب العالمية الأولى، مجموعة ولايات تابعة له. ولدى الشروع ببناء الدولة العصرية في العراق بدأت الملامح الفنية والثقافية تتشكل في العاصمة بغداد بصورة نشاط فردي وجماعي، فكانت فنون الرسم والنحت في طليعة هذه النشاطات، خاصة وأن الدولة الفتية أولت الفنون الجميلة اهتمامها وباشرت بعد العقد الأول من تأسيسها إرسال البعثات الدراسية إلى أوروبا. وما أن حل العقد الرابع من القرن العشرين حتى أصبح في العراق نخبة من الفنانين الذين درسوا الفن في المعاهد المتخصصة واستأنفوا نشاطهم من خلال التدريس أو العمل في محترفاتهم الخاصة.

في مطلع عقد الخمسين من القرن العشرين بدأت الجماعات الفنية تتشكل في العراق على غرار ما جاءت عليه هذه التكتلات الفنية في أوروبا. فتكونت جماعة «الرواد» بقيادة فائق حسن في عام ١٩٥٠، و«جماعة بغداد» بقيادة جواد سليم في عام ١٩٥١، وكان كلا الفنانين الرائدين قد درس الفن في أوروبا، ولهما يعود الفضل لا في إرساء قواعد الفن الحديث في العراق فحسب، بل في تأسيس قسمي التصوير والنحت في معهد الفنون الجميلة في بغداد (١٩٣٩). وفي عام ١٩٥٣ قام الفنان حافظ الدروبي، الذي عاد من إيطاليا، وأقام أول مرسم حر في بغداد، بتأسيس جماعة «الانطباعيين». كان لكل جماعة توجهها الفني، غير أن جواد سليم تميز عنهم بطرح ذي بعد فكري وأسلوبي معاً، فقد كان أول من تنبه إلى قيمة التراث في فنون العراق عبر مراحله التاريخية المختلفة، وسعى إلى

إيجاد منهج فني ذي طابع عربي. وحققت الحركة الفنية في العراق ذروة نشاطها وإبداعها في عقد الخمسين، ثم مرت بشيء من التلكؤ والارتباك والتكرار مع مطلع الستين. ولكن في النصف الثاني من عقد الستين شهدت الحركة الفنية نشاطاً وتحركاً جريئاً مع ظهور جيل جديد من المبدعين تعزز بعودة عدد من الفنانين الذين درسوا الفن في دول العالم المختلفة غرباً وشرقاً، واكتسبوا مهارات متنوعة، فكان ذلك أحد الأسباب المهمة وراء غنى الحركة التشكيلية العراقية وتنوع الأساليب فيها. كما أن تعاضد المثقفين من مختلف الاختصاصات، خاصة المعماريين، أسهم إسهاماً كبيراً في الترويج للحركة الفنية الحديثة وتقريبها إلى أذهان الجمهور وذوقه. وسرعان ما أصبح نتاج الفنانين التشكيليين العراقيين مع نهاية الستين مصدر دهشة وتساؤل من خلال حضوره المميز في العالم العربي.

كان، ولا يزال، لهذا الجيل الذي أصبح يعرف بجيل الستين الفضل الكبير في دفع الحركة الفنية في العراق إلى مدى أوسع، مستنداً إلى الركائز والتقاليد الفنية التي وضعها الرواد: فائق حسن وجواد سليم وشاكر حسن آل سعيد ومحمود صبري على وجه خاص. وعلى الرغم من ظهور أجيال لاحقة من المبدعين العراقيين، لا تزال أعمال جيل الستين، على الأغلب، نموذجية في عطائها المتواصل وتكريسها للعمل الفني والالتزام بمبادئه والحفاظ على مستوياته. ولهذا الجيل يعود الفضل في مد جسور التواصل مع العالم العربي والعالم برمته.

رافع الناصري، إذن، واحد من أعلام جيل الستين. اختار، بعد تخرجه في معهد الفنون الجميلة في بغداد عام ١٩٥٩، دراسة الفن في جمهورية الصين الشعبية من بين خيارات أخرى كانت أمامه لدراسة الفن في المعاهد الأوروبية. ولعل انغماسه في فنون الصين وعشقه لها ترك تأثيره الإيجابي على أعماله الفنية سواء الغرافيكية أو الزيتية؛ بل كان الخيط السري الذي غذى تجربته الفنية على امتداد مراحلها. والمتابع لمسيرته الفنية بوسعه أن يضع يده على سلسلة متواصلة من التجارب المتوالدة التي تسعى إلى تطوير الشكل الفني دون التنازل عن الأسس العلمية التي قامت عليها تجربته بدءاً من أعماله الأكاديمية الأولى وانتهاء بأعماله التجريدية المحض.

المقابلة

مي مظفر: كيف وجدت طريقك إلى الفن؟

رافع الناصري: كان درس الرسم في المدارس العامة في العراق درساً منهجياً وكنت أتعلم الرسم وأمارسه بمحبة كبيرة، وكنت متفوقاً في الأداء بين زملائي حتى أنني لمست اهتماماً خاصاً من مدرس الرسم وهو الذي شجّعني على استئناف هذا الطريق. فاخترت الدراسة في معهد الفنون الجميلة في بغداد، وفضّلته على اختيارات أخرى كانت أمامي. وفي المعهد اندمجت مع الحياة الفنية، وأصبحت جزءاً منها، كما أدركت أنني أملك

البذرة الصالحة للنمو في هذه التربة، ولنقل إنني أدركت قدراتي الأولية. كان القبول في معهد الفنون الجميلة يتم عن طريق اختبار الكفاءات، وعلى توافر عناصر أساسية لدى المتقدم. كان اختباراً صعباً، وكان ذلك، فلأول مرة وجدت نفسي أمام «موديل» حي، وكان ذلك فرّاش المعهد، وقد جلس أمامنا مرتدياً بذلة رمادية مع قميص أبيض وحذاء أسود، وقد وضع على رأسه «سدارة» [السدارة هي غطاء يوضع على الرأس، على شكل نصف دائرة بيضاوية، وتسمى «الفيصلية» نسبة إلى الملك فيصل الأول الذي شاع على زمنه هذا الشكل المبتكر من غطاء الرأس]. كان المتقدمون لهذا الاختبار كثيرين، ولكن عدد المقبولين منهم لم يزد على ستة عشر شخصاً بينهم فتاتان.

كان ذلك هو التحدي الأول الذي فجَّر لدي الرغبة في التفوق ومواصلة هذا الطريق من أصعب مساراته. فكنت أعمل بجهد وتركيز كبيرين لتحقيق المستوى الذي يجعلني في طليعة زملائي. كما كان طموحي نيل استحسان أساتذتي الذين كانوا قادة الفن في العراق: فائق حسن وجواد سليم وخالد الرحال وعطا صبري وإسماعيل الشيخلي. وجميعهم عراقيون، فضلا عن فالنتينوس القبرصي الذي كان له فضل تطوير دراسة الفخار والخزف في المعهد. بعد تخرجنا في عام ١٩٥٩، كنت وزملائي المتفوقون أمام اختيار دراسة فنية متقدمة في شرق العالم وغربه. وكنت أمام اختيارين: إما الذهاب إلى إحدى الدول الأوروبية، أو الذهاب إلى الصين، فاخترت الصين.

مي مظفر: كيف اخترت الصين، ولماذا؟

رافع الناصري: جاء اهتمامي بفنون الصين التقليدية من خلال مشاهدتي لمعرض فني كبير أقيم في معهد الفنون الجميلة في بغداد في ربيع عام ١٩٥٩، أي قبل تخرجي بشهرين. لقد أدهشني المعرض، وأُخذت به. وحين وجدت الفرصة أمامي للذهاب إلى الصين اخترتها بدون تردد. فقد أحسست أنني في هذا الاختيار ستكون أمامي فرصة الاطلاع على فنون الشرق ودراستها، بدلاً من فنون الغرب التي تتلمذنا عليها في أثناء دراستنا في معهد الفنون.

مي مظفر: كيف كانت تجربتك في الصين؟

رافع الناصري: أمضيت في الصين أربع سـنـوات (١٩٥٩-١٩٦٣) حيث درست في الأكاديمية المركزية في بكين، وهي أعلى مؤسسة فنية في الصين عامة. كانت الدراسة فيها مكثفة، والتعليم يسير وفق الأسس الغربية في الفنون إلى جانب تدريس الفن الصيني التقليدي، وكان المستوى الدراسي يتطلب قدرات فنية هائلة، ناهيك عن التفوق فيه. وبطبيعة الحال كان الأساتذة القائمون عليها من صفوة الفنانين الصينيين، وهم معروفون من قبل العالم مثل الفنان خوان يو يي والفنان لي خوا والفنان غو يوان، وغيرهم. وكما كنت محظوظاً حين تتلمذت على يد كل من فائق حسن وجواد سليم في معهد الفنون في بغداد،

كنت أكثر حظاً لأنني درست على يد كبار الفنانين في الصين. كان الجو الدراسي مليئاً بالتحدي والجدية، فبذلت قصارى جهدي لأتميز عن زملائي من طلاب الفن في الأكاديمية وأكون في الطليعة بينهم. وفعلاً كنت الأول على دفعتي. ونتيجة لذلك أقمت معرضاً شخصياً في هونغ كونغ بتوصية من أستاذي خوان يو يي، كان أول معرض شخصي لي. فأحسست في هذا المعرض ولأول مرة طعم النجاح من خلال ما لقيته من تكريم لي ولفني عبرت عنه المقالات النقدية والصحفية التي تحدثت عن المعرض. وفي الوقت نفسه أحسست بحجم المسؤولية الملقاة على عاتقي في مواجهة المستقبل.

مي مظفر: عدت إلى بغداد في صيف عام ١٩٦٣، فكيف اتخذت موقعك في الحركة الفنية في العراق، وكيف تصف لنا حالة الفن آنذاك؟

رافع الناصري: في الصين درست، إلى جانب فن التصوير، فن الحفر والطباعة (graphic art) وتخصصت به. ولدى عودتي عينت مدرساً في معهد الفنون الجميلة لأدرس فن الحفر إلى جانب تدريس فن الرسم. وأصبحت زميلاً لأساتذتي. ثم أقمت أول معرض لي في عام ١٩٦٥ في قاعة المركز الثقافي التشيكوسلوفاكي، وكانت قاعة جيدة معروفة بنشاطها الفني والثقافي، ومعروفة باستقبالها للمعارض ذات المستوى الجيد. كان ذلك هو معرضي الأول في بغداد، وأسعدني الإقبال الجيد عليه لجدة الأعمال المعروضة. فلأول مرة في بغداد جرى عرض أعمال منفذة بتقنية الحفر على الخشب وبالألوان المائية، وهذه تقنية صينية تقليدية. وفي هذا المعرض حصلت على اعتراف فني من الفنانين الشباب الذين هم من جيلي، وكذلك اعتراف الفنانين الرواد.

أما عن الوضع الفني آنذاك فإن منتصف الستين يعد نقطة انطلاق جديدة في الحياة الفنية في العراق. ففي ذلك الوقت كان معظم الذين أوفدوا للدراسة خارج العراق قد عادوا بعد أن أكملوا دراستهم في المعاهد الفنية المختلفة في العالم. وبعودتهم، مع وجود الجيل السابق من الفنانين الذين كان لهم الفضل في إرساء قواعد الفن في العراق وتقاليده، تغلغلت في الحياة الفنية دماء جديدة تحمل شحنة عالية من النشاط والرؤى لتدفع الحركة الفنية دفعاً أقوى باتجاه الحداثة. فقد عاد الفنانون محملين بتجاربهم الجريئة وباشروا يعرضون أعمالهم في القاعات الرسمية والخاصة القليلة التي كادت تضيق بهذا الإنتاج الغزير. كانت القاعات الرسمية المتوفرة آنذاك تقتصر على قاعة المتحف الوطني للفن الحديث (افتتح عام ١٩٦٢)، وقاعة جمعية الفنانين التشكيليين العراقيين في مبناها الجديد آنذاك، إلى جانب قاعتين خاصتين هما: قاعة «الواسطي» (للمعماريين هنري زفوبدا وسعيد علي مظلوم)، وقاعة «إيا» (للمعماري رفعت الجادرجي). وكانت هناك المراكز الثقافية التابعة لبعض السفارات الأجنبية. وقد أقمت معرضي الشخصي الثاني في قاعة «إيا». ولا بد من التنويه هنا أنه في النصف الثاني من عقد الستين تعززت مكانة الفنان العراقي لدى الأوساط العربية لما أظهرته هذه التجارب بمجملها من غزارة في الإنتاج وتنوع في الأساليب فضلاً عن

قوة التعبير والاستخدام الجريء للألوان والأشكال، وفوق هذا وذاك ما حملته هذه الأعمال إجمالاً من قدرة على توظيف البعد الفكري دون التنازل عن الشرط الفني. وكانت بيروت بوابة العراق الواسعة التي انطلقنا منها إلى العالم العربي.

مي مظفر: في عام ١٩٦٧ حصلت على زمالة إلى لشبونة (البرتغال) لتطوير مهاراتك الفنية في فنون الحفر والطباعة. أمضيت سنتين وعدت بعد ذلك وقد تغير أسلوبك تغيراً جذرياً؛ هجرت التشخيص والتشخيص المؤسلب الذي ظهرت عليه أعمالك الأولى، لتتبنى التجريد لغة تعبير لم تزل ملتزما بها، كما اعتمدت هناك الحرف العربي بوصفه جزءاً أساسياً من التكوين. كيف تصف لنا ذلك التحول؟

رافع الناصري: حصلت على هذه الزمالة من مؤسسة كولبنكيان Gulbenkian، وهي مؤسسة عالمية مركزها في البرتغال، ترعى مجموعة مؤسسات ثقافية من ضمنها جمعية الحفّارين البرتغاليين (Gravura) ولدى هذه الجمعية مشاغل (ستوديوهات) كبيرة لفنون الحفر (غرافيك)، كالحفر على الزنك والنحاس، والطباعة الحجرية (Lithograph). وتضم هذه المشاغل فنانين من شتى أنحاء العالم، ويشرف عليها الفنانان البرتغاليان أليس جورج Alice George وجوان أوغن Joan Hogan. استمرت الدورة سنتين أقمنا في نهايتها معرضاً على قاعة الجمعية Gallaria Gravura، وهي قاعة معروفة في لشبونة، ومن هذا المعرض اختارت الجمعية ثلاثة من أعمالي المحفورة (prints) لغرض النشر والتسويق، وأنجزت ١٥٠ طبعة (edition) من كل عمل.

أما عن الأسلوب التجريدي الذي تبنيته فهو لم يأت على نحو مفاجئ. لقد كنت دائماً أنزع نحو التجريد منذ دراستي الأكاديمية، وقد ظهرت لدي هذه النزعة سواء أثناء دراستي في بغداد أو بكين. ذلك أنني كنت أقدم على تجاربي الحرة خارج الأساليب الدراسية الصارمة. وحين عدت من الصين بدأت أرسم الموضوعات العراقية بأسلوب تعبيري ورمزي، فأبسط الشكل لأضفي عليه دلالات رمزية تخرجه بعض الشيء عن واقعيته. فكنت مهيئاً في الأساس للمغامرة نحو المزيد من التجريد. وعندما جئت إلى البرتغال ووجدت نفسي في خضم التجارب الحداثية في أوروبا، ومنها الحروفية التي كان يمارسها عدد من الفنانين المعروفين في العالم، رأيت أن أمامي مجالاً واسعاً لإدخال الحرف العربي بجمالياته وقدراته الكبيرة على التشكيل. كما أنني استندت في استخدامي للحرف العربي إلى الكتابة الصينية وجمالياتها، خاصة عند استخدام الفرشاة في الأداء. من هذه الخلفية البصرية المركبة شرعت في تجاربي لاعتماد الحرف بوصفه عنصر تعبير خطي مجرد. كانت تلك هي بداية تعاملي مع الحرف العربي، وسرعان ما وجدت الحرف يتسلل إلى أعمال الحفر (الغرافيك) أيضاً، لما فيه (أي الحرف) من إمكانيات خطيّة (غرافيكية) عالية.

وفي تلك الأثناء كنت قد اهتديت إلى ألوان الأكريليك كبديل للألوان الزيتية، وهي مادة سريعة الجفاف. فأعانني استخدام هذه المادة على ملاحقة الأفكار والصور التي تتوالد بسرعة أثناء العمل على الورق أو القماش. وهذه طريقة شرقية تقليدية في الأداء – الصين مثلاً – وتتطلب السرعة الشديدة في العمل مع ضبط النفس بسبب طبيعة المواد المستخدمة. وهكذا كنت محكوماً بهذه المادة (الأكريليك).

مي مظفر: ونحن لا نزال في معرض الحديث عن الحرف العربي واستخداماته في العمل الفني، قل لي ما مدى قربك أو بعدك آنذاك عن التجارب العراقية التي بدأت منذ نهاية الأربعين (من القرن العشرين) مع مديحة عمر التي كانت في واشنطن، وجميل حمودي في باريس، ثم عصام السعيد في لندن بعدهما بعقد تقريباً. وبين هذا وذاك كان جواد سليم قد أدخل بعض الكتابات العربية في لوحاته التي أنجزها خلال عقد الخمسين في بغداد، وجميع هذه المحاولات، على ما فيها من تفاوت في المستوى، نمّت عن رغبة في مزج المحلي بالعالمي؟

رافع الناصري: في البدء أود أن أبين أنني كنت في البرتغال معزولاً عزلة تامة عما كان يدور آنذاك في العالم العربي، لا بسبب العزلة الجغرافية للبرتغال فحسب، وإنما لأنني كنت منغمراً في متابعة عملي ضمن المحيط الأوروبي الذي وجدت نفسي في خضمّه. أما قبل عام ١٩٦٧، أي قبل ذهابي إلى البرتغال، فلم أشاهد من هذه التجارب إلا أعمال جواد سليم. ثم علمنا، آنذاك، بأن ثمة فنانين عراقيين مقيمين خارج العراق أقدموا على محاولات لإدخال الكتابة العربية إلى اللوحة، مثل مديحة عمر وجميل حمودي ولم نكن في العراق قد اطلعنا على تلك التجارب إلا من خلال بعض الصور لها. أما تجربة عصام السعيد في استخدام الكتابة العربية في اللوحة، والتي ظهرت في مطلع الستين حسب علمي، فلم تُعرف إلا في أواسط الستين عندما أقيم معرض شخصي له هناك في عام ١٩٦٥. غير أن تجربتي في استخدام الحرف العربي جاءت من رغبتي في تكوين لوحة تجريدية ذات ملامح خاصة بي، بوصفي فناناً له خلفية ثقافية مغايرة للمحيط الذي كنت فيه، أي في البرتغال. فجاء الحرف العربي ملائماً لتحقيق هذا العمل.

لقد استغرق هذا التحول وقتاً طويلاً. كنت أرسم في البداية موضوعات واقعية بأسلوب تعبيري رمزي، ثم أحسست فجأة برغبة في التحول كلياً إلى الأسلوب التجريدي. كان علي أن أبحث عن عناصر جديدة، ووجدت ضالتي في الحرف العربي. استخدمت الحروف ذات الامتدادات والانحناءات المناسبة كالواو والهاء والميم والسين.

مي مظفر: وحين عدت إلى بغداد في عام ١٩٦٩، وعرضت أعمالك في بغداد ثم بيروت، كيف استقبلت هذه التجربة؟

رافع الناصري: في بداية الأمر لابد من توضيح. كان فن الحفر والطباعة (غرافيك) عامة قد شاع في أوروبا وراج كثيراً بعد الحرب العالمية الثانية. وعلى الرغم من أن هذه التقنية تمارس

على امتداد قرون قبل ذلك، فإنها ظلت مقتصرة على عدد قليل نسبياً من الفنانين في العالم. أما في العالم العربي فلم يكد يُعرف هذا الفن قبل عقد الستين من القرن العشرين. تضمن المعرض الشخصي الذي أقمته في بغداد ثم في بيروت أعمالاً غرافيكية فقط. كما أن هذه الأعمال جاءت بصياغة جديدة لم تكن معروفة في عالمنا العربي. وهي تقنية اكتشفها الفنان البريطاني هيتر، وتعلمتها في البرتغال، وتعتمد استخدام الألوان في الحفر على الزنك باستخدام «كليشيه» واحد، مع استخدام بكرات حديدية مختلفة (rollers). والذين استخدموا طريقة هيتر هم هذه قلة في العالم. فحين التحقت بالأكاديمية الصيفية في سالزبورغ (النمسا) في صيف ١٩٧٤، كنت الوحيد في مشغل الحفر التابع للأكاديمية الذي يستخدم هذه التقنية، وقد طلب مني الأستاذ المشرف على المشغل، وكان ألمانياً، أن أقدم ورشة عمل لإطلاع الفنانين المشاركين، وكانوا من جنسيات مختلفة، على هذه التقنية الجديدة.

مي مظفر: ظلت تجربتي الرسم والحفر (الغرافيك) متلازمتين لديك؛ ما مدى تأثير بعضهما في البعض الآخر، وإلى أي من الفنين تشعر بانتماء أكبر؟

رافع الناصري: هما تجربتان متلازمتان. حين كنت في معهد الفنون الجميلة درست فن التصوير وكنت منذ البداية أقوى أداء في الخط من اللون، وحين تعرّفت على فن الحفر في الصين وجدته منسجماً معي، وتخصصت به. ومع استخدامي الحرف العربي وجدت في الحرف ما يمكن أن يضيف إلى تجربتي تميّزاً.

الحفر في الأساس يعتمد على الرسم دون التلوين. كانت أعمالي الأولى حفراً على الخشب (woodcut) بالأبيض والأسود. والبعض منها كان ملوناً، وأحب أن أؤكد هنا أن فن الحفر على الخشب في الصين تستخدم فيه الألوان المائية، وهي تقنية خاصة بهم. وكانت المرة الأولى التي أتفرغ فيها للرسم بانتظام، وفي عزلة عن الغرافيك، أثناء إقامتي في البرتغال عام ١٩٦٨، وذلك بعد اكتشافي لمادة الأكريليك التي وجدت فيها قدرة هائلة على تنفيذ أفكاري بسرعة وشفافية. لذلك فإنني أستطيع القول إن تجربتي في الرسم بالمعنى الاحترافي بدأت من ذلك التاريخ. ومن هنا أيضاً بدأ التأثير المتبادل بين الرسم والحفر: بين اللون والخط، بين الكتلة والفراغ، بين الظل والضوء.

مي مظفر: عدت من البرتغال إلى بغداد في صيف عام ١٩٦٩، وعدت إلى التدريس في معهد الفنون الجميلة في بغداد، وكانت معك حصيلة كبيرة من أعمال الحفر، فهل تواصلت مع الفنين معاً؟

رافع الناصري: في بغداد لم تكن لدي أية وسيلة لممارسة الحفر والطباعة (غرافيك) آنذاك، فانغمرت في الرسم. وفي هذه المرحلة بدأت اتصالاتي مع زملائي الفنانين. تعرفت إلى ضياء العزاوي وسرعان ما وجدنا انسجاماً في توجهاتنا وتطلعاتنا، كما كان محمد مهر الدين زميلي

في المعهد، وكنا لم نزل نعيش صدمة الخامس من حزيران [١٩٦٧] وتداعياتها. فشكلنا معاً مجموعة ضمت إلينا، إضافة للعزاوي ومهر الدين، كلا من هاشم سمرجي وصالح الجميعي وإسماعيل فتاح، وأصدرنا بياناً فنياً يحدد مواقفنا من عدد من القضايا الفنية كقضية الحرية في الفن، والتواصل مع التراث والتعامل معه بحرية وشفافية. وكان القصد من البيان دفع الحركة الفنية إلى مدى أبعد، وتحفيز الجهود بعد الهزة التي تعرضنا لها على أثر النكسة. وبدأت المجموعة أول نشاطاتها بمعرض مشترك أقيم على قاعة المتحف الوطني للفن الحديث في بغداد عام ١٩٧١ ضم أربعة من هذه المجموعة فقط، إذ لم يشارك في المعرض كل من محمد مهر الدين وإسماعيل فتاح. كان لكل منا تجربته الجديدة التي شكلت بمجموعها في هذا المعرض حدثاً فنياً في الحياة الثقافية أثار اهتمام المشاهدين والنقاد لما تضمنه من توجه جديد، سواء في التعبير أو التقنيات.

مي مظفر: لنقف عند هذه التجربة التي تعد أول ظهور لتجربة الرسم لديك. في هذا المعرض بالتحديد عرضت مجموعة أعمال تعتمد في تكويناتها مساحات لونية كبيرة صافية تقاطعها خطوط أفقية أو طولية على لوح (board) معيني الشكل، وقد أثارت أعمالك الكثير من التساؤلات. كانت تلك أعمالا تجريدية هي أقرب إلى فن التصميم منها إلى الرسم. واستمرت معك هذه النزعة التجريدية الحادة لسنوات لاحقة. فمتى انتهت هذه المرحلة؟

رافع الناصري: في البدء أحب أن أبيّن أن أي لوحة فنية مرسومة سواء بأسلوب أكاديمي أو غير أكاديمي، ذات أشكال مشخصة أو خالية من أية شخوص، تعتمد في الأساس على كمٌ من التصميم يزيد أو ينقص تبعاً لطبيعة التكوين والأسلوب الذي رسمت به اللوحة. في تلك التجربة عمدت إلى إنتاج لوحة حديثة لا تضع حدوداً بين الأساليب والتقنيات. وأعترف بأن السمة الغرافيكية قد طغت في تلك المرحلة على روحية اللوحة المرسومة.

مي مظفر: كان في تلك التكوينات ذات المساحات الفارغة والخطوط الحادة التي تقطع اللوحة بشكل ما الكثير من الانضباط والتقسيم المدروس (الذي يميز الأعمال الهندسية مثلا)، بينما يتطلب فن الرسم حرية أكبر في الأداء؛ كما أن اللوحة بألوانها الصافية فوق سطح اللوحة كادت تخلو من الظلال، من هذا المنطلق بدت اللوحة لديك وكأنها تفتقر إلى مقومات فن التصوير (painting). وأذكر أن الفنان الكبير فائق حسن عندما زار معرضك الذي أقمته في بغداد عام ١٩٧٩، علّق قائلاً:«هذا تصميم وليس رسماً»؛ علماً بأن لوحتك في ذلك المعرض الذي قدمت فيه مشاهد ذات طبيعة كونية، كانت قد تحررت كثيراً من تلك التقاطعات الحادة، ومضت، في جزء كبير منها، نحو تمازج لوني كثير الظلال، واقتصرت على خط قاطع واحد هو خط الأفق الذي بنيت عليه تجربتك لسنوات عدة فاصلاً ما بين الأرض والسماء. فماذا تقول عن تلك الملاحظة؟

رافع الناصري: فائق حسن أستاذ كبير. ورسام يقف في طليعة الفنانين العرب، كما أنه لا يقل مكانة عن أي فنان عالمي في قدراته الأدائية العالية. ولكن فائق حسن كان رساماً أكاديمياً ظل متمسكا بمفاهيمه التقليدية للوحة المرسومة. لقد نشأ عليها وبرع فيها، ولم يستطع تجاوزها. ربما من أجل ذلك كان من الصعب عليه تقبل تجربة تنزع هذا النزوع الحاد نحو الخروج من التقاليد الأكاديمية ولم أخرج. لقد نشأت على أصول أكاديمية محض، في دراستي في معهد الفنون الجميلة أولاً، ثم رسخت بقوة في الأكاديمية المركزية في بكين بعد ذلك. وعملي الأكاديمي في بداية تجربتي الفنية يشهد على ذلك. ولكن من خلال وجودي في البرتغال وعودتي إلى الرسم بعد سنوات من الانقطاع، عمدت إلى الذهاب إلى أقصى حدود التجريد، مع ذلك فأنا لم أفرط قط بالمبادئ الأساسية لبناء اللوحة الفنية بمفهومها الأكاديمي. وهو ما أحرص عليه لغاية اليوم.

من تلك الأرض المجردة التي بنيت عليها تجربتي الفنية الأولى في التصوير نشأت لوحتي وتطورت على مدى ما يقرب الآن من أربعين عاماً. شيئاً فشيئاً تحولت الخطوط القاطعة إلى عالمين متقابلين: المساحة المجردة إزاء كتلة بارزة ملموسة، يفصل بينهما خط واضح، هو الأفق الوهمي الذي يفصل ما بين الأرض والسماء. وفي الوقت الذي ظلت فيه مساحة السماء مجرد فضاء فارغ إلا من بُقَع لونية شفافة، انشغلت مساحة الكتلة الأرضية بإشارات رمزية كالحرف والرقم والعلامة للدلالة على البعد الإنساني أو أثره. ومع الوقت، واستمرار التجربة تلاشى خط الأفق كلياً، وامتزجت المساحات امتزاجاً كلياً، واكتسبت المشاهد الطبيعية في لوحاتي شكلا مغايراً لما كانت عليه، متصلة جذراً بماضيها على الرغم مما يبدو عليها من انفصال تام عن ذلك الماضي.

مي مظفر: اختفى الحرف العربي من لوحاتك الزيتية والمحفورة (غرافيك) في بعض مراحل عملك، ثم عدت مؤخراً إلى إدخال نصوص مطبوعة جاهزة داخل التكوين، مستخدماً اللصق (collage)، كما ظهر في مجموعة أعمالك الحفرية والزيتية التي تحمل عنوان «تحية إلى المتنبي»، وكذلك في مجموعة أعمالك الأخيرة المسماة «تحية إلى بغداد». فما هو سر هذه العودة؟

رافع الناصري: الحرف العربي لم يغب قط عن عملي. ولكنه يتجلى بأشكال مموهة ومجازية. فهو إشارة وهو رمز وهو جزء من كتلة أو حركة، أحياناً يظهر كاملاً، وقد يختصر إلى مجرد نقطة. في مجموعة «تحية إلى المتنبي» استخدمت صفحات مطبوعة لشعر المتنبي مستلة من طبعة قديمة، واستخدمت هذا العنصر الغرافيكي للخط العربي في هذه النصوص، ووظّفته لخدمة اللوحة. ثم أغراني هذا الاستخدام إلى تجربة أخرى ما زلت اليوم في خضمها، وهي استخدام جزئيات من نصوص مكتوبة بخط الثلث نفذها

خطاطون معاصرون كبار. فأنا أستخدم كلمات هذه النصوص أو أجزاء من الكلمة بوصفها عنصراً غرافيكياً داخل التكوين، بوصفها صورة رمزية دالة بعيداً عن دلالاتها اللغوية، إلا للعين التي تدرك هذه الحروف. وأحب أن أوضح هنا أن استخدامي للحرف كان دائماً ينبع من هذا المفهوم. فالحرف في جميع لوحاتي ليس عنصراً مضافاً إلى التكوين ولا هو قيمة زخرفية، بل هو عنصر خطي من صلب التكوين، ومركز يتمحور عليه الموضوع.

مي مظفر: في بعض تكويناتك تظهر بين حين وآخر أشكال توحي بأنها جزء من أثر يعود لمراحل حضارية قديمة من تاريخ العراق. فما مدى ارتباطك بحضارات وادي الرافدين؟

رافع الناصري: يتضح اليوم تمام الوضوح مدى ارتباطي البصري والنفسي بالآثار العراقية. ففي طفولتي كان لي اتصال بشكل من الأشكال بالآثار الإسلامية من خلال زيارات متكررة لأثر معماري إسلامي يدعى «مرقد الأربعين». وهو جامع ومرقد لأربعين صحابياً استشهدوا على تخوم مدينتنا، تكريت. كنا نتسلق قبابه الحصّية وأسواره، ونلعب الكرة في فنائه. أما رائحة البخور المنسابة من سردابه فما زال شذاها يأتيني بين الحين والآخر. وفي بغداد زرت متحف الآثار أيام دراستي في معهد الفنون الجميلة ولكنني لم أستوعب القطع الفنية بالعمق الكافي. بينما سُحرت بالآثار الصينية كما أدهشني فنها، وتابعتها بحكم دراستي، ولتفتح مدركاتي أكثر وأكثر هناك. وانعكس هذا الاهتمام على الآثار العراقية واهتمامي الشديد بها بعد عودتي من الصين إلى بغداد. ولم يقتصر اهتمامي على مقتنيات المتحف العراقي، أو مقتنيات المتاحف العالمية من آثارنا، وإنما سعيت إليها في مواقعها الأصلية في أنحاء العراق كافة. وعلى غفلة مني وجدتها تتسلل إلى لوحاتي تدريجيا، بدءاً من أواخر السبعينيات حتى تجلت بصورة واضحة في لوحة كبيرة (٣م×٥م) بعنوان **الزقورة**، وهو اسم يطلق على معابد العراقيين القدماء. وقد عرضت هذه اللوحة في مهرجان بغداد العالمي للفنون ١٩٨٦، وحازت الجائزة الأولى.

مي مظفر: منذ بضعة عقود يعيش الفنانون العراقيون في مناطق شتى من العالم، وقد انقسموا إلى داخل وخارج، هل بالإمكان حصر مشهد تقريبي لطبيعة أعمال الفنانين العراقيين ونشاطهم، وكيف تنظر إلى التجربة العراقية اليوم في ظل هذه الظروف الصعبة التي مرّ ولا يزال يمر بها العراق؟

رافع الناصري: يعاني الفن في العراق في الوقت الحاضر من نتائج الحروب والحصار وتبعاتها من تشتت الكثير من المواهب والقدرات وتشرذمها. فقد دفعتها الظروف الصعبة إلى أن تصبح هامشية وغير مؤثرة في مسيرة الحركة عامة. ولو عاشت هذه المواهب في ظروف طبيعية متواصلة مع ماضيها وحاضرها لأعطت نتائج مختلفة، إن لم أقل باهرة. وعلى الرغم من

ذلك فقد تبلورت داخل العراق وخارجه تجارب شابة رائعة، وتعمّقت تجارب فنانين مكرسين. باختصار، عندما ننظر الآن إلى أعمال الفنانين العراقيين بمنظار نقدي موضوعي سنجد أنه تطور كثيراً خلال السنوات العشر الأخيرة ممثلاً بنخبة من الفنانين الرائعين، في الوقت الذي نرى فيه الكثير من الإنتاج السطحي بل التجاري الذي يفتقر إلى أية قيمة فنية أو تاريخية، والذي قلما وجد في المراحل السابقة. ولكن هذا أمر طبيعي في بلد تفكك وتدهورت أحواله كما هو العراق اليوم.

صور المقابلة
(مـن أعـمـال رافـع الناصـري)

رسم، ٦٠ X ٨٠ سم، بكين، ١٩٦٢.

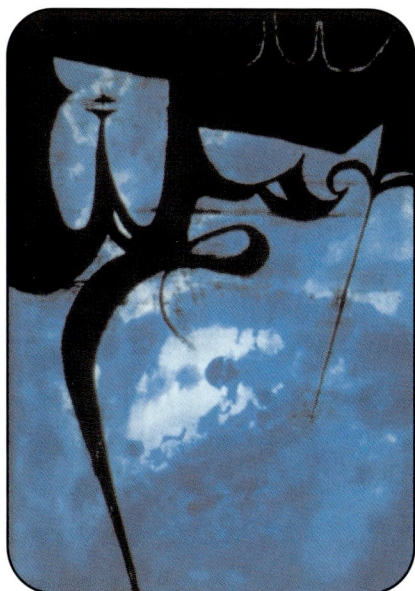

حفر ملون على الزنك، ٢٥ X ٣٥ سم، لشبونة، ١٩٦٨.

طباعة حجرية، ٣٥ X ٥٠ سم، لشبونة، ١٩٦٨.

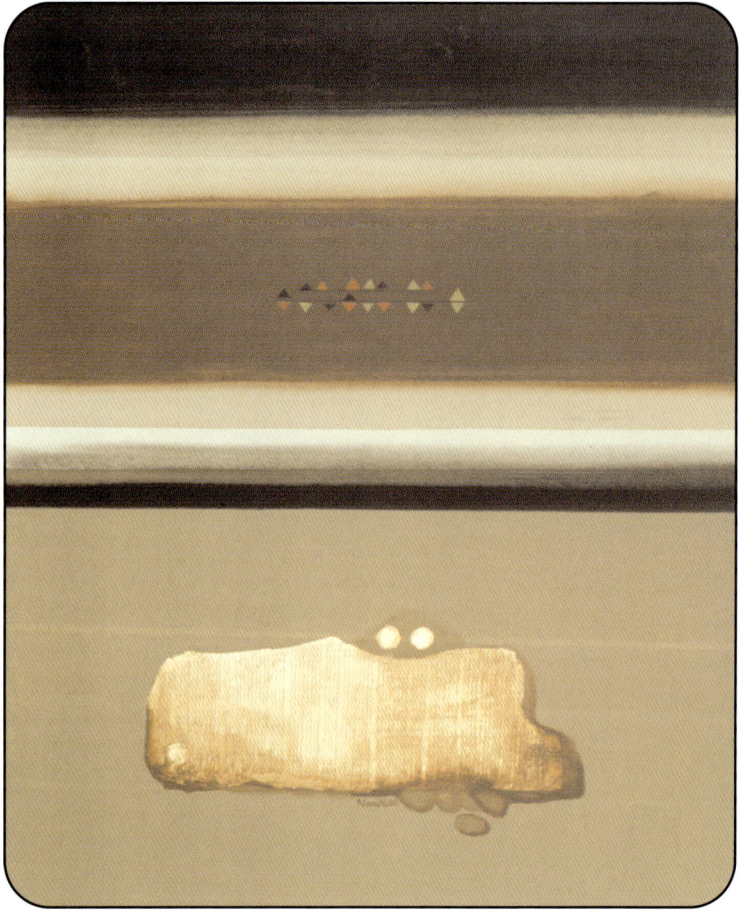

أكريليك على قماش، ١٠٠ X ١٢٠ سم، بغداد، ١٩٨٠.

حفر ملون على الزنك، ٣٥ X ٥٠ سم، بغداد، ١٩٨٨.

أكريليك على ورق، ٥٠ X ٥٠ سم، عمّان، ١٩٩٦.

أكريليك على ورق، ٥٦ x ٥٦ سم، البحرين، ٢٠٠١.

ألف ٢٤ (٢٠٠٤)

٢٢٢

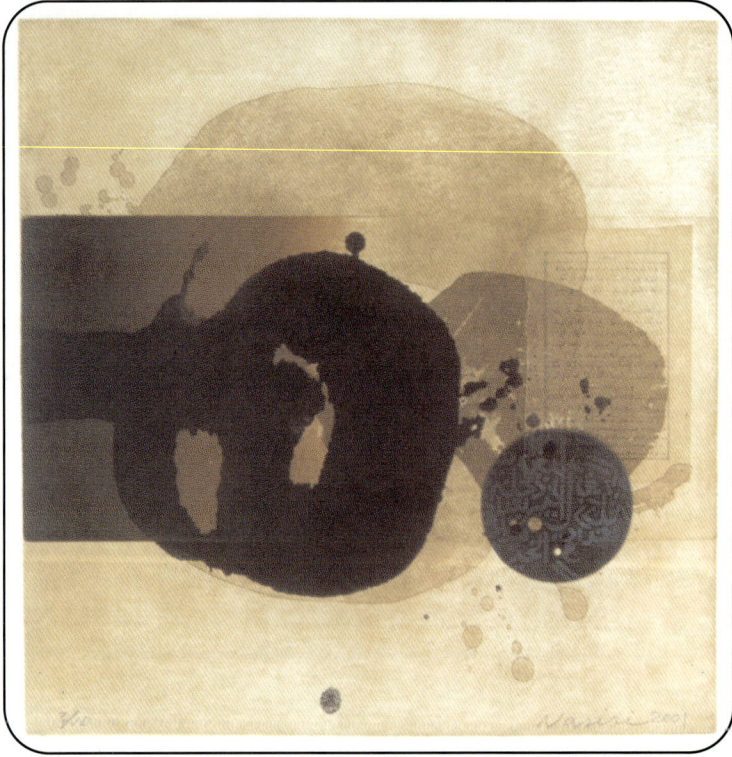

حفر ملون على الزنك، ٥٠ X ٥٠ سم، عمّان، ٢٠٠١.

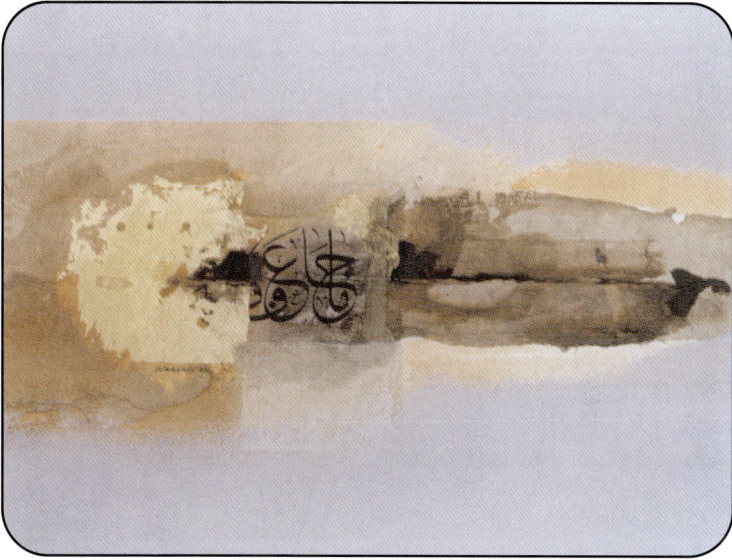

خامات متنوعة على ورق، ٥٦ X ٧٦ سم، البحرين، ٢٠٠٢.

القضاء والقدر:
بحث في التراسل بين القديم والجديد

محمد بريري

تهدف هذه الدراسة إلى إماطة اللثام عن بعض النصوص التحتية التي تتضمنها نصوص شعرية حديثة حين تتطرق، في سياقات متباينة، لموضوعات بعينها، مثل موضوع القدر. ومن جهة ثانية تتلمس الدراسة الطبيعة الاستمرارية لهذا الموضوع الذي تداوله الشعراء منذ الجاهلية حتى عصرنا الحديث. وقد انتهت الدراسة إلى أن الشعر الحديث تفاعل مع موضوع القدر بطريقتين مختلفتين. ففي الحقبة الرومانتيكية تغلب الطابع التأملي الوجودي، بينما أنزل شعراء الحداثة موضوع القدر من المستوى الميتافيزيقي إلى مستوى النظر في الممارسات الاجتماعية الدينية السائدة، معلنين عن موقف نقدي متمرّد. أما الشاعر الجاهلي فقد سلّم مع الشاعر الرومانتيكي بالحتمية الميتافيزيقية للقدر، لكنه تماس مع الشاعر الحداثي حين أثار في تناوله للموضوع حسّاً واضحاً بالمقاومة وعدم الاستسلام للأقدار، فكأنه يؤمن بحتميتين لا حتمية واحدة؛ حتمية القدر، وحتمية المقاومة.

التاريخ والشعر

وليد بيطار

يتمحور التاريخ حول البحث والتحليل، ومن ثم فهو يوضح ويصنف، أما الشعر فمهمته توصيف تلك الفوضى التي يحاول المؤرخون محوها. والكاتب هنا، في محاولته لإيضاح الفارق بين التاريخ والشعر، يسبر أغوار ذلك «التأثير التاريخي» في شعره؛ أي الدروس والرؤى المستقاة من العديد من المصادر المتنوعة مثل «أوتوسيكوجرافيا» لفرناندو بيسوا، و«النمر» لريلكه، ولوحات جورجيو دي تشيريكو الميتافيزيقية، وقصيدة والاس ستيڤنز «يوم صاف ولا ذكريات»، وقصيدة سويفت «مرثاة ساخرة». ويعتقد الكاتب

أن اتخاذ موقف لاتاريخي قد يرسي مكانة الفنان في الزمن على نحو أبلغ في تأثيره من مجرد محاولة واعية لأن يكون تاريخياً، كما يناقش المصادر البيروتية لاستلهام مجموعته الجديدة التي تحمل عنوان *Bastardi Puri*، ليخلص في النهاية إلى أن المدينة ذاتها - تماماً كشعره - تعرض بجلاء طبيعة التاريخ ذات الطابع المتلون المراوغ.

عزفاً على أُصابع اليد:
حفريات في الذاكرة الشعرية

حسب الشيخ جعفر

في هذه الشهادة الذاتية والتأملية، يسترجع الشاعر العراقي جعفر فترة دراسته في موسكو في الستينيات وعودته إلى بغداد. فهو يصور لقاءاته بالشعراء والأدباء وجهاً لوجه أو عبر نصوصهم المكتوبة، ومنهم الجواهري، توفيق الحكيم، بوشكين، وألكساندر بلوك - إضافة إلى أناس عاديين أحدثوا تأثيراً واضحاً فيه. والشعري عند جعفر لا يقتصر على المنظوم، بل إنه يجد أن بعض كتابات تشيخوف، وكافكا، والتكرلي شعرية محضة رغم كونها تصنف كتابة نثرية.

الموسيقى العربية الكلاسيكية
ومكانتها في المجتمع العربي المعاصر

شهرزاد قاسم حسن

تصف هذه المقالة الأركان الأساسية التي يعتمد عليها التراث المديني الفني العربي بصيغته المتوارثة، ثم الأولويات التي تعتمد عليها الحداثة، والتساؤل عن مفهومها ومكوناتها وعما احتفظت به من الأفكار و القواعد والأصول «القديمة» من ناحية، ومن ثم التساؤل عن ماهية وأصول العناصر الجديدة التي لجأت إليها الحداثة من ناحية أخرى. تنطلق أسئلة هذا المقال من واقع الطرح الذي جاءت به المؤسسات العربية في الموسيقى خلال القرن العشرين عن علاقة التراث (القديم) بالحداثة (الجديد) على صعيدي المفاهيم والممارسة. وهو طرح يرى أن هذين المفهومين، إذا ما تم النظر إليهما بشكل مطلق، يمثلان ضدين لابد لهما من التصارع. إلا أن الواقع الميداني يرينا أن هذا الصراع أحادي الجانب تمثله المؤسسات التعليمية والإدارية والإعلامية التي ترى أن مفهوم الحداثة يكمن أولا في التغلب على خزين العالم التقليدي وتعبيراته، على اعتبار أنه لا يمثل الواقع الحالي، وبالتالي تهدف إلى نفيه خارج الحيز الحديث ما لم يذعن إلى التطويع وتغيير المعالم ولبس حلل جديدة تؤهله للدخول في المشهد الموسيقي المعاصر.

القص والاقتصاص بين قديم اللحظة وجديد التاريخ:
قراءة في رواية «متون الأهرام» للغيطاني

أيمن الدسوقي

تتناول هذه الدراسة رواية **متون الأهرام** للغيطاني (١٩٩٤) بالتحليل في محاولة لتتبع أثر القديم، الذي هو قديم اللحظة، والتي تأتي في شكل ذكرى شخصية مرتبطة بموضع بعينه، في جديد التاريخ. تخرج **متون الأهرام** في شكل عربي سليم وإن كان محتواها ينزع إلى رغبة المصري القديم في حفظ لحظته التاريخية التي هي أيضاً قوام صوته المتفرّد وشخصيته التي عاش بها، وذلك بتسجيلها في حروف مقدسة تتغلب على «تاريخية» اللحظة بقوة اللغة ونموذجية تراكيبها وأساليبها الموروثة. يردُ الراوي في **متون الأهرام** بكل شخصية إلى الهرم حيث تمر بتجربتها الفريدة وتكتشف أو يُكتَشف لها عن كنه غموض قدرها الذاتي، ثم هو يردُ بها إلينا، في شكل التأريخ أو أدب الحوليات وأنساق تراثية أخرى، وقد سجلها على بنية الهرم أو بنيانه والذي يشكل بدوره بنية الرواية. يتناول البحث بالتحليل بنية الرواية الشكلية ثم بنيتها الداخلية أو حركية السرد ثم نمطية الشخصية، ويختتم البحث بعرض لأساليب استيحاء مصادر الرواية ولنظرية الغيطاني حول الاستمرارية التاريخية، متطرقاً إلى رواية لاحقة للغيطاني، **سفر البنيان** (١٩٩٨) التي تعبر روائياً عن جماليات الفن المعماري الإسلامي.

المرتحلون من أرض بائدة:
مصادر الوحي عند شيلي في نظمه لقصيدة «أوزيماندياس»

جون رودنبك

يحاول الكاتب في هذه المقالة أن يبحث في الأصول التي استوحى منها شيلي قصيدة «أوزيماندياس» "Ozymandias"، وهي أسطورة صامدة عن فنانين من كل الضروب تنطلق إبداعاتهم من تجارب شخصية معيشة. في هذا الصدد تبدو سونيتة شيلي السياسية العظيمة التي تحمل عنوان «أوزيماندياس» ذات صلة وثيقة بهذه الأسطورة؛ إذ جرى العرف على اعتبارها «مستوحاة» من تمثال مصري قديم. لم يرتحل شيلي يوماً إلى مصر، ومن ثم فهو يقيناً لم يرَ مطلقاً تلك المناظر الطبيعية التي يصفها في قصيدته، وعلى النقيض من الاعتقاد الشائع، فإنه لم يرَ تلك الرأس المنحوتة والموصوفة زعماً بكلماته، والتي لم تصل إلى إنجلترا إلا عقب يوم أو اثنين من نزوحه هو وعائلته إلى إيطاليا وإقامته بها بشكل دائم، وبعد أكثر من ستة أشهر من نشره للقصيدة. وكافة المصادر والتأثيرات الواضحة بجلاء في «أوزيماندياس» هي أدبية محضة، ولعل جميعها جزء من عملة رائجة إبان ذلك

العصر. وفضلاً عن ديودوروس سيكولوس Diodorus Siculus والسونيتات السياسية التي نظمها ووردزورث Wordsworth وميلتون Milton فإن تلك المصادر تضم أيضاً كلاسيكيات عدة من أدب الرحلات بالإنجليزية والفرنسية، أبرزها أعمال ڤولني Volney.

الذاكرة واللامساواة والقوة:
فلسطين وعالمية حقوق الإنسان

إدوارد سعيد

يؤكد سعيد على دور الذاكرة الجماعية في بقاء الفلسطينيين واستمرارهم كشعب على الرغم من توزعهم في الشتات، ويطرح ضرورة الاعتراف بهم كشعب؛ حيث إن حقوق الإنسان تنطبق على البشر جميعاً دون تمييز. وليس هناك استثناء دنيوي أو إلهي يمنح البعض حق قهر الآخرين متذرعين بأنهم كانوا ضحيةً. ويناهض سعيد الفكر المبتسر والسطحي وراء صراع الحضارات، ويؤيد معرفة الآخر والاعتراف بالحق التاريخي للفلسطينيين في وطنهم. ويرى أن من الممكن أن يكون العلم والمعرفة وسيطين في فهم المقهورين واحترامهم. وهو يدعو إلى استبدال المصالحة بالعداوة، انطلاقاً من نموذج جنوب أفريقيا التي تجاوزت التمييز العنصري. فبالنسبة لسعيد لا يمكن حلّ الخلاف الفلسطيني-الإسرائيلي عسكرياً، بل بالاعتراف الديمقراطي بالمساواة والتعايش الجمعي عوضاً عن نفي الآخر. فالماضي الفلسطيني لا يمكن محوه ولا يصح تجاهله عند البحث عن سلام حقيقي.

من الماضي إلى الحاضر والمستقبل:
الروح المتجددة للـ«أبيكو»

منيرة سليمان

تبحث هذه المقالة تمثيل ظاهرة «الأبيكو» الغرب أفريقية الشهيرة في ثلاثة أعمال أبدعها ثلاثة كتاب نيجيريين، وهي قصيدة ج. ب. كلارك-بيكيديريمو التي تحمل عنوان «أبيكو» (١٩٦٥)، وقصيدة وول سوينكا التي تحمل العنوان ذاته، «أبيكو» (١٩٦٧)، ورواية بن أوكري **الطريق الجائع** (١٩٩١). تطرح الدراسة قراءة اجتماعية سياسية لظاهرة «الأبيكو» (المرتبطة بالطفل المكتوب له الموت) حسبما يتناولها الكتاب الثلاثة ووفقاً لرؤية غرب أفريقية تقليدية للعالم، كما تستكشف كيفية اجتذاب ظاهرة «الأبيكو» للعديد من الكتاب المهتمين بقضايا القومية الثقافية وتشكيل الهوية، وتبرز المقالة أيضاً كيف أن القراءة الدقيقة لأعمال هؤلاء الكتاب تؤدي حتماً إلى التعرف على همومهم الإيديولوجية والجمالية.

«ليس إلا سطوراً صغيرة»

شتيفن شتيلزر

هذه المقالة الفلسفية مصوغة بأسلوب مبتكر يندرج تحت التلاعب الإبداعي، متخذاً شكل الحوار مع صديقة ومع فلاسفة آخرين بدءاً من سقراط وانتهاءً بالفيلسوف الفرنسي جيل دولوز. وتطرح المقالة سؤالاً جوهرياً عن معنى الفلسفة ولماذا يرد هذا السؤال في ذهن المفكر في مرحلة الشيخوخة. وعلى نهج هيجل وهيدجر وأرندت، يقوم صاحب المقالة باستكشاف دلالة الشيخوخة، فيتداخل نثره مع استشهادات من كتاب جيل دولوز وفيليكس جواتاري بعنوان **ما هي الفلسفة؟** (١٩٩٣)، والذي ترجمه مطاع صفدي (مركز الإنماء العربي). إن الإشارة العابرة في هذا الكتاب إلى «الحكيم الشرقي» تأخذ موقع الصدارة في المقالة حيث يتم استنطاقها. ويرى صاحب المقالة أن الحكمة الشرقية كما يعبّر عنها جلال الدين الرومي تتمثل في الشيخ بشعره الأشيب (حيث الكلمة تشير إلى شخص مسن وإلى معلم حكيم في آن واحد). ويقوم صاحب المقالة بتأويل منطق الرومي مقارناً بينه وبين الفكر الأوروبي في علاقة الفلسفة بالشيخوخة.

الرواية ومساءلة التاريخ

نجوى شعبان

تتناول هذه الشهادة ارتباط تفتح وعي الكاتبة بالبحر وذكريات الجدة عنه، فتلتقط ذاكرتها مباني حجرية قديمة في دمياط ودراستها، مما دفعها إلى التعلق بالكتابة والتاريخ وممارسة مهنة الصحافة. ابتعدت عن كتابة الذات، وكتبت عن مصر/التاريخ. ففي رواية **الغُر** تعود إلى الربع الأخير من القرن التاسع عشر حيث تختطف سرية نوبية/بجاوية وتهرب إلى مصر وتستقر في دمياط. ودمياط نفسها في القرن السادس عشر كانت نموذجاً لمجتمع الدولة العثمانية متعدد الجنسيات والديانات. وتبرز رواية **نوة الكرم** التفاعل الخلاق بينهم ومتاعبهم التي تشاركوا فيها، مستائين من ظروف اقتصادية ضاغطة وقرارات تعسفية. ويحظى البحر المتوسط بحضور ميتافيزيقي ودور مركزي حيث القرصنة والثقافة والتجارة المتبادلة. تضع الرواية علامات استفهام حول مفهوم أن «للتاريخ القول الفصل» فلصناع التاريخ وبنائيه، أي «عامة الناس»، حكايات أخرى مغايرة لما حفظته لنا كتب رسمية.

شجن ملتاع لفقدان لايسترَد

دوريس شكري

في هذه الشهادة، تسترجع الكاتبة، محاطة بالمعابد المصرية القديمة، ذكريات الماضي متأملة مغزاه في الوعي الشخصي والجماعي. وترى الكاتبة، استناداً إلى خبرتها الشخصية، أن كل بحث هو في جوهره مرتبط حتمياً بتوق إلى انطباع أول لا يسترَد، وهو ما تطلق عليه «المشهد البدائي». فلم يتعارض تخصصها في الأدب اللاتيني الوسيط مع شغفها بالأدب الحديث. فالنصوص الحديثة تستحوذ على القارئ مرددة أصداء موتيفات من الأدب الكلاسيكي والوسيط ونصوص عصر النهضة. فحتى يقدّر المرء قيمة الحديث، عليه أن يستشف ثراء الماضي فيه.

تجربتي في الجامعة ورؤيتي لدورها التعليمي

دوريس شكري
(ترجمة ليس النقاش)

ألقت دوريس شكري هذه الكلمة في حفل تخرج طلاب الدراسات العليا في الجامعة الأمريكية (٢٠٠٢) بعد أكثر من أربعة عقود عملت فيها أستاذة في تلك الجامعة. وتعبر فيها عن آرائها حول دور الجامعة، وهو الدور الذي تكمن قيمته في رأيها في توفير مكان تتفتح فيه العقول على المعرفة وإعادة الاكتشاف، لا في كونها مؤسسة ذات توجه نفعي تلبي للمجتمع احتياجاته المادية المباشرة. وتؤكد شكري من موقعها كعضو هيئة تدريس في مؤسسة أمريكية للتعليم العالي في مصر على أن تعدد وجهات النظر واختلاف الثقافات دافع لجدل مثمر بين العقول الحرة. كما ترى في الأدب تحديداً طريقاً لإثراء العقل وفرصة لدارسيه من الشباب للتعلم من كبار الكتاب والمفكرين من دون التقيد برؤاهم.

حفريات أدبية في شعر محمود درويش:
مشروع قراءة في قصيدة «الهدهد»

محمد عجينة

تمثل المقالة حفراً استبطانياً في قصيدة «الهدهد» لمحمود درويش – ضمن بحث في علاقة الأساطير بالثقافة عامة وبالأدب والشعر خاصة – انطلاقاً من الهدهد كرمز أسطوري يتجاذب النص في اتجاهين اثنين: أ– اتجاه جدولي، يصل القصيدة – عبر

الزمن – بعالم الكون وعالم المنام وعالم الشعر في لغة اللمح والإشارة. ب- اتجاه أفقي قصصي، يجعل من القصيدة – عبر رحلات نموذجية سابقة ومن خلال نصوص حاضرة غائبة للجاحظ، وابن سينا، والسهروردي، والحلاج، وأرسطوفان، وفريد الدين العطار، وغيرهم – رحلة في أعماق الذات الفردية، وفي أعماق الذات الجماعية ذاكرة وتاريخاً. تجمع قصيدة درويش بين «الشعر» و«النثر» والمسرحية والملحمة، كما أنها أسطورة أدبية تقص علينا قصة بحث عن زمن مقدس هو زمن البدايات والطفولة.

ذاكرة الأ(د)ب في «ذاكرة الجسد»

فريال جبوري غزّول

تقدم هذه المقالة في جزئها الأول الرواية الأولى للروائية الجزائرية أحلام مستغانمي **ذاكرة الجسد** (١٩٩٣) التي عرفت عربياً بالرواية النسائية الأولى في الجزائر المكتوبة بالعربية ونالت جائزة نجيب محفوظ عام ١٩٩٨؛ وقد لاقت هذه الرواية إقبالاً جماهيرياً منقطع النظير بينما كان تلقيها عند النقاد متبايناً بين إعجاب وانصراف وتجريح. وتناقش المقالة آراء النقاد حولها وترد على الاتهامات الجارحة حولها. ثم تنتقل في جزئها الثاني إلى تحليل مستويات الرواية مقدمةً رؤية تأويلية لها. فهناك ثلاثة مستويات يمكن قراءة العمل انطلاقاً منها، ففيها أولاً حكاية حب بين خالد الرسام وبطلة الرواية ذات الاسم المزدوج حياة/أحلام. وهناك ثانياً الوطن المفقود الذي يستدعيه خالد وهو في منفاه الباريسي. وهناك ثالثاً حكاية الحكاية في الرواية والتساؤل عن ماهية القص وما هي دوافع الأديب لاختيار الرواية نمطاً للبوح وما الفرق في التعبير بين الصورة والكلمة. وتقتفي المقالة أثر القديم في الجديد عبر حضور الأب في وعي ابنته ورفاقه بعد استشهاده، وعبر التناص مع الأب الروحي لأحلام مستغانمي، مالك حداد الروائي الجزائري الفرانكفوني وعبر استدعاء نضال الثوار الجزائريين في حاضر الجزائر الموجع.

الاستدعاء الموسيقي:
الذاكرة الما بعدية والشتات البنجابي

أنانيا جاهانارا كبير

كان لتقسيم شبه القارة الهندية في عام ١٩٤٧ بالغ الأثر في تغيير الملامح الجيوبوليطيقية والديموجرافية لمنطقة جنوب آسيا؛ فقد خلّف حركات شتات ونزوح واسعة النطاق إلى بريطانيا قادمة من المناطق التي تأثرت بذلك التقسيم على نحو عميق مثل البنجاب. من خلال نزوع الكاتبة هنا إلى سوق نماذج من دراسات الهولوكوست نجدها تربط بين الشتات وحالة الصدمة بغية تحليل عمل الذاكرة المحفور بعمق بين ثنايا الموسيقى

المعاصرة التي يبدعها ويستمتع بها البنجابيون البريطانيون في بريطانيا، وتطرح أيضاً قضية مفادها أن مثل هذه الموسيقى ما هي إلا تعبير عن «ذاكرة ما بعدية» بنجابية «إثنية جديدة» ترنو إلى استدعاء بنجاب ما قبل التقسيم، ومن ثم فهي تقترح أن ذلك «الاستدعاء الموسيقي» ينطوي على إمكانية خلاصية تذكارية تكمن في قدرته على مجاوزة قصص العنف والقومية وتجنبها، وإبراز صور ما بعد وما وراء قومية لمفهوم تشكيل الهوية والانتماء الثقافي.

استخدامات التأويل في مسرحية «هاملت»

ليزلي كروكسفورد

تثير مسرحية **هاملت** من الجدل ما لم تثره أي كتابة مسرحية أخرى. فقد نشأ عن تعدد مصادرها، التي تعود إلى القرون الوسطى وعصر النهضة، بعض التعارضات، التي نتجت أيضاً عن التضارب بين الطبعات المختلفة لتراث شكسبير المسرحي، وعن ذلك الحشد من المشكلات التي لا حل لها. تتعلق تلك المشكلات بموضوع المسرحية حيناً، وبالمسائل النفسية حيناً آخر. من ذلك، على سبيل المثال، التساؤل الذائع عن العلة وراء تأجيل الأمير لانتقامه. وقد أفضى هذا كله إلى ألا ينقطع تأويل تلك المسرحية. على أن التأويل لم يكن شأناً من شئون النقاد والدارسين فحسب، بل انهمك فيه الأمير وسائر الشخصيات الرئيسية. يعد التأويل، إذن، موضوعاً محورياً في المسرحية، وهو بالتالي يمثل إشارة تلميحية لأولئك الذين يطمحون إلى تأويل **هاملت**. ولكي يمنح شكسبير موضوع التأويل هذا المغزى المهم، قام بتطويرات في بعض الروايات السابقة للقصة. إن هناك عاملين كان لهما معاً تأثير على التحويلات التي مرت بها **هاملت**؛ الأول هو المناخ العقلي الذي أحاط بكتابة المسرحية، والثاني هو الطبيعة السياسية لعالم القرن السادس عشر. منح شكسبير عبر **هاملت** صوتاً درامياً مهماً للذات الأوروبية الحديثة التي كانت في طور النشوء آنذاك.

ڤالانتينوس والأسماء:
سوسور، أفلاطون، والمغزى

روندو كيل

تزخر أسطورة ڤالانتينوس الغنوصي المسيحي بذلك الطرح الرائع الذي يؤكد أن الأسماء تتمتع بقوة الخلاص؛ فهو يقول في **إنجيل الحقيقة** The Gospel of Truth إن الله يستخدم أسماء لكي يدعو الكائنات إلى الولوج إلى حيز الوجود، ويذهب أيضاً إلى أن «اسم الأب هو الابن»، ولعل مفهوم «الاسماء المقدسة» هذا قد أثبت أنه يستعصي بحق على الفهم، ويُرجع الكاتب في مقالته بعضاً من أسباب تلك الصعوبة إلى الإطار ما بعد السوسوري الذي نتحرك بداخله؛ إذ نجد صعوبة بالغة في أن نجعل مثل تلك الادعاءات

متسقة مع مبدأ سوسور القائم على اعتباطية العلامات. وعلى النقيض تماماً من هذا المبدأ، يفترض ڤالنتينوس وجود صلة مسبقة بين الأسماء والكائنات، وطالما يعتمد الأمر – على هذا النحو – على هذه النزعة الجوهرية يصبح من العسير أن نطرح تأويلاً ما بعد سوسوري يتسم بالدقة والمباشرة للطابع الصوفي المغلف للاسم في مفهوم ڤالنتينوس عن «الخلاص بالأسماء» *salus per nomina*. ولكن ثمة الكثير من المعلقين حاولوا طرح مثل هذه التأويلات، منحين جانباً ذلك التوتر من خلال جعله جزءاً لا يتجزأ من قراءتهم. بيد أن هذه المحاولات تنتهي غالباً بالغموض واليأس؛ فلا تميط اللثام إلا عن قليل. يتناول كاتب المقالة بالنقد جزءاً من هذا التقليد التأويلي المعتاد، ويحاول التغلب على الصعاب الأكبر عبر طرح يعيد بناء مفهوم «الخلاص بالأسماء»، معتمداً على منهج أفلاطوني في التسمية، ليصل بذلك إلى تأويل بديل قابل للتطور ذي صبغة جوهرية.

الكتابة خارج المكان:
«الحب والفانتازيا» لآسيا جبار و«خارطة الحب» لأهداف سويف

سامية محرز

إن القصة الرسمية عن التاريخ ووقائعه مرتبطة دائماً بالسلطة وبنظامها وقيمها بشكل عام. لذا، فإن هيمنة القصة/الحبكة الرسمية على المعرفة تضع معاً المؤرخ والأديب في موقع الاختيار والاختبار. إما أن يخضعا لسلطة الحبكة الرسمية فتتطابق روايتهما/حبكتهما معها وإما أن يثورا عليها فيتعارض إنتاجهما للحبكة مع القصة الرسمية. يتناول هذا المقال موقع المبدعين العرب مزدوجي الثقافة من هذه المنظومة متخذاً من الكاتبتين آسيا جبار (الجزائر) وأهداف سويف (مصر) – الأولى تكتب بالفرنسية والثانية بالإنجليزية – نموذجاً لمواجهة «الحبكة» الرسمية سواء كانت تلك التي تتسلط على الثقافة الأم أو تلك التي تسيطر على الثقافة المكتسبة/المضيفة. وينتهي المقال إلى أن هاتين الكاتبتين اللتين تكتبان «خارج المكان» هما بصدد استكشاف معالم جديدة، «حبكة» جديدة في إمكانيات كتابة اللقاء عبر الحضارات، انطلاقاً من موقعيهما الاستثنائي الـ«بين-بين».

الخيط السري بين القديم والحديث في الفن:
مقابلة مع رافع الناصري

مي مظفَّر

رافع الناصري فنان عراقي معاصر اشتهر بأعماله في الرسم وفنون الحفر والطباعة (غرافيك). درس فن الرسم في بغداد، ودرس فنون الحفر والطباعة في الصين، ثم في لشبونة. توصل إلى أسلوبه الخاص في الفن التجريدي عندما اكتشف سحر الحرف العربي

وطواعيته في الرسم فأخضعه إلى مهاراته في استخدام الفرشاة والضربات اللونية التي اكتسبها من دراسته في الصين. تعكس أعمال الناصري، سواء أكانت لوحات مرسومة بمادة الأكريلك أو مطبوعة (باستخدام الحفر على النحاس)، اهتماماته بحضارة وادي الرافدين على تعاقب حضاراتها بما في ذلك جماليات الفنون الإسلامية، فهو يستعير منها رموزه وعناصر تكويناته التي تتجلى في أسلوبه الحداثي المفعم بالحيوية. أجرت الشاعرة والناقدة التشكيلية مي مظفر مقابلة مع الفنان رافع الناصري تحدث فيها عن مراحل عمله المختلفة وتطور تجربته الفنية بدءاً من مرحلته الأكاديمية التشخيصية. كما ننشر مع المقابلة مجموعة من الصور التي تمثل مراحل العمل خلال السنوات ١٩٦٢-٢٠٠٢، لإعطاء لمحة عن طبيعة تطور هذه الأعمال التي تجمع بين التقنيات الفنية المبتكرة، وفلسفته في العمل التي تتخذ من التصميم نقطة مركزية في تنفيذ العمل الفني التشكيلي.

تجاذب القديم والجديد في شعر نازك الملائكة ونظريتها الشعرية

سامي مهدي

تتناول هذه المقالة مواقف الشاعرة العراقية نازك الملائكة (١٩٢٣-) من التجديد في شعرها وفي نظريتها الشعرية وتكشف عن بصمات القديم وعلاقته بالجديد في أعمالها الأدبية والنقدية. تركز الدراسة على استفادة نازك الملائكة من الشعر الأجنبي وأثره على تجديدها في الأسلوب والعروض، وبشكل خاص علاقتها بقصائد إدغار ألان پو وتنظيره حول بنية الشعر. وتتخذ الدراسة من التكرار الشعري منطلقاً للكشف عن هذه العلاقة بين الشاعرة العراقية والشاعر الأمريكي، كما تتابع المقالة تراجع نازك الملائكة عن ثوريتها الأولى، ومن ثم ترددها بين القديم والجديد، وتنتهي الدراسة بالإشارة إلى الأسباب الإيديولوجية والذاتية والاجتماعية التي أدت إلى توقف الملائكة عن تطوير تجربتها الرائدة في الشعر.

مصر في التاريخ والرواية عند الإغريق والرومان

ستيفن نيميس

تتعرض هذه المقالة للرؤى الإغريقية والرومانية إزاء المصريين القدماء كتوطئة لاستكشاف ذلك الصدى المجازي لمصر في القصص التي أُبدعت إبان الحقبة الاستعمارية في الأدب القديم. كتب كل من الإغريق والرومان عن مصر كشكل من أشكال تناول هموم وقضايا معينة في ثقافتيهم اللتين تُصوّر مصر فيهما على أنها ذلك «الآخر» المروّع للثقافة الإغريقية-الرومانية، كما يُحتفى بها في الوقت نفسه كبقعة قديمة من بقاع الغموض والتجدد. وتلك ما هي إلا ازدواجية متناقضة يتم تطويعها في الروايات القديمة بغية صياغة آراء وأقوال عن العلاقات والحقائق المعاصرة.

ديزموند أوجرادي شاعر إيرلندي درس في جامعتي دبلن وهارڤارد. درّس في روما وباريس والقاهرة. له خمس عشرة مجموعة شعرية، كما ترجم قصائد شعرية من اللغات المختلفة، ومنها الويلزية والعربية والإيطالية والفرنسية واليونانية.

محمد بريري يدرّس الأدب العربي القديم والحديث بجامعتي القاهرة والجامعة الأمريكية بالقاهرة. صدر له كتاب عن الشعر العربي القديم بعنوان **الأسلوبية والتقاليد الشعرية: دراسة في شعر الهذليين**. له دراسات منشورة في حقل الأدب العربي القديم، شعره ونثره، وأيضاً في الأدب الحديث (الشعر والرواية والقصة القصيرة). له ترجمات من الإنجليزية إلى العربية في مجالي النظرية النقدية والأدب العربي القديم. يقوم بتقديم ومناقشة الأعمال الأدبية العربية المعاصرة من خلال أنشطة المجلس الأعلى للثقافة والجمعية المصرية للنقد الأدبي.

وليد بيطار درّس الإنجليزية في الجامعة الأمريكية في بيروت. صدر له ديوان شعر بعنوان Two Guys on Holy Land، عن دار نشر جامعة ويزليان (١٩٩٣). تصدر مجموعته الشعرية الجديدة بعنوان Bastardi Puri قريباً.

حسب الشيخ جعفر شاعر عراقي درس في موسكو وحصل على الليسانس في الأدب من معهد جوركي. له ثماني مجموعات شعرية، وعملين نثريين، وترجمات لأهم الشعراء الروسيين. نشر بشكل منتظم في مجلة **عمّان** الثقافية الشهرية. حصل مؤخراً على جائزة مؤسسة العويس في الشعر.

شهرزاد قاسم حسن باحثة في الإثنوميوزيكولوجي (علم موسيقى الشعوب). درّست في جامعتي بغداد وباريس. تبحث في التقاليد الموسيقية لمنطقة الشرق الأوسط وقامت بدراسات ميدانية في كل من العراق وسوريا وقطر والبحرين والإمارات العربية المتحدة واليمن. نشرت عدداً من الكتب والمقالات والبحوث.

أيمن الدسوقي أستاذ محاضِر بكلية الدراسات الشرقية والأفريقية بجامعة لندن. درس الأدب المقارن بالجامعة الأمريكية بالقاهرة وجامعة تكساس في أوستن، ودرّس اللغة والأدب العربي

في جامعة جونز هوبكنز وجامعة هارفارد بالولايات المتحدة الأمريكية. يعمل الآن على مشروع لكتاب حول مفاهيم اللغة والخطاب المقدس في الأدب العربي الحديث.

جون رودنبك حصل على الليسانس من جامعة هارفارد، والماجستير والدكتوراه من جامعة فيرجينيا. أستاذ متفرغ بقسم الأدب الإنجليزي والمقارن بالجامعة الأمريكية بالقاهرة حيث درّس لأكثر من عقدين ورأس دار نشر الجامعة الأمريكية، ١٩٧٤–١٩٨٣. نشر أكثر من مائة كتاب ومقالة في موضوعات تتنوع ما بين الأدب الإنجليزي في القرن التاسع عشر وفن المعمار الوسيط في القاهرة. يعيش حالياً بفرنسا.

إدوارد سعيد تلقى تعليمه في القدس والقاهرة وجامعتي برنستون وهارفارد. درّس الأدب الإنجليزي والمقارن في جامعة كولومبيا وله عشرون كتاباً في الأدب والنقد والقضية الفلسطينية، بما في ذلك كتابه المرجعي **الاستشراق**. حصل على عشرات الدرجات العلمية الشرفية والجوائز.

منيرة سليمان مدرسة الأدب الإنجليزي بقسم اللغة الإنجليزية بجامعة القاهرة. كتبت رسالة دكتوراه بعنوان «الواقعية السحرية في الرواية الأفريقية والأفريقية–الأمريكية المعاصرة». تعمل حالياً على مشروع بحثي يتمحور حول الأدبين اليهودي–الأمريكي والعربي–الأمريكي في سياق الثقافة الأمريكية.

شتيفن شتيلزر درس الفلسفة والأدب المقارن في جامعات ألمانيا وفرنسا. درّس بجامعة جونز هوبكنز بالولايات المتحدة الأمريكية، وحاضر في جامعتي هارفارد ونيويورك. يعمل حالياً أستاذاً للفلسفة في الجامعة الأمريكية بالقاهرة. نشر كتاباً حول الجانب الزماني للفكر، بالإضافة إلى العديد من المقالات حول القضايا الإبستمولوجية في الفلسفة والأدب. وقد تحولت اهتماماته البحثية مؤخراً إلى دراسة الجوانب الإبستمولوجية للصوفية الإسلامية.

نجوى شعبان محررة ثقافية بوكالة أنباء الشرق الأوسط. صدرت لها ثلاثة أعمال إبداعية: مجموعة قصصية، **جدائل التيه** (١٩٩٥)؛ رواية **الغُر** (١٩٩٨) والتي فازت بجائزة أندية فتيات الشارقة؛ ورواية **نوة الكرم** (٢٠٠٢؛ ٢٠٠٣). أنجزت دراستين عن الفن التشكيلي في الولايات المتحدة الأمريكية. لها العديد من المقالات في النقد التشكيلي والرواية. ترجمت العديد من الأعمال في مجالات علم النفس، والسياسة، والأنثروبولوجيا، والفن التشكيلي، والتاريخ، من الإنجليزية إلى العربية.

دوريس شكري أستاذة متفرغة رأست قسم الأدب الإنجليزي والمقارن بالجامعة الأمريكية بالقاهرة. حققت وترجمت أعمالاً لاتينية، كما نشرت دراسات عديدة عن

فرجينيا وولف ويونسكو وكونديرا ومارجريت دوراس وعن البعد الفلسفي في الحداثة وفي ما بعد الحداثة.

محمد عجينة حصل على درجتي الماجستير والدكتوراه في اللغة العربية وآدابها من تونس. كتب أطروحة الدكتوراه حول أساطير العرب في الجاهلية ودلالاتها. ترجم العديد من الكتب إلى العربية، ومنها **دروس في الألسنية العامة** لفردينان دي سوسير (بالاشتراك). له عدد من المقالات حول الشعر، ويدرّس بجامعة تونس.

فريال جبوري غزول أستاذة الأدب الإنجليزي والمقارن في الجامعة الأمريكية بالقاهرة. لها العديد من الكتابات والمقالات حول الأدب الوسيط والشعر ونقد ما بعد الكولونيالية. ترجمت أعمالاً أدبية ونقدية من وإلى العربية والإنجليزية والفرنسية، منها **رباعية الفرح** لمحمد عفيفي مطر و**رامة والتنين** لإدوار الخراط، ودراسات لألتوسير وريكور وريفاتير وبيرس وإدوارد سعيد.

أنانيا جاهانارا كبير تدرّس الأدب الإنجليزي في جامعة ليدز بالمملكة المتحدة. عملت باحثة في ترينيتي كوليدج وفي مركز التاريخ والاقتصاد التابعين لجامعة كمبريدج، وباحثة زائرة في قسم اللغة الإنجليزية بجامعة كاليفورنيا في بيركلي. تلقت تدريبها البحثي وتخصصت في الأدب الوسيط ثم بدأت البحث في العلاقة بين تشظي الذات والانتماء الثقافي والتعبير الخيالي، خاصة في سياق منطقة جنوب آسيا ما بعد الكولونيالية وما يرتبط بها من حالات شتات. تشمل اهتماماتها البحثية بشكل خاص المناطق والثقافات التي تم تقسيمها في جنوب آسيا: البنجاب، البنغال (مسقط رأسها)، وكشمير. تبحث حالياً في الأدب والفن النابعين من الصراع السياسي في منطقة كشمير الخاضعة للحكم الهندي.

ليزلي كروكسفورد أستاذ الإنسانيات بجامعة سفولك ببوسطن بالولايات المتحدة الأمريكية ويدير فرعها بمدريد. حصل على الدكتوراه في دراسات القرن السادس عشر من جامعة كمبريدج، حيث درّس. كما قام بالتدريس في جامعة هارفارد، وفي الجامعة الأمريكية بالقاهرة، وفي جامعات أخرى ببريطانيا وأمريكا واليابان. له كتابات قصصية ومسرحية. وتقع أحداث رواية *Solomon's Folly* في الإسكندرية، مسقط رأسه. وقد عرضت مسرحيته *Confessions* على مسرح إيموري بأطلنطا بالولايات المتحدة الأمريكية في عام ٢٠٠٣.

روندو كيل مدرس الفلسفة في الجامعة الأمريكية بالقاهرة. تركّز اهتماماته البحثية على الميتافيزيقا، والنظرية الدلالية، والمنطق في أواخر العصور الوسطى. له أيضاً اهتمامات بفلسفة الدين، وتاريخ الرياضيات، والمنطق الحديث. نشرت أبحاثه في عدد من الدوريات الأكاديمية.

سامية محرز درست الأدب الإنجليزي والعربي في مصر والولايات المتحدة وتعمل الآن أستاذة مساعدة في قسم الدراسات العربية بالجامعة الأمريكية بالقاهرة. لها كتاب بالإنجليزية، **الأدب المصري بين التاريخ والرواية (١٩٩٤)**، إلى جانب عدة مقالات عن الأدب العربي والفرانكوفوني المعاصر نشرت في مجلات أجنبية وعربية. تعد كتاباً عن الروائية العربية والوطن.

مي مظفر حصلت على بكالوريوس الأدب الإنجليزي من جامعة بغداد. صدر لها أربعة دواوين شعرية، وأربعة مجموعات قصصية، وخمسة كتب مترجمة من الإنجليزية إلى العربية في مجال التقابل بين الفنون التشكيلية والأدب. لها دراسات مقارنة في الأدب والفن. عملت محررة فنية في مجلة Iraq الصادرة باللغة الإنجليزية عن وزارة الثقافة العراقية، ومديرة التحرير لمجلة **ثقافات** الصادرة عن جامعة البحرين. كما عملت باحثة في المجمع الملكي لبحوث الحضارة الإسلامية (مؤسسة آل البيت). ترجم لها عدد من القصائد والقصص القصيرة إلى اللغات الإنجليزية والفرنسية والإيطالية. تقيم حاليا في الأردن.

سامي مهدي شاعر عراقي، درس الاقتصاد في بغداد، وعمل في حقل الصحافة والثقافة، فكان رئيس تحرير جريدة **الثورة** العراقية. له دواوين عديدة منها **أسفار جديدة، أوراق الزوال، بريد القارات، حنجرة طرية، الخطأ الأول**، كما له دراسات نقدية منها **الثقافة العربية من الشفاهية إلى الكتابة والموجة الصاخبة: شعر الستينيات في العراق**.

رافع الناصري درس فنون الرسم والحفر والطباعة في بغداد ثم الصين ثم البرتغال تباعاً. عمل مدرساً للفنون في معهد الفنون الجميلة في بغداد، وأسس خلالها قسم الحفر والطباعة (الغرافيك)، كما درّس في جامعة اليرموك (الأردن)، ثم جامعة البحرين. أقام محترفاً لفن الغرافيك خاصاً به في بغداد والعشرات من المعارض الشخصية في العراق وعواصم العالم المختلفة، كما شارك في العديد من المعارض الدولية، ونال عدداً من الجوائز العالمية في مجالي الرسم والحفر (الغرافيك). اختير عضو لجنة تحكيم في بيناليات وترناليات عالمية في كل من القاهرة وباريس ولندن وبرلين وفردريكشتاد. أصدر كتابا بعنوان **فن الغرافيك المعاصر (١٩٩٦)**، كما له قيد الطبع كتاب بعنوان **آفاق ومرايا** (مجموعة مقالات فنية).

لميس النقاش مدرسة مساعدة بقسم اللغة الإنجليزية بجامعة القاهرة. تخصصت في الأدب المقارن بعد حصولها على درجة الماجستير عن رسالة بعنوان «المادة الوثائقية في الرواية: دراسة مقارنة لهيرمن ميلفل وصنع الله إبراهيم». تعمل بالترجمة ولها عدد من المقالات والكتب المترجمة، منها **النهضة النسائية في مصر** لبث بارون.

ستيفن نيميس أستاذ الدراسات الكلاسيكية بجامعة ميامي بأوهايو بالولايات المتحدة الأمريكية. عمل أستاذاً زائراً بقسم الأدب الإنجليزي والمقارن بالجامعة الأمريكية بالقاهرة، ٢٠٠٢-٢٠٠٣. من أبحاثه المنشورة **السيميوطيقية السردية في التراث الملحمي**، وله مقالات أخرى عديدة حول الرواية القديمة.

نهاية القسم العربي